THE
NEW INTERNATIONAL
LESSON ANNUAL
1999–2000

September–August

THE
NEW INTERNATIONAL
LESSON ANNUAL
1999–2000

September–August

Abingdon Press
Nashville

THE NEW INTERNATIONAL LESSON ANNUAL 1999–2000

Copyright © 1999 by Abingdon Press

All rights reserved.

This book is printed on recycled, acid-free paper.

ISBN 0-687-02303-3

ISSN 1084-872X

99 00 01 02 03 04 05 06 07 08—10 9 8 7 6 5 4 3 2 1

MANUFACTURED IN THE UNITED STATES OF AMERICA

PREFACE

Welcome to an exciting journey through the Scriptures in 1999–2000! Thank you for choosing *The New International Lesson Annual* to guide you in your study of God's word as contained in both the Hebrew Scriptures and the New Testament. We trust that this resource, illumined by God's grace through the power of the Holy Spirit, will enable you to study the Scriptures so that you "may be proficient, equipped for every good work" (2 Timothy 3:17).

In order to help you grow toward spiritual maturity, the lessons you will find here are designed to inform you, transform you, and enable you to be conformed to the image of Christ. Here's how each lesson works to achieve that purpose:

- **Previewing the Lesson** spotlights the focus and direction of the lesson.
- **Focusing on the Main Question** introduces the scripture for the lesson by raising a question that encourages you to think about how the passage relates to your own life.
- **Reading the Scripture** highlights the biblical passage for the day's lesson as it appears in both the New Revised Standard Version (NRSV) and the New International Version (NIV).
- **Understanding the Scripture** delves into the entire background scripture to shed light on its meaning.
- **Interpreting the Scripture** looks at the lesson scripture to discern how the early hearers and readers, as well as modern Christians such as yourself, might interpret it.
- **Sharing the Scripture** provides teaching suggestions for class leaders. This section begins with *Preparing to Teach*, which offers ideas for the teacher's own spiritual and mental preparation, along with a list of supplies. *Leading the Class*, which is divided into an introduction and subheadings that correspond to those under Interpreting the Scripture, offers questions, lecture ideas, and activities designed to meet a wide range of classroom styles and interests.
- **Helping Class Members Act** gives three options that will enable the students to put what they have learned into practice once they leave the classroom.
- **Planning for Next Sunday** concludes the lesson with information that will help teachers and students prepare for the next session.

The writer of each quarter's lessons provides you with the material found in Focusing on the Main Question, Understanding the Scripture, and Interpreting the Scripture. To keep the teaching plan consistent throughout the year, editor Nan Duerling writes the Sharing the Scripture, Helping Class Members Act, and Planning for Next Sunday portions of all of the lessons.

We want to thank each of you who have taken your valuable time to write and share your ideas with us. We do respond personally to all of your letters. If you have any comments, questions, or stories you want to share, please write to:

Dr. Nan Duerling, Abingdon Press, P.O. Box 801, Nashville, TN 37202.

From your correspondence we know that our readers represent a variety of denominational heritages, though many of you are United Methodists. Moreover, some of you meet with a small discussion group on Sunday morning while others of you are members of very large lecture classes. You hail from all parts of the country and attend churches that vary greatly in size. You approach Bible study from diverse theological perspectives. To honor this rich diversity, we try to offer ideas appropriate for different teaching and learning styles. We also invite our writers to present a spectrum of viewpoints when such interpretations are held by reputable scholars. We encourage you to be open to new angles of vision as you study, for while you may disagree with some ideas and set them aside, others that you haven't thought of before may broaden and deepen your faith. That willingness to grapple continually with our beliefs is how we keep growing as disciples! And that's exactly what we pray that you will do. May God richly bless you as we walk together in faith through the Bible in the coming year.

Nan Duerling, Ph.D.
Editor, *The New International Lesson Annual*

CONTENTS

SECOND QUARTER

Studies in Matthew
(December 5–February 27)

UNIT 1: BEGINNINGS: BIRTH AND MINISTRY
(December 5–26)

UNIT 2: JESUS' TEACHINGS AND MINISTRY
(January 2–30)

UNIT 3: FULFILLMENT OF JESUS' MISSION
(February 6–27)

THIRD QUARTER

Continuing Jesus' Work
(March 5–May 28)

UNIT 1: CHRIST THE BASIS OF UNITY
(March 5–26)

UNIT 2: UNITY IN HUMAN RELATIONSHIPS
(April 2–30)

UNIT 3: THE GLORY OF CHRISTIAN MINISTRY
(May 7–28)

FOURTH QUARTER

New Life in Christ
(June 4–August 27)

UNIT 1: LIVING IN CHRIST
(June 4–25)

UNIT 2: CALLED TO BE A NEW HUMANITY
(July 2–30)

UNIT 3: CHRIST ABOVE ALL
(August 6–27)

FIRST QUARTER
From Slavery to Promised Land

SEPTEMBER 5, 1999—NOVEMBER 28, 1999

The lessons for the fall seamlessly follow the study of Genesis during the summer. During this quarter we will see how the people whom God fashioned move from bondage in Egypt to the promised land in Canaan. Our study focuses on God's liberation of Israel from slavery, the making of a covenant with them, and the fulfillment of the promise of land first made to Abraham. Key themes in this study are freedom, covenant, obedience, and faithfulness.

The first unit, "Liberation and Covenant," surveys the stories of the Exodus and the making of the covenant at Mount Sinai. On September 5 we will overhear God call Moses to lead the Israelites out of Egypt. "Called to Involvement" tells the familiar story from Exodus 3:1-12 that features a burning bush. "Called to Deliverance," the lesson for September 12, examines the amazing crossing of the Red Sea as recorded in Exodus 13:17-22 and 14:26-31. The following week our attention will turn to the covenant that God made with the people on Mount Sinai. Exodus 19:3-6 and 20:2-4, 7-8, and 12-17 is the foundation for our session on the Ten Commandments, "Called to Covenant." The final lesson in this series, "Called to Obedience," concerns the consecration of the tabernacle of the tent of meeting that God instructed Moses to have built, as recorded in Exodus 40:1-9 and Leviticus 26:2-6 and 11-13.

The five sessions in Unit 2, "Wilderness Wanderings," show how God leads the people in the desert, though they choose to rebel and bring punishment upon themselves. Despite their disobedience, God does not abandon them or cease to love them. This unit begins with a study of Exodus 40:34-38 and Numbers 9:15-19 and 22-23. In this lesson, "Follow Day by Day," we see God leading the people as a pillar of cloud by day and a pillar of fire by night. On October 10 we will look at "A Missed Opportunity," based on Numbers 13:1-3, 32–14:4, and 20-24. This passage tells the story of the spies sent out to reconnoiter the promised land and the Israelites' response to their report. Because they would not follow the Lord, the people had to spend years "In the Wilderness." This lesson, rooted in Deuteronomy 1:41–2:8, shows how God provides everything the people need in the midst of a barren land. On October 24, we will study the Great Commandment that the people must learn and teach their children. This lesson is found in Deuteronomy 6:1-9 and 20-24. Unit 2 concludes with "Don't Lose Perspective," based on Deuteronomy 8:7-20. Before they enter the promised land, Moses warns the people not to forget God by failing to obey the commandments.

In "Entering the Promised Land," the final unit of this quarter, we will follow the people from the death of Moses to their entry into the promised land and the renewal of their covenant under Joshua's leadership. The lesson for November 7 from Deuteronomy 31:1-8 and 34:5-9 records the death of Moses and Joshua's assumption of leadership. "Going Forward in Faith" looks at Joshua 3:7-17 where the people cross the Jordan River into Canaan. On November 21 we will see how the people destroy Jericho so as to have a place to live in the already occupied land that God has given them. This story of "Overcoming Obstacles" is found in Joshua 6:1-5 and 15-20. Our last lesson of this quarter, entitled "Making the Right Choice," looks at the renewal of the covenant as recorded in Joshua 24:1-2, 14-22, and 25. Here, Joshua says that he and his house will serve the Lord, and he calls the people to make that same commitment to God and God alone.

MEET OUR WRITER

THE REVEREND DR. REBECCA ABTS WRIGHT

Rebecca Abts Wright grew up in a series of United Methodist parsonages in Ohio. She went to college at The American University in Washington, D.C. and sometime later to Wesley Theological Seminary, also in Washington. She is an elder in the Baltimore-Washington Annual Conference of The United Methodist Church and has served churches in West Virginia, Maryland, and Connecticut. After several years in parishes, she returned to school and earned a Ph.D. in Old Testament from Yale. She now teaches Old Testament and Biblical Hebrew at the School of Theology, University of the South, Sewanee, Tennessee, where she lives with her two daughters, Anna and Helen Kate, and their dog, Gailor.

UNIT 1: LIBERATION AND COVENANT
CALLED TO INVOLVEMENT

PREVIEWING THE LESSON

Lesson Scripture: Exodus 3:1-12
Background Scripture: Exodus 3
Key Verse: Exodus 3:14

Focus of the Lesson:
God called Moses to become involved by leading the people out of slavery in Egypt.

Main Question of the Lesson:
How does God act in our world and include us in those activities?

This lesson will enable adult learners to:
(1) hear God calling Moses to become involved in God's work.
(2) discern God's call in their own lives.
(3) respond by taking a step to make a difference in the world.

Today's lesson may be outlined as follows:
(1) Introduction
(2) Attention!
(3) Who?
(4) What to Do

FOCUSING ON THE MAIN QUESTION

Does God know what is going on in the world today? If God knows, does God care? If God knows and cares, does God become involved? Such questions are as current as daily news broadcasts and as old as the story of the Israelite slaves in Egypt. Many thoughtful people wonder about God's presence and concern today. Some church folk are afraid that such questions indicate a lack of strong faith, but the Bible is clear that neither God nor Jesus ever scolds anyone for asking honest questions.

Sometimes when we say we want God to be involved in our world what we may really mean is that we want God to step into a particular situation and *fix* whatever the problem is. Then, we imagine, God will step back out and we can continue to run our own lives much as before. We tend to assume at times that in turning a problem over to God, we can "wash our hands of it." Alas, for those of us who want to be able to get off any hook of responsibility, that is not the way the Bible shows God's involvement.

The three verses that come immediately before today's passage say that when the slaves "groaned...and cried out," God "heard...remembered...looked...and was concerned" (Exodus 2:23-25 NIV) or "took notice" (NRSV). This sounds like a good introduction for saying something like, "Then God reached out and delivered the slaves from Egypt, led them to the promised land, and they all lived happily ever after." But even without reading ahead in this lesson, you know that is not how the story goes. God acts, yes. But God chooses human beings, individual people, through whom to act. In this case Moses and Aaron will be the leaders. We can see clearly the interaction between God and Moses throughout the book of Exodus. In today's lesson God calls Moses to become involved in the freeing of his people from Egypt. As we study this lesson we will ask: **How does God act in our world and include us in those activities?**

READING THE SCRIPTURE

NRSV

Exodus 3:1-12, 14

1 Moses was keeping the flock of his father-in-law Jethro, the priest of Midian; he led his flock beyond the wilderness, and came to Horeb, the mountain of God. 2 There the angel of the LORD appeared to him in a flame of fire out of a bush; he looked, and the bush was blazing, yet it was not consumed. 3 Then Moses said, "I must turn aside and look at this great sight, and see why the bush is not burned up." 4 When the LORD saw that he had turned aside to see, God called to him out of the bush, "Moses, Moses!" And he said, "Here I am." 5 Then he said, "Come no closer! Remove the sandals from your feet, for the place on which you are standing is holy ground." 6 He said further, "I am the God of your father, the God of Abraham, the God of Isaac, and the God of Jacob." And Moses hid his face, for he was afraid to look at God.

7 Then the LORD said, "I have observed the misery of my people who are in Egypt; I have heard their cry on account of their taskmasters. Indeed, I know their sufferings, 8 and I have come down to deliver them from the Egyptians, and to bring them up out of that land to a good and broad land, a land flowing with milk and honey, to the country of the Canaanites,

NIV

Exodus 3:1-12, 14

¹Now Moses was tending the flock of Jethro his father-in-law, the priest of Midian, and he led the flock to the far side of the desert and came to Horeb, the mountain of God. ²There the angel of the LORD appeared to him in flames of fire from within a bush. Moses saw that though the bush was on fire it did not burn up. ³So Moses thought, "I will go over and see this strange sight—why the bush does not burn up."

⁴When the LORD saw that he had gone over to look, God called to him from within the bush, "Moses! Moses!"

And Moses said, "Here I am."

⁵"Do not come any closer," God said. "Take off your sandals, for the place where you are standing is holy ground." ⁶Then he said, "I am the God of your father, the God of Abraham, the God of Isaac and the God of Jacob." At this, Moses hid his face, because he was afraid to look at God.

⁷The LORD said, "I have indeed seen the misery of my people in Egypt. I have heard them crying out because of their slave drivers, and I am concerned about their suffering. ⁸So I have come down to rescue them from the hand of the Egyptians and to bring them up out of that land

the Hittites, the Amorites, the Perizzites, the Hivites, and the Jebusites. 9 The cry of the Israelites has now come to me; I have also seen how the Egyptians oppress them. 10 So come, I will send you to Pharaoh to bring my people, the Israelites, out of Egypt." 11 But Moses said to God, "Who am I that I should go to Pharaoh, and bring the Israelites out of Egypt?" 12 He said, "I will be with you; and this shall be the sign for you that it is I who sent you: when you have brought the people out of Egypt, you shall worship God on this mountain."

Key Verse
14 God said to Moses, "I AM WHO I AM." He said further, "Thus you shall say to the Israelites, 'I AM has sent me to you.'"

into a good and spacious land, a land flowing with milk and honey—the home of the Canaanites, Hittites, Amorites, Perizzites, Hivites and Jebusites. ⁹And now the cry of the Israelites has reached me, and I have seen the way the Egyptians are oppressing them. ¹⁰So now, go. I am sending you to Pharaoh to bring my people the Israelites out of Egypt."

¹¹But Moses said to God, "Who am I, that I should go to Pharaoh and bring the Israelites out of Egypt?"

¹²And God said, "I will be with you. And this will be the sign to you that it is I who have sent you: When you have brought the people out of Egypt, you will worship God on this mountain."

¹⁴God said to Moses, "I AM WHO I AM. This is what you are to say to the Israelites: 'I AM has sent me to you.'"

Key Verse

UNDERSTANDING THE SCRIPTURE

Exodus 3:1. After the excitement of his life in Egypt, having been brought up in the palace of Pharaoh by Pharaoh's own daughter, Moses has had to flee Egypt for his life when he killed an Egyptian overseer. Now his life is far different from the one he knew in the court. He is alone, tending sheep in the wilderness, far away even from his new Midianite family.

Exodus 3:2-4. In the midst of his ordinary work as a shepherd, Moses' attention is caught by a bush that is on fire and yet does not seem to be burned up. The sight is strange enough that he goes over to investigate. As soon as he turns aside to "look at this great sight" (3:3), the bush's job is over and the miraculous blazing is never mentioned again. That is, the point of the bush is not to proclaim a God who is able to work mighty wonders—there are many other events in the book of Exodus which can do that!—but rather to com-

mand Moses' undivided attention. Once Moses is paying attention, God begins to speak to him.

Exodus 3:5. God's first command is for Moses to keep a certain distance and take off his sandals. In some cultures, people take their shoes off before entering a house, in part to keep it clean. But that cannot be the meaning here, for how would sandals get even "holy" ground dirty? To the ancient Israelites and their neighbors, going barefoot was a sign of being a slave whereas wearing sandals or shoes was reserved for free people. Thus, Moses is being told that in this place he is not the one in charge; God is. In God's presence, all humans are servants; no one is master of God.

Exodus 3:6-10. God next tells Moses that it is the same God of Abraham, of Isaac, and of Jacob who is speaking to him. This is not a new deity, even though Moses is not in the land where his ancestors lived, nor in the country where the majority of Israelites are. God has seen and heard what is going on in Egypt. The suffering of the Israelites has come to God's attention, and in response God is going to deliver them and take them to a "good and broad land" (3:8) where they can be free. In verse 10 God announces that it is Moses who will be sent to Pharaoh "to bring my people, the Israelites, out of Egypt."

Exodus 3:11-15. Is Moses startled? Is he alarmed? Is he merely being polite when he asks, "Who am I that I should go to Pharaoh, and bring the Israelites out of Egypt?" (3:11). We have no indication in the Bible of his tone of voice as he asked this question. We do know that many times in the Bible when God calls someone to a particular task, the first response is to ask, "Who am I to do such a thing?" or, in simpler terms, "Why me?"

God's answer to Moses is the same as God's answer to others who are called, from Abraham to Gideon to Jeremiah to Mary the mother of Jesus. God's first promise is always "I will be with you" (3:12). That is rarely enough to satisfy the person and usually another question is asked immediately. In Moses' case, he asks what God's name is. This may seem like a silly question. Isn't God's name just that: "God"? Actually, no. "God" is a job description, not a name. "God" is like "mother," "teacher," "mailman," "grocer." Every mother and teacher and mailman and grocer also has a name, and probably more than one name. But in many cases, when there is only one person filling that particular role, the job description is enough. "Teacher," the child says, and the teacher in the room answers, whether that person is Mrs. Wilkinson or Mr. Jones. Only if Mrs. Wilkinson and Mr. Jones are team-teaching in the fourth-grade classroom is it necessary to know the individual names in order to get the attention of the specific individual wanted.

Well then, what about "Lord"? Is that God's name? No again. "Lord" is a title, similar to "Mr.," "Mrs.," "Ms.," "The Honorable," or "Dr." Kings and other high officials are routinely addressed as "lord" by other people in the Bible. We are likely to say "Miss" instead of "Waitress," for example, if we wish to get that person's attention but do not know her name.

Why does Moses ask to know God's name? If Abraham, Isaac, Jacob, and all their descendants up to this point have gotten along without that knowledge, why is Moses asking now? There are many parts to the answer to this question, or many separate answers. Maybe Moses believes that God will not disclose the divine personal name and thus Moses will be "off the hook" so far as going to Pharaoh is concerned. Or perhaps Moses wants to know God more intimately than is possible without knowing God's name.

Whatever the reasons, Moses asks and God answers. But God's answer is strange: "I AM WHO I AM" (3:14). Is this an answer? Is this really a name at all? The Hebrew language is quite different from English in several ways. When the Bible was penned, no vowels were written. With only consonants recorded, it is possible to use different sets of vowels and have different words, and thus different meanings. What God says can be translated many ways, depending in part on the vowels one inserts between the Hebrew consonants. (Your English Bibles may give some of the other possibilities in a footnote.) The most likely include "I AM," "I WILL BE," and "I WILL CAUSE TO BE." God's self-identification includes being and becoming and creating.

God also makes it clear that Moses has not met a new God out in the wilderness. This new name—usually represented in English Bibles by using the word LORD with small capital letters—is specifically equated with "the God of your ancestors, the God of Abraham...Isaac...and Jacob" (3:15). Moses may have learned a new name, but it is the same God as the God of the ancient covenant.

Exodus 3:16-22. Then God gives Moses specific instructions. He is to go back to Egypt, but he is not to go first to Pharaoh. First he is to tell the Israelite leaders that God has heard them and is going to act on their behalf. Moses is to tell the elders that God will act not only through him, Moses, but also through them. All of them are instructed to go to Pharaoh. Moses, and through him the elders, are also warned from the very beginning that Pharaoh is not going to be happy about this turn of events. It will take "wonders" from God to compel Pharaoh to release the slaves. It may be a long and difficult process, but God's first promise to Moses in verse 12 stands: "I will be with you."

INTERPRETING THE SCRIPTURE

Attention!

Often even people who know little about the Scriptures have heard of the "burning bush." And yet the bush itself is about the least important feature of this chapter. It is understandable, though, that we would remember the bush because it is so different from what we see in our regular lives. We tend to remember what is special, what is out of the ordinary. There may also be another reason why we tend to remember the things we can call miracles: as long as we are focusing on the bush itself, we may not be able to hear what God is saying.

God sometimes uses the unusual to get our attention. But I do not believe that the point of these encounters, whether in the Bible or in our own lives, is the spectacular manifestation of God. I believe the point of the encounter is the encounter itself—the relationship that God desires to have with us. I believe also that God wants us to be involved in God's own life with the world. God calls us not only to contemplation and worship but also to responsibility and service. It is good to pray for God to deliver those in bondage or suffering. But God may well treat us as Moses was treated; we may be called to participate in that deliverance.

Who?

The question of identity in this chapter has two parts. First, Moses asks "Who am I?" If you have ever felt the call of God to some particular work—to speaking a word of apology or of forgiveness, to going out of your way to help a neighbor, to changing your entire lifestyle or profession—you may have asked this same question. Compared with God, compared with all the powerful people in the world today, compared with the people whose spiritual lives are much more robust than mine, who am I that God would call *me* to some work of deliverance? The biblical witness and the witness of the saints throughout the centuries is that such a question is met with the same answer from God: "I will be with you." The specific objections we raise are seldom answered right away. Instead, there is just that stark assurance, "I will be with you."

This question and response leads, inevitably, to the other identity question: "Who is this God?" Again there is a cryptic answer. God says "I AM WHO I AM"; "I CREATE ALL THAT I CREATE"; "I WILL BE WHAT I WILL BE." Jesus, of course, uses this "I am" terminology to speak of himself, especially in the Gospel of John. (See, for example, John 6:35, 48, 51; 8:12; 9:5; 10:7, 11, 14; 11:25.) Both Jesus and God give the same underlying assurance of presence with us (compare Matthew 28:20). We learn who God is the same way we learn who Jesus is, by following. For God is supremely involved with this world and desires to be involved with us in our lives in this world. I suppose God could simply snap a finger or shout out a pronouncement and *fix* all our problems. But for as long as we have known anything about God, we have seen that this is not the way of the Lord. Rather, God desires our involvement. God is one who desires relationship. God does not work miracles as "flashy tricks" to evoke our awe or our terror. What miracles there are often serve the same purpose as the burning bush—to get our attention. Then, when we are receptive to God's message, we are invited into involvement with God and our world.

What to Do

All right. Suppose we have had our attention grabbed and we realize that the encounter is with God. How are we to proceed? Here is where the biblical witness is clear in a frustrating way. We have hints, but not rigid recipes. Look, for example, at what Moses is told. He is to go back and work with the leaders of the Israelite people. As God works through Moses, so Moses is to work through the people. As God does not promise to set things right with the flick of a magic wand, neither does God propose that any one human being shoulder the entire responsibility.

God is also honest and realistic about the probable outcome. In the short run, Pharaoh is not going to go along with God's plan. The struggle will likely be long. We know from reading on in the book of Exodus that there were times when the elders of the people abandoned Moses, times when Moses himself wanted to give up, times when the whole host of Israelites said they would rather be slaves in Egypt than continue the struggle to be God's freed people. But God's vision is not limited by what we can see in the short run. In the long run, God promises, the Israelites will be freed from Egypt and will live in the land God has promised to their ancestors.

We pray in the Lord's Prayer that God's will will be done. We believe the day will ultimately dawn when God's will will be a reality. In the meantime we believe that God works in and through regular human beings toward that day. God takes each of us as we are, with our interests and talents, our shortcomings and weaknesses. And God says to us, "Take off your shoes. This is holy ground. I have a job for you to do and I will be with you through it all." God calls us to become involved. Then we must decide, just as Moses did, how we will respond.

SHARING THE SCRIPTURE

PREPARING TO TEACH

Preparing Our Hearts

Teaching Sunday school is a challenge, a privilege, and a responsibility. Whether you are a novice instructor or a seasoned teacher, you will likely experience the excitement of the first lesson in the new Sunday-school year. As we move into this new year, the waters are both familiar and uncharted—familiar because this quarter's lessons focus on some beloved biblical stories, and uncharted because we cannot know how God's Spirit is going to speak and move us as we encounter these scripture passages afresh. Pray that God will speak to you so that you might share the story of God's interaction with humanity in ways that uplift, encourage, and confront the students.

Begin your devotions by reading Exodus 6:2-8. As you hear the words God gave Moses to share with the people, think about how Moses' God is your God. Also ponder the ways in which God has "freed you from the burdens" that weigh you down (6:7). Offer a prayer of thanksgiving for God's gracious work in your own life.

Now read today's lesson from Exodus 3. Imagine yourself in Moses' position. What might have drawn you to the burning bush? In what ways has God called you? How have you responded to God's call upon your own life? How has your response been similar to or different from Moses' response? You may want to record answers to these questions in a spiritual journal. If not, spend time quietly reflecting on your responses.

Preparing Our Minds

Read this lesson and review Exodus 3, particularly verses 1-12. As you delve into this material, ask yourself these questions: How is God identified? Why is God calling Moses? What does God intend to do for the people? What concerns/questions does Moses raise with God?

You may also want to review Exodus 1 and 2 so that you will be able to bridge the gap between Genesis and Exodus. Here are a few points to keep in mind:

- Joseph's family had come to Egypt during a severe famine and settled in the land.
- About four hundred years have elapsed since the days of Joseph.
- The Israelites are now slaves oppressed by the Egyptian king who was probably Seti I (who ruled circa 1308-1290 B.C.). They endured hard labor to build cities for Pharaoh.
- Pharaoh was concerned that the Israelites had become so numerous that they would form political alliances with his enemies and help to overthrow him. Therefore, he ordered that all male Israelites be killed at birth.
- The midwives ignored this royal decree, so the king ordered anyone who saw a male Hebrew baby to throw the infant into the Nile.
- Moses was born in this environment but escaped death because his mother hid him in a basket and set him afloat in shallow waters.
- Pharaoh's daughter discovered Moses and rescued him. Unbeknown to her, she returned him to his own mother to be nursed until he was weaned.
- As an adult, Moses responded to the killing of a Hebrew slave by killing the Egyptian taskmaster who had taken the slave's life. His act was intentional for he had "looked this way and that" (2:12), but he thought no one had seen him.
- When he learned that two Hebrews had seen the crime, he fled to Midian, where he married Zipporah, daughter of a Midianite priest. They had two sons.
- Moses was engaged in his regular work of tending the sheep when God appeared to him.

Preparing Our Learning Space

Prior to class, set out a candle and be prepared to light it during the scripture reading if that is possible in your space. Have on hand:

- several Bibles
- candle and matches
- paper and pencils.

LEADING THE CLASS

(1) Introduction

Begin today's lesson with the three questions, listed below, that open the Focusing on the Main Question section. Be aware that people's responses to these questions may vary widely. Accept these diverse answers. Someone, for example, may say that God is in charge of all things, while another student will counter that if God knows and cares, then God should intervene to stop natural catastrophes, illness, and other causes of suffering. Allow for disagreement but don't get bogged down in it. By the end of the lesson students should be able to recognize that God is indeed concerned about—and involved with—humanity. Moreover, God calls us to be involved as well, just as Moses was called.

(1) Does God know what is going on in the world today?

(2) If God knows, does God care?

(3) If God knows and cares, does God become involved? Give reasons to defend your answer.

Conclude this discussion by lifting up today's main question: **How does God act in our world and include us in those activities?**

(2) Attention!

If possible, darken the room and light a candle to set the mood. Then read Exodus 3:1-6 and ask these questions:

(1) Would Moses have been expecting God to call him that day? Give reasons for your answer. (Note that in all likelihood, the idea of being called by God was the furthest thing from Moses' mind. He was going about his ordinary business as a shepherd, tending his father-in-law's flock, when God surprisingly came to him. Had Moses been seeking God, or had reason to believe that God was seeking him, he likely would have planned to be in a place that he knew was sacred.)

(2) Why might God have used a burning bush to get Moses' attention? (The unusualness of a bush burning without being consumed surely would have grabbed Moses' attention in ways that an ordinary event would not have.)

(3) How does Moses respond to God at this point? (Note that while he responds in verse 4 with "Here I am," he also hides his face in verse 6 because he is afraid to look at God.)

(4) Under what circumstances have you directed your wholehearted attention to God? (Here students might mention some crisis, such as the loss of a job, a divorce, the death of a loved one, or a serious illness of their own.)

(3) Who?

Direct the class to look again at verse 6. Note that this God who speaks to Moses is the same one who is the God of the patriarchs Abraham, Isaac, and Jacob.

Now ask the class to listen carefully for additional information they can glean about who God is as you read 3:7-15. Discuss their observations. Note that we now have some idea of who God is.

Next, notice that Moses also asks, "Who am I?" (3:11). Distribute paper and pencils. Ask each class member to write an imaginary dialogue between themselves and God that is focused on the question "Who am I that I should be involved in your affairs?" Some members may have specific concerns about work that they may feel God is calling them to do. Let this be a silent, confidential activity.

Finally, encourage the students to discuss the following questions with a partner or small team:

(1) What does God intend to do in response to the Israelites' cries? (God will liberate them from their oppressor and take them into the land that was promised to Abraham.)

(2) Do Moses' concerns about going to the Pharaoh and leading the Israelites out of Egypt seem reasonable to you, or is he just trying to set up an excuse for not getting involved? Explain reasons for your answer.

(3) Could God have liberated the Hebrew slaves without help from anyone? If so, why did God choose to work through Moses? (Point out, as found in the Interpreting the Scripture section, that God wants a relationship with Moses and with us as well. Thus, God invites Moses into a relationship that will allow him to get involved with the world and with God.)

(4) What to Do

If time permits, read aloud the rest of the background scripture through verse 22. Use the information in the Interpreting the Scripture portion to help the students understand what God wants Moses to do in order to bring about liberation. Be sure to point out that God offers Moses a realistic appraisal of the outcome: Pharaoh won't go along with God's plan and the Hebrew elders will be discouraged. However, in the long run the people will be liberated, just as God promised.

Provide a few moments of meditation time for students to ponder these questions.

(1) What is God calling me to do?

(2) How will I respond?

(3) If I believe that God wants me to respond in a certain way and I am not doing so, what barriers hold me back from responding as I would like to?

Close with a prayer that God will empower each class member to hear the divine voice and respond as Moses did, "Here I am."

Before dismissing the class, suggest at least one action below so that the students may put their faith into action this week.

HELPING CLASS MEMBERS ACT

Encourage students to identify one injustice and take at least one step toward helping to free people from it.

Suggest that class members consider their own identity before God by asking, as Moses did, "Who am I?" and also, "How can I become involved in the things that concern God?" Then urge them to take one action to become involved wherever God calls them.

Invite the students to write a journal entry about a time when they, like Moses, felt very inadequate. Suggest that they recall what this task or challenge was, any difficulties they had in discerning God's will in regard to this challenge, what resources they had to meet it, and how they may have surprised themselves by rising to the occasion.

PLANNING FOR NEXT SUNDAY

During next week's lesson, "Called to Deliverance," we will journey with the Israelites as they make their escape from Egypt and cross over the waters of the Red Sea that have miraculously parted. Invite the students to prepare for this lesson by reading Exodus 13:17–14:31.

CALLED TO DELIVERANCE

PREVIEWING THE LESSON

Lesson Scripture: Exodus 13:17-22; 14:26-31
Background Scripture: Exodus 13:17–14:31
Key Verse: Exodus 14:13

Focus of the Lesson:
God miraculously delivered the Israelites from bondage.

Main Question of the Lesson:
What role do miracles play in shaping the faith commitments of people, both those whose stories are recorded in the Bible and us today?

This lesson will enable adult learners to:
(1) hear the story of God's miraculous deliverance of the Israelites.
(2) enter into the anxiety felt by the Israelites as they fled from the Egyptians.
(3) respond by helping someone in the midst of a life transition.

Today's lesson may be outlined as follows:
(1) Introduction
(2) Marching Orders
(3) Second Thoughts
(4) God Acts, but Not Alone
(5) Is Everything Clear?

FOCUSING ON THE MAIN QUESTION

People are rarely neutral about miracles. Some say they are impossible and never happened, period. Others believe that every miraculous event in the Bible did happen exactly as narrated in the Scriptures and that God continues to perform similar acts today. A great number of people find themselves somewhere between those positions—entirely willing to believe that God acted in the past as the Bible declares, but not so sure that similar actions can be seen all around us now.

Would attitudes toward miracles necessarily have been any different for the Israelites of Moses' day? They certainly had experienced strange events in the weeks and months leading up to their escape from Egypt. All the water in the land turned to blood (Exodus 7:17-21); hordes of frogs had appeared, cavorting everywhere—including in people's beds (8:2-15); there had been a violent hailstorm that somehow spared the Israelites' portion of the land (9:18-34); and there was a deep darkness that lasted for three days (10:21-23).

Moses and Aaron said these plagues as well as all the others had come from God. Maybe Moses could do tricks, but did that necessarily mean that God had sent him? After all, Pharaoh's court magicians had been able to duplicate the first feats (7:11-12, 22). Even when there were plagues that Pharaoh's servants could not create (beginning with 8:18), was it possible that Moses was just a better magician? Or, even if God had been behind all the plagues, was there any assurance that God could rescue Israel from the whole Egyptian army? It is one thing to be safe at home during a storm. It is quite something else to find yourself caught between an advancing army and a body of water!

Questions of faith are not limited to those of us living long after Bible times. When Moses tells the people, "Do not be afraid" (14:13), he is speaking to folks as terrified as I am sure I would have been in their situation. We are not automatically weaker in faith if we ask questions about God's actions, both in the Bible and in our own lives. Today's lesson is an appropriate time to ponder the relationship between biblical miracles and our lives. This lesson prompts us to ask: **What role do miracles play in shaping the faith commitments of people, both those whose stories are recorded in the Bible and us today?**

READING THE SCRIPTURE

NRSV
Exodus 13:17-22

17 When Pharaoh let the people go, God did not lead them by way of the land of the Philistines, although that was nearer; for God thought, "If the people face war, they may change their minds and return to Egypt." 18 So God led the people by the roundabout way of the wilderness toward the Red Sea. The Israelites went up out of the land of Egypt prepared for battle. 19 And Moses took with him the bones of Joseph who had required a solemn oath of the Israelites, saying, "God will surely take notice of you, and then you must carry my bones with you from here." 20 They set out from Succoth, and camped at Etham, on the edge of the wilderness. 21 The LORD went in front of them in a pillar of cloud by day, to lead them along the way, and in a pillar of fire by night, to give them light, so that they might travel by day and by night. 22 Neither the pillar of cloud by day nor the pillar of fire by night left its place in front of the people.

NIV
Exodus 13:17-22

[17]When Pharaoh let the people go, God did not lead them on the road through the Philistine country, though that was shorter. For God said, "If they face war, they might change their minds and return to Egypt." [18]So God led the people around by the desert road toward the Red Sea. The Israelites went up out of Egypt armed for battle.

[19]Moses took the bones of Joseph with him because Joseph had made the sons of Israel swear an oath. He had said, "God will surely come to your aid, and then you must carry my bones up with you from this place."

[20]After leaving Succoth they camped at Etham on the edge of the desert. [21]By day the LORD went ahead of them in a pillar of cloud to guide them on their way and by night in a pillar of fire to give them light, so that they could travel by day or night. [22]Neither the pillar of cloud by day nor the pillar of fire by night left its place in front of the people.

Exodus 14:13, 26-31

13 But Moses said to the people, "Do not be afraid, stand firm, and see the deliverance that the LORD will accomplish for you today; for the Egyptians whom you see today you shall never see again."

26 Then the LORD said to Moses, "Stretch out your hand over the sea, so that the water may come back upon the Egyptians, upon their chariots and chariot drivers." 27 So Moses stretched out his hand over the sea, and at dawn the sea returned to its normal depth. As the Egyptians fled before it, the LORD tossed the Egyptians into the sea. 28 The waters returned and covered the chariots and the chariot drivers, the entire army of Pharaoh that had followed them into the sea; not one of them remained. 29 But the Israelites walked on dry ground through the sea, the waters forming a wall for them on their right and on their left.

30 Thus the LORD saved Israel that day from the Egyptians; and Israel saw the Egyptians dead on the seashore. 31 Israel saw the great work that the LORD did against the Egyptians. So the people feared the LORD and believed in the LORD and in his servant Moses.

Exodus 14:13, 26-31

13Moses answered the people, "Do not be afraid. Stand firm and you will see the deliverance the LORD will bring you today. The Egyptians you see today you will never see again."

26Then the LORD said to Moses, "Stretch out your hand over the sea so that the waters may flow back over the Egyptians and their chariots and horsemen." 27Moses stretched out his hand over the sea, and at daybreak the sea went back to its place. The Egyptians were fleeing toward it, and the LORD swept them into the sea. 28The water flowed back and covered the chariots and horsemen—the entire army of Pharaoh that had followed the Israelites into the sea. Not one of them survived.

29But the Israelites went through the sea on dry ground, with a wall of water on their right and on their left. 30That day the Lord saved Israel from the hands of the Egyptians, and Israel saw the Egyptians lying dead on the shore. 31And when the Israelites saw the great power the LORD displayed against the Egyptians, the people feared the LORD and put their trust in him and in Moses his servant.

UNDERSTANDING THE SCRIPTURE

Exodus 13:17-22. If your Bible has some maps, there is probably one that shows the route of the Exodus, the way the Israelites left Egypt and traveled to the promised land. If you look at such a map—and especially if you compare your map to others printed in other places—you will probably notice several things right away. First, the paths drawn on the maps will likely differ from each other in some places. Indeed, some place names may even be in different locations. Do not fret about these differences. We simply do not know today exactly where some places

were more than three thousand years ago.

A second thing you may notice is that however the route is drawn, it probably will not look like the shortest way to get from Egypt to the land of Canaan. This reflects what our text says. Out of concern for the people, lest they be faced with war with the Philistines and decide to go back to Egypt, God led them along a different, though longer, route.

Then there is the matter of the body of water the Israelites faced. Most of us remember it from childhood Sunday-school lessons as the "Red Sea." At Exodus

13:18, both the NRSV and the NIV have a footnote that gives an alternative reading, "Sea of Reeds." The Hebrew does actually say "Sea of Reeds," using the same word for "reed" here as when the infant Moses is in his little basket in the reeds at the edge of the Nile River (Exodus 2:3, 5). For some reason, the ancient Vulgate version of the Bible translated the crossing place into Latin as the "Red Sea" rather than the "Sea of Reeds."

Two companions for the entire journey, the pillar of fire and pillar of cloud, are introduced in verse 21. Fire and clouds are often used in the Bible as symbols of God's presence. (Remember the fire at the burning bush in last week's lesson, for instance.) To make sure that we do not miss the point, verse 21 says the Lord went with the Israelites in the cloud and fire, "to lead them along the way."

Exodus 14:1-14. God warns Moses that Pharaoh is going to have a change of heart and will send his army to try to recapture the fleeing Israelites. Sure enough, not only Pharaoh but also his high officials say, "What have we done? We have let the Israelites go and have lost their services!" (14:5 NIV). The army assembles and the chariots set out in hot pursuit. Naturally enough, when the Israelites see the Egyptians coming after them, they are afraid. In their great fear, they turn on Moses. "Why have you done this to us?" they wail. "Didn't we tell you to leave us alone so we could continue to serve Pharaoh? Don't you realize being a living slave is better than ending up as a dead runaway?"

Moses' response to their terror is striking. His answer has three parts. First, in verse 13 he tells them not to be afraid. Then he tells them what to do. Finally, he assures them that the Lord has already won the victory. These three parts happen together many times in the Bible. There is a word of calm assurance that the victory belongs to the Lord. Because of God's presence, fear is unnecessary. And there is something for the people to do. (There is a

very similar sequence when Israel takes the city of Jericho in Joshua 6 and again when Gideon and his little band defeat the Midianites in Judges 7:9-23.)

It is important to see the similarities of these events when they occur. God decides what the people are to do, not the people themselves. And the instructions are different every time. Consequently, the people must be willing to wait on the Lord and to follow directions, rather than trying to think up solutions on their own. Furthermore, the instructions God gives are well within the range of possibility for those being addressed, if they decide to obey. In the case of today's key verse, Exodus 14:13, the instruction is "Stand firm." That is, "Stop running around in a panic. Do not even try to fight. Let God take care of this battle while you watch calmly." The pattern is important, I believe. We are called to turn over to God those things that we cannot do for ourselves and at the same time to obey what God tells us to do.

Exodus 14:15-28. Then God instructs Moses to tell the Israelites to take up the march again. Moses is directed to raise his staff over the water, which will cause it to divide and create a path for the people to cross over. The text also tells us that "The LORD drove the sea back by a strong east wind all night" (14:21). Israel was able to cross on dry ground. But when the Egyptians pursued them into the sea, the chariots were bogged down. Did the chariot wheels "come off" as the NIV says, or were they "clogged" as the NRSV has it? Does it really matter? Isn't the greater point of Exodus 14:25a that the army was stopped in its tracks by the Lord's doing? When all Israel was on the other side Moses again stretched out his hand over the sea so that it came back to its normal depth, covering the entire Egyptian army.

Exodus 14:29-31. Israel traveled on dry ground between two walls of water, according to verse 29, and all Pharaoh's army and charioteers and horses were drowned. But then verse 30 says, "Israel saw the Egyptians dead on the seashore." How can that be? And if the east wind blew the water away from the Israelites, how could the water be standing up in two walls for them to pass between? Again, to draw a picture of the event is not the point, and at this great distance we cannot say *how* the escape happened. Even when Exodus was written down there clearly were different viewpoints about how the great event had taken place. The climax of the story, and what I believe is the point of it, comes in the final verse. By God's action, Israel escaped the Egyptian army. They had reverence for ("feared") the Lord and trusted both God and God's servant Moses.

INTERPRETING THE SCRIPTURE

Marching Orders

Sometimes God's ways seem unfair, or unduly hard on humans. Since God has all the power that has been demonstrated to Egypt in the plagues, why not just somehow pick up the people and plop them down in Canaan? Or if that is not possible, why not give them superhero weapons to zap the Philistines? Why make them go the long way around to avoid the Philistines?

"Why" questions are often the most interesting ones, but they are equally often impossible to answer. What we can see from these verses is that God can see more than we can. God can see dangers and potential dangers ahead of us well before we are aware of them. Because of our limited vision we cannot always recognize that God's plans are better than we think at the moment. There is nothing wrong with questioning God's "marching orders," but it is to our benefit to follow them even before we understand all their whys and wherefores.

God gives us marching orders but does not send us out on our own. That double sign of God's presence and protection— the pillar of cloud by day and pillar of fire by night—is a sign of the constancy of God's care. God doesn't keep office hours; God's presence may be experienced in different ways under different conditions.

And then there is that wonderful and curious notice about the bones of Joseph.

Those few words constitute a link with the past—not only with the past as long-ago events, but with the vibrancy of past faith. Joseph was so sure that the people would eventually return to Canaan that he said he wanted his bones to go back with them. How do the people honor that request made so long ago? They carry their history into their future. That is, they are not content to sit around the bones in Egypt, remembering the "good old days" when there were real heroes like Joseph, but they carry them along the journey toward the promised land.

It is not always easy to strike a healthy balance between future and past. Each one has the potential to hold the other hostage. I have worshiped in churches where the literal bones of literal ancestors, right outside the backdoor in the cemetery, hindered the congregation's faith and witness as so much time and money and energy was focused on the upkeep of those graves. On another hand, I also know of a congregation that came alive in the Lord as they discovered some ancient graves in a nearby grove and pitched in together to clean up the area. The fellowship they found as they worked together on that project was then channeled into other mission efforts. Bones in and of themselves are neutral, as is both the past and the future. What counts is what we do with them—how we respond to them in the light of how our Lord is calling us.

Second Thoughts

Poor, short-sighted Pharaoh. He cannot even remember back to Exodus 12:31-32 when he was desperate to get rid of Israel. As soon as the crisis has passed, he is ready to go back to his old ways. During a plague, he will say whatever he thinks Moses wants to hear; as soon as the plague is gone, he reneges on whatever he had promised. Even the death of his first-born son is not enough to break the cycle. We should not be too hard on Pharaoh alone, of course. His officials, who had also lost firstborn sons on the Passover night, were equally eager to recapture their slaves.

Nor should we be too hard on Egyptians alone. Once they were out of Egypt and then when they felt themselves in grave danger, the Israelites were also eager to go back to the old ways. Freedom can be hard work. Being responsible adult human beings is hard work. Sometimes I think I would rather go back to childhood, when my parents took care of me and made all the major decisions for my life. All by ourselves we are weak. We too need to hear Moses' words: "Do not be afraid, stand firm, and see the deliverance that the LORD will accomplish" (14:13).

God Acts, but Not Alone

All right. Let's take the situation of the last paragraph a little farther. When it is difficult to act responsibly, can I just turn everything over to God? Well, yes and no. Look how God rescues Israel in this case. The people have to "stand firm." Then Moses has to raise his hand over the water and the people have to start marching forward. There is a Midrash (an ancient Jewish story) about this episode that, in question and answer form, asks when was the moment God parted the waters.

Was it when the Israelites got their toes wet? No, they had to keep walking.
Was it when their ankles were wet? No,

they had to keep walking.
Was it when their knees were wet? No, they had to keep walking.
Was it when the water was up to their waists? No, they had to keep walking.
Was it when they were shoulder-deep in the water? No, they had to keep walking.
Was it when they were neck-deep or chin-deep in the water? No, they had to keep walking.
When was it that God parted the waters? Only when Israel was walking on tiptoe with the water up to their noses.

There is a kind of cooperation God requests of the people in the Bible and, I think, of people today. God also used the strong east wind in saving Israel, not just a miracle of Moses' hand. God is neither a mechanical force nor a despotic ruler. We cannot automatically *make* God act on our behalf, nor does God count up our good deeds and only after we have enough come to our aid. Deliverance comes, I believe, when we go ahead and do what we believe God wants us to do, even if we cannot see the end from the beginning. We trust that the Lord will come to do the parts we cannot do.

Is Everything Clear?

Rarely does the Bible present a straightforward, plain "miracle." There are always alternative explanations possible or multiple descriptions given that cannot be made to agree with each other. Israel has been called to freedom and to trust in the Lord. Having been delivered from Egypt in a way that we can neither describe in its entirety nor duplicate, they now believe in the Lord and in the divinely called servant Moses. This result is more important than the manner in which it happened. Is this explanation a "cop-out" on my part? Perhaps. But just maybe one sort of bondage we who live in the industrial and scientific twentieth century need to break as we move into the twenty-first century is the necessity of understanding everything, of explaining everything, before we will trust it and live by it. God will not force us to believe or compel us to trust. God does, however, continue to invite our belief and our trust.

SHARING THE SCRIPTURE

PREPARING TO TEACH

Preparing Our Hearts

Prepare your heart to teach today's lesson by reading the devotional scripture from Psalm 106:1-12. As you ponder the great deeds of God in saving the Israelites from the Egyptians, meditate on reasons that you have to give thanks and praise to God. Have you had any "Red Sea experiences" in your own life, situations in which God has acted to deliver you from seemingly hope-less circumstances? What happened? How did you know that God was present with you? Offer a prayer of praise and thanks for God's saving activity in your own life.

Now read today's background scripture from Exodus 13:17–14:31. Try to imagine yourself as one of the fleeing Israelites. How would you have felt about leaving Egypt? What worries or concerns might you have had? What hopes would have been in your heart? Think about your own understanding of this story and what it says to you about God's willingness and ability to free people from that which oppresses them.

Preparing Our Minds

Read today's lesson and look again at the scripture, focusing this time on Exodus 13:17-22; 14:26-31; and the key verse, 14:13. If you have access to *Bible Teacher Kit* (available from Cokesbury), you may want to read the article "Life in Egypt" (pp. 15-18) for additional background. You may also want to consult commentaries for more information about this critical period in the history of the Hebrew people.

As you prepare to teach today's lesson, remember that class members' perceptions of the crossing of the Red Sea may range from complete acceptance of the biblical story to total skepticism that such an event could have ever occurred. Do not let the class get bogged down in a scientific analysis of the events. Instead, try to focus on the fact that, whether or not the events happened exactly as the Bible says, what is important here is that the Israelites under-stood that God was responsible for deliv-ering them from the Egyptians. This belief was crucial in shaping their faith commit-ments to God.

Preparing Our Learning Space

If possible, have a map that shows Egypt and Canaan at the time of the Exodus. *Bible Teacher Kit* includes a reproducible map (p. 137) that shows the traditional route and alternate routes of the Exodus.
Have on hand:
- several Bibles
- optional hymnals
- optional map.

LEADING THE CLASS

(1) Introduction

Begin the session by singing a familiar spiritual, "Go Down, Moses" (*The United Methodist Hymnal*, no. 448). Before class, select the verses you will use, but be sure to include verses 5 and 6, which refer to the parting of the Red Sea. If singing is not possible in your space, ask the class to read the verses responsively and the cho-rus in unison.

Next, read or retell the first three paragraphs in the Focusing on the Main Question section. Ask the class these questions:

[?]

(1) **What questions would you have raised had you been one of the Israelites?**

(2) **How do you feel when you move from a familiar situation to one that is completely unknown, maybe even from one home to another?**

(3) **What is your attitude when you read about a miracle in the Bible or when someone credits God with a miraculous deliverance, perhaps from critical illness or accident or natural catastrophe?**

Close this part of the lesson by lifting up today's main question: **What role do miracles play in shaping the faith commitments of people, both those whose stories are recorded in the Bible and us today?**

(2) Marching Orders

Move into the lesson by showing the group a map of Egypt and Canaan at the time of the Exodus. Make these points in a brief lecture:

- Place names have changed since the time of the Exodus, making it impossible to trace the route with accuracy. Hence, different maps may show different routes.
- The route of the Exodus definitely was not the shortest one possible. According to Exodus 13:17, God led the Israelites the long way around so that they would not have to encounter the fearsome Philistines.
- In Hebrew, the body of water that we traditionally call the Red Sea is actually the "Sea of Reeds."

Choose a volunteer to read Exodus 13:17-22. Also read aloud "Marching Orders" from the Interpreting the Scripture section. Then ask:

[?]

(1) **How do you carry your past into the future?**

(2) **God led the Israelites as a pillar of cloud**

and a pillar of fire. How do you experience God's protection and leading?

[?]

(3) Second Thoughts

Briefly retell the story from the background scripture in Exodus 14:1-25. Make these points:

- God directed Moses to lead the people in such a way that Pharaoh would think they were wandering aimlessly.
- Once the Israelites were gone, Pharaoh changed his mind and sent his army in pursuit.
- The Israelites began to complain, telling Moses that they would have preferred to remain in Egypt.
- Moses reassured the people: "Do not be afraid, stand firm, and see the deliverance that the LORD will accomplish for you today; for the Egyptians whom you see today you shall never see again" (14:13, key verse).
- As the Israelites moved forward, God's presence illuminated their path.
- During the night, as Moses stood with his hand outstretched, God parted the waters of the sea.
- With their chariot wheels clogging in the mud of the sea, the Egyptians wanted to flee because they realized that God was fighting for Israel.

(4) God Acts, but Not Alone

Select a volunteer to read aloud the exciting conclusion of this story, found in Exodus 14:26-31. Ask:

[?]

(1) **Had you been an Israelite, what would you have thought about God?**

(2) **What would you have thought about Moses?**

(3) **What would you have thought about God had you been an Egyptian?**

(4) **What does this story say to you as a Christian about how God works through humans to accomplish divine purposes?**

(5) **What troubles or puzzles you about this story?**

(5) Is Everything Clear?

Read the paragraph under this heading in the Interpreting the Scripture portion. Emphasize this observation: "But just maybe one sort of bondage we who live in the industrial and scientific twentieth century need to break as we move into the twenty-first century is the necessity of understanding everything, of explaining everything, before we will trust it and live by it. God will not force us to believe or compel us to trust. God does continue to invite our belief and our trust." Then ask:

(1) What tensions do you personally experience between our culturally instilled need to understand and explain things and our faith-based need to trust and believe?

(2) Have you known of or experienced anything that you would term a miracle? If so, state what happened and why you believe it was a miracle.

Close this portion of the lesson by lifting up a prayer that all might believe that God has the power and desire to deliver us from bondage if we will but call upon the name of the Lord.

Before dismissing the class, lift up at least one activity below so that students will have some ideas for putting what they have learned today into practice.

HELPING CLASS MEMBERS ACT

Invite students to seek God's guidance through prayer, meditation, and journaling about a situation in which they feel trapped. Ask them to recall how God led the Israelites out of circumstances that appeared hopeless and relate that victory to their own situation.

Suggest that members offer support to someone who is facing a life transition, perhaps moving from their own home to a retirement community.

Encourage students to be aware of people they feel are inspirational leaders. What characteristics do these leaders possess? How can class members be more like them?

PLANNING FOR NEXT SUNDAY

Next week's lesson will focus on God's covenant with the people. To prepare for this session, ask the students to read Exodus 19:3-6; 20:2-4, 7-8, 12-17; or, if possible, the entire background scripture from Exodus 19:1–20:21.

CALLED TO COVENANT

PREVIEWING THE LESSON

Lesson Scripture: Exodus 19:3-6; 20:2-4, 7-8, 12-17
Background Scripture: Exodus 19:1–20:21
Key Verse: Exodus 19:5

Focus of the Lesson:
In the covenant given at Sinai, the people were called to give their full allegiance to God and to live righteously with one another.

Main Question of the Lesson:
How is it possible to give our full allegiance to God and to live righteously with one another?

This lesson will enable adult learners to:
(1) examine God's covenant with the people given at Sinai.
(2) consider how God calls them into a covenant relationship.
(3) respond by making a commitment to serve God in a specific way.

Today's lesson may be outlined as follows:
(1) Introduction
(2) Enthusiasm of the Moment
(3) Take Care and Prepare
(4) God's Words
(5) Too Much of a Good Thing?

FOCUSING ON THE MAIN QUESTION

Human communities tend to draw together during times of crisis. As the rivers rise, strangers work as one to fill and deploy sandbags. When a toddler wanders away from a picnic into the woods, strangers abandon their own leisure activities in order to search for the child. Such cooperation is not limited to short-term emergencies. Many people who are reading this lesson can remember World War II and how people on the home front as well as the soldiers in combat all did their part for the war effort—an effort that spread over several years.

Eventually the crisis passes. The water recedes; the child is found; peace treaties

---

are signed. And, usually, most people go back to lives very similar to what they were before the emergency. Sometimes, though, they will remember the crisis almost wistfully. "We were really *alive* in those days." "We all felt like *family*." "Why can't it be like that more often?" Is there, indeed, some way we could live with that sense of unity, that genuine cooperation, which an emergency situation frequently brings forth in a community? Isn't that sense of common purpose, of shared labor to a good end, what we want in our lives?

The Israelites have gone from the sorrow of generations of slavery to the excitement and anger of God's rescuing them from Pharaoh's army. They have thought themselves without drinkable water (Exodus 15:22-25). They have thought they were going to starve out in the wilderness, but have seen God's provision of daily manna (16:12-35). It has been about three months since their daring escape, and they have arrived at Mount Sinai. After suitable preparations, God through Moses is going to offer them a special agreement, a covenant. It is offered as a gift from God, precisely to try to keep that spirit of cooperation alive by spelling out the ways Israelites are to live in relationship to God and to each other. God asks only for their allegiance as their part of this covenant.

Realistically, though, aren't we sinful human beings? Aren't we going, inevitably, to sin, both against God and against each other? Yes, given life in this world as we know it, we all sin. We cannot automatically lead righteous lives with our full allegiance to the one true God. It is for this very reason that God gives the people the commandments at Sinai. The law is a gift from our gracious God to show us how to live, to enable us to live as is best for us and for our world. Still, given what we see around us and what we know in our own hearts, the question is inescapable: **How is it possible to give our full allegiance to God and to live righteously with one another?**

READING THE SCRIPTURE

NRSV

Exodus 19:3-6

3 Then Moses went up to God; the LORD called to him from the mountain, saying, "Thus you shall say to the house of Jacob, and tell the Israelites: 4 You have seen what I did to the Egyptians, and how I bore you on eagles' wings and brought you to myself. **5 Now therefore, if you obey my voice and keep my covenant, you shall be** Key Verse **my treasured possession out of all the peoples.** Indeed, the whole earth is mine, 6 but you shall be for me a priestly kingdom and a holy nation. These are the words that you shall speak to the Israelites."

Exodus 20:2-4, 7-8, 12-17

2 I am the LORD your God, who brought

NIV

Exodus 19:3-6

³Then Moses went up to God, and the LORD called to him from the mountain and said, "This is what you are to say to the house of Jacob and what you are to tell the people of Israel: ⁴'You yourselves have seen what I did to Egypt, and how I carried you on eagles' wings and brought you to myself. ⁵**Now if you obey me fully and keep my covenant, then out of all** Key Verse **nations you will be my treasured possession.** Although the whole earth is mine, ⁶you will be for me a kingdom of priests and a holy nation.' These are the words you are to speak to the Israelites."

Exodus 20:2-4, 7-8, 12-17

²"I am the LORD your God, who brought

you out of the land of Egypt, out of the house of slavery; 3 you shall have no other gods before me.

4 You shall not make for yourself an idol, whether in the form of anything that is in heaven above, or that is on the earth beneath, or that is in the water under the earth.

7 You shall not make wrongful use of the name of the LORD your God, for the LORD will not acquit anyone who misuses his name.

8 Remember the sabbath day, and keep it holy.

12 Honor your father and your mother, so that your days may be long in the land that the LORD your God is giving you.

13 You shall not murder.

14 You shall not commit adultery.

15 You shall not steal.

16 You shall not bear false witness against your neighbor.

17 You shall not covet your neighbor's house; you shall not covet your neighbor's wife, or male or female slave, or ox, or donkey, or anything that belongs to your neighbor.

you out of Egypt, out of the land of slavery.

³"You shall have no other gods before me.

⁴"You shall not make for yourself an idol in the form of anything in heaven above or on the earth beneath or in the waters below.

⁷"You shall not misuse the name of the LORD your God, for the LORD will not hold anyone guiltless who misuses his name.

⁸"Remember the Sabbath day by keeping it holy.

¹²"Honor your father and your mother, so that you may live long in the land the LORD your God is giving you.

¹³"You shall not murder.

¹⁴"You shall not commit adultery.

¹⁵"You shall not steal.

¹⁶"You shall not give false testimony against your neighbor.

¹⁷"You shall not covet your neighbor's house. You shall not covet your neighbor's wife, or his manservant or maidservant, his ox or donkey, or anything that belongs to your neighbor."

UNDERSTANDING THE SCRIPTURE

Exodus 19:1-9. Three months—"the third new moon"—after their miraculous escape from Pharaoh's army and from their lives of slavery in Egypt, the Israelites arrive at the foot of Mount Sinai. They stop traveling for the time being and set up camp there at the bottom of the mountain. Moses goes up to speak with God and the Lord gives him a message for all Israel. In Exodus 19:4, God begins by reminding them what they have just experienced: they are free from Egypt. In the next verse, God offers them a continuation of their special relationship. But this offer is conditional as seen in the "if ... then ..." form of verse 5 (NIV): "If you obey ... then ... you will be my treasured

possession." At the same time God is offering this special relationship, however, the Israelites are reminded that "the whole earth is mine." That is, God will still be God of other people, whether or not they acknowledge the Lord—whether or not they even know the Lord.

In verse 6, God spells out a little more what being a "treasured possession" will mean. Israel will be a "kingdom of priests and a holy nation" (NIV). Does this mean that all of them are supposed to be ordained? Not at all. Does being a holy nation mean they will never sin? Hardly. God is saying that as an individual priest functions within the community, so the nation of Israel is to function among all the nations of the world, all of which belong to God. What does the individual priest do within the community? In this early time in Israel's life, the priest was an intermediary, functioning as a channel of communication between God and the people and also as one who made available God's blessings to the community as a whole. This is how Israel is to function among the nations—as a channel of God's blessings and as a source of God's word. This is not a new role, but another spelling out of the third portion of the ancient covenant God made with Abraham in Genesis 12:3: "In you all the families of the earth shall be blessed."

When Moses returned to the people and told them what God had said, they responded enthusiastically: "We will do everything the LORD has said" (19:8 NIV). Moses dutifully reported this to God, who then promised to come and speak so that *everyone* could hear.

Exodus 19:10-25. God gives Moses instructions to carry to the people for their preparations. Some of these directions may seem odd. What difference does the state of their clothing make—for example, that they should have to wash their clothes? It certainly wasn't easy for them to do laundry. And why should the people and their animals have to be so careful about not even touching the mountain? Whether they understood or not, the people prepared as they had been told.

On the third day, as promised, God came to the top of the mountain. The description of the sights and sounds, of thick clouds and lightning and fire, of rams' horns or trumpets has sometimes been taken to mean that the mountain was a volcano and what the people thought was God's presence was "really" just the eruption of a volcano. Remember, however, that fire and cloud are used in many places in the Bible as symbols of God's presence. God's leading for the three months between Egypt and Sinai has been symbolized by the pillar of cloud by day and the pillar of fire by night. So it would actually be surprising if suddenly God used some other symbols of presence with the people. God has used cloud and fire before (for example, Genesis 15:17 and Exodus 3:2), and God will use cloud and fire many other times. Maybe the mountain was a volcano. Maybe that is one of the reasons God is so strict that the people not climb up it, lest they be injured. The point is not *how* God spoke to Israel, but rather *that* God spoke.

Exodus 20:1-17. God begins the core of the law with a self-introduction, reminding the people of the grace they themselves have experienced. Exodus 20:2 says two things: the God speaking to them is not some new God, and this God has already done things for them that they could not do for themselves. Because of this, God demands exclusive loyalty. Verses 3-6 do not present a case for monotheism but are much more practical in a world where many cultures believe in many gods. Regardless of what other people may do, this commandment says, *you* are to worship only one God.

One word in verse 5 is troublesome, in that it is usually translated "jealous": "for I the LORD your God am a jealous God." The difficulty here can be traced to changes in the English language. A few hundred years ago, "jealous" and "zealous" were used nearly interchangeably in English, and both are used to translate the particular Hebrew word here. "Jealous" and "zealous" no longer mean the same thing, and we would do better to use "zealous" in Exodus 20:5 as it is used in many other places in our standard translations. (See, for example, Numbers 25:13; 2 Kings 19:31; Isaiah 9:7; 37:32.) God is zealous; God cares passionately about things, including whether or not we live according to the covenant.

Verses 8-11 concern the Sabbath and the weekly day of rest and refreshment. Note carefully that it is a commandment and gift to everyone. Adults and children, masters and slaves, natives and strangers—even animals—are all included.

We might paraphrase Exodus 20:12 as, "Honor your parents so that you will have a long life." What is the connection between honor and long life? Does it mean that people who are nice to their parents will be rewarded by God? Probably not in such a simplistic way. Rather, the word translated "honor" means, at its root, "make heavy." Perhaps—and I will readily admit this is conjecture on my part—what this commandment is getting at is that elderly parents are to be fed ("made heavy") even when they can no longer contribute to the economic well-being of the family unit. What would this have to do with the children's long life? Just this: If I continue to take care of my parents in their old age, my children will learn from my example and will take care of me when I become too feeble to do any work, thus lengthening my life. Remember also that the Israelites did not live in isolated "nuclear families" but in extended families of three and even four generations.

The next three verses are short, even stark, being only two words each in Hebrew: Don't kill. Don't commit adultery. Don't steal. Exodus 20:16 is only slightly longer: Don't answer with falsehood. This terminology is from the legal system and has two sides. Not only are we not supposed to lie about someone but also when we know something to someone's credit we are not to keep it secret.

Finally, we are not to "covet." Coveting also has two sides. It means to want what someone else has *and* to want that person not to have it. To say, "Gee, I wish I had a car like yours" is not coveting. To say, "Gee, I wish I had *your* car and you had none" is what this commandment is about.

Exodus 20:18-21. How do the Israelites react to all this? They are obviously terrified. The Hebrew wording makes it clear they have just experienced something quite out of the ordinary. The King James Version captures this sense by beginning verse 18 with "And all the people saw the thunderings," but most modern translations try to tame it into something that sounds more reasonable, such as "all the people witnessed the thunder." Although the impulse to make the Bible understandable is a good one, I think we need to pause at places such as this and realize that some things are simply beyond our understanding.

The people are so afraid that they plead with Moses to be their intermediary. They promise to listen to him if only they do not have to hear God directly again. God and Moses are both willing to go to "Plan B," as it were, on account of Israel's fear. We need to remember, though, that at first God spoke to everyone, not just to their leader, and that the arrangement was changed at the request of the people.

INTERPRETING THE SCRIPTURE

Enthusiasm of the Moment

God is always clear that grace comes before law. God freed Israel from Egypt before giving them the law. Then God offers to continue the relationship but does not make the people agree. At first the people are enthusiastic and they say,

almost without thinking, "Yes, yes, yes. We agree to everything." This can be similar to an individual's enthusiasm after a personal encounter with the Lord. Everything seems possible; everything is agreed to immediately. Then when disappointment comes—and in this fallen world, disappointment is almost inevitable—the individual may be crushed, may feel cheated or defeated.

Take Care and Prepare

The three days of preparation that God prescribes are, in part, a time for the people to consider what they are about to do. God is gracious and God's covenant is wonderful beyond anything we could imagine on our own. But God does not want to coerce us or rush us into making a commitment we really do not mean to live up to. God knows us so much better than we know ourselves.

The covenant is serious; those who enter into it are bound by its stipulations. But God never threatens. God doesn't say to Israel, "Agree to this covenant or I'll abandon you here in the wilderness," nor "Abide by this covenant or I'll send you back to Egypt." God does not say to us, "Abide by the covenant or I'll make bad things happen to you," nor "If you do enter into the covenant, only good things will happen." The Lord wants us to live righteously, that is, in right relationships, and offers us the means to do so. But the decision is always left to us.

God's Words

The Ten Commandments are well known, of course. But can anyone live only by them? I ask this question not just because we are sinners who cannot perfectly uphold the commandments, but rather because they do not seem to cover every situation. Indeed, they are not specific enough for the daily decisions of human life. We may make a comparison with the Constitution of the United States. The Constitution is the basic foundation of our laws, but it is certainly not our only law. Congress, state legislatures, county commissioners, local school boards, and many other governmental bodies have added tens of thousands of specific bits of legislation to cover specific situations. But

if any law is found by the court system to contradict the Constitution, it is null and void. We might consider the Ten Commandments to be Israel's "Constitution." There are hundreds of other laws in the Bible, because life is lived in particular situations, not "in general," but none of the additional laws contradict the basic commandments.

How can we give our allegiance to God alone? How can we live righteously? In one sense, we need keep only the first and tenth commandments, for if we have only one God and if we do not want anything at the expense of our neighbor, then it follows we will not make and worship idols, we will not steal or kill or do any of the other things the commandments enumerate. So ten commandments are more than we need. On the other hand, ten are far from enough. What does the Bible know of traffic laws and stock markets, of genetic engineering and mass media entertainment? The Bible itself has many more laws, some of which we will look at in other lessons this quarter. Many of them apply only in some situations. For example, only people who own cultivated fields are required to leave the corners and edges unharvested and allow the poor to glean. But all of us who choose to enter into covenant with God are called to see how the laws fit our own situations. I own no real estate, but do I have other things I should share? Unquestionably!

Too Much of a Good Thing?

The people who were so enthusiastic in Exodus 19:8 changed their tune when they actually heard God speaking to them. And God, ever gracious, is willing to communicate with them by way of Moses. What of us? When we pray the Lord's Prayer and say, "Thy kingdom come, Thy will be done on earth...," how soon do we really want it to happen? The good news is that the day will come when God's will is done on earth as it is done in heaven. The good news is also that God works with us, remembering our frailties, pushing and nudging and coaxing us forth into the future, but neither crushing us nor abandoning us if we cannot keep up a particular pace. We need not be afraid.

SHARING THE SCRIPTURE

PREPARING TO TEACH

Preparing Our Hearts

Start your preparations by reading Deuteronomy 4:32-40. Here Moses reminds the people of how God spoke to them from Mount Sinai. This remarkable event prompted the people to acknowledge that the Lord is God. What events in your own experience have led you to recognize that God is the Lord of your life?

Now read the complete background scripture from Exodus 19:1–20:21. Here you will see the event about which Moses spoke in Deuteronomy 4:32-40. Try to imagine yourself as the Israelites. What would you have thought about God? Why would you have been willing (or unwilling) to obey Moses?

Now look especially at today's key verse, Exodus 19:5. How well do you obey God's voice? Is God the first priority in your life? What signs do you have that you are indeed God's "treasured possession"?

Preparing Our Minds

Look again at the scripture, focusing this time on 19:3-6; 20:2-4, 7-8, and 12-17. Be sure to read all of this lesson, especially the Understanding the Scripture section.

Note that in today's lesson you are reading an account of a theophany, which is a visible appearance of God. Just as God appeared and spoke to Moses out of the burning bush (see Exodus 3:1-12 from the lesson for September 5), God also continues to speak with Moses. In addition, God delivers the Ten Commandments to the people without using Moses as an intermediary. Notice in Exodus 20:1 that "God spoke all these words." While Moses gives directions from God to the people concerning appropriate preparations, God comes "in person" to speak the covenant. Signs of God's presence—such as thunder, lightning, and smoke—are recorded as well (20:18). God's presence frightens the people so much that they ask Moses to be the covenant mediator so that they do not need to hear directly from God.

Preparing Our Learning Space

Have on hand:
- several Bibles
- hymnals
- paper and pencils
- optional list of Ten Commandments as suggested under Helping Class Members Act.

LEADING THE CLASS

(1) Introduction

During this session the class will examine the covenant that God made with the Israelites while they were being led through the desert by Moses. The heart of this Mosaic covenant is the Ten Commandments. Read or retell the third and fourth paragraphs under Focusing on the Main Question.

Then ask the class to read aloud Psalm 19, which is a hymn to God who is the Creator and the giver of the law. If you have access to *The United Methodist Hymnal*, you'll find Psalm 19 as a responsive reading on page 750. After the reading provide a few moments of silence for the class to ponder what God's covenant and law mean in their lives.

Close this segment by lifting up the main question: **How is it possible to give our full allegiance to God and to live righteously with one another?**

(2) Enthusiasm of the Moment

Choose a volunteer to read Exodus 19:3-6. Point out that the people answer enthusiastically in verse 8 that they will do everything that God has said. Ask these questions:

(1) **Which comes first, God's grace or God's law?** (Note that in verse 4 Moses is to remind the people that God first saved them from the Egyptians. Now God offers to continue that relationship by making a covenant.)

(2) **What does God offer to the people?** (They are to be God's treasured possession.)

(3) **What are the conditions of this offer?** (They must obey God and keep the commandments.)

(4) **What does this passage tell you about who God is?**

(5) **What does this passage tell you about how God views the Israelites?**

(3) Take Care and Prepare

If you have time, read the dramatic scene in the background scripture from Exodus 19:7-25. Encourage the class to imagine themselves on the mountain with the Israelites. Ask them to close their eyes as you read and to imagine the sights, sounds, and smells that are recorded here. You may want to discuss the students' perceptions.

If time permits, use information from both the Understanding the Scripture and the Interpreting the Scripture sections. Emphasize that God commands the people to prepare, in part, so that they have time to consider what they are being asked

to do and decide whether or not they really want to enter into a covenant with God.

(4) God's Words

Ask someone to read the Ten Commandments from Exodus 20:2-4, 7-8, and 12-17. Include the intervening verses (5-6 and 9-11) if time permits. Ask the following questions. Use information from the Interpreting the Scripture portion to augment the discussion as needed.

(1) **How do the Ten Commandments help you to live daily as a faithful Christian?**

(2) **What guidelines do you use in applying these commandments when they do not specifically address a difficult moral or ethical dilemma (such as surrogate motherhood or cloning or legalized gambling) that you as a Christian may want to take a stand on?**

(3) **God said, "You shall have no other gods before me" (20:3), and yet we often find ourselves in situations where conflicting voices and influences hinder us from making God our first priority. What other "gods" compete for your allegiance? How do you keep these "gods" at bay?**

(5) Too Much of a Good Thing?

We want to know how to live and yet the commandments seem so impossible to follow. They're almost too much of a good thing. What if I can't measure up to God's expectations? This excerpt from Exodus reminds us that God is a gracious lawgiver who will help us. God is not waiting like a crouching tiger to attack at the first hint of failure to obey. But God does want us to obey, for if we do we are God's "treasured possession" (19:5).

Distribute paper and pencils. Ask the students to open their Bibles to Exodus 20. Make sure that everyone has, or at least can see, a Bible. Then direct the class members to choose one or more commandments that challenge them personally. For example, someone may have committed (or been tempted to commit) adultery, or stolen, or given false testimony. Suggest that they write about why this commandment seems so difficult to obey and how God empowers them to uphold the covenant. If you choose this option, tell the students that they will not be asked to discuss their ideas with anyone. Those who prefer not to write can simply meditate.

As an alternative, students may want to write about a commandment that raises questions for them. For example, what does it mean to say "you shall not murder" (or "kill," KJV) (20:13) when the Bible also speaks of stoning people as punishment for certain crimes and condones war? If time permits, allow class members to talk about what they have written with a partner or small group.

Close this section with a prayer asking for God to help us to first understand the limits that the covenant sets before us, second, to live within them, and third, to continue to focus on what God would have us to do.

Suggest at least one of the activities below so that students will have an opportunity to put into practice what they have learned.

HELPING CLASS MEMBERS ACT

Encourage class members to consider their priorities this week. Do they really have no other gods? Is their relationship with God their first priority, or is God relegated to leftover time and space in their lives? One way to determine their priorities is to keep a log of how they spend their time and then review their entries. Did they really spend their time and energy on what they professed was important to them? Suggest that each person pray and meditate on this issue and, if need be, make necessary changes.

Recommend that students be especially alert for God's voice this week. They may want to keep a journal record of ways in which God spoke to them and how they responded. Make clear that most of us certainly do not hear God on a smoking mountain but instead must be alert for subtle ways that God comes to us.

Challenge class members to memorize the Ten Commandments as found in Exodus 20:2-4, 7-8, and 12-17. Or here is an alternative, perhaps easier to remember, list that you may want to post on newsprint or make available as a handout:

- I am the eternal, your God.
- Do not make idols.
- Do not blaspheme.
- Sanctify the Sabbath.
- Honor your father and mother.
- Do not kill.
- Do not commit adultery.
- Do not steal.
- Do not lie.
- Do not envy your neighbor.

PLANNING FOR NEXT SUNDAY

Ask the students to prepare for next week's lesson, "Called to Obedience," by reading the background scripture from Exodus 40:1-33 (especially verses 1-9) and Leviticus 26 (especially verses 2-6 and 11-13).

CALLED TO OBEDIENCE

PREVIEWING THE LESSON

Lesson Scripture: Exodus 40:1-9; Leviticus 26:2-6, 11-13

Background Scripture: Exodus 40:1-33; Leviticus 26

Key Verse: Leviticus 26:2

Focus of the Lesson:
God promised blessings to those who remained faithful and obedient to the covenant.

Main Question of the Lesson:
Is religious life truly a matter of grace, or is it primarily a matter of obeying rules?

This lesson will enable adult learners to:
(1) hear the blessings God promises to those who are faithful.
(2) consider their own willingness to be obedient to God.
(3) respond by acting in accord with Jesus' call on their lives to be obedient to him.

Today's lesson may be outlined as follows:
(1) Introduction
(2) More Instructions Given and Carried Out
(3) The "Carrot"
(4) The "Stick"
(5) The Outcome

FOCUSING ON THE MAIN QUESTION

The issues of this lesson are among the most important of any we might study. Last week we looked at the Ten Commandments and emphasized that the law is the gift of a gracious God who wants the very best for all people. In today's readings, God promises blessings to those who obey and grave punishments to any who refuse to obey. These promises prompt us to ask today's main question: **Is religious life truly a matter of grace, or is it primarily a matter of obeying rules?** Moreover, we wonder if faithful obedience to the covenant results in blessings and punishments immediately, or if God saves up the rewards and punishments and doles them out after death, in either heaven or hell.

If we do not think about these ideas very carefully, we can end up with the picture of a deity as a cosmic bookkeeper, keeping meticulous track of each individual's good and bad deeds and sending blessings and curses to match the obedience tally. In reaction to such a rigid, even mechanical, view, some people tend to go to another extreme. For some, God is an indulgent figure, like a beloved grandmother who relaxes the parents' rules and "spoils" her grandchildren whenever they come to visit her.

When we consider God's relation to us and our level of obedience, the picture is even more complicated than these two extremes and all the positions between them. Can God be both just and fair at the same time? If I have worked hard all week and been faithful to God, but my neighbor has been terrible, how will God decide whether or not to make Saturday a clear, sunny day? I deserve good weather for my picnic, but my neighbor deserves a hailstorm (at the very least!).

READING THE SCRIPTURE

NRSV
Exodus 40:1-9

1 The LORD spoke to Moses: 2 On the first day of the first month you shall set up the tabernacle of the tent of meeting. 3 You shall put in it the ark of the covenant, and you shall screen the ark with the curtain. 4 You shall bring in the table, and arrange its setting; and you shall bring in the lampstand, and set up its lamps. 5 You shall put the golden altar for incense before the ark of the covenant, and set up the screen for the entrance of the tabernacle. 6 You shall set the altar of burnt offering before the entrance of the tabernacle of the tent of meeting, 7 and place the basin between the tent of meeting and the altar, and put water in it. 8 You shall set up the court all around, and hang up the screen for the gate of the court. 9 Then you shall take the anointing oil, and anoint the tabernacle and all that is in it, and consecrate it and all its furniture, so that it shall become holy.

Leviticus 26:2-6, 11-13

2 You shall keep my sabbaths and reverence my sanctuary: I am the LORD.

3 If you follow my statutes and keep my commandments and observe them faithfully, 4 I will give you your rains in their season, and the land shall yield its produce,

NIV
Exodus 40:1-9

[1]Then the LORD said to Moses: [2]"Set up the tabernacle, the Tent of Meeting, on the first day of the first month. [3]Place the ark of the Testimony in it and shield the ark with the curtain. [4]Bring in the table and set out what belongs on it. Then bring in the lampstand and set up its lamps. [5]Place the gold altar of incense in front of the ark of the Testimony and put the curtain at the entrance to the tabernacle.

[6]"Place the altar of burnt offering in front of the entrance to the tabernacle, the Tent of Meeting; [7]place the basin between the Tent of Meeting and the altar and put water in it. [8]Set up the courtyard around it and put the curtain at the entrance to the courtyard.

[9]"Take the anointing oil and anoint the tabernacle and everything in it; consecrate it and all its furnishings, and it will be holy."

Leviticus 26:2-6, 11-13

[2]"'Observe my Sabbaths and have reverence for my sanctuary. I am the LORD.

[3]"'If you follow my decrees and are careful to obey my commands, [4]I will send you rain in its season, and the ground will yield its crops and the trees of the field their fruit. [5]Your threshing will continue

Key Verse

Key Verse

and the trees of the field shall yield their fruit. 5 Your threshing shall overtake the vintage, and the vintage shall overtake the sowing; you shall eat your bread to the full, and live securely in your land. 6 And I will grant peace in the land, and you shall lie down, and no one shall make you afraid.

11 I will place my dwelling in your midst, and I shall not abhor you. 12 And I will walk among you, and will be your God, and you shall be my people. 13 I am the LORD your God who brought you out of the land of Egypt, to be their slaves no more; I have broken the bars of your yoke and made you walk erect.

until grape harvest and the grape harvest will continue until planting, and you will eat all the food you want and live in safety in your land.

⁶" 'I will grant peace in the land, and you will lie down and no one will make you afraid.

¹¹" 'I will put my dwelling place among you, and I will not abhor you. ¹²I will walk among you and be your God, and you will be my people. ¹³I am the LORD your God, who brought you out of Egypt so that you would no longer be slaves to the Egyptians; I broke the bars of your yoke and enabled you to walk with heads held high.'"

UNDERSTANDING THE SCRIPTURE

Exodus 40:1-33. Several chapters of planning for the building of the tabernacle (or tent of meeting), of receiving instructions from God, and of gathering the materials have taken place as reported in Exodus 25–31. The contributions are used and the plans carried out in chapters 35–39. There has been something for everyone to do, from ordinary labor to skilled craftsmanship. Now we come to the summary of the whole project and its culmination with Moses. Moses is necessary for the consecration of place and space and all the equipment of liturgy. Moses is necessary for the ordination of Aaron and his sons for priesthood. (This ordination does not contradict the "kingdom of priests" of last week's lesson, but represents a division of labor for the good of the community. Remember that the "kingdom of priests" is for the benefit of the entire world; this priesthood of Aaron and his sons is internal to Israel.)

Leviticus 26:1-13. The results of worshiping the Lord alone and not turning aside to any false gods are spelled out. If people follow God, then the natural world will work the way God intended from the very beginning of creation. The rains will fall in the rainy seasons; the fruit trees will

yield fruit and the grapevines will be full of grapes. Peace will prevail, for the people will neither be afraid of predatory animals nor cowed by their enemies. The people will be fruitful and will multiply, in an echo of Genesis 1:28. (See also the repetitions at Genesis 8:17; 9:1, 7; 35:11.) Note two more things: there is nothing magical here. God does not say, "If you obey me, you'll never have to work another day in your life." Rather, the verses speak of sowing and reaping and other normal activities of good human labor. That labor will produce abundantly, to be sure, with each crop's reaping lasting until the harvesting of the next crop. The conditions seem almost as good as in Eden, and this goodness includes the gift of fruitful work.

Second, God's presence is promised in a continuing relationship: "I will walk among you, and will be your God, and you shall be my people" (Leviticus 26:12). This is not the picture of a kindly uncle showering presents from afar, nor of an important person having to do with no one except other equally important persons, but of a God who desires an intimate relationship with the entire community. And the desired relationship is one of mutual respect and activity toward common ends. God will do those things that the Israelites could not: removing dangerous wild animals and ensuring peace with surrounding neighbors, as well as sending rain at the appropriate seasons.

Key to this entire passage is the repeated refrain "I am the LORD your God" (26:1, 2, 13, 44, 45). God has the right to establish these laws. Even more important, God reminds the people of the grace they have seen already in God's freeing them from captivity in Egypt (26:13, 45). This is not a new deity, not a god they have not known before, but the God of creation and liberation, the God who invited them to enter into a covenant relationship, as we saw in last week's lesson.

Leviticus 26:14-39. What if the Israelites do not do what their part of the covenant stipulates? What will happen then? This next section spells out in horrifying detail six curses to match the six blessings of verses 1-13. (Similar passages may be found in Deuteronomy 28:15-68 and 29:18-28.) These dire things will not happen if people accidentally break a law, or if they inadvertently stray, but specifically if they turn away from the Lord. Turning away is the foundational sin, the sin that can lead to any and all of the others.

Our verses are clear that these terrible things that are threatened when Israel abandons the Lord are things that God will do. They are an escalating series of calamities, and each ensuing disaster results only when Israel continues in its willful disobedience. For example, as God promises the rain when Israel lives under the covenant, the rain will be sealed up in the sky if they rebel, so that their farming will yield no grain, their trees no fruit (26:19-20). If, even under these conditions, they do not return to the Lord, then the wild animals God promised in verse 6 to remove will be let loose again on the countryside. The curses, the punishments, are in many instances the undoing of the previous blessings. That is, God does not threaten "fairy-tale" punishments. There is no talk here of turning people into frogs or having sinners fall asleep for hundreds of years. As God is the ruler of the natural world and its benefits, God can also cause those benefits to be withheld.

What could Israel—what could anyone—do that would bring about such dire consequences? The Bible describes the sin this way: "If you will not obey me...if you remain hostile toward me and refuse to listen to me...if you do not accept my correction..." (26:18, 21, 23 NIV). What this wording also shows is that the curses, the punishments, are not intended only to be punitive but also to be corrective.

Leviticus 26:40-46. Once the relationship is broken, once Israel has, for whatever reason, turned away from the Lord, is the inevitable result this horrific escalating catalogue of curses? Not at all. At any time the downward spiral can be stopped. "If they confess their iniquity...and they make amends for their iniquity, then will I remember my covenant..." (26:40, 42). Whenever the people signal that they want to restore the disrupted relationship with God, and when they want to enough to make amends for their sins, then God is eager to accept them back.

INTERPRETING THE SCRIPTURE

More Instructions Given and Carried Out

You have probably heard the quip that the human race is divided into two groups: those who divide everyone into two groups and those who don't. We have a tendency to make many issues either/or, to see situations as all good or all bad. Time after time the Bible indicates that God is much less either/or and much more both/and. With a whole nation out in the wilderness, wouldn't physical safety and getting to the promised land seem more important than fancy worship space and complicated forms for worship services? Wouldn't it make more sense to take care of physical life first and then, when things are going well in their new land, to attend to liturgical space and ceremonies? It might seem so, but God tells Moses and the Israelites that worship is important no matter where they are.

Interestingly, the people do not argue this point with God. They do not ask how they can possibly be expected to come up with all the required materials out in the middle of nowhere. Indeed, they are such eager givers that Moses has to tell them to stop bringing contributions, that they have all that they need! (See Exodus 36:2-7.) Is God trying to tell the Israelites that proper worship can take place only in certain spots with particular equipment? Not at all. But we humans tend to better remember God and remember the relationship we can find in worship if we set aside particular times and spaces and have ordered ways of going about it.

The "Carrot"

With the tabernacle finished and Aaron and his sons newly ordained, there is a reminder of God's primary requirement: they are to be faithful and obedient to the Lord and to no one and nothing else. If they will do that, God reminds them, then their lives will be as blessed as God's original intention described in Genesis 1 and 2. There will be satisfying work for everyone and more than enough food. They will not have to be afraid of wild animals; they will not have any human enemies to fear. This is what God holds out to them as a promise.

Does this sound like blessing? Where does it say they will all be rich? Where does it say they will get to trample on their enemies or lord it over other peoples?

Where does it promise lives of endless luxury and ease with someone else to do the necessary but boring or dangerous or unpleasant jobs? You know the answer, of course: there are no such texts in the Bible. Many of us in this country, however, might consider these promises pretty pale blessing. Many of us have more food than we should eat and have houses that seem small and cramped only because we have more "stuff" than we can cram into them comfortably. Some of us need to reconsider our idea of "blessing."

For others, including many Americans, having enough food and having satisfying work to do would be experienced as the greatest blessing imaginable. This is what God promises to those who keep the covenant and live in relationship with the Lord. Even today, with the world's population hundreds of times larger than it was in Moses' day, the earth produces enough food for everyone to have enough for a healthy life. What the earth does not produce, what the earth is incapable of producing, is enough for all of us to have too much and to be wasteful. We have enough for everyone's need but not enough for everyone's greed. God's promise is "enough," not "more than you can possibly know what to do with."

The "Stick"

What happens if we decide not to accept God's offer of covenant, or if we accept it in lip service but ignore it in the majority of our living? Then we will reap the curses. And they will come to us as they did to Israel, not as fairy-tale punishments. In essence God says, "If you think you can live without me, if you would rather try to live without me, then that is what I will let you do."

So where are we in relation to the main question of this lesson? Is the religious life one of rule-keeping or of grace? If we keep the rules for the sake of external rewards, then we are missing God's point. For the greatest blessing God bestows is to live in covenant relationship. People who do not want that—people who want to be rewarded with having more money than all their neighbors, or with some sign that God loves them more than anyone else, or proof that they are more important than other people—are following other gods than the Lord of Israel.

The Outcome

None of us manages to keep the covenant entirely; none of us escapes sin. And therefore the promise of Leviticus 26 needs to be there for us also. When we repent and turn back to God, God is there, eagerly meeting us to reestablish that promised relationship.

It is frustrating to try to write at length about this, and yet it is just about the most important topic for people who take the Bible and the God of the Bible seriously. The people who have experienced God know what it is about without endless words. The people who have not had such a relationship with God—people who are still following assorted gods proposed by the culture we all live in—may have trouble understanding any of this.

SHARING THE SCRIPTURE

PREPARING TO TEACH

Preparing Our Hearts

Set aside some quiet time to read and meditate on this week's devotional passage, Psalm 84. As you reflect on this hymn of praise, think about your relationship with the church building in which you worship. Is it a place that you long for, a place where you find God's presence? You may want to write in your journal about what the house of the Lord means to you.

Now turn to today's background passages from Exodus 40:1-33 and Leviticus 26. Notice in Exodus the detailed directions that God gives to Moses concerning the building and furnishing of the tabernacle, as well as the consecration of the "perpetual priesthood" (Exodus 40:15) of Aaron and his family. Note in 40:16 that "Moses did everything just as the LORD had commanded him." Moses' obedience to God's commands is also referenced in verses 19, 21, 23, 25, 27, 29, and 32. Ponder Moses' obedience to God even in matters that may seem trivial to us. As you read

Leviticus 26, with its description of blessings and curses, think about how God is calling you to obedience right now. What do you need to do? How will you respond?

Preparing Our Minds

Review the scripture lesson, this time focusing on Exodus 40:1-9 and Leviticus 26:2-6 and 11-13. Read the lesson carefully, paying particular attention to the Understanding the Scripture section.

The chapter from Leviticus is part of what scholars refer to as the Holiness Code, which is found in chapters 17–26. God who is holy has come to dwell amid sinful humanity. The provisions set forth in this section are intended to help the people know how they can maintain ritual purity to fulfill the command to "be holy, for I the LORD your God am holy" (19:2). To be holy is to be set apart. People (for example, the whole nation of Israel and their priests) and objects (such as those found in the tabernacle) can be set apart for God's service and worship. Leviticus 26, which is part of today's lesson, concludes the Code with God's promises and warnings of punishment.

Preparing Our Learning Space

Have on hand:
- ✔ several Bibles
- ✔ hymnals
- ✔ paper and pencils
- ✔ newsprint and marker.

LEADING THE CLASS

(1) Introduction

Begin today's lesson by singing or reading responsively a familiar old hymn, "Trust and Obey" (*The United Methodist Hymnal*, no. 467).

Spend a few moments talking about what it means to trust and obey God. Perhaps some volunteers will share stories of times when they have trusted and obeyed God. Encourage the students to talk about how God apparently responded to their obedience. Ask them to comment on whether they felt rewarded in any way. Perhaps the reward was simply the satisfaction of knowing that they had faithfully obeyed God, regardless of the outcome of the situation.

Lift up today's main question: **Is religious life truly a matter of grace, or is it primarily a matter of obeying rules?**

(2) More Instructions Given and Carried Out

Select a volunteer to read Exodus 40:1-9. As an option, distribute paper and pencil to each student. Ask them to draw what they hear as this passage about the building and furnishing of the tabernacle is being read. Ability as an artist is unimportant. What you want the group to gain from this experience is an understanding of all the details God so meticulously set forth in creating this worship space in the desert.

Ask these questions:

(1) **What do God's detailed directions say to you about the importance of sacred space for worship?**

(2) **Had you been one of the Israelites, what would you have thought about God's directions, given the fact that you were in the middle of the wilderness and didn't have a permanent home?**

(3) **How might this sacred space have helped you become more aware of God's presence in an otherwise hostile environment?**

If time permits, you may want to have the class compare and contrast the description in Exodus with their description of the worship space in your own congregation. Ask these questions:

(1) **What features make a space sacred for you?**

(2) **If a fire or other catastrophe were to destroy your sanctuary, what one object would you try to save? Why?**

(3) **If you could make one comment to your church's trustees or building maintenance committee, what would you say about your own sanctuary?**

(4) **How do you feel when you worship in another sanctuary?**

(3) The "Carrot"

Invite the students to read in unison today's key verse from Leviticus 26:2: "You shall keep my sabbaths and reverence my sanctuary: I am the LORD." Here you may want to use information under Preparing Our Minds to set this verse within the context of the Holiness Code. Emphasize that obedience to the Lord enables one to be holy as God is holy.

Now continue reading from Leviticus 26:3-6 and 11-13. Ask the students to identify what God promises. Write their answers on newsprint. The list will include seasonal rain, abundant harvest, security, peace, freedom from fear, the removal of predatory animals from the land, the ability to overcome their enemies, an increase in their population, and God's continuing presence.

Ask the following questions:

(1) Does God promise all of these blessings unconditionally? (No.)

(2) What are God's terms or conditions for bestowing these blessings? (Verse 3 states that the people must observe God's statutes and faithfully keep the commandments. In other words, the blessings are contingent upon obedience to God. If the people obey, then God will pour out these blessings.)

(3) What specifically are the people called to do here? (They are to keep the sabbath and show reverence for the sanctuary, per verse 2. Verse 1 reiterates the prohibition of idols and images stated in the Ten Commandments.)

(4) Had you been one of the ancient Israelites, how would you have felt about granting God authority over your life and promising to obey God? Conclude this section by asking the students to think about the following questions. Provide a few moments for silent reflection.

(1) Who or what has authority over your own life?

(2) If your answer to the previous question was not "God," name some reasons why you are reluctant to give God complete control over you.

(3) How do you personally feel about being obedient to God?

(4) The "Stick"

Like other ancient covenants, curses as well as blessings are spelled out here. If time permits, have someone read the background scripture from Leviticus 26:14-39. Note that these terrors are brought about because people refuse to obey God.

Such prospects remind us that Christ calls us to obedience as well. We cannot just say, "Yes, Lord," and then go about our business as we choose. Jesus said, "You are my friends if you do what I command you" (John 15:14).

You may want to do a Bible study concerning obedience by having the class check the references listed below. Consider having the students work in teams or with a partner. You may want to assign a different reference to each group and then have them report back to the whole class. The point here is to see and understand that obedience is crucial for a right relationship with God. This point is made throughout the Bible, not just in the Holiness Code. Here would be an appropriate place to remind the class of the main question and point out that if we keep the rules for the sole purpose of being rewarded, we are missing the point, for the greatest blessing that God bestows is for us to live in covenant relationship with God.

- Matthew 28:18-20—Jesus gives the Great Commission.
- Mark 1:27—Even unclean spirits obey Jesus.
- Luke 11:28—Jesus blesses those who obey God.
- Acts 5:29, 32—Peter tells the religious leaders that Jesus' followers must obey God rather than human authority.
- Romans 6:16—We can choose to obey sin, which leads to death, or obey righteousness.
- Hebrews 5:8-10—The Son of God learned obedience through his suffering.
- 1 John 2:3-6—God's love reaches perfection in those who are obedient.
- 1 John 3:21-24—Those who obey Christ's commandments abide in him as he abides in them.
- 1 John 5:1-5—Those who love God obey the commandments.
- Revelation 3:3—The church is called to obey the gospel.

To reinforce the importance of obedience, consider reading aloud one or more of the following quotations. Encourage the class to respond to the reading(s) as they feel led:

I find the doing of the will of God leaves me no time for disputing about His plans. (George MacDonald, *The Marquis of Lossie*)

Every revelation of God is a demand, and the way to knowledge of God is by obedience. (Archbishop William Temple)

What we did today was not the negative thing of saying we disobeyed. It was the positive thing of saying we obeyed God. (Archbishop Desmond Tutu, February 29, 1988)

(5) The Outcome

The background scripture from Leviticus 26:40-46 closes with a promise that if the people confess their sins, God will remember the covenant and not forget or destroy the people even though they have disobeyed. Provide a few moments for class members to meditate silently on this question that you will need to read aloud: How is God's promise good news for you?

Before you dismiss the class, be sure to lift up at least one idea below so that the students will have ideas for embodying this lesson in their own lives during the coming week.

HELPING CLASS MEMBERS ACT

Suggest that individual students visit the sanctuary during the week when they can be alone there with God. Tell them to be alert for the stirrings of God's presence in that sacred space.

Recommend that students spend some time this week writing in their journals concerning how they feel about needing to abide by God's rules. Do they find obedience restrictive, or does it give them freedom?

This week's lesson has spoken of earthly rewards and punishments to be meted out by God according to whether one has obeyed or disobeyed. Suggest that students reflect on their understanding of such rewards and punishments. Do they expect to receive their due on earth or in an afterlife? If God were to give them what they deserve right now, what do they think they would receive?

PLANNING FOR NEXT SUNDAY

Next week the class will begin a new unit entitled "Wilderness Wanderings." To prepare for the first lesson, "Follow Day by Day," ask the students to read the background scripture from Exodus 40:34-38 and Numbers 9:15-23. Encourage class members to think about what it means to follow God faithfully.

UNIT 2: WILDERNESS WANDERINGS
FOLLOW DAY BY DAY

PREVIEWING THE LESSON

Lesson Scripture: Exodus 40:34-38; Numbers 9:15-19, 22-23
Background Scripture: Exodus 40:34-38; Numbers 9:15-23
Key Verse: Exodus 40:38

Focus of the Lesson:
The Israelites obediently followed God, who led them day and night in a pillar of cloud and a pillar of fire.

Main Question of the Lesson:
After the excitement and crises in our own lives, what does God want from us and how are we able to respond?

This lesson will enable adult learners to:
(1) examine how God faithfully led the Israelites in the wilderness.
(2) consider how they follow God daily.
(3) respond by seeking God's guidance.

Today's lesson may be outlined as follows:
(1) Introduction
(2) The Glory of the Lord
(3) Divine Traffic Signals
(4) Waiting on the Lord

FOCUSING ON THE MAIN QUESTION

The lessons thus far have been exciting and full of danger, with close calls and the nearly overwhelming presence of God. The people have been given the law as a guide for their life together and their ongoing relationship with their Lord. They even have the laws that will begin to structure their community's life when then finally reach the promised land. But they are still far from that land. They still have much weary plodding ahead of them through this boring wilderness. (They do not yet know that they will be spending forty years in the wilderness. We will come to that part of the story in a subsequent lesson.)

In some ways it may be easy for us to put ourselves out there with Israel in our imaginations. Few people reach adulthood without having a crisis or two during which they call upon God for deliverance. Most of us have experienced God's grace, which one way or another may have led us to this particular community of faith in which we come together to study God's Word. And yet few of us live lives of daily crisis. This is not to say that there are not people whose lives are an ongoing series of emergencies, but that most of us who participate in this class are not homeless, are not destitute, do not have to spend all our meager energies trying to find food for our children.

We have seen in the previous lessons how God over and over again "comes through" for Israel—by delivering them from bondage, rescuing them from Pharaoh's army, giving them food and drink in the wilderness, teaching them the proper way to relate to God and to one another, and calling them into covenant relationship. When life seems to have settled into a daily regularity, what does God want from them? **Similarly, after the excitement and crises in our own lives, what does God want from us and how are we able to respond?** In this lesson we will explore how God faithfully leads the Israelites—and us—and how people of faith are to follow.

READING THE SCRIPTURE

NRSV
Exodus 40:34-38

34 Then the cloud covered the tent of meeting, and the glory of the LORD filled the tabernacle. 35 Moses was not able to enter the tent of meeting because the cloud settled upon it, and the glory of the LORD filled the tabernacle. 36 Whenever the cloud was taken up from the tabernacle, the Israelites would set out on each stage of their journey; 37 but if the cloud was not taken up, then they did not set out until the day that it was taken up. **38 For the cloud of the LORD was on the tabernacle by day, and fire was in the cloud by night, before the eyes of all the house of Israel at each stage of their journey.**

Numbers 9:15-19, 22-23

15 On the day the tabernacle was set up, the cloud covered the tabernacle, the tent of the covenant; and from evening until morning it was over the tabernacle, having the appearance of fire. 16 It was always so: the cloud covered it by day and the appearance of fire by night. 17 Whenever the cloud lifted from over the tent, then the Israelites would set out; and in the

NIV
Exodus 40:34-38

³⁴Then the cloud covered the Tent of Meeting, and the glory of the LORD filled the tabernacle. ³⁵Moses could not enter the Tent of Meeting because the cloud had settled upon it, and the glory of the LORD filled the tabernacle.

³⁶In all the travels of the Israelites, whenever the cloud lifted from above the tabernacle, they would set out; ³⁷but if the cloud did not lift, they did not set out—until the day it lifted. **³⁸So the cloud of the LORD was over the tabernacle by day, and fire was in the cloud by night, in the sight of all the house of Israel during all their travels.**

Numbers 9:15-19, 22-23

¹⁵On the day the tabernacle, the Tent of the Testimony, was set up, the cloud covered it. From evening till morning the cloud above the tabernacle looked like fire. ¹⁶That is how it continued to be; the cloud covered it, and at night it looked like fire. ¹⁷Whenever the cloud lifted from above the Tent, the Israelites set out; wherever the cloud settled, the Israelites encamped.

Key
Verse

Ke
Ver

place where the cloud settled down, there the Israelites would camp. 18 At the command of the LORD the Israelites would set out, and at the command of the LORD they would camp. As long as the cloud rested over the tabernacle, they would remain in camp. 19 Even when the cloud continued over the tabernacle many days, the Israelites would keep the charge of the LORD, and would not set out.

22 Whether it was two days, or a month, or a longer time, that the cloud continued over the tabernacle, resting upon it, the Israelites would remain in camp and would not set out; but when it lifted they would set out. 23 At the command of the LORD they would camp, and at the command of the LORD they would set out. They kept the charge of the LORD, at the command of the LORD by Moses.

18At the LORD's command the Israelites set out, and at his command they encamped. As long as the cloud stayed over the tabernacle, they remained in camp. 19When the cloud remained over the tabernacle a long time, the Israelites obeyed the LORD's order and did not set out.

22Whether the cloud stayed over the tabernacle for two days or a month or a year, the Israelites would remain in camp and not set out; but when it lifted, they would set out. 23At the LORD's command they encamped, and at the LORD's command they set out. They obeyed the LORD's order, in accordance with his command through Moses.

UNDERSTANDING THE SCRIPTURE

Exodus 40:34-35. The work on the tabernacle was finished in Exodus 39:33. Using the same verb, the author tells us that Moses' work of ordaining and consecrating is also finished. Everything the people can do has been done. They have all followed the Lord's instructions, and the sanctuary for their God is complete. What will happen now? Anything? Yes. Another of God's promises is now being fulfilled in a new way. God has always promised to be with the people, even before they were a nation. (See, for example, Genesis 28:15 and 46:4.) Now there is a physical place for a visible reminder of the presence of God. The cloud, which has been mentioned before as going ahead of them by day (Exodus 13:21-22) and as signaling the Lord's presence at Mount Sinai (24:16), now settles on the newly completed tabernacle. In addition, the inside of the tent of meeting is said to be filled with God's glory. Thus the promise made in Exodus 25:8 is fulfilled in the presence of all Israel.

We cannot draw a portrait of this moment. The cloud means more than just an overcast sky or a particularly thick bit of ground fog. And the glory is described as light, but as more than just light, for its presence within the tent is so vast that even Moses is not able to enter. This passage uses *symbols* for God's presence. Does this mean they aren't really real? Not at all. It means that once more we have come to the limits of our language to describe in scientific terminology what Israel experienced. Their experience is not captured on videotape to be shared with us. But some of the sense of it *is* captured in the words they use, for cloud and fire are often indicators of God's presence. God could have chosen any number of ways to assure Israel of the divine presence, I believe. They had the experience that we refer to symbolically by the words *cloud* and *fire*.

Exodus 40:36-38; Numbers 9:15-17. These symbols of God's presence served another function as well, besides being visible symbols that the Lord was indeed with them. As long as the cloud stayed over the tent of meeting, the people remained in camp. When it lifted and started ahead, then they would break camp and continue their journey, led by the signs of the Lord's presence. When the cloud stopped again, the Israelites would stop and set up camp.

An important point not to be overlooked is that *all* the people witness God's presence in the cloud and the glory. This is not a special "reward" for Moses, nor something limited to the leaders. It is not a tiny special object that can be seen by only a few people at a time. The signs of God's active presence are available to anyone who chooses to look toward the tent of meeting. Nor must someone look at a special time. The cloud is there during all the daylight hours; there is "fire in the cloud" during the night to continue its visibility. The reassurance is there for everyone and it is available at any hour.

Numbers 9:18-23. These verses repeat and expand what we have seen in the previous section. Israel uses the cloud to tell them when to break camp and when to stop and make a new camp. There seems to be no way for them to tell ahead of time how long they will remain in any particular place. The report is simply that as long as the cloud was stationary, Israel did not move. As soon as the cloud resumed its journey, so did Israel.

What we may not think about because it seems so simple is the notion that God is with them all the time. God stays with them in the camp; God travels with them as they move. God never expresses boredom. God doesn't tell Israel to hurry up or say, "I'll meet you when you make it to the next oasis," and then zip on ahead of them. This is also a way of teaching Israel that God is not limited to any particular place. Many of the surrounding nations had national gods whose powers apparently stopped at the border between nations. One of the things that made traveling so dangerous, some thought, was that to leave home was also to leave one's gods behind. Not so for Israel. Their God is not limited by national borders.

On the other hand, Israel did not take the idea of God's ability to move to mean there was not specific presence in a specific place. This can be seen in the symbolism of the tent of meeting. God is indeed seen to be specifically located there in awesome particularity. God is always willing to "pull up stakes" and leave a spot.

INTERPRETING THE SCRIPTURE

The Glory of the Lord

"The glory of the Lord" has such a nice ring to it! Maybe you have felt God's presence strongly in a particular place, whether in church or in some glorious scenery outside. From one perspective, we can see the glory everywhere—in a leaf, a mountain, the majestic ocean, the unrestrained laughter of little children. But aren't these "normal" things, "natural" things? How can they be "the glory of the Lord"? Once again we have come upon the matter of our freedom of choice in the realm of faith. We may choose to see God in the world around us or in the people near us. Or we may choose not to see God in such ordinary matters.

God's reasoning, as it is expressed in the Bible, seems to go like this. If people have no choice but to believe that something is a manifestation of God, then their belief will not be the result of their genuine free choice. Since God desires our free and willing relationship in faith and belief, there will always be an "alternative" explanation for God's appearances. But I do not think we have to make such stark distinctions. I believe that God can be seen in a rainbow and heard in the screechy squawk of sandhill cranes alongside the "natural" explanations for such sights and sounds. All of the world is open to many interpretations. The correctness of any one interpretation does not necessarily make all other interpretations wrong. God can be seen nearly everywhere we look, if we choose to look with the desire or expectation of finding a glimpse of the Lord.

Think again of the relationship of parents and their children. My daughters have made me presents in school; they have saved up their money and bought gifts for me. I enjoy such indications of their love for me. But I also know of their love from shared jokes, from particular family phrases that have extra meaning only to us because they speak of our history together, from the daily, normal, ordinary ways we relate to each other. The spectacular gifts would not mean much at all if we did not have the daily, normal, ordinary relationship of days that are not a birthday or graduation or Christmas.

The cloud over the tent of meeting may be compared with the hugs or grins or silly words we exchange with friends and family members. A hug is "no big deal," and yet it stands for a relationship that sometimes cannot be contained in mere words. A cloud is "no big deal," and yet it stands for a relationship between God and Israel that cannot be contained in mere words.

Divine Traffic Signals

Like the Israelites, we too have had wilderness experiences. We wander around, having lost our way for any number of reasons. Perhaps the death of a loved one has turned our life upside down. Maybe a child's continuing misbe-havior has not only broken our hearts but left us feeling adrift and alone. Possibly a serious illness and hospitalization have made us feel as if we were in exile. Our routine, familiar surroundings, and sense of control over our lives are all gone. Similarly, a fire or natural catastrophe can cause dislocation and disorientation.

The Israelites have been displaced from their familiar, albeit oppressive, situation. They need guidance, just as we do. They want a dependable source of information, and they find that in God. According to the verses in today's lesson, Israel follows the lead of the cloud without any complaints. When the cloud says go, they go. When the cloud says stay here, they stay.

We may want such direct, unmistakable guidance in our own lives. We read the story of the Israelites in the wilderness and think that it certainly would be easier today if there were some tabernacle somewhere where we could look to get our signals. I would feel easier about waiting and then moving out in a specific direction if I could actually *see* God's presence. Wouldn't it be wonderful if we had such clear directions from God? Actually, we probably have clearer directions than we are comfortable admitting. We have divine guidance in ways Israel did not.

A prime example of the guidance God gives us is the Bible itself. Not one of those Israelites had a Bible to read in the wilderness. We are jealous, sometimes, of the biblical characters, thinking they had a much easier time of understanding God. But they might think that we have a clearer picture of what God wants because we have the stories of those who went before us. We know what they were told; we know what they did; we know what the result was. We have our own moving and resting cloud, just in different forms. We have the Scriptures as a guide. We also have the community of faith—the communion of saints—of all the generations before us, and those in the room with us each week. Hearing their stories helps us to recognize patterns of ways that God acts in our lives. Furthermore, we are guided through the worship service as we sing the songs of our faith, turn to God in prayer, and hear the word of God proclaimed in the sermon. In addition, we are guided by our conscience or a fear of being caught that keeps us from doing something we know is wrong. Or we may see such nudges away from the wrong and toward the right to be our own versions of the cloud over the tabernacle. As we see the divine traffic signals that God so clearly placed before the Israelites, we can recognize and give thanks for the many ways in which God guides us as well.

Waiting on the Lord

There is nothing wrong with ordinary life. It is daily, weekly, yearly life that is blessed by God—not just the spectacular, once-in-a-lifetime events. God is seen by Israel in cloud and fire, not just in a comet or solar eclipse. God feeds Israel in the wilderness with water and manna/bread, not with endless four-course banquets.

God's ancient blessing to Abraham, to Isaac, to Jacob, to all Israel, and even to the church is the promise of a place to belong and people to belong to and work to do.

God shows that ordinary life is not only all right, it is good. God shows that rest and waiting and just "hanging around" can be good too. God waits in the wilderness for the sake of Israel. Numbers 9 never tells us why the cloud rested over the tent of meeting for long periods, so we are free to use our imaginations to think of possible reasons. Maybe some children were tired from walking. Maybe some newlyweds needed a bit of time apart with each other just to enjoy their new life together. Maybe you can think of other possibilities. What seems very possible is that God wanted Israel to learn that pushing themselves at top speed was not a good idea. There was no more pursuing army; they were free to enjoy the portion of God's creation they saw each day. Waiting on the Lord does not mean marking time until "real life" begins. The waiting itself, the quietness, the very ordinariness of daily life is also a divine gift.

SHARING THE SCRIPTURE

PREPARING TO TEACH

Preparing Our Hearts

To begin your personal preparations, turn to Psalm 107:1-9. This song of thanksgiving mentions those who "wandered in desert wastes" (107:4). Think about times that you have wandered in a spiritual desert. List the ways that you sought guidance. How did God work through the Bible, the church, other people, your own conscience, and circumstances to guide you out of the wilderness? Based on your own experience, what advice would you give to other pilgrims who are journeying through uncharted territory in their own lives?

Now read today's background scripture from Exodus 40:34-38 and Numbers 9:15-23. As you read, imagine that you are one of the Israelites. How would you feel knowing that God was continually present with you? Do you feel that God is always present with you? If so, what might that constant presence suggest to you about God's ability and willingness to guide and comfort you in all situations?

To conclude your own spiritual preparations, offer a prayer asking God to help you follow faithfully, day by day, wherever the Holy Spirit may lead you.

Preparing Our Minds

Review the scripture passages for today, along with this lesson. You may also wish to consult a Bible dictionary about the tent of meeting, which may be discussed under *tabernacle*. In short, this structure was a movable sanctuary that was designed to be assembled, disassembled, and transported to a new location where it would be reassembled. The people voluntarily gave materials that were used to construct the tent of meeting and its furnishings. It was very sacred space, for here God met and communicated with the people.

Preparing Our Learning Space

Prior to class, you may want to write on newsprint the meditation questions for use under "Divine Traffic Signals."
Have on hand:
- several Bibles
- paper and pencils
- newsprint and marker
- optional hymnals.

LEADING THE CLASS

(1) Introduction

One way to begin today's session is to read or retell the Focusing on the Main Question portion.

Another way to begin is to ask volunteers to share stories of times when they needed clear-cut guidance from God. Encourage them to explain how they knew that God was present with them. Also ask them to report on their response to God's guidance. Provide time for each person to reflect quietly on current situations in their own lives that call out for God's direction.

Move to today's lesson by noting that even though the Egyptian crisis had passed, the Israelites faced a difficult situation in the wilderness. They needed God's direction, and so do we. Lift up today's main question: **After the excitement and crises in our own lives, what does God want from us and how are we able to respond?**

(2) The Glory of the Lord

You may want to distribute paper and a pencil to each student. Ask them to draw their interpretation of the tabernacle and the cloud that settled over it as you read Exodus 40:34-38 aloud. Then either invite students to show their picture to a partner or describe what they have drawn for the class. Emphasize that artistic ability is unimportant. The point here is to allow the scripture passage to come alive by imagining what this sacred, portable space in the wilderness must have been like.

Now read the second paragraph in the Understanding the Scripture segment under Exodus 40:34-35. Note that no matter how good our drawings may be, we cannot truly envision the scene because the Israelites' description of cloud and pillar are inadequate to express what the presence of God must have been like. Ask the group these questions:
(1) **God gave the Israelites a clear, visible reminder of the divine presence in their midst. What symbolizes God's presence for you?**
(2) **What feelings or emotions do you experience when you are especially aware of God's abiding presence?**
(3) **Had you been one of the Israelites, how might you have responded to the pillar and cloud of God's presence?**

(3) Divine Traffic Signals

Choose a volunteer to read aloud Numbers 9:15-19 and 22-23. Ask the class to brainstorm answers to the following questions. List their ideas on newsprint. Ideas to augment the discussion are found under this heading in the Interpreting the Scripture portion.

(1) How did God direct the Israelites?

(2) How did they respond to these divine signals? (Be sure to note that the people did not set out until the cloud moved from its post at the tabernacle. Only then did they proceed to break camp.)

(3) What kinds of signals does God give to direct us?

(4) Not everyone seeks guidance from God. What are some other sources of direction that people turn to in our day? (Answers may include horoscopes, people who claim to foretell the future, self-help books, or secular support groups.)

(5) God directed the people by having them follow the cloud. What advantages do you see in having such a clear-cut signal? What disadvantages do you see?

Provide some quiet time, along with paper and a pencil for each student. Ask them to meditate on these questions, which you may either read aloud or post on newsprint. Some students may want to record their thoughts on paper, while others may prefer just to think.

(1) Suppose you lived each day completely under God's direction. In the words of a familiar spiritual you said, "I'm goin' a sing when the Spirit says sing . . . and obey the Spirit of the Lord." How might your life be different than it is now?

(2) What changes do you need to make to follow God more closely every day?

(3) What first step will you make in the week ahead to bring about these changes?

Close this portion of the lesson with a brief prayer, asking God to empower each person to live according to God's direction.

(4) Waiting on the Lord

Point out Numbers 9:22, which states in essence that the Israelites had to wait upon the Lord. They could not just take off whenever they felt like moving. Instead, they had to wait until God gave the signal for them to move on. Discuss these questions:

(1) How do you feel about waiting?

(2) How do you explain the fact that most people in our society feel that they are accomplishing something only if they are taking action, as opposed to waiting patiently for God's direction? (You may want to point out that the drive to achieve, to be busy constantly, is rooted in American heritage in what is commonly called the Puritan work ethic. Oft-repeated sayings of older generations, such as "idle hands do the devil's work," have prompted many folks to disdain quiet waiting and meditation as "a waste of time." Moreover, in this age of high tech and high speed, waiting is just not an acceptable alternative to instant gratification.)

Isaiah has words to counter our rush and busyness. We need to wait in the camp until God tells us to move on. Tell the class to be in an attitude of prayer and meditation as you read these familiar words from Isaiah 40:28-31:

Have you not known? Have you
  not heard?
The Lord is the everlasting God,
  the Creator of the ends of the
  earth.
He does not faint or grow weary;
  his understanding is
  unsearchable.
He gives power to the faint,
  and strengthens the powerless.
Even youths will faint and be
  weary,
  and the young will fall
  exhausted;
but those who wait for the Lord
  shall renew their strength,
  they shall mount up with
  wings like eagles,
they shall run and not be weary,
  they shall walk and not faint.

When you have finished reading, ask the class members to ponder these questions and, if possible, talk about them with a partner:

(1) When was the last time you waited for the Lord?

(2) Are there circumstances in your life right now that cry out for you to wait upon the Lord, rather than rush head-long according to your own plan and schedule? If so, what are those circumstances?

(3) How will today's lesson help you to face a difficult situation?

As an option, close the session with a hymn that speaks of obedience. "Jesus Calls Us" (*The United Methodist Hymnal,* no. 398) or "Take Up Thy Cross" (*UMH,* no. 415) would be especially appropriate. Before you dismiss the class, be sure to suggest at least one of the activities below so that students may begin to incorporate today's lesson into their own lives.

HELPING CLASS MEMBERS ACT

Encourage students to write entries in a spiritual journal this week concerning times when they have needed God's guid-ance. In some cases, they may have waited patiently for the symbolic cloud of God's presence to guide them to the next place. In other instances, they may have tried to plan their own itinerary and timetable. Ask them to be aware of how their will-ingness to let God lead them makes a dif-ference in their lives.

Recommend to students who have a scholarly interest in the Bible that they look up *tent of meeting* (usually found under *tabernacle*) in a Bible dictionary. This information is interesting because scholars have raised questions about the appear-ance and portability of the tent as described in the Bible.

Suggest that students who have an artistic bent may want to use whatever medium they prefer to illustrate the tent of meeting and cloud. They can use a con-cordance to find references to the tent in addition to those they encountered in this lesson. Perhaps some who do this activity will bring their work to class next week.

PLANNING FOR NEXT SUNDAY

Next week's lesson, "A Missed Opportunity," looks at Numbers 12:1–14:25, especially verses 13:1-3, 32–14:4, 8-9 (key verses) and 20-24. Ask the class to read these passages to see how the people rebelled against God and the price that they had to pay for their rebellion.

A MISSED OPPORTUNITY

PREVIEWING THE LESSON

Lesson Scripture: Numbers 13:1-3, 32–14:4, 20-24
Background Scripture: Numbers 12:1–14:25
Key Verses: Numbers 14:8-9

Focus of the Lesson:
Because they rebelled and disobeyed God, the people who left Egypt with Moses would not live to see the promised land.

Main Question of the Lesson:
Is it ever possible to "push God too far," to disobey past the point of God's forgiveness?

This lesson will enable adult learners to:
(1) hear the reports of the Israelite spies and the rebellious response of the people.
(2) examine their own willingness to obey God.
(3) respond by standing up for the minority view when they feel it is right.

Today's lesson may be outlined as follows:
(1) Introduction
(2) The Scouts and Their Mission
(3) What They Saw and What They Said
(4) The People's First Response
(5) Minority Report
(6) God's Last Word

FOCUSING ON THE MAIN QUESTION

People often seem to position themselves at one extreme or the other of most any question. We have such a strong tendency to reduce every issue to yes/no dimensions, to make every issue all or nothing. It should be no surprise that this happens with religious questions too. Some people focus so heavily on God's grace and forgiveness that it almost seems sin doesn't really matter at all. Yes we sin, but God's job is to forgive. So, as long as we make sure we ask for forgiveness, then it hardly matters what we do. Off the other end of the scale are those who preach about (or worry about) the "unforgivable sin." They emphasize God's absolute right to punish sinners for every single infraction that is not properly repented of or atoned for.

There are, of course, biblical passages

that seem to support each of these positions, especially if the passages are read all by themselves. But what we have in the Bible is not simply a collection of independent sayings that can be shuffled and put together like a "mix and match" flower garden from which we can pluck whatever color of flowers we want on a particular day. To continue the figure of speech, the Bible is the entire garden, not just the parts we tend so carefully. My daughters came back home to Tennessee from a visit to relatives in Maryland with the amazed report that a particular plant that grows in our yard and is routinely mowed with the grass is, up there, cultivated in gardens and used in bouquets. They were surprised to see it inside people's houses; their friends in Maryland were amazed that we consider it a weed.

Instead of playing "dueling verses" with the Bible, I think it is more profitable to our spiritual health to consider whole stories and the flow of the narrative within one book and from one book to the next. Although for the purpose of a Sunday-school series such as this one it is necessary to skip some passages, there are times when it is equally necessary to remember some of the things that have been skipped. In the case before us today and the issue of God's punishments, we need to remember that there were several times after the Israelites had witnessed and experienced God's mighty acts on their behalf that they renewed their complaints. Taking Numbers 14 all by itself, it might seem that God is being arbitrary and unfair. Looking at the number of times the people complained, it might seem that God is justified in being "fed up" with these "stiff-necked" people. But that raises a frightening question for us today: **Is it ever possible to "push God too far," that is, to disobey past the point of God's forgiveness?**

READING THE SCRIPTURE

NRSV
Numbers 13:1-3

The LORD said to Moses, 2 Send men to spy out the land of Canaan, which I am giving to the Israelites; from each of their ancestral tribes you shall send a man, every one a leader among them." 3 So Moses sent them from the wilderness of Paran, according to the command of the LORD, all of them leading men among the Israelites.

Numbers 13:32–14:1-4, 8-9, 20-24

32 So they brought to the Israelites an unfavorable report of the land that they had spied out, saying, "The land that we have gone through as spies is a land that devours its inhabitants; and all the people that we saw in it are of great size. 33 There we saw the Nephilim (the Anakites come from the Nephilim); and to ourselves we

NIV
Numbers 13:1-3

¹THE LORD said to Moses, ²"Send some men to explore the land of Canaan, which I am giving to the Israelites. From each ancestral tribe send one of its leaders."

³So at the LORD's command Moses sent them out from the Desert of Paran. All of them were leaders of the Israelites.

Numbers 13:32–14:1-4, 8-9, 20-24

³²And they spread among the Israelites a bad report about the land they had explored. They said, "The land we explored devours those living in it. All the people we saw there are of great size. ³³We saw the Nephilim there (the descendants of Anak come from the Nephilim). We seemed like grasshoppers in our own eyes,

OCTOBER 10

seemed like grasshoppers, and so we seemed to them."

14.1 Then all the congregation raised a loud cry, and the people wept that night. 2 And all the Israelites complained against Moses and Aaron; the whole congregation said to them, "Would that we had died in the land of Egypt! Or would that we had died in this wilderness! 3 Why is the LORD bringing us into this land to fall by the sword? Our wives and our little ones will become booty; would it not be better for us to go back to Egypt?" 4 So they said to one another, "Let us choose a captain, and go back to Egypt."

Key Verse

8 If the LORD is pleased with us, he will bring us into this land and give it to us, a land that flows with milk and honey. 9 Only, do not rebel against the LORD; and do not fear the people of the land, for they are no more than bread for us; their protection is removed from them, and the Lord is with us; do not fear them."

20 Then the LORD said, "I do forgive, just as you have asked; 21 nevertheless—as I live, and as all the earth shall be filled with the glory of the LORD—22 none of the people who have seen my glory and the signs that I did in Egypt and in the wilderness, and yet have tested me these ten times and have not obeyed my voice, 23 shall see the land that I swore to give to their ancestors; none of those who despised me shall see it. 24 But my servant Caleb, because he has a different spirit and has followed me wholeheartedly, I will bring into the land into which he went, and his descendants shall possess it."

and we looked the same to them."

14.1 That night all the people of the community raised their voices and wept aloud. [2]All the Israelites grumbled against Moses and Aaron, and the whole assembly said to them, "If only we had died in Egypt! Or in this desert! [3]Why is the LORD bringing us to this land only to let us fall by the sword? Our wives and children will be taken as plunder. Wouldn't it be better for us to go back to Egypt?" [4]And they said to each other, "We should choose a leader and go back to Egypt."

Key Verse

[8]If the LORD is pleased with us, he will lead us into that land, a land flowing with milk and honey, and will give it to us. [9]Only do not rebel against the LORD. And do not be afraid of the people of the land, because we will swallow them up. Their protection is gone, but the LORD is with us. Do not be afraid of them."

[20]The LORD replied, "I have forgiven them, as you asked. [21]Nevertheless, as surely as I live and as surely as the glory of the LORD fills the whole earth, [22]not one of the men who saw my glory and the miraculous signs I performed in Egypt and in the desert but who disobeyed me and tested me ten times—[23]not one of them will ever see the land I promised on oath to their forefathers. No one who has treated me with contempt will ever see it. [24]But because my servant Caleb has a different spirit and follows me wholeheartedly, I will bring him into the land he went to, and his descendants will inherit it."

UNDERSTANDING THE SCRIPTURE

Numbers 12:1-16. Moses, Miriam, and Aaron are all leaders of the Israelites as well as being brothers and sister. Miriam and Aaron are jealous of Moses' position, though they use his marriage to a Cushite (that is, foreign) woman as a pretext for

their complaints. God hears their fussing and calls all three of them out to the tent of meeting. The Lord, represented by the pillar of cloud, reaffirms Moses' special role and scolds Miriam and Aaron.

Once the cloud has departed, Miriam is

seen to be leprous. What the Bible traditionally calls "leprosy" is not what medicine used to call "leprosy" and now terms "Hansen's Disease." We cannot say with assurance what Miriam's malady was. It is clear, however, that she had been afflicted with some sort of skin condition. Aaron pleads to Moses on her behalf and Moses in turn prays to the Lord. God is willing to heal her, although requiring her to be quarantined for a week. All the Israelites wait until the seven days are over before setting out once again on their journey.

Numbers 13:1-20. At the direction of God, Moses appoints one leading man from each of the tribes to reconnoiter the land of Canaan, the land long promised to Abraham, Isaac, and Jacob and to their descendants, this huge, straggly group of Israelites. Moses gives them specific questions to answer as well as the general instruction "see what the land is like" (13:18). His questions have to do with military and agricultural matters. Are the towns fortified? Does the land yield good crops? He also asks them to bring back some samples of whatever fruit they find.

Numbers 13:21-33. From the first verses that report the spying mission, all seems to be well. In fact, a single cluster of grapes is so big two men have to carry it on a pole between them (13:23). They also find other fruit: pomegranates and figs. After a forty-day expedition the explorers return and show everyone the fruit they have gathered. They describe the land first in the very terms of God's promise: "it flows with milk and honey" (13:27; see also Exodus 3:8; Leviticus 20:24; Jeremiah 11:5, 32:22; Ezekiel 20:6, among many others). The happy report, however, soon turns grim. The spies proclaim that the people who live in the land are much too strong for the Israelites and that their towns and cities are heavily fortified. Caleb is the one voice of encouragement, urging Israel forward. His voice is lost in the dismay of the other explorers. Not only are there well-fortified cities and many people, some of

the people are actually giants! (The "Nephilim" in verse 33 are legendary gigantic people. To speak of seeing Nephilim would be similar to our saying we came across a town inhabited by Paul Bunyan and his family.)

Numbers 14:1-4. The Israelites are distraught. They cry all night. Then they take their familiar complaints to Moses and Aaron, saying they wish they had died in Egypt instead of coming out into this wilderness. (See, for example, Exodus 16:3 and Numbers 11:18.) They decide that Egypt would indeed be better than where they are now, and they talk of electing a new leader and heading back.

Numbers 14:5-10. Joshua, who had also been on the spying mission, joins his voice with Caleb's and they say again that the land is indeed very good, just as the Lord promised it would be. Along with Moses and Aaron they urge the people to put their trust in the Lord, saying that if God is with them then whatever obstacles may appear to be before them can be removed by the Lord. "Do not be afraid," they urge repeatedly. But the Israelites are not listening. In their distress they threaten to stone those who are urging them on.

Numbers 14:11-19. It seems the Lord has had enough of the people's complaining. God appears at the tent of meeting and proposes to Moses to get rid of them and make an even greater nation from Moses. As Moses prayed for Miriam's healing in chapter 12, now he intercedes to God for all Israel.

Numbers 14:20-25. Once again God listens to Moses' prayer. But there are limits to the Lord's patience, it seems. Over and over again the people have fussed and complained about water, about lack of food, about the manna God sends them, now about the inhabitants of the land where the Lord is taking them. Although they saw God's mighty acts on their behalf when they escaped from Egypt, although they have seen God's provisions of water and bread and meat, they still are not able to trust God's continuing ability to care for them. So God tells them that they are free *not* to enter the promised land; indeed, they are forbidden to. Only their children will be able to enter it. Only Joshua and Caleb—who, although they saw the same frightening sights as the other spies, continued to urge the people to follow the Lord—will be able to enter into the land. Everyone else will wander about in the wilderness until the entire first generation has died.

INTERPRETING THE SCRIPTURE

The Scouts and Their Mission

God has been with Israel constantly. The Lord saved them from Pharaoh's army and has fed them daily with manna. God is doing for the people things that they could not do for themselves. At the same time, God wants them to shoulder responsibility for those things that are within their power to do. Thus, in this case, Moses is to send a group of men representing all the tribes to see what lies ahead of them. They are to spy out the land not because God is not going to give it to them and so they must seize it on their own, and certainly not because God doesn't know what is in it, but because God is not taking away their human freedoms and responsibilities. Even with God at the head of their company, the Israelites should know what they face. Thus the men are told to bring back word about the defenses of the towns, as well as the produce of the land.

It is a delicate balance sometimes to trust God while also acting ourselves. We are more likely to keep our balance when we are honest in the endeavor. The scouts were not told to bring back a particular sort of report. That is, they did not have instructions either to sugarcoat a bad situation or to make easy prospects look grim, but to go and look and then tell what they had seen.

What They Saw and What They Said

The scouts' report is a blend of hope and fear. The land is indeed good—but is it too good to be true? One verse of positive report (13:27) is overwhelmed by five verses of fearful news (13:28-29, 31-33). In their fear the spies are not even logical in what they say. If the land is so bad that it "devours those living in it" (13:32 NIV), how can it also be a land of giants (13:32-33)? Caleb's voice is lost in the fear of the others' voices. But note well what Caleb says. He does not dispute the facts of the majority report. He does not say, for instance, that the towns are not fortified. Rather, he says that "we can certainly do it" (13:30 NIV). It is not the facts that are in dispute, but the interpretation of those facts.

And thus it often is in our own decision-making. We often have an accurate grasp of the situation at hand, but fear makes us believe the future to be too grim. Compared to the size of the problem—whether it is countering institutional racism, fostering world peace, meeting the local church's budget, or finding time for daily devotions—we feel like mere grasshoppers.

The People's First Response

Several times the people have said, in effect or in so many words, "Let's just go back to Egypt." Now once again they complain about their leaders, accuse God of treachery, and say they want a new leader who will return them to Egypt. It is harder to live a life of responsible freedom than to give up all one's initiative to an authority figure. Maturity takes more work and thought than immaturity. "For freedom Christ has set us free," writes Paul (Galatians 5:1). All the same, there are days when I'd just as soon stay at home reading novels than face the responsibilities and choices of life as an adult. I have known people who say that once they made the momentous decision to surrender to Jesus Christ, they have not had to make any other decisions in their lives. I do not doubt their sincerity. But my experience has been different. I know that God is "alive and well and living in this world," but sometimes I feel like a grasshopper and would prefer to return to the security of slavery in Egypt—or back to childhood.

Minority Report

Joshua and Caleb repeat the news that the land God has promised them is a good land. They do not make light of the practical difficulties ahead but remind the people of the original promise of God to be with them. Note again that they do not try to diminish any part of the situation. But God's presence is the counter force that should tip the balance. "The Lord is with us," they say. "Do not fear them" (that is, the people in the land) (Numbers 14:9).

Yet, as it is easier to worship the golden calf that we can see rather than the God whom our eyes cannot behold; it is easier to fear the visible threat than to trust the assurance of our invisible God. "We can't afford it" or "We don't have enough people to do that" or "We have to be realistic about our situation" are sentiments that can be heard in countless church meetings. And in many circumstances, they may be exactly right. God certainly does not call us to be blind to the realities of our situations. Jesus himself spoke about "counting the cost" before committing oneself to a project

(Luke 14:28-33). And over and over again we find ourselves in that uncomfortable position. Logic and comfort tell us to go back to Egypt; a few voices urge us to continue to follow the Lord into a new land. It is easy for a minority to be shouted down.

God's Last Word

"In spite of all the signs that I [God] have done among them" (Numbers 14:11), they refuse to believe. In a conversation similar to that on Sinai (Exodus 32:10-14), God proposes to Moses to destroy the people and begin anew with Moses as patriarch. Using arguments similar to those he said on Sinai, Moses once again intercedes on behalf of the people. God again forgives them, "stiff-necked" though they are.

This time there is a difference from the events at Sinai. God forgives and punishes simultaneously. God will not refuse to forgive the penitent sinner (although here the people are not repenting, but Moses is praying on their behalf). God does not, however, make everything come out just the way we wanted it to in the first place. We may, by our choices or by our refusing to make choices, miss out on some of the things God has prepared for us. If the Kingdom of God begins in this life, as Jesus repeatedly taught (Luke 17:21, for example), then for as long as we refuse to live a kingdom life here on earth, we are missing what cannot be gotten back. God does not kill the people for their rebellion, but only gives them what they say they want. It is a grave punishment.

SHARING THE SCRIPTURE

PREPARING TO TEACH

Preparing Our Hearts

Today's devotional reading is actually part of the background scripture. Read

Numbers 14:5-19. Here, Joshua and Caleb urge the people not to rebel against God. What are the "giants" (13:33 KJV) in the land of your own life that cause you to fear? Why might these large problems or conflicts prompt you to rebel against God? How do you try to guard against such rebellion?

Now read the entire background scripture from Numbers 12:1–14:25. Make a list of the major events that occur in this lengthy passage. What does this story say to you about how God has acted in the past? How would the outcome of the story have been different had the people trusted God rather than rebelled? What lesson is in this story for your own life?

Conclude your personal preparation time with a prayer asking God to help you face difficulties with confidence, to go against the crowd if necessary in order to be faithful to God's leading.

Preparing Our Minds

Read this lesson in its entirety. Look again carefully at today's scripture passage. Note an important point made in the lesson: the facts reported by both the minority and majority were the same. Where the ten spies differed from Joshua and Caleb was in their *interpretation* of the facts. Whereas the majority of spies believed that the obstacles were insurmountable, Joshua and Caleb essentially told the people to trust God and not rebel so that God would give them the promised land. Perhaps you can think of other situations in which both parties agreed upon the facts but recommended very different action based on their interpretation of the data.

Preparing Our Learning Space

You may want to write the suggested quotations concerning opportunity on newsprint prior to the session for use during the Introduction. You may also want to write the questions that appear under "Minority Report."

Have on hand:

✔ several Bibles
✔ newsprint and marker
✔ paper and pencils.

LEADING THE CLASS

(1) Introduction

Since today's lesson is entitled "A Missed Opportunity," plan to begin the session with one or more of these quotations about opportunities. If possible, write them on newsprint prior to the session so that everyone can see them.

The most magnificent opportunities come into our lives disguised as problems. (John Powell)

To recognize opportunity is the difference between success and failure. (author unknown)

We are all faced with a series of great opportunities brilliantly disguised as impossible situations. (Charles R. Swindoll)

The pessimist sees the difficulty in every opportunity; the optimist sees the opportunity in every difficulty. (Lawrence Pearsall Jacks)

Invite class members to comment on any of these quotations by asking these questions:

(1) **Why do you think people miss opportunities?** (Be sure to note that the facts of the situation may be agreed upon, but the person who takes advantage of the opportunity likely interprets those facts differently from the one who dismisses the situation as impossible.)

(2) **Do any of these quotations reflect an incident in your own life? If so, briefly describe what happened.**

Move to today's lesson from Numbers by pointing out that when the Israelites heard reports of the spies who had been sent to reconnoiter the land, the people relied upon the majority report that said the situation was impossible, rather than trusting God as Joshua and Caleb urged them to do. Lift up today's main question: **Is it ever possible to "push God too far," to disobey past the point of God's forgiveness?**

(2) The Scouts and Their Mission

Choose someone to read Numbers 13:1-3. Ask:

[?]
(1) **Why might God have specified that a leader from each ancestral tribe be appointed to the reconnaissance mission?**
(2) **Why do you think a reconnaissance mission was necessary in the first place?** (Note the ideas given in the first paragraph of this section in the Interpreting the Scripture portion.)
(3) **Had you been one of the twelve spies, what might your expectations have been as you set off from the wilderness toward Canaan?**
(4) **Had you been one of the Israelites, what hopes, dreams, and fears might you have had as the spies embarked on their mission?**

(3) What They Saw and What They Said

Have someone read Numbers 13:17-33, which includes background about what the spies were asked to do and a full report of their findings. Note that the Nephilim, who are also mentioned in Genesis 6:4, were said to be extremely tall people with superhuman power.

Help to interpret the Bible reading by retelling or reading aloud the information in the two paragraphs of this section of the Interpreting the Scripture portion of the lesson.

If time permits, discuss with the class some modern-day problems that the church could confront if we would listen to those who say "we can certainly do it" (13:30 NIV), rather than to the pessimists who believe that tackling a huge problem is futile.

(4) The People's First Response

Read aloud Numbers 14:1-4. Discuss with the group the ways in which the Israelites responded to the reports. On newsprint, list these responses, which include crying, complaining, wanting to go back to their old situation, and considering the possibility of choosing a new leader to take them back to Egypt. Ask:

(1) **Why do you think the people seem so fearful and unwilling to trust God for their future?** [?]
(2) **What might your response to the news have been had you been in their situation?**
(3) **Can you think of other situations in the church when the congregation had stepped out in faith, become fearful, and wanted to return to their old ways? What happened?** (Such a discussion about events in your own church may be helpful as long as it does not become a "gripe and blame" session.)

(5) Minority Report

Read aloud Numbers 14:5-12. This passage includes both background information and today's key verses, 8-9. Distribute paper and pencils and invite class members to write a private response to these questions, which you may want to write on newsprint prior to class:

(1) **When you are faced with difficulties, do you truly believe that God is with you? If so, how does God's presence empower and embolden you so that you do not fear what lies ahead?** [?]
(2) **Think of a time when you heeded a minority report, rather than going along with the crowd. What was the outcome?**

(6) God's Last Word

Choose a reader for Numbers 14:20-24. Ask:

(1) **If you had been one of the Israelites, what good news would you hear in God's words?**

(2) **What words of punishment would you hear?**

(3) **What does the story of the opportunity that the Israelites missed because of their rebellion say to modern Christians about how we approach or turn away from opportunities?**

Before you dismiss the group, be sure to lift up at least one of the activities suggested below.

HELPING CLASS MEMBERS ACT

Tell the students to be aware of situations where they disagree with the majority view and yet are afraid of going against the crowd. Suggest that they use part of today's key verses, "Do not rebel against the Lord," as words of encouragement to stand up for the minority opinion.

Recommend that class members write journal entries about times when they faced difficult challenges. Did they embrace these challenges as opportunities, or withdraw from them in fear? If this opportunity were to present itself again, how would they respond?

Suggest that students do whatever they can to support someone who is willing to face uncertainty now for the promise of a better life ahead. For example, perhaps a middle-aged worker is changing careers, or an older adult is moving into a retirement community.

PLANNING FOR NEXT SUNDAY

During next week's session we will look at the Israelites' experience of wandering in the desert. Ask the class to prepare for the lesson by reading Deuteronomy 1:41–2:25, paying particular attention to 1:41–2:8.

IN THE WILDERNESS

PREVIEWING THE LESSON

Lesson Scripture: Deuteronomy 1:41–2:8
Background Scripture: Deuteronomy 1:41–2:25
Key Verse: Deuteronomy 2:7

Focus of the Lesson:
Despite God's gracious care, the Israelites disobeyed and had to pay the price for their impetuous actions.

Main Question of the Lesson:
Is there life after punishment?

This lesson will enable adult learners to:
(1) learn about the Israelites' sojourn in the desert.
(2) consider their own "wilderness" experiences.
(3) respond by being aware of God's presence in times of trouble.

Today's lesson may be outlined as follows:
(1) Introduction
(2) Too Little, Too Late
(3) Strange Protection
(4) Forty Years Later
(5) God's Long Memory

FOCUSING ON THE MAIN QUESTION

The main question of this week's lesson, **Is there life after punishment?** may sound too flippant for Bible study, but I mean something quite serious by it. We saw last week that the Israelites were persuaded by the scary reports brought to them by their frightened spies that the promised land was already inhabited by people they could not conquer. Disregarding the pleas of Moses and Aaron and the urging of two of the scouts, Caleb and Joshua, the Israelites said they would rather go back to Egypt than try to go into the promised land, even with God leading them. By that time God had heard them complaining needlessly about many things and decided that since they did not want to enter the land, they would indeed not enter it. God threatened to destroy the people and start over again with Moses as the sole patriarch, but Moses interceded and God relented. Still, the people's determined faithlessness is punished, for the Lord maintains that the entire first generation will be kept out of the promised land.

If this were a moral tale we were writing for children, we might end it here and say, "See: this is what happens to people who disobey! They missed out on all the good things God had promised them in their own land. So you had better be careful always to obey God lest you be punished too!" That wouldn't be wrong, exactly, but it is far from right enough. Yes, the punishment is real. God did not suddenly take it all back, or say, "Oh, that's OK. I didn't really mean it. I'll pretend you never really disobeyed."

What is to become of Israel? Will God send them back to Egypt, back to their slavery under Pharaoh? Or will God leave them to their own devices in the wilderness, to make their way as best they can on their own? Using theological terms we phrase the question as one of the relationship between "judgment" and "grace." These are not just historical matters or issues of interest only to theologians. What is to become of us when we sin? Even after we repent, can God take us back, or have we lost out on God's good promises? Is there life after punishment?

READING THE SCRIPTURE

NRSV
Deuteronomy 1:41–2:8

41 You answered me, "We have sinned against the LORD! We are ready to go up and fight, just as the LORD our God commanded us." So all of you strapped on your battle gear, and thought it easy to go up into the hill country. 42 The LORD said to me, "Say to them, 'Do not go up and do not fight, for I am not in the midst of you; otherwise you will be defeated by your enemies.'" 43 Although I told you, you would not listen. You rebelled against the command of the LORD and presumptuously went up into the hill country. 44 The Amorites who lived in that hill country then came out against you and chased you as bees do. They beat you down in Seir as far as Hormah. 45 When you returned and wept before the LORD, the LORD would neither heed your voice nor pay you any attention.

46 After you had stayed at Kadesh as many days as you did, 2:1 we journeyed back into the wilderness, in the direction of the Red Sea, as the LORD had told me and skirted Mount Seir for many days. 2 Then the LORD said to me: 3 "You have been skirting this hill coun-

NIV
Deuteronomy 1:41–2:8

41Then you replied, "We have sinned against the LORD. We will go up and fight, as the LORD our God commanded us." So every one of you put on his weapons, thinking it easy to go up into the hill country.

42But the LORD said to me, "Tell them, 'Do not go up and fight, because I will not be with you. You will be defeated by your enemies.'"

43So I told you, but you would not listen. You rebelled against the LORD's command and in your arrogance you marched up into the hill country. 44The Amorites who lived in those hills came out against you; they chased you like a swarm of bees and beat you down from Seir all the way to Hormah. 45You came back and wept before the LORD, but he paid no attention to your weeping and turned a deaf ear to you. 46And so you stayed in Kadesh many days—all the time you spent there.

2:1 Then we turned back and set out toward the desert along the route to the Red Sea, as the LORD had directed me. For a long time we made our way around the

try long enough. Head north, 4 and charge the people as follows: You are about to pass through the territory of your kindred, the descendants of Esau, who live in Seir. They will be afraid of you, so, be very careful 5 not to engage in battle with them, for I will not give you even so much as a foot's length of their land, since I have given Mount Seir to Esau as a possession. 6 You shall purchase food from them for money, so that you may eat; and you shall also buy water from them for money, so that you may drink. **7 Surely the LORD your God has blessed you in all your undertakings; he knows your going through this great wilderness. These forty years the LORD your God has been with you; you have lacked nothing."** 8 So we passed by our kin, the descendants of Esau who live in Seir.

Key Verse

hill country of Seir.

²Then the LORD said to me, ³"You have made your way around this hill country long enough; now turn north. ⁴Give the people these orders: 'You are about to pass through the territory of your brothers the descendants of Esau, who live in Seir. They will be afraid of you, but be very careful. ⁵Do not provoke them to war, for I will not give you any of their land, not even enough to put your foot on. I have given Esau the hill country of Seir as his own. ⁶You are to pay them in silver for the food you eat and the water you drink.'"

⁷The LORD your God has blessed you in all the work of your hands. He has watched over your journey through this vast desert. These forty years the LORD your God has been with you, and you have not lacked anything.

⁸So we went on past our brothers the descendants of Esau, who live in Seir.

Key Verse

UNDERSTANDING THE SCRIPTURE

Deuteronomy 1:41-45. The major part of the book of Deuteronomy is set as a series of addresses or sermons Moses makes to the Israelites when they are at the Jordan River, on the verge of entering into the promised land. In these speeches, Moses tells them again the history of their life over the past forty years. (We even call the book *Deuteronomy* from two Greek words that mean "second law," referring to a retelling of the law already given.) Verse 41 picks up the action immediately after the point where we left things in Numbers 14 last week—only this time it is in the form of Moses' reciting the story, rather than an account of things as they are going on.

When Moses told the people that God wouldn't make them go into the land, indeed would not even *allow* them to, they immediately changed their minds. Sud-denly they were eager to fight; they grabbed their weapons and started out against the Amorites. Moses warned them not to try, saying that the Lord was not with them and that they were sure to be defeated. But they paid no attention to Moses and "presumptuously" (1:43 NRSV) or "in [their] arrogance" (NIV) marched over into the hill country. And, sure enough, they were defeated. They ran away as from swarming bees. When they finally turned to the Lord, God paid no attention to them.

Deuteronomy 1:46–2:15. The Israelites stayed in Kadesh for awhile and then returned to the "wilderness" (2:1 NRSV) or "desert" (NIV). Because most of us tend to picture a desert as trackless wastes of sand, endless dunes, and no vegetation, we probably should use the word "wilderness" instead of "desert." The land into which the Israelites returned was more like the steppe regions of central Asia than the desert of the Sahara. It is without marked roads, but has scrub vegetation and intermittent streams (called *wadis*) so that a nomadic life is possible.

The Lord is no longer ignoring them but, through Moses, again gives them directions. When they come to the territory of their relatives, the descendants of Esau, God commands them to be careful not to start a fight and to pay them for what they eat and drink from their territory. This is not the promised land, and even if they go to war for it, God will not let them have any of it. God gave similar instructions to pass peaceably through the territory of Moab (2:8-9) and of the Ammonites (2:18-19).

Moses sums up the history of their past forty years by reminding them that during all that time "the LORD your God has blessed you . . . has watched over your journey through this vast desert . . . has been with you, and you have not lacked anything" (2:7 NIV).

Deuteronomy 2:16-18. God had said that the wilderness wandering would last until all the original adult men—those who had refused to follow Moses and Aaron, Caleb and Joshua, into the new land—had died. Now when the original generation has died, God instructs Moses to give the Israelites their marching orders. It has been a long time, but God has not forgotten them.

Deuteronomy 2:19-25. The instructions show that God's memory is longer even than the forty years of going about in the wilderness. In one sense, it is as if no time had passed at all. What the first generation would have gotten, their children may now receive. When the time of punishment is over, the Israelites can go on into the future with God. (In some ways this is similar to all Israel waiting seven days for the time of Miriam's punishment as we read in last week's scripture lesson from Numbers 12:14-16.)

Just as God told Israel not to harass the descendants of Esau or the Moabites during their journeying because God had promised those lands to the people in them, so God now tells Israel not to fight with the Ammonites. God's promise to Israel is going to be fulfilled, but it will not be carried out at the expense of others who have been given lands by God. That is, the Lord's promises to one group will not be broken in order to care for another group.

We often read over passages such as Deuteronomy 2:19-25 in great haste, in part because it is studded with very many difficult names. Also, it is a "sidebar" to the main story we are following; these verses are not specifically about the Israelites. Yet we should slow down long enough to remember that God's concern is not only for us and our spiritual ancestors. Even peoples we know nothing else about except that their names appear in the Bible are beloved children of God. When God makes a promise, as to Lot and his descendants (2:19), God continues to honor that promise.

INTERPRETING THE SCRIPTURE

Too Little, Too Late

When the Israelites saw that they had gone too far with God in refusing to go over into the promised land, they then changed their minds. But it was too late for them. They made matters worse by disobeying yet again and trying to mount an invasion after God had specifically told them not to. This is such a human way to behave. How often we push and push and push against limits, not stopping until we have gone too far. Children test their parents' limits with whining; students push teachers by talking among themselves instead of paying attention to the lessons. There are even cases when parishioners habitually fuss about their pastor. Then a line is crossed. The parents decree no television for a week; the teacher springs a pop quiz; the pastor requests a move. All of a sudden it is as if the complainers "wake up." "We'll be good, we promise," say the children. The students are suddenly models of attentive interest. The parishioners start to talk about the minister's strengths. Often, though, it is too late to undo the effects of the previous behavior.

We have all been in similar situations, I am sure. Not one of us has likely spent forty years in the wilderness as a result. Often we have learned from such experiences so that our treatment of other people or of God is improved as a result of a difficult lesson.

Strange Protection

What we often fail to see is God's presence with us even through judgment. We have gotten the idea that God is present in good times and that bad times mean the Lord is somehow absent, perhaps punishing us by such absence. God did not abandon Israel, however. God did not make their punishment anything other than what was said the first time on the edge of the promised land: they would not be allowed to enter. As you read the rest of the Bible you will see that God doesn't continue to throw this incident up to the Israelites.

I call this section "strange" protection because God's behavior is so different from what we tend to do and how we tend to think God ought to behave. When I am right it can be such a delicious feeling, such an inviting temptation to continue to tell those in the wrong that I was right. But when I succumb to those temptations, hard as they are to resist, what am I doing except perpetuating the original quarrel?

Whatever the nature of the incident, we cannot get past it if the "winner" is unwilling to leave it in the past. God demonstrates this better way of being throughout the wilderness journeying, continuing to bless Israel so that they have "lacked nothing" (Deuteronomy 2:7).

Forty Years Later

When the punishment is over, it is over. God does not tell Israel they will get only part of the land originally promised, or that it will not be "flowing with milk and honey" after all. No, the covenant that was made is upheld. When the punishment has run its course, God moves on into the future without continuing to hark back to the people's failures.

Think of our own criminal justice system. When it works as it is supposed to, the person who commits a crime is apprehended, tried, found guilty, and if the crime is of a serious enough nature, sentenced to a term in prison. After the required amount of time has been served, the person is set free, presumably to pick up the pieces of life disrupted by the arrest and all that followed it. We say such people have "paid their debt to society." And yet it doesn't always work out that way. I am not thinking here of unsolved crimes or plea-bargains or such. Rather, society often does not consider the debt paid, regardless of how much prison time has been served. A convicted felon may not vote, may not hold most public offices, may not follow many professions. Family members, former neighbors, old employers and coworkers—most people will continue to see a "criminal" rather than someone who has paid the societal debt in full. There is physical life after the punishment, but it may be greatly curtailed and cramped compared with what had been before, to the point that it may not feel like life at all.

We do not have to look at such drastic cases as people arrested and jailed. Many friendships and family relationships are disrupted and never allowed to get back on track because we are unwilling to pick up the relationship "forty years later" and continue on.

God's Long Memory

The Old Testament is primarily about Israel, just as the New Testament tells of the earliest Christians. It is a mistake, however, for us to think that Israelites and Christians are the only people God cares for and the only ones with whom covenants are made and kept. Land promised by God to the descendants of Lot may not be violated by Israel. God promised Esau's descendants a place of their own, and Israel is not allowed to violate that.

Some Christians believe that God's covenant in Jesus Christ is the only one in effect today. I think that is not the case.

Our Lord *keeps* promises. Israel is reminded in these verses in Deuteronomy that, although God does indeed care for them, they are neither the only people on earth nor the only ones under God's care. This may be a difficult idea for some persons even to consider. But I would ask you to think about the alternative: what would it be like if God did break promises? What if God forgot about the Ammonites (2:19) and Moabites (2:18), both of whom were traditionally related through Abraham's nephew Lot, and others who had been given promises when Moses came along? What if God grew so tired of Israel's sins that the Mosaic covenant was thrown out? Would that not say that God might become so tired of Christians' sins that our covenant in Jesus Christ could be done away with? No, I think our Lord is a promise keeper, even to people we do not know. Even with people we may not like.

SHARING THE SCRIPTURE

PREPARING TO TEACH

Preparing Our Hearts

Isaiah 35, today's devotional reading, speaks of what life will be like when the people return home to Zion. After the wilderness experience, which in this chapter probably refers to Israel's exile in Babylon, there will come a time of joy and gladness, a time when "sorrow and sighing shall flee away" (Isaiah 35:10). As you read this passage, imagine what it must have been like to march into Zion after a "wilderness" experience, wherever that might have been.

Now turn to Deuteronomy 1:41–2:25, which is the background scripture for today's lesson. Here Moses rehearses the story of the people's presumptuousness

in trying to claim the promised land on their own after they had refused to heed the claims of Joshua and Caleb, who believed that God would give the people the victory. As a result, God would not let the people go into their new land but sent them instead into the wilderness. Beginning in Deuteronomy 2:16 we learn that the first rebellious generation has died and the Israelites are now going to resume their journey toward the promised land.

Think back in your own life to a time when you had rebelled against God and then decided to take matters in your own hands. What happened? How did this situation work itself out? What did you learn about how God works? You may want to meditate on these questions or write about them in your spiritual journal.

Preparing Our Minds

Review the scripture and this lesson. You may also want to consult a map, though you may not be able to locate all of the places mentioned in the lesson on a single map. The map of the Exodus in *Bible Teacher Kit* (available from Cokesbury, p. 137) is helpful, as is the one entitled "Israel in Canaan" (p. 139). Look at the Exodus map to locate the King's Highway where the people traveled.

The Deuteronomistic historian clearly shows that the upshot of rebellion against God is diaster. In this section of scripture the reader is also introduced to themes that, according to *Harper's Bible Commentary*, occur later in Deuteronomy: "God's anger with Moses (3:26; 4:21; 34:4), faith and courage in war (7:17-21; chapter 20), and Israel's unworthiness (8:11-18; 9:1-9)."

Preparing Our Learning Space

Have on hand:
- several Bibles
- optional maps
- hymnals.

LEADING THE CLASS

(1) Introduction

One way to begin the session is to read or retell the Focusing on the Main Question portion of the lesson. Be sure to lift up today's main question.

Another way to begin is to invite students to recall incidents from their youth (or the early years of someone they know but do not mention by name) when they acted impetuously against authority and then lived to regret it, possibly because they incurred punishment for their action. If the class needs help in getting started, here are possible scenarios that may jog some memories:
- a young driver took the car out after being told specifically that he or she was

not to do so. Possibly an accident ensued or the driver received a ticket.
- a teenager continued to hang around with the wrong crowd, despite stern warnings from parents to stay away from this group, and wound up in serious trouble.
- a high school student dated someone that parents did not approve of, possibly with serious consequences, such as a pregnancy.

After a few volunteers have shared their stories, ask these questions:

(1) **How does impetuous behavior, especially if it causes unalterable situations, affect our lives?**

(2) **Are you able to wait for things? If not, how might your impatience cause needless suffering and mistakes for you?**

(3) **What clues have you had as to God's presence, even in the throes of a difficult situation?**

Close this portion of the lesson by lifting up today's main question: **Is there life after punishment?**

(2) Too Little, Too Late

Note that this week's reading follows the action of last week's events as recorded in Numbers 12:1–14:25. Review that lesson if you think it is necessary. If time permits, you may want to use some information from Understanding the Scripture to help orient the class as to what is happening. Make sure the group understands that the "you" refers to the Israelite people and "me" refers to Moses. Next, choose a volunteer to read Deuteronomy 1:41-46. Then ask:

(1) **What is the people's sin?** (The sin in 1:41 is named in 1:32. The people did not trust God. Consequently, they rebelled. They were afraid and did not go up to Canaan as the Lord had commanded. Their lack of trust prompted God to punish the people by saying that "not one of this evil generation—

?

shall see the good land that I [God] swore to give to your ancestors" (1:35).

(2) How did the people try to express regret for their sin? (Note in 1:41 that the people had reversed their decision and were now ready to fight. They thought they would be following God's command to do so, but they did it in their own time and way.)

(3) How did God respond to their change of heart? (The people were warned that God would not be in their midst (1:42). They were told not to fight, but they would not listen, according to 1:43.)

(4) What happened? (The people rebelled by presumptuously going against the Amorites, but they were quickly routed and God paid no attention to their cries.)

Conclude this part of the lesson by asking the class to meditate silently on times when they have rebelled against God, perhaps acting presumptuously against God's will. You may want to close the meditation period with a brief prayer, asking God's forgiveness for times when we have failed to be obedient.

(3) Strange Protection

Now choose someone to read Deuteronomy 2:1-8. If you have a map showing the time of Exodus, you may want to locate some of the places so that the students can see how the Israelites wandered in the desert. If you use a wall map, be sure everyone can see it; if you photocopy handouts (which is legally allowable if you use maps from *Bible Teacher Kit*), be sure you have an ample supply to distribute.

Note that their wandering was a direct result of their rebellion against God when the people refused to accept the minority report of Joshua and Caleb and move into the promised land.

Also remind the class that this account is "after the fact." In Deuteronomy Moses is helping the people to recall their journey with God. It is a kind of historical review of their journey with God.

Now ask these questions:

(1) As you look at Deuteronomy 2:7, what does this key verse tell you about God? (God has been with the people and blessed them so that they lacked nothing.)

(2) Does this information in verse 7 surprise you in any way? If so, how?

(3) How is God's behavior different from what most of us would do? (See "Strange Protection" in the Interpreting the Scripture portion of the lesson for ideas to augment the discussion.)

(4) How does God's behavior with the Israelites reassure you as you face your own "wilderness" experiences?

Close this part of the lesson by asking the students to share with the class, or a small group, or a partner, a time when they felt abandoned by God but later realized that God had been with them all along.

(4) Forty Years Later

As we look back on today's scripture, we are aware that God has punished the people by forcing them to march in the desert for forty years until the generation of rebels died out. Yet, when the punishment is over, it is over. As Moses is speaking to the people, they have completed their forty years. At this point the Israelites are poised to take possession of the land God had promised to them since the days of Abraham (1:8). God is giving them the land despite the disobedience that prompted the forty years of punishment.

Ask these questions:

(1) How would our family relationships be different if people were able to let the punishment be over when it is over? Give examples, if possible.

(2) How would our local, national, and international relationships be different?

As you conduct this discussion, note that God does not bring up the people's failure to obey. Instead, God acts justly, for the people were punished, but God is also merciful, for they will have a chance to move into the land that their ancestors had been promised, despite their disobedience.

(5) God's Long Memory

Ask the class to look again at Deuteronomy 2:2-6. Then ask these questions:

(1) What were God's instructions regarding how the Israelites should act in Seir, the home of Esau's descendants? (Recall that the biblical story continues through Esau's brother, Jacob. Esau's people, however, are descendants of Abraham and Isaac and, therefore, have also given land by God. The Lord says that the Israelites will not possess "even so much as a foot's length of their land" (2:5). Moreover, they are to pay their kindred for any supplies they take from the land.)

(2) What does God's careful protection of the descendants of Esau say to you about God as a keeper of promises? (Refer to "God's Long Memory" in the Interpreting the Scripture section for discussion ideas.)

To bring the lesson to a close, distribute hymnals if yours includes a psalter. Ask students to turn to Psalm 90 (*The United Methodist Hymnal*, p. 809) and read it responsively.

Before you dismiss the class, be sure to lift up at least one of the activities below.

HELPING CLASS MEMBERS ACT

Suggest that students privately review some "wilderness" experiences in their own lives. What had happened to cause such an experience? How was God present?

Recommend that class members memorize today's key verse, Deuteronomy 2:7. This is a helpful verse to remember, especially when one feels that life is going badly and that God is nowhere to be found.

Encourage students to try to act as God does, meting out punishment as necessary but then forgetting the offense when the punishment is over.

PLANNING FOR NEXT SUNDAY

Next week's lesson focuses on the Great Commandment, as found in Deuteronomy 6:4-5. This commandment was not just for the people who heard it originally but was intended to be passed from generation to generation. In preparation for next week's lesson, "Teach Your Children Well," ask the students to read Deuteronomy 6, especially verses 1-9 and 20-24.

TEACH YOUR CHILDREN WELL

PREVIEWING THE LESSON

Lesson Scripture: Deuteronomy 6:1-9, 20-24
Background Scripture: Deuteronomy 6
Key Verses: Deuteronomy 6:4-5

Focus of the Lesson:
Through Moses, God gave the people commandments to live by and pass on to their children.

Main Question of the Lesson:
How are we to pass on to the next generation what we have learned about God so that the community of faith will continue?

This lesson will enable adult learners to:
(1) hear God's great commandment.
(2) consider how faith is transmitted from one generation to the next.
(3) respond by passing their beliefs on to the next generation.

Today's lesson may be outlined as follows:
(1) Introduction
(2) The Great Commandment
(3) The Great Temptation
(4) Unto the Next Generation

FOCUSING ON THE MAIN QUESTION

Have you ever heard the saying, "Christianity is never more than one generation away from extinction"? It may be said to shock people into thinking, and there is a good bit of truth in it. We see the same phenomenon most starkly with individual congregations in areas of diminishing population. Many tiny rural congregations will go out of existence as separate churches when the last of their elderly members die. Whether the younger population attends different churches or no church at all—or perhaps the area has no younger population anymore—their absence in a particular place may mean the demise of a once thriving congregation.

Some congregations who see this future ahead of themselves in a few years may hire a youth director to attract new teenagers or start a daycare center in the hopes of gaining more young adult members. The realities of shifting populations throughout the country means that some areas will not be able to sustain the same number of individual congregations as they have previously. The reality of the total population of the country is enough to sustain all we have and more, if people choose to make a commitment to a community of faith.

Many reasons are given for declining numbers besides people's moving away to follow the jobs to distant areas. "People are just too busy," we hear, or "People don't believe faith is relevant anymore." Busy-ness is certainly real and goodness knows there are enough competing "faiths" to attract our potential members.

One would think that Moses and the Israelites wouldn't have either of these problems. Out in the wilderness, everyone was there—where else would they be? And out there in the wilderness, the Lord didn't seem to have very attractive competition. But the issue was just as real in that generation as in ours, and has been in all the generations in between. Today's lesson prompts us to ask: **How are we to pass on to the next generation what we have learned about God so that the community of faith will continue?**

READING THE SCRIPTURE

NRSV
Deuteronomy 6:1-9, 20-24

1 Now this is the commandment—the statutes and the ordinances—that the LORD your God charged me to teach you to observe in the land that you are about to cross into and occupy, 2 so that you and your children and your children's children may fear the LORD your God all the days of your life, and keep all his decrees and his commandments that I am commanding you, so that your days may be long. 3 Hear therefore, O Israel, and observe them diligently, so that it may go well with you, and so that you may multiply greatly in a land flowing with milk and honey, as the LORD , the God of your ancestors, has promised you.

4 Hear, O Israel: The LORD is our God, the LORD alone. 5 You shall love the LORD your God with all your heart, and with all your soul, and with all your might. 6 Keep these words that I am commanding you today in your heart. 7 Recite them to your children and talk about them when you are at home and when you are away, when you lie down and when you rise. 8 Bind them as a sign on your hand, fix them as an emblem on your forehead,

Key Verses

NIV
Deuteronomy 6:1-9, 20-24

[1]These are the commands, decrees and laws the LORD your God directed me to teach you to observe in the land that you are crossing the Jordan to possess, [2]so that you, your children and their children after them may fear the LORD your God as long as you live by keeping all his decrees and commands that I give you, and so that you may enjoy long life. [3]Hear, O Israel, and be careful to obey so that it may go well with you and that you may increase greatly in a land flowing with milk and honey, just as the LORD, the God of your fathers, promised you.

[4]Hear, O Israel: The LORD our God, the LORD is one. [5]Love the LORD your God with all your heart and with all your soul and with all your strength. [6]These commandments that I give you today are to be upon your hearts. [7]Impress them on your children. Talk about them when you sit at home and when you walk along the road, when you lie down and when you get up. [8]Tie them as symbols on your hands and bind them on your foreheads. [9]Write them on the doorframes of your houses and on your gates.

Key Verses

9 and write them on the doorposts of your house and on your gates.

20 When your children ask you in time to come, "What is the meaning of the decrees and the statutes and the ordinances that the LORD our God has commanded you?" 21 then you shall say to your children, "We were Pharaoh's slaves in Egypt, but the LORD brought us out of Egypt with a mighty hand. 22 The LORD displayed before our eyes great and awesome signs and wonders against Egypt, against Pharaoh and all his household. 23 He brought us out from there in order to bring us in, to give us the land that he promised on oath to our ancestors. 24 Then the LORD commanded us to observe all these statutes, to fear the LORD our God, for our lasting good, so as to keep us alive, as is now the case."

20In the future, when your son asks you, "What is the meaning of the stipulations, decrees and laws the LORD our God has commanded you?" 21tell him: "We were slaves of Pharaoh in Egypt, but the LORD brought us out of Egypt with a mighty hand. 22Before our eyes the LORD sent miraculous signs and wonders—great and terrible—upon Egypt and Pharaoh and his whole household. 23But he brought us out from there to bring us in and give us the land that he promised on oath to our forefathers. 24The LORD commanded us to obey all these decrees and to fear the LORD our God, so that we might always prosper and be kept alive, as is the case today.

UNDERSTANDING THE SCRIPTURE

Deuteronomy 6:1-9. Forty years have passed since God led Israel into freedom from their slavery in Egypt. The people are now at the very brink of crossing over into the promised land. Moses gathers them together and retells the story of their salvation. Why does he do such a thing? Because during their wandering in the wilderness, all those who were adults in the Exodus have died. Moses tells the story again to people who were not eyewitnesses of the great events. And Moses gives them the law again. (This is what the name we use for the book, *Deuteronomy*, means: "Second Law.")

Moses begins the recital with the most basic premise of Judaism, which continues into Christianity: there is one God. And that one God demands our undivided loyalty: loyalty of mind and life. That is what Deuteronomy 6:5 says. I know that is not what your English translation says. You read the more familiar words, "You shall love the LORD your God with all your

heart, and with all your soul, and with all your might." That is what the Hebrew words say when you translate them into English. But some of the English words don't mean the same things. (Before you give up in confusion, please read a couple more sentences.) The word we translate as "love" means "be loyal to" in Hebrew. (Loyalty is not a bad definition for love in any language, I think.) It has nothing to do with emotions. It doesn't mean to feel nice about or to be all emotionally attached to God. It means to be loyal to God, regardless of how we are feeling toward God on a particular day. Indeed, one can be loyal to God even without liking God.

But doesn't the verse say to love God with all your heart? Yes, it does. But the Hebrews divided the body symbolically in different ways than we are used to. To us, *heart* refers to emotions. Now if you stop and think about it for a moment, you can see that that is a symbolic usage even for us, because we all know that the heart is a pump to keep the blood moving in our bodies and isn't *really* where we feel our emotions. To say *heart* is just how we express this image in English. For the Israelites, however, *heart* meant the place where decisions are made and where one thinks. So the verse is saying we are supposed to "be loyal to God with all our thinking and all our decision making." And to say that this is to be done "with all your might" indicates right at the start that it may sometimes be hard work. You don't have to use any might, let alone "all your might," to do something that is simple and pleasant. Things that are hard, things that are sometimes what we'd rather not do, those are things for which we have to use might.

These words are to be kept in our heart, says Moses in verse 6. *Heart* here means the same thing it does in verse 5: mind. We are to remember and to think about God's law. And these laws are not to be kept privately inside each individual. Verse 7 tells us to talk about them to our children and at home and away from home, the last thing in the evening and the first thing the next morning. In Hebrew, a writer can name two extremes and the reader understands that everything between them is also included. So "at home" and "away from home" includes *all* places we could ever be. The first thing in the morning and the last thing at night includes *all* times we are awake. Lest you begin to think that Hebrew is a strange language, remember the English expression "from A to Z," which is a similar way of saying "everything."

When Israel enters the promised land and they build houses, these words are to be put on the doorposts of the houses. When they build cities, the words are to be put on the gates of the cities. That is, just in case anyone forgets what they are supposed to be keeping in mind, there will be physical reminders of this great commandment: "Love the LORD your God with all your heart. . . ."

Deuteronomy 6:10-19. God is keeping a promise made long ago to Abraham and repeated to Isaac and Jacob and down through the generations to Moses and the people listening to him. With the promise and with the reminder of the great commandment comes a warning. It is possible, human nature being what it is, that once the people have taken possession of their new land with all its houses and vineyards, its rain cisterns and olive groves, they will forget God. They may even begin to think that they have achieved all this by themselves. Or they may begin to think that the Lord is fine for rescuing slaves from Egypt, but maybe the local gods would be better for them to worship now that they are in a new land. Such a turning away from God to false gods would be disastrous to them, Moses warns. The only way they can live securely in their new land is to continue to follow the Lord.

Deuteronomy 6:20-25. Then Moses turns to a practical question. When the children start to ask why they have to obey all "the decrees and the statutes and the ordinances" (6:20), the adults are to be ready to tell the whole story to the next generation. They are to begin, according to Deuteronomy 6:21, "We were Pharaoh's slaves in Egypt, but the LORD brought us out of Egypt with a mighty hand." As literal, factual truth, that is not correct. The adults whom Moses is instructing at this point, the ones who are to say, "We were Pharaoh's slaves," were not themselves slaves at all. Their parents were the ones freed from Egypt. Moses is not interested in literal, factual truth here as much as theological truth. In their actual bondage in Egypt, that generation stood for all their descendants and all future bondages. Israel remembers and recites and lives the story of their rescue and incorporates future generations into the narrative. The narrative is not only of the rescue but also of the giving of the gift of the law. The relationship begun in the previous generation is continued by the present generation's keeping of God's commands.

INTERPRETING THE SCRIPTURE

The Great Commandment

How can love be commanded? Love is an emotion, and emotions either happen or they don't happen. We are not responsible for the emotions we feel—although we do bear responsibility for what we *do* with those emotions. This commandment, whether the version here in Deuteronomy or Jesus' quotation of it in the New Testament (Matthew 22:37; Mark 12:30; see also Luke 10:27), has caused genuine difficulty for many Christians. Because we hear the word *love* and do not realize it means "be loyal to," we may fear that questioning God or being angry with God is breaking this most important law. But you can see that questions and even stark emotions are not necessarily out of place. Indeed, there are times when the greatest loyalty is shown by being honest about one's questions.

To be loyal to God and to keep God in your thoughts and decisions, however, does not mean the matter has become simple. For what God is asking—actually, requiring of all who wish to live within the covenant—is that we consider the Lord and the Lord's ways in all the decisions we make. That would have to include how we spend our money, for instance, or whether or not we pass on the latest bit of gossip or the clever racist put-down we heard at the office. To maintain our loyalty to God in all aspects of our life will indeed take "all our might."

The Great Temptation

"Be careful," God warns through Moses. And the content of this warning is just as apt for us today as it was all those centuries ago. Here is an area where we and the Israelites may be seen as very close kin indeed. Whether by training or habit or even instinct, we are likely to turn to God in a moment of crisis. We may even promise faithful obedience if only God will do what we need done. When things are going well for us, however, we are tempted to forget about God and God's ways. Or we may see God's hand in the rescue of Israel from Egypt, but congratulate ourselves on what we have accomplished by our own hard work. Or we may give in to some of those around us and decide that religion is nice "in its place" but that there are more important things to spend our time and energy on in "real life."

Regardless of how hard I work, there is no way I could live in a house with electricity and running water and a telephone—to say nothing of a computer—if I had had to build it all with my own two hands. I could not invent the automatic washing machine; I could not grow all the food my family eats nor make all the cloth to make all the clothes we wear. You get the idea. We all have been helped by many people who have gone before us. We are all helped daily by people we will never know. How much more have we been helped by the God who created this entire universe in the first place! Yet how seductive the temptation to "outgrow" the need for God. How easy it is to transfer our loyalties to other "gods"—hard work, or family, or whatever.

Unto the Next Generation

Moses' "religious education" program is as simple and as difficult as the other portions of this reading. We are to talk to our children about God. And there are no limits on the times or the places where that is to be done. But you can see how this portion follows from the other two. If our supreme loyalty is to God and if that loyalty is to be a part of all our thoughts and decisions, then of course the results will be seen by our children. If we are to talk about God not only within the family circle but also out in the community, then our children will hear about God from other people too. And if even the gates of our cities have reminders of God's law, then there is no part of life that can be separated off as "religious," leaving the rest for us to use as we please.

The talking that we do about God is not an explanation of some theory, doctrine, or theology. No, we are to tell the children how God has been with us. We are to recite the history of God's involvement with the people, for God has brought about great wonders in the lives of the people. This God that we are to teach our children about is the same one who liberated the slaves from Egypt and performed signs and wonders. This is the God who not only freed us from bondage but led us along the road that would take us to the land that had been promised generations ago to the descendants of Abraham and Sarah. Faith is built on a trusting relationship between people and God. That relationship is nurtured as we obey God.

Now there is nothing wrong with youth ministers and church daycare centers in and of themselves. But if we want to make sure that the faith is passed on, then it has to be something that is alive, something that is *lived* and not something that is shut away in a special room of a special building for a couple of hours once a week or so. Only if our faith is something that those not currently in the circle of our faith can see as vibrant and alive is it likely that children will ask us about it. And when they ask, we must have our story ready to tell: "We were slaves and God freed us. What we could not do for ourselves, the gracious God did for us. And in response to God's love and grace, we try to live by God's law."

Note that the older generation is not responsible for the children's response to the story. Moses seems to assume that those who hear the story of God's gracious presence and see how significant adults in their own lives act toward God will choose to abide by the sacred truths of the faith community because of what they have heard and seen. Yet, the children cannot know God unless the adults bear witness to God's saving action. That message is as relevant to the church today as it was to the community of faith in Moses' time.

SHARING THE SCRIPTURE

PREPARING TO TEACH

Preparing Our Hearts

Prepare yourself spiritually for this week's lesson by reading Deuteronomy 30:11-20. This passage speaks of obedience to God's commands. We are called to love God, to walk in God's ways, and to observe all that God has commanded. That may sound difficult, but it is not. Obedience is a choice, but that choice, like all others, has consequences. Those who choose to obey will reap blessings and life. Those who serve other gods—whether they be idols made by human hands or the power, status, and money that entices us— will perish. In your prayer time, ask God to show you how you are obedient and disobedient. Seek God's wisdom and guidance so that you may make the right choices.

Now turn to the lesson in Deuteronomy 6. Read these words carefully. Take a few moments to turn to Jesus' quotation of verses 4-5, as found in Matthew 22:37 and Mark 12:30; see Luke 10:27. What does Jesus' acknowledgment of these words as God's great commandment mean in your own life? How do you live out this command? What changes do you need to make to be more faithful to the Great Commandment, or the Shema, as it is known in Jewish tradition? You may want to write your thoughts in a spiritual journal.

Preparing Our Minds

Reread Deuteronomy 6, this time focusing on verses 1-9 and 20-24. Pay particular attention to the key verses, 4-5. Note in verse 3 the idea, also seen in today's devotional reading, that obedience to divine commandments results in blessings, especially the blessing of land promised to ancestors centuries before. Remember that as Moses is speaking these words, the people are not yet in the promised land (see 6:10). Imagine what you might be thinking if you had been one of the Israelites who heard this message from Moses.

This passage and this lesson deal not only with the commandment but also with how it is to be taught to the next generation. Adults are instructed to tell the children of God's mighty deeds on other occasions, and children are called to listen to this teaching. If time permits you may want to check these references:

- Exodus 10:1-2; 12:26-27
- Deuteronomy 4:9; 11:18-19; 31:12-13; 32:46
- Joshua 4:6-7, 21-22
- Psalm 34:11; 78:1-8
- Proverbs 4:1-2; 5:1-2; 7:1, 24; 8:32.

Preparing Our Learning Space

Have on hand:
- several Bibles
- newsprint and marker
- paper and pencils
- optional hymnals.

LEADING THE CLASS

(1) Introduction

You may want to begin today's session by reading or retelling the material in the

Focusing on the Main Question portion of the lesson.

Another way to help the class get into the lesson is to lead a discussion of the following questions:

(1) **How does our congregation educate its children? Do we offer Sunday school, Vacation Bible School, a preschool, daycare, parents' day out groups, children's choirs, and/or fellowship groups?**
(2) **How do we help parents communicate the gospel to their children?**
(3) **How do we include children and teens in our worship services?**
(4) **What else could we be doing to help the next generation to know the good news about God and Jesus Christ?**

Conclude the discussion by noting that in today's lesson we find the order to teach the next generation God's commandment. Lift up today's main question: **How are we to pass on to the next generation what we have learned about God so that the community of faith will continue?**

(2) The Great Commandment

Choose a volunteer to read Deuteronomy 6:1-9. Ask the students to close their Bibles as the passage is being read so that they, like the Israelites, will actually *hear* what is being said.

Then ask them to call out as many verbs (action words) as they can remember. List their answers on newsprint. Direct them to open their Bibles and find any other verbs in this passage to add to the list. Lists will vary, depending upon the Bible translations that are used, but be sure to include the words *hear, observe, love,* and *keep.* The action words tell us what God expects us to do.

Next, read or retell the information for verses 1-9 found in the Understanding the Scripture portion. The main point that you want to make here is that there is one God and this God demands our undivided loyalty. One who loves God is loyal to God.

Now tell each person to work with a partner or small group. Assign one third of the pairs or groups to work on verses 1-3, another third to consider verses 4-5, and the final third to study 6-9. Distribute paper and pencils. Direct the groups to complete the following tasks:

• The groups working on verses 1-3 are to try paraphrasing these verses, that is, writing them in their own words.

• The groups working on verses 4-5 are to figure out how to explain these two verses so that a five-year-old child could understand them.

• The groups working on verses 6-9 are to decide how parents (and others who influence children) can keep the commandment in their own hearts and by word and deed teach it to their children.

Set a time limit. When you call time, ask persons from the various groups to share what they have written and discussed. Encourage reaction from the class when all of the groups have had an opportunity to report.

(3) The Great Temptation

Note that in the background scripture, verses 10-19, Moses warns the people not to forget God when they come into the prosperous land that God had promised them. The concern is that the people will turn to the gods of their neighbors, forgetting the one God who delivered them from slavery. Moses clearly states that the God they worship will not tolerate divided loyalties.

Ask the class these questions:

(1) Why do you think that people who are doing well—that is, those who are healthy, prosperous, well-fed, and not in danger—forget God?

(2) What kinds of blessings have you received because you have loved God faithfully? (Some students may respond with a litany of material blessings, but other blessings are just as important, likely more so. These may include good health, friends, family, a church home, a sense of mission in life, and meaningful paid or unpaid work.)

(4) Unto the Next Generation

Select a volunteer to read Deuteronomy 6:20-24.

Note that the passage includes a review of the mighty deeds of God in delivering the people from bondage in Egypt. It also reminds the people of the covenant promise of land made with Abraham centuries before Moses' time. Ask the class to brainstorm answers to the following questions. Record their answers on newsprint.

(1) What are the most important points of our heritage as Christians that our children need to hear?

(2) What are the distinctive points of our denominational heritage that our young people need to know?

(3) What special events in the life of our congregation do we want to teach our children?

As an option, create a task force to meet outside of class to refine the list. Consider passing it on to your church's education committee or Sunday school superintendent. Perhaps a special heritage Sunday could be planned with lessons for students of all ages that touch on the important points the class has raised.

You may want to conclude the lesson by reading Psalm 78:1-4, which speaks of teaching the younger generation.

If time permits, distribute hymnals and invite the class to sing a hymn related to today's lesson. "Tell Me the Stories of Jesus" (*The United Methodist Hymnal*, no. 277) or "O Lord, May Church and Home Combine" (*UMH*, no. 695) would be particularly appropriate.

Before you dismiss the class, suggest at least one of the activities below so that students will be able to relate this Bible lesson to their lives.

HELPING CLASS MEMBERS ACT

Challenge class members to speak to at least one child this week about God. Ask the students to point out, preferably in the course of a casual conversation, something that God has done. For example, an adult might share how Jesus healed him or her. Or the adult might use a child's curiosity about nature to talk about God as Creator.

Recommend that class members find appropriate opportunities to share with children what life was like when they were children. Include in the discussion comments about what they remember about attending Sunday school and church during their childhood and teen years. Some of the students may want to put together a scrapbook that includes pictures, perhaps bulletins or other programs they have saved, and written recollections to present to a special child in their lives.

Suggest that the students review the key verses from Deuteronomy 6:4-5 and consider how they are fulfilling this commandment. Encourage them to seek God's counsel in prayer so that they might learn how to be more faithful to it.

PLANNING FOR NEXT SUNDAY

Next week we will turn our attention to a warning that is just as applicable to us as it was to the Israelites. Moses warned the people not to forget God's commandments once they reached the land of milk and honey. When the people became prosperous, they could be tempted to credit themselves for their good fortune rather than give God the glory. In preparation for this lesson, ask the students to read Deuteronomy 8, noting especially verses 7-20.

DON'T LOSE PERSPECTIVE

PREVIEWING THE LESSON

Lesson Scripture: Deuteronomy 8:7-20
Background Scripture: Deuteronomy 8
Key Verse: Deuteronomy 8:11

Focus of the Lesson:
Moses warned the people not to lose their perspective, lest their future prosperity in the promised land cause them to forget their total dependence upon God in the wilderness.

Main Question of the Lesson:
What can we do to keep from forgetting our obligations to God?

This lesson will enable adult learners to:
(1) hear Moses' word of warning to the people not to forget God.
(2) remember what God has done for them.
(3) respond by remembering how God and other people have helped them.

Today's lesson may be outlined as follows:
(1) Introduction
(2) Remember the Past
(3) Look Toward the Future
(4) The Great Temptation Revisited
(5) The Protection of Memory

FOCUSING ON THE MAIN QUESTION

At first glance, this lesson may seem to be quite similar to the previous one. And in many ways it is. Moses recites to the people once again the great acts and gracious care God has shown for Israel during their sojourn in the wilderness. Moses warns them yet again not to forget the Lord once their lives have become prosperous and easy.

Perspective makes a great difference. Moses seems to be concerned that once the people are settled in their new land, they will lose the proper perspective of life in the wilderness. In the wasteland they have been crossing, it is obvious that God is caring for the people. They do not know where they are. They do not know where to find water, where to obtain food. All the necessities of life must be provided for them. Even before they reached the wilderness, their very escape from Egypt was something they could not accomplish by themselves. Their escape was so amazing, such a miraculous event in their lives, that they had no trouble remembering that God was acting on their behalf. They have needed to rely on God for their food and for their direction. God has given them more than mere food and water. God has also taught them, has given them the covenant by which they will be able to live righteously with each other and with their Lord, even after they are settled in the promised land.

Moses is still concerned that in their new situation their continuing dependence on the Lord may not be as obvious and they may forget God. When they grow their own food, will they remember the Lord? And if they do not remember their dependence on God, will they give in to the temptation to follow other gods—those fascinating and alluring gods worshiped by some of their new neighbors? Many centuries later we face the same issues that concerned Moses. With our mostly secure lives, with our abundant food, it is easy to assume that we are self-made people who have no need of God, except of course in case of emergency. Moses' words to the Israelites remind us to ask ourselves: **What can we do to keep from forgetting God and our obligations to God?**

READING THE SCRIPTURE

NRSV
Deuteronomy 8:7-20

7 For the LORD your God is bringing you into a good land, a land with flowing streams, with springs and underground waters welling up in valleys and hills, 8 a land of wheat and barley, of vines and fig trees and pomegranates, a land of olive trees and honey, 9 a land where you may eat bread without scarcity, where you will lack nothing, a land whose stones are iron and from whose hills you may mine copper. 10 You shall eat your fill and bless the LORD your God for the good land that he has given you.

11 Take care that you do not forget the LORD your God, by failing to keep his commandments, his ordinances, and his statutes, which I am commanding you today. 12 When you have eaten your fill and have built fine houses and live in them, 13 and when your herds and flocks have multiplied, and your silver and gold is multiplied, and all that you have is multiplied, 14 then do not exalt yourself, forgetting the LORD your God, who brought you out of the land of Egypt, out of the house of slavery, 15 who led you through

NIV
Deuteronomy 8:7-20

7For the LORD your God is bringing you into a good land—a land with streams and pools of water, with springs flowing in the valleys and hills; 8a land with wheat and barley, vines and fig trees, pomegranates, olive oil and honey; 9a land where bread will not be scarce and you will lack nothing; a land where the rocks are iron and you can dig copper out of the hills.

10When you have eaten and are satisfied, praise the LORD your God for the good land he has given you. **11Be careful that you do not forget the LORD your God, failing to observe his commands, his laws and his decrees that I am giving you this day.** 12Otherwise, when you eat and are satisfied, when you build fine houses and settle down, 13and when your herds and flocks grow large and your silver and gold increase and all you have is multiplied, 14then your heart will become proud and you will forget the LORD your God, who brought you out of Egypt, out of the land of slavery. 15He led you through the vast and dreadful desert, that thirsty and waterless land, with its venomous snakes

Key Verse

Ke Ver

the great and terrible wilderness, an arid wasteland with poisonous snakes and scorpions. He made water flow for you from flint rock, 16 and fed you in the wilderness with manna that your ancestors did not know, to humble you and to test you, and in the end to do you good. 17 Do not say to yourself, "My power and the might of my own hand have gotten me this wealth." 18 But remember the LORD your God, for it is he who gives you power to get wealth, so that he may confirm his covenant that he swore to your ancestors, as he is doing today. 19 If you do forget the LORD your God and follow other gods to serve and worship them, I solemnly warn you today that you shall surely perish. 20 Like the nations that the LORD is destroying before you, so shall you perish, because you would not obey the voice of the LORD your God.

and scorpions. He brought you water out of hard rock. ¹⁶He gave you manna to eat in the desert, something your fathers had never known, to humble and to test you so that in the end it might go well with you. ¹⁷You may say to yourself, "My power and the strength of my hands have produced this wealth for me." ¹⁸But remember the LORD your God, for it is he who gives you the ability to produce wealth, and so confirms his covenant, which he swore to your forefathers, as it is today.

¹⁹If you ever forget the LORD your God and follow other gods and worship and bow down to them, I testify against you today that you will surely be destroyed. ²⁰Like the nations the LORD destroyed before you, so you will be destroyed for not obeying the LORD your God.

UNDERSTANDING THE SCRIPTURE

Deuteronomy 8:1-5. Moses begins the section of scripture we are studying today by reminding the people once again that the law, and their observance of the law, is for a specific purpose: "so that you may live and increase" (8:1) in the land that God had promised to their ancestors. Keeping the law is not necessary just to satisfy a despotic deity. Keeping the law is not a magic charm to coerce God into blessing them. Keeping the law is, instead, the best way for the entire community to live that full and abundant life that God has intended since the beginning of creation.

Moses reminds Israel of some of the incidents of their past forty years in the wilderness. God allowed them to get hungry and then provided for them abundantly with manna. Why? "In order to make you understand that one does not live by bread alone, but by every word that comes from the mouth of the

LORD" (8:3b). These words may sound familiar to you because they are part of what Jesus said to Satan when he was being tempted in the wilderness (Matthew 4:4; Luke 4:4). Once again we do not have an either/or decision to make. One does not live either by bread or by God's word. Human life requires both. In the wilderness God graciously provided both food and instruction to the people. The food wasn't "just there." It wasn't something Israel was counting on finding. Moses is careful to remind them of God's part in their feeding when he describes the manna as something "with which neither you nor your ancestors were acquainted" (8:3a).

We do not have other texts that relate stories about the forty-year life of the Israelites' clothing, nor other accounts of their non-swelling feet, as we do have other manna stories (Exodus 16; Numbers 11). There are, however, two other references to their clothing and feet in very similar terms (Deuteronomy 29:5; Nehemiah 9:21). Again, the major point is not "magic clothes" but rather the combination of God's care and discipline, using the familiar biblical metaphor of parents and children (8:5).

Deuteronomy 8:6-10. Verse 6 acts as a hinge between remembering how God has led them and looking forward to their new life in the promised land. The land is described in compelling terms. First it is called "a good land." Then that generic description is filled out with the mention of abundant water and abundant food. Those who live in arid regions may understand the reasons for describing the water as flowing streams and springs and underground streams better than those of us who have water in such abundance that we are prone to waste it.

Deuteronomy 8:10 begins with three verbs that form an important sequence: you will eat, you will be satisfied, you will bless the Lord. There will be not only food, but enough food. There will be not only abundant food, but food that satisfies. Eating one's fill will lead to blessing the Lord for bringing the people into a land with such rich resources that they no longer fear being hungry.

Deuteronomy 8:11-13. The definition of "forgetting the Lord" given in verse 11 may seem odd. To forget the Lord is to fail to live out the covenant life, to fail to live

by the law. That means that remembering the Lord is something different from, something more than, just thinking about God in our mind. To remember is to act. To remember God is, for Israel, to remember the covenant they entered into at Mount Sinai and to keep it diligently. In the words of last week's "Great Commandment," to remember the Lord is to be loyal to God with one's entire mind and life. Moses is not concerned that the people are forgetting as he speaks to them. He is concerned that once they have achieved their dreams, once their lives are more secure and more comfortable than they have been in the wilderness, then they will think they have no more need for God. In their improved situation, they will congratulate themselves for their good life, forgetting what God had done for them.

Deuteronomy 8:14-20. Yet again Moses repeats the outline of their story. It is the Lord and no other who brought Israel out of their bondage in Egypt. It is the Lord and no other who has led them throughout their wanderings in the wilderness and fed them and protected them along the way. Moses even warns Israel explicitly not to say, "My power and the might of my own hand have gotten me this wealth" (8:17). The equation is simple and stark. If Israel forgets the Lord, they will worship other gods. If they worship other gods, Israel will surely perish.

INTERPRETING THE SCRIPTURE

Remember the Past

Remember is one of the most important verbs in the whole Bible. Remembering is essential to our identity as God's people. Remembering is necessary if we are to keep the covenant and live in righteousness with God and with one another. *Remember* is also a special verb in the Bible

in that its meaning is not exactly what we may mean when we use it in other ways.

First, our remembering is not to be a sort of longing for the "good old days." For one thing, those "good old days" were not as golden in the living as the glow our nostalgia puts over them. Nor is our remembering supposed to be an endless moaning over our past mistakes. Of course we are sinners. But when we have been forgiven, then we no longer need to dwell on the errors of our past. Finally, biblical remembering is not something that we do only in our minds. It is, rather, a sort of "anti-amnesia" by which we incorporate ourselves into the continuing community of faith, the communion of saints.

Look Toward the Future

Looking toward the future, eagerly awaiting God's reign, can also be tricky for us as we are living in this world. The future we await is not only whatever God has prepared for us after this life. God is not telling us to ignore earthly life and focus entirely on what is to come. In fact, that is nearly a very unbiblical viewpoint. The promised land in Deuteronomy is some very particular real estate. The houses and vineyards and olive groves Moses mentions are not in the spiritual realm, but earthly, physical realities. God's promises may need the next life to come to their full fruition, but if we are to believe Jesus, then the reign of God begins within and among us (Luke 17:21). Right here and right now is when we can begin to experience at least a tiny taste of God's kingdom.

The Great Temptation Revisited

I sometimes think that it would be much easier to be a faithful Christian if I lived in poverty. Study after study has shown that the poor are more likely to be faithful attendees of worship; as an individual's income rises, the proportion of that income that is given to all charities combined declines. At least if I were poor, I would not be so easily distracted from gratitude to God by my own cleverness in having arranged for such a comfortable life. But as soon as I start thinking in such directions, I know I am wrong. If I weren't sure from day to day how I was going to feed my daughters, if I were afraid of being evicted from our house, if I lost my job—those also would be "distractions" and potential roadblocks to a faithful life. There is no perfect situation that makes faith automatic, just as there is no circumstance that makes faith impossible. Moses' point, and mine too, is captured well in two verses from the book of Proverbs: "Remove far from me falsehood and lying; give me neither poverty nor riches; feed me with the food that I need, or I shall be full, and deny you, and say, 'Who is the LORD' or I shall be poor, and steal, and profane the name of my God" (30:8-9).

The Protection of Memory

The heading for this section has two meanings. We need to be sure that memory is protected, and memory has protective powers for us. Episode after episode in the Bible tells of the dire results when someone forgets what should be remembered. One of the most poignant verses comes in the first chapter of Exodus: "Now a new king arose over Egypt, who did not know Joseph" (1:8). From that ignorance, from that loss of memory of who Joseph had been and what he had done for all Egypt—to say nothing of what the Pharaoh had promised him and his family in gratitude for his wisdom in coping with the famine—came fear and oppression. Israel was enslaved because of historical amnesia. Egypt suffered the series of plagues, climaxing with the death of the firstborn, because of historical amnesia. Memory might have protected Israel and Egypt alike, had memory itself been protected and kept alive.

The tricky part is to combine living memory with eager anticipation of God's future. It is ridiculously easy to worship the past while thinking we are keeping memory alive. "Our dear Pastor Previous was so wonderful. If only our current pastor could be like that. . . ." How many congregations spin their collective wheels with such thinking!

Although it comes well after the time of

Moses and the entry into the promised land, I want to call to mind a later biblical example that shows both sides of this issue. When Jesus began his public ministry, many faithful Jews were remembering what God had done in the past and were looking for God's coming deliverance in their future. They used that great "memory aid" of the Scriptures and found verses that they used as clues for identifying the Messiah when he should appear. People lined up passages and compared them to what Jesus said and did. Some people found passages that led them to believe he was indeed the Messiah. Other people, using the same holy writ, found passages that led them to believe Jesus was not the Messiah, but that they were supposed to wait for another. The point is not that some people were simply wrong, or that they had been looking at the wrong passages. There are indeed some verses that Jesus seems not to have fulfilled, and yet Christians acclaim him as God Incarnate, the promised Savior.

"Do this in remembrance of me" (Luke 22:19; 1 Corinthians 11:24-25) is a way for us to combine the biblical ideas of remembering—Jesus and what he taught and how it was built on the ancient scriptures that we now name the Old Testament—with our ongoing life in the present and in anticipation of God's future. God's promises are still valid; our covenant obligations still hold. By telling each other the story of our faith, we may be better able to avoid being led astray by false gods.

SHARING THE SCRIPTURE

PREPARING TO TEACH

Preparing Our Hearts

Begin your study of this week's lesson by reading Psalm 85. Today's devotional reading is actually a lament of the people who are praying to God to deliver the nation from difficulties. The psalmist recounts memories of God's gracious favor toward the people.

Now turn to Deuteronomy 8. Here Moses reminds the people of God's favor, for it was God—not the people—who empowered them to escape from the clutches of Egyptian slavery. It was God who led them through the wilderness, providing food and water in the midst of a hostile environment. God has cared for the people constantly. And yet Moses is deeply concerned that as the people prepare to move into the promised land, they will forget the wilderness experience. Instead of relying on God in their new homeland, as they did in the wilderness, they may be tempted to become proud of their own self-sufficiency.

As you read Deuteronomy 8, consider how this passage may apply to your own life and the life of your church. Recall a time when you had to depend totally upon God, perhaps because of a serious illness or some other upheaval in your life. Examine your life now to see if you are continuing to depend upon God, or if you have become so self-reliant that you only call upon God in case of emergency. Pray that you might always rely on the gracious hand of God. In response to that graciousness, give thanks and praise the Lord.

Preparing Our Minds

Review Deuteronomy 8, this time focusing on verses 7-20. If time permits, you may want to check some of the stories referred to in this passage:
- God's continuing care of the people: Exodus 12:37–17:16.
- manna in the wilderness: Exodus 16 and Numbers 11:7-9.

- poisonous snakes: Numbers 21:6-9.
- water from the flint rock: Numbers 20:2-13.

Preparing Our Learning Space

Prior to the session, you may want to write the second set of discussion questions under "Look Toward the Future" on a sheet of newsprint.
Have on hand:
✔ several Bibles
✔ newsprint and marker
✔ hymnals.

LEADING THE CLASS

(1) Introduction

One way to begin the session is to read or retell the Focusing on the Main Question portion of the lesson.

Another way to get into today's lesson is to call for volunteers to tell stories of times, perhaps in their younger days, when they had to struggle. Some may recall working hard to start a business, or putting in long hours to earn money while going to college, or being young and married with few amenities in a small apartment. After a few folks have shared their accounts, ask these questions:

(1) **What words or phrases come to mind when you remember challenging times and the generosity of others that helped to see you through?**

(2) **How did you view God's role in your life during those challenging times?**

(3) **Once you made it over the rough places, were you likely to forget how others and God helped you? Why or why not?**

Conclude this part of the lesson by telling the class that in our scripture passage for today we will hear Moses warning the people not to forget all that God has done for them once they get to the promised land. We too can be guilty of that. Our main question for today asks:

What can we do to keep from forgetting our obligations to God?

(2) Remember the Past

In Deuteronomy 8, Moses is calling the people to remember the past, to recall how God has led and cared for them. In verse 2 Moses says: "Remember the long way that the LORD your God has led you these forty years in the wilderness, in order to humble you, testing you to know what was in your heart, whether or not you would keep his commandments."

Discuss with the class their definitions of the word *remember*. After they have shared their ideas, note these points about *remember* as it is used in the Bible:

- Remembering the Lord is something different from, something more than, just thinking about God in our mind.
- To remember is to act.
- Remembering is essential to our identity as God's people.
- To remember God is, for Israel, to recall the covenant they entered into at Mount Sinai and, more important, to keep it diligently.
- Remembering is necessary if we are to keep the covenant and live in righteousness with God and with one another.
- In the words of last week's "Great Commandment," to remember the Lord is to be loyal to God with one's entire mind and life.
- To remember is a sort of "anti-amnesia" by which we incorporate ourselves into the continuing community of faith.

Ask the class to read in unison today's key verse from Deuteronomy 8:11. Then turn it into a positive statement by saying: Take care that you remember the Lord, by keeping God's commandments, ordinances, and statutes, which I am commanding you today.

Pause for a few moments of silent reflection by encouraging the class members to remember God's mighty actions in their own lives and their responses to God. If time permits, invite a few volunteers to share their reflections.

(3) Look Toward the Future

Choose a reader for Deuteronomy 8:7-13. Remind the class that Moses is speaking to the people before they enter the promised land. He is looking toward the future with them. Ask these questions:

(1) **How does Moses describe the land to which the people are going?**

(2) **Suppose you had been with the Israelites, wandering in the hostile desert environment for forty years. What expectations would you have about this land that God had promised to give?**

(3) **What would this glowing description of the land say to you about the kind of life God desires for you?**

Direct the students to work with a partner or small group. Tell them to talk about the kind of future they long for. Ask them to address these questions, which you may want to write on newsprint prior to the session:

(1) **Ideally, what kind of future do you envision for yourself?**

(2) **How do you perceive this kind of future to be in keeping with God's will for you?**

(3) **What do you need to do in order to experience this kind of future?**

(4) The Great Temptation Revisited

Select a reader for Deuteronomy 8:14-20. Then ask:

(1) **What is Moses' point here?** (Be sure that students understand that Moses is warning the Israelites not to forget God once they become prosperous. In the wilderness they had to depend solely on God for everything, but surrounded by all the fine amenities the promised land has to offer, the people may easily forget God and assume that they are responsible for their own good fortune.)

(2) **Moses recounts specific actions of God in the wilderness. What specific actions of God on behalf of your own community, state, or nation can you recall?**

(3) **Why do you think that people who have great needs often rely heavily upon God, whereas those who are prosperous are more likely to forget God and assume they are self-sufficient?**

Again read aloud Deuteronomy 8:18: "But remember the LORD your God, for it is he who gives you power to get wealth, so that he may confirm his covenant that he swore to your ancestors, as he is doing today." Encourage the class to comment on the following statement, which you will need to read aloud: **If more Christians realized that all that they have and all that they are is a gift from God who gives us the power to get wealth, our individual lives and our churches would be vastly different in many ways.**

(5) The Protection of Memory

Ask the students to look again in their Bibles at Deuteronomy 8:19-20. Note the punishment for those who forget the Lord. Ask:

(1) **What Bible stories can you think of where failure to remember resulted in serious consequences?**

(2) **Similarly, what examples from your own life can you recall where failure to remember caused real problems?**

(3) **Sometimes we need to be protected from a faulty memory, just as the Israelites who were now on the journey erroneously recalled the "good life" in Egypt, complete with fleshpots of food. When you have looked back on a chapter in your own life, what faulty memories do you have?** (If students seem reluctant to share this information aloud, invite them to think silently about this question for a few minutes.)

Wrap up this part of the lesson by offering a prayer that we might not yield to the temptation of self-sufficiency but instead remember God and keep the divine commandments that the Lord has set before us.

If your class likes to sing, consider "Let My People Seek Their Freedom" (*The United Methodist Hymnal,* no. 586), based on Deuteronomy 8:14-18. If the tune is unfamiliar, either read the hymn in unison or assign different groups to read each verse.

Before you say good-bye, be sure to suggest at least one of the activities below to help students live out what they have learned from the Scriptures this week.

HELPING CLASS MEMBERS ACT

Suggest that students remember one or more persons who helped them to achieve an important life goal. Encourage them to make a phone call or write a letter to each of these persons thanking them for the role he or she played in the student's life. If the person is deceased, class members can still write a letter in which they acknowledge, perhaps to a relative, how much this person's help meant.

Recommend to the class that they examine circumstances in their own lives to see what kinds of warnings God is giving them. For some, the warnings may manifest themselves in physical problems, or ruptured family relationships, or distance from God. Suggest that they prayerfully consider how they will respond to these warnings.

Encourage the students to recall the commandments that God has given, especially the Ten Commandments and the Great Commandment to love God totally, that is, to be loyal to God. Ask them to measure their own obedience to these commands. What changes do they need to make to be more faithful to God?

PLANNING FOR NEXT SUNDAY

In our lesson for November 7 we will move with the Israelites from the wilderness into the promised land. This lesson, "Maintaining Continuity," begins the final unit of the this quarter, entitled "Entering the Promised Land." Ask the class members to read Deuteronomy 31:1-8 and 34, paying particular attention to 31:1-8 and 34:5-9.

UNIT 3: ENTERING THE PROMISED LAND
MAINTAINING CONTINUITY

PREVIEWING THE LESSON

Lesson Scripture: Deuteronomy 31:1-8; 34:5-9
Background Scripture: Deuteronomy 31:1-8; 34
Key Verse: Deuteronomy 31:8

Focus of the Lesson:
Before his death, Moses passed the mantle of leadership to Joshua, who was an able leader.

Main Question of the Lesson:
How can we maintain continuity in a community and give their appropriate due to both the retiring leader and the new leader?

This lesson will enable adult learners to:
(1) see how God provided continuity for the people by raising up Joshua to succeed Moses as leader.
(2) explore their own understandings of leadership in the church.
(3) respond by recognizing the importance of leaders, both those who are retiring and those who are coming on board.

Today's lesson may be outlined as follows:
(1) Introduction
(2) The Lord's Promise
(3) Moses' Final Charge
(4) Moses' Reward
(5) Moses' Legacy

FOCUSING ON THE MAIN QUESTION

Most people who have been associated in any way with United Methodist churches for any length of time know about saying good-bye to their pastor one Sunday and greeting a new one the very next week. Some denominations that "call" their ministers usually have an interim period between permanent appointments.

Unlike these—Episcopalians, Lutherans, and Baptists, for instance—United Methodists most often go from one permanent minister to the next with no interruption of pastoral leadership. Having experienced these transitions myself from a variety of vantage points—as the daughter of a departing and then new minister, as a parishioner saying good-bye and then hello, and as the departing and arriving minister myself—I know that these can be difficult times as well as times of great opportunity both for congregations and for the parsonage families.

Rarely is a transition as dramatic as Moses' passing the leadership on to Joshua. Most of our pastoral changes do not come about because of death. Usually the former pastor goes to a new church or charge, or leaves for retirement. But the changes can feel as wrenching as if someone had died. It is inevitable for some members to remember dear Pastor Previous so fondly that they expect to find fault with most things the new minister does. Others will expect the Reverend Newcomer to "fix" whatever they think needs

fixing—immediately! Transitions can be rocky for all concerned. It is hard for a congregation to see people they admire and enjoy move away; it can be difficult for the minister's family to uproot themselves and come to a new community.

What does this have to do with Moses and the Israelites? Surely their situation at the Jordan River, on the verge—finally—of entering into the promised land was far different from what goes on in United Methodist churches in June and July, isn't it? Yes, their situation may have been more dramatic. Yet it illustrates ways of coping with a question we approach today: **How can we maintain continuity in a community and give their appropriate due to both the retiring leader and the new leader?**

NOVEMBER 7

READING THE SCRIPTURE

NRSV

Deuteronomy 31:1-8; 34:5-9

1 When Moses had finished speaking all these words to all Israel, 2 he said to them: "I am now one hundred twenty years old. I am no longer able to get about, and the LORD has told me, 'You shall not cross over this Jordan.' 3 The LORD your God himself will cross over before you. He will destroy these nations before you, and you shall dispossess them. Joshua also will cross over before you, as the LORD promised. 4 The LORD will do to them as he did to Sihon and Og, the kings of the Amorites, and to their land, when he destroyed them. 5 The LORD will give them over to you and you shall deal with them in full accord with the command that I have given to you. 6 Be strong and bold; have no fear or dread of them, because it is the LORD your God who goes with you; he will not fail you or forsake you."

7 Then Moses summoned Joshua and said to him in the sight of all Israel: "Be strong and bold, for you are the one who

NIV

Deuteronomy 31:1-8; 34:5-9

¹Then Moses went out and spoke these words to all Israel: ²"I am now a hundred and twenty years old and I am no longer able to lead you. The LORD has said to me, 'You shall not cross the Jordan.' ³The LORD your God himself will cross over ahead of you. He will destroy these nations before you, and you will take possession of their land. Joshua also will cross over ahead of you, as the LORD said. ⁴And the LORD will do to them what he did to Sihon and Og, the kings of the Amorites, whom he destroyed along with their land. ⁵The LORD will deliver them to you, and you must do to them all that I have commanded you. ⁶Be strong and courageous. Do not be afraid or terrified because of them, for the LORD your God goes with you; he will never leave you nor forsake you."

⁷Then Moses summoned Joshua and said to him in the presence of all Israel, "Be strong and courageous, for you must go with this people into the land that the

will go with this people into the land that the LORD has sworn to their ancestors to give them; and you will put them in possession of it. **8 It is the LORD who goes before you. He will be with you; he will not fail you or forsake you. Do not fear or be dismayed."**

LORD swore to their forefathers to give them, and you must divide it among them as their inheritance. **8The LORD himself goes before you and will be with you; he will never leave you nor forsake you. Do not be afraid; do not be discouraged."**

Key Verse

Deuteronomy 34:5-9

5 Then Moses, the servant of the LORD, died there in the land of Moab, at the LORD's command. 6 He was buried in a valley in the land of Moab, opposite Beth-peor, but no one knows his burial place to this day. 7 Moses was one hundred twenty years old when he died; his sight was unimpaired and his vigor had not abated. 8 The Israelites wept for Moses in the plains of Moab thirty days....

9 Joshua son of Nun was full of the spirit of wisdom, because Moses had laid his hands on him; and the Israelites obeyed him, doing as the LORD had commanded Moses.

Deuteronomy 34:5-9

5And Moses the servant of the LORD died there in Moab, as the LORD had said. 6He buried him in Moab, in the valley opposite Beth Peor, but to this day no one knows where his grave is. 7Moses was a hundred and twenty years old when he died, yet his eyes were not weak nor his strength gone. 8The Israelites grieved for Moses in the plains of Moab thirty days....

9Now Joshua son of Nun was filled with the spirit of wisdom because Moses had laid his hands on him. So the Israelites listened to him and did what the LORD had commanded Moses.

UNDERSTANDING THE SCRIPTURE

Deuteronomy 31:1-6. Moses has now finished retelling the grand story of the Exodus to the next generation of Israel. In Deuteronomy 30 he has reminded them once again of the covenant to which they have committed themselves, and reminded them of the blessings that accompany faithful living and the curses they will experience if they abandon the Lord. Now in chapter 31 he tells them what is going to happen in the immediate future. God has told Moses that he cannot cross over the Jordan. Moses makes haste to assure the people that God will continue to go with them even when he is no longer their leader. God's presence with Israel does not depend on Moses' presence with them. They will not be without a human leader either, for Joshua is to take Moses' place, in accordance with what the

Lord has said, both earlier (Deuteronomy 18:15, 18) and again here.

What of the people who are already living in the land? Have they disappeared since the spies brought back such a terrified report some forty years before? No, they are still there. But Moses assures the people that God will take care of them on behalf of Israel. The very same word Moses spoke at the beginning of the adventure of the Exodus, he speaks now to the next generation: "Do not be afraid or terrified because of them" (Deuteronomy 31:6 NIV; see also Exodus 14:13). The reason the people need not fear is the same now as it was then: "It is the LORD your God who goes with you" (31:6). This was God's promise to Moses as an individual (Exodus 3:12) and God's promise to all the people. God has kept that promise so far, and assures the whole people that it continues to be in force.

Deuteronomy 31:7-8. After telling all the people to be strong and bold, Moses turns to Joshua and in the presence of all Israel, tells him the same thing. (In Hebrew also the words are the same.) Moses ties together the ancient promise to the ancestors, to Abraham and Isaac and Jacob, with the very near future. It is the same Lord who made the promise in the past who will now carry it out. It is the same Lord who continues to go before the people, as the pillar of cloud and of fire has done throughout the wilderness years. Because God will be with Joshua, with all Israel, Moses repeats, "Do not fear or be dismayed" (31:8).

Deuteronomy 34:1-4. We move now from the very public appearance of Moses to the most private of moments. Moses leaves the plain and goes to the top of Pisgah where "the LORD showed him the whole land" (34:1). If a miracle is defined as something that cannot happen in any ordinary way, then what follows is a miracle. For God shows Moses more than can be seen with the unaided human eye. Moses gets a glimpse of the entirety of the promised land, to Dan in the far north, Judah in the south, the Mediterranean Sea to the west. Although Moses will not be able to cross into the land himself, God has shown it to him, declaring that it is indeed "the land of which I swore to Abraham, to Isaac, and to Jacob, saying, 'I will give it to your descendants'" (34:4).

Deuteronomy 34:5-12. Moses died and was buried and no one knows where. Here we see another example of a different way of looking at experiences than we are accustomed to. Think of famous people who have died in the last generation or so: President Kennedy, Elvis Presley, Princess Diana. Not only do we know where they are buried, their burial sites have become secular shrines. Tens of thousands of tourists make pilgrimages to Arlington National Cemetery and to Graceland. Hundreds of thousands of people lined the route of Princess Diana's funeral cortege and have made her Kensington Palace home a much-visited site in London. Or think of what happens when an airplane crashes over an ocean or in nearly inaccessible mountains. Extreme effort is expended to recover the bodies of the victims and return them to their families for burial.

For the most important people within the Bible, however, while death is noted and burial place may be mentioned (for example, Sarah and Abraham, Genesis 23:19 and 25:9-10, respectively), the location does not become a focus of interest. Even Jesus' tomb receives no more mention once he has left it at the Resurrection. More important than geographical place is *relationship*, and that relationship is often perpetuated by continuing in the line of covenant and following the promises and teachings of God as given through particular individuals. God's continued self-identification as "the God of Abraham, of Isaac, and of Jacob" (Genesis 28:13; Exodus 3:6, 15, 16; 4:5, among many others) is a part of this way of thinking. We also see the weight of relationship over place in the fact that the conversation between God and Moses at the burning bush (Exodus 3) is remembered to this day, although the precise location was never kept as a holy place.

All Israel mourns for Moses for thirty days. They do not immediately set out under Joshua, but give Moses a period of honor. And then, when "the period of mourning for Moses was ended" (Deuteronomy 34:8*b*), Joshua son of Nun does take over the leadership and Israel does obey him, for he is the duly appointed successor to Moses. The final three verses could be considered Moses' epitaph, summarizing his relationship to the Lord and his leadership in God's freeing Israel from Egypt. From the time of Moses' death until the writing of Deuteronomy, it is asserted, there has never been another "prophet in Israel like Moses" (34:10).

INTERPRETING THE SCRIPTURE

The Lord's Promise

God's presence with Israel is not dependent on Moses' presence with them. Moses has played a crucial role in the life of the nation, but Israel's life does not depend on Moses' life. The only one who is indispensable is the Lord. Lest the people become distraught at his death, Moses reassures them yet again that the Lord has promised to continue with them, to go before them into their new life in their new land. The early church remembered this part of their heritage and saw Jesus Christ as one "like Moses" as part of God's continuing promise of leadership. (Acts 3:22 and 7:37, for instance, make specific reference to our passage in Deuteronomy.)

I doubt if any of this story from Deuteronomy sounds strange to class members. And yet, it is sometimes so hard for *us* to see a change of leadership without becoming very upset about the possibility of the life of our own group. Whether the change comes about because of death, retirement, resignation, or move, it is easy to wonder how the group can continue without its leader. God's promise to Israel was not that the covenant relationship would last as long as Moses lived. No, God's promise is not dependent upon any human's lifespan. Why should we fear it will be different for us? If the Lord is with us now and has promised to be with us in the future, we need not be anxious when our human leadership changes.

Moses' Final Charge

Now it might be fun to play with this text and our contemporary United Methodist polity and draw a detailed analogy with God as the district superintendent, Moses as the current pastor, and Joshua as the new pastor. But that would be to limit the meanings of this text too much. For the critical issue is not one of human leadership at all. Yes, Moses did publicly pass his authority on to Joshua. But in what Moses said to Joshua and to all the company of Israel, the emphasis was on the Lord's continuing leadership. We humans are faithful and unfaithful; we act as fine leaders and shoddy leaders. The only factor that can assure the maintenance of the community of faith is the God whom we trust and who has promised to lead us. Think of all the things Moses could have said, but didn't. There is no mention of "Don't forget to do things *my* way." There is no hint of "Now, Joshua isn't quite as good as I am, but do the best you can with him." Rather, the emphasis throughout is that the community's continuance and stability rests on their covenant relationship with God and not on the vagaries of human leadership.

Moses' Reward

Church leaders never see all their dreams come true any more than Moses did. But we can have glimpses. We experience times when it truly does seem that the kingdom of God has come near. The Reverend Dr. Martin Luther King, Jr. had this very passage of Deuteronomy in mind when he said that although he "might not get there with you," he had "been to the mountaintop" and had "seen the promised land." The Lord grants glimpses of the Beloved Community not only to leaders but to all who are hungry and thirsty for righteousness, to all who are peacemakers, to all who are persecuted for the sake of their faith.

Moses' Legacy

Although Moses publicly proclaimed that Joshua was to be his successor, although the community did not build a monument at the place of Moses' burial, Moses was not forgotten as soon as he died. The transition to Joshua's leadership was not in doubt, but the transition was not a matter of forgetting Moses as though he had never been. We do not see Joshua barging in after a couple of days saying, "You've been weeping for Moses for long enough now. Life goes on. Get over it. Let's go," or any of the similar messages our culture blares to those in mourning. Death is inevitable. Leadership change is inevitable. Neither of those facts, however, means that grieving the loss of what we have known in the past is a bad thing or in any sense unfaithful either to God or to the new leader.

Perhaps it is a sign of Joshua's being "full of the spirit of wisdom" (34:9) that the mourning for Moses is allowed to run its entire thirty days. Continuity is maintained when the honesty of emotional life is allowed. Part of that honesty means that mothers may be weepy when their children go off to school for the first time; children may be scared when they make the transition from elementary to junior high school; employees may be anxious when a new supervisor replaces one who retires. And of course congregations are full of a jumble of emotions when they must bid farewell to one pastor and welcome another. In the face of the new life—at school or work or home or church—there may still be sadness for what is no more.

The new supervisor may have a different attitude toward coffee breaks; changing classes in a noisy school building may be intimidating after years of being in one classroom all day. Even though the new situations bring with them new opportunities, they also signal losses. Healthy continuity includes finding appropriate ways for mourning what is no more.

The time of mourning ends. The new life at home, at school, at work, at church, unfolds before us. We may be better able to move into that new life when we remember that our ultimate leader is the Lord, and that God's promises do not expire as we move from one stage of life to another or from one form of human leadership to another. We may also be able to maintain continuity when we remember that no human goal is a worthy *ultimate* goal. If it is the kingdom of God in all its fullness, the reign of the Lord in all of creation, that we are seeking and striving toward, then we can better say good-bye and say hello as our human situations change. Moses dies before the people enter the promised land. Joshua takes over the human leadership with many of the promises still unfulfilled. But the community of Israel does not fragment or splinter into various factions at the death of their original leader, because they know their ultimate leader is the Lord, and that the Lord continues with them.

SHARING THE SCRIPTURE

PREPARING TO TEACH

Preparing Our Hearts

Today's devotional reading is quite poignant. In Numbers 27:12-23 we hear God tell Moses that because of his rebellion (see Numbers 20:2-13, especially verse 12) he will not be allowed to enter into the promised land. Moses does not try to plea-bargain with God. Instead, he asks God to raise up a leader so that the people will not be lost like sheep without a shepherd. God agrees and says that Joshua, "a man in whom is the spirit" (27:18), is to be commissioned. Moses does as God commands.

Think about how various organizations you are affiliated with, especially the church, might be different if all the leaders were truly called and commissioned by God.

Now turn in your Bible to today's lesson from Deuteronomy 31:1-8 and 34, especially verses 5-9. How would you have felt had you been Moses? What would you have thought about God had you been one of the Israelites hearing Moses' announcement in Deuteronomy 31:1-8? How would you have felt had you been Joshua, both at that time and again after Moses' death (34:5-9) when you were expected to assume the mantle of leadership?

God has called you to a position of leadership within the Sunday school. Perhaps you serve in other areas of the church as well. Why did you accept your position(s)? How did the former leader help (or hinder) you in your new job? What will you do to help make a smooth transition when it is time for a new leader to assume your role? Pray that God will give you insight so as to lead your class wisely.

Preparing Our Minds

Review the entire background scripture for today's lesson. Also read the account of Moses' rebellion in Numbers 20:2-13 and Deuteronomy 32:48-52. This incident at Meribah caused God to bar Moses from entering the promised land.

You may want to read a commentary to become familiar with Joshua. Here is some information about his life prior to the time that he assumed leadership.
- Nothing is known of Joshua's early life except that he was the son of Nun, an Ephraimite (Numbers 13:8, 16).
- Joshua distinguished himself as a military leader during a battle with the Amalekites in the wilderness soon after the Israelites had left Egyptian captivity (Exodus 17:8-16).
- Referred to as Moses' assistant, Joshua accompanied Moses on a trek up God's mountain when Moses received the law (Exodus 24:12-14).
- Joshua, who accompanied Moses down the mountain, heard the noise of the throng that was worshiping the golden calf (Exodus 32:17).
- Joshua was with Moses at the tent of meeting (Exodus 33:7-11).
- Joshua was one of the twelve chosen to reconnoiter the promised land. His report agreed with the others, though he believed that God would bring the Israelites into this land. He urged the people not to rebel (Numbers 14:5-10).
- During a ceremony at the tabernacle, Moses laid hands on Joshua and conferred leadership responsibilities upon him (Deuteronomy 31:7-8; 34:9).

Preparing Our Learning Space

Have on hand:
✔ several Bibles
✔ paper and pencils.

LEADING THE CLASS

(1) Introduction

Begin today's lesson by brainstorming with the class ways in which transitions of leadership take place in politics, business, and the church. Five common ways are election, appointment, promotion, retirement, and military overthrow.

Invite the group to zoom in on changes of leadership within the church. Ask these questions:
(1) **Why do laypersons assume volunteer jobs in the church?**
(2) **Why do laypersons leave volunteer jobs in the church?**
(3) **How do ordained clergy in your denomination assume a new position?** (Note that in The United Methodist Church clergy are appointed by a bishop. In other words, they have agreed by virtue of their ordination to

?

be sent. In some other denominations, such as the Baptist, Lutheran, and Episcopal churches, individual congregations call a pastor to minister among them.)

(4) **What kinds of problems can occur when a layperson or clergy member comes into a new position?** (Try to keep this discussion generic. This is not the appropriate time or place for an airing of grievances or criticism of a church leader, lay or clergy.)

(5) **What new opportunities does a change of leadership offer to a church?**

Close this introduction to the lesson by noting that today we will be studying the passing of leadership from Moses to Joshua as the Israelites prepare to move into the promised land. The main question that will guide us this week is this: **How can we maintain continuity in a community and give their appropriate due to both the retiring leader and the new leader?**

(2) The Lord's Promise

Encourage the students to listen carefully as someone reads Deuteronomy 31:1-6. Then ask:

?

(1) **What does Moses say about himself in this passage?**

(2) **What does Moses say about God?**

(3) **What does Moses say to the people?**

Be sure to point out that neither God's presence nor covenant relationship with the people was dependent upon Moses' leadership. God will continue to be the Sovereign, even after Moses dies. Thus, a change in human leadership does not have an impact on our relationship with God or God's relationship with us. Continue the discussion by raising these questions:

?

(1) **What governs your attitude toward a change of leadership in your church, business, or other organization?**

(2) **Do you believe most people welcome change or fear it? Explain your answer.**

?

(3) **Some groups, including churches, falter and die when a particular leader is no longer present. Why do you think that is the case?**

(3) Moses' Final Charge

Now read aloud Deuteronomy 31:7-8. Note that verse 8 is today's key verse. Here we see Moses passing the mantle of leadership to Joshua. Ask:

?

(1) **How would you have felt had you been one of the Israelites witnessing this scene?**

(2) **What concerns would you have if you were Joshua?** (Joshua could have been concerned about how the people would receive him after the long, distinguished tenure of Moses. He might have feared that no one would follow him. He might have felt that he was "in over his head.")

(3) **What words of reassurance does Moses offer?** (Moses assures Joshua, and the people who are listening, that God is still in charge. God is the One who will give the people possession of the land. God will neither fail nor forsake Joshua or the Israelites. Since God will continue to lead, Joshua and those who follow him need not fear.)

(4) **What did Moses fail to say that some lesser leaders might want to make clear to their followers and their successor?** (He does not suggest that Joshua will—or should—do things Moses' way. Nor does Moses imply that Joshua lacks the experience or ability to do the job.)

(4) Moses' Reward

Deuteronomy 34:1-4, part of our background scripture, recounts how God took Moses up a mountain and showed him the promised land. Though Moses will not enter this land, he is rewarded by seeing it.

Distribute paper and pencils. Tell the students not to put their names on the paper. Ask them to head one side of the paper "Dreams Fulfilled" and then list one or two dreams that they have had for their church that have come to fruition. Next, ask the class members to flip their papers over and head this side "Dreams Deferred." Invite them to list one or two dreams for the church that have not yet become reality. Collect the anonymous papers. Read aloud all (or some, if the class is large) of the "Dreams Fulfilled." Also read some of the "Dreams Deferred."

Conclude this part of the lesson by offering a prayer that class members will be in tune with God's promises for them and will be able to see and identify God's dreams for them.

(5) Moses' Legacy

Choose someone to read Deuteronomy 34:5-9. Ask:

(1) How might the transition from Moses to Joshua be different from most leadership changes in our society and/or churches? (Note that Joshua did not hurry the people to accept his leadership. He wisely gave them time to mourn the loss of Moses. In con-

trast, we often expect an instant shift of allegiance from one leader to the next.)

(2) How could a period of "mourning" for the leader who is stepping down facilitate a change in leadership?

(3) What can you do personally to ease the transition from one leader to another?

Before you dismiss the class, lift up at least one of the activities below.

HELPING CLASS MEMBERS ACT

Suggest that students contemplate leadership positions they have held. How did they feel when they had to relinquish a post? What help did others offer to them? What other help would have been useful? How might they use their own experience to support another leader?

Encourage students who like to read to select a biography of a famous leader. Suggest that they look for characteristics that made this person an effective leader.

If this is the time of year in your denomination when nominations committees are seeking new leaders, urge students to consider prayerfully the leadership roles that they might play in your congregation.

PLANNING FOR NEXT SUNDAY

Next week's lesson, "Going Forward in Faith," is taken from Joshua 3. Encourage the class to read that chapter, especially verses 7-17. Also tell them to look at the key verse, Joshua 1:9. Ask them to consider the impact that a leader has in guiding people through the unknown territories of life.

GOING FORWARD IN FAITH

PREVIEWING THE LESSON

Lesson Scripture: Joshua 3:7-17
Background Scripture: Joshua 3
Key Verse: Joshua 1:9

Focus of the Lesson:
Led by priests bearing the ark of the covenant—a sign of God's presence—the people crossed the Jordan River at Joshua's command.

Main Question of the Lesson:
As we move by faith into new regions of life, are there any indicators we can look for to assure us we are going in the right direction?

This lesson will enable adult learners to:
(1) witness the people crossing the Jordan River.
(2) consider their own willingness to step out in faith and venture into new territory.
(3) respond by taking a risk of faith.

Today's lesson may be outlined as follows:
(1) Introduction
(2) Preparations
(3) Signs and Symbols
(4) Even the Waters Obey

FOCUSING ON THE MAIN QUESTION

Change is a normal part of our lives. Decisions about which path to take have to be made over and over through the years. I don't find it at all surprising that some people read the daily horoscopes "religiously" and never start a new undertaking unless the stars are favorable, or that "psychic" telephone services are springing up and making great sums of money for their owners. One can buy secret systems for picking winning lottery numbers and surefire ways to win at casino gambling. There are many newsletters telling investors which stocks to buy and which to sell, and it doesn't take much looking to find stocks that appear on both lists at the same time. Much is at stake in the daily decisions of life. People want to do the best they can and to avoid all the trouble that is avoidable.

There are times when I too long for a straightforward sign, times when I can feel jealous of Gideon, as he asked God first for one sign—which was granted—and then for its opposite—which was also granted to him. (See the story of Gideon and his signs in Judges 6:36-40.) One thing I learn from Gideon's story is that God is patient with our uncertainties. Another thing I have to remember is that even when Gideon was convinced that the messenger who had come to him was really and truly from God, he still had to decide whether or not he was going to follow that messenger's direction. That is, God does indeed give hints and signs to people in the Bible, but the individuals still have to decide the course of action they will follow. The signs are there for all who will look; they are not reserved for the select few any more than God's word was reserved for Moses and the elders instead of being for all the children of Israel. Does God still give signs today? Can they be as clear as the priests bearing the ark of the covenant before all the people? **As we move by faith into new regions of life, are there any indicators we can look for to assure us we are going in the right direction?**

READING THE SCRIPTURE

NRSV
Joshua 1:9

Key Verse

9 "I hereby command you: Be strong and courageous; do not be frightened or dismayed, for the LORD your God is with you wherever you go."

Joshua 3:7-17

7 The LORD said to Joshua, "This day I will begin to exalt you in the sight of all Israel, so that they may know that I will be with you as I was with Moses. 8 You are the one who shall command the priests who bear the ark of the covenant, 'When you come to the edge of the waters of the Jordan, you shall stand still in the Jordan.'" 9 Joshua then said to the Israelites, "Draw near and hear the words of the LORD your God." 10 Joshua said, "By this you shall know that among you is the living God who without fail will drive out from before you the Canaanites, Hittites, Hivites, Perizzites, Girgashites, Amorites, and Jebusites: 11 the ark of the covenant of the Lord of all the earth is going to pass before you into the Jordan. 12 So now select twelve men from the tribes of Israel, one from each tribe. 13 When the soles of the feet of the priests who bear the ark of the LORD, the Lord of all the earth, rest in

NIV
Joshua 1:9

9 "Have I not commanded you? Be strong and courageous. Do not be terrified; do not be discouraged, for the LORD your God will be with you wherever you go."

Key Verse

Joshua 3:7-17

7 And the LORD said to Joshua, "Today I will begin to exalt you in the eyes of all Israel, so they may know that I am with you as I was with Moses. 8 Tell the priests who carry the ark of the covenant: 'When you reach the edge of the Jordan's waters, go and stand in the river.'"

9 Joshua said to the Israelites, "Come here and listen to the words of the LORD your God. 10 This is how you will know that the living God is among you and that he will certainly drive out before you the Canaanites, Hittites, Hivites, Perizzites, Girgashites, Amorites and Jebusites. 11 See, the ark of the covenant of the Lord of all the earth will go into the Jordan ahead of you. 12 Now then, choose twelve men from the tribes of Israel, one from each tribe. 13 And as soon as the priests who carry the ark of the LORD —the Lord of all the earth—set foot in the Jordan, its waters

the waters of the Jordan, the waters of the Jordan flowing from above shall be cut off; they shall stand in a single heap."

14 When the people set out from their tents to cross over the Jordan, the priests bearing the ark of the covenant were in front of the people. 15 Now the Jordan overflows all its banks throughout the time of harvest. So when those who bore the ark had come to the Jordan, and the feet of the priests bearing the ark were dipped in the edge of the water, 16 the waters flowing from above stood still, rising up in a single heap far off at Adam, the city that is beside Zarethan, while those flowing toward the sea of the Arabah, the Dead Sea, were wholly cut off. Then the people crossed over opposite Jericho. 17 While all Israel were crossing over on dry ground, the priests who bore the ark of the covenant of the LORD stood on dry ground in the middle of the Jordan, until the entire nation finished crossing over the Jordan.

flowing downstream will be cut off and stand up in a heap."

¹⁴So when the people broke camp to cross the Jordan, the priests carrying the ark of the covenant went ahead of them. ¹⁵Now the Jordan is at flood stage all during harvest. Yet as soon as the priests who carried the ark reached the Jordan and their feet touched the water's edge, ¹⁶the water from upstream stopped flowing. It piled up in a heap a great distance away, at a town called Adam in the vicinity of Zarethan, while the water flowing down to the Sea of the Arabah (the Salt Sea) was completely cut off. So the people crossed over opposite Jericho. ¹⁷The priests who carried the ark of the covenant of the LORD stood firm on dry ground in the middle of the Jordan, while all Israel passed by until the whole nation had completed the crossing on dry ground.

UNDERSTANDING THE SCRIPTURE

Joshua 1:9. Last week's lesson included the death of Moses, Israel's mourning for him, and the installation of Joshua, son of Nun, as the new leader in Moses' place. Today's key verse comes at the conclusion of God's commission to Joshua. In last week's passage we heard Moses proclaim to Joshua that God would be present with him and, therefore, he had nothing to fear because God would not fail or forsake him. Similarly, in this verse we hear God tell Joshua not to be afraid, for God will be present wherever Joshua goes.

Joshua 3:1-6. Now the people are camped just across the Jordan River from the promised land. At last it is in sight! Joshua prepares the people for the crossing, having leaders go throughout the camp and tell everyone to wait until they see the ark of the covenant being carried by the priests. The priests and the ark,

which is a symbol of the covenant relationship between the Lord and Israel, are to lead the procession. As Moses told the people to prepare or "sanctify" themselves in order to receive the law from God at Mount Sinai (Exodus 19:10-11, 14-15), so now Joshua tells them to sanctify themselves in preparation for the new wonders the Lord will do among them (Joshua 3:5).

Joshua 3:7-13. Parallels between this passage and previous events during the Exodus continue. God gives Joshua a personal word of reassurance. Joshua will be exalted "in the sight of all Israel, so that they may know that I will be with you as I was with Moses" (3:7). Joshua calls the assembly together to "hear the words of the LORD your God" (3:9) as Moses had assembled them to hear God at Mount Sinai (Exodus 19:9). Once again, *all* the community is to witness what God will do. The victories that will come are said even at this early moment to be victories of God. There is nothing here along the line of "Be strong and of good courage so that you will fight bravely." No, it is entirely "the living God who without fail will drive out from before you the Canaanites, Hittites, Hivites, Perizzites, Girgashites, Amorites, and Jebusites" (3:10).

(As an aside, note that the text doesn't say that God is going to destroy or to kill all those people, but rather "drive them out." Now of course that is not a friendly thing to do. But it isn't as violent and death-dealing as we sometimes assume. This is not the appropriate place to enter into a long discussion of the "God of violence" found in the Bible. Do, however, note that moving people from one place to another is far different from slaughtering them. This issue will come up again next week.)

Twelve ark-bearers are to be chosen to carry the ark into the Jordan River. When they enter the water, Joshua says, the water will stop flowing and will "stand in a single heap" (3:13). This again echoes the crossing of the Red Sea during the Exodus when the water is also described as being heaped up (Exodus 15:8). Over and over

we hear echoes of the past. Twelve sons of Jacob, twelve tribes of Israel, twelve bearers of the ark of the covenant. What God did for Moses, God will do for Joshua. Those who have listened to Moses as he retold the story of their parents' escape from Egypt will not miss these (and other) connections to their own past in what they will now see with their own eyes.

Joshua 3:14-17. The Jordan River should not be confused with the mighty Nile or the Mississippi or the Amazon. There are times in the dry season when the title *river* seems an exaggeration, when *stream* or *creek* would do just fine. At such times, fording the river is done without difficulty. But we are told specifically in Joshua 3:15 that this crossing is going to take place at harvesttime when "the Jordan overflows all its banks." There was no bridge for Israel, of course, and to get everyone and everything across at the time of high water would be well-nigh impossible. But, true to what God had said through Joshua, when the men bearing the ark set foot in the water, the flow stopped and the water piled up, leaving dry ground for Israel to walk upon.

INTERPRETING THE SCRIPTURE

Preparations

We want to know what God wants of us. We want to know what we, as a community of faith, should be doing with our time and our energies. There are some hints in this story of Joshua and the Israelites crossing the Jordan that we may use as we go forward in faith.

First, there are preparations to be made, and they involve the entire community. When Joshua tells the people to sanctify themselves because "tomorrow the LORD will do wonders among you" (Joshua 3:5), he is speaking to everyone, not just the

priests, not just the elders, not just the "important" people. There are indeed different gifts and different jobs and functional hierarchies among the community, but preparations to discern God's leading cannot be limited always to a small group.

Second, the people are given clear directions. Joshua tells the ark-bearers to pass in front of all the people. They need to see what they are to follow. They need to be able to recognize what and whom they are to follow.

Two ways we can begin to prepare ourselves to go forward in faith are to involve the whole community and to give clear directions to everyone. Does this sound like it involves a contradiction? If everyone is involved, then why is someone giving directions to the others? It is not a contradiction, although for us sinful humans it is sometimes a delicate balance to try to keep. Yes, there are leaders, and yes, God works through leaders. But leadership does not hide from the community. And leaders try very hard not to confuse themselves with God. (You might want to read Numbers 11:26-29 to see an example of a time when some of the Israelites didn't follow what others thought were the proper procedures—and what Moses said about it.)

Signs and Symbols

Symbols are both useful and dangerous. At this time in Israel's history, the ark of the covenant is an important symbol. It plays the practical role of being the focal point for their march. The people look for the ark of the covenant and they follow it. In following the ark, they are acting out its symbolic meaning of God's presence with them. It is also the symbol of their promises to God, their promises to obey the law given at Sinai and to live in righteous relationship with their Lord and with each other. Many years later the ark was captured in battle (1 Samuel 4:17). After awhile it was recovered from the Philistines (1 Samuel 6:21). Then, in still another battle, it was lost forever. If Israel had confused the ark of the covenant with actually *being* God, they would have been in bad shape indeed when it was no longer in their possession. But because Israel knew that the ark was a symbol of God and was not itself God, they were not utterly bereft when the ark was captured.

The Understanding the Scripture section lists some comparisons between this passage and others in Exodus. Did the Israelites under Joshua make those same connections? We cannot know whether they did or not. We do know, of course, that they did not have the book of Exodus

with them as the events it relates were going on. What we can say with some certainty is that when Israel came to write down some of their history with the Lord, the writers saw connections between events because they saw the Lord as being in charge of those events. By looking at what God had said and done in the past, they believed they could better understand what God was doing in their present. This, then, can give us another way we can discern God's will for our own community. We can search the Scriptures, not to find exactly the same situation we are in—the Bible knows nothing of the trappings of our industrial life, after all— but to find the same God who is still with us and still leading us. If we see that over and over again God tells the people to prepare themselves before meeting with the Lord, then we might say that serious preparation is a good idea. If we see that time and again God repeats the promises of old, extending them to new situations, then we might expect those promises still to be in force. If we see that the promise God gives most often is "I will be with you," then we can take comfort that the Lord is still with us—in our deliberations and in our steps, whether hesitant or eager, as we go forward in faith.

Even the Waters Obey

This section title may remind you of the story of Jesus' stilling the storm on the lake (Matthew 8:27; Mark 4:41; Luke 8:25). You will remember that the disciples were terrified by the storm, and not a little upset that Jesus didn't seem at all worried about it or about what was going to happen to them. If they hadn't wakened him, would the boat have capsized and drowned some of them? If they had let him sleep, would the storm have blown itself out without any harm to anyone? There is no way we can know the answers to such questions. As we have the story now, they did wake him up and he did calm the storm. They were amazed, and somewhat frightened of him too, for "even the winds and the sea obey him" (Matthew 8:27). They got the result they wanted, but it was scary. I think if I were to receive some spectacular sign from God, I would be more than a little frightened.

Take it another way: the waters obey—what about the people? It can border on the simplistic to say that "all we need to do" is go forward in faith. Which way is forward? Where is the visible symbol, such as the ark of the covenant, for us to follow? And yet it is too easy for us to give up and say following in faith is too hard. For we have God's promises in the Bible, we have the stories of others who asked and watched and listened. And we have each other. The religion of the Bible is not a private affair, strictly between the individual and God, but rather it is lived out amid other people. The church and the Sunday school class you are in are also sources of guidance and strength as you attempt to live faithful lives, going forward in faith.

SHARING THE SCRIPTURE

PREPARING TO TEACH

Preparing Our Hearts

Prepare to teach this week's lesson by reading the account of the crossing of the Jordan found in Joshua 3. Note the people's preparations for this historic event. Look for similarities between this crossing and the crossing of the Red Sea, as recorded in Exodus 14:10-31, which we studied on September 12. Consider how the people are going forward in faith. Think about your own faith journey. When has a major barrier threatened to impede your progress? How did you get over or around that barrier with God's help? What "leap of faith" was needed on your part to continue the journey? What signs assured you that you were going in the right direction? You may want to write answers to these questions in your spiritual journal.

Now turn in your Bible to today's devotional reading from Joshua 4:15-24. This passage brings us to the point in the story where the crossing is complete. Joshua commands the people to set up twelve stones as a memorial of their crossing. How does remembrance of what God has done for you in the past help you deal with a difficult situation in the present?

Offer a prayer that God will continue to guide you in all that you do, especially in your ministry of teaching.

Preparing Our Minds

Review Joshua 3. Locate Shittim, which is the place from which the people set out to cross the Jordan River (Joshua 3:1). If you have Bible Teacher Kit, look at the map entitled "Israel in Canaan," found on page 139. Note the proximity of Mount Pisgah to Shittim. Recall from last week's lesson that God showed Moses the promised land from the top of Mount Pisgah (Deuteronomy 34:1).

Note in Joshua 3:10 the names of the peoples that God will drive out from the promised land: Canaanites, Hittites, Hivites, Perizzites, Girgashites, Amorites, and Jebusites. Although we will not be studying any of these cultures, you may want to consult a commentary to learn more about them for your own background information.

As you read this lesson, be alert for parallels between the crossing of the Jordan under Joshua's leadership and the crossing of the Red Sea at Moses' direction. Some of these parallels are discussed in the Understanding the Scripture portion.

Preparing Our Learning Space

You may want to write on newsprint the second set of questions, which will be used for a written activity, found under "Signs and Symbols."
Have on hand:
- several Bibles
- newsprint and marker
- paper and pencils
- optional hymnals.

LEADING THE CLASS

(1) Introduction

Open today's session by talking with the class about ministries that your church is (or could be) planning to offer to meet specific needs. Perhaps you have looked into opening a Christian preschool, or serving meals two days a week for the hungry, or working with other congregations in your area to house the homeless, or inviting a self-help group such as Alcoholics Anonymous or Narcotics Anonymous to meet in your building. Brainstorm a list of these potential ministries and list them on newsprint.

Continue the discussion by asking the class to identify the barriers that prevent the church from offering these new programs and services. Some reasons may include fear of change, uncertainty about where the funding will come from, a desire to keep the building for the exclusive use of church members, or a lack of faith.

Move to today's lesson by noting that as we pick up the story in Joshua we find the people again facing some barriers in their journey. The promised land is not uninhabited, though God has promised to drive out the Canaanites, Hittites, Hivites, Perizzites, Girgashites, Amorites, and Jebusites who live there. Likewise, just as the people faced the Red Sea as they fled from Egypt, the Jordan River, said to be overflowing its banks at this time of the year, poses an obstacle for them. The people must decide whether they will stay in the wilderness or take the risk necessary to move forward in faith. Clearly, they needed God's guidance as well as Joshua's leadership. Our main question for today asks: **As we move by faith into new regions of life, are there any indicators we can look for to assure us we are going in the right direction?**

(2) Preparations

Invite the class to read aloud in unison today's key verse, Joshua 1:9.

If you have ample class time, ask someone to read the background scripture from Joshua 3:1-6. This passage outlines the preparations the people are called to make and sets the stage for their crossing of the Jordan River.

Discuss these questions:

(1) **Recall a difficult time in your life when the knowledge of God's presence with you, as promised in Joshua 1:9, gave you courage. What happened? How did God's presence empower you to get through this situation?**

(2) **What are some examples of preparations you have had to make in order to venture into unknown territory, however you may define that in your own life?** (Examples of unknown territories could include moving to a new home, regrouping after the death of a spouse, facing major surgery or serious illness, or retiring from a career. Preparations may vary widely and include physical, mental, emotional, and intellectual changes.)

(3) **What directions were you given to help you prepare for your venture?**

(4) **Why did you believe that the person who gave you the directions had the authority and/or knowledge to help you make preparations?**

(3) Signs and Symbols

Choose two persons to read Joshua 3:7-13: one to read God's words to Joshua (3:7-8), and one to read Joshua's speech to the Israelites (3:9-13).

Now ask class members to recall similarities between the crossing of the Jordan and the crossing of the Red Sea. List the comparisons on newsprint as students call them out. If you take into account the entire crossing, which includes some verses we have not yet read from today's lesson, your chart might look like this:

- God spoke directly to Joshua or Moses (Joshua 3:7/Exodus 14:15).
- The leaders (Joshua and Moses) spoke reassuringly to the gathered people (Joshua 3:9-10/Exodus 14:13-14).
- God was visibly present as a sign to the people in the ark of the Lord or the pillar of cloud (Joshua 3:11/Exodus 14:19-20).
- God gave directions as to how the people were to proceed (Joshua 3:12-13/Exodus 14:15-16).
- The waters obeyed God (Joshua 3:16/Exodus 14:21-22).
- The people were able to cross safely despite apparently insurmountable obstacles (Joshua 3:17/Exodus 14:29).

After you have listed the comparisons, ask these questions:

(1) **Had you been one of the Israelites crossing with Joshua, do you think you would have recognized the similarities between the crossing that Moses led and the one Joshua was leading? Why or why not?** (No one can answer this question definitively, of course, but the people may have realized the connection. Remember that those who crossed with Joshua are not the same generation as those led by Moses.)

(2) **Why might the historian who wrote the book of Joshua have gone to such lengths to show similarities between the two crossings?** (Such linkages could help the people recognize that God was in their midst and in charge of both the past and the present. Israel's God was trustworthy and could therefore be depended upon to take care of the people in whatever situation they found themselves.)

(3) **What might the similarities between these two ancient stories say to us today?** (Note that God is still present, still in charge. We too can trust God to be available and ready to act on our behalf.)

Distribute paper and pencils and ask the students to consider the following questions, which you may want to write on newsprint and post where everyone can see them. Tell the group in advance that they will not be asked to share their responses.

(1) **What "Jordan River experience" are you facing right now in your own life? That is, what overwhelming problem confronts you right now?**

(2) **How do you experience God's presence in this situation?**

(3) **What does the fact that the Israelites were willing to venture into unknown, perilous territory say to you as you venture forward in your own faith journey?**

Conclude this silent activity by reading again the words of today's key verse from Joshua 1:9: <u>"Be strong and courageous; do not be frightened or dismayed, for the LORD your God is with you wherever you go."</u>

(4) Even the Waters Obey

Choose a volunteer to read Joshua 3:14-17. Ask the class to close their eyes and imagine themselves in the midst of the crowd. After the reading, ask these questions:

(1) **What expectations might you have had if you were one of the first people to step into the Jordan?** (Note that we know the end of the story—the people arrived safely on the opposite shore. However, those who crossed first might have assumed they were facing death. They had to have real courage to take this risk.)

(2) **What indications would you have had that stepping into the river was**

?

the right thing to do? (The fact that the ark of the covenant was leading the way would have been a positive indication that this was the right thing to do because the ark was the sign of God's presence.)

(3) What would you have said, done, or thought after you safely reached the other side of the river? (Class members will not be reading the story in Joshua 4 concerning the setting up of memorial stones. However, one possible action is to build a monument to remind future generations of what God has done.)

(4) What might you have thought about God at this point? (One answer, found in Joshua 4:24, is that God is mighty and, therefore, to be feared—i.e., the people are to stand in awe of God.)

If time permits, close today's session by singing an old familiar hymn, "On Jordan's Stormy Banks I Stand," which is number 724 in *The United Methodist Hymnal*.

Before you say good-bye, be sure to lift up at least one of the activities below so that class members will have a chance to put what they have learned today into practice.

HELPING CLASS MEMBERS ACT

Challenge students to memorize today's key verse, Joshua 1:9. Suggest that they call it to mind when they are faced with a situation that requires them to take a risk in order to move ahead in faith.

For the Israelites who accompanied Joshua, the ark of the covenant was a sign of God's presence. Encourage the students to think of signs of God's presence in their own lives. Suggest that they keep a list of these signs for several days and then give thanks for the myriad of ways that God uses to guide them even when they are in unfamiliar territory.

The crossing of the Jordan appears to be a liturgical celebration. Recommend that the class members think of a liturgical celebration that has special meaning for them, such as a Christmas Eve service that includes the lighting of candles. Ask the students to consider why the event or ritual they have identified is meaningful for them.

PLANNING FOR NEXT SUNDAY

Next week's lesson is entitled "Overcoming Obstacles." During this session students will read about the Israelites' siege of Jericho. Ask the class to read Joshua 6, paying particular attention to verses 1-5 and 15-20.

OVERCOMING OBSTACLES

PREVIEWING THE LESSON

Lesson Scripture: Joshua 6:1-5, 15-20
Background Scripture: Joshua 6
Key Verse: Joshua 6:16

Focus of the Lesson:
Following the plan that God had given to Joshua, the people conquered the city of Jericho.

Main Question of the Lesson:
How does God work with people to overcome daunting obstacles?

This lesson will enable adult learners to:
(1) overhear God's marching orders for the Israelites.
(2) examine their own courage as they work with others to surmount a problem.
(3) respond by trying to overcome obstacles to obtain a victory in their own lives.

Today's lesson may be outlined as follows:
(1) Introduction
(2) God's Marching Orders
(3) God's Orders Are Carried Out
(4) Beyond God's Orders
(5) Another Promise Kept

FOCUSING ON THE MAIN QUESTION

A number of lessons in this series have looked at questions of discerning God's will, at sorting out competing claims from other powers that would have us treat them as gods, and at giving our ultimate allegiance to the Lord alone. We have read of blessings that will be the lot of those who keep God's law and of horrific curses that will fall on those who turn aside to other gods. We have seen that God does indeed keep promises even from generation to generation, that punishments are meted out to sinners, that forgiveness is offered to those who repent. We have read stories of human faithfulness and human sin and the never-ending faithfulness of God even in such circumstances.

Today's text is the account of Joshua and the Israelites and how, following God's directions, they are able to capture the walled city of Jericho. You have probably been familiar with this story since your childhood. It is a story with a "happy ending" in that the people obey God and achieve their goal. It is a miracle story in that it appears impossible at the beginning that Israel could ever capture a fortified city. It is also a miracle story because what the people do certainly doesn't sound like shrewd military tactics! Admittedly, this story is troubling for me, and perhaps for you as well, because of the violence perpetrated in the name of God. The directions given to Joshua (Joshua 6:2-5) say that God has handed over the city of Jericho. God makes no mention of killing all the inhabitants, though Joshua gives instructions to do so in verse 17. Israel certainly did achieve a victory, but we have to question whether Joshua overstepped his bounds in

overcoming the obstacle that was before him by annihilating the populace.

Joshua's story has much to say to us. Likely we won't be asked to circle a city and watch in amazement as its walls collapse. Yet all of us face obstacles in our lives that are apparently as insurmountable as the walls of Jericho. Sometimes we act like Joshua and the Israelites. We seek God's guidance and follow those directions, even when they make no sense to us. How often, though, do we ignore God's leading and try to solve the problem in our own way? As we study today's lesson, ask yourself: **How does God work with people to overcome daunting obstacles?**

READING THE SCRIPTURE

NRSV
Joshua 6:1-5, 15-20

1 Now Jericho was shut up inside and out because of the Israelites; no one came out and no one went in. 2 The LORD said to Joshua, "See, I have handed Jericho over to you, along with its king and soldiers. 3 You shall march around the city, all the warriors circling the city once. Thus you shall do for six days, 4 with seven priests bearing seven trumpets of rams' horns before the ark. On the seventh day you shall march around the city seven times, the priests blowing the trumpets. 5 When they make a long blast with the ram's horn, as soon as you hear the sound of the trumpet, then all the people shall shout with a great shout; and the wall of the city will fall down flat, and all the people shall charge straight ahead."

15 On the seventh day they rose early, at dawn, and marched around the city in the same manner seven times. It was only on that day that they marched around the city seven times. **16 And at the seventh time, when the priests had blown the trumpets, Joshua said to the people, "Shout! For the LORD has given you the city.**

NIV
Joshua 6:1-5, 15-20

¹Now Jericho was tightly shut up because of the Israelites. No one went out and no one came in.

²Then the LORD said to Joshua, "See, I have delivered Jericho into your hands, along with its king and its fighting men. ³March around the city once with all the armed men. Do this for six days. ⁴Have seven priests carry trumpets of rams' horns in front of the ark. On the seventh day, march around the city seven times, with the priests blowing the trumpets. ⁵When you hear them sound a long blast on the trumpets, have all the people give a loud shout; then the wall of the city will collapse and the people will go up, every man straight in."

¹⁵On the seventh day, they got up at daybreak and marched around the city seven times in the same manner, except that on that day they circled the city seven times. **¹⁶The seventh time around, when the priests sounded the trumpet blast, Joshua commanded the people, "Shout! For the LORD has given you the city!**

17 The city and all that is in it shall be devoted to the LORD for destruction. Only Rahab the prostitute and all who are with her in her house shall live because she hid the messengers we sent. 18 As for you, keep away from the things devoted to destruction, so as not to covet and take any of the devoted things and make the camp of Israel an object for destruction, bringing trouble upon it. 19 But all silver and gold, and vessels of bronze and iron, are sacred to the LORD; they shall go into the treasury of the LORD." 20 So the people shouted, and the trumpets were blown. As soon as the people heard the sound of the trumpets, they raised a great shout, and the wall fell down flat; so the people charged straight ahead into the city and captured it.

[17]The city and all that is in it are to be devoted to the LORD. Only Rahab the prostitute and all who are with her in her house shall be spared, because she hid the spies we sent. [18]But keep away from the devoted things, so that you will not bring about your own destruction by taking any of them. Otherwise you will make the camp of Israel liable to destruction and bring trouble on it. [19]All the silver and gold and the articles of bronze and iron are sacred to the LORD and must go into his treasury."

[20]When the trumpets sounded, the people shouted, and at the sound of the trumpet, when the people gave a loud shout, the wall collapsed; so every man charged straight in, and they took the city.

UNDERSTANDING THE SCRIPTURE

Joshua 6:1-5. The very first verse sets the situation before us. Jericho's being "shut up inside and out" means that it was a city with a fortified wall around it. The inhabitants were relatively safe from any advancing army because few weapons in those days could wreak destruction across such walls, let alone penetrate the walls or knock them down. Of course, if a hostile force surrounded such a town and was well supplied with food and water, it could try to wait out the shut-up population. Centuries later, Jerusalem came under such siege and was able to outlast the army because of King Hezekiah's conduit that brought fresh water to the city from a spring outside the walls (2 Kings 20:20).

Joshua and Israel will not have to wait out Jericho, however. Everyone knows from the very beginning that this is not going to be the usual sort of fight, for the Lord tells Joshua immediately that "I have handed Jericho over to you" (Joshua 6:2). What this means is that if Israel follows God's directions, then the outcome is not in doubt. There are four things to notice about the directions: (1) they include everyone at some level; (2) they are possible for everyone at the appropriate level; (3) they are odd; and (4) they are unique in the Bible. Warriors and priests, as would be expected, are given a task. There is no difficulty in their walking around the city each day for six days. But on the seventh day, "all the people shall shout with a great shout" (6:5). There were undoubtedly people who couldn't have walked around the city even once, let alone seven times on the seventh day. But everyone could make noise. Thus, God gives everyone in the community a task in this enterprise.

Do the directions sound odd? Maybe we are so familiar with this story that they sound normal. But what I mean by *odd* is that no one using common sense or great military acumen would have come up with the idea of marching around the city and then shouting and expect the walls to collapse as a result. This is the only time in the entire Bible when God helps Israel win a battle with circular marching and shouting. God's instructions to Joshua end with the falling of the walls.

Joshua 6:6-16. In great detail we are told of Joshua's passing along the instructions to the priests and warriors and all the rest of the people. We read in detail how they obeyed on the first day, and then the rest of the first six days are summarized. On day seven, everyone takes part in the shouting, just as they were supposed to.

Joshua 6:17-21. "The city and all that is in it shall be devoted to the LORD for destruction" (6:17a). This idea is new. We did not read any such instruction from God to Joshua. (Of course it is possible that God said many things that were not recorded in the Bible. But we cannot treat as biblical some possible text we do not have in the Bible.) This is the final part of what is sometimes called a "War of the Lord" or a "holy war," although that latter term does not appear in the Bible. Not only is the victory supposed to be proclaimed as God's alone, no human is to profit personally from it. When the time came that there was a Temple in Jerusalem, all the valuable goods would be taken there. At this point, the valuables are said to "go into the treasury of the LORD" (6:19). Animals would be sacrificed to

God. What about the people? This is the difficult aspect. According to Joshua 6:21 they were all killed along with the animals. Indeed, the verse treats the people no differently from the animals. It is not only the soldiers who are killed. It is not only those who could, potentially, be warriors. No, "men and women, young and old" (6:21) are all killed.

Joshua 6:22-27. The only exception to this mass slaughter is Rahab and her family. Rahab is the prostitute who hid the Israelite spies when they had come to see about the city and its fortifications (2:1-24). In return for saving their lives she extracts the promise from them that when Israel captures Jericho—and, since the Lord is with Israel, she has no doubt that will happen—she and her family be allowed to live. The writer of this passage steps into the time of its writing in Joshua 6:25 to tell us that Rahab's "family has lived in Israel ever since." She is also mentioned in the New Testament, in the genealogy of Jesus (Matthew 1:5).

The final verse of today's passage sums up the matter with the simple words "So the LORD was with Joshua." This has been God's great promise all along, to be with the people. And with God with them, then God's promises do come to pass.

INTERPRETING THE SCRIPTURE

God's Marching Orders

As mentioned in the Understanding the Scripture section, God's instructions at times can seem odd. Such strangeness is within our perception, I think, because we do not perceive as God does. And such strangeness is not limited to battle accounts. We humans have a tendency to measure God's ideas by our own interests. Where they agree, where they make sense to us, we follow them. Where they are in conflict, we are much more likely to say

the Lord's notions are "unworkable" or "utopian" or some such way of trying to get ourselves off the hook of obeying. Whether the Ten Commandments (Exodus 20:1-17; Deuteronomy 5:6-21), the Beatitudes (Matthew 5:1-12), or even the Great Commandment (Matthew 22:37; Mark 12:30; Luke 10:27; Deuteronomy 6:4-5; Leviticus 19:18), we may give them lip service, but we are also quick to say that they cannot "work" in the "real world."

As mentioned above, I think God's solutions may be both "odd" and "one-time-only" in part so that we will recognize our need to rely on the Lord. It is equally important to see that whatever it is God tells the people to do, they are capable of doing it if they choose to. God sets no impossible tasks, no mighty feats of strength or valor or cunning, which must be accomplished before God will act on behalf of Israel. At the Red Sea, they had to "stand firm, and see the deliverance that the LORD will accomplish" (Exodus 14:13). I resolutely believe that God will never demand that we do something impossible. Difficult perhaps, or even distasteful in that it may set us apart from our neighbors, but God knows our limits and does not taunt us by requiring the impossible. In some situations, we may have to face the fact that the biggest obstacle in front of us is our own unwillingness to be faithful to the Lord.

God's Orders Are Carried Out

Joshua and the Israelites were willing to do as God told them. We hear no complaints that marching around Jericho is too hard or too silly. God speaks. They follow. The walls fall down. So far, so good. Not all the stories in the Bible flow so smoothly. There is the account of Naaman, for instance, a Syrian general who had leprosy and is sent to the prophet Elisha to be healed. When Elisha sends word that Naaman should bathe in the Jordan River, he is outraged and starts back home. His servants remind him that if Elisha had told him to do something very difficult, he would have attempted the task. Why not do the simple thing and see what happens? Naaman follows Elisha's orders and is healed. (You can read the entire account in 2 Kings 5.)

There is a wonderful story told about Dorothy Sayers, an English theologian and mystery writer in the first half of this century. It is said that once when she was invited to preach before a college congregation, she stood up at the pulpit and said,

"You are all Christians. You know what you are supposed to do. Now go home and do it." And then she sat down. I do not know whether that story is true or not, but couldn't something similar be said to most of our congregations on most Sundays? We know what God has told us to do. We should go home and try it and see what happens. Now, I do not mean to make light of the real difficulties that confront many people. My point is, rather, that for some of us it is easier to think up reasons why we cannot follow the Lord's teachings than to work at living faithfully.

Beyond God's Orders

This lesson is about overcoming obstacles. Sometimes the biggest obstacle is not even our unwillingness to try to live faithfully, but our own lack of imagination. Because we can see what God has done in the past, we demand that God act in just that same way in the future. This, I believe, is one reason that the Lord's specific directions are different every time they are given in the Bible, and also why they are outside of the realm of what we would likely define as common sense. If, having seen how God works, we decide we now know how the "trick" works, we will not think we need to go to God for guidance. If the tactics were commonsensical, we wouldn't even need to go to God the first time. But creation is much more complex than we can understand, even though we are much more advanced scientifically than the Israelites were under Joshua. And God still wants to be in continuing relationship with us. These two things, I believe, are why the directions are "nonsensical" and unique.

Israel needed to get past Jericho's walls. God told them how. Israel needed to be sure they were not slaughtered by the inhabitants of Jericho once they entered the city. Joshua didn't bother to ask God about this matter because he knew (or thought he knew) the solution himself.

Everyone knows, even today, that the best thing to do to an enemy population is kill everyone. That way, no one will cause any trouble. Right? I may be overstating it somewhat, but I do want to make a point here. Yes, of course killing all the people in Jericho kept them from harming Israel. But stop and think for a moment. If God could make those fortified walls fall down just from a week's worth of marching and a final loud shout, is it not possible that God could make peace between the two populations without having one wipe out the other? Distressingly often we turn to God only for those things we cannot solve ourselves. We might be surprised if we also asked for guidance even in instances where we didn't think we needed it. We might discover that God has even better ideas than we do! Sometimes—not always, but sometimes—our biggest obstacles are ourselves.

Another Promise Kept

Rahab and her family could have been killed in the general slaughter. After all, when everything was finished, who would have known there was a broken promise? And Rahab wasn't an Israelite. And she was a prostitute. On all those counts it wouldn't have been surprising for that little promise the spies made to be overlooked. They could have gotten away with forgetting. But they remembered, and centuries and centuries later her name appears in the genealogy of Jesus. I am scarcely saying that Jesus wouldn't have been born had Rahab's life not been spared. But this is an example of the durability of a good deed. It is often easier to do what we think is right when we assume someone will notice. The story of Rahab may be a reminder that the results of a good deed may echo through centuries.

SHARING THE SCRIPTURE

PREPARING TO TEACH

Preparing Our Hearts

For our devotional scripture today, read Psalm 47, which celebrates God's enthronement as the Sovereign of all nations. Read this passage aloud and hear the psalmist summon all the world to praise God. Do you believe that God is the ruler of all? If so, how do you praise God as the incomparable Sovereign?

Now turn to this week's background scripture, found in Joshua 6. Connect this reading to the devotional passage by considering how the Israelites' triumph over Jericho reflects God's sovereignty. Consider how this passage reminds you of some kind of religious ritual, complete with a procession.

Meditate on the following questions: Under what circumstances have you struggled to achieve a worthwhile goal? How did God empower you in that situation? With whom did you need to cooperate to win the victory? How did the remembrance of that victory give you courage to face another difficult obstacle? (Perhaps you will want to write answers in your spiritual journal.)

Conclude your devotional time by praying that God will guide you and that you will be receptive to such guidance as you struggle with your own "Jerichos."

Preparing Our Minds

Read this lesson and review Joshua 6.

Note that Joshua 6 is not so much a description of a historical battle as it is a recollection of what happened. Many scholars believe that this excerpt from Joshua records a religious ritual. Here are some details that suggest this passage documents a liturgical celebration: the priests are carrying the Ark; the ram's horn is blown; specific instructions are given for circling the city; and the sacred number seven is used repeatedly. In addition, verse 17 speaks of the total destruction of the city and all that is in it, which is a formula referring to a ritual act of a holy war.

If you have time, you may want to consult a Bible dictionary to learn more about the city of Jericho. This ancient city was first occupied nine thousand years before Jesus lived. Located six miles north of the Dead Sea and irrigated by a spring, Jericho was an important site because of its vegetation and its strategic location as an entrance from the Transjordan into the highlands of Judah. For the people of Joshua's time, Jericho was an ideal base from which to launch an attack on Canaan.

Preparing Our Learning Space

If possible, duplicate or post a map of Israel at the time of Joshua. *Bible Teacher Kit* includes a map of Israel in Canaan on page 139.
Have on hand:
✔ several Bibles
✔ map showing Jericho
✔ optional large cardboard box and markers
✔ newsprint and marker.

LEADING THE CLASS

(1) Introduction

To introduce today's session, set out a cardboard box (several boxes if the class is large) and markers. Ask the students as they enter the room to write on the box an obstacle that they are facing right now. They need not be specific but could simply list a broad category, such as illness, family problems, or job. When people have finished writing, place the box on a table or somewhere that it can easily be seen. Read aloud a few of the obstacles that have been written. Then discuss these questions with the group:

(1) Are there ever times when you will just let an obstacle defeat you? If so, give an example.

(2) What role do other people play in helping you meet a challenge?

(3) What role does one's own courage play in overcoming an obstacle?

(4) What role does God play in overcoming an obstacle?

Close this segment by noting that Joshua and the Israelites had a huge obstacle to overcome if they were to take possession of the walled city of Jericho. They had to listen to Joshua who was directed by God, work together, and use some rather unorthodox means to achieve the outcome that God promised. Lift up today's main question: **How does God work with people to overcome daunting obstacles?**

(2) God's Marching Orders

Choose a volunteer to read Joshua 6:1-5. Discuss these questions:

(1) What do you know about Jericho? (Use information you have learned about the city to augment the discussion. If you have a map available, help the class locate Jericho. Note that the people were evidently prepared for an attack, because the city was barricaded so that no one could enter or leave.)

(2) How would you have felt had you been Joshua and heard God's words in verse 2? (God's words likely inspired great confidence and hope, for the Lord proclaimed to Joshua that Jericho and its leaders were delivered into the hands of the Israelites.)

(3) Had you been an Israelite, what would you have thought of God's directions as recorded in verses 3-5? (These instructions seem ludicrous from a military point of view. The people are not to storm the city. Rather, they are simply to march around, listen for the ram's horn, and then shout. God tells them that the wall of this fortified city will just fall down.)

(4) Joshua seems to include everyone in his directions. Why do you think that was the case? (Everyone had to work together to achieve the goal that God had for them.)

(3) God's Orders Are Carried Out

If time permits, read Joshua 6:6-14 from the background scripture. Here you will find the account of the Israelites following through on God's orders. When we humans follow God's orders, things go well. You may want to look briefly at one or more of the following stories concerning people who follow God's directions and overcome obstacles. Many other stories could be used here.

• Judges 7:1–8:12—Gideon leads a small army against the Midianites and God wins the victory.

• 2 Kings 5:1-14—Naaman is healed.

• Daniel 1:1-21—Daniel insists on eating a proper Jewish diet while held captive by King Nebuchadnezzar and is remarkably healthy because he upholds his dietary laws.

As you review these stories, consider these questions:

(1) What is the obstacle that must be faced?

(2) What means does God use for overcoming the problem?

(3) What difference does the person's obedience to God make?

(4) Beyond God's Orders

Select a reader for Joshua 6:15-20. Ask:

(1) How are God's orders fulfilled here? (You may want to go back to the beginning of the chapter and look again at verses 2-5 to see what God said was to be done.)

(2) What did Joshua do that seems to go beyond God's orders? (Notice that

God says that the city, its king, and soldiers will be handed over. Joshua, however, leads the people in a holy war wherein the city and all that is within it is destroyed. Verse 17 makes reference to what is to be done; verse 21 records the destruction.)

(3) Why do you think Joshua ordered this total destruction? (Perhaps Joshua wanted to be sure that there were no traces of Jericho's Canaanite culture left that could create problems for the Israelites. He certainly wanted to somehow sanctify the city. Joshua also may not have considered that God could deal with the inhabitants in ways other than death.)

If time permits, brainstorm answers to one or both of the following scenarios that you will need to read aloud. If you want, you may record ideas on newsprint.

Scenario 1: Several members of your congregation feel strongly that God is calling you to offer substantial support to a missionary. Church members like the idea but believe that no money is available for such a project. What could be done?

Scenario 2: Elected officials have taken a stand that is in opposition to your church's beliefs. For example, a need to raise money to fund schools and other projects has made casino gambling an attractive alternative, but your denomination opposes gambling. What can you and your church do?

(5) Another Promise Kept

Look back at Joshua 6:17b. You may also want to look at the rest of the chapter, namely, verses 22 through 27, which also speak of Rahab, as well as at Joshua 2:1-21, which tells the story of Rahab's assistance to the Israelite spies. Then ask:

(1) What does the fact that the promise of safety to Rahab and her family was kept say to you about God?

(2) What does it say to you about Joshua and the Israelites?

(3) **What does the fact that Rahab is not only remembered but listed in the genealogy of Jesus (Matthew 1:5) say to you about the importance of one person doing a good deed to help others overcome obstacles?**

Conclude today's session by returning to the cardboard box(es) on which obstacles were written at the beginning of the session. Offer a prayer in which you name these obstacles and ask God to empower those who face them to overcome them.

Before you dismiss the group, lift up at least one of the activities below so that students will have ideas for relating this lesson to their daily lives.

HELPING CLASS MEMBERS ACT

Tell students to pray fervently and listen for any directions that God gives them for surmounting an obstacle in their own lives. Suggest that they write down what-ever they understand God to be telling them and then that they act on those directions. Have them further note how their obedience to God's leading ultimately allows the obstacle to be overcome.

Recommend that students read one or more books that speak of courage and survival in difficult circumstances, such as a natural catastrophe, war, plane crash, or serious illness. Tell class members to be alert for indications that the survivor(s) felt led to take a particular course of action that turned out to be the right thing to do. *The Survivor Personality* by Al Siebert (ISBN 0-399-52230-1, published by Perigree Books) presents a fascinating discussion of this topic.

Encourage class members to search their Bibles this week for occasions when God gave someone apparently strange directions to overcome a problem. Some examples are listed above under "God's Orders Are Carried Out."

PLANNING FOR NEXT SUNDAY

We will conclude this quarter's lessons with another session from the book of Joshua. Ask the students to read Joshua 24. This familiar passage includes a challenge to the Israelites, and to us as well, to choose to serve God.

MAKING THE RIGHT CHOICE

PREVIEWING THE LESSON

Lesson Scripture: Joshua 24:1-2, 14-22, 25
Background Scripture: Joshua 24
Key Verse: Joshua 24:24

Focus of the Lesson:
Joshua called the people together at Shechem and challenged them to choose whether they would serve God or other gods, and they pledged themselves to serve God.

Main Question of the Lesson:
How can we help ourselves and one another to make the right choices in the important matters of our lives?

This lesson will enable adult learners to:
(1) listen to Joshua's challenge to the Israelites and their response.
(2) choose for themselves whom they will serve.
(3) respond by keeping a promise.

Today's lesson may be outlined as follows:
(1) Introduction
(2) "Their" History
(3) "Your" History
(4) Choose, Think, Choose
(5) The Witnesses

FOCUSING ON THE MAIN QUESTION

There is a public service ad on television from time to time that shows a boy, ten years old or so, at an urban playground. We can hear an older person who is out of camera range offering him some drugs. The man says the boy will feel good if he does it and that the first time will be absolutely free. To every suggestion, the boy answers resoundingly that he is not interested. The man is persistent. The boy continues to say, "Leave me alone" and "I'm not interested." Then the man says, "That's just what you do if this ever happens to you." In the last picture we see the two of them walking off together, the man's arm around the boy's shoulder, and the man saying, "I like how you handled yourself, son."

When I was a child my parents didn't have to help me practice saying "no" to drug dealers. Things have certainly changed, haven't they? And yet, parents have always tried to protect their children from dangers. Part of that protection includes teaching the children how to protect themselves when the parents are not around. Ultimately the children have to learn how to protect themselves and be responsible for themselves as they become adults. Most matters of safety can come down to making the right choices: wearing a helmet when bike-riding or stopping the car at the red light even if no other cars are in sight. Spiritual and moral safety are also connected with making choices: not looking on another student's paper while taking a test, or going swimming after church and not instead of church.

As adults, we recognize that life is a daily round of choices. Some are inconsequential: Do I write my grocery list on an index card or the back of an envelope? Other choices apparently make no immediate difference but do have effects over time: Knowing that food choices will affect my health, do I eat meat and potatoes with gravy three nights a week, or do I select vegetarian dinners? One choice echoes throughout eternity: Will I serve God, or will I look out only for myself? God certainly does not coerce us into making the right choice, but we must accept the consequences of our decision. The Israelites also had to make this decision as they stood poised at the edge of the promised land. As we study today's lesson we will ask: **How can we help ourselves and one another to make the right choices in the important matters of our lives?**

READING THE SCRIPTURE

NRSV
Joshua 24:1-2, 14-22, 24-25

1 Then Joshua gathered all the tribes of Israel to Shechem, and summoned the elders, the heads, the judges, and the officers of Israel; and they presented themselves before God. 2 And Joshua said to all the people,

14 "Now therefore revere the LORD, and serve him in sincerity and in faithfulness; put away the gods that your ancestors served beyond the River and in Egypt, and serve the LORD. 15 Now if you are unwilling to serve the LORD, choose this day whom you will serve, whether the gods your ancestors served in the region beyond the River or the gods of the Amorites in whose land you are living; but as for me and my household, we will serve the LORD."

16 Then the people answered, "Far be it from us that we should forsake the LORD to serve other gods; 17 for it is the LORD our God who brought us and our ancestors up from the land of Egypt, out of the

NIV
Joshua 24:1-2, 14-22, 24-25

1Then Joshua assembled all the tribes of Israel at Shechem. He summoned the elders, leaders, judges and officials of Israel, and they presented themselves before God. 2Joshua said to all the people,

14"Now fear the LORD and serve him with all faithfulness. Throw away the gods your forefathers worshiped beyond the River and in Egypt, and serve the LORD. 15But if serving the LORD seems undesirable to you, then choose for yourselves this day whom you will serve, whether the gods your forefathers served beyond the River, or the gods of the Amorites, in whose land you are living. But as for me and my household, we will serve the LORD."

16Then the people answered, "Far be it from us to forsake the LORD to serve other gods! 17It was the LORD our God himself who brought us and our fathers up out of Egypt, from that land of slavery, and per-house of slavery, and who did those great signs in our sight. He protected us along all the way that we went, and among all the peoples through whom we passed; 18 and the LORD drove out before us all the peoples, the Amorites who lived in the land. Therefore we also will serve the LORD, for he is our God."

19 But Joshua said to the people, "You cannot serve the LORD, for he is a holy God. He is a jealous God; he will not forgive your transgressions or your sins. 20 If you forsake the LORD and serve foreign gods, then he will turn and do you harm, and consume you, after having done you good." 21 And the people said to Joshua, "No, we will serve the LORD!" 22 Then Joshua said to the people, "You are witnesses against yourselves that you have chosen the LORD, to serve him." And they said, "We are witnesses."

Key Verse

24 The people said to Joshua, "The LORD our God we will serve, and him we will obey." 25 So Joshua made a covenant with the people that day, and made statutes and ordinances for them at Shechem.

formed those great signs before our eyes. He protected us on our entire journey and among all the nations through which we traveled. 18And the LORD drove out before us all the nations, including the Amorites, who lived in the land. We too will serve the LORD, because he is our God."

19Joshua said to the people, "You are not able to serve the LORD. He is a holy God; he is a jealous God. He will not forgive your rebellion and your sins. 20If you forsake the LORD and serve foreign gods, he will turn and bring disaster on you and make an end of you, after he has been good to you."

21But the people said to Joshua, "No! We will serve the LORD."

22Then Joshua said, "You are witnesses against yourselves that you have chosen to serve the LORD." "Yes, we are witnesses," they replied.

Key Verse

24 And the people said to Joshua, "We will serve the LORD our God and obey him." 25On that day Joshua made a covenant for the people, and there at Shechem he drew up for them decrees and laws.

UNDERSTANDING THE SCRIPTURE

Joshua 24:1-6. Joshua does at the end of the book of Joshua something similar to what Moses did at the end of Deuteronomy. Joshua summons the entire community to gather at Shechem, the site of their first holy place in the promised land. Joshua is more succinct in his sermon than Moses was in his, but Joshua, like Moses, repeats the history of Israel. God, through Joshua, begins the story all the way back with Abraham and his father Terah in a time when they still worshiped other gods. Joshua reminds the people of God's promises and how they were carried out, how Abraham had Isaac and Isaac fathered Jacob and Esau. Even Esau, who

was not the favored son through whom the main covenant would continue, was given a land of his own. The history is summarized quickly, getting to the plagues of Egypt and the chariots and horsemen of Egypt pursuing "your ancestors" (Joshua 24:6). Joshua is relating again the story of God's faithfulness that had all happened before any of his hearers had been born.

Joshua 24:7-13. Now Joshua shifts pronouns. He says, "When *they* cried out to the Lord, he put darkness between *you* and the Egyptians..." (24:7, italics added). From now on, he relates the account in terms of "you" rather than "them." Historically, he is incorrect, for many of those listening to him would be the second generation after the Exodus. Theologically, however, Joshua is doing the same thing Moses did in teaching the people to remember the story as their own story and not just something that happened to someone else. The history of God with the people of God cannot be thought of in terms of "long ago and far away." Over and over God says, "I brought *you*..." (24:8), "I rescued *you*..." (24:10), "I gave *you* a land..." (24:13, italics added). God's actions have not been vague; God has not acted "in general" but quite specifically with particular deeds for this particular people. What Joshua is recounting is not history in general but God's history with them.

Joshua 24:14-25. Because of what the Lord has done for Israel, says Joshua, the people should respond by being completely faithful to the Lord. It is time for them to put away their false gods. They cannot continue trying to serve the old gods they and their ancestors worshiped years ago—gods who are not gods—if they want also to serve the Lord. It is time for them to choose and to make a break with one or the other. Joshua is emphatic that he and his household will serve the Lord.

The people's first response is immediate and clear. They too repeat parts of the history, and they too recite it in terms that begin with "them" and soon change to "us." Look, for example, at Joshua 24:17, which refers to "us and our ancestors" together being brought out of slavery in Egypt by God. Joshua does not accept their first quick response. Instead, he reminds the people that it is a grave matter to agree to be loyal to the Lord and then to fall away. The Lord is "a holy God. He is a jealous God..." (24:19). The word rendered "jealous" here is the same one discussed in the lesson for September 19 on the Ten Commandments. Here too, it is closer to the Hebrew meaning to say *zeal-*

ous rather than *jealous*. (Remember that it is English that has changed. Some three centuries ago, *jealous* and *zealous* could be used interchangeably.)

Remember also that the divisions of the text into verses happened many, many centuries after the Bible was first written down. We really should not make a stop at the end of verse 19, but carry it on into verse 20. The "not forgiving" in verse 19 is the result that will come "if you forsake the Lord and serve foreign gods" (24:20). Joshua 24:19 is not saying that God simply "will not forgive your transgressions or your sins," period, but that there will not be forgiveness to those who say they will be loyal to the Lord and then leave to serve other gods instead.

After hearing Joshua's warnings, the people still promise to remain faithful and to serve the Lord. Joshua tells them they are witnesses themselves to their promises. As a result of their decision, Joshua says they must put away all other gods and turn their "hearts" to the Lord. Again we have the word *heart*, which, in Hebrew, stands for thinking and decision making rather than for emotions, as it does in English. What Joshua is telling the people, therefore, is that they are to keep the Lord in their thoughts and their decisions. This is another way of stating the Great Commandment. The people answer as one that they will be faithful to God.

Joshua 24:26-27. Joshua's next action seems sensible to us: he "wrote these words in the book of the law of God." But the very next thing he did seems curious. He took a big stone and set it up in the sanctuary at Shechem and told the people the stone would be the witness against them. It was common among the surrounding cultures to set up a statue of a god to be a witness to important treaties and other agreements. Since Israel has only one God, they can hardly set up a statue of another god to serve as a witness. Joshua uses a stone, which will serve as a visual reminder of the agreement the people have made, but without any danger that they will think there is another god involved.

Joshua 24:28-33. These final verses in today's lesson conclude the book of Joshua. They serve to tie up any loose ends. Joshua dies and is buried. Unlike Moses, Joshua not only has been able to come into the land but has "his own inheritance" along with the rest of Israel. Joseph's bones, which the Israelites carried with them from Egypt (Exodus 13:19), are finally buried at Shechem, in the very plot of ground his own father had purchased. Finally, notice is given of the death of Aaron's son Eleazar.

INTERPRETING THE SCRIPTURE

"Their" History

We have considered the matter of history and remembering before in this quarter's lessons. The fact that it comes up yet again is another indication of how very important it is. The stories of what has gone on before serve as a way of identifying both the people and God. The history of Israel and the history of God are caught up in the stories of what happened between them. Israel's story cannot be told without mentioning God.

We tell family stories today for similar reasons of identity. For example, my brothers are not interchangeable parts. It was Howard who, at about twelve years old, got up in the middle of a winter night and shoveled the sidewalks of an elderly neighbor without realizing until he got home that it was only three o'clock in the morning. It was toddler Jonathan who took his favorite toy over to a visiting child who had fallen and was crying— while the adults all stood around trying to figure out something to do. It was the youngest, Tim, who—but you get the idea. We remember and tell particular stories not so much for their specific content as to get to know the people involved.

In Joshua 24:1-2, Joshua gathers the Israelites together so that everyone will hear the story. All of the tribes have gathered under Joshua's leadership. Now, at Shechem, they have come together to hear their leader tell the story of their journey with God.

"Your" History

For the telling of stories, for the remembering of history, to have a significant impact on our lives, they must somehow bridge the gap from "their" story to "your" story or "our" story. This is probably one reason children are so keen to hear tales about their parents' escapades as youngsters. It is a way of making connections, of becoming a part of a group. For children, it is a matter of learning how to live.

Why do we teach our children history in school if not to incorporate them into the community and the nation? Why did I study Ohio's history in seventh grade and my daughter Tennessee's history if not to incorporate us more deeply into the areas where we were living at the time? What is dangerous—and not a little sad—is when we try to slant the story or omit significant parts. If we do not remember and pass on our history accurately, people will find it much more difficult to make good choices as a community. For instance—and I know this is an area of great controversy, but that does not mean it should be ignored!—I still remember a Thanksgiving program my daughter's fourth-grade class put on for parents and the rest of the school. There were songs and skits and poems recited; there was turkey and Pilgrims and the *Mayflower*. But there was no mention at all of God or religion. No, I do not want the public school to take over the role of family and church. Nor is it necessary to recite all the sociopolitical-economic circumstances of the early seventeenth century. But, after a while, without those deeper understandings of reasons and causes, all our holidays may merge into each other as undifferentiated marketing days.

In today's lesson, Joshua's telling of the story is preliminary to asking the people to commit themselves to a choice. He tells the Israelites' story by rehearsing the wondrous deeds that God has done on their behalf.

What helps us make right choices? Knowing who we are and whose we are, knowing what has happened in the past and what has been promised for the future.

Choose, Think, Choose

In Joshua 24:14-15, Joshua calls the people to choose whether they will revere and serve the Lord or continue to worship the same false gods that their ancestors worshiped. Although the Israelites clearly must choose for themselves, Joshua announces that he and his family will serve the Lord.

At once the people respond that they will not forsake the Lord to serve other gods. After all, it was God who led them out of bondage in Egypt. It was God who performed miracles. It was God who guided and guarded them throughout their entire journey. And it was God who drove people out of the land so that the Israelites could possess it. This choice was, in modern terms, a no-brainer. The people definitely wanted to remain faithful to this God of their ancestors, for this God had done mighty deeds for them.

In verses 19-20, Joshua seems harsh when he first responds to their enthusiasm for choosing the Lord. But such momentous choices are not to be made lightly. You can likely come up with many examples of choices that need to be carefully weighed. Marriage, for instance, needs to be considered beyond the first excitement of "We're so in love!" Confirmation, or reaffirmation of the baptismal covenant, is another serious step that requires preparation, thought, and the support of the community of faith.

What helps us make good choices? Having the support of the community as we ponder our decisions, having honest people who will ask us hard questions and thus assist our considerations.

The Witnesses

We may agonize long and hard over a decision, or we may make a choice quickly. However, if we don't follow through on the option we've selected, we have, in essence, chosen to do nothing or perhaps just to preserve the status quo rather than make a significant change. One way to avoid this failure to act is to tell others, even just one person, what our decision is. That person can then help us to act on the choice we have made.

We also may use objects as symbols and witnesses of our commitments. For example, many married persons wear wedding rings as visible reminders of the vows they made at the altar. Similarly, Joshua wrote the words of the covenant in the book and then set up a large stone to prompt the people to remember their promise to serve God. A ring, a book, a stone—such reminders are witnesses not only to those who have made the promises but also to anyone else who sees the symbol.

Persons can serve as living witnesses, as Joshua 24:31 states: "Israel served the LORD . . . all the days of the elders who . . . had known all the work that the LORD did for Israel." As these persons know and share the stories, they are visible witnesses to us as we journey on together toward the fullness of God's kingdom.

What helps us make good choices? Having witnesses that attest to our decisions, having visible reminders to be faithful to the choices we have made, listening to witnesses recall the shared stories of our journey with God.

SHARING THE SCRIPTURE

PREPARING TO TEACH

Preparing Our Hearts

Today's devotional reading is actually taken from the lesson itself. Read Joshua 24 in its entirety. Imagine yourself among the Israelites, listening intently as Joshua rehearses the history of your people's relationship with God. What details are most important to you? Had you been asked to tell the story, what other details might you have included? Which details would you have omitted? What does Joshua's account say to you about God? How would you respond to his challenge to "choose this day whom you will serve" (24:15)?

Now think about this story in the context of your own life. God continues to call each of us to choose whom we will serve. Is God your one and only choice, or do you divide your loyalties? What changes do you need to be more faithful? Pray that God might show you what you need to do and empower you to do it.

Preparing Our Minds

Look again at Joshua 24. Note this long and impressive list of things that God has done, according to Joshua's account in 24:1-13. Although verses 3-13 are simply background reading for this lesson, it is important to note all that God has done, for Joshua's call to the people to choose whom they will serve is rooted in their history with God.

- God called Abraham from his home and led him to Canaan.
- God gave Abraham (and Sarah) numerous offspring, beginning with Isaac.
- God gave Isaac Jacob and Esau.
- God gave Esau the land of Seir, even though the covenant promise was to follow Jacob's line.

- God sent Moses and Aaron to Egypt and, after plagues, brought the people out of bondage.
- God led the people to the Red Sea and safely through it, though their Egyptian pursuers were drowned.
- God guided the people in the wilderness.
- God handed over the land of the Amorites to the Israelites.
- God rescued the people from the Moabites.
- God gave the people the victory at Jericho and also against other enemies.
- God gave the people the promised land, which included towns they had not built and food from crops they did not plant.

Preparing Our Learning Space

Prior to the session, write the questions suggested in the Introduction on newsprint.
Have on hand:
- several Bibles
- newsprint and marker
- optional Advent wreath, matches, and blue or purple cloth for classroom altar or worship table
- optional hymnals.

LEADING THE CLASS

(1) Introduction

Since this is the first Sunday in Advent, you may want to light an Advent wreath and sing an appropriate hymn as the class gathers, such as "Blessed Be the God of Israel" (*The United Methodist Hymnal*, no. 209).

Begin today's session by asking the students to work with a partner or small group to answer these questions that you wrote on newsprint prior to class:

?

(1) **Recall a difficult choice you had to make. What were your options?**

(2) **How did you decide which option was best for you?**

(3) **In retrospect, which choice would you have made if you had the opportunity to make the decision again?**

At a time that you designated at the start of the activity, call the group back together. Note that making the right choice is sometimes very difficult. Point out that in today's lesson Joshua calls the people to choose whom they will serve. On one hand, that should not be a hard choice, given all that God has done for the people. On the other hand, the people have opted to serve foreign gods throughout the history of their relationship with the Lord. To serve God means that they cannot divide their loyalties. They will have to give themselves to the Lord unreservedly. As we consider today's scripture lesson, we will ask this main question: **How can we help ourselves and one another to make the right choices in the important matters of our lives?**

(2) "Their" History

Ask the group to talk about why we gather together to tell stories. You'll find ideas in the "Their History" section of Interpreting the Scripture to augment the discussion.

Then choose someone to read Joshua 24:1-2. Be sure to note that Joshua is reviewing events that took place years before. He himself is now old, and the people have lived in the promised land for many years. Ask the class to consider these questions:

?

(1) **Why do you think it was important for Joshua to tell the story at this point in Israel's history?** (Note that Israel had grown and changed. Surely younger members needed to hear the story. Perhaps the stories of their ancestors' enslavement in Egypt or their triumphs over enemies on the

way to the promised land were just dimly recalled tales in the minds of the younger generation.)

?

(2) **How do you feel when someone tells a story to remind those present at a family or community event of what has happened and why they have come together?**

(3) **When has your church (or denomination) gathered to hear the story of how God has dealt with you?** (Note that sometimes stories are told in preparation for a financial stewardship campaign. Some churches even include pictures to show whatever is happening. Such storytelling can have a very positive effect.)

(3) "Your" History

Joshua 24:3-13 recounts the history of God's dealings with the Israelites. If time permits, you may want to use the list found under "Preparing Our Minds" to review this history with the class in a brief lecture.

(4) Choose, Think, Choose

To read Joshua 24:14-22, 24-25 (or if you prefer, 24:14-28), select someone to recite Joshua's words and someone to serve as a narrator. Invite the rest of the class to respond in unison in verses 16-18, 21, 22*b*, and 24.

Provide some quiet time for group members to meditate on the choices they have made regarding their relationship with Jesus Christ. If you have access to a hymnal that includes "Your Love, O God" (*The United Methodist Hymnal*, no. 120), invite the class to sing this hymn. Or, you might want to read it expressively as they close their eyes and listen. This hymn speaks in the first verse about the freedom we have to accept or reject God.

Allow time for meditation and gently bring the group back together with words such as, "when you are ready, open your eyes."

(5) The Witnesses

Note that in verse 22 Joshua says, "You are witnesses against yourselves." The stone referred to in verses 26 and 27 is also a witness. Use information from "The Witnesses" in the Interpreting the Scripture portion to consider the importance of having persons and/or symbols that bear witness to our commitments.

Point out that just before Jesus' ascension, he commanded his followers to be "witnesses in Jerusalem, in all Judea and Samaria, and to the ends of the earth" (Acts 1:8). Discuss these questions:

(1) **Just as Joshua told the people that they were their own witnesses to the choice that they had made to serve God, our decisions regarding discipleship bear witness as to who we are and whose we are. As outsiders look at the Christian church in general (or our congregation in particular), what might they say about the kind of witness we are making? Are we, in other words, being faithful to our commitments?**

(2) **What do we need to do to be more faithful, to keep the promises of our baptism?**

Close with a word of prayer, asking for help in making choices that are pleasing to God and then in following through with whatever commitments we make.

Before dismissing the group, be sure to lift up at least one of the ideas below so that students can put this week's lesson into action.

HELPING CLASS MEMBERS ACT

Encourage students to think about one long-term serious commitment they have made, such as marriage, the raising of children, or employment with a certain company. Suggest that they take a walk or sit in a quiet space where they can think undisturbed about their faithfulness to this commitment. How have they upheld it? How have they broken it? What have been the consequences of their actions?

Advise class members to tell at least one other person about an important choice they have made. Recommend that this person be asked to help hold the student accountable for following through on the commitment.

Encourage each individual to consider his or her personal relationship with Jesus Christ. How has this relationship been nurtured by the telling of stories about the history of one's own people with God? Reaffirm this choice by repeating the key verse, Joshua 24:24, daily.

PLANNING FOR NEXT SUNDAY

Next week we will begin our winter quarter, which focuses on the Gospel of Matthew. These sessions will look at Jesus' ministry, particularly in light of how he was received by those to whom he ministered. To prepare for the opening lesson in Unit 1, "Beginnings: Birth and Ministry," ask the students to read Matthew 3. This session on preparing for Jesus' birth looks especially at verses 1-8 and 11-17.

SECOND QUARTER
Studies in Matthew

DECEMBER 5, 1999–FEBRUARY 27, 2000

All of the lessons during the winter quarter will be from Matthew's Gospel. Although we will follow Jesus from his birth through his resurrection, most of the sessions focus on aspects of his ministry and how he was received by those to whom he ministered.

The four lessons of Unit 1, "Beginnings: Birth and Ministry," introduce John the Baptist as the herald of Jesus' ministry, recount Jesus' temptations in the wilderness, give an account of Jesus' birth, and describe the visit of the Magi. The unit opens on December 5 with "Time of Preparing." This lesson explores the ministry of John the Baptist as recorded in Matthew 3:1-8 and 11-17. "Time of Testing," based on Matthew 4:1-14, shows Jesus overcoming Satan's temptations. The lesson for Christmas, which we will study on December 19, looks at the account of Jesus' birth as found in Matthew 1:1-6 and 18-25. We are called to a "Time of Rejoicing" because God is now with us in Emmanuel. In "Time of Worshiping," from Matthew 2:1-12, we accompany the Magi as they follow the star to pay homage to Jesus and then return home a different way so as not to encounter Herod again.

"Jesus' Teachings and Ministry" is a five-session unit that includes the account of Jesus calling the twelve disciples, his teachings on prayer, examples of his miracles of compassion, a glimpse at the growing opposition toward Jesus, and his parable of the laborers in the vineyard. In "Thinking About Commitment," based on Matthew 4:18-22, 9:9-12, and 10:1-4, we will hear Jesus calling disciples to follow him and fish for people. The lesson for January 9, "Thinking About Prayer," examines not only Jesus' teachings about prayer but also the beloved model he has given us, as recorded in Matthew 6:1-15. The lesson for January 16, "Thinking About Wholeness," looks at several miracles of compassion found in Matthew 9:18-31 and 35-36. Here we see Jesus raise the synagogue leader's daughter from the dead, heal the woman who had suffered from hemorrhages, and heal two blind men. "Thinking About Jesus' Power," which we will study on January 23, reveals the growing opposition to Jesus as seen in Matthew 12:22-32 and 38-40. The unit ends on January 30 with the familiar parable of the laborers in the vineyard from Matthew 20:1-16. In this session, "Thinking About Rewards," we will hear Jesus say that "the last will be first, and the first will be last" (20:16).

Unit 3, "Fulfillment of Jesus' Mission," delves into the closing days of Jesus' life. We begin with his triumphal entry into Jerusalem and then hear him prepare us for his return. The third session focuses on his crucifixion, while the final lesson celebrates his resurrection and commission to his followers. In "The Guidance of the Word" we see how Jesus' entry into the Holy City is rooted in prophecy. This lesson for February 6 is found in Matthew 21:1-13. The following lesson, "The Joy of Being Prepared," considers Jesus' teachings in Matthew 24:45–25:13. Here Jesus tells us to "keep awake" because we do not know when he will return. To illustrate his point, he tells the parable of the wise and foolish bridesmaids, also known as the parable of the wise and foolish virgins. "The Death in Our Behalf," which we will study on February 20, looks at Matthew 27:38-54. Here we will witness Jesus' final hours and hear the Roman soldiers who participated in these events declare that Jesus was indeed God's Son. The final lesson for this quarter, "The Basis of Our Authority," looks first at the account of the empty tomb on Easter morning as found in Matthew 28:1-10 and concludes with the commission to the disciples in verses 16-20.

MEET OUR WRITER

DR. CHARLES E. WOLFE

Charles E. Wolfe, a retired Methodist minister, has a B.A. from Northern Iowa University, a B.D. from Austin Presbyterian Theological Seminary, and a D.Min. from Wesley Theological Seminary. He has been a pastor in Texas, New York, and Maryland, and an Army chaplain. Dr. Wolfe taught Old and New Testament courses at Western Maryland College. At Wesley Theological Seminary he taught the Bible in various programs, including Course of Study for local pastors, the Lay Resource Institute, and the certification program for diaconal ministry. For sixteen years he edited *Exegetical Resource*. Dr. Wolfe is married and the father of four sons. He lives in Westminster, Maryland.

UNIT 1: BEGINNINGS: BIRTH AND MINISTRY
TIME OF PREPARING

PREVIEWING THE LESSON

Lesson Scripture: Matthew 3:1-8, 11-17
Background Scripture: Matthew 3
Key Verse: Matthew 3:11

Focus of the Lesson:
John preached repentance so that the people would be prepared to receive Jesus, whom John baptized.

Main Question of the Lesson:
What does "Joy to the World" have to do with repentance?

This lesson will enable adult learners to:
(1) hear John the Baptist as he preaches and baptizes.
(2) repent of their own sins.
(3) respond by preparing themselves during this season of Advent for the One who is to come.

Today's lesson may be outlined as follows:
(1) Introduction
(2) Kingdom
(3) Repentance
(4) Baptism
(5) Fulfillment

FOCUSING ON THE MAIN QUESTION

By now, on this second of the four Sundays of Advent, we are in the midst of our preparations for Christmas. The stores and the malls have already been decorated, and lights begin to appear on some of the houses in the neighborhood. We have been making our gift list and checking it twice. We've been busy addressing cards to all the people on our list. Music fills the air. Parties are planned. There is a smile on every face—or at least on many faces. We meet Rudolph the Red-Nosed Reindeer one more time, and imagine Santa's bustling workshop at the North Pole. The manger scene touches our hearts again. It is the happiest time of the year as we sing "Joy to the World."

Today's text intrudes upon this pleasant holiday season with an alien harshness that is hard to take. For John the Baptist's Christmas has no room for Rudolph or the manger. And this gives us pause because Christmas, of course, is God's entrance into our world. Yet the manger scene is only one of the ways in which the New Testament describes the Christmas event—from the abstractions of Titus 3:4 ("when the goodness and loving kindness of God our Savior appeared") to the mythological struggle against the dragon in Revelation 12.

Christmas for John the Baptist is the Last Judgment. And so instead of hearing about the baby Jesus, we hear from John about a Messiah who is the Grim Reaper at harvesttime, separating out the wheat from the chaff. Instead of hearing about the Little Drummer Boy, we hear about

unfruitful trees being cut down and burned to ashes. The approach of Christmas is so frightening that people run before it like snakes trying to escape a prairie fire. We are to get ready by repenting. But that is not so easy. The *Peanuts* comic strip character Lucy strikes a responsive chord when she explains to Linus that she has a knack for seeing other people's faults and overlooking her own!

In some ways, our mirthful enthusiasm seems diametrically opposed to John's call for repentance. Today's lesson prompts us to ask: **What does "Joy to the World" have to do with repentance?**

READING THE SCRIPTURE

NRSV

Matthew 3:1-8, 11-17

1 In those days John the Baptist appeared in the wilderness of Judea, proclaiming, 2 "Repent, for the kingdom of heaven has come near." 3 This is the one of whom the prophet Isaiah spoke when he said,

"The voice of one crying out in
    the wilderness:
'Prepare the way of the Lord,
    make his paths straight.' "

4 Now John wore clothing of camel's hair with a leather belt around his waist, and his food was locusts and wild honey. 5 Then the people of Jerusalem and all Judea were going out to him, and all the region along the Jordan, 6 and they were baptized by him in the river Jordan, confessing their sins.

7 But when he saw many Pharisees and Sadducees coming for baptism, he said to them, "You brood of vipers! Who warned you to flee from the wrath to come? 8 Bear fruit worthy of repentance.

11 "I baptize you with water for repentance, but one who is more powerful than I is coming after me; I am not worthy to carry his sandals. He will baptize you with the Holy Spirit and fire. 12 His win-

NIV

Matthew 3:1-8, 11-17

[1]In those days John the Baptist came, preaching in the Desert of Judea [2]and saying, "Repent, for the kingdom of heaven is near." [3]This is he who was spoken of through the prophet Isaiah:

"A voice of one calling in the desert,
'Prepare the way for the Lord,
    make straight paths for him.' "

[4]John's clothes were made of camel's hair, and he had a leather belt around his waist. His food was locusts and wild honey. [5]People went out to him from Jerusalem and all Judea and the whole region of the Jordan. [6]Confessing their sins, they were baptized by him in the Jordan River.

[7]But when he saw many of the Pharisees and Sadducees coming to where he was baptizing, he said to them: "You brood of vipers! Who warned you to flee from the coming wrath? [8]Produce fruit in keeping with repentance.

[11]"I baptize you with water for repentance. But after me will come one who is more powerful than I, whose sandals I am not fit to carry. He will baptize you with the Holy Spirit and with fire. [12]His

Key
Verse

Key
Verse

nowing fork is in his hand, and he will clear his threshing floor and will gather his wheat into the granary; but the chaff he will burn with unquenchable fire."

13 Then Jesus came from Galilee to John at the Jordan, to be baptized by him. 14 John would have prevented him, saying, "I need to be baptized by you, and do you come to me?" 15 But Jesus answered him, "Let it be so now; for it is proper for us in this way to fulfill all righteousness." Then he consented. 16 And when Jesus had been baptized, just as he came up from the water, suddenly the heavens were opened to him and he saw the Spirit of God descending like a dove and alighting on him. 17 And a voice from heaven said, "This is my Son, the Beloved, with whom I am well pleased."

winnowing fork is in his hand, and he will clear his threshing floor, gathering his wheat into the barn and burning up the chaff with unquenchable fire."

[13]Then Jesus came from Galilee to the Jordan to be baptized by John. [14]But John tried to deter him, saying, "I need to be baptized by you, and do you come to me?"

[15]Jesus replied, "Let it be so now; it is proper for us to do this to fulfill all righteousness." Then John consented.

[16]As soon as Jesus was baptized, he went up out of the water. At that moment heaven was opened, and he saw the Spirit of God descending like a dove and lighting on him. [17]And a voice from heaven said, "This is my Son, whom I love; with him I am well pleased."

UNDERSTANDING THE SCRIPTURE

Matthew 3:1-4. The prophet Malachi had asserted that the Lord would send a messenger (Malachi 3:1), Elijah, to prepare Israel for the day of the Lord (Malachi 4:5-6). In John the Baptist this forerunner has appeared (Matthew 11:14 and 17:11-14). And so the Baptist dresses like Elijah (2 Kings 1:8) and eats the food of a desert prophet (Matthew 3:4). The desert recalls the wilderness wandering that culminated in the Sinai covenant, and especially the forgiveness that lay behind the return from exile across the Syrian desert. For the "comfort" that results in the voice of verse 3 is the forgiveness (Isaiah 40:1-2) that makes the repentance meaningful.

Matthew 3:5-12. We are not told whether the people are baptized as individuals or in groups. Nor do we know whether they immerse themselves or are immersed by John or by his disciples. There is a darkness on the edge of the crowd, however, for the Pharisees and Sadducees, who will become Jesus' deadly opponents, come (3:7a). Calling them poi-

sonous snakes trying to escape a field fire, John tells them to act like people who really have repented (3:7b-8). There is no substitute for this total personal commitment to God—not synagogue or church membership, and not even the faith of a loved one (3:9). God has already laid the ax at the tree's root, to mark the spot where the cut is to be made (3:10). The "already" (NIV) stresses that there is no time for us to fool around with our response to the crisis. We are offered the opportunity to be wheat rather than chaff (3:12)—but only if our repentance is verified by our conduct. Then we may seal our commitment by baptism.

Matthew 3:13-17. There are two views of the dove symbolism in verse 16: On one hand, it may be a simple comparison with the gentle movement of the dove as it sinks down to its place of rest. On the other, it may be a deliberate symbol that intends to evoke a new layer of meaning. If Noah's dove (Genesis 8:9-11) is in view, the idea is God's intention to provide salvation. If it is Hosea's dove (Hosea 7:11 and 11:11), the stress is upon identification with Israel. If it is the Spirit moving over the waters (Genesis 1:2), which, according to rabbinical tradition, was a dove, the idea here is God's Spirit at work in a new creation. In any case, the dove must be understood as empowerment for mission.

It is not clear whether the heavenly voice is a public or a private revelation. In the parallels at Mark 1:11 and Luke 3:22, the voice clearly speaks to Jesus ("you are my Son"), but here the voice seems to speak to others about Jesus ("this is my Son"). If the voice's words had been intended as a public announcement, however, it is difficult to understand why no crowd later in Matthew ever knows that Jesus is the Son of God and why John himself needs reassurance later on (11:2-3). We are told, furthermore, that "he saw" the dove rather than "they saw." In this case the revelation lies completely within the consciousness of Jesus, so that a bystander would not have seen or heard anything.

The revelation, which will shape the ministry about to begin, flows out of the combination of texts quoted by the heavenly voice. The "Son" echoes Psalm 2:7 at the coronation of the king. Since the ideal king—ruling God's people by God's commission—shapes the idea of the Messiah, the beginning of the reign, marked by the coronation, is an apt image for the commencement of the messianic ministry, marked by the baptism. In addition to the King/Messiah typology, however, the Son also suggests Israel as a whole. (See Exodus 4:22 and Hosea 11:1.) The stress here is on Jesus' identification with Israel. We'll see this again in the lesson for December 19 in the genealogy. Finally, beyond even the Israel/Messiah typology, which in Paul will become the body of Christ, the church has understood the Son in terms of the Trinity.

The "whom I love; with him I am well pleased" (3:17 NIV) then defines the King/Messiah as the Suffering Servant of Isaiah 53. For surely the reference to Isaiah 42:1 in verse 17 intends to call to mind the Servant passages as a whole. (See the four servant songs in Isaiah 42:1-4; 49:1-6; 50:4-11; and 52:13–53:12.) As the Servant is endowed with the Spirit in order to fulfill his mission of bringing forth justice to the nations, so the Spirit descends upon Jesus to strengthen him for his task.

INTERPRETING THE SCRIPTURE

Kingdom

John's dramatic announcement in Matthew 3:2 introduces a major theme: the Kingdom appears dozens of times throughout the Gospel. So we shall encounter it in virtually every lesson this quarter. Matthew has "kingdom of heaven" where the other three Gospels have "kingdom of God," but the interchangeability in the manuscripts demonstrates that for Matthew the two phrases are equivalent.

We often think of a kingdom as a territory ruled over by a king, but we can also think of it as the exercise of regal power, the action of "kinging." Here the "of heaven" indicates that God is the King in question, and so it is the kingdom of God. Heaven, as the location of the divine throne, is the source of the authority as well as the sphere within which it is exercised. If source is stressed rather than sphere, the Kingdom is the reign of God—wherever and however that reign expresses itself.

John's announcement, flowing out of the prophetic expectation of the Day of the Lord, taps into the hope that God will one day come forth as King in our world as well as in heaven. But such a hope—the salvation of the age to come that will put a stop to the drive-by shootings—is pretty abstract and far-off. The Kingdom or reign is there, of course, somewhere, somehow—but we don't have to deal with it today. Closer concerns crowd it to the bottom of our "must do" list. So it isn't a pressing topic—unless it is at hand (RSV), near (GNB), upon you (REB). Then we might have to deal with it.

Repentance

Since the Kingdom is of heaven rather than of earth, we can't evolve into it or bend it to our will. It comes to us as a gift, always remaining beyond our control, offering us a blessing and at the same time mandating the terms upon which it may be accepted. "Joy to the World" requires repentance.

To repent is to reform our lives, to turn away from our sins (GNB). The basic idea in the Greek word for repentance is a change of mind. But this doesn't carry us far enough; for we can change our minds from good to evil as easily as from evil to good—and back again—many times! New Testament usage, therefore, has been influenced by the Old Testament idea that to repent is to turn, to make an about-face, from the world to God.

Repentance is described in verse 3 as preparing the way for the Lord, as straightening out the road. The image is based upon the requirement in ancient times to build or rebuild the highway upon which the king would travel to make a visit to a city or province. The Baptist who tells us to do this has the authority of a prophet, for he is the voice of Isaiah 40:3. The original voice announces that Yahweh is bringing the people back home from Babylon, and so a road is to be prepared in the wilderness for that purpose. Now the Lord comes again and another herald speaks to us. But this time it is the voice that is in the wilderness—for the road leads into our hearts and minds.

It is possible to ignore the voice. A television commentator once quipped, "Thanks to the interstate highway system, it is now possible to travel from coast to coast without seeing anything!" We can also hear without hearing anything. But it is also possible to sense the nearness of the Kingdom. What if the holy really is near? What if, like those who went out to the Jordan River, we too were to repent? If we were to begin the highway construction at the near end? To straighten out our lives so that they conform to the divine will? To clear away the obstacles within ourselves to the gospel? And to assist others with their own construction?

The "about-face" leads to confession of sin (3:6) and then to fruit that is worthy of repentance (3:8). The image of fruit suggests growth from a soil and correspondence between the soil and the fruit. The change of attitude is to result in a change of conduct. "Go and do something to show that your hearts are really changed" (JBP). "Produce fruit in keeping with repentance" (NIV). "Do those things that will show that you have turned from your sins" (GNB).

Baptism

Baptism presupposes and expresses repentance (3:11) as the proper response to the nearness of the Kingdom, but the Coming One marks its arrival. The difference between nearness and arrival is such that the herald is not even fit to do the work of a slave for the Coming One; and water baptism yields to a baptism with the Holy Spirit and fire. In that final searing examination, the Coming One will show us who we really are—wheat or chaff.

John's baptism, the first of three in a progressive series of baptisms in Matthew, within a context of approaching wrath (3:7), prepares us for that ultimate examination. The Kingdom's arrival triggers a separation into two groups: those who may enter to claim the blessing and those who are denied entrance. Such a separation, of course, is judgment. Advent, accordingly, involves threat as well as promise. If the Kingdom's arrival is imminent, then so is the judgment. The winnowing fork already is in the hand of the Coming One (3:12). The stalks have already been threshed and are on the floor. At any moment the cleansing will begin—the wheat to be preserved in the granary and the chaff to be burned up as useless.

Moved by the desert prophet's preaching, many people present themselves for baptism (3:6). This baptism, flowing out of Old Testament water purification rites and the idea of the faithful remnant within the faithless whole, is a recommitment to the Sinai covenant. Thus it is preparation for the Coming One who will bring that covenant to its ultimate completion. But it is not Christian baptism. So the contrast in verse 11 between water baptism and baptism with the Holy Spirit indicates preparation to fulfillment, rather than Christian water baptism followed by a special presence of the Holy Spirit.

Fulfillment

When the excitement generated by John the Baptist reaches Galilee, Jesus knows that God is at work; and so he travels to the Jordan River to be part of it (3:13). But John is reluctant to baptize him, sensing the inappropriateness of the prophetic symbol in this case. Since the Coming One is now here, water baptism no longer serves its preparatory function. Instead, the Baptist himself is not complete until he has been baptized with fire and Spirit (3:14). Jesus tells John to proceed with the baptism, however, for in this action they will both fulfill all righteousness (3:15). Righteousness is God's whole purpose for the covenant people, and so it is what God requires (GNB) as well as the promised blessing. The righteousness is primarily known from the Scriptures, where the divine purpose is spelled out. Fulfillment is the final development of what is inherent in the beginning. In some way, therefore, this baptism plays a vital role in salvation history.

Jesus' own baptism, starting out like all the others, is generally understood in terms of his identification with the people he came to save. But with the dove and the heavenly voice it acquires such additional meaning that it becomes the second of the baptismal types in Matthew's series. The voice in verse 17 echoes Isaiah 42:1, which begins the prophet's discussion of the Servant of the Lord. This reference suggests that the baptism is Jesus' entrance into the messianic ministry. Isaiah 53 defines the mission of the Servant as redemptive suffering on behalf of the people, and Mark 10:38 understands the baptism in terms of the cross. We have here, then, Jesus' acceptance of the cross as the way to accomplish God's ultimate purpose for his people. The opening of the heavens, the descent of the Spirit, and the heavenly voice place the seal of divine approval upon this inauguration of the messianic ministry. Its fulfillment, evidenced in the Resurrection, then leads to the third and final baptismal type in Matthew's progression, the seal of our salvation. (See also Romans 6:1-4 and the key verses of our final lesson, Matthew 28:19-20.)

The heavenly voice has offered its identification. Now a response is required. We are like that couple who visited the Salon Carre at the Louvre in Paris. Surrounded by world-famous masterpieces, the husband commented superciliously to a museum guard, "Well, I don't think they are so wonderful." The guard replied, "They are not on trial. You are!" The baptism launches the public ministry, and Matthew will proceed to detail responses of hostility, of faith, and of indifference.

SHARING THE SCRIPTURE

PREPARING TO TEACH

Preparing Our Hearts

Turn to the story of the chief priests and elders questioning Jesus' authority, as found in Matthew 21:23-27. This devotional passage for the week's lesson comes, of course, long after the events of Matthew 3 that are the focus for this first session of the winter quarter. The link between the two readings is John the Baptist—his standing as a prophet and his baptism of Jesus. As you read, consider what you know about John the Baptist. Do you believe the baptism he offered was of human or divine origin? What difference does your answer make in terms of your understanding of who Jesus was?

Now read Matthew 3 in its entirety. Try to put yourself in the scene. Ask yourself, how would I have responded to John? Would I have sought baptism from him? Why or why not?

Preparing Our Minds

This week we begin a new quarter of study focused on the Gospel of Matthew. If your schedule permits, you may want to read the entire Gospel prior to teaching the first lesson. You need not study the Gospel in depth at this point, but read simply to get an overview and remind yourself of the way Matthew tells the good news. Remember that Matthew portrays Jesus as the Messiah whose coming and actions fulfill God's will as revealed in the Hebrew Scriptures. For the benefit of the Jewish readers for whom he is writing, Matthew often identifies events or actions that were undertaken so that the Scriptures (that is, the Old Testament) might be fulfilled.

Read this lesson. Review Matthew 3, looking especially at verses 1-8 and 11-17.

Write down any questions you have about who John the Baptist is or what he does. As you study, be alert for answers to your own questions.

You may also want to read about John's activities in Mark 1:1-8; Luke 3:1-18; and John 1:6-8 and 19-28 in order to compare and contrast Matthew's account of John with those of the other Gospel writers.

Preparing Our Learning Space

Prior to the session, you may want to write the questions you will use under "Repentance" on newsprint.
Have on hand:
- several Bibles
- optional Advent wreath, candles, matches, blue or purple cloth for classroom altar or worship table
- hymnals
- newsprint and marker
- paper and pencils.

LEADING THE CLASS

(1) Introduction

One way to begin the session is by lighting an Advent wreath in your learning area. Check with your pastor about a litany that will tie in with the congregational lighting of the wreath during worship. You may also want to sing an Advent carol, such as "O Come, O Come, Emmanuel" (The United Methodist Hymnal, no. 211).

Then ask the class to brainstorm answers to these questions. If you choose, record their responses on newsprint:
(1) What preparations have you made for Christmas?
(2) How do you help others prepare for Christmas?

Note that John the Baptist comes in Matthew's Gospel to call us to make preparations that are quite different from what we have likely done. While we're preparing for a joyous celebration, John is calling us to repent.

Close the introduction by lifting up today's main question: **What does "Joy to the World" have to do with repentance?**

(2) Kingdom

Choose a volunteer to read Matthew 3:1-8. Use information in Understanding the Scripture to show how John the Baptist was foretold by the prophet Malachi and came dressed like Elijah.

Note the importance of the theme of "kingdom of heaven" (or "kingdom of God" as it appears in the other Gospels). You may want to read or retell the information found under "Kingdom" in the Interpreting the Scripture section.

Reiterate these sentences: "The Kingdom or reign is there, of course, somewhere, somehow—but we don't have to deal with it today. Closer concerns crowd it to the bottom of our "must do" list. So it isn't a pressing topic—unless it is at hand (RSV), near (GNB), upon you (REB). And then we might have to deal with it." Ask:

(1) **How do you understand the kingdom of heaven to have "come near"?**
(2) **What difference does the Kingdom's nearness make in the way you live your life?**
(3) **How might John the Baptist's message jolt you out of complacency in this season of Advent?**

(3) Repentance

Ask the students to look again at verse 3. In response to the nearness of the kingdom of God, John challenges each of us to repent. That is, we are to do an "about-face," to turn 180 degrees around, so that we are facing God and not the world.

Read or retell the section entitled "Repentance" under Interpreting the Scripture. Post on newsprint the following questions, which are intended for meditation or personal written responses only. Assure the class that their answers will not be discussed. Then distribute paper and pencils.

(1) **What would happen if I were to repent so that my life conforms to God's will?**
(2) **What obstacles need to be cleared from my life so that I may more readily hear and respond to the gospel?**
(3) **How can I help others repent and turn toward God?**

(4) Baptism

Have someone read Matthew 3:11-12. Direct the students to listen for images that they can see in their mind's eye as this passage is being read. Likely they will suggest the following:

- someone baptizing another with water, perhaps by immersion, pouring, or sprinkling;
- the Holy Spirit coming upon persons with a blaze of fire;
- Jesus holding a winnowing fork;
- Jesus clearing the threshing room floor by gathering wheat;
- Jesus burning the chaff.

Now ask the class:

(1) **How are these images similar to the ones that usually come to your mind when the word *baptism* is mentioned?**
(2) **How are these images different from your own?**
(3) **What does this passage reveal to you about the nature of baptism as John the Baptist interpreted it?**

Conclude this section by asking the class to read in unison the key verse from Matthew 3:11.

(5) Fulfillment

You may want to choose four students to read the parts of the narrator, John the Baptist, Jesus, and the voice from heaven in Matthew 3:13-17. Ask the class to imagine themselves on the scene at the Jordan. Tell them to pay attention to what they hear, see, smell, taste, and touch. Then ask:

?

(1) **Suppose you had been John the Baptist. How would you have felt about baptizing Jesus, especially after you saw the dove and heard the voice?**

(2) **Suppose you had been Jesus. Your baptism started out the way any other baptism would have, but the appearance of the dove and sound of the voice made it different. How did baptism affect and influence you?** (For help in answering this question, look at the second paragraph under "Fulfillment" in Interpreting the Scripture.)

(3) **Now recall what it means to you to be a baptized member of Christ's holy church. How has baptism prepared you to be a faithful disciple of Jesus Christ?**

Close today's lesson with these words taken from the Baptismal Covenant of The United Methodist Church, or use words from your own church tradition, to remind the students of how their own baptism identifies them as a follower of Jesus, who himself sought baptism by John: Brothers and sisters in Christ: Through the Sacrament of Baptism we are initiated into Christ's holy church. We are incorporated into God's mighty acts of salvation and given new birth through water and the Spirit. All this is God's gift, offered to us without price.

Before dismissing the students, be sure to suggest at least one of the activities below so that they may act on what they have learned this week.

HELPING CLASS MEMBERS ACT

Encourage the students to think about the changes they need to make in their own lives as they prepare for the coming of Jesus. Suggest that they take one specific step this week to initiate a change they decide to make.

Recommend that class members spend time in prayer recalling and admitting their own recent shortcomings and sins, and then offering a penitent and contrite heart to God, who will forgive them.

The season of Advent is a fitting time for new beginnings. Suggest that students who have been estranged from a family member or friend contact that person and make overtures toward reconciliation.

PLANNING FOR NEXT SUNDAY

Next week's lesson, "Time of Testing," focuses on the temptations of Jesus and his move to Capernaum after John the Baptist's arrest. Ask the students to prepare for this lesson by reading Matthew 4:1-17, especially noting verses 1-14.

TIME OF TESTING

PREVIEWING THE LESSON

Lesson Scripture: Matthew 4:1-14
Background Scripture: Matthew 4:1-17
Key Verse: Matthew 4:10

Focus of the Lesson:
Tempted for forty days in the wilderness, Jesus was able to overcome Satan's lures.

Main Question of the Lesson:
How can we turn a temptation into a test?

This lesson will enable adult learners to:
(1) study the temptations that Jesus faced.
(2) confront the temptations in their own lives.
(3) respond by immersing themselves in scripture passages that model how we are to deal with temptation.

Today's lesson may be outlined as follows:
(1) Introduction
(2) Tested
(3) Tempted
(4) Wilderness

FOCUSING ON THE MAIN QUESTION

On the last day of professional golf's 1996 Masters Tournament in Augusta, Georgia, Greg Norman woke up with such a commanding lead that everyone thought it was in the bag. They could engrave his name on the trophy and write the check. When he went to bed that night he had made history. But it was not the history he had expected. He played so badly that he lost his six-stroke lead and then went down another five strokes. His humiliation on national television was complete when he hooked a midiron shot into the pond.

But the real story is what happened next. As Colman McCarthy tells it in the *Washington Post*, "Norman revealed the extra reserves of his character. He accepted the embrace of the man he had just been trounced by. In the week following Augusta, Norman could have holed up in self-absorbed misery and given the world a no-comment. Instead, he went on to the next tournament and answered all questions from all askers." So many people told him that his demeanor in defeat had helped them that Norman later spoke of a conversion that "changed my total outlook on life and on people. There's no need for me to be cynical anymore.... It's extraordinary how I reached out and touched people by losing." McCarthy concluded that "his blowing the tournament was not a fall from grace, it was a finding of grace."

That's how it is supposed to be when we are tested—to discover who we are and then to shape our future attitudes and actions accordingly. Such testing is the core meaning of the verb we translate as "tempt" in Matthew 4, verses 1 and 3, and as "test" in verse 7. If temptation and testing are two sides of the same coin, and if temptation intends to hurt us but the test intends to reveal to us our strengths and weaknesses, then the main question is this: **How can we turn a temptation into a test?**

READING THE SCRIPTURE

NRSV
Matthew 4:1-14

1 Then Jesus was led up by the Spirit into the wilderness to be tempted by the devil. 2 He fasted forty days and forty nights, and afterwards he was famished. 3 The tempter came and said to him, "If you are the Son of God, command these stones to become loaves of bread." 4 But he answered, "It is written,
　'One does not live by bread alone,
　　but by every word that comes from
　　　the mouth of God.'"

5 Then the devil took him to the holy city and placed him on the pinnacle of the temple, 6 saying to him, "If you are the Son of God, throw yourself down; for it is written,
　'He will command his angels
　　concerning you,'
　　and 'On their hands they will bear
　　　you up,
　so that you will not dash your foot
　　against a stone.'"
7 Jesus said to him, "Again it is written, 'Do not put the Lord your God to the test.'"

8 Again, the devil took him to a very high mountain and showed him all the kingdoms of the world and their splendor; 9 and he said to him, "All these I will give you, if you will fall down and worship me."

10 Jesus said to him, "Away with you, Satan! for it is written,
　'Worship the Lord your God,
　and serve only him.'"

NIV
Matthew 4:1-14

[1]Then Jesus was led by the Spirit into the desert to be tempted by the devil. [2]After fasting forty days and forty nights, he was hungry. [3]The tempter came to him and said, "If you are the Son of God, tell these stones to become bread."

[4]Jesus answered, "It is written: 'Man does not live on bread alone, but on every word that comes from the mouth of God.'"

[5]Then the devil took him to the holy city and had him stand on the highest point of the temple. [6]"If you are the Son of God," he said, "throw yourself down. For it is written:
　"'He will command his angels
　　concerning you,
　　and they will lift you up in their hands,
　　so that you will not strike your foot
　　　against a stone.'"
[7]Jesus answered him, "It is also written: 'Do not put the Lord your God to the test.'"

[8]Again, the devil took him to a very high mountain and showed him all the kingdoms of the world and their splendor. [9]"All this I will give you," he said, "if you will bow down and worship me."

[10]Jesus said to him, "Away from me, Satan! For it is written: 'Worship the Lord your God, and serve him only.'"
[11]Then the devil left him, and angels came and attended him.

Key
Verse

Ke
Vers

11 Then the devil left him, and suddenly angels came and waited on him.

12 Now when Jesus heard that John had been arrested, he withdrew to Galilee. 13 He left Nazareth and made his home in Capernaum by the sea, in the territory of Zebulun and Naphtali, 14 so that what had been spoken through the prophet Isaiah might be fulfilled.

[12]When Jesus heard that John had been put in prison, he returned to Galilee. [13]Leaving Nazareth, he went and lived in Capernaum, which was by the lake in the area of Zebulun and Naphtali—[14]to fulfill what was said through the prophet Isaiah.

UNDERSTANDING THE SCRIPTURE

Matthew 4:1-11. To be led by the Spirit is to be faithful and obedient to the divine will; and so the end result is foreshadowed in the beginning. God tests, as with Abraham in Genesis 22:1, but in order to teach (Deuteronomy 8:3), not to entice to sin (James 1:13). The forty days is best taken as a period of communion with God rather than as a time of continuous temptation. Whether the fasting is strict or reflects what little food is available, genuine hunger results. The temptations then occur at the conclusion of the fast, when Jesus is at his weakest and most vulnerable. Trust and faithful obedience are tested. The devil leaves and the angels come (4:11) to attend or wait on Jesus. The Greek verb, from which the word *diaconate* enters English, from its background of a table waiter, suggests that the angels bring food. Their appearance verifies Jesus' identity as the Son.

Matthew 4:12-17. The preparation for the Coming One is as complete as it ever will be. This One sent by God had been confirmed at the baptism and defined in the temptations, and is now ready to begin a public ministry. John's arrest is the trigger for Jesus' move to Galilee to begin the messianic ministry (4:12). We are not told the reason for the move. To withdraw for the purpose of fulfilling prophecy would be a meaningless manipulation; and so some scholars assume that it is to avoid the danger of a premature arrest as a known associate of the troublemaker. Prominent disciples in the immediate area might be scooped up, but distance would provide a measure of security; for although Herod Antipas also controlled Galilee, it is doubtful that he would scour the realm looking for a relatively unknown carpenter from Nazareth. As it turned out, of course, Herod's interest, at least initially, is only in John, and that for personal reasons.

Other scholars stress the movement from Nazareth to Capernaum. Although John 2:12 might suggest that Mary and her sons had moved to Capernaum, Matthew 13:54-56 implies that the family had remained in Nazareth. Luke 4:16-30 explains the move on the basis of hometown rejection. Still other scholars find a symbolic finality in Jesus' leaving home, never to return. Declaring independence from family and friends, he begins to set out on his own course.

Whatever the historical reasons for the move, Matthew finds a surplus of meaning. It results in the fulfillment of prophecy (4:13-16). Capernaum is located within the ancient tribal boundaries of Naphtali, and this recalls Isaiah 9:1-2. The point is that Galilee is identified as "of the Gentiles" because of its mixed population. Surrounded by Gentiles—Phoenicians to the west, Syrians to the north and east,

Samaritans to the south—Galilee is the obvious choice for the Great Commission to all the world (Matthew 28:16-20). To begin the ministry in Capernaum, therefore, is to reveal its ultimate focus.

Isaiah 9:1-7 begins with the Assyrian conquest of the northern kingdom in 733-32 B.C. The people have been broken and deported, but their helpless misery is not forever. Deliverance is promised at the hands of the house of David (Isaiah 9:6-7). Even far-off Galilee is to share in the coming bliss. In fact, the first to go into exile is the first to return. Matthew, of course, takes the "child who has been born for us" as Jesus the Messiah. Isaiah's darkness, reflective of the misery of a defeated people, is now the hopelessness of sin. And Isaiah's light, reflective of restoration to prosperity in their own land, is now Jesus' gospel or good news that admits to the kingdom of heaven.

The dawning of the light (Matthew 4:16) is Jesus' preaching (4:17). The NRSV, with "proclaim" in verse 17, recalls the root idea in the verb, the herald's announcement. This announcement is the nearness of the kingdom of heaven. As we saw last week, the Kingdom is the divine sovereignty rather than a stretch of real estate. It is at the door because Jesus is its herald, but its completion is yet to come. Its imminence means that God is about to rule on earth, and that means judgment—and so repentance is the appropriate response. Note, however, that since this announcement is identified as gospel, as good news (4:23), rather than as the wrath of an approaching judgment, as in the preaching of John the Baptist, repentance here is in order to receive a blessing rather than a fearful attempt to avoid a disaster.

INTERPRETING THE SCRIPTURE

Tested

Last week we heard the heavenly voice at the baptism define the messianic ministry in terms of Isaiah's Suffering Servant. The Transfiguration (Matthew 17:1-8), which is not included in our lessons this quarter, picks up the heavenly voice again and then speaks very specifically about the suffering of the Son of Man. Any effort to keep Jesus from the cross, furthermore, is a temptation by Satan (16:23). Gethsemane, as the final effort to avoid the cross, is then the conclusion to the struggle begun in the wilderness. Assuming this general movement toward the cross, therefore, one reading of today's text is that it begins the process that gives precise definition to the messianic ministry. At the baptism the Spirit descends upon Jesus while the heavenly voice proclaims him to be the Son of God. The Spirit immediately

leads him up from the lower ground at the river bank to the higher ground in the adjacent wilderness in order that he might be tempted by the devil (4:1).

When we stress the leading of the Spirit, the focus is upon the core meaning of the Greek verb peirazo, to test. Its intention is to discover something's true nature, whether the gold content of a metal or the purity of water or the power of a battery or the strength and weakness of a human character. The testing thus defines and shapes our attitudes and conduct. We may well find in these three tests those things that affect us all—the pressures that physical pain places upon the mind and spirit, the lust for power, the tendencies toward doubt and idolatry. After all, Hebrews 4:15 points out that Jesus was tested in all things, as we are. But here, following immediately upon the baptism, we may also understand the test in terms of explaining just what kind of Son of God Jesus is. What is the Messiah's mission and how is it to be fulfilled?

Some scholars have suggested that the point of the bread test is not so much Jesus' own hunger as that of the world's poor. Is it the primary mission of the Servant to solve the world's economic problems, even if this hardly leaves any room for the "Suffering" part of the Suffering Servant? Or if not that, what about a miracle so that the crowds will flock to the Wonder Worker? Angels flying about the Temple catching a falling body in midair will certainly attract an audience for a sermon on repentance and the kingdom of heaven, even if faith must take a back seat. And if not even this, then what about a military Messiah who meets the world's evil head on and destroys it? So many of the people are ready to follow such a Messiah into battle against Rome even if this leads away from the cross.

Tempted

A second reading of the text, however, translating *peirazo* as "tempt" rather than as "test," introduces the theme of struggle or combat with evil; for now the emphasis is upon the devil's effort to interfere with the messianic work. The character of this tempter (4:3) is sketched out for us by his various names or titles in Matthew. In the Lord's Prayer he is called simply the Evil One (Matthew 6:13 GNB; see also the lesson for January 9). As the devil (4:1), he is the slanderer; for the Greek word, which has entered English as *diabolical*, starts out as anyone who slanders anyone else. At last the slanderer above all other slanderers emerges, and we have the devil.

A satan, in Old Testament usage, is an adversary, an opponent, an enemy. The Enemy, accordingly, who consistently tries to separate us from God, aiming at our destruction in order to frustrate the divine intention to bless us, is Satan. That Satan, both in Job and here, is ultimately con-

trolled by God, with however long a leash, spells his final defeat—but it does not lessen his enmity or predict a bloodless fight. Satan, in fact, has his own kingdom, composed of demons (Matthew 9:34; 12:26), at war with the kingdom of heaven. Beelzebul (Matthew 12:24, 27; see also the lesson for January 23), whether understood as "Master of the Household" or derisively as "Lord of the Flies," is his special name in this regard.

During the ministry itself combat with the Enemy revolves around demon possession. The exorcisms foreshadow the turning of the tide. Jesus binds the strong man and plunders his house (Matthew 12:29) and Satan falls like lightning from heaven (Luke 10:18). The Normandy landings on D day in World War II come to mind. When the Germans failed to drive the Allied troops off the beaches and back into the sea, an eventual Allied victory was no longer in doubt—even though a long and bloody struggle remained. In like manner, the Good Friday/Easter Sunday event guarantees the final conclusion of this war. But here too a long and bloody struggle remains. For the devil is a devouring lion—even though his time is limited (1 Peter 5:8). Satan never lets up in the effort to gain an advantage over us (2 Corinthians 2:11). The tempter continues to tempt (1 Thessalonians 3:5).

Wilderness

A third reading of the text begins with the wilderness or desert and recalls that critical period of Israel's history from the Exodus to the conquest. God led Israel, whom God calls "my son" (Hosea 11:1), out of Egypt through the Red Sea and into the wilderness to be tested for forty years. So now the Spirit leads God's Beloved Son, the Servant, through the Red Sea's baptismal waters (see 1 Corinthians 10:1-5) into the wilderness for forty days to be tested. Jesus embodies Israel (see the lesson for December 5 for the fulfilling righteousness at the baptism) and fulfills its hopes. Therefore he repeats Israel's experiences, erasing each failure with a success. (Note Matthew's use of the Jesus/Israel typology in the Hosea 11:1 quotation in 2:15.) And so Jesus counters each of the temptations with a quotation from Deuteronomy.

The background to the first temptation is the manna. The grumbling in Exodus 16:3 reveals that Israel does not trust God to provide the necessities of life. Deuteronomy 8:1-10 reflects upon this experience. The Lord placed Israel in such a perilous situation in order to humble the covenant people, to test whether they would keep the commandments (8:2). They must be disciplined (8:5) to trust the Lord (8:3) so that they might enter the blessing intended for them (8:7-10). The entire passage is in mind even though Jesus quotes only Deuteronomy 8:3b in verse 4. Jesus, unlike Israel, will not doubt the divine willingness and power to provide. There is another dimension, however, based upon the assumption that Jesus really could change the stones into bread. Since the hunger is the Father's will for him, will the Son accept it? Will he embrace the Servant ministry that is to climax on the cross—even if he doesn't have to?

The background to the second temptation is the crisis posed by the lack of water in the desert. At Rephidim the covenant people failed the test; for, unable or unwilling to trust, they tested the Lord (Exodus 17:1-7). Although the Lord passed the test when Moses struck the rock and they got what they wanted, their relationship was damaged. Deuteronomy 6:16, quoted by Jesus in verse 7, reflecting upon this incident, urges the people not to do it again. The devil, however, tries to mask a temptation to test God by quoting Psalm 91:11-12 in Matthew 4:6. There is, in fact, no doubt in Jesus' mind that the Father would send angels if asked (see Matthew 26:53); but this would be a demand for a confirmation of his Sonship, for the sign that he refuses to give others (see Matthew 12:38-42). Here the jump is to safety—as the devil knows—and so to refuse to jump is to choose the cross.

The background to the third temptation is the golden calf (Exodus 32), the "bird in the hand worth two in the bush" idolatry to which Israel turned in its fear. Now idolatry offers another shortcut, this time to achieve a good result in the easiest and most efficient way. We might state the same principle as "the end justifies the means" or "nothing gets done without compromise." If Jesus will only grant the devil a little respect, he can have his paradise here on earth, right now. Who needs the cross when you can get what you want without it? Deuteronomy 6:13, which Jesus quotes in Matthew 4:10, warns against leaving God out of our plans. And so, trusting God even when the end is beyond sight, Jesus does receive the kingdoms of the world on another high mountain—but from the Father rather than from the devil, and through the cross rather than by avoiding it (Matthew 28:16). And because Jesus embodies Israel, and because we who believe are Israel (Galatians 3:7), then we too can trust God.

SHARING THE SCRIPTURE

PREPARING TO TEACH

Preparing Our Hearts

Begin your personal preparation for this week's lesson by reading the account of Jesus' return to Galilee after his temptation as found in Luke 4:14-21. Think about how the temptations strengthened Jesus for his ministry. What is the substance of Jesus' ministry, as indicated in his reading from Isaiah? Consider examples of the ways in which Jesus fulfilled this ministry.

Look now at the background scripture from Matthew 4:1-17. Look again at the temptations the devil flings before Jesus, as well as at our Lord's responses. Imagine how he might respond to a temptation that you are facing. Then pray for the wisdom and strength to face your own temptations as Jesus faced his.

Preparing Our Minds

Read this lesson in its entirety. Review today's scripture reading, focusing on Matthew 4:1-14. Spend time contemplating the nature of each of the three temptations. Look at the verses from Deuteronomy that Jesus quotes. Matthew 4:4 is from Deuteronomy 8:3; 4:7 is from 6:16; 4:10 is from 6:13. Note that the devil begins by saying to Jesus "if you are the Son of God." In Matthew 3:17, we are told that a voice from heaven said that Jesus was "my Son, the Beloved." Think about how the devil's temptations are designed to sow seeds of doubt within Jesus about his divine identity and to undermine Jesus' mission.

Preparing Our Learning Space

Prior to class, you may want to write the questions under "Tested" as well as the group assignments under the section entitled "Wilderness" on newsprint or notebook paper.
Have on hand:
- several Bibles
- optional Advent wreath, candles, matches, blue or purple cloth for classroom altar or worship table
- paper and pencils
- optional hymnals.

LEADING THE CLASS

(1) Introduction

One way to begin the session is by lighting an Advent wreath in your learning area. Check with your pastor about a litany that will tie in with the congregational lighting of the wreath during worship on this third Sunday in Advent. You may also want to sing an Advent carol, such as "Hail to the Lord's Anointed" (*The United Methodist Hymnal,* no. 203).

Move into the lesson by reading aloud the first two paragraphs under Focusing on the Main Question. When you have finished this story about golfer Greg Norman, ask the class these questions:
(1) **How did Greg Norman's defeat tempt him?**
(2) **What discoveries did Norman make about himself?**
(3) **How did this humiliating loss shape Norman's actions and attitudes?**
(4) **What experiences have you had that may have seemed at first like a fall from grace but turned out to be a means of finding grace?**

Close this portion of the lesson by lifting up today's main question: **How can we turn a temptation into a test?**

(2) Tested

Choose three students to read Matthew 4:1-14. One is to read the narration in verses 1-2, 5, 8, and 11-14; a second will read the tempter's words in verses 3, 6, and 9; and a third will respond as Jesus in verses 4, 7, and 10. As this passage is being read, ask the students to close their eyes and try to envision the scene. Then ask:
(1) **How do you picture the wilderness and the one who is doing the tempting?** (There are no definitive answers here. Encourage students to describe what they imagine.)
(2) **What names did you hear for the one who is doing the tempting?** (Answers include "devil" in verses 1, 5, 8, and 11; "tempter" in verse 3; and "Satan" in verse 10.)
(3) **How do you think Matthew understands the Spirit's purpose in leading Jesus "to be put to the test by the devil," as the New Jerusalem Bible**

states in verse 1? (Read or retell the second paragraph under "Tested" in the Interpreting the Scripture portion for an explanation of the possible reason for testing.)

Now direct class members to work with a partner or small group. Ask each student to discuss with his or her group these questions, which you may want to write on newsprint. If you feel that class members do not know one another well enough to share this information, distribute paper and pencils and ask them to write answers for their private use only.

(1) **Recall one experience that God used to test your mettle. What was the situation?**

(2) **What do you think this test revealed about you to God?**

(3) **What did this test tell you about yourself?**

(3) Tempted

Point out that although the Greek word *peirazo* can mean "test," it can also mean "tempt." Ask:

(1) **Why would the devil want to test Jesus?** (Students may have a variety of ideas here, but be sure they realize that a major purpose is to interfere with Jesus' work as Messiah.)

(2) **What does the Bible tell us about the devil?** (Here you will want to refer to the paragraphs under "Tempted" in Interpreting the Scripture. Be sure to note the ideas of Evil One, slanderer, adversary, opponent, and enemy who tries to separate us from God.)

(3) **What does Jesus' strength in overcoming the devil's temptations say to you about your own ability to do so?**

(4) Wilderness

As noted in the Interpreting the Scripture portion, the temptations set forth by the devil recall Israel's sojourn in the wilderness after the Exodus. Have the class do a Bible study, perhaps by dividing them into three groups. Distribute Bibles as needed. You may want to write each group's assignment on paper or newsprint prior to class. Do not include the suggested answers (in parentheses), but use this information as needed for the class discussion that will follow the group work.

Group 1 is to examine the first temptation, which is based on Israel's lack of trust in God to provide food in the wilderness. Direct this group to read Matthew 4:3-4; Exodus 16; and Deuteronomy 8:1-10. They are to answer these questions:

(1) **Why did God allow the people to be in such a precarious position in the wilderness?** (God wants to test the people, to see if they will keep the commandments and trust God to meet their needs.)

(2) **What does Jesus' refusal of bread from the devil say about his relationship with God?** (Jesus knows that God will provide for him. He is willing to accept the servant ministry that will eventually lead him to the cross.)

Group 2 is to consider the second temptation, which is rooted in the crisis brought about by the lack of water in the desert. Tell this group to read Matthew 4:5-6; Deuteronomy 6:16-19; Exodus 17:1-7; and Psalm 91:11-12. Have them consider these questions:

(1) **What did Moses say to the covenant people when they quarreled with him about water?** (He asked why they tested God, according to Exodus 17:2.)

(2) **What is Jesus' point in quoting Deuteronomy 6:16?** (He is saying that people are not to test God as they did when water seemed scarce.)

(3) **What is the devil trying to accomplish by quoting Psalm 91:11-12 in Matthew 4:6? Why does Jesus respond as he does?** (This quote is a veiled temptation to test God, but Jesus doesn't fall for it because he has no need of a sign to confirm his Sonship.)

Group 3 will look at the temptation to idolatry that has its roots in the incident with the golden calf. Tell this group to read Matthew 4:8-10; Exodus 32:1-14; and Deuteronomy 6:10-15. Have them address these questions:

(1) What does the devil want from Jesus? (He wants Jesus to worship him.)

(2) Why does Jesus refuse to compromise his principles? (Jesus worships only God, just as God had commanded the Israelites to do in Exodus 20:3.)

(3) What is the upshot of Jesus' responses to the devil? (Jesus receives a kingdom, but his is from God, not the devil.)

At a time that you have set, call the groups back together and ask each one to report their findings. Close the discussion by asking a few volunteers to summarize in a sentence or two what they have learned about Jesus' temptation.

To conclude the session, ask the class to join hands and pray the Lord's Prayer, focusing especially on the words "lead us not into temptation." If possible in your setting, invite the group to sing Jesus' prayer as it appears in *The United Methodist Hymnal* (no. 271). This lively West Indian folk tune is very easy to follow even if students have not sung it before.

Before dismissing the class, be sure to tell them about at least one of the suggestions below so that they might respond actively to this week's lesson.

HELPING CLASS MEMBERS ACT

Encourage class members to keep a list of temptations they face and how they handle each one.

Suggest that students call to mind (or use a concordance to find) appropriate scripture verses to counteract the temptations that confront them.

Recommend that students meditate on a time of testing they underwent in their own lives. What happened? How was their character and/or faith tested? What was the outcome? How did they see God at work in them?

PLANNING FOR NEXT SUNDAY

On December 19 we will study a lesson entitled "Time of Rejoicing." This is Matthew's account of the Christmas story. Ask students to prepare for class by reading the familiar words of Matthew 1, especially verses 1-6 and 18-25.

TIME OF REJOICING

PREVIEWING THE LESSON

Lesson Scripture: Matthew 1:1-6, 18-25
Background Scripture: Matthew 1
Key Verse: Matthew 1:21

Focus of the Lesson:
As Isaiah had prophesied, and as Joseph was told by an angel in a dream, Mary had a son.

Main Question of the Lesson:
How do we respond to the Savior's birth?

This lesson will enable adult learners to:
(1) hear again Matthew's account of Jesus' birth.
(2) consider anew their understanding of Jesus as Son.
(3) respond by rejoicing that God Incarnate has come to earth.

Today's lesson may be outlined as follows:
(1) Introduction
(2) Son of David, Son of Abraham
(3) Son of Joseph
(4) Son of Mary
(5) Son of God

FOCUSING ON THE MAIN QUESTION

Some years ago when I was a pastor in Texas, the chamber of commerce of my town sponsored a parade. Our church decided to enter a float. It is the only float I have ever helped to build. On each side, in great red letters, we had the legend "Joy to the World." In order for the red letters to stand out, we created a white background with thousands and thousands of white tissues stuffed into the holes of the chicken-wire frame. My work started with the white tissues—and I never got to do anything else! So when I stood on the curb to watch the float pass by, I could only think of all those white tissues—even if others in the crowd didn't realize they were even there. They only served to make the red letters noticeable.

And so it is when we read the genealogy of Jesus. Some names jump out—David, Abraham, Jacob, Ruth, Solomon. Some names we can sort of remember—or at least find if we look them up—Perez, Josiah, Jeconiah. But others—like Azor,

Eliud, Eleazar—don't ring any bells for us. They are like those nameless, faceless white tissues on the side of the float. Yet Matthew somehow thought they were too important to leave out. For the Messiah who emerged from this list of names was to explain to us that even the hairs on our head are numbered (Matthew 10:26-33), that the obscure names mean as much as the famous names. For the God who cares for the sparrow loves each one of us. We see a blur of white tissues going by; but our heavenly Father sees beloved children, each one an individual, each one important, each one loved. And that, of course, is the central point of the Christmas event. The baby is to be named Jesus, that is, as the Savior, for he will save people from their sins. Those who understand that they need to be saved from their sins and who embrace this offered salvation will call him Emmanuel, that is, God with us. So our main question is: **How do we respond to the Savior's birth?**

READING THE SCRIPTURE

NRSV
Matthew 1:1-6, 18-25

1 An account of the genealogy of Jesus the Messiah, the son of David, the son of Abraham.

2 Abraham was the father of Isaac, and Isaac the father of Jacob, and Jacob the father of Judah and his brothers, 3 and Judah the father of Perez and Zerah by Tamar, and Perez the father of Hezron, and Hezron the father of Aram, 4 and Aram the father of Aminadab, and Aminadab the father of Nahshon, and Nahshon the father of Salmon, 5 and Salmon the father of Boaz by Rahab, and Boaz the father of Obed by Ruth, and Obed the father of Jesse, 6 and Jesse the father of King David.

And David was the father of Solomon by the wife of Uriah.

18 Now the birth of Jesus the Messiah took place in this way. When his mother Mary had been engaged to Joseph, but before they lived together, she was found to be with child from the Holy Spirit. 19 Her husband Joseph, being a righteous man and unwilling to expose her to public

NIV
Matthew 1:1-6, 18-25

[1]A record of the genealogy of Jesus Christ the son of David, the son of Abraham:

[2]Abraham was the father of Isaac,
    Isaac the father of Jacob,
    Jacob the father of Judah and his
        brothers,
[3]Judah the father of Perez and Zerah,
    whose mother was Tamar,
    Perez the father of Hezron,
    Hezron the father of Ram,
[4]Ram the father of Amminadab,
    Amminadab the father of Nahshon,
    Nahshon the father of Salmon,
[5]Salmon the father of Boaz, whose
        mother was Rahab,
    Boaz the father of Obed, whose mother
        was Ruth,
    Obed the father of Jesse,
[6]and Jesse the father of King David.
David was the father of Solomon, whose
        mother had been Uriah's wife.
[18]This is how the birth of Jesus Christ came about: His mother Mary was pledged to be married to Joseph, but before they came together, she was found to be with child through the Holy Spirit. [19]Because Joseph her husband was a righteous man and did not want to expose her

disgrace, planned to dismiss her quietly. 20 But just when he had resolved to do this, an angel of the Lord appeared to him in a dream and said, "Joseph, son of David, do not be afraid to take Mary as your wife, for the child conceived in her is from the Holy Spirit. **21 She will bear a son, and you are to name him Jesus, for he will save his people from their sins."** 22 All this took place to fulfill what had been spoken by the Lord through the prophet:

23 "Look, the virgin shall conceive
     and bear a son,
    and they shall name him
      Emmanuel,"

which means, "God is with us." 24 When Joseph awoke from sleep, he did as the angel of the Lord commanded him; he took her as his wife, 25 but had no marital relations with her until she had borne a son; and he named him Jesus.

to public disgrace, he had in mind to divorce her quietly.

[20]But after he had considered this, an angel of the Lord appeared to him in a dream and said, "Joseph son of David, do not be afraid to take Mary home as your wife, because what is conceived in her is from the Holy Spirit. **[21]She will give birth to a son, and you are to give him the name Jesus, because he will save his people from their sins."**

[22]All this took place to fulfill what the Lord had said through the prophet: [23]"The virgin will be with child and will give birth to a son, and they will call him Immanuel"—which means, "God with us."

[24]When Joseph woke up, he did what the angel of the Lord had commanded him and took Mary home as his wife. [25]But he had no union with her until she gave birth to a son. And he gave him the name Jesus.

Key Verse

Ke Ver

UNDERSTANDING THE SCRIPTURE

Matthew 1:1-17. Although we end up with a Jesus/Savior who is still our Emmanuel even today, we begin with a Jewish Messiah—the son of David, son of Abraham. Such a Messiah sums up Israel; and so, in order to understand his ministry, the genealogy rehearses the history of the Israel that produced him. That history is divided into three periods: (1) from Abraham to David; (2) the Davidic kings who reigned in Jerusalem, from David to Jeconiah; and (3) from the Babylonian captivity to the birth of Jesus. There are fourteen names in each of these periods; and since some names had to be left out in order to make the scheme work, it is clear that the balanced arrangement is artificial. Because of its symmetry, the genealogy is often analyzed according to what is called a three-by-fourteen pattern. The clue to its meaning is usually found in Matthew's opening stress on "the son of David" as the controlling name. Gematria, popular in

those days, is the system that assigns a numerical value to each letter. In Hebrew "David" adds up to fourteen. So it is a subliminal reinforcement of Jesus' Davidic descent.

There are four women in the genealogy, and this is sufficiently unusual that it calls attention, like waving a flag or blowing a whistle. Tamar (1:3) was a Canaanite who disguised herself as a prostitute in order to have a son by Judah, her own father-in-law. (See Genesis 38.) Rahab (1:5) was the prostitute in Jericho who saved Joshua's spies. (See Joshua 2:1-21.) Ruth (1:5) was the Moabite who virtually seduced Boaz. (See Ruth 3.) The wife of Uriah (Bathsheba, 1:6) was a Hittite whose beauty led David to adultery and murder. (See 2 Samuel 11.) These four women, despite their sexual improprieties (and sometimes because of them), enabled the line of Judah, which was to culminate in the Messiah, to continue. Do they somehow prepare for an ambiguity in

Mary's pregnancy? Note also that these women are all Gentiles. This fact may be a subtle indication that the ministry of Jesus is to extend beyond Israel to the whole world.

Luke's genealogy, by going all the way back to Adam, more obviously emphasizes that Jesus' ministry is for the benefit of the whole world. Note also that Luke has seventy-seven names, almost twice as many as Matthew lists. Although this difference is partly due to Luke's going back to Adam, it is mostly because he is not bound by the three-by-fourteen pattern. For Luke the most important name is "son of God," whereas for Matthew it is "son of David." This distinction is clear from the location of the genealogy. Matthew has it where we expect it to be, at the beginning. But Luke places it between Jesus' baptism and temptation, after the birth stories and after John the Baptist. The son of God of the genealogy thus picks up after the son of God of the heavenly voice, and the son of Adam introduces the temptation. This son of God/son of Adam will reverse the failure at Eden.

Matthew 1:18-25. Mary and Joseph are betrothed (NKJV) or engaged (NRSV) or pledged to be married (NIV). Betrothal had a legal standing then that an engagement does not have today; for it was a formal, legal contract entered into before witnesses. During the year between engagement and marriage the woman lived at home with her parents. Although the couple did not have sexual relations, they were considered virtually as man and wife in that she would be a widow if the groom died before the wedding. Likewise, a formal divorce was required if the wedding were to be called off. By the terms of biblical betrothal, Mary would have been viewed as an adulteress rather than as an unwed mother in our sense of the term. Joseph really has no choice about whether or not to divorce her, for a man must divorce a wife who slept with another man—even if she had been forcibly raped. His only option, therefore, is the manner in which he will divorce her. He could accuse her in public and demand a trial to determine whether she had been raped or whether she had given her consent. Or he could draw up the divorce himself before two or three witnesses and forgo the trial. This would avoid the public disgrace for her.

However, before Joseph can take any action, an angel appears to him in a dream and tells him to wed Mary because the child she is carrying is of the Holy Spirit. In typical fashion, Matthew quotes from the Hebrew Scriptures to underscore how Jesus is the fulfillment of prophecy.

The one who is born is Emmanuel, meaning God with us (1:23); and the Great Commission concludes with the promise that Emmanuel continues with us (Matthew 28:20).

INTERPRETING THE SCRIPTURE

Son of David, Son of Abraham

Jesus is the Messiah (Matthew 1:1 NRSV) or the Christ (NIV) or the Anointed, according to Hebrew or Greek or English terminology. This means that he is the son of David, the son of Abraham. John Mark Jones suggests that "the very names David and Abraham create character for Jesus, just as the names Babe Ruth and Mickey Mantle evoke character for a baseball player. To say that a baseball player is another Babe Ruth is to suggest that he has extraordinary hitting power. Similarly, to say that Jesus is the child of David is to indicate that he has royal authority and the capacity to overthrow Rome just as David conquered Goliath and, later in his life, the enemies of Israel."

Yet there is more to David than Goliath

and success in battle. Above all else is the prophecy in 2 Samuel 7:16 that the Davidic throne will be established forever. Since the forever could not describe a political throne, it must refer to the Messiah; and so the Messiah is the last son of David and the forever throne is the kingdom of God. People anticipated that this warrior king would surely lead the angels in battle against Rome.

As the son of Abraham, moreover, Jesus is the embodiment of Israel, as we saw last week in the temptation scene. As with David, there is a promise to be fulfilled—the blessing for the nations (Genesis 12:3). Abraham, therefore, introduces the theme of salvation for the Gentiles. Gentiles come from the east and west to sit at the banquet table with Abraham (Matthew 8:11) because disciples obey the Great Commission (Matthew 28:19).

Son of Joseph

So we begin the story of this son of David, son of Abraham, with wedding plans. Mary and Joseph have planned a very ordinary sort of family life together; but everything turns topsy-turvy when she gets pregnant after the engagement but before the wedding—and Joseph knows that he is not the father. The "was found" in verse 18 highlights the unexpectedness of it all. However Joseph deals with this distressing information, it will be as a man who is righteous, that is, as one who always does what is right (GNB). Rightness for him, of course, is defined by the law; and since the law views Mary's condition in terms of adultery, he cannot overlook it. He must, therefore, break the engagement, which is pretty much the equivalent of a divorce. But there are divorces and then there are divorces. He determines, out of consideration for her future, to do it as painlessly as possible.

Joseph's uprightness also serves to reinforce the virgin birth. If such a man accepts the creative power of the Holy Spirit as the source of the pregnancy, then Mary's conception cannot be the result of adultery.

The two major interpretations as to why Joseph is not to fear to take Mary as his wife flow out of knowledge and suspicion. If Joseph already knows that the Holy Spirit is the source of the pregnancy before the angel speaks, the fear is the awe or reverence that must draw him away from Mary because she is within the sphere of the sacred. To touch such a one would be sacrilege. The angel then reassures him that God wills him to be Mary's husband. If, on the other hand, the angel is the source of this new information, then we must assume that Joseph had actually suspected her of having committed adultery. In this case the angel reassures him that he is not, as John Calvin explained it, committing a sin by condoning adultery.

Joseph enables Davidic descent to be linked with the virgin birth; for at that time and in that place what mattered was public acceptance of responsibility rather than biology. And so in a dream the angel tells Joseph to take Mary home with him as his wife (1:20). It is as his wife, accordingly, that Mary gives birth; and by naming the child, Joseph publicly acknowledges the baby as his own son. Jesus thus becomes the son of David because he is the son of Joseph.

Son of Mary

This son of David, son of Joseph, reflecting the theme of continuity with the past, is to be named according to his life's work (1:21). "Jesus" is the Greek for the Hebrew "Joshua," which in the popular etymology of the time was connected with the verb "to save." Joshua is a Savior—"for he will save." He is, therefore, a proper son of the David who saved Israel from its enemies. At the same time, however, this son of David is so different that a theme of discontinuity emerges from within the continuity itself. For now the enemies are sins rather than oppressing nations; and so the messianic salvation is spiritual rather than political. Furthermore, since this son of Abraham has now brought the blessing to the world, the "his people" includes Gentiles as well as Jews.

Although we are not told how Jesus saves from sins, the cross must be in view; for in Matthew 26:28 Jesus' blood is poured out in order to effect the forgiveness of sins. We read Christmas, therefore, in the light of Good Friday. But we cannot read Good Friday in isolation from Easter Sunday, for the cross and empty tomb depend upon each other for their meaning. So Christmas promises the Savior who brings life through the gospel (2 Timothy 1:10). And this is our blessed hope (Titus 2:13), for now the possibility of our salvation has been given to us. We can turn to God—or away. The current is there—but we can short it out. We can unplug our ears to hear the music, unbandage our eyes to see the dawn—but we don't have to. The new wine has been offered to us—but we can leave the cork in the bottle.

It is, then, the son of Mary who is to be the Savior. Joseph will serve *in loco parentis*, but God is the true Father, by means of or through the agency of the Holy Spirit. The Spirit, of course, is not the male partner in a sexual union, as if the Spirit were some Jupiter in the form of a swan making love to a good-looking young woman. The New Testament never considers the Holy Spirit to be Jesus' father. Instead, the Spirit is to be identified with the creative power of God, as in Genesis 1:2. Since, furthermore, the messianic era is a re-creation, this same Spirit is to be at work again. (Compare Isaiah 11:2; Ezekiel 37:1-14; and Joel 2:28.) And so this son of Mary, bracketed by the Spirit from birth to rebirth (Romans 1:4), is David's Lord (Matthew 22:45-46), and those who come to faith in him are new creatures (John 3:3-7 and 2 Corinthians 5:17).

Son of God

This son of Mary, as we saw two weeks ago, is identified at his baptism by the heavenly voice as the Son of God. And thus we have Emmanuel, "God with us." The newness of the birth, emphasized in the implied comparison with the creation of the world, is, however, at the same time the completion of the old. For, as verse 23 affirms, the Christmas event fulfills the prophecy embedded in Isaiah 7:14. But controversy over the tightness or looseness of the "fit" has sometimes been a rabbit trail leading away from the central focus upon Emmanuel.

In Isaiah the sign is the period of babyhood rather than the birth. God will deliver Israel from her enemies by the time the child is weaned. But we have to know which "young woman" is going to have which baby in order to know when to start the clock. So she must be known to Isaiah and to King Ahaz—or else the sign could never be verified and thus would be meaningless. The Septuagint, the Greek Old Testament, for reasons that remain unknown in spite of all the speculation, translated Isaiah's "young woman" from the Hebrew into "virgin" in the Greek. This translation allowed Matthew to use the text as a prophecy of the birth of Christ.

The Isaiah text is not, however, the source of our information about Mary's virginity. That is spelled out clearly in the narrative itself (Matthew 1:25). The importance of the citation lies rather in the church's appropriation of the Old Testament, as in Luke 24:27 and Galatians 3:14, which then validates the church's claim to be the covenant people. So, as Eduard Schweizer notes, "When Matthew finds this prophecy fulfilled in the birth of Jesus, he is right, not in the sense that precisely what Isaiah expected has come true—Isaiah expected something different and sooner—but in his sense of the continuity of God's providence, operating coherently from the past and on into the future."

This means that we too are part of those who "shall name him" in verse 23, for we too have been saved from our sins and therefore live in Emmanuel. Such good news causes us to rejoice with praise and thanksgiving.

SHARING THE SCRIPTURE

PREPARING TO TEACH

Preparing Our Hearts

This week's devotional reading is taken from the prologue of John's Gospel. As you read John 1:1-14, note how this Gospel writer sets Jesus' coming within a cosmic background, rather than writing a birth story as Matthew and Luke have done. Ponder the purpose of Jesus' coming in the flesh as set forth in the Gospel of John.

Now turn to today's reading from Matthew 1. Be sure to read over the genealogy. Note the women who are mentioned. If time permits, you may want to look up some of the names in a concordance to trace the lineage through the Hebrew Scriptures.

Think about the characters in this story. How would you describe Joseph? What role does the angel play in this story? Although Mary does not actually appear here, she is mentioned prominently. What do you know about her? What can you surmise about Matthew and his purposes from the way he structured chapter 1?

Spend some quiet time in this week before Christmas giving thanks to God for the great gift of Emmanuel, for God is truly with us.

Preparing Our Minds

In addition to reading Matthew 1 and John 1:1-14 as noted above, try to read Luke 1:26-38 and 2:1-20. The purpose of this additional reading is to heighten your awareness of the similarities and dissimilarities among the Gospel writers' stories of Jesus' coming into the world. You may need to help class members who confuse the details of these stories. If mention is made of a detail that does not appear in Matthew (such as the shepherds), be ready to note where the detail may be found.

Preparing Our Learning Space

Prior to class, set up a genealogical display. Perhaps this will include a Bible from your family or from families of the students. Maybe you will have one or more family trees to hang on the wall. Consider contacting someone in the class or church who you know has this kind of material for this display.

Have on hand:
- several Bibles
- optional Advent wreath, candles, matches, blue or purple cloth for classroom altar or worship table
- optional hymnals
- optional family Bible that includes a genealogy or other genealogical record
- paper and pencils
- optional newsprint and marker.

LEADING THE CLASS

(1) Introduction

One way to begin the session is by lighting an Advent wreath in your learning area. Check with your pastor about a litany that will tie in with the congregational lighting of the wreath during worship on this fourth Sunday in Advent. You may also want to sing one or more carols appropriate to the season. Perhaps you will need to distribute hymnals if you think that some class members will not know the words to the hymn you have selected.

You may want to begin the lesson by reading or retelling the Focusing on the Main Question portion of the lesson.

Or, if you have been able to bring (or have students bring) any genealogical material, direct the class members' attention to the family tree(s) and/or Bible(s). Discuss these questions:

[?]

(1) **Why is it helpful to have information about one's ancestors?**
(2) **What are some types of traits that may be seen from one generation to the next?**
(3) **What makes some members of a family stand out from others?**

Move into today's lesson by pointing out that Matthew traces Jesus' family back to Abraham. Some of the names on the family tree stand out, while others we don't remember. Ultimately, the tree includes Jesus, the Messiah, whom God sent to be with us as our Savior. Lift up today's main question: **How do we respond to the Savior's birth?**

(2) Son of David, Son of Abraham

Make sure that everyone has a Bible. Instead of reading aloud Matthew 1:1-16, ask the students to turn to that passage and read it silently. Distribute paper and pencils. Ask the class to list all the names in the left-hand column of the paper and then write what they know, if anything, about each person. To expand the study, you may want to divide the class into thirds and ask one group to take verses 2-6*a* (Abraham to David), a second group to examine the era of David to the deportation to Babylon in verses 6*b*-11, and the last group to look at the time from the deportation to Jesus' birth in verses 12-16.

Ask each group to report on any names that seemed to be unusual for any reason. Supplement their findings with information from Understanding the Scripture for

verses 1-17 and "Son of David, Son of Abraham" under Interpreting the Scripture. Ask:

(1) **What value do you attach to Jesus' genealogy?** **[?]**
(2) **Why do you think Matthew is so intent on tracing Jesus back to Abraham?** (As he writes his Gospel for an audience of Jews and Gentiles, Matthew takes great pains to show that Jesus fulfills the Hebrew Scriptures for a Messiah. Relating Jesus both to the house of David, who was promised a successor on his throne forever, and to Abraham, who was the first to receive the covenant promise of land, offspring, and a people who would bless others, was an important strategy for Matthew.)

(3) Son of Joseph

Choose a volunteer to read aloud Matthew 1:18-25. Note that Matthew focuses on Joseph's response. Invite the students to hear this story through Joseph's ears. Then ask:

(1) **Why does Joseph plan to dismiss Mary quietly rather than bring her to a public trial?** (Use information for these verses in the Understanding the Scripture portion to augment the discussion. Underscore the meaning of betrothal.) **[?]**
(2) **What does Joseph's response to the angel's command say to you about his spiritual relationship with God?**
(3) **If you have time, ask the class to turn to Luke 1:26-38, where the angel Gabriel appears to Mary. How is this angelic appearance different from the one in Matthew?**

(4) Son of Mary

Ask the class these questions:

(1) **From the reading in Matthew 1:18-25, what do you know about who Mary's baby will be and what he will do?** **[?]**

(2) How has Jesus fulfilled these roles in your life? (Here you will want to discuss his role as Jesus, who saves people from sins, and as Emmanuel, through whom humanity experiences God's presence.)

Read or retell "Son of Mary" in the Interpreting the Scripture portion. If time permits, direct the students to look up the scripture references noted in this section.

If you have hymnals available, ask the students to turn to "O Come, O Come, Emmanuel" (*The United Methodist Hymnal*, no. 211). Work in small groups and assign each group to one of the verses (and the corresponding antiphon if it is included in your hymnal). Direct the groups to discuss what their assigned portion of the hymn says about who Jesus is and what he was expected to do. Call the groups back together and make a list of the findings. You may want to record these ideas on newsprint.

(5) Son of God

Note that Jesus is the Son of God—Emmanuel—"God with us." Remind the class that at Jesus' baptism (which we studied on December 5) "a voice from heaven said, 'This is my Son, the Beloved, with whom I am well pleased'" (Matthew 3:17).

Make sure that everyone has paper and a pencil. Then ask them to write their own words of praise to God, rejoicing that this Beloved Son has come to earth to be with us. Perhaps several students will be willing to read what they have written to bring the lesson to a close.

Before you dismiss the class, lift up at least one of the activities below so that students will have some ideas for relating this lesson to their lives this week.

HELPING CLASS MEMBERS ACT

Since Christmas is a time of family memories, encourage students to recall and give thanks for ancestors who helped shape them into who they are. Perhaps they will do this by reviewing a family genealogy.

Christmas is also a time when memories of hurts and wrongdoing come to the forefront as people anticipate family reunions. Suggest that class members pray about how they can act with sensitivity and kindness toward someone who has wronged them.

Recommend that students spend some time considering the miraculousness of Jesus' birth. They may want to think through their own beliefs about angelic appearances and the virgin birth.

PLANNING FOR NEXT SUNDAY

Next Sunday the class will focus its attention on the visit of the Magi, as recorded in Matthew 2, especially verses 1-12. Encourage the students to pay particular attention to how these Magi from the East respond to Herod and to Jesus.

TIME OF WORSHIPING

PREVIEWING THE LESSON

Lesson Scripture: Matthew 2:1-12
Background Scripture: Matthew 2
Key Verse: Matthew 2:2

Focus of the Lesson:
Having seen a star, the Magi came from the East to find and worship the newborn king.

Main Questions of the Lesson:
(1) Has Epiphany lifted my Christmas from Santa's North Pole to Bethlehem's manger?
(2) What am I doing to help others gain this same insight?

This lesson will enable adult learners to:
(1) see the Magi's reactions to both Jesus and Herod.
(2) take a step forward in their own faith adventure.
(3) respond by worshiping God.

Today's lesson may be outlined as follows:
(1) Introduction
(2) Guiding Light
(3) Bethlehem
(4) The Dreams
(5) Herod

FOCUSING ON THE MAIN QUESTION

After the state funeral that culminated in Charles Darwin's burial in London's Westminster Abbey, while the bells were still tolling his death, someone asked Thomas Huxley if Darwin had been right. Huxley replied, "Of course he was right." The questioner observed in a low voice, "But couldn't he have kept it to himself?" In the light of the bitter controversy generated by Darwin's insight into evolution, the remark is understandable. In the light of Hiroshima, who has not wondered if the atomic scientists could not have kept their discoveries to themselves? Similarly, the grieving mothers of the slain infants in Bethlehem must have wondered why the Magi could not have kept their news to themselves.

But of course they could not; for, once discovered, truth must come out—even if that truth should be a mixed blessing, a two-edged sword. That "out" is the epiphany—the appearance or manifestation, the sudden intuitive insight into meaning. In the church year Epiphany is January 6, or the first Sunday in January when the sixth is not on a Sunday. Epiphany Sunday, arising from today's lesson, celebrates the revelation of the Jewish Messiah to the Gentiles, as we today follow the star along with the Magi.

If the biblical idea of truth as reality is correct, then the truth is independent of its recognition. Until truth is recognized, we cannot make a morally responsible response to it. Cholesterol is clogging our arteries whether we understand it or not, whether we admit it or not. When heart

trouble induces epiphany, however, we are able to choose whether to alter our diet or to continue on in the same old way. Heart patients make both choices. Atomic power can light up a city or blow it up according to our reaction to its reality. Likewise, Christmas is the eternal reality and Epiphany is the revelation of that truth to the world of men and women blessed (or cursed?) with free will. That revelation has been denied, ignored, and embraced.

This leads to a double-edged main question: **Has Epiphany lifted my Christmas from Santa's North Pole to Bethlehem's manger? What am I doing to help others gain the same insight?**

READING THE SCRIPTURE

NRSV
Matthew 2:1-12

1 In the time of King Herod, after Jesus was born in Bethlehem of Judea, wise men from the East came to Jerusalem, 2 asking, **"Where is the child who has been born king of the Jews? For we observed his star at its rising, and have come to pay him homage."** 3 When King Herod heard this, he was frightened, and all Jerusalem with him; 4 and calling together all the chief priests and scribes of the people, he inquired of them where the Messiah was to be born. 5 They told him, "In Bethlehem of Judea; for so it has been written by the prophet:

6 'And you, Bethlehem, in the land
      of Judah,
   are by no means least among
      the rulers of Judah;
for from you shall come a ruler
   who is to shepherd my
      people Israel.' "

7 Then Herod secretly called for the wise men and learned from them the exact time when the star had appeared. 8 Then

NIV
Matthew 2:1-12

[1]After Jesus was born in Bethlehem in Judea, during the time of King Herod, Magi from the east came to Jerusalem [2]and asked, **"Where is the one who has been born king of the Jews? We saw his star in the east and have come to worship him."**

[3]When King Herod heard this he was disturbed, and all Jerusalem with him. [4]When he had called together all the people's chief priests and teachers of the law, he asked them where the Christ was to be born. [5]"In Bethlehem in Judea," they replied, "for this is what the prophet has written:

[6]" 'But you, Bethlehem, in the land of
      Judah,
   are by no means least among the rulers
      of Judah;
for out of you will come a ruler
   who will be the shepherd of my
      people Israel.' "

[7]Then Herod called the Magi secretly and found out from them the exact time the star had appeared. [8]He sent them to

Key Verse

Ke Ver

he sent them to Bethlehem, saying, "Go and search diligently for the child; and when you have found him, bring me word so that I may also go and pay him homage." 9 When they had heard the king, they set out; and there, ahead of them, went the star that they had seen at its rising, until it stopped over the place where the child was. 10 When they saw that the star had stopped, they were overwhelmed with joy. 11 On entering the house, they saw the child with Mary his mother; and they knelt down and paid him homage. Then, opening their treasure chests, they offered him gifts of gold, frankincense, and myrrh. 12 And having been warned in a dream not to return to Herod, they left for their own country by another road.

Bethlehem and said, "Go and make a careful search for the child. As soon as you find him, report to me, so that I too may go and worship him." 9After they had heard the king, they went on their way, and the star they had seen in the east went ahead of them until it stopped over the place where the child was. 10When they saw the star, they were overjoyed. 11On coming to the house, they saw the child with his mother Mary, and they bowed down and worshiped him. Then they opened their treasures and presented him with gifts of gold and of incense and of myrrh. 12And having been warned in a dream not to go back to Herod, they returned to their country by another route.

UNDERSTANDING THE SCRIPTURE

Matthew 2:1-12. Most of us have a composite Christmas story, with Matthew's words welded onto a framework provided by Luke. But it doesn't quite fit, for the movement in Luke is from Nazareth to Bethlehem and back again. Matthew's movement, in contrast, is from Bethlehem to Egypt to Nazareth. In Luke we have a manger, shepherds, and the angelic chorus; while in Matthew we have a house, a star, Magi, and the massacre of the innocents. The comparison is inevitable, but we can make too much of the discrepancies. Perhaps it is best to say that we have two versions of the same event and not try to harmonize the disparate elements into a single story. Matthew is less interested in the birth itself than in its impact upon the world, and so the birth is assumed rather than described. The book of Matthew stresses that God is in control; and so, if Herod suggests the coming Crucifixion, the fulfillment of prophecy implies that the Resurrection will also be inevitable.

Matthew 2:13-15. The Exodus from Egypt is the defining moment in which Israel becomes the people of God. Their continuing experience of the saving divine presence in their midst gives them the confidence by which they may appeal to the compassion of a Parent. For Yahweh has adopted Israel as a firstborn son (Exodus 4:22-23) and called that son out of Egypt (Hosea 11:1) to the promised land. When that adoption is extended (Galatians 4:5), when on a new level the promised land is understood as the kingdom of heaven, then that Son must again be called out of Egypt (Matthew 2:15).

There is an interesting reversal in the play on Egypt and Israel. Egypt is the land of bondage from which Moses fled and to which he returned in order that the people might escape. Now, however, the danger is in the land of promise and Egypt is the safety net. So Jesus flees from Israel to Egypt in order to return to Israel to lead the people forth in a new Exodus to a new promised land. Jesus, therefore, is both Israel and the Moses who delivers Israel. Because he is the one he can be the other.

Matthew 2:16-18. "The massacre of the

innocents," ordered by Herod the Great who reigned as king of the Jews from 37 to 4 B.C., likely involves fewer than twenty boys, given birth and infant mortality rates in a village of Bethlehem's size. The Herod who would murder his own wife and three of his sons because of a paranoid suspicion that they are a threat to his hold on power would not stick at the slaughter of twenty babies in an unimportant village. The weeping mothers of Bethlehem remind Matthew of Rachel weeping for her children as they pass by her grave on their way into the Babylonian exile (Jeremiah 31:15). Some scholars, considering the citation in terms of its context in Jeremiah, suggest that the upbeat promise of the return from exile in Jeremiah 31:16 implies that God will overcome evil. In any case, Herod bears responsibility for his own actions.

Matthew 2:19-23. With Herod's death the danger is removed, and so, at the angel's command, the Holy Family returns to the land of Israel, but to Nazareth rather than to Bethlehem. Judea had been given to Archelaus, and he would act just like his father if he suspects the baby's identity. Galilee, under his milder brother Antipas, is safer. So Jesus grows up in Nazareth. The choice of this insignificant small town is not by chance. It is, rather, to fulfill the prophecies that he will be called a Nazorean (2:23 NRSV) or a Nazarene (NIV). The resident of Nazareth is a Nazarene. From a linguistic point of view, the pun doesn't quite work. But from a practical point of view, it is close enough to press some buttons. Perhaps Matthew does not even want to be pinned down by modern scholars, for he cites "the prophets" rather than a specific text. The source of the pun has been explained in several ways. Perhaps the Nazirite is in mind. Although Jesus is not a Nazirite in the same sense as Samson and Samuel, he shares the idea of being set aside for holiness from the womb. Or perhaps the netzer is in mind, the branch from the root of Jesse in Isaiah 11:1. Or perhaps the remoteness and unimportance of Nazareth is intended to suggest prophecies that the Messiah will be humble and unrecognized, despised and rejected. Or perhaps "all of the above" is the right answer, such that one allusion suggests another.

INTERPRETING THE SCRIPTURE

Guiding Light

However reluctantly, we must remove "We Three Kings of Orient Are" from the traditional manger scene. The star presumably first appears at the birth; and time must then be allowed for the trip from Babylonia or Arabia. Herod at least thinks that Jesus might be nearly two years old by now. It is no later than 4 B.C., for that is the year in which Herod dies. Luke's shepherds have long since returned to their flocks and the angelic chorus is a fading memory. Mary and Joseph are living in a house (2:11). Now at last we have the wise men (2:1 NRSV) or Magi (NIV), astrologers from the East. We cannot identify their number, their national origin, or their rank; but they are wealthy enough to make the trip and influential enough to be taken seriously by Herod. The primary point is that outsiders have been invited to the Great Supper (Luke 14:16-24). The star is the invitation, and they show up because they are willing to follow their guiding light. They are "the world" that God so loved (John 3:16) and the "all nations" into which the disciples are to go (Matthew 28:19).

Last week we saw that part of the meaning of "son of Abraham" in the genealogy is the promised blessing to the world

(Genesis 12:2-3). The Gentiles, in order to be included in the blessings associated with Zion, will come, in the last days, from near and far, to worship God and bring tribute. (See Isaiah 60:1-7.) If, then, the child is Emmanuel, the Magi at the Messiah's crib fulfill this prophecy.

The prophecy includes the flow of wealth to Zion; and so it is not enough for the Magi to come. They must bring gifts. The gifts, in accordance with Eastern custom, indicate submission to royal authority. The tribute, therefore, introduces the theme of Jesus' kingship. Incense is associated with worship. Myrrh suggests cosmetics, perfumes, pain killers (as offered to Jesus in wine), and preparing corpses for burial. Sometimes the gifts are assigned specific meanings: gold as to a king, incense as to God, myrrh as to one destined to die. And sometimes their value is seen as financing the flight to Egypt. Since such explanations are not based in the text, however, it is best to take the gifts simply as part of the prophecy.

The star of Jacob (Numbers 24:17) had, before Jesus' time, already been interpreted as heralding the appearance of the Messiah. When the Magi observe the "star at its rising" (Matthew 2:2), they understand the birth of a Jewish king whose impact upon the world warrants their journey.

Bethlehem

The star leads them to Jerusalem, perhaps as the pillars of fire and cloud had led Israel to the promised land. But then they lose sight of it; for another guiding light, the Scriptures (Psalm 119:105), points them to Bethlehem. The universality of salvation is to be funneled through the particularity of Israel's covenant. Thus, in Matthew 2:5-6, by a combination of texts, these Gentiles are brought to the forever throne of David (see the lesson for December 19). Micah 5:2 prophesies that from little Bethlehem will come the one who is to rule over Israel. Since David is from Bethlehem, Micah is speaking of a Davidic king. As Herod is to demonstrate, however, there are kings and then there are kings. This one, as Matthew explains by adding 2 Samuel 5:2 to Micah 5:2, is to shepherd God's people. The shepherd is to feed the sheep and protect them from danger. Jesus, who is to save his people from their sins, will echo the shepherd theme at the Mount of Olives as he prepares to go to the cross (Matthew 26:31).

So the Magi head out for Bethlehem, "following yonder star." Since it is revelation rather than astronomy, however, instead of remaining a distant pinprick, our star swings low and hovers over a particular house. The Magi rejoice at the sight of the child, sensing that they are to be included in whatever meaning this has for the world. Matthew, in fact, cannot restrain himself at the thought of salvation, and so he piles up expressions: they rejoice an exceedingly great joy, that is, "they were overwhelmed with joy" (2:10 NRSV) or "overjoyed" (NIV). Compare the joy of the shepherds in Luke 2:10. They have felt in Jesus the wholeness and goodness of life. Naturally, they worship.

Several years ago at Niagara Falls I visited the Turtle, the museum of the Iroquois Indians, and was struck by the explanation of the drumbeat for the dances. It represents the heartbeat of the earth, and when the dancers place themselves in rhythm with the drum they are in harmony with the universe. The drumhead is a circle to represent the unity of Creator, nature, and people. The Magi, so to speak, have heard the very heartbeat of God in the child. They have altered themselves to conform to the rhythm of that beat, and then they know the joy of oneness in God's purpose.

The Dreams

In addition to the star and the Scriptures, today's lesson has one more guiding light—the dream in verse 12. Matthew, the only New Testament writer to use the Greek word for dream *(onar)*, records six dreams in which God gives instructions, and in each case the dreamer takes appropriate action. Joseph is told to take Mary as his wife, for she has not committed adultery (1:20). The Magi are warned not to return to Herod, for he intends harm to the child (2:12). Joseph is commanded to flee to Egypt with Mary and Jesus (2:13). Joseph is told to return home (2:19) and then is warned not to return to Bethlehem (2:22). Because of her dream, Pilate's wife tries to stop her husband from condemning Jesus (27:19).

Note that in each case the dreamer obeys. And since a change of plan is involved, the obedience is deliberate. Moreover, since there is no compulsion, the obedience is freely willed. The dreams, furthermore, never contain any revelation of doctrinal substance. They are, instead, providential in nature, the guiding light for an individual in a particular situation. Their importance, therefore, is that God does not leave us alone to fend for ourselves. Consequently, they are to be considered along with all the other ways in which we are led and strengthened in and by the Spirit. This means that the New Testament dream is not a hope for the future, not some shaping "impossible dream" to which we may aspire, but rather it is empowerment for today's discipleship.

Herod

In what amounts to a witness or testimony, the Magi tell Herod that they have followed their guiding light to Jerusalem. When the birth prophecy is explained to them, they understand a new guiding light in the Scriptures and eagerly go to Bethlehem where they worship and experience great joy. Herod, of course, understands the Scriptures as well as they do; but he reacts differently. Instead of joining the Magi in pilgrimage to Bethlehem to worship, he sends them on ahead and then plots how he will kill the Messiah. Herod perceives the Messiah to be a political rival and thus a threat to his throne. This interpretation of his messiahship is to plague Jesus throughout his entire ministry and at last it will lead to his death at the hands of Pontius Pilate. Joseph fears the Judean ruler (2:22), yet there will always be a Herod or an Archelaus or a Pilate or a whoever who will resist even God.

In spite of all the pain and heartache that he causes, Herod is unable to derail the divine intention to bless the world through the Bethlehem child. Herod's ace, so to speak, is trumped by the obedience of the Magi. The trickster is "tricked" (2:16 NRSV) or "outwitted" (NIV) in a scene reminiscent of the mockery of human pretentiousness at the Tower of Babel. And so we have two responses to the Christ event, with no middle ground. Matthew implies that either we kill Jesus, as Herod would, or we worship him, as the Magi do.

Instead of rejoicing at the news of the birth, therefore, as do the Magi, Herod is "disturbed" (2:3 NIV) or "frightened" (NRSV). Because of his Edomite background, he is especially vulnerable to any messianic movement that could challenge the legitimacy of his holding the Jewish throne. It is possible that all Jerusalem is troubled with him because of the fear that a struggle for the throne would plunge the nation into the horror of civil war, or that Herod's fury would impose terrible retaliations against the people out of his paranoid fear that they would support his rival. Most likely, Jerusalem is ranged on Herod's side against Jesus.

SHARING THE SCRIPTURE

PREPARING TO TEACH

Preparing Our Hearts

Begin your preparation by meditating on today's devotional reading from Psalm 98. What phrases in this psalm call you to praise and worship God? What images prompt you to think of God as Sovereign over all creation? In what ways might this psalm make you think of Jesus?

Now turn your attention to Matthew 2. Note that verses 1-12, which are the focus of this week's lesson, record the story of the Magi and their encounters with both Herod and Jesus. Verses 13-23 report on the Holy Family's escape to Egypt and their subsequent return to Galilee after the death of Herod the Great.

Ponder how you are like the Magi. What kinds of gifts do you bring to worship Jesus? Such offerings may include money or other material goods, but think especially about how you give yourself to God. What lengths will you go to in order to find God?

Contemplate how you may be like Herod. What are you trying to hold on to or protect? What hidden agendas might you have that cause you to misrepresent your motives to others?

Conclude your time with a prayer that God will give you wisdom to lead the class and insight into how you can become a more faithful worshiper.

Preparing Our Minds

Read again the story of the visit of the Magi as found in Matthew 2:1-12, preferably from at least two Bible translations. Read this lesson in its entirety.

You may want to check a Bible dictionary or commentary for information about the wise men. Note that they are learned Gentiles, possibly from Persia, but they are not kings as one of our familiar seasonal carols claims. The Bible makes no mention of the number of Magi, their names, or their national origin.

You may also want to look up Herod. The dynasty members that concern us in this lesson are Herod the Great and one of his sons, Archelaus. Do not be confused by the fact that Herod the Great died in what we now call 4 B.C. Remember that the division between the years "before Christ" (B.C.) and "anno Domini" (A.D., "in the year of the Lord," a Latin term first used in the sixteenth century) was not made until a Scythian monk and scholar, Dionysius Exiguus (500?-560? A.D.), introduced a calendar change that calculated the time of the Christian era beginning with the birth of Christ. He apparently made a mistake in computing the first year of the Christian era as it related to the calendar of the Roman Empire. Hence, although our common understanding of the time division would lead us to believe that Herod died prior to Jesus' coming, he actually died several years after Jesus' birth.

Preparing Our Learning Space

Have on hand:
- several Bibles
- hymnals or other songbooks that include "We Three Kings"
- newsprint and marker
- paper and pencils.

LEADING THE CLASS

(1) Introduction

To begin today's lesson, distribute hymnals and ask the students to turn to "We Three Kings" (*The United Methodist Hymnal*, no. 254). Invite the class to tell you what this carol says to them about the

Magi. You may want to list their ideas on newsprint. Compare that carol with a traditional Puerto Rican carol, "De Tierra Lejana Venimos" ("From a Distant Home," *UMH*, no. 243, verses 1-4). Again list ideas on newsprint.

Point out that Epiphany, which is celebrated on January 6 or the Sunday closest to it, is the time when the church has traditionally said that the Magi came to worship Jesus. Also note that the Magi probably arrived at Jesus' home when he was about two years old (see Matthew 2:11, 16).

If time permits, tell the group to read through the other carols in their hymnbook in search of additional references to the Magi. Here are some carols that do include such allusions: "What Child Is This" (*UMH*, no. 219, verse 3); "Angels from the Realms of Glory" (*UMH*, no. 220, verse 3); "In the Bleak Midwinter" (*UMH*, no. 221, verse 4); "Sing We Now of Christmas" (*UMH*, no. 237, verses 4-5); "The First Noel" (*UMH*, no. 245, verses 4-5); and "On This Day Earth Shall Ring" (*UMH*, no. 248, verse 3).

As an alternative, plan to do a carol-sing using as many of the hymns listed above as time permits. The singing would fit nicely with the title of today's lesson, "A Time of Worshiping," for through music we can indeed worship God.

Note that today's lesson focuses on the Magi. Lift up our main questions: **(1) Has Epiphany lifted my Christmas from Santa's North Pole to Bethlehem's manger? (2) What am I doing to help others gain this same insight?**

(2) Guiding Light

Select a volunteer to read Matthew 2:1-12. Then ask:
(1) We have already discussed what some familiar carols say about the Magi. Some of that information, however, comes from tradition. What does the Bible tell us about them? (Note that all the biblical information we have about the Magi is found in Matthew, for they are not mentioned elsewhere. We know that they must have been Gentiles because they came from the East, possibly Persia, though their country of origin is never identified. The word *magi* means astrologer. They were led to Jesus by a star. These men would have been sages but they were not kings. They were important enough that Herod wanted to talk with them, but they were neither taken in by his hidden motives nor afraid to disobey his request. They were overjoyed to find Jesus and brought him gifts.)

(2) What is the significance of the gifts they bring? (Note the third paragraph under "Guiding Light" in Interpreting the Scripture.)

(3) Read Isaiah 60:1-7. How do the Magi fulfill this prophecy?

As an option, distribute paper and pencils. Direct the students to write a paragraph or two as if they were one of the Magi writing a journal entry. They may want to record why they were seeking the child, how they went about locating the child, their impressions of Herod, and their response to Jesus. Encourage a few volunteers to read what they have written. They, like those who wrote the carols you studied and/or sang earlier, may describe what happened and also express their own attitudes toward the events.

(3) Bethlehem

Read aloud or create a brief lecture from the section entitled "Bethlehem" in the Interpreting the Scripture portion. Then ask:
(1) How might the journey to Jerusalem and then on to Bethlehem be an adventure in faith for the Magi?

(2) We know nothing about the Magi once they leave Jesus, except that they did not return to Herod. How do you think their lives might have been changed by this encounter with the Messiah?

?

(3) How is your own journey with Christ an adventure in faith?

(4) The Dreams

Point out that the Magi obey the warning of the dream and do not return to Herod (Matthew 2:12). This dream, like the star and the Scriptures, is a guiding light for the Magi.

Invite the class to recall the other dreams that Matthew records in chapters 1 and 2. You may want to list them on newsprint. (You'll find the dreams listed in the first paragraph of "The Dreams" in Interpreting the Scripture. Note that there is a dream recorded in 27:19, which we have not studied.)

Encourage the students to share ways in which dreams have been guiding lights from God in their own lives.

(5) Herod

Note that the Magi have come to pay homage to Jesus, the one they understand to be the king of the Jews (2:2). Ask:

?

(1) How does Herod react when he hears about this newborn king? (Note that he is frightened, so he calls in experts on the Scriptures to learn where this child was to have been born. He obviously has a hidden agenda when he tells the Magi to return and let him know where the child is so that he can worship. When he realizes that he has been tricked by the Magi, who never returned to see him, Herod orders the massacre of boys under age two, according to verses 16-18.)

?

(2) Why do you think Herod reacted this way? (Herod wanted to be sure that his own throne and dynasty were not jeopardized by this newborn king. He needed to kill this threat to his power.)

(3) How is your emotional response to Jesus different from Herod's reaction? How is it similar?

You may want to sing a carol to close the lesson, possibly one from the list above if you did not sing all of them earlier.

Before you dismiss the group, tell them about at least one of the ideas below so that they can put their faith into action this week.

HELPING CLASS MEMBERS ACT

Encourage students to think about the gifts they have given and received and what these gifts mean. What gifts will they give to the Christ Child?

The Magi clearly set out on an adventure in faith, for they followed a star not knowing where it would lead but believing that something very important was happening. Suggest that class members spend some quiet time reviewing their own faith journey. What surprises have they had along the way? How has God been present with them in all situations?

Recommend that adults examine their own motives for hidden agendas. What good things are they doing for the wrong reasons? What changes do they need to make?

PLANNING FOR NEXT SUNDAY

On January 2 we begin not only a new year but also a new unit, "Jesus' Teachings and Ministry." The first lesson, "Thinking About Commitment," focuses on Jesus' calling of the disciples and equipping them for service. To prepare for this lesson, ask the students to read Matthew 4:18-22; 9:9-12; and 10:1-4.

UNIT 2: JESUS' TEACHINGS AND MINISTRY
THINKING ABOUT COMMITMENT

PREVIEWING THE LESSON

Lesson Scripture: Matthew 4:18-22; 9:9-12; 10:1-4
Background Scripture: Matthew 4:18-22; 9:9-12; 10:1-4
Key Verse: Matthew 4:19

Focus of the Lesson:
Jesus called and empowered his disciples for ministry.

Main Question of the Lesson:
What do we do with Jesus' call to "Follow me!"?

This lesson will enable adult learners to:
(1) witness Jesus' calling and equipping of his disciples.
(2) consider their own commitment to Jesus.
(3) respond by answering Jesus' call in their own lives.

Today's lesson may be outlined as follows:
(1) Introduction
(2) Called
(3) Called to Follow
(4) Called to Fish
(5) Called to Heal

FOCUSING ON THE MAIN QUESTION

In endeavors that enjoy public support—athletics, art, music, theater, dance, whatever—the difference between the amateur and the professional is most often the level of commitment to the activity. There are talented and dedicated amateurs in every field—who are just as good as and who work just as hard as the professionals in that field. But, as a character in Mordaunt Shairp's play *The Green Bay Tree* puts it, "It doesn't really matter whether the amateur gets there or not." For the professional, however, it does matter; for it is the livelihood itself which is at stake. Amateurs give their best if they feel like it. Professionals must always produce up to capacity, whether or not they feel like it.

The Green Bay Tree struggles with our arrival at a critical fork in the road. A young man has been adopted by a wealthy dilettante. He enjoys a luxurious but useless life until he falls in love with a veterinarian. She wants him to get a job: "you can't live an amateur life." He is drawn to her idea of a professional life, one that means something, and he takes a few tentative steps. But when the dilettante threatens to cut him off without a penny, so that it really will matter whether he gets there or not, he draws back. He is nearly there, but never; almost, but not quite. His real father, who had given him up for adoption because he had been unable to support him, then makes the supreme sacrifice. He kills the dilettante in order to free his son, and goes to prison for it. In the closing scene, however, we see that the sacrifice is in vain. The young man is the dilettante's heir, and he has chosen the amateur life after all.

So what do we do when we come to this critical fork in the road? Whether or not we ever have to choose between the love of a veterinarian and a life of luxury, we do have to determine the quality of our discipleship. Does it really matter whether we get there or not? Are we to be amateur or professional Christians? Thus our main question asks: **What do we do with Jesus' call to "Follow me!"?**

READING THE SCRIPTURE

NRSV

Matthew 4:18-22

18 As he walked by the Sea of Galilee, he saw two brothers, Simon, who is called Peter, and Andrew his brother, casting a net into the sea—for they were fishermen. **19 And he said to them, "Follow me, and I will make you fish for people."** 20 Immediately they left their nets and followed him. 21 As he went from there, he saw two other brothers, James son of Zebedee and his brother John, in the boat with their father Zebedee, mending their nets, and he called them. 22 Immediately they left the boat and their father, and followed him.

Matthew 9:9-12

9 As Jesus was walking along, he saw a man called Matthew sitting at the tax booth; and he said to him, "Follow me." And he got up and followed him.

10 And as he sat at dinner in the house, many tax collectors and sinners came and were sitting with him and his disciples. 11 When the Pharisees saw this, they said to his disciples, "Why does your teacher eat with tax collectors and sinners?" 12 But when he heard this, he said, "Those who are well have no need of a physician, but those who are sick."

NIV

Matthew 4:18-22

18As Jesus was walking beside the Sea of Galilee, he saw two brothers, Simon called Peter and his brother Andrew. They were casting a net into the lake, for they were fishermen. **19"Come, follow me,"** **Jesus said, "and I will make you fishers of men."** 20At once they left their nets and followed him.

21Going on from there, he saw two other brothers, James son of Zebedee and his brother John. They were in a boat with their father Zebedee, preparing their nets. Jesus called them, 22and immediately they left the boat and their father and followed him.

Matthew 9:9-12

9As Jesus went on from there, he saw a man named Matthew sitting at the tax collector's booth. "Follow me," he told him, and Matthew got up and followed him.

10While Jesus was having dinner at Matthew's house, many tax collectors and "sinners" came and ate with him and his disciples. 11When the Pharisees saw this, they asked his disciples, "Why does your teacher eat with tax collectors and 'sinners'?"

12On hearing this, Jesus said, "It is not the healthy who need a doctor, but the sick."

Key Verse

Matthew 10:1-4

1 Jesus summoned his twelve disciples and gave them authority over unclean spirits, to cast them out, and to cure every disease and every sickness. 2 These are the names of the twelve apostles: first, Simon, also known as Peter, and his brother Andrew; James son of Zebedee, and his brother John; 3 Philip and Bartholomew; Thomas and Matthew the tax collector; James son of Alphaeus, and Thaddaeus; 4 Simon the Cananaean, and Judas Iscariot, the one who betrayed him.

Matthew 10:1-4

¹He called his twelve disciples to him and gave them authority to drive out evil spirits and to heal every disease and sickness.

²These are the names of the twelve apostles: first, Simon (who is called Peter) and his brother Andrew; James son of Zebedee, and his brother John; ³Philip and Bartholomew; Thomas and Matthew the tax collector; James son of Alphaeus, and Thaddaeus; ⁴Simon the Zealot and Judas Iscariot, who betrayed him.

UNDERSTANDING THE SCRIPTURE

Matthew 4:18-22. The Sea of Galilee, an important source of fresh water for Israel, is a large inland lake, pear-shaped, thirteen miles long north to south and seven miles wide east to west. In the time of Jesus, according to Josephus, nine cities lined its shores and its waters were crowded with fishermen. Peter, Andrew, James, and John seem to be in business with Zebedee. They are successful enough to have two boats and to employ several men. (See also Mark 1:16-20 and Luke 5:1-11.) The net is circular, weighted with stones at the edges and controlled with a draw rope in the center. It would sink rapidly, trapping fish on its way down. The rope, when pulled, gathers the stones together at the bottom and the fish are held in place. Since James and John are already in the boat, they are preparing (NIV) the nets for use (Matthew 4:21). Any mending (NRSV) is at most a last-minute minor repair. Simon, of course, will not be Peter until 16:18.

Matthew 9:9-12. Even though the translations use "tax collector" for the convenience of the modern reader, Matthew is, strictly speaking from the original Greek word, a toll collector. The tax booth (9:9) or table at which he sits is probably the customhouse of Capernaum. It would be located on the highway at the edge of town to collect the tolls for Herod Antipas from the caravans passing through from Damascus to Egypt and back again. The toll collectors are despised and often lumped together with sinners because only sinners will associate with them. They have two strikes against them. Their occupation, by its very nature, leads them into dishonesty. And their work brings them into close contact with Gentile traders. This inevitably triggers ceremonial defilement. They have the reputation, in fact, of being little better than the Gentiles in their observance of the law. To associate with them defiles and to eat with them is to accept their friendship. Jesus shares this negative view of the toll collector. If a person refuses to be reconciled, let him/her be as a Gentile or as a toll collector (Matthew 18:15-17). Even if the toll collectors and the prostitutes believed in John the Baptist (Matthew 21:31-32), this is regarded as unusual and surprising. Here, however, they are the sick to be healed rather than the sinners to be condemned. (See also Luke 5:29-32.)

Matthew 10:1-4. Matthew 9:35 is almost identical with 4:23. Such repetition, called an inclusio, is intended to tie materials together. The earlier summary, following the baptism, temptations, and initial calling of disciples, describes the beginning of Jesus' ministry. The summary is given definition by the Sermon on the Mount and a cycle of healing miracles. Now we start over with a repetition of the summary, but with a new twist. Hitherto the disciples have been relatively passive spectators of what Jesus has said and done. Now they are to say and do themselves, to imitate the Master. Because of the inclusio, therefore, we look backwards as well as forward, each section interpreted in the light of the other. Jesus' ministry is not complete until the disciples can carry it on, but their ministry has meaning only because of his.

There are too many synagogues, too many fields, too many sick (9:37). There is a limit to Jesus' energy. And so the workforce needs to be enlarged. But we cannot make a unilateral decision to work someone else's fields. So we are to pray (9:38) that the Lord

of the harvest, who has already sent Jesus, now will send additional workers. The continuing supply of witnesses, beginning with the commissioning of the Twelve and continuing, generation by generation, even unto our own time, is grounded in this prayer. Our commission, however, like that of the Twelve, is from Jesus (10:1). The Son deals directly with the Father and we deal with the Son. Thus the Mediator sends us to the Father's flock.

The Twelve are called disciples in 10:1 and apostles in 10:2. The idea behind "disciple" is learner, pupil, apprentice, and then one who acts according to what he or she has learned. It is, therefore, especially apt for the lifelong growth in grace of one who follows Jesus. An apostle is sent to do something and acts with the authority of the sender. The Twelve, as apostles, are sent to do what Jesus does—to cast out demons and heal (10:1) and to preach (10:7). So apostleship is task-oriented rather than a promotion to a higher status.

INTERPRETING THE SCRIPTURE

Called

Picking up the baton from the imprisoned Baptist, Jesus begins his own preaching ministry (4:17; see the lesson for December 12). The kingdom of heaven is at the door because Jesus is its herald, but its completion is yet to come. Its imminence means that God is about to rule on earth, and that means judgment. So repentance is the appropriate response. Since this announcement is identified as gospel, as good news (4:23), rather than as the wrath of an approaching judgment, as in John's preaching, the repentance here is a blessing rather than a fearful attempt to avoid a disaster. And so, in Matthew 9:13, we have the basic call, the offer of salvation to all who will respond. Those called

are described as sinners, for the righteous do not need salvation. Some manuscripts, including those used by the NKJV, have "call . . . sinners to repentance." If we are the righteous, the call is not for us. If we identify ourselves as sinners, we respond by repenting, thereby claiming the salvation that is offered us.

So we, along with the Twelve and all other Christians, are called to repentance in order to receive salvation. In addition to the basic summons to the Christian life, however, the Twelve are called to full-time service. They are thereby set apart from most of us, for not many sinners receive this second call. But their experience is not completely irrelevant to the rest of us either, for on that shore so long ago our own commitment was shaped. It is, in fact, demanded by a Lord with the authority to do so. In 4:19 the translations generally render the command as "follow" or "come." The Greek is even stronger. It is an adverb of place: "here, after me." The fact that the call comes to people at work rather than at prayer in the synagogue defines our discipleship as a seven-day-a-week affair.

The locus of the authority is shown in the call-response sequence. Only the one who can create the conditions under which this kind of life-transforming relationship is possible can initiate the relationship. And so, as John 15:16 puts it, we do not choose Jesus, but Jesus chooses us. The "after me" explains the relationship in terms of obedience. The walking away from nets and boat in 4:21-22 provides perspective, for this earthly life must fit itself into our greater commitment to Christ's kingdom. Discipleship cannot be pushed to the periphery by a crowded schedule. The "immediately" of verse 22, furthermore, contains an implied warning that postponing a response may well end up as a rejection.

Called to Follow

The "after me" introduces the theme of "following" as a basic definition of discipleship. The Greek verb appears more than twenty times in Matthew, generally with a surplus of meaning. The command to Matthew (9:9) stresses the element of undeserved grace in the call; for we, like the despised tax collector, have not earned our salvation. Such grace, however, requires in response a commitment that relativizes everything else (8:22; 19:21; 19:27). But if the sacrifice is great (16:24), the reward is even greater (19:28). And so disciples follow Jesus (4:20-22; 8:23; 20:34; 27:55)—even if on occasion somewhat tentatively (26:58). The crowds are attracted (4:25; 8:1; 8:10; and others), perhaps out of a sense of need (9:27), perhaps intending more than they can deliver (8:19), always on the verge of falling away or plunging ahead into genuine commitment.

The commitment goes beyond intellectual assent into a faith that entrusts life and welfare to the person of Jesus Christ. In *Returning God's Call*, John C. Purdy has pointed out that if we read the text forward rather than backwards these disciples do not know how it is going to turn out. "That end, however, is not visible from the beginning. All that Andrew, Peter, John, and James can hear is 'Follow me.' They go after Jesus with little knowledge of what it is they have signed on to do. They are like soldiers who have enlisted in an army to fight in a war yet to be declared; like actors who have signed up to perform roles in a play that is still being written. Jesus' call to them is a summons to step out into the unknown; it is a call to adventure." And so it is for us too.

Called to Fish

These first disciples—and we along with them—are called to a task. And that task, in the words of the old Fanny Crosby gospel hymn, is to "Rescue the perishing, care for the dying, snatch them in pity from sin and the grave; weep o'er the erring one, lift up the fallen, tell them of Jesus, the mighty to save" ("Rescue the Perishing").

The scene is a familiar one on the Sea of Galilee of a man standing on the shore watching two professional fishermen casting their net into the water. The phrase "fishers of people" is commonly explained as a wordplay based upon their occupation. If they had been soldiers, Jesus might have said "I will make you a regiment for me," or if they had been teachers, "I will make you teachers."

A second explanation searches for an Old Testament source. Sometimes Ezekiel 47:10 is cited as the basis of the image, for fishermen are standing on the shore catching many kinds of fish. But the context is totally different. They are fishing in the river of life and it is the messianic era. So the fish, as part of paradise, compare with the fruit on the trees rather than with lost souls to be saved. More likely the source of the image is Jeremiah 16:15-16, within the context of restoration from exile: "I am now sending for many fishermen, says the LORD." The fish are the lost Israelites in exile. They are caught at God's command and returned to the promised land.

The third major interpretation begins with the biblical symbolism of the sea as the place of rebellion against God and therefore the home of sin and death. So the beast comes from the sea (Revelation 13:1), and because the sea is a place of revolt it cannot participate in the world of the future (Revelation 21:1). To fish, therefore, is to rescue from darkness. This interpretation also fits the Jeremiah text, where Israel is fished out of the sea of separation from God and brought home. So the image of fishing fits a carpenter or a tax collector as well as a professional fisherman.

Note the future tense in Matthew 4:19. "I will make you" fish. We are probably to think of Jesus' teachings during the earthly ministry and also of the Holy Spirit equipping them—and us—for the task. We are not on our own, therefore, but directed and empowered.

Called to Heal

With the introduction of the physician in 9:12 the fishing is more closely defined as healing, for the fish are now the sick. Some of the sick, of course, have physical and mental illnesses; but all of them are sick with sin (9:13) and thereby excluded from the blessings of the Kingdom— unless they are healed. And so the Physician mingles among the sick with the cleansing call. We, along with the Twelve,

by repenting, have already responded (the "freely you have received" of 10:8 NIV). Now, in the authority of 10:1, comes the "freely give" as we share our own joy in the Savior. The healing power that we are to mediate is as unrestricted as the list of illnesses. Even if we should be uncomfortable with formal healing ceremonies involving oil or the laying on of hands, we nevertheless pray for the sick to be healed. In addition, at the most basic level, we witness to the healing power of God's forgiving love through Christ.

The healing comes with that proximity to the Physician that is symbolized by the table fellowship of the banquet scene. The haphazard guest list stretches far enough in each direction to include all of us. Jesus, here acting as host of the messianic banquet, has authority over the guest list. The background text is Isaiah 25:6-9, in which heaven is portrayed as a great party with God as the host. The New Testament makes use of this imagery to describe eternal life. Abraham, Isaac, and Jacob are fellow guests (Matthew 8:11), those invited to eat bread in heaven are blessed (Luke 14:15), and eternal life is attendance at the marriage supper of the Lamb (Revelation 19:9). One dimension of the Lord's Supper is this kind of anticipation of eternal life.

The twelve tribes became a symbol for the covenant people as a whole. So the twelve tribes of the first covenant are matched by the twelve disciples of the new covenant. The twelve tribes and the twelve disciples then represent the entire people of God, and so there are twenty-four elders in heaven (Revelation 4:4). In this corporate sense, therefore, you and I are to be located among the Twelve.

SHARING THE SCRIPTURE

PREPARING TO TEACH

Preparing Our Hearts

Begin to study for this week's lesson by reading Matthew 10:5-15. Note that our devotional passage follows the lesson scripture found in Matthew 10:1-4. As you read Jesus' instructions to the disciples, envision yourself among the Twelve. What would these directions look like if they were modernized? What would you be called to do? Where would you do your work? How would you respond to those who refused to hear the message you had been sent to proclaim? Meditate on how (even if!) you would go forth in Jesus' name. What changes do you need to make to be more faithful to Jesus' mission for your life?

Turn to today's lesson by reading the three brief passages from Matthew 4:18-22; 9:9-12; and 10:1-4. You may want to jot down notes about the kind of people Jesus called and the work that he expected them to do. How are you similar to or different from the disciples? How is your work similar to or different from theirs?

Pray that God will guide you into making a commitment to Jesus with no strings attached, if you have not already made such a commitment.

Preparing Our Minds

Review today's scripture passages. Read this lesson. Check the Bible references made throughout the lesson. Look especially at the verses from Matthew cited in the first paragraph of "Called to Follow" in the Interpreting the Scripture portion. These passages will be studied in the class session.

If time permits, check a Bible dictionary or who's who to learn more about at least one of the disciples.

Preparing Our Learning Space

Prior to class, write on newsprint the following citations from Matthew as noted in the first paragraph of "Called to Follow" in the Interpreting the Scripture portion.

- The grace of Jesus' call is unmerited: Matthew 9:9.
- Grace requires a commitment that puts everything else in proper perspective: Matthew 8:22; 19:21; 19:27.
- Sacrifice is great for those who follow: Matthew 16:24.
- Reward is greater than the sacrifice: Matthew 19:28.
- Disciples do in fact follow Jesus: Matthew 4:20-22; 8:23; 20:34; 27:55.
- Sometimes the following is tentative: Matthew 26:58.
- Crowds are attracted to Jesus: Matthew 4:25; 8:1; 8:10.
- Some come because they have a need: Matthew 9:27.
- Some have good intentions but cannot deliver what they intend: Matthew 8:19.

Have on hand:
- several Bibles
- optional picture of the Sea of Galilee
- newsprint and marker.

LEADING THE CLASS

(1) Introduction

You may want to begin today's session by reading or retelling the Focusing on the Main Question portion.

Another way to begin is to discuss these questions:

(1) **Have you, or someone you know, ever changed careers?**

(2) **What prompted the change?**

(3) **What sacrifices did you have to make to pursue this new vocation?**

(4) **How did you or your friend feel about engaging in work that was different from that previous career?**

Segue into the Bible lesson by pointing out that Jesus' disciples made career changes when he called them to follow him. Several were fishermen. One was a tax (or toll) collector. Their way of life would be radically altered. Yet each one answered and moved out into uncharted waters, following closely behind the Lord who had called them.

Close the Introduction by reading aloud today's main question: **What do we do with Jesus' call to "Follow me!"?** Provide a few moments of silence so that the students can begin to think about how they have responded to Jesus' call.

(2) Called

Read Matthew 4:18-22 aloud yourself. If you have a picture of the Sea of Galilee, show this to the class prior to the reading to set the scene. Ask the students to close their eyes and imagine themselves in the scene as you read. Then ask the following questions. Encourage class members to participate because this type of activity helps readers to engage the Scriptures more fully than simple comprehension of the words themselves will allow.

(1) What did you see? (Examples include Jesus walking, the men fishing, the men getting out of the boat.)

(2) What did you hear? (Examples include Jesus' call to "follow me," waves splashing, water lapping against the boat.)

(3) What could you touch? (Examples include the nets, the fish, the boat, one of the people.)

(4) What did you smell? (Examples include fish, the water.)

(5) What could you taste? (Examples include the fish, the water, perspiration dripping off your head as you stood in the sun.)

(3) Called to Follow

First, show the class the list of Bible citations you have copied onto newsprint prior to class (see Preparing Our Learning Space). Ask for a different volunteer to look up each citation.

Next, read aloud these words: **In Matthew 4:19 the translations generally render the command as "follow" or "come." The Greek is even stronger. It is an adverb of place: "here, after me."**

Then read aloud the first paragraph in "Called to Follow" under Interpreting the Scripture. As you get to the appropriate place in your reading, pause and ask the assigned volunteer to read the passage.

When you have finished, ask the class:

(1) What do these verses reveal to you about what it means to follow Jesus?

(2) How do you perceive yourself to be similar to any of the persons who followed Jesus?

Conclude this portion of the lesson by asking the students to think about how they would finish this sentence stem: **To be a follower of Jesus means that I . . . .** Do not discuss their answers, but ask them to pray that their answers reflect God's will for their lives.

(4) Called to Fish

Jesus called the professional fishermen to be "fishers of people." In a brief lecture explain the three interpretations of this image, using the information under "Called to Fish" in Interpreting the Scripture. To help the class follow the explanation, you may want to write the following headings on newsprint as you speak:

- One Interpretation: "Fishers of people" is a play on words based on the occupations of Peter, Andrew, James, and John.
- A Second Interpretation: An image from the Hebrew Scriptures, possibly Ezekiel 47:10 or, more likely, Jeremiah 16:15-16, is Jesus' source.
- A Third Interpretation: Since the sea symbolized the place of rebellion against God, one who fishes rescues people from darkness.

Point out that Matthew 4:19 is written in the future tense: "I will make you fish."

Here we are to understand that Jesus not only calls us but by the power of the Holy Spirit equips us to do the work. This idea is reinforced by Matthew 10:1, where Jesus gives the disciples authority to accomplish the work.

Ask these questions. Perhaps you will want to have students discuss them in small groups, or you may prefer to do this activity as a silent meditation.

(1) **How has Jesus called and equipped you?**

(2) **How is work for the Kingdom a significant part of your life?**

(3) **Why are you willing to make the necessary sacrifices to follow Jesus?**

(5) Called to Heal

Select a volunteer to read Matthew 9:9-12 and 10:1.

Invite a few volunteers to tell of an experience of healing in their own lives. Ask them to include how they perceived God and those called by God, such as medical professionals, to be involved in this healing.

Relate the idea of Jesus as physician to the idea of Jesus eating with "tax collectors and sinners," presumably at Matthew's home. Use the information in the second paragraph of "Called to Heal" under Interpreting the Scripture to make the connections between an earthly meal and Jesus as the host of the messianic banquet that those who respond to his call will one day attend.

If possible with the size of your group, ask the students to be ready to say their names, in turn, when you give them the cue at the close of the reading you will do in a moment. Perhaps you will be able to stand in a circle and designate someone to begin the list of names at the appropriate time.

Now read aloud Matthew 10:2-4. Then say: **These are the names of some of Jesus' current disciples.**

Before you say good-bye, offer at least one of the suggestions below so that students will have a concrete way to live out what they have learned today.

HELPING CLASS MEMBERS ACT

Challenge students to examine their own commitment to Jesus this week. Suggest that they pull out their calendars and see how much time they really devote to prayer and other spiritual disciplines, worship, serving others, and proclaiming the good news. Encourage them to allow God's Spirit to work in them to reorder their priorities if necessary.

Jesus must have had a special "spark" that drew people to him. Recommend that class members ponder the qualities that make for an effective leader. Which of these traits do they have? Which ones could they develop?

Encourage students to offer whatever help they can to those who need healing. Perhaps they come into contact with people who are sick, lonely, victims of violence or abuse, lacking in confidence, or overwhelmed by the problems of life.

PLANNING FOR NEXT SUNDAY

Next week we will consider Jesus' teachings on prayer. He not only gave us a model prayer but also offered directions on how we should pray. Ask the students to read Matthew 6:1-15 in preparation for the lesson.

THINKING ABOUT PRAYER

PREVIEWING THE LESSON

Lesson Scripture: Matthew 6:1-15
Background Scripture: Matthew 6:1-15
Key Verse: Matthew 6:6

Focus of the Lesson:
To show his followers how to pray effectively, Jesus taught them a model prayer.

Main Questions of the Lesson:
(1) Why do we pray?
(2) What do we hope to accomplish?

This lesson will enable adult learners to:
(1) study Jesus' teachings on prayer.
(2) consider their own practices of prayer.
(3) respond by offering prayers to God.

Today's lesson may be outlined as follows:
(1) Introduction
(2) The Hallowing
(3) The Bread
(4) The Forgiveness
(5) The Trial

FOCUSING ON THE MAIN QUESTION

C. S. Lewis, the Oxford professor who is best known for his book on temptation, *The Screwtape Letters*, was a confirmed bachelor. Startling his friends, he married Joy, an American woman with a young son. Not long after the marriage they discover that Joy has a bone cancer that is so far advanced that she cannot survive. The movie *Shadowlands* is the deeply moving story of that marriage and how the three of them—Joy, Lewis, and her son, Douglas—deal with her illness and death. Joy herself provides the insight that allows them to cope. In the film she tells her husband, "I am going to die and I want to be with you then. But I can be with you then only if I talk about it with you now." The point, she feels, is that "We can't have the happiness of yesterday without the pain of today. That's the deal." And so, after her death, Lewis explains to Douglas, "The pain now is part of the happiness then. That's the deal."

At one point in the movie, after Joy

undergoes intense chemotherapy, there is the good news of a temporary remission. A colleague remarks to Lewis, "I know how hard you've been praying; and now God is answering your prayer." Lewis's answer, at first blush, is pretty surprising. "That's not why I pray. I pray because I can't help myself...because I'm helpless. . . . It doesn't change God, it changes me." This exchange highlights our main questions: **Why do we pray? What do we hope to accomplish?** Naturally we identify our own needs—heal-ing, guidance, whatever—and ask God to satisfy them. When our prayer turns out the way we hope, when Joy's cancer is cured, we say that the prayer has been answered.

But when it doesn't work out, when Joy dies anyway, do we say that our prayer was not answered? Even though God knows well enough what we need (Matthew 6:8)? What of our promised reward (6:6)? Can we then trust God's will, even when we don't understand it? Can we affirm that "That's the deal!"?

READING THE SCRIPTURE

NRSV
Matthew 6:1-15

1 "Beware of practicing your piety before others in order to be seen by them; for then you have no reward from your Father in heaven.

2 "So whenever you give alms, do not sound a trumpet before you, as the hypocrites do in the synagogues and in the streets, so that they may be praised by others. Truly I tell you, they have received their reward. 3 But when you give alms, do not let your left hand know what your right hand is doing, 4 so that your alms may be done in secret; and your Father who sees in secret will reward you.

5 "And whenever you pray, do not be like the hypocrites; for they love to stand and pray in the synagogues and at the street corners, so that they may be seen by others. Truly I tell you, they have received their reward. **6 But whenever you pray, go into your room and shut the door and pray to your Father who is in secret; and your Father who sees in secret will reward you.**

7 "When you are praying, do not heap up empty phrases as the Gentiles do; for they think that they will be heard because of their many words. 8 Do not be like

NIV
Matthew 6:1-15

[1]"Be careful not to do your 'acts of righteousness' before men, to be seen by them. If you do, you will have no reward from your Father in heaven.

[2]"So when you give to the needy, do not announce it with trumpets, as the hypocrites do in the synagogues and on the streets, to be honored by men. I tell you the truth, they have received their reward in full. [3]But when you give to the needy, do not let your left hand know what your right hand is doing, [4]so that your giving may be in secret. Then your Father, who sees what is done in secret, will reward you.

[5]"And when you pray, do not be like the hypocrites, for they love to pray standing in the synagogues and on the street corners to be seen by men. I tell you the truth, they have received their reward in full. **[6]But when you pray, go into your room, close the door and pray to your Father, who is unseen. Then your Father, who sees what is done in secret, will reward you.** [7]And when you pray, do not keep on babbling like pagans, for they think they will be heard because of their many words. [8]Do not be like them, for your

Key
Verse

Key
Vers

them, for your Father knows what you need before you ask him.

9 "Pray then in this way:
Our Father in heaven,
    hallowed be your name.
10 Your kingdom come.
    Your will be done,
        on earth as it is in heaven.
11 Give us this day our daily
        bread.
12 And forgive us our debts,
        as we also have forgiven our
        debtors.
13 And do not bring us to the
        time of trial,
        but rescue us from the evil
        one.

14 For if you forgive others their trespasses, your heavenly Father will also forgive you; 15 but if you do not forgive others, neither will your Father forgive your trespasses."

Father knows what you need before you ask him.

9"This, then, is how you should pray:

" 'Our Father in heaven,
    hallowed be your name,
10your kingdom come,
    your will be done
        on earth as it is in heaven.
11Give us today our daily bread.
12Forgive us our debts,
        as we also have forgiven our debtors.
13And lead us not into temptation,
        but deliver us from the evil one.'

14For if you forgive men when they sin against you, your heavenly Father will also forgive you. 15But if you do not forgive men their sins, your Father will not forgive your sins."

UNDERSTANDING THE SCRIPTURE

Matthew 6:1-6. "Piety" (NRSV) or "righteousness" (NIV) in verse 1 is the exercise of religion ("religious duties" GNB) expressed in concrete actions. In today's lesson, righteousness is defined in two particulars—charitable giving and prayer. There is the assumption that Christians will engage in both of these activities, but we are to be careful that they are done in the proper spirit. They must not be done for the purpose of being seen by others. The Greek verb has come into English as *theatrical*. It has the nuance of that which attracts attention as interesting, such as a tourist attraction or an entertainment. Here the purpose of attracting attention is to win approval, and so actions that are good in themselves may become a form of self-seeking that detracts from the glory of God.

The desire to receive a reward from God is affirmed (6:4, 6). What is condemned is the desire to receive a reward from men and women now, that is, their approval. There is only one reward for a given set of deeds, and so to gain the reward from society is to lose it from God. The phrase "they have received" in verse 2 has a specialized meaning in the papyri to indicate a receipt for rent, taxes, or purchase of goods. "I have received" whatever it is that is involved in the business transaction. This word ironically places charitable giving on the level of a business transaction rather than a good deed motivated by a compassionate desire to relieve human suffering. They have been praised, and so their account is marked "paid in full."

The hypocrites blow their own horns and want their names on plaques as big givers (6:2). In contrast, our own left hand is not to know what our own right hand has done (6:3). Then our mind also does not know, and so there is not even a trace of self-satisfaction. We do what there is to do and then we forget it. Compare Matthew 25:37, where the righteous are not aware that they have performed any good deeds. Christ has kept track, but they have not. The interpretation of the reward must begin from the premise that the Christian is the slave of God (Luke 17:7-10) and therefore not entitled to a reward for obedience. So if God rewards the obedience that is owed, it is a gift of grace and not payment for services rendered. The reward is then eternal life in heaven. (See also 6:19-21.)

Verses 5-6 do not relate to public and private prayer, but to private prayer that is addressed to bystanders rather than to God in order to secure a reputation for piety. The "room" in verse 6 is in the interior of the house. The door of the retreat is closed in order to exclude all but the Father. The specific reward here is the reality of the desired communion with God. Note, however, that in Matthew 5:16 we are to let our light shine so that people may see our good works and be moved to glorify God—not us.

Matthew 6:7-15. When the pagans pray they keep on babbling (6:7 NIV). This rare word is cognate to the one for stammer or stutter. Are we to think of the stammering "many words" as unintelligible sounds, as "meaningless words" (GNB)? Or are we to think of the many words as intelligible but "empty" (NRSV) of any real meaning, or as "vain repetitions" (NKJV), unable to move a nonexistent idol to action? Pagans must pile up the names of gods and goddesses, together with flattering invocations, in the hope of pressing all the right buttons and avoiding any wrong button that might anger some deity. It is, of course, a counsel of anxious desperation. The Christian prayer may or may not be appreciably shorter, but the ambiance is totally different. For we come with the confidence that our Father already knows our needs and wants to meet them. (See also Matthew 7:9-11.)

When we call the model the "Lord's Prayer," the emphasis is upon Jesus as the authority by which we use it, for it belongs to him. When we call it the "Disciples' Prayer," the emphasis is upon our obedience. The doxology at the end of verse 13, relegated to the margin by the NRSV and the NIV although placed in the text by the NKJV, is not in the best of the early manuscripts. It is generally considered to be a liturgical addition.

INTERPRETING THE SCRIPTURE

The Hallowing

The basic biblical Creator/creature equation is here crowded to a back burner by the Parent/child image. Jesus used the Aramaic "Abba" in his own prayers (as in Mark 14:36). This is what young children call their fathers within the family circle—"daddy." Since Jesus is the Son, by means of our faith in him we too become the children of God (Galatians 3:26). We are, however, children by adoption (Romans 8:15), for by nature we remain creatures. So the invitation to call God "our Father" is an assurance of salvation. The "our," furthermore, is a reminder that we are not only children, that we have brothers and sisters, and that we cannot turn our back on them at the same time that we call upon their Father.

To call God "Father" is to confess that salvation is of grace, for the child is dependent upon the parent for the necessities of life. This confession is the childlikeness that is required of those who would enter the Kingdom (Matthew 18:3). There is always a potential problem with images, however, because even though they offer powerful dramatic insight, they do not always transfer easily from one culture to another. In our child-oriented society, for example, we often assume that the focal point is the "innocence" of the child rather than the dependence that an adult-oriented society stresses. "Father"—or "Mother" for that matter—is also a problematic image for those who have had mostly negative experiences with their own parents.

To call God "Father" is to trust that the promised salvation is actually ours, just as the child trusts the parent to provide for his or her needs. The "Father" image, therefore, represents the willingness, the immanence of the divine will within our "now" world. But, lest we bet the farm on good intentions, the "in heaven" stresses the transcendence, the power to implement the will, the "forever" of our life in the Kingdom. And so we dare pray for the hallowing of the name, for the Kingdom to come in its fullness, for the divine will to be obeyed as completely on earth as it is in heaven. When good has won out over evil, when all of God's creatures sing praises because the blessed purpose of creation has been realized, then there is no room for a despairing "what's the use?" The hallowing is God's business, even though our discipleship fits into it.

The Bread

The word translated as "daily" in verse 11 is so rare—occurring in the New Testament only here and in Luke 11:3 and at best only a couple of times in secular Greek—that scholars are not sure of its exact meaning. Depending upon derivation from "day" or from "existence," the two leading guesses are "daily" (NRSV and NIV) and "needed" (GNB). The bread itself stretches

out to include all of our necessities, physical as well as spiritual and emotional—from food and clothing to faith and courage. Both ideas are implicit in the prayer, of course, regardless of which translation we adopt. If we pray for what we need, the "daily" is in the "today"; and if we pray for the "daily" bread, the "this day" limits us to current necessities.

The Old Testament background is the story of the manna in Exodus 16. Israel is to learn, as the old gospel hymn has it, to "trust and obey, for there's no other way" ("Trust and Obey"). Each morning the manna is to be gathered according to the day's need, and it always comes out exactly right (16:16-18)—unless the fear of the "rainy day" overwhelms our trust in the Lord (16:20). The point is guaranteeing freedom from anxiety rather than forbidding prudent planning. We are to pray for the resources to make the day's witness, trusting that what we need will be provided when we need it. We do not pray for that extra margin of safety beyond the requirements of the task. And we do not pray for luxuries just because we are tired of the manna (Numbers 11:1-6). Since, furthermore, we are to get out each morning to gather, we don't just sit back and wait for pennies from heaven to fall into our lap. But no matter how hard we work, we still understand that the Lord has provided.

This interpretation of the bread in terms of the immediacy of earthly life breaks the pattern of the Lord's Prayer. So far—in the petitions for the hallowing, the Kingdom, and the will—our eye has been on the final consummation at the end of time. Now, however, we have narrowed our perspective to the next twenty-four hours. Some scholars, uncomfortable with such a shift, struggle for consistency by understanding the bread of salvation rather than the necessities of ordinary life. They get there from the sabbath in the manna story (Exodus 16:5, 23, 26) and then from the sabbath as a symbol for eternity. But whether—

[handwritten margin note: Daily as manna in O.T.]

here, as well as in the forgiveness and temptation petitions—our emphasis is upon the end or the road to the end, it is a "both/and" rather than an "either/or." The hallowing energizes and directs a discipleship that is enabled by this morning's breakfast, and that hallowing guarantees the bread of salvation.

The Forgiveness

Like the bread, which is triangular in its movement, from God to the disciple to the one in need—for surely the bread petition includes feeding the hungry—so also forgiveness has its three points: God, disciple, neighbor. By the terms of our Creator/creature relationship, we owe God perfect obedience. To come short is to incur a debt; and since perfection is the required standard, we can never repay that debt by an extra bit of goodness. So we sink deeper and deeper into a sea of red ink. Then possibility comes our way in the gospel. So we pray to be forgiven. The Last Judgment at the end of the road is the climax, of course, but we also pray to get started again when we stumble along the way.

Forgiveness is of grace, and that means that we don't earn it. But just as electricity cannot flow until the circuit is completed, so we also cannot receive forgiveness without repentance. Obviously this involves a recognition of our need, a confession of sin. More than this, however, is the reality that sin is social as well as individual, that it wraps us up together as if rolled in barbed wire. Wire cutters, so to speak, come in two sizes, and they must be used together. It is forgiveness that frees us and heals our scars, that which God grants us and that which we grant each other. The refusal to forgive is the evidence that we have not repented. Note, furthermore, that sins against God and against the neighbor are defined in the same language, debts in Matthew 6:12, false steps in 6:14-15 (NRSV's "trespasses," NIV's "sins," GNB's "wrongs"). (See also Matthew 18:23-35 and Colossians 3:13.)

The Trial

It is unthinkable, according to James 1:13-14, that God would lead us into temptation to see what we're made of. It makes no sense, therefore, to ask God not to do what God would never do anyway. More promising is NRSV's "trial" in Matthew 6:13 and the "hard testing" of the GNB. The reference is to the resistance to our discipleship that we encounter in the world, ranging from indifference to the active hostility of persecution. The resistance is not a test ginned up to determine the authenticity of our faith. It is, instead, a threat to our Christian life. What matters is that the divine will be done, and so it is proper for us to pray that the cup of suffering pass us by (26:39).

But the prayer always includes the "nevertheless," as we pledge our lives to the "your will be done on earth." So when we must drink the cup, when the trials are unavoidable except at the cost of our faith and witness, the prayer is for the strength to endure. The Greek verb translated as "rescue" (NRSV) or "deliver" (NIV) occurs only once more in Matthew. It is the mocking shout to Jesus on the cross, "He trusts in God; let God deliver him now!" (27:43). The taunters assume, like so many people today, that the deliverance is *from* suffering rather than *through* it. The promise, however, as 1 Corinthians 10:13 assures us, is that the trial will never be more than we can bear, that God will provide a way of escape from its threat to our faith, so that we may be enabled to endure.

The deliverance, therefore, is from the evil one rather than from the pain. We are delivered from the triumph over us that the evil one would enjoy were we to renounce our faith in order to avoid the trial, or if under the pressure of the pain we were to break down and loosen our hold on the Savior.

SHARING THE SCRIPTURE

PREPARING TO TEACH

Preparing Our Hearts

Begin to center yourself by sitting quietly, contemplating these questions and listening for God's voice. What praises, petitions, and intercessions do you need to bring to God right now? What do you think happens when you pray? How do you decide if your prayers have been answered, especially when an outcome is not at all what you had desired?

When you are ready, read Luke 11:1-13. Here, Jesus provides the disciples with a model prayer and tells a parable to encourage them to be persistent in prayer. Compare verses 2-4 to the version of this prayer that you regularly say.

Now turn to today's lesson from Matthew 6:1-15. Note Jesus' teachings about piety in verses 1-8. Now look at Matthew's rendering of Jesus' prayer. Again, compare verses 9-13 to the version of the prayer that is most familiar to you.

Close this time by offering a prayer that the Holy Spirit will continue to lead you in praying according to God's will.

Preparing Our Minds

Review Matthew 6:1-15. Read this lesson carefully. You may want to consult additional commentaries.

One word of caution: When we are called upon to teach a familiar scripture passage, we may not study it as thoroughly as a passage that is less well-known to us. As you read this week's lesson, be on the lookout for new insights that will bring fresh meaning to this beloved prayer.

Preparing Our Learning Space

You may want to write the questions for contemplation under "The Bread" on newsprint prior to class.

Have on hand:
- ✔ several Bibles
- ✔ newsprint and marker
- ✔ paper and pencils.

LEADING THE CLASS

(1) Introduction

Open the session with today's main questions:
(1) **Why do we pray?**
(2) **What do we hope to accomplish?**

Encourage the students to answer these questions aloud. List their ideas on newsprint. If the class is large, divide it into small groups so that as much discussion as possible can be generated in response to these questions.

Now ask these questions:
(1) **What practices or rituals do you observe when you pray?**
(2) **How do you understand the giving of alms and praying to be related?**

Ask the class members to turn in their Bibles to Matthew 6:1-8. Select a volunteer to read this passage aloud. Then use the information from Understanding the Scripture to illuminate Jesus' teachings. This explanation will help you set the Lord's Prayer into the appropriate context. Emphasize that prayer and almsgiving are both acts of piety.

Conclude the Introduction by inviting the class members to pray together the Lord's Prayer. Join hands, if possible.

(2) The Hallowing

Having just prayed the Lord's Prayer using the customary language of your congregation, ask the students to turn now to Matthew 6:9-10. Invite several persons to read these verses from different Bible translations. Then make these points in a brief lecture:

- Jesus often called God "Abba," which means "daddy," thus indirectly referring to himself as God's Son.
- Through faith in Christ, we too become children of God (Galatians 3:26).
- Unlike Jesus, who was one with the Father, we are children by virtue of adoption (Romans 8:15).
- Jesus uses the plural pronoun "our," rather than the singular "my," to begin this prayer.
- Since a child depends upon a parent, when we confess that God is "our Father," we acknowledge that we are saved by grace. We depend upon God.
- By calling God "Father," we demonstrate that, like children, we trust in God to care for us.
- God is not only as close as a father but also "in heaven."
- God has the power to bring about the divine will.
- We pray that God's name will be "hallowed" or made holy.

If time permits, you may want to ask the class to do a comparative study of the prayer by turning to Luke 11:2-4.

(1) **How are Matthew and Luke's versions similar?**
(2) **How do they differ?**
(3) **How do each of these versions differ from the one you traditionally say in your congregation?** (If you get into this discussion, you may also want to note that while most Protestants include the doxology found in the KJV, only later manuscripts had some form of "for the kingdom and the power and the glory are yours forever. Amen." Consequently, translations that use the oldest manuscripts generally relegate the doxology to a footnote.)

(3) The Bread

Ask the students to recite Matthew 6:11 in unison. Note that the idea of daily bread comes from the story of the Hebrew people in the wilderness. Recall the terms under which the people were to gather manna, according to Exodus 16. (See also "The Bread" under Interpreting the Scripture.)

Point out that "bread" here means all of the necessities of life, not just literal food.

Distribute paper and pencils. Ask students to make a confidential list of all that they need today. The list may include specific foods, articles of clothing, and shelter, as well as whatever is needed to satisfy spiritual, emotional, and intellectual needs.

When they have finished, ask them to review their lists and silently answer these questions, which you will read aloud. Pause after each one to allow time for the students to contemplate their responses. Or, if you prefer, write the questions on newsprint in advance and post them at this point in the lesson.

(1) **Do I really need all of the items on my list?**
(2) **How does my list of needs compare to the resources that I have at hand to meet my needs?**
(3) **In what areas do I have an overabundance of riches?**
(4) **In what areas of my life do I need to place more trust in God to meet my needs?**

Close this part of the lesson by offering this prayer: <u>**God, you know what I need. You also know that I rely on myself too often, forgetting that I am your child. Help me to trust you to meet my needs today, just as you sent manna to the Hebrew children in the wilderness each day. Amen.**</u>

(4) The Forgiveness

Encourage a few persons with different Bible translations to read aloud Matthew 6:12, 14-15. Then ask:
(1) **Why is the phrase "as we also" (6:12 NRSV) so important in this sentence?** (It reminds us that God expects us to forgive others even as God forgives us. Forgiveness is a triangle that includes God, others, and ourselves.)

(2) What do these verses say to you about God?

(3) What do they say to you about your relationship with God?

(4) What do they say to you about your relationship with other people?

Tell the class to think silently about these two questions.

(1) If God were to ask you to rate yourself on your ability to forgive, what would you say?

(2) If this is not the answer you think God expects, what changes do you need to ask God to help you make?

(5) The Trial

After allowing a few moments for personal reflection on the questions above, bring the class back together by asking someone to read aloud Matthew 6:13.

Note that we usually say "lead us not into temptation." Ask:

(1) Do you believe that God actually tempts people? (Note the reference to James 1:13-14 in Interpreting the Scripture that teaches that God "tempts no one.")

(2) Rather than the word "temptation," the words "trial" (NRSV) or "hard testing" (GNB) are more helpful in understanding what Jesus is saying here. To what might these words refer? (Again, note the information under "The Trial" in Interpreting the Scripture. See especially the first paragraph.)

(3) When and how has God rescued you, someone you know, or someone you've heard about from trials?

Distribute paper and pencils. Direct each person to work with a partner or small team. Each group is to write the Lord's Prayer in their own words. They can amplify or explain meanings, based on what they have learned.

To conclude the lesson, ask a few volunteers to read their paraphrases aloud. If possible, direct the class to gather in a circle or hold hands across the aisles as these prayers are being read.

Following the prayer, offer at least one of the suggestions below so that students can live out what they have studied.

HELPING CLASS MEMBERS ACT

Challenge class members to give a sacrificial amount of money to a charitable organization or individual in need, without telling anyone except a spouse that they have done so.

Suggest that students begin a prayer log this week, if they do not already keep one. In the log they are to write a few words about what (or who) they are praying for and the date of the prayer. When the prayer is answered, they are to write the date and a few words about how the situation was resolved, whether it was the hoped for outcome or not.

Encourage individuals to pause each time they pray "forgive us our debts, as we also have forgiven our debtors." Ask them to think not only of their own sins but also of the people whom they need to forgive. Such forgiveness may be difficult, but Christians cannot expect to ask God for something that they will not give to others.

PLANNING FOR NEXT SUNDAY

Next week's lesson, "Thinking About Wholeness," is a familiar story of Jesus' compassion. In Matthew 9:18-31 and 35-36 students will read about how Jesus raised a leader's daughter from the dead, how he healed a woman who had been hemorrhaging for twelve years, how he healed two blind men, and how he met the needs of others who needed healing.

THINKING ABOUT WHOLENESS

PREVIEWING THE LESSON

Lesson Scripture: Matthew 9:18-31, 35-36
Background Scripture: Matthew 9:18-38
Key Verse: Matthew 9:36

Focus of the Lesson:
Jesus demonstrated compassion by restoring to wholeness the sick who had faith in Him.

Main Question of the Lesson:
How interruptible am I?

This lesson will enable adult learners to:
(1) observe Jesus' compassion and its effect on people.
(2) feel Jesus' compassion in their own lives.
(3) respond by offering Jesus' compassion to others.

Today's lesson may be outlined as follows:
(1) Introduction
(2) Compassion
(3) Saved
(4) Faith
(5) Miracles

FOCUSING ON THE MAIN QUESTION

In his book *There's a Lot More to Health Than Not Being Sick*, Bruce Larson tells the story about the time he almost drowned in the Gulf of Mexico. Several days after being rescued by a tugboat crew after spending hours trying to keep afloat in tumultuous seas, Larson met an old friend he hadn't seen in years. Chatting briefly, the old friend asked, "What's new with you?" Larson replied, "Well, you won't believe this, but two days ago I almost drowned in the Gulf of Mexico. I was res-

cued by a tugboat after four hours in the sea." There was no reaction to this dramatic news. As Larson recalls the scene, "My friend and I stood there for awhile and he didn't say anything. He was looking at his shoes. Eventually, though, he looked up and said, 'By the way, how's fishing these days?' You can guess what my reaction was. To say the least I felt unloved and put down."

Whenever I mention this story in conversation there is almost always an immediate sense of identification. "People don't mean it when they say 'How are you?' They don't really care. So you say 'Fine' even when you aren't." In the case of the old friend, we automatically assume that the inappropriate response indicates an uncaring attitude. And perhaps that is true. But not necessarily. Suppose that he just didn't know what to say, that he has great difficulty expressing emotion, that he is just trying to get past his own awkwardness, that his apparent unresponsiveness does not give a clue about his real feelings.

Why not, for a change, try on the old friend's shoes and see if they fit? Larson himself found a better fit than he had hoped. He began to think of all the "my wife is sick" and "I lost my job" comments that he had turned aside with a pleasantry as he hurried about his business. These shoes fit so well that they prompt us to pose our main question: **How interruptible am I?** We expect Christ to be interruptible when we express our needs, to give us his full attention. Does that mean that Christ expects us to be equally interruptible for our brothers and sisters—to give them our full attention whenever and wherever?

READING THE SCRIPTURE

NRSV
Matthew 9:18-31, 35-36

18 While he was saying these things to them, suddenly a leader of the synagogue came in and knelt before him, saying, "My daughter has just died; but come and lay your hand on her, and she will live." 19 And Jesus got up and followed him, with his disciples. 20 Then suddenly a woman who had been suffering from hemorrhages for twelve years came up behind him and touched the fringe of his cloak, 21 for she said to herself, "If I only touch his cloak, I will be made well." 22 Jesus turned, and seeing her he said, "Take heart, daughter; your faith has made you well." And instantly the woman was made well. 23 When Jesus came to the leader's house and saw the flute players and the crowd making a commotion, 24 he said, "Go away; for the girl is not dead but sleeping." And they laughed at him. 25 But when the crowd had been put outside, he went in and took her by the hand, and the girl got up. 26 And the report of this spread throughout that district.

27 As Jesus went on from there, two blind men followed him, crying loudly, "Have mercy on us, Son of David!"

NIV
Matthew 9:18-31, 35-36

[18]While he was saying this, a ruler came and knelt before him and said, "My daughter has just died. But come and put your hand on her, and she will live." [19]Jesus got up and went with him, and so did his disciples.

[20]Just then a woman who had been subject to bleeding for twelve years came up behind him and touched the edge of his cloak. [21]She said to herself, "If I only touch his cloak, I will be healed."

[22]Jesus turned and saw her. "Take heart, daughter," he said, "your faith has healed you." And the woman was healed from that moment.

[23]When Jesus entered the ruler's house and saw the flute players and the noisy crowd, [24]he said, "Go away. The girl is not dead but asleep." But they laughed at him. [25]After the crowd had been put outside, he went in and took the girl by the hand, and she got up. [26]News of this spread through all that region.

[27]As Jesus went on from there, two blind men followed him, calling out, "Have mercy on us, Son of David!"

[28]When he had gone indoors, the blind

28 When he entered the house, the blind men came to him; and Jesus said to them, "Do you believe that I am able to do this?" They said to him, "Yes, Lord." 29 Then he touched their eyes and said, "According to your faith let it be done to you." 30 And their eyes were opened. Then Jesus sternly ordered them, "See that no one knows of this." 31 But they went away and spread the news about him throughout that district.

35 Then Jesus went about all the cities and villages, teaching in their synagogues, and proclaiming the good news of the kingdom, and curing every disease and every sickness. **36 When he saw the crowds, he had compassion for them, because they were harassed and helpless, like sheep without a shepherd.**

Key Verse

men came to him, and he asked them, "Do you believe that I am able to do this?"

"Yes, Lord," they replied.

²⁹Then he touched their eyes and said, "According to your faith will it be done to you"; ³⁰and their sight was restored. Jesus warned them sternly, "See that no one knows about this." ³¹But they went out and spread the news about him all over that region.

³⁵Jesus went through all the towns and villages, teaching in their synagogues, preaching the good news of the kingdom and healing every disease and sickness. **³⁶When he saw the crowds, he had compassion on them, because they were harassed and helpless, like sheep without a shepherd.**

Key
Vers

UNDERSTANDING THE SCRIPTURE

Matthew 9:18-19, 23-26. While Jesus is explaining the Kingdom's approach in terms of the new wine and the old skins, he is interrupted by a grief-stricken father. It is an elder, no less, the supervisor of the synagogue worship, a rich and important person in that community. In front of everyone this VIP kneels before Jesus in supplication. Note that the girl is not sick and in danger of dying. According to Matthew's account, she is already dead. The father is asking for a resurrection. His faith is shown in his coming to Jesus like this, and in the confident "she will live" if only Jesus will lay hands upon her. (See also Mark 6:5 and Luke 4:40 for the laying on of hands within the context of the healing miracles.) Without comment Jesus goes with the man and the disciples trail along.

By the time they get to the house, funeral preparations are already pretty far along, for burial takes place a few hours after death. The hired flute players and the professional mourners are there, together with friends and neighbors and whoever

else wants to come. The commotion they make correlates with the social standing of the dead girl's family. Jesus tells the crowd to leave. There will be no funeral today. To say that she is asleep, of course, is not to deny that she is dead, but it is to affirm life beyond death. (See also 1 Thessalonians 5:10 and Ephesians 5:14 for images of death as sleep pending resurrection.) Note the contrast between the faith of the father and the mocking laughter of the crowd. Apparently, since neither parents nor disciples are mentioned and the crowd has been cleared out, there are no witnesses to the miracle. Naturally the story spreads. Christians can hardly help looking past a resurrection in this life to their own resurrection to the eternal life.

Matthew 9:20-22. The woman has been suffering from "hemorrhages" (NRSV) or "bleeding" (NIV) for twelve years. She is obviously not in danger of bleeding to death, but there must at least be chronic fatigue from a persistently low blood count. More serious even than her fatigue, however, is its impact upon her social life. For a bodily discharge is one of only three forms of uncleanness considered serious enough to exclude the infected person from society. (The other two are leprosy and contact with a corpse.) Her case is detailed in Leviticus 15:25-27. The problem is that uncleanness is contagious. Anyone or anything that comes in contact with her becomes unclean. So she can't go to the synagogue. No one will come to her house for a visit or invite her to go anywhere until she has been purified. But she can't begin the purification process until the bleeding stops.

Since, therefore, she can hardly confront Jesus face to face, she comes up behind him, hoping that no one will notice. The word translated as "edge" (NIV) or "fringe" (NRSV) in verse 20 may be used to indicate the tassel at each corner of the cloak that reminds the wearer of the commandments. This detail, stressing Jesus as a Jew faithful to the law, highlights the tension over the uncleanness. But the contagion is reversed. Instead of Jesus becoming unclean she is healed.

Matthew 9:27-31. The woman's uncleanness invites a look past a specific illness to Jesus' power to transform the whole of life. And just as blindness symbolizes unbelief, so for Matthew's readers the opening of the eyes suggests the insight of faith. This point is hammered home in the narrative. The two blind men demonstrate their faith by calling Jesus the Son of David (Matthew 1:1; see the lesson for December 19) and by their persistence, following after him even though he had apparently ignored their first prayer. They then confess their faith (9:28) and give public testimony (9:31). The reader's expectation is that his or her life experience also will be "according to faith."

The general explanation for the stern injunction to silence in verse 30 is the fear that the reputation as a miracle worker would detract from the preaching and teaching ministry. Since the text makes no comment on the disobedience, we should probably not make anything of it either. Those who have been healed are just so bursting with the good news that they can't keep still.

Matthew 9:32-34. The blind men hardly clear the doorway (the "while...going" of the NIV in verse 32), however, before friends enter with a mute demoniac. He is healed and he speaks. But we are not told what he says. Perhaps the reader is expected to use his or her own tongue to praise God.

Matthew 9:35-38. Matthew records that as Jesus travels throughout the region, He teaches, preaches, and heals. The motivation for His action is compassion. Moreover, others are needed to "harvest" souls for the Kingdom.

INTERPRETING THE SCRIPTURE

Compassion

Jesus goes around the cities and villages in a threefold ministry that engages the human condition as a whole—teaching in the synagogues, proclaiming the good news of the Kingdom's approach, and healing the sick (Matthew 9:35). The motive for this ministry is defined in verse 36 as compassion or pity (GNB) or feeling sorry for (JB). This particular verb occurs five times in Matthew. Twice it leads to healing the sick (14:14 and 20:34), once to feeding the hungry (15:32), and once to forgiveness (18:27). Here, of course, it leads to teaching, preaching, and healing. Note that, in Matthew at least, it always begins with some human distress and then stimulates some action to relieve that distress.

In view of the prayer in verse 38 and the commissioning of the Twelve in 10:1, it seems clear that we are expected to imitate

Jesus' ministry in all three particulars—teaching, preaching, healing—and from the same motive. Remember Eliza Doolittle in the Broadway musical *My Fair Lady*? She tells a young man that she is sick of words, words, words! "If you love me, show me!" In a very real sense, Jesus does more than tell us that God loves us. He shows us. And we are to show that we love Him by our efforts to carry on His ministry with those around us.

The distress that triggers the compassion is the unsatisfied spiritual needs of the people; for according to verse 36, they are as bedraggled as sheep trying to survive by their own wits—and making a bad job of it. Footsore and fleece-worn after a frustrating and unsuccessful search for pasture, they feel harassed or worried (GNB). The verb translated as "helpless" means "thrown." If they are thrown apart they are scattered (NKJV). If they can't get up again they are helpless (NRSV and NIV), and so they can hardly help feeling dejected (JB). Where are their shepherds? How could the flock get into such a fix?

Ezekiel 34 is the Old Testament background, for the sheep are the covenant people (34:31). Their shepherds, the religious leaders, have mishandled the flock (34:1-10); and so God will take back control through the Davidic Messiah (34:23). Jesus, reflecting God's own compassion for the flock's distress, is that promised Shepherd. He is identified at his birth (Matthew 2:6), and he himself verifies that identification (Matthew 14:14; 15:24, 32; 18:12-14; 26:31-32). He shepherds by teaching, preaching, healing, and getting disciples to extend that ministry.

Saved

In Matthew 9:35 Jesus cures (NRSV) or heals (NIV) every kind of sickness. The Greek word commonly found in the healing miracles is the one from which *therapy* has entered English. (See 4:23; 8:16; 10:1; and 14:14 for examples.) A second word for physical healing occurs in 8:13; 13:15;

15:28; and so on. It is, therefore, surprising to see the verb that is used in relation to the woman with a flow of blood in verses 21-22. Translated here as healed (NIV) or made well (NRSV) or restored to health (JB), the normal meaning of this third verb in Matthew is "save." Of its fourteen occurrences in Matthew, in fact, only in this passage does it involve physical healing. Its very unusualness is thus a flashing light inviting a closer look.

The verb *(sozo)* means to rescue from a threat. When the threat is physical death, the salvation is the preservation of physical life, whether from drowning (8:25 and 14:30) or from the cross (27:40-49). When, however, the threat is condemnation at the Last Judgment, the salvation is the preservation of eternal life. (See 1:21; 10:22; 16:25; 18:11; and so on.) Salvation is entrance into the kingdom of God or the inheritance of eternal life. So, to use such a high-powered word, and to connect it so clearly with faith, is to suggest that more has happened here than the stoppage of a flow of blood. We are expected to see past the healing of the body to the healing of the soul. Such a layered interpretation is supported by the play on saving and losing life in earthly and eternal terms in 16:25.

Faith

Faith is a key component in all of the miracles in today's lesson, even though it is spelled out in only two of them. The beginning point, of course, is a need that cannot be met with our own resources—death, bleeding that does not respond to medical treatment, demon possession, or whatever the need may be. Instead of toughing it out or giving up in despair, however, we ask for help. But we don't just ask anybody. We turn to the one we think can help, and in New Testament terms that one is the Christ. Faith, then, is the confidence that Jesus Christ can meet our needs, whatever they are.

The "can" doesn't mean much if it keeps

company with a "won't." Thus, in addition to confidence in Christ's power, faith has confidence in his willingness to use it on our behalf. It is the assurance that the King of kings and Lord of lords is never too busy to listen to us. He is so interruptible because he cares for us. Therefore, faith knows a predisposition to respond to our prayer. That predisposition, furthermore, is always toward what is best for us in the long run. And so faith trusts the ability and the will to do right by us—even when an answer to prayer is not quite what we had hoped for. Faith does not dismiss out of hopelessness (9:24), or look for a dark purpose beneath the surface of an apparent good (9:34).

The trust factor in faith impels us to take some action, to commit ourselves, to depend upon Another. The ruler of the synagogue kneels down before Jesus. A woman touches his garment. Blind men follow him. Friends bring a demoniac. They—and we who imitate them—do this in the certainty that something will come of it, not with some vague "what have you got to lose?" attitude. What comes of it, as verse 29 points out, is "according to your faith." The woman has been saved by her faith (9:22), for it has connected her with Jesus. Matthew elsewhere calls attention to the faith of the centurion (8:10), of the paralytic's stretcher bearers (9:2), and of the Syrophoenician woman (15:28). And, lest we fear that we can't measure up to such company, Christ offers to work with whatever we have (17:20 and 21:21).

The faith that connects us with Christ then shades into the faithfulness that maintains the connection. Since our fortunes are now bound up with his, the Lord tells us to take heart when we have to swim against the stream. Twice in Matthew 9 (verses 2 and 22), for example, Jesus tells the sick to have courage. When fear grabs hold of us, his reassuring voice comes to us out of the darkness (14:27). But the most powerful encouragement is the pledge, given at the Last Supper, that our destinies are linked

(John 16:33). Such a faith enables faithfulness in good times and bad times alike.

Miracles

Jesus answers the jailed Baptist's question by describing his ministry: "the blind receive their sight, the lame walk, the lepers are cleansed, the deaf hear, the dead are raised, and the poor have good news brought to them" (Matthew 11:5). This is the sort of thing that Isaiah expected to happen when the Lord at last leads the people home again to the promised land for their eternal blessing. The blind, the deaf, the crippled, and the mute will all be healed (Isaiah 35:5-6). Isaiah's list is now complete—the crippled in 9:2-7 and the blind, the deaf, and the mute in today's lesson. So if such things indicate the age to come, then the one who does them is the Coming One. Prophecy has been fulfilled, but with a surplus; for to Isaiah's list Jesus adds cleansing the leper (8:2-3), raising the dead (9:25), and exorcising demons (9:33).

Even though, as given in Jesus' answer to John's question, the primary function of the miracles is verification of messianic identity by fulfilling prophecy, that does not exhaust their meaning. The nature miracles—stilling a storm, walking on water, raising the dead—suggest the power of the Creator. Such a one preaches and teaches with a unique authority. The healing miracles reveal the divine intent to bless. The exorcisms, part of the deadly combat between good and evil, predict the victory upon which our salvation is based. The miracles, furthermore, are not to be taken in isolation from the ministry, for Jesus himself links them with the preaching. The miracles therefore focus on faith and the forgiveness of sins (9:2-7) in the light of the Kingdom's approach. The result, accordingly, is a demonstrated concern for the wholeness of the human condition, body and soul. Our faith in this concern is what sees us through—even if the cup of suffering does not pass us by.

SHARING THE SCRIPTURE

PREPARING TO TEACH

Preparing Our Hearts

Today's devotional reading from Matthew 11:2-6 will help you to center yourself spiritually as you begin to prepare this lesson. It points out how Jesus described the work of his ministry. Is Jesus the one to come, or is there another who is yet to come? Jesus does not respond defensively to the query by John's disciples. Instead, he enumerates what he has done. Jesus leaves it to these disciples and their imprisoned teacher, John the Baptist, to determine the answer to the question. His response, however, demonstrates that he is performing the work of the Messiah whose coming was prophesied (see Isaiah 35:5-6). Think about how you would answer John's question. Are you unshakably certain that Jesus is the Messiah?

Now turn to Matthew 9:18-38. Here you will find several miracles. Jesus not only teaches about the Kingdom (see the Sermon on the Mount, Matthew 5:1–7:27) but by his compassionate healing of others he also demonstrates what life in the Kingdom is like. In your spiritual journal, you may want to consider these questions: How do you experience Jesus' compassion? How do you extend that compassion to others? Pray that God will give you the wisdom, love, and grace to be a good and compassionate shepherd for the adults in your class.

Preparing Our Minds

Look especially at Matthew 9:18-31 and 35-36. Notice the structure of verses 18-31. The religious leader's urgent plea interrupts Jesus as he is responding to a question from one of John's disciples as to why Jesus and his disciples do not fast often (Matthew 9:14-17). Then, while on the way to the synagogue leader's house, Jesus is again interrupted by the woman who touches his garment so that she might be healed of her hemorrhage. Finally, Jesus reaches the home and restores the religious leader's daughter to life. While on his way from the leader's home, Jesus is interrupted by two blind men. Today's main question deals with our willingness to be interrupted. Clearly, Jesus was willing to be interrupted, even to allow interruptions to pyramid one atop of the next. Instead of complaining about how busy he was, Jesus seemed to welcome such opportunities to show compassion by doing whatever was needed to make people whole.

Preparing Our Learning Space

Have on hand:
- several Bibles
- hymnals.

LEADING THE CLASS

(1) Introduction

Begin today's session by reading Bruce Larson's story as found in the first paragraph of the Focusing on the Main Question part of the lesson.

Invite volunteers to share similar experiences when friends seemed to ignore their pain and hurry on to the next topic of conversation or depart from the scene. Now ask students to recall an experience when someone did enter into their pain and responded compassionately.

Then ask these questions:
(1) **What difference did a friend's caring attitude and willingness to take the time to be with you make in your ability to deal with the problem?**
(2) **Do you have anyone you can contact who will drop everything in order to**

take the time to be present with you if a need arises?

Recognizing that there are folks who are willing to come to our aid whenever necessary, we ask today's main question: **How interruptible am I?** In today's lesson we will see that Jesus, the compassionate shepherd, is indeed willing for people to call upon him at any time or place. His compassionate response to their needs brings about wholeness and healing.

(2) Compassion

Ask a volunteer to read aloud Matthew 9:18-19 and 23-26. Use these questions, or create a brief lecture to make the points that the questions raise.

?

(1) **What was Jesus doing when the synagogue leader interrupted him?** (Jesus was busy instructing John's disciples about the Kingdom, according to verses 14-17. Note that verse 18 begins with "while he was saying these things.")

(2) **What was the daughter's condition?** (She was already dead.)

(3) **How did this father's expectations differ from those of the crowd who had gathered at his home?** (The crowd had come to mourn, for the girl was indeed dead, but the father had faith that she would be resurrected if Jesus would just lay his hand upon her.)

(4) **How are you similar to the girl's father?**

(5) **How are you different from him?**

(3) Saved

Invite someone to read Matthew 9:20-22. You may want to note the structure of this passage as outlined under Preparing Our Minds. Point out how often Jesus is interrupted.

Use the portion entitled "Saved" in the Interpreting the Scripture section to explain three Greek words, one of which has entered English as *therapy*, a second that is

usually translated "healed" or "cured," and a third word that means "saved." The Greek language does not describe the woman with the hemorrhage as having been healed but rather as having been saved.

Ask the class these questions:

(1) **What relationship do you see between the salvation of one's soul and the healing of one's body?** **?**

(2) **Until recent years modern Western medicine viewed the body as a machine, independent of its emotional and spiritual side. How is this view different from Jesus' perspective?**

(3) **What experiences have you had that would confirm or deny this relationship between soul and body?**

(4) Faith

Now choose someone to read the story of the blind men that is found in Matthew 9:27-31. For a more dramatic effect, have one person read the narrator's part, another Jesus' words, and a third (or third and fourth) read the blind men's response.

Note that Jesus again is interrupted, for he was leaving the synagogue leader's home when these two men cried out to him for healing. Point out that in response to Jesus' question, "Do you believe that I am able to do this?" they responded, "Yes, Lord." They neither hesitated nor wavered. Ask these questions:

(1) **What does Jesus say in response to the men's affirmation of faith?** (See verse 29.) **?**

(2) **What does this response say to you about the role one's own faith plays in the healing process?** (This verse implies that the men are healed because they affirmed faith in Jesus. Faith can often have amazing results. Be careful, though, as you discuss this section with the class not to create the impression that those who are not healed lack faith. No one knows exactly why some persons recover from a critical illness while others—

even those who appear to be less sick—do not recover from a similar illness.)

(5) Miracles

Begin to wrap up the lesson by asking a volunteer to read Matthew 9:35-36. Ask:

(1) **What does this passage say to you about Jesus?**
(2) **What does this passage say to you about Jesus' concern for humanity?** (Point out that Jesus is interested in our physical bodies, for he heals people. But he is also very concerned about our souls, for he teaches and proclaims the good news. He has compassion and seeks laborers for the harvest. If we are to be like Jesus, we too must do all we can to help people find the wholeness that only God can give. Moreover, we must be willing to be as interruptible as Jesus was to allow this to happen.)

Spend some time now praying for persons who are ill. If your group is small, gather in a circle and hold hands. Invite students to pray just a sentence or two, such as "Healing God, I lift up my friend Jim who has cancer. I believe that you are present, willing, and able to heal him if that is your will." Do not press anyone to pray aloud by insisting that each student take a turn around the circle, but do encourage each one to do so. End the prayer with a thanksgiving for God's healing mercies.

Conclude this part of the lesson by distributing hymnals and asking students to sing or read in unison a song that relates to healing. If you have access to *The United Methodist Hymnal*, consider using "Heal Us, Emmanuel, Hear Our Prayer" (no. 266, based in part on Matthew 9:20-22), "Heal Me, Hands of Jesus" (no. 262), or "When Jesus the Healer Passed Through Galilee" (no. 263).

Before dismissing the group, be sure to offer at least one of the ideas below so that students can live out today's lesson in the week ahead.

HELPING CLASS MEMBERS ACT

Suggest that students pay particular attention this week to someone who is ill or grieving the loss of a loved one. Encourage them to do some act of kindness, which may be as simple yet meaningful as taking the time to listen to this person's concerns and respond appropriately.

Since this week's readings have focused on healing miracles, ask the students to contemplate what they really believe about these miracles. Have they, or someone they know, ever experienced a healing that doctors did not expect? Would they describe these events as miraculous? Why or why not? What role do they believe Christ played in such situations?

Recommend that students block out some time to write in their spiritual journals. Tell them to think about areas in their own lives where they need to experience Christ's compassionate touch so that they might be made whole. Encourage them to pour their hearts out, just as the people we studied today did.

PLANNING FOR NEXT SUNDAY

Next week's lesson, "Thinking About Jesus' Power," looks at selected verses from Matthew 12:22-45. In this scene, the question of the source of Jesus' power arises. Is he able to cast out demons because, as the Pharisees believe, evil forces empower him? Or does Jesus' power come from somewhere else, as his own response to their accusations makes clear?

THINKING ABOUT JESUS' POWER

PREVIEWING THE LESSON

Lesson Scripture: Matthew 12:22-32, 38-40
Background Scripture: Matthew 12:22-45
Key Verse: Matthew 12:30

Focus of the Lesson:
Some people opposed Jesus because they thought that one sent by God could not have miraculous power over demons.

Main Question of the Lesson:
If we really had our druthers, what would we do with them?

This lesson will enable adult learners to:
(1) overhear the exchange between Jesus and his opponents.
(2) consider their own resistance to Jesus' power.
(3) respond by acting in accordance with their decision to be "for" Jesus.

Today's lesson may be outlined as follows:
(1) Introduction
(2) Resistance
(3) Sign
(4) Emptiness

FOCUSING ON THE MAIN QUESTION

In the Broadway musical of the same name, Li'l Abner sings, "If I had my druthers...I'd rather have my druthers ...than anything else I know." He defines his druthers in negative terms—not having to do anything he doesn't want to do. So he makes no commitment to a job or to Daisy Mae. This then frees him up to do anything he wants to do—go fishing, lie in the sun, whatever. It sounds so good that probably most of us resonate with Li'l Abner. To have our druthers means that we can play golf or bridge or travel or garden or what-

ever—as long as it is what we want to do, when we want to do it, with no external compulsion to interfere.

If we really had our druthers, what would we do with them? That is our main question.

The druthers, of course, are always affected by some external force or other. Our health permits some things and denies others, as do our financial resources, the situation of loved ones, and a dozen other factors. With whatever grace we can muster, we at last make our peace with

---

these realities. The trick is to want what we can have, to want to do what we must do, to want what is best. But this is easier said than done, for all too often we read life the way a person who has dyslexia reads a page. The letters and words are all there, but putting them in the correct order to draw the right conclusion is the difficulty.

This is the problem the Pharisees have in today's lesson. The power of Christ is there in the exorcism, but to read it properly would result in a commitment they were unable to make. That power is enabling and transforming, but it is not coercive. The Pharisees could walk away from it as easily as we can ignore the cross. When we read it properly, however, when we understand that our ultimate welfare is bound up in it, then we commit to it. Such a commitment, as our key verse has it, places us "with" Christ. That is where we want to be. Then, strengthened and inspired by the Spirit, gathering with Christ turns out to be our druthers.

READING THE SCRIPTURE

NRSV

Matthew 12:22-32, 38-40

22 Then they brought to him a demoniac who was blind and mute; and he cured him, so that the one who had been mute could speak and see. 23 All the crowds were amazed and said, "Can this be the Son of David?" 24 But when the Pharisees heard it, they said, "It is only by Beelzebul, the ruler of the demons, that this fellow casts out the demons." 25 He knew what they were thinking and said to them, "Every kingdom divided against itself is laid waste, and no city or house divided against itself will stand. 26 If Satan casts out Satan, he is divided against himself; how then will his kingdom stand? 27 If I cast out demons by Beelzebul, by whom do your own exorcists cast them out? Therefore they will be your judges. 28 But if it is by the Spirit of God that I cast out demons, then the kingdom of God has come to you. 29 Or how can one enter a strong man's house and plunder his property, without first tying up the strong man? Then indeed the house can be plundered. **30 Whoever is not with me is against me, and whoever does not gather with me scatters.** 31 Therefore I tell you, people will be forgiven for every sin and blasphemy, but blasphemy against the Spirit will not be forgiven. 32 Whoever

Key Verse

NIV

Matthew 12:22-32, 38-40

22Then they brought him a demon-possessed man who was blind and mute, and Jesus healed him, so that he could both talk and see. 23All the people were astonished and said, "Could this be the Son of David?"

24But when the Pharisees heard this, they said, "It is only by Beelzebub, the prince of demons, that this fellow drives out demons."

25Jesus knew their thoughts and said to them, "Every kingdom divided against itself will be ruined, and every city or household divided against itself will not stand. 26If Satan drives out Satan, he is divided against himself. How then can his kingdom stand? 27And if I drive out demons by Beelzebub, by whom do your people drive them out? So then, they will be your judges. 28But if I drive out demons by the Spirit of God, then the kingdom of God has come upon you.

29"Or again, how can anyone enter a strong man's house and carry off his possessions unless he first ties up the strong man? Then he can rob his house.

30"He who is not with me is against me, and he who does not gather with me scatters. 31And so I tell you, every sin and blasphemy will be forgiven men, but the blas-

Ke
Ve

speaks a word against the Son of Man will be forgiven, but whoever speaks against the Holy Spirit will not be forgiven, either in this age or in the age to come."

38 Then some of the scribes and Pharisees said to him, "Teacher, we wish to see a sign from you." 39 But he answered them, "An evil and adulterous generation asks for a sign, but no sign will be given to it except the sign of the prophet Jonah. 40 For just as Jonah was three days and three nights in the belly of the sea monster, so for three days and three nights the Son of Man will be in the heart of the earth."

phemy against the Spirit will not be forgiven. ³²Anyone who speaks a word against the Son of Man will be forgiven, but anyone who speaks against the Holy Spirit will not be forgiven, either in this age or in the age to come."

³⁸Then some of the Pharisees and teachers of the law said to him, "Teacher, we want to see a miraculous sign from you."

³⁹He answered, "A wicked and adulterous generation asks for a miraculous sign! But none will be given it except the sign of the prophet Jonah. ⁴⁰For as Jonah was three days and three nights in the belly of a huge fish, so the Son of Man will be three days and three nights in the heart of the earth."

UNDERSTANDING THE SCRIPTURE

Matthew 12:22-24. The miracle itself is so briefly mentioned in verse 22 that we are given no details; for the point is the varying reactions, and so it functions as a trigger. The people are so amazed that they begin to wonder if Jesus could be the Son of David, even if He doesn't quite fit their notion of a proper Messiah. Lest they be gathered, however, the Pharisees step in to scatter—to use the symbolism of our key verse—nipping such speculation in the bud with the accusation of sorcery.

Matthew 12:25-29. Jesus replies with a four-point argument, from the premise that Satan controls lesser devils, much as God controls angels, and that a state of war exists between the two kingdoms. It is a truism that no organization, from the largest to the smallest, from the nation to the family, can remain intact in the face of civil war. If, then, the charge of sorcery were to be true, Satan would be working against himself, which is absurd; for the possessed represent the growing edge of his kingdom.

Jesus' second point begins with the Jewish exorcists who are recognized as legitimate by the Pharisees (12:27). His com-

ment means that if they cast out demons by the power of God, then Jesus also must do it by the power of God. Unless they do in fact operate through Beelzebul, the exorcists will judge the Pharisees for attributing their good work to an evil power. The critics can't have it both ways, giving one power to their own exorcists and an opposite power to Jesus. Beelzebul obviously is Satan, even though the exact derivation is not clear. The "Beel" is from "Baal," of course, which means "master" or "lord" and then is the name of the Canaanite god. At issue is the "zebul"—whether Lord of the House, or of Dung, or of the Flies (the Baal-zebub of 2 Kings 1:2).

Since the Pharisees can't admit that their own exorcists work by the power of Beelzebul, they must admit that Jesus also works by the Spirit of God. The third point in the argument moves from the Spirit to the kingdom of God (12:28). Note that the Kingdom's presence is not inferred from exorcisms as such. After all, the Pharisees have their own exorcists. It is, rather, the "I" that is significant; for the exorcisms do not stand alone. They are part of the package, supporting, along with the other miracles, the preaching.

The presence of the Kingdom, bound up as it is with the person of Jesus, leads into the fourth point, that Jesus has defeated Satan (12:29). The exorcisms demonstrate the victory, for the strong man must be rendered powerless before his house can be plundered. Isaiah had posed a similar question: "Can the prey be taken from the mighty?" (Isaiah 49:24). If Satan is the strong man, then Jesus, as John the Baptist has declared, is the more powerful one (Matthew 3:11). The binding occurs at the temptation (4:11), and so Satan falls like lightning from heaven (Luke 10:18).

Matthew 12:30-37. Even though the ultimate victory is not in doubt, a hard, dangerous struggle yet remains. Verse 30 requires us to throw our weight to one side or the other. Our words and deeds flow out of that decision. Just as fruit reveals the kind of tree (12:33), so the words we speak reveal our nature, whether good or evil. The treasure (12:35) is the inner nature, "the real me." We can only speak according to what is there. To call good evil, as in the accusation of sorcery, therefore, is to be evil. If our words reveal us, then by our words we are justified or condemned (12:37). Verse 36 goes beyond out-and-out evil speech to include the words that are merely careless. These words are idle, useless, ineffective. Nothing comes of them. They reflect the lost opportunities of a wasted discipleship.

Matthew 12:38-45. The title "teacher" in verse 38 is a negative clue. Although a term of respect, in Matthew it is used by those who are not likely to become disciples. (See, for example, 9:11; 17:24; and 19:16.) The adultery in verse 39 is symbolic rather than realistic. When the covenant relationship is described as a marriage (see Hosea 2 and Revelation 19:7), then faithlessness or apostasy is adultery. For the house in verse 44 as a symbol for a human being, compare 1 Corinthians 3:16.

INTERPRETING THE SCRIPTURE

Resistance

Something makes an impression—a blind, mute demoniac is healed before our very eyes, a prayer uttered more out of desperation than out of faith has been answered, a power to endure is attributed to Christ, whatever—and we begin to wonder what it all means. Like the crowd that presses close to watch in Matthew 12:23, we too are surprised. Is there even more here than meets the eye? Could this one really be the Son of David, the promised one who will actualize our dreams? The crowd is not there yet. There is no confession of faith in Jesus. But they keep on saying (which is the intent of the verb tense in Greek that is translated as "said" in the NRSV and NIV) "it can't be? . . . can it? . . . perhaps?" They are on the verge, edging closer to faith. Will they go ahead or back away?

Then the bystanders, in this case the Pharisees, act quickly to tip the balance against any forward movement into faith. For in verse 24 they speak to the awed crowd. The reality of the miracle itself is not the issue. What does it mean? Jesus cannot be the Son of David, doing these things by the power of God; for then, as verse 28 notes, they would have to confess that the kingdom of God actually is involved in this radical teacher from Nazareth. Moreover, they would have to take his teaching seriously. But his new wine puts an intolerable strain upon the old bottles. So if he dazzles by means of Beelzebul, who is identified as Satan in verse 26, then the miracles are discredited and the teaching is nullified.

The general forgiveness of verse 31 highlights the single exception, thereby stressing the seriousness of the warning concerning the unforgivable sin. The sin is very narrowly defined as the deliberate confusion of good and evil. The light is called darkness. This means that no other sin, however serious, can be called unforgivable. The parallel statement at Mark 3:30, moreover, suggests that the key is persistence in the behavior. The opponents "were saying" that Jesus has an unclean spirit. The verb tense in the Greek indicates repetition and therefore expresses a fixed attitude. No single instance is decisive, but at last the settled outlook is condemned because it is impervious to grace. We can't make this point from Matthew's verb, but we can make it from last week's background scripture.

Forgiveness, of course, is the nexus of repentance and grace. If the grace is through Christ, and if the sin is the refusal of that grace on the score that it is demonic, then obviously there will be no repentance, and therefore no forgiveness. The existence of such a sin, furthermore, is denied by those who will not repent; and so Christ's warning is nonsense. For those who do repent, however, and who claim that grace in Christ, the wideness of God's mercy and the broad dimensions of the divine pardon are words of comfort. Anyone who worries about it can be sure that he or she has not committed the unforgivable sin.

Sign

The high point of the resistance is the accusation of sorcery, turning good into evil. But there is another resistance, not so overt but no less deadly to faith—the request for a sign to help us overcome our unbelief (12:38). A sign, of course, is anything that points beyond itself to something else. It may be as neutral as a kiss to identify a person (26:48) or an overcast sky to warn of an impending storm (16:2-3). Mostly, however, it has the more dynamic sense of pointing to God. Although these pointers tend to be miracles, it is important to note that Matthew, Mark, and Luke use other words for the actual miracles. They become signs only when they reveal—and things other than miracles can also be signs if they reveal. This pointing feature highlights the problem with signs: they can lead us away from (24:24) as well as toward God.

At any rate, who can blame the scribes and Pharisees for wanting some help with their faith? For which of us has not wondered how much more vibrant our discipleship would be if only we had seen with our own eyes? Except that they saw, and apparently it did them no good. For in verse 38 they "answer" (NKJV; NRSV and NIV omit this verb) by asking for a sign. They have seen the healing miracle and responded to the crowd by accusing Jesus of sorcery. They have heard Jesus' rebuttal in verses 25-37. Now they answer the rebuttal by asking for something more impressive than an exorcism or a healing miracle. We can always hope that their request is a genuine search for help against unbelief (as Mark 9:24); but Matthew's characterization in 16:1 as a hostile test or challenge explains Jesus' anger.

The "signs of the times" (16:3) are obvious—the gospel is preached, people are healed in body and soul, the Spirit is active. The kingdom of God is casting its shadow ahead of its arrival, and faith is the freely given commitment to the Agent through whom it comes. Last week we saw that faith precedes the miracle. So whatever generates the faith is not the kind of sign the scribes and Pharisees are demanding. Such a sign, in fact, by inducing an inescapable knowledge actually prevents faith. For when the sign from heaven comes (16:1), when the sign of the Son of Man appears in the sky (24:30), it is too late for a response. Meanwhile, to ask for the sign that proves Jesus' identity is to repeat the devil's effort in the wilderness. (See the lesson for December 12.) Thus, those who demand such a sign are described as evil (12:39). We are, instead, to content ourselves with the drawing to Christ that is mentioned in John 6:44. For us, after the Pentecost event of Acts 2, that drawing is through the Holy Spirit.

There is, however, a sign for us after all—the sign of Jonah. The first aspect of that sign compares the whale's belly with the tomb (12:40). Just as Jonah was swallowed and vomited up again, so the Son of Man will be buried and then will be raised from the dead. This is the first prediction of the death and resurrection. For us at least, after the fact, the sign is foundational; for it points the cross and empty tomb toward God. The second aspect of the sign demonstrates the possibility of faith as a response to preaching. If a prophet brought Ninevites to repentance, surely the Son of Man should bring us to faith (12:41). The empty tomb and the testimony of believers, therefore, are all the sign we'll ever need.

Emptiness

The empty house in the parable of the unclean spirit (12:43-45) suggests yet another resistance, no less deadly to the spiritual life than the others, even if less overt. Douglas R. A. Hare has pointed out that "the word here translated 'empty' is not the ordinary Greek word with this meaning but a most unusual one; it is not an adjective but a participle meaning 'having leisure,' that is, not occupied with work. Perhaps our English word 'unoccupied' should be used to preserve the wordplay. The house is carefully cleaned and decorated in preparation for a special visitor or new tenant, the Messiah perhaps, but it remains unoccupied. It is 'at leisure,' that is, uninvolved and unresponsive, unwilling to take the risk of a commitment."

Hare's point is nailed down by the only other occurrence of the verb in the New Testament. When we have, as Li'l Abner calls them, our druthers, when no external pressure schedules our day, what do we do with our time and energy? Do we remain "at leisure"? Paul thought we might use that leisure to "devote" ourselves to prayer (1 Corinthians 7:5). "Empty" and "devote," therefore, different translations for the same verb, suggest positive as well as negative potentials. In the parable the exorcism creates the possibility for blessing. Unless we take advantage of the demon's absence to repent and to strengthen our commitment to the Lord, we end up frittering away that possibility. A nominal conversion, therefore, that does not fill the vacuum with faithful discipleship never quite grasps the blessing.

Our key verse, Matthew 12:30, is to be seen against the background of this fight to the death between Jesus and the strong man. We are all swept up into this "winner-take-all" struggle; for because of its ultimacy, we all have a stake in its outcome. Therefore, we are not allowed to remain on the sidelines. Indifference to Christ thus turns out to be hostility rather than indifference. There are two possible referents for the gathering and scattering—a flock of sheep or a grain harvest. In either case the gathering is to salvation and the scattering is to condemnation. Since scattering is whatever inhibits gathering, indifference qualifies by adding a drag to the more active resistance. So we really have chosen sides after all—even if we deny it.

SHARING THE SCRIPTURE

PREPARING TO TEACH

Preparing Our Hearts

Our devotional reading for this week is from Matthew 12:1-14, which precedes today's scripture lesson. This passage, like the one you will read for today, shows Jesus in conflict with the religious leaders. They deem him a lawbreaker because he apparently breaks the sabbath laws. Jesus, however, responds with examples from the Hebrew Scriptures to demonstrate the priority of human need and service to God. As you read this passage, see yourself as one of Jesus' opponents. How are you similar to the opponents? Before you answer, recall that these folks were upstanding members of the Jewish community who took their beliefs and relationship with God very seriously. Pray that God will lead you to be more open to persons who, for whatever reason, do not appear to you to be "church-member material."

Now turn to today's lesson in Matthew 12:22-45, paying particular attention to verses 22-32 and 38-40. Here the crux of the problem is the source of Jesus' authority. Does he get his power from God or from Satan? Again, put yourself in the shoes of the religious leaders. From their perspective, does their argument make sense? How does Jesus try to counter their insistence that "only by Beelzebul" can he do what he is doing? Think about what you would say to someone who asked you about the source of Jesus' power. Pray for the Spirit's guidance as you prepare to lead the class.

Preparing Our Minds

Review Matthew 12:22-45. Read this lesson carefully. As you prepare for this week's session, be aware of the terms "Beelzebul" and "the strong man" that are discussed in the Understanding the Scripture section, as well as the unforgivable sin that is described under "Resistance" in the Interpreting the Scripture section. You may want to get additional information on these terms from a Bible dictionary or commentary.

Preparing Our Learning Space

Have on hand:
- several Bibles
- optional paper and pencils.

LEADING THE CLASS

(1) Introduction

Begin the session by lifting up the main question: **If we really had our druthers, what would we do with them?** Encourage class members to state what they would do if they could do anything they wanted. Tell them that time, money, age, health, and geographic location do not matter.

Then read or retell Focusing on the Main Question. Be sure to point out, as this section concludes, that being "with Christ" (as the key verse from Matthew 12:30 indicates) is where we who are Christian really want to be. Gathering with Christ, then, is our druthers.

Provide a few moments for silent reflection. Ask students to meditate on the question of whether or not being with Christ is truly their heart's desire.

(2) Resistance

Choose a volunteer to read Matthew 12:22-32. Encourage the students to imagine themselves in the crowd as Jesus healed the demoniac. Ask:
1. **What would you have thought about Jesus had you seen this miracle?**
2. **Would you have seriously considered the possibility that Jesus was the**

?

Messiah, or would you have denounced him as a servant of Satan? Explain the reason for your answer.

(3) **What motive do you think the Pharisees have for attributing Jesus' power to Satan?**

Call attention to the argument that Jesus makes in verses 25-30. You may want to present the following information in a brief lecture using material for these verses as found in the Understanding the Scripture portion. Or you may prefer to ask these questions.

?

(1) **What four points does Jesus give to refute the Pharisees' idea that he is an agent of Satan?**

(2) **Do you find Jesus' argument credible? If you do not, where do you believe the logic breaks down?** (Allow students their own opinions, but as you will note, Jesus' points are tightly reasoned.)

(3) **What do you understand about the unforgivable sin that Jesus speaks of in verses 31-32?** (The point here is that Jesus is talking about the deliberate confusion of good and evil, where good is seen as evil and evil is seen as good. This kind of thinking constitutes rebellion against God.)

Now direct the students to read aloud, in unison if possible, today's key verse from Matthew 12:30. Provide meditation time for the students to each consider how they are—or are not—with Christ. As an option, distribute paper and pencils so that they may write down their thoughts.

(3) Sign

Ask someone to read Matthew 12:38-40. Note that a sign can be anything that points beyond itself. For example, a decorated tree can be a sign of Christmas, while a robin is a sign of spring. Clarify that in the context of our lesson a sign is something that points toward God. What the scribes and Pharisees were requesting was some tangible indication of who Jesus really was. Ask:

?

(1) **Why won't Jesus honor the scribes and Pharisees' request for a sign?** (What they are really trying to do is test him. They were obviously looking for something more than a healing or exorcism.)

(2) **What point is Jesus making when he calls his questioners "an evil and adulterous generation"?** (They were adulterers because they had turned away from God. The prophets had also used the image of adultery to describe the Israelites because they had turned from God and worshiped idols. You can find some references to this adultery in Jeremiah 3:8; Ezekiel 23:37; and Hosea 2:2-9. Jesus' questioners were evil because they wanted some sign to prove his identity.)

(3) **What is the sign of Jonah to which Jesus refers?** (Check the comparison between Jonah's three days in the belly of the whale and Jesus' three days in the tomb. Jesus is saying, in effect, that his empty tomb is all the sign that will ever be needed to demonstrate who he is.)

Divide the class into pairs or teams. Ask each group to think about the needs that people have today for a sign of God's presence. You may want to suggest that they think about specific situations in which people seek signs of assurance that God really is with them. Such circumstances might include serious illness, the death of a loved one, mental or emotional distress, financial problems, family discord, or an unwanted job loss or change. Encourage the groups to share examples of how they have seen God at work in these challenging situations in their own lives and/or in the lives of others.

If time permits, you may want to have each group share an example or two with the entire class.

(4) Emptiness

Read the parable in Matthew 12:43-45, part of today's background scripture. Next, read or retell "Emptiness" as it appears in Interpreting the Scripture. Be sure the class understands that the word *empty* is better translated as "unoccupied" in this context. Encourage a few volunteers to restate the meaning of this teaching in their own words. They might say something like this: "We can let go of evil, but when we fail to replace it with good, the evil will soon return to manifest itself within us."

Now ask the students to look again at verse 30, our key verse. Note that the teaching illustrates the point of the key verse. The person from whom evil had been exorcised may not appear to be against Jesus. However, because this individual did not replace the evil with the good that Jesus has to offer, he or she really is against Jesus. The person does not "gather" with Jesus unto salvation but instead "scatters" unto condemnation. Neutrality (that is, simply the absence of evil) is insufficient. Indifference to Christ is actually hostility.

As time permits, ask these questions:

[?]

(1) **What would you say to those who claim that they don't need Christ in their lives because they live good moral and ethical lives?**

(2) **What does this passage suggest to the church in general and to your own congregation in particular about its need to be proactive in trying to bring unchurched persons to Christ?**

[?]

Before the class leaves, lift up at least one of the suggestions below so that students will have some specific ideas for putting the lesson into action this week.

HELPING CLASS MEMBERS ACT

Challenge class members to examine their own commitment to Christ. Do their thoughts, words, and deeds reflect a strong commitment, or do they need to make some changes in order to be "for" Christ? Suggest that as they prayerfully consider this challenge they write their reactions in a spiritual journal.

Encourage students to listen with an open mind to people who claim to have experienced a miracle (perhaps an unexpected healing) in their lives. Have them think about how this miracle is a sign of God's presence.

Tell the class to be alert this week for examples of resistance to Christ in themselves and in others. Recommend that they find ways, possibly through prayer and other spiritual disciplines, to overcome this resistance so as to draw closer to Christ.

PLANNING FOR NEXT SUNDAY

Next week you will study the final lesson in this unit, "Thinking About Rewards." The familiar parable of the laborers in the vineyard will be our focus. Ask students to read Matthew 19:16–20:16. Encourage them to think honestly about how they would have felt had they come early in the morning or late in the afternoon.

THINKING ABOUT REWARDS

PREVIEWING THE LESSON

Lesson Scripture: Matthew 20:1-16
Background Scripture: Matthew 19:16–20:16
Key Verse: Matthew 20:16

Focus of the Lesson:
The parable of the laborers in the vineyard shows how those who are in the Kingdom, regardless of when they arrived, will be rewarded by God.

Main Question of the Lesson:
If we can't earn our salvation, if it is a gift unrelated to our conduct, then what motivates us to work at a decent life?

This lesson will enable adult learners to:
(1) encounter one of Jesus' teachings about the kingdom of God.
(2) confront their own concerns about inequity.
(3) respond by treating others with generosity.

Today's lesson may be outlined as follows:
(1) Introduction
(2) The Evil Eye
(3) The Vineyard
(4) The Goodness
(5) The Reward

FOCUSING ON THE MAIN QUESTION

In *The Great Divorce* C. S. Lewis describes a group of ghosts who take a bus from hell to heaven. At the bus stop each one is met by a heavenly escort and must decide whether to go on ahead into heaven or get back on the bus and return to hell. Big Ghost is pretty upset when his escort turns out to be a fellow he had known, one Len who had murdered Jack. He bursts out, "I gone straight all my life. I don't say I was a religious man and I don't say I had no faults, far from it. But I done my best all my life, see? I done my best by everyone, that's the sort of chap I was. I never asked for anything that wasn't mine by rights."

Len replies that he didn't get his rights or he wouldn't be in heaven. "You will not get yours either. You'll get something far better." But Big Ghost thinks he has earned the blessing. "I only want my rights. I'm not asking for anybody's bleeding charity." Len advises him to "ask for the Bleeding Charity. Everything is here for the asking and nothing can be bought." Big Ghost is bitter at such unfairness. "That may be very well for you, I daresay. If they choose to let in a bloody murderer all because he makes a poor mouth at the last moment, that's their lookout. But I don't see myself going in the same boat with you, see? Why should I? I don't want charity. I'm a decent man and if I had my rights I'd have been here long ago . . . ."

Len makes one more effort. "You weren't a decent man and you didn't do your best. We none of us were and we none of us did." Unfortunately Big Ghost insists upon justice rather than mercy. "I'd rather be damned than go along with you. I came here to get my rights, see? Not to go snivelling along on charity tied onto your apron-strings."

And this dialogue leads us into our main question: **If we can't earn our salvation, if it is a gift unrelated to our conduct, then what motivates us to work at a decent life?**

READING THE SCRIPTURE

NRSV
Matthew 20:1-16

1 "For the kingdom of heaven is like a landowner who went out early in the morning to hire laborers for his vineyard. 2 After agreeing with the laborers for the usual daily wage, he sent them into his vineyard. 3 When he went out about nine o'clock, he saw others standing idle in the marketplace; 4 and he said to them, 'You also go into the vineyard, and I will pay you whatever is right.' So they went. 5 When he went out again about noon and about three o'clock, he did the same. 6 And about five o'clock he went out and found others standing around; and he said to them, 'Why are you standing here idle all day?' 7 They said to him, 'Because no one has hired us.' He said to them, 'You also go into the vineyard.' 8 When evening came, the owner of the vineyard said to his manager, 'Call the laborers and give them their pay, beginning with the last and then going to the first.' 9 When those hired about five o'clock came, each of them received the usual daily wage. 10 Now when the first came, they thought they would receive more; but each of them also received the usual daily wage. 11 And when they received it, they grumbled

NIV
Matthew 20:1-16

[1]"For the kingdom of heaven is like a landowner who went out early in the morning to hire men to work in his vineyard. [2]He agreed to pay them a denarius for the day and sent them into his vineyard.

[3]"About the third hour he went out and saw others standing in the marketplace doing nothing. [4]He told them, 'You also go and work in my vineyard, and I will pay you whatever is right.' [5]So they went.

"He went out again about the sixth hour and the ninth hour and did the same thing. [6]About the eleventh hour he went out and found still others standing around. He asked them, 'Why have you been standing here all day long doing nothing?'

[7]"'Because no one has hired us,' they answered.

"He said to them, 'You also go and work in my vineyard.'

[8]"When evening came, the owner of the vineyard said to his foreman, 'Call the workers and pay them their wages, beginning with the last ones hired and going on to the first.'

[9]"The workers who were hired about the eleventh hour came and each received a

against the landowner, 12 saying, 'These last worked only one hour, and you have made them equal to us who have borne the burden of the day and the scorching heat.' 13 But he replied to one of them, 'Friend, I am doing you no wrong; did you not agree with me for the usual daily wage? 14 Take what belongs to you and go; I choose to give to this last the same as I give to you. 15 Am I not allowed to do what I choose with what belongs to me? Or are you envious because I am generous?'

Key Verse **16 So the last will be first, and the first will be last."**

denarius. ¹⁰So when those came who were hired first, they expected to receive more. But each one of them also received a denarius. ¹¹When they received it, they began to grumble against the landowner. ¹²'These men who were hired last worked only one hour,' they said, 'and you have made them equal to us who have borne the burden of the work and the heat of the day.'

¹³"But he answered one of them, 'Friend, I am not being unfair to you. Didn't you agree to work for a denarius? ¹⁴Take your pay and go. I want to give the man who was hired last the same as I gave you. ¹⁵Don't I have the right to do what I want with my own money? Or are you envious because I am generous?'

¹⁶"So the last will be first, and the first will be last." Key Verse

---

UNDERSTANDING THE SCRIPTURE

Matthew 19:16-22. "Teacher, what good deed must I do to have eternal life?" is no trick question, such as those the Pharisees and Sadducees will pose about taxes and resurrection (22:15-32). The rich young man is sincere, and therein lies the point of the passage. He has already done everything the law expects him to do (19:20). But somehow he senses that there is something else and that Jesus knows what it is. So what is that final good deed that will nail down eternal life as its reward (19:16)? Jesus picks up on the "good" in the good deed and reminds the young man that only God is good. So if God is the very definition of the good, the "good deeds" are spelled out in the commandments (19:17-19).

Jesus takes at face value the young man's statement in verse 20 that he has actually kept the commandments. If he has not measured up to the intensity of the Sermon on the Mount, he has nevertheless done as well as anyone could reasonably expect. Far from challenging this assess-

ment, Jesus calls the man into discipleship (19:21), perhaps even to join the Twelve. The perfection is a radical commitment to God that does not have to compete with any worldly attachment. The young man, unfortunately, cannot make such a commitment. His money stands in the way. Recognizing the critical importance of the choice, he regrets his inability to rise to the occasion (19:22).

Matthew 19:23-26. The sight of the rich young man sadly walking away moves Jesus to comment that it is hard for a rich person to enter the kingdom of God (19:23). It is, in fact, about as hard as trying to squeeze a camel through the eye of a needle (19:24). The disciples are dismayed. If such a fine young man as this can't make it, who can (19:25)? Jesus agrees that it is beyond the reach of human effort (19:26). But it is well within God's reach, and so salvation is possible only when we trust our all to the divine grace. It is especially difficult to have money and not to depend upon it—but not impossible, as the case of Zacchaeus demonstrates (Luke 19:1-10). For this young man, however, the money interferes with his commitment.

Matthew 19:27-30. The Twelve, in contrast, have walked away from their worldly possessions. What are they walking toward (19:27)? Jesus points to the climax of all things, the renewal (19:28) at the Last Judgment, when the rabbi from Nazareth is enthroned in glory. Those who share Jesus' fate now will also share his fate then. (See also Luke 22:27-30.) Eternal life will more than compensate for whatever sacrifices are required along the way (19:29).

Matthew 20:1-16. Note that the parable is bracketed by the saying about the first and the last, 19:30 and 20:16, thereby shaping its interpretation. The saying also links the parable to the preceding material about rewards. Scholars have placed it within a number of contexts. Are the first and the last (1) those who have rejected Jesus and those who have followed him, or (2) the scribes and Pharisees objecting to Jesus' inclusion of tax collectors and other sinners, or (3) Jewish versus Gentile Christians, or (4) those who have been Christians all their lives wondering about the "Johnny-come-latelies" with their last-minute conversions, or even (5) a warning to the church leadership about pride?

The parable is not about judgment, for none are sent away empty-handed. The critical point, therefore, is that they all receive the same wage and that the wage does not correlate with their labor. No one is favored over anyone else. Some scholars stress the hiring as the invitation to enter the Kingdom, while others emphasize the undivided denarius as the redemptive work of the cross. The parable's punch, of course, is its insistence that you and I have not deserved our salvation either. Perhaps we can't help wondering why those fellows stood about all day without getting hired when there is so much work to be had. Maybe, we think, there is a reason why no one wanted to hire them.

If the elder brother (see Luke 15:11-32) really doesn't want to work for his father, he naturally resents the reception given the younger brother. But suppose, just for the sake of argument, that it is a privilege to work in the vineyard, that the work of discipleship is a joy rather than a burden. Then perhaps we can be glad at the final inclusion of the "last"—just sorry that they missed out on so much joyous discipleship.

INTERPRETING THE SCRIPTURE

The Evil Eye

The point of the parable flows out of the complaint made by the first workers. They had worked hard all day long and received the same wage as those who had put in a single hour. This strikes us as unfair because we think that reward should correlate with effort. But it is this very desire for justice or fair play that is condemned in Matthew 20:15 as the evil eye (NKJV). The eye enables us to see and thereby to understand. The eye becomes good or evil according to what it sees and the behavior that it stimulates. So the eye can be associated with adultery (2 Peter 2:14) and hatred (1 John 2:11). The evil eye is especially dangerous because it blocks the light (Matthew 6:23). Here most of the translations interpret the evil eye as envy (NIV and NRSV) or jealousy (GNB).

In *The Bible in the Pulpit*, Leander E. Keck has suggested that the

> story illumines who we are by the way it exposes our sympathies. The way we relate to those who worked most and to those who worked least shows us the truth about ourselves.

Most of us identify with those who worked longest not simply because we think *they* got a raw deal but because we think *we* get one too. Like the day-long workers in the story, even though we get exactly what we bargained for, we begin to feel gypped when we see someone do better. The farmer pointed out, you recall, that he was not unfair to them, because he paid them exactly what he said he would. It is the sight of others, who worked less for the same reward, that first makes us feel cheated, then feel sorry for ourselves.... We assume that if God is...fair...we will come out ahead because we deserve more.... Few of us identify with those who were hired near quitting time and got paid more than they earned. These are the men who expected fairness but benefitted from goodness, from a sheer generosity that ignored achievement....

We resist identifying with those who benefit from goodness because we hate to acknowledge that we did not deserve the goodness we ourselves received. We tell ourselves that we deserve even our good fortune. "It couldn't have happened to a nicer guy." The idea that in the mystery of things we get better than we deserve is too disturbing to our way of valuing ourselves.

The Vineyard

Such disturbance, however, is the critical foundation for spiritual growth. The last hired are paid first, therefore, so that the first hired will be sure to know how much they receive. This rubs their noses in the unfairness, so to speak, thereby shocking us into reexamining our relationships with God and with our fellow believers. For the work is in the vineyard. This means that it has nothing to do with management or unions or labor law or welfare reform. In a real work-a-day vineyard—or office or factory—such action would be a recipe for disaster. Sometimes we turn the parable's vineyard into a real vineyard by stressing the pressure to get the harvest in, the tough economic conditions, and even the need to overpay workers on occasion in order to have a labor force available when needed.

Actually, it is not a real vineyard at all. It is, rather, a symbol for the blessing that God intends for us. The covenant people, in fact, are the vine that the Lord brought forth out of bondage in Egypt and planted in the promised land (Psalm 80:8). Unfortunately, however, the vine produced worthless wild grapes instead of the expected good fruit (Isaiah 5:1-7). This is the vineyard that appears twice more in Matthew (21:28-32 and 21:33-41). In all three cases, from the vine in the vineyard as the covenant people in the promised land, the vineyard has become the kingdom of God that houses the fruitful vine. John 15:1-11 defines this vine as Christ; and then, by extension as the branches, those who are "in Christ."

Matthew's three vineyard parables deal with the kind of branches that can draw their sustenance from this Vine. We must learn the lesson embodied in Jack Benny's famous quip when he was given an award: "I don't deserve this, but I have arthritis, and I don't deserve that either!" When finally we identify with the last hired instead of with the first hired, with the prodigal son instead of the elder brother, understanding the blessing as a gift rather than as payment for services rendered, we are grateful for the grace flowing into us from our Vine. The parable of the two sons (21:28-32) offers us a second chance, but the parable of the tenants (21:33-44) warns us that there is a limit to God's patience.

The Goodness

The complaint of the first hired, labeled the evil eye, contrasts in Matthew 20:15 with the goodness (NKJV) of the landowner. Most of the English translations interpret goodness here as generosity. But it is a lopsided generosity that bends our word *generosity* all out of shape. For the money involved is the minimum wage for unskilled labor. How strange to call this "generous"! And the generosity to some is at the expense of discriminating against others—for the argument in verse 13 is hardly reflective of generosity. We would expect a generous man to give a bonus to the first hired rather than to stick within the letter of contractual law. This translation, moreover, unduly narrows our focus by obscuring for the English reader a whole range of passages that suggest that goodness is a wider concept than generosity.

The good is the useful, that which makes life pleasant and agreeable, while evil is the useless, that which makes life unpleasant and disagreeable. So a good tree produces edible fruit, but inedible fruit comes from a useless tree (7:17). And nourishing food is good for children (7:11). People also are good or evil according to whether they improve or degrade the quality of life for others (12:33-37). Our goodness, however, is relative; for the standard of goodness itself is the character of God (19:17). This means that the good offers to make our life pleasant and agreeable by giving us the useful gifts from heaven (7:11) that will make us fit for residence in the kingdom of heaven.

If the offer comes to us all, good and bad alike (22:10), then we have not earned the heavenly gifts. They are based on need rather than on merit. And this leads us to the problem of the first and the last. They all need a day's wage in order to provide for their families, and that need is satisfied. Rent is to be paid and groceries are to be bought, to be sure, but the parable is about entrance into the kingdom of God. This point directs our attention to a still more basic need, that of salvation through Christ. None needs more and none needs less. So all receive the same because all need the same.

The Reward

The emphasis upon need, of course, is what leads us to grace. And this runs counter to the whole idea of reward; for a reward is something that is due us, something that we have earned. But then there is no place for a Savior—unless we postulate a two-tiered blessing, greater for those who have worked their way into heaven, lesser for the undeserving lost sheep, prodigals, and debtors who have to be saved if they are to make it at all. But this kind of thinking is condemned as the evil eye. There is but a single blessing, and all receive it as a gift.

The vineyard parables all expect hard labor. But if there is no correlation between labor and reward, what happens to motivation? If everyone gets the same reward, if no one can get ahead by hard work, why not just slide by? Imagine, however, that the labor is itself the reward (25:14-30) and the discipleship is an unconscious response to the grace (25:31-46).

Leander E. Keck has pointed out the difference that the parable's teaching about grace would make in our lives. "We would understand that God is for us, whether we win, lose, or draw, and that he is for us because he wants to be, not because we maneuver him into paying us off." Keck explains that our relationship is based on God's goodness, not ours. Such knowledge frees us from delusions and helps us to accept our shadowy side. We know that success is not necessary. God will love and care for us, no matter what.

SHARING THE SCRIPTURE

PREPARING TO TEACH

Preparing Our Hearts

Today's lesson focuses our attention on rewards. Before you study the familiar parable of the vineyard, look at the devotional reading from Matthew 20:20-28. In the midst of Jesus' somber discussion with his disciples about his impending passion and death, the mother of James and John asks Jesus to reward her sons by allowing one to sit on his right and the other on his left when Jesus takes his place in the Kingdom. We may shake our heads in disgust that anyone would be so brash as to expect such rewards. Yet, take a few minutes to think about your own expectations. Do you expect to be lauded for your work as a Sunday school teacher, or as a leader in some other capacity? Why do you think you deserve accolades? As you read Jesus' answer in verses 22-23, consider what he might say to you about your own desire for special recognition.

Now read all of this week's background scripture from Matthew 19:16–20:16. Here you will first meet a rich young man who asks Jesus about the good deed he must do to inherit eternal life. Soon after he leaves, Peter asks Jesus how those who have left everything to follow him will be rewarded. Note that it is in the context of this discussion that Jesus tells the parable of the vineyard, which is the story that we will be focusing on. Again, listen for what Jesus is saying to you personally.

Preparing Our Minds

Read again all of the scripture from Matthew 19:16–20:16. Then check two subsequent references to the vineyard found in Matthew 21, the first parable in verses 28-32 and the second in verses 33-41. Also look up the references to the vineyard mentioned in John 15:1-11 and Isaiah 5:1-7.

Preparing Our Learning Space

Have on hand:
- ✔ several Bibles
- ✔ optional sack of pennies.

LEADING THE CLASS

(1) Introduction

One way to begin this week's lesson is to read or retell the information in Focusing on the Main Question.

Another way to begin is to use the fol-

lowing case study. Read it aloud and then ask these questions:

(1) Does Emily deserve what she received? Why or why not?

(2) How would you have felt had you been Tom?

(3) How would you have felt had you been Emily?

(4) In reality, was Tom short-changed? Why or why not?

Tom has worked at his job for nearly twenty years. He has been a faithful, effective worker, seldom missing a day even for illness. When a supervisory position came open in his department, he assumed that he had the inside track. Tom was really caught off guard when the management announced that Emily, a young employee with a master's degree but only five years of experience, would be his new boss.

Close this segment of the lesson by noting that Jesus tells a parable about workers in a vineyard who also are upset by perceived inequities in their workplace. Jesus uses their reaction to make a point about life in the kingdom of God. Lift up today's main question: **If we can't earn our salvation, if it is a gift unrelated to our conduct, then what motivates us to work at a decent life?**

(2) The Evil Eye

One way to make this parable come alive is to pantomime it. Indicate that a certain area of the room is the vineyard. First, ask a large group to stand together as if they are aimlessly milling around outside the vineyard area. Tell these students that they must remember the time (from early in the morning until 5 at night) that they are brought into the vineyard. Next, select one volunteer to play the part of the landowner who will invite a few persons at a time into the vineyard at each point in the story until the entire group is there by the end of verse 7. Choose a manager and, if possible, give that volunteer a sack of pennies that will be used as the payroll in verses 9-10, with each student receiving one penny.

When you have finished reading, ask the class these questions after they have returned to their seats.

(1) **If you were one of the first workers hired, how did you feel about your good fortune in being hired to earn the full day's pay that was needed to feed your family?**

(2) **If you came into the vineyard later in the day, what was your attitude toward a landowner who was willing to pay you a full day's wage for a partial day's work?**

(3) **If you had been one of the early hires, what expectations would you have had as you saw those who came later get a full paycheck?**

(4) **Try to put yourself in the landowner's place. Why do you think he paid everyone equally?**

(5) **How would you have responded to his explanation in verses 13-16?**

Conclude this segment of the lesson by reading aloud the quotation from Leander Keck's book *The Bible in the Pulpit,* found in the Interpreting the Scripture portion under "The Evil Eye." Provide a few moments for the students to meditate on their own response to Keck's observation that "The idea that in the mystery of things we get better than we deserve is too disturbing to our way of valuing ourselves."

(3) The Vineyard

Indicate that since this is a parable, not a record of a "real" situation, Jesus must be talking about something other than workers receiving a denarius in a vineyard. Ask:

(1) **To what does the vineyard refer?** (Look at the second paragraph under this heading in Interpreting the Scripture. You may want to have the students turn to other references concerning the symbolic use of "vineyard" and "vine" as

found in Psalm 80:8; Isaiah 5:1-7; Matthew 21:28-32; Matthew 21:33-41; and John 15:1-11.)

(2) **What is the meaning of this parable?** (Students may state their ideas in different words, but the idea is this: When we can identify ourselves with the last hired instead of with the first hired, we can begin to understand that our invitation to enter into the vineyard (kingdom) of God is a gift of blessing, rather than payment for services rendered. In response, we are grateful for the grace flowing into us from our Vine, Jesus Christ.)

(4) The Goodness

Use this section from the Interpreting the Scripture portion to prepare a brief lecture about "goodness," which is a much broader concept than the idea of "generosity" that is used in verse 15 of many translations.

Invite the class to respond to this idea: <u>All of us need salvation through Christ. None needs more and none needs less. So all receive the same because all need the same.</u>

(5) The Reward

Invite a few students to comment on how they feel when they work hard but do not reap the kinds of rewards they would expect from their labor. Likely you will be able to draw a parallel between their feelings and those of the workers hired early to work in the vineyard. Then ask:

(1) **If there is no correlation between labor and reward, what happens to motivation?**

(2) **If everyone gets the same reward, if no one can get ahead by hard work, why not just slide by?** (Point out that the labor itself, that is, discipleship, is its own reward.)

To conclude the lesson, you may want to read the last paragraph of "The Reward" in the Interpreting the Scripture section.

Before the students leave, offer at least

one of the activities below so that they can put the theory into practice this week.

HELPING CLASS MEMBERS ACT

Recommend that students be alert for instances when others may perceive them as acting unfairly, though they do not believe they are doing so. For example, a mother may spend more time with one child because he needs extra attention at this time, though the other children view her behavior as a show of favoritism that is unfair to them.

Encourage class members to meditate seriously this week on their attitudes toward people who they believe do not "deserve" God's love and care. How do such biases impair their ability to accept God's grace in their lives and in the lives of others?

Suggest that students take note of inequalities in the workplace. Are these real problems, or is the person who feels shabbily treated simply responding to a distorted view of his or her own self-worth? How do the students rate the kind of treatment they receive? Are they treated like everyone else, or do they receive more or less? Tell them to pray that God will help them in this situation to recognize what is fair from God's point of view.

PLANNING FOR NEXT SUNDAY

Next week we will begin the final unit for this quarter, entitled "Fulfillment of Jesus' Mission." The lesson for February 6, "The Guidance of the Word," includes Jesus' triumphal entry into Jerusalem on Palm Sunday and his astonishing act of overturning the money changers' tables. Ask the students to read Matthew 21:1-17 to prepare for the session.

UNIT 3: FULFILLMENT OF JESUS' MISSION
THE GUIDANCE OF THE WORD

PREVIEWING THE LESSON

Lesson Scripture: Matthew 21:1-13
Background Scripture: Matthew 21:1-17
Key Verse: Matthew 21:5

Focus of the Lesson:
Jesus' humble arrival in Jerusalem had been foretold in the Scriptures.

Main Question of the Lesson:
Where among those bystanders on the road to Jerusalem do we place ourselves?

This lesson will enable adult learners to:
(1) connect the story of Jesus' Palm Sunday entry into Jerusalem with scripture passages from the prophets.
(2) examine their own hearts to see where they would stand in the crowd in relation to Jesus.
(3) respond by seeking to be guided by God's word.

Today's lesson may be outlined as follows:
(1) Introduction
(2) The Earthquake
(3) The Humility
(4) The Hosanna
(5) The Temple

FOCUSING ON THE MAIN QUESTION

A couple of months before the writing of this lesson, I revisited the Maryland and West Virginia sites associated with John Brown's 1859 raid on Harper's Ferry—from the Kennedy Farm House where the raid was planned to the fire house where he was captured to the courthouse where he was tried to the field where he was hanged. The pikes with which he planned to arm the slaves enraged the South and

his demeanor on the scaffold inspired the North. The Civil War swirled out of the mix of "John Brown's body lies a'mouldering in the grave,...but his soul goes marching on" ("John Brown's Body" by Thomas Bishop).

In the Charles Town museum the wagon that carried him to the place of execution is on display. Stonewall Jackson, in command of the troops sent to keep order, had spent the night praying for the soul of the man who was to be hanged—but that's a different story for another day. The docent at the museum explained that the memory of John Brown can still evoke contradictory assessments. She told the story of a Northerner who asked a local Charles Town man, "Can you tell me where the martyr John Brown was executed?" The local replied, "No. But I can tell you where the traitor John Brown was hanged."

These differing perspectives concerning an event with significant consequences echo the varying attitudes toward an earlier event with even more awesome consequences. For here too there are those who shout "Hosanna" and will come to revere this man on a donkey as a martyr. But there are also those there who object to the Hosanna. And then there are those who wish it hadn't happened, who would rather go on with their buying and selling, like the museum docent who admitted that she really would prefer that we stop coming to Charles Town.

These perspectives lead us to our main question: **Where among those bystanders on the road to Jerusalem do we place ourselves?** Do we shout Hosanna, or do we object to those who are shouting? The event itself won't go away because its consequences have forever changed our lives. America is different because of the Civil War, and religion because of Palm Sunday. Do we rejoice or disapprove?

READING THE SCRIPTURE

NRSV
Matthew 21:1-13

1 When they had come near Jerusalem and had reached Bethphage, at the Mount of Olives, Jesus sent two disciples, 2 saying to them, "Go into the village ahead of you, and immediately you will find a donkey tied, and a colt with her; untie them and bring them to me. 3 If anyone says anything to you, just say this, 'The Lord needs them.' And he will send them immediately." 4 This took place to fulfill what had been spoken through the prophet, saying,

Key Verse

**5 "Tell the daughter of Zion,
   Look, your king is coming to
      you,
   humble, and mounted on a
      donkey,
   and on a colt, the foal of a
      donkey."**

6 The disciples went and did as Jesus had directed them; 7 they brought the donkey and the colt, and put their cloaks on them, and he sat on them. 8 A very large crowd spread their cloaks on the road, and others

NIV
Matthew 21:1-13

[1]As they approached Jerusalem and came to Bethphage on the Mount of Olives, Jesus sent two disciples, [2]saying to them, "Go to the village ahead of you, and at once you will find a donkey tied there, with her colt by her. Untie them and bring them to me. [3]If anyone says anything to you, tell him that the Lord needs them, and he will send them right away."

[4]This took place to fulfill what was spoken through the prophet:

Key Verse

[5]**"Say to the Daughter of Zion,
   'See, your king comes to you,
   gentle and riding on a donkey,
      on a colt, the foal of a donkey.'"**

[6]The disciples went and did as Jesus had instructed them. [7]They brought the donkey and the colt, placed their cloaks on them, and Jesus sat on them. [8]A very large crowd spread their cloaks on the road, while others cut branches from the trees and spread them on the road. [9]The crowds that went ahead of him and those that fol-

cut branches from the trees and spread them on the road. 9 The crowds that went ahead of him and that followed were shouting,

"Hosanna to the Son of David!
Blessed is the one who comes in
the name of the Lord!
Hosanna in the highest heaven!"

10 When he entered Jerusalem, the whole city was in turmoil, asking, "Who is this?" 11 The crowds were saying, "This is the prophet Jesus from Nazareth in Galilee."

12 Then Jesus entered the temple and drove out all who were selling and buying in the temple, and he overturned the tables of the money changers and the seats of those who sold doves. 13 He said to them, "It is written,

'My house shall be called a
house of prayer';
but you are making it a den
of robbers."

lowed shouted,

"Hosanna to the Son of David!"
"Blessed is he who comes in the name of
the Lord!"
"Hosanna in the highest!"

[10]When Jesus entered Jerusalem, the whole city was stirred and asked, "Who is this?"

[11]The crowds answered, "This is Jesus, the prophet from Nazareth in Galilee."

[12]Jesus entered the temple area and drove out all who were buying and selling there. He overturned the tables of the money changers and the benches of those selling doves. [13]"It is written," he said to them, " 'My house will be called a house of prayer,' but you are making it a 'den of robbers.' "

UNDERSTANDING THE SCRIPTURE

Matthew 21:1-7. Jesus and his disciples approach Jerusalem from Jericho (Matthew 20:29). When they reach Bethpage (21:1), on the Mount of Olives, they see the holy city below, to the west across the Kidron Valley. The unnamed village of verse 2 is probably the Bethany of Mark 11:1. Jesus has walked all the way from Galilee and is certainly able to make these last two miles on foot. This is, in fact, the only recorded instance of Jesus riding rather than walking; and so our attention is drawn to the prophecy, which is deliberately fulfilled.

There is only one animal in Zechariah 9:9, a donkey that is described as a colt. But in Matthew there are two animals, the colt and his mother. The two disciples place their cloaks on both donkeys and Jesus sits upon "them" (21:7). Some scholars believe the word "them" refers to the garments, whereas other commentators believe it refers to the animals. If the refer-

ence is to the animals, as seems more likely, he is riding the colt of Mark 11:4, not straddling them both like some circus rider. Matthew is often accused of making a stupid mistake, of inventing the mother because he thought Zechariah had two donkeys. But it is a stretch to assume that Matthew would not understand the simple poetic device of Hebrew parallelism. It is more likely that Matthew thought there really were two animals when Jesus made his entry into Jerusalem. It would not be unusual to bring the mother along in order to steady the unbroken colt, especially when the shouting crowd would make him nervous. Since the focus is on the colt that is actually ridden, Mark could well ignore the mother and Matthew could conceive of the "them" as a single unit. In this way the two can fulfill a prophecy that has only the one.

Matthew 21:8-13. The cleansing of the Temple, which many scholars consider the precipitating trigger for the arrest, follows immediately upon Jesus' entrance. The authority/obedience equation in verses 3 and 6 prepares us for such audacity. The authority is reinforced by the crowd of excited pilgrims who spot a series of Old Testament passages in this event. In addition to Zechariah 9:9 and Isaiah 62:11 in verse 5, 2 Samuel 7:12-16 lies behind the Son of David in verse 9 and Psalm 118:26 presents the one coming in the name of the Lord. These are all royal texts that at last came to be understood of the messianic king. In the crowd's identification of Jesus as the prophet (21:11), there is perhaps an allusion to Deuteronomy 18:15. If so, the messianic interpretation of the prophet like Moses whom God will raise up from among the people completes the list.

By their citation of Jeremiah 7:11, Matthew (21:13), Mark (11:17), and Luke (19:46) explain the cleansing of the Temple as a prophetic sign of judgment against religious hypocrisy. Two additional motives have been suggested. First, in his book *Reading Matthew*, David E. Garland understands this cleansing in terms of a fundamental shift in the way we approach God. "Jesus' prophetic protest is not directed against any so-called abuses but against the normal functioning of the temple as a place of sacrifice. If sacrificial victims cannot be purchased, then sacrifice must end. If money cannot be exchanged into the holy currency, then monetary support for the daily sacrifices that effect atonement between Israel and God...must end....Jesus is to be the ransom for the people (Exodus 30:12-13) for the forgiveness of sins (26:28) whose death will make the cult of animal sacrifice obsolete, and the temple will lie desolate (23:38). The *locus* of salvation and the hope of the nations is not to be the temple in Jerusalem...it has lost its capacity to bring the unholy into communion with the holy God. That power will shift to Jesus through his death and resurrection." A different motive for the cleansing suggested by other scholars is that Jesus wanted to move the buying and selling off the temple grounds rather than eliminate it.

Matthew 21:14-17. The buyers and sellers of verse 12 correlate with the chief priests and scribes of verse 15, while the blind and the lame of verse 14 correlate with the children of verse 15. The lame and the blind—seeking out Jesus in their need, becoming like the children who shout "Hosanna" (see 18:3)—are healed. The buyers and sellers, too intent upon their business to shout "Hosanna," are rejected. Moreover, the chief priests and scribes are rebuked for their angry response. For it is not the Father's will that one of these little ones be lost (18:14).

INTERPRETING THE SCRIPTURE

The Earthquake

Jesus' entourage—blanketing the road with clothing and branches and shouting "Hosanna"—makes an impression as he enters Jerusalem. The whole city, in fact, is moved (21:10 NKJV) or stirred (NIV), in turmoil (NRSV), thrown into an uproar (GNB), wild with excitement (REB). The Greek word behind all of these translations has entered English as *seismic*. The whole city, therefore, is shaken by an earthquake. Only Matthew uses this specialized verb to describe the reaction of the people; and since there is no indication that this earthquake would register on the Richter scale, the translations, considering it to be purely symbolic, do not present it to the English reader.

Matthew has another earthquake, however, which is not translated for the English reader either, and for the same reason.

At 8:24 the furious storm (NIV) or wind-storm (NRSV) actually is an earthquake of the sea. Such an odd expression for a storm, coupled with the Palm Sunday language, suggests a closer comparison with the other two earthquakes in Matthew that are translated as such and that do not appear in the other Gospels—those at the empty tomb (28:2) and at the crucifixion (27:54).

The earthquake at the empty tomb doesn't do anything. There is no damage to the tomb. The guards are not hurt. No danger prevents the return of the women. Matthew continues the story, in fact, as if it had not happened. Often it is assumed that the seismic tremor pops the stone out of the groove. But note what Matthew actually says: the angel rolls the stone away. That is a very different idea. The earthquake at the cross, in contrast, does seem to do something. The centurion notices it. It splits open the tombs. And perhaps it can be related to the tearing of the Temple curtain. But even this one is strange. No fissures open up in the earth. The cross doesn't topple over. No other Gospel writer knows about it.

The earthquake has two meanings in the Bible. First, it is a sign of God's appearance to men and women. This may be seen in the mild quaking at Mount Sinai that signals Yahweh's approach to Moses and in Elijah's surprise that the Lord is not in the earthquake, for that is where he would be expected (1 Kings 19:11). Second, it is also a sign of the divine judgment at the end of the world. On that day there will be a great quaking (Ezekiel 38:19). These earthquakes have eternal implications, however, and so they are not simply geological tremors. This end-of-the-world earthquake, found in Matthew 24:7 (see next week's background scripture), is the only earthquake in the other Gospels. It is clear, therefore, that Matthew has used the earthquake to symbolize God's special presence in Jesus Christ at critical points in the narrative—control over nature, entrance into the Holy City, death, resurrection, and Last Judgment. At each point we are reminded of the awesome significance of Christ—for judgment as well as for salvation.

The Humility

The earthquake language, leading all the way to the Last Judgment by stressing the cosmic significance of the Palm Sunday entrance, lays the foundation for discipleship. But the humility of verse 5, by its connection with the third Beatitude (5:5), defines the discipleship itself. This linkage of humility and earthquake thereby gives an eternal dimension to our everyday Christian life. There are three key texts. First, in Matthew 21:5, Jesus' attitude is gentle, humble, lowly, or without display. Second, at Matthew 11:29 the English translations agree that the one commanding obedience is gentle. Third, in the Beatitudes at 5:5, the blessed are meek, humble, lowly, or gentle.

In classical Greek the word (praus) means gentle, as of a breeze or a soft voice. When used of people it means mild and gracious. According to Aristotle it is the mean between too much anger and too little anger. It describes the person who is never angry at the wrong time but has anger at appropriate times. The word was also used to describe a beast who is gentle because it has been tamed, as a wild horse has been broken to bit and bridle. In this case the idea is strength that has been brought under control. Meekness or humility, therefore, is not being nice or easygoing. It is not the spirit of compromise, but is strength such as that of the martyr, controlled by God.

From the Hebrew comes the special idea of our relationship to God rather than to other people. The meek or the humble are those who will possess the land (Psalm 37:11). The Greek Old Testament (the Septuagint) has translated the Hebrew by our word. In the psalm they are those who have submitted themselves to the leadership of God during the desert wandering. In the English language we often think of meekness or humility as weakness and deficiency in courage or spirit. The Hebrew, however, suggests people who are strong enough to suffer wrong without becoming bitter or consumed by a thirst for vengeance. Because they hope in God rather than in their own power, they are able to serve others. We, in short, can leave it all in God's hands because Jesus did.

The Hosanna

If the humility is the strength engendered by our faith in God, the Hosanna is our joy that this should be so. But it is a joy flowing out of our sense of salvation; for Hosanna starts out as a prayer to Yahweh for rescue, help, deliverance. (See Psalms 12:1; 20:9; 28:9; 60:5; 108:6; and 118:25.) The experience of answered prayer, coupled with confidence in God for the future, then adds to the cry for help a second meaning, that of praise, the shout of jubilation. Matthew, reflecting upon the scene from our side of the empty tomb, retains both meanings. We can cry out "save us" to this Jesus and then shout "praise" precisely because He has.

The Hosanna, occurring in the New Testament only in the Palm Sunday narratives, is to Jesus as the Son of David, thereby identifying him as the Messiah (see the lesson for December 19); and its echo in the highest heaven reflects Yahweh's approval. Jesus' defense of the children in verses 15-16 indicates his acceptance of the messianic title. The Hosanna is Zion's welcome to its king as he enters the holy city. This is highlighted in the two texts that are fulfilled in the entrance, Zechariah 9:9 in verse 5 and Psalm 118:26 in verse 9.

The welcome is given by the Passover pilgrims who are streaming into Jerusalem. Psalm 118, originally a royal psalm and thus capable of an allusion to the messianic king, is now associated with Passover. By evoking the spectacular escape from Egypt, the Passover constantly refurbishes the hope for national independence. And so the crowd welcomes a Messiah who will throw off the Roman yoke. But this one comes in the name of the Lord to die on a cross for the sins of the world. Matthew 23:39, however, speaks of a second coming in the name of the Lord. And that coming, finalizing salvation on a cosmic scale, will indeed be as Victor. The Palm Sunday Hosanna, meanwhile, is the pledge that the messianic hope has already begun the process that will lead to such an ultimate realization.

The Temple

This One who comes in the name of the Lord gets off the donkey and heads straight for the Temple, where he causes a ruckus in the Court of the Gentiles. Here are the licensed merchants who make it possible for people to worship in the Temple. Money changers exchange the ordinary money, with its unacceptable pagan symbols, for the special coin with which the Temple tax can be paid. Moreover, the proper animals for sacrifice do not have to be brought all the way from home because they can be purchased at the Temple. So it is a large, active bazaar, with dozens of dealers and crowds of customers.

Jesus makes a demonstration at the edge of the bazaar—it is too big to shut down—as a prophetic sign. Verse 13 explains the sign in the light of two Old Testament texts that interpret each other. The purpose of the Temple, according to Isaiah 56:7, is to provide an environment in which prayerful communion with God occurs. Instead of this, however, as Jeremiah 7:11 has it, both buyers and sellers have turned the Temple into a den of robbers. The Temple is not where the robbery takes place, as if dealers are cheating customers or customers are cheating dealers.

It is, rather, the hideout where they go to be safe after they have committed their crimes. In calling the Temple a hideout, Jeremiah accused the people of hypocrisy. They feel safe in the Temple (Jeremiah 7:10), as if the liturgy compensates for behavior. (See also Isaiah 58:5-10.) The prophetic sign, therefore, is the summons to hunger and thirst for righteousness. It is for buyer and seller alike, and also for us.

SHARING THE SCRIPTURE

PREPARING TO TEACH

Preparing Our Hearts

Today's devotional reading is Luke's record of Jesus' Palm Sunday entrance into Jerusalem. Read this account from Luke 19:29-44. As you read, you may want to list in your own words what is happening with Jesus, the disciples, the crowd, the religious leaders. Try to imagine yourself somewhere in the scene.

Now read Matthew 21:1-17. You may want to make another list of events to compare Matthew's account with Luke's account. As you read, notice the quotations Jesus uses from God's word (which, of course, did not at that time include what we know as the New Testament). Ponder how these quotations may have guided his listeners to understand who he was and the mission that he had come to fulfill.

Close your quiet time with prayer, asking God to reveal the message of the Scriptures to you through the power of the Holy Spirit that you might share this good news with those you teach.

Preparing Our Minds

As you read the passage from Matthew and this lesson, note the numerous references to the Hebrew Scriptures. Allow enough study time to look up these citations, perhaps in more than one translation. Consider how God's word guided both Jesus and his listeners.

If possible, have a map of Jerusalem and the surrounding area available to point out the places mentioned in Matthew 21:1. A map will help students envision Jesus' entry. If you can find some pictures of the Mount of Olives and/or Jerusalem itself, those visual aids would be helpful as well.

This week's study focuses on the Palm Sunday narrative, even though we will not be entering into Lent until March 8. This unit, "Fulfillment of Jesus' Mission," also includes the Crucifixion and Resurrection. Be sure to help students understand that these lessons are an appropriate conclusion to our study of the Gospel of Matthew, despite the fact that they are not in sync with the seasons of Lent and Easter.

Preparing Our Learning Space

Have on hand:
- several Bibles
- hymnals
- newsprint and marker
- optional map and pictures of Jerusalem.

LEADING THE CLASS

(1) Introduction

To begin today's session, read or retell the Focusing on the Main Question segment. This example of different perspectives as seen during the Civil War in our own country's history may be very helpful in understanding a variety of reactions to Jesus' entry into Jerusalem.

You may also want to spend a few moments discussing other examples of widely divergent perspectives on the same issue. Some of these may be biblical issues (such as the question found in Acts 15 of whether one had to become a Jew before becoming a Christian), or issues affecting the modern church, or secular issues that affect the social and political discourse of a society.

Close this portion of the lesson by lifting up today's main question: **Where among those bystanders on the road to Jerusalem do we place ourselves?**

(2) The Earthquake

Ask the class to sing "Hosanna, Loud Hosanna" (*The United Methodist Hymnal*, no. 278) and/or "Mantos y Palmas" ("Filled with Excitement," *UMH*, no. 279), both of which are based on Matthew 21:8-9. If singing is not possible in your learning space, divide the class in half and have each group read one line alternately.

Next, invite the class members to state what they would know about Palm Sunday if they only had the hymn(s) they have just sung. Reflect on how accurately they believe the hymn portrays the events as we recall them from the Scriptures.

Ask a volunteer to read aloud Matthew 21:1-11. Encourage the students to close their eyes and imagine the scene by using all of their senses. Have them consider the sights, sounds, tastes, smells, and touches they might have experienced had they been present. You may want to list their ideas on newsprint. The more the students can sense, the more easily they can put themselves into this important story and see themselves in relation to Jesus. If time permits, ask the students to compare the scriptural account with the hymn(s).

Finally, direct the group's attention to verse 10. Use several translations of the Bible to help the class see that Jesus' entry shook the city, as if an earthquake had occurred. Note the translations in the first paragraph of this section under Interpreting the Scripture. Use whatever other information from "The Earthquake" that you deem helpful to your class, being sure to point out that the earthquake is a sign of God's presence and of judgment at the end of the world. Thus, Matthew's use of the verb that we would translate as *seismic* indicates that Jesus has come both as the divine judge over us and as Emmanuel, "God with us." For a few moments, let the class ponder the awesome significance of Christ's coming.

(3) The Humility

Read again Matthew 21:5, today's key verse. Ask the students to think of other instances of Jesus' humility and/or the humility to which he calls his disciples. Examples include Matthew 5:5 and 11:29. Explain the meaning of the Greek word *praus*, which you will find in the second paragraph under "The Humility" in the Interpreting the Scripture section. Contrast the meaning of humility in English (weak, lacking in courage or strength) with the meaning in the Hebrew (strong enough to suffer wrong without becoming bitter or consumed by a thirst for vengeance).

Invite the students to turn to Zechariah 9:9. Ask:

(1) **If you had been a Jewish person standing among the crowd as Jesus rode by on a donkey, what would this quotation from Zechariah 9:9 in Matthew 21:5 say to you about Jesus?**

(2) **Why do you suppose that Matthew included this quotation from Zechariah, along with a description of Jesus' entry in verses 6-7?** (Remember that Matthew, more than any of the Gospel writers, wanted to show clearly that Jesus of Nazareth is the fulfillment of prophecy. The writer uses God's word to buttress his argument that Jesus is, in fact, the promised Messiah.)

(3) **What difference would it make in your own Christian discipleship if you began to think of humility as strength rather than weakness?**

(4) The Hosanna

Look next at another quotation from the Hebrew Scriptures found in Matthew 21:9. Here the Gospel writer quotes from Psalm 118:26. Have someone read both quotations aloud. Point out that the word *Hosanna* originally meant "save us" and later was used as a jubilant shout of praise. Ask:

?

(1) What might the bystanders have meant when they shouted to Jesus? (Note that by identifying Jesus as the Son of David, they likely viewed him as the Messiah. They welcome him as the Sovereign as he enters the Holy City.)

(2) If you were to shout "Hosanna" to Christ right now, what would you mean to say?

(5) The Temple

Have a volunteer read the conclusion of today's lesson from Matthew 21:12-13. Use the information under "The Temple" in Interpreting the Scripture to help the students understand what is going on here.

Also read aloud the second paragraph in the section labeled Matthew 21:8-13 in Understanding the Scripture, which includes the quotation from David Garland about Jesus' motivation for his actions in the Temple. Ask:

(1) Why do you think Jesus overturned the tables?

(2) How does the quotation from Jeremiah 7:11 in verse 13 help you interpret Jesus' motivation?

(3) How does this action move Jesus toward the fulfillment of his mission?

?

Close with a prayer asking that we will be guided by God's word to fulfill our own mission, just as the word guided Jesus in fulfilling his.

Before you dismiss the class, be sure to suggest at least one of the activities below.

HELPING CLASS MEMBERS ACT

Challenge the students to think about how they allow God's word to guide their own lives. What barriers prevent them from receiving even more guidance from the word?

Suggest that the class members look for instances in their own lives that demonstrate humility as Jesus practiced it—strength that can suffer wrong without seeking vengeance. Encourage them to pray for this kind of humility.

Encourage the students to think of practices in the modern church that need to be challenged and perhaps overturned. Recommend that class members take whatever steps they can to bring about needed changes and reforms.

PLANNING FOR NEXT SUNDAY

The lesson for February 13, "The Joy of Being Prepared," calls Jesus' followers to keep awake for we do not know when he will return. Ask the students to prepare for this lesson by reading Matthew 24:1–25:13. Matthew 24:45– 25:13, the focus of our lesson, includes the parable of the wise and foolish bridesmaids.

THE JOY OF BEING PREPARED

PREVIEWING THE LESSON

Lesson Scripture: Matthew 24:45–25:13
Background Scripture: Matthew 24:1–25:13
Key Verse: Matthew 25:13

Focus of the Lesson:
Jesus told parables to teach his followers that they must be prepared at all times for his return.

Main Question of the Lesson:
What do we need to do while there is still time?

This lesson will enable adult learners to:
(1) hear Jesus' parables about the coming of the kingdom of God.
(2) think about how prepared they are to meet the risen Christ.
(3) respond by overcoming procrastination in their spiritual lives.

Today's lesson may be outlined as follows:
(1) Introduction
(2) The Wedding
(3) The Banquet
(4) The Insomnia
(5) The Oil

FOCUSING ON THE MAIN QUESTION

On a warm August morning, some forty-six years after the crucifixion of Christ, Mount Vesuvius begins to rumble. The people of Pompeii do not pay much attention. The volcano had often growled and nothing much had ever happened. There is no reason to assume that it will be any different this time. When the first soft ash begins to fall, there is still no cause for alarm. It can easily be brushed off. People first realize that there is danger when pumice stones begin falling in the streets and on the roofs. They rush to gather their valuables in order to flee, exactly as we would do. Unfortunately, by now it is already too late. The ash becomes thick and sulfurous fumes develop with blinding speed. The only people who escape from Pompeii are those who run at the first warning of danger and never stop to pick up anything they own or even look for friends or relatives. There really is no margin for error this time, and everyone dies who counts on even a small margin.

Today's lesson suggests that we too, as it were, develop this mentality of those who live in the shadow of a volcano that often growls but never erupts. Even if someday it should erupt, the lava will come down so slowly that we can make our last-minute preparations. Tragically, we have not allowed for the sudden sulfurous fumes and the thick ash. We lose our alertness and the Kingdom will arrive and separate us as suddenly as Vesuvius divides Pompeii into the living and the dead. There will be no margin for error, no time for last-minute preparation. This is the difference between the wise and foolish virgins. The wise had been alert to the possibility of delay and had taken extra oil, but the foolish had not. Until the sudden climax it is not clear who are the wise and who are the foolish. They all look and act about the same. But the foolish girls can't get their oil any more than the foolish builder can strengthen the foundations during the storm (Matthew 7:13-27).

Preparedness is all-important, so our main question asks: **What do we need to do while there is still time?**

READING THE SCRIPTURE

NRSV
Matthew 24:45–25:13

45 "Who then is the faithful and wise slave, whom his master has put in charge of his household, to give the other slaves their allowance of food at the proper time? 46 Blessed is that slave whom his master will find at work when he arrives. 47 Truly I tell you, he will put that one in charge of all his possessions. 48 But if that wicked slave says to himself, 'My master is delayed,' 49 and he begins to beat his fellow slaves, and eats and drinks with drunkards, 50 the master of that slave will come on a day when he does not expect him and at an hour that he does not know. 51 He will cut him in pieces and put him with the hypocrites, where there will be weeping and gnashing of teeth.

25:1 "Then the kingdom of heaven will be like this. Ten bridesmaids took their lamps and went to meet the bridegroom. 2 Five of them were foolish, and five were wise. 3 When the foolish took their lamps, they took no oil with them; 4 but the wise took flasks of oil with their lamps. 5 As the bridegroom was delayed, all of them became drowsy and slept. 6 But at midnight there was a shout, 'Look! Here is the bridegroom! Come out to meet him.' 7 Then all those bridesmaids got up and

NIV
Matthew 24:45–25:13

45"Who then is the faithful and wise servant, whom the master has put in charge of the servants in his household to give them their food at the proper time? 46It will be good for that servant whose master finds him doing so when he returns. 47I tell you the truth, he will put him in charge of all his possessions. 48But suppose that servant is wicked and says to himself, 'My master is staying away a long time,' 49and he then begins to beat his fellow servants and to eat and drink with drunkards. 50The master of that servant will come on a day when he does not expect him and at an hour he is not aware of. 51He will cut him to pieces and assign him a place with the hypocrites, where there will be weeping and gnashing of teeth.

25:1 "At that time the kingdom of heaven will be like ten virgins who took their lamps and went out to meet the bridegroom. 2Five of them were foolish and five were wise. 3The foolish ones took their lamps but did not take any oil with them. 4The wise, however, took oil in jars along with their lamps. 5The bridegroom was a long time in coming, and they all became drowsy and fell asleep.

trimmed their lamps. 8 The foolish said to the wise, 'Give us some of your oil, for our lamps are going out.' 9 But the wise replied, 'No! there will not be enough for you and for us; you had better go to the dealers and buy some for yourselves.' 10 And while they went to buy it, the bridegroom came, and those who were ready went with him into the wedding banquet; and the door was shut. 11 Later the other bridesmaids came also, saying, 'Lord, lord, open to us.' 12 But he replied, 'Truly I tell you, I do not know you.' **13 Keep awake therefore, for you know neither the day nor the hour."**

Key Verse

[6] "At midnight the cry rang out: 'Here's the bridegroom! Come out to meet him!'

[7] "Then all the virgins woke up and trimmed their lamps. [8] The foolish ones said to the wise, 'Give us some of your oil; our lamps are going out.'

[9] " 'No,' they replied, 'there may not be enough for both us and you. Instead, go to those who sell oil and buy some for yourselves.'

[10] "But while they were on their way to buy the oil, the bridegroom arrived. The virgins who were ready went in with him to the wedding banquet. And the door was shut.

[11] "Later the others also came. 'Sir! Sir!' they said. 'Open the door for us!'

[12] "But he replied, 'I tell you the truth, I don't know you.'

[13] **"Therefore keep watch, because you do not know the day or the hour."**

Key Verse

UNDERSTANDING THE SCRIPTURE

Matthew 24:1-14. The coming (Matthew 24:3, 27, 37, and 39), the *parousia* in Greek, is so decisive that it can be called the end of the age (24:3). Therefore, it is inevitable and inescapable, hanging over our heads like a dark cloud casting its shadow before it in the form of the tribulations (24:6-28). It culminates in judgment (24:40-41) and it is dangerous, like a thief breaking into a house (24:43). Nevertheless, the writer of Revelation, considering it to be the ultimate blessing, urges us to pray for it (22:20). *Parousia* means arrival or presence, especially the visit of a king to a province; and so the idea is that we are waiting for the arrival of the King of kings. The mixture of tribulation and blessing appears in the birth pains of 24:8. Just as a woman's labor precedes the birth of a child, so the tribulations precede the birth of the new age. Meanwhile, pending that birth, there is work for us to do because the purpose of the delay is to enable mission (24:14).

Matthew 24:15-31. The desolating sacrilege (24:15 NRSV) or the abomination that causes desolation (NIV) is a reference to Daniel 12:11. In 167 B.C. Antiochus built a pagan altar to Zeus within the Temple itself. (See 1 Maccabees 1:54.) What happened once will happen again, this time at the hands of the Romans. But instead of being cleansed as it was after a successful Maccabean revolt, the Temple will be destroyed. Such bold and chilling idolatry, challenging holiness itself, brings to mind the Antichrist of the last days. (See 2 Thessalonians 2:3-4.) The destruction of Jerusalem, verses 15-28, foreshadows the coming of the Last Judgment. The mourning of verse 30 is an allusion to Zechariah 12:10, where, due to the gift of grace, Israel grieves for the one they had martyred. The grief, therefore, is repentance; and in Zechariah 13:1 it is followed by forgiveness. So here humanity repents; and here also the forgiveness is implied, for the gathering in verse 31 is to the Kingdom. Judgment for those who refuse to repent is passed over in silence. (See also Revelation 1:7.)

Matthew 24:32-51. We don't know when the end will come; not even the Son of Man who will at last effect it knows ahead of time (24:36). Such ignorance, revealing Jesus' limitations, stresses the completeness of the Incarnation. The interest of the text, however, is in the implication of this ignorance for discipleship in the here and now. If no one can know when, then it will be sudden and unexpected—like the way the flood caught Noah's generation (24:37-39). They did not expect it to happen at all, or at least not yet, and so they concentrated upon the daily routine. There really isn't anything wrong with what they are doing—eating, drinking, getting married, and all the other things that people do in the pursuit of happiness. That's pretty much what we'll be doing—working in the fields (24:40), grinding at the mill (24:41), trying to protect our property (24:43).

The problem is not that we are doing such things. The problem, rather, is that that's all that we're doing, that God has been crowded off the front burner, and maybe even off the stove entirely. The note of judgment in the text, however, insists that it really does matter whether or not God is on the front burner. The flood, the taking/leaving, and the thief are all images of judgment. Note also the following four parables in Matthew: faithful and evil servants (24:45-51); wise and foolish virgins (25:1-13); talents (25:14-30); and sheep and goats (25:31-46).

Matthew 25:1-13. Of the several possibilities, it is easiest for me to see the unmarried girls as invited guests. They have not been at the wedding ceremony but have gone to the house of the bride's father. The newly married couple will be coming here for the party. This interpretation is supported by a number of manuscripts that indicate that the girls went forth to the meeting of the bridegroom and of the bride. The girls have gathered here with their torches to honor the couple with the dance of the torches. The torches were probably made by wrapping rags around a stick and pouring oil over the rags. They would burn brightly for about fifteen minutes. The girls expected the arrival of the couple momentarily and so the torches have been lit. There is an unexpected delay and the girls put out their torches. But then the rags must be resoaked with oil. Only those who are prepared are able to do this.

INTERPRETING THE SCRIPTURE

The Wedding

In the lesson for January 30, we encountered the vineyard as a symbol for the kingdom of God. The biblical writers are never satisfied that they have caught the essence, however, and so they constantly search for new images to express the relationship of the faithful with their God. Like the facets of a diamond, none of which is adequate by itself and yet each of which affords its own unique avenue into the whole, the piling up of images creates an overarching concept from many specific angles. And so in today's lesson we see two more of these images, the wedding and the banquet.

The dominant Old Testament image, the Sinai or Mosaic covenant, is political in nature. But several prophets, desiring something more personal than law, use marriage as a way of describing Yahweh's bond with Israel. (See Hosea 2:16; Isaiah 54:6; and Ezekiel 16:8.) Note that Israel as a whole, men and women alike, is the bride and that Yahweh is the Husband. This new picture changes idolatry from a violation of law into the adultery that breaks the relationship. These texts use the universal dimensions of human marriage—love, faithfulness, betrayal, divorce, reconciliation—in order to gain new insight into God's reaction to the varying quality of our ongoing discipleship.

Matthew picks up this image in the parable, comparing the kingdom of heaven with the wedding. Christ, of course, is the Bridegroom, as in Matthew 9:15, but there is no bride; for we all, as the church, are the bride, represented here by the ten virgins and in 9:15 by the wedding guests. Compare also the wedding background in Matthew 22:1-10. Ephesians 5:25-33 clearly reveals this process of image formation. In verse 25 Christ's love for the church is set within the context of the ideal marriage, and in verses 31-32 the Adam and Eve story (Genesis 2:24) is applied to Christ and the church. Revelation 19:7-9 describes our eternal life in heaven in two ways. First we are the bride and then we are the guests at the marriage supper.

The wise and foolish virgins (NIV) support this understanding of the background symbol for the parable. Note the use of "virgin" in 2 Corinthians 11:2 and Revelation 14:4 to indicate the saints in heaven. We, then, are the virgins, using our time wisely or foolishly, pending the final consummation. This dimension is obscured for the English-speaking reader when the word for "virgins" is translated as "bridesmaids" (NRSV) or as "young women" (GNB). These translations reflect our inability to nail down the exact scene. Are they village girls waiting to go to the party? Or bridesmaids waiting to go to the wedding ceremony? Where are they waiting? But it doesn't matter, for the point is the wedding banquet. And to get in is to be "in Christ" (2 Corinthians 5:17).

The Banquet

Table fellowship, especially on a regular basis, establishes a relationship with mutual obligations. The willingness to eat together, even more so in antiquity than today, reflects a deliberate acceptance of such a bond. The dramatic touch of the two hands on the table at the Last Supper, therefore, heightens the heinousness of Judas' betrayal. It is worse than it would have been if he had not eaten with Jesus. This creation of community by "who eats what with whom" is a major biblical theme. It is the horizontal bonding of people with a common purpose.

Not only does eating together cement interpersonal relationships on the human level, but the sacred meal adds a vertical dimension to the horizontal one because eating with deity creates community with deity. Note, for example, Paul's argument in 1 Corinthians 10:16-21. The Christian Eucharist, obviously, is a sharing in the body of Christ. Those who eat the Old Testament sacrifices become partners in the altar (that is, with Yahweh). But the identification with deity in the sacred meal extends also to the pagan rites, though it is a partnership with demons that is created.

When the bonding occurs in both directions at once, vertically with God and horizontally with fellow worshipers, and when the time frame is changed from this life to eternity, the image of the messianic banquet becomes possible. The classic text is Isaiah 25:6-9, in which heaven is portrayed as a great party with God as the Host. The guests do not know that they have been invited to a party, and so they are covered by a veil of mourning. God rips away the veil and dries their tears so they can rejoice. The New Testament makes use of this symbolism to describe eternal life. Abraham, Isaac, and Jacob are fellow guests (Matthew 8:11); those invited to eat bread in heaven are blessed (Luke 14:15); and the faithful will eat and drink at Christ's table (Luke 22:30). When the two streams merge, the wedding and the messianic banquet, we have the party in our parable.

The Insomnia

On my last visit to Texas, as we dropped my little grandson off at the day-care center on the way to the airport, my son remarked that the boy would be upset when he figured out that I had gone. I said, "Because the party's over?" He replied, "No. He's afraid it will go on without him!" And that, of course, is precisely the point of Matthew 25:10—that the party will go on. Therefore we are to keep watch (25:13 NIV) or keep awake (NRSV) in order to make sure that we are included. The Greek verb means to keep awake, to be on the alert, to be watchful, to keep a sharp eye peeled, to be alive. Matthew uses the verb six times in two different contexts. In 24:42-43 the context is discipleship under the shadow of the end of the age, and in 26:38-41 it is the crisis at Gethsemane.

Since "birds of a feather flock together," we can learn something about this insomnia by the company it keeps. It is defined by prayer, which is the sentry duty that guards against temptation (Matthew 26:41). This alertness (NRSV) in prayer is further characterized by an attitude of thanksgiving (Colossians 4:2).

Watchfulness is also associated with soberness. In the first instance, soberness means not having alcohol in the system to slow down reaction times. Soberness then acquires two further meanings. Since the sober are not drunk and disorderly in public, they are circumspect or serious. And since their senses are not dulled, they are vigilant or alert. (See 1 Thessalonians 5:6 and 1 Peter 5:8.)

Watchfulness or readiness or alertness as a description of discipleship in the here and now involves endurance for the long (or short?) haul, standing firm. In order to be firm we must have courage and strength (1 Corinthians 16:13); and therefore we are to strengthen ourselves (Revelation 3:2). This courage and strength to watch enables us to defend our brothers and sisters from attack—from without and also, sad to say, from within (Acts 20:29-31). Furthermore, even though the word itself is not used, is it too much to understand the alertness in terms of the Great Commission (Matthew 28:16-20; see the lesson for February 27)? Aren't we always to be on the lookout for any opportunity to make the witness?

Again, even though the word itself is not used, doesn't Matthew imply that the alertness is also to be understood in terms of actions? Matthew 25:31-46 clearly indicates that we are to feed the hungry that we can see, to clothe the naked that are in our town, to care for the sick and the homeless. Christ apparently expects us to do something while we are waiting for his return.

The Oil

There are limits even to spiritual insomnia, however, and so we come to the sleepiness and the oil. Five of the girls want to go to the party more desperately than do the other five. This is seen not only in their foresight in bringing the extra oil, but also in the frantic actions of the five without the oil. They had lost sight of their goal, which is to go to the party. There is no reason to assume from the parable that they would have been denied entrance if they had remained where they were with unlit torches. The point then is keeping the ultimate purpose in mind and not allowing ourselves to be sidetracked. We must identify our primary goal and then stick to it.

Some scholars have found meaning in the oil that cannot be transferred. Does the oil fit into any sort of pattern in Matthew? Can we relate the torchlight here to the light that enables people to see our good works (5:14-16)? Or to the wedding garments in 22:11-14, which seem to indicate righteousness? Or perhaps, as Luther thought, the oil represents faith rather than works. The difference then is between going part of the way and all of the way.

SHARING THE SCRIPTURE

PREPARING TO TEACH

Preparing Our Hearts

Start your time of spiritual preparation for this week's lesson by reading Matthew 24:36-44. This passage, which immediately precedes our lesson scripture and is included in the background reading, speaks about the importance of being prepared for Christ's return. No one knows when it will come. One thing, however, is known: when the end does come, we will not have time to prepare. We must be watchful and ready at all times. Think about your own degree of readiness to meet Jesus, whether at his second coming or your own death. What do you need to do in order to be better prepared?

Now look at the lesson scripture in Matthew 24:45–25:13. As you read, jot down any ideas about the coming of the kingdom that you derive from this passage. How do these ideas square with your own beliefs about Jesus' coming? Pray that God will lead you to make your Christian discipleship and preparedness for the kingdom your number-one priority.

Preparing Our Minds

Read the entire background scripture from Matthew 24:1–25:13. Study this lesson carefully. You may find it helpful to read additional commentaries to expand your interpretations of this material.

Preparing Our Learning Space

Have on hand:
- ✔ several Bibles
- ✔ paper and pencils
- ✔ hymnals.

LEADING THE CLASS

(1) Introduction

Begin today's session by reading or retelling the first paragraph in the Focusing on the Main Question section. Then ask:

(1) **Suppose you lived in the shadow of a volcano that often rumbles but doesn't erupt. What preparations would you make for an eruption?**

(2) **If you were not ready for an eruption, what would you do when such an event occurred?**

(3) **Even as you took whatever last-minute action you could, what chance for survival do you think you would have?**

Now read aloud Matthew 24:45-51 and ask:

(1) **How does Jesus' teaching here relate to the story of Mount Vesuvius?**

(2) **Why do you suppose people tend to think something will not happen just because it is delayed?** (This question may be especially difficult to address in our "instant society" where we expect immediate replies to e-mail, faxes, and voice mail, as well as overnight delivery of even nonessential items.)

(3) **In verse 46 Jesus says, "Blessed is that slave whom his master will find at work when he arrives." What implication might this verse have for us two thousand years after Jesus' crucifixion?** (Jesus expects us to continue working for the good of the Kingdom, rather than fritter away our time in the false belief that he will not return at all because he has not done so yet.)

Close the introduction by stating today's main question: **What do we need to do while there is still time?**

(2) The Wedding

Spend a few moments discussing these questions with the class:

(1) What are some preparations that modern couples normally make for a wedding?

(2) What might happen if things are not ready when the wedding is to take place?

Choose a volunteer to read Matthew 25:1-13, the parable of the wise and foolish virgins.

Set this passage within the context of the marriage imagery found in the Bible by creating a brief lecture using points in the Interpreting the Scripture portion under "The Wedding." Cite the passages from Hosea 2:16; Isaiah 54:6; and Ezekiel 16:8 that show how the Israelites understand that God was their Husband. Also use the New Testament references in this section to demonstrate how the early Christians understood the church to be the bride of Christ. Finally, link the students (and all Christians) to the virgins in the parable who use their time wisely or foolishly. Note that there is no middle ground. These women either are or are not prepared for the wedding festivities. Similarly, either we are or are not prepared for the coming reign of God.

(3) The Banquet

Ask the students:

(1) What is the point of Jesus' parable? (Jesus is calling us to be prepared for the coming of the kingdom of God.)

(2) The wedding and its association with God as the Husband and the church as the bride is an important image in this parable. What other image does Jesus allude to that links this parable to the kingdom? (The banquet mentioned in verse 10 would have been understood as a reference to the messianic banquet. Point out that Isaiah 25:6-9 clearly states the idea of God hosting a great party. See "The Banquet" in Interpreting the Scripture for additional references.)

Divide the students into groups or ask them to work with a partner in order to write their own version of this parable. They may select whatever images that seem most helpful to them, but the point of their story must be that we are to be prepared for the sudden coming of the kingdom of God. Distribute paper and pencils and set a time to work. Choose a few volunteers to read their stories.

(4) The Insomnia

Direct the group's attention to the key verse, Matthew 25:13. Have them look especially at the words "keep awake," which also may mean to be on the alert, to be watchful, to keep a sharp eye peeled, to be alive. Then ask the students to do a Bible study in which they see what this alertness entails. You will find this information in Interpreting the Scripture.

- Matthew 26:41—Alertness is defined by prayer.
- Colossians 4:2—Alertness in prayer is characterized by an attitude of thanksgiving.
- 1 Thessalonians 5:6—Watchfulness is associated with soberness.
- 1 Peter 5:8—Those who are alert are vigilant.
- 1 Corinthians 16:13—Those who are alert have courage and strength.
- Revelation 3:2—God's people are called to awaken and strengthen themselves.
- Acts 20:29-31—The church needs to keep alert for attacks from without and within.
- Matthew 25:31-46—Those who are alert show their readiness by their actions.

(5) The Oil

Note that the frantic behavior of the foolish virgins focuses on their lack of oil. Ask:

[?]

(1) **How do the foolish ones try to obtain oil?**

(2) **Is the oil really necessary? If not, what function does the oil serve in this parable?** (Nothing in the text says that the girls would not be allowed to join the party if they had unlit torches. Thus, the girls were diverted from their real goal—attending the party—to seek the oil they had foolishly forgotten to bring.)

Provide a few moments for silent meditation on these questions that you will need to read aloud slowly:

[?]

(1) **How are you like the foolish bridesmaids?**

(2) **How are you like the wise ones?**

(3) **What action will you take this very day to be more prepared for the coming of God's reign?**

(4) **How might such preparations make you more joyful?**

You may want to conclude the session by singing "Wake, Awake, for Night Is Flying" (*The United Methodist Hymnal*, no. 720). This 1599 hymn, based on Romans 13:11-12 and Matthew 25:1-13, refers to the virgins awaiting the Bridegroom.

Prior to dismissing the group, offer at least one idea from the list below to help the students respond to the lesson in the coming week.

HELPING CLASS MEMBERS ACT

Suggest that students examine how they are obeying Christ's call to stay alert for his coming. Will they be ready at a moment's notice? Or do they put off preparations because they assume they have plenty of time to do whatever they want? Encourage them to consider prayerfully what they need to do to be ready, and then to take whatever actions are necessary.

Recommend that class members explore their human tendency to procrastinate. Ask them to think about why they put things off, how they could reschedule their lives, and what their priorities are in relation to what they really want their priorities to be. Suggest they make whatever changes they can this week.

Promote the idea that we need to be prepared for our own death. Suggest that students assign a current power of attorney and a power of attorney for healthcare, and write a living will and a last will and testament. Remind the class that though some adults find it difficult to discuss such matters, as Christians we can confront our own mortality with confidence. Therefore, we need to do whatever we can to make our final days as easy for our surviving loved ones as possible.

PLANNING FOR NEXT SUNDAY

Next week we will study Matthew's account of Jesus' death. Ask the students to read Matthew 27:32-61, paying particular attention to verses 38-54. Encourage them to confront their own beliefs about Jesus' death. Can they, like the centurion, assert that Jesus was God's Son?

THE DEATH IN OUR BEHALF

PREVIEWING THE LESSON

Lesson Scripture: Matthew 27:38-54
Background Scripture: Matthew 27:32-61
Key Verse: Matthew 27:54

Focus of the Lesson:
Jesus accepted death on the cross for the sake of the world.

Main Question of the Lesson:
How can we "faith" our way through life when knowledge fails?

This lesson will enable adult learners to:
(1) witness Jesus' crucifixion as Matthew reports it.
(2) explore their own beliefs about the purpose of Jesus' death.
(3) respond by confessing their own faith.

Today's lesson may be outlined as follows:
(1) Introduction
(2) Mockery
(3) Godforsakenness
(4) Curtain
(5) Confession

FOCUSING ON THE MAIN QUESTION

Recently one of my granddaughters introduced me to Hank the Cowdog, whose adventures as head of security on a western cattle ranch are chronicled by John R. Erickson. One day Hank orders Drover, his young subordinate, to go bark at the mailman. Drover wonders why he is to bark at the man who is bringing mail to the ranch. An exasperated Hank simply repeats the order more forcefully, and Drover dutifully heads out to do his barking. But then Hank himself begins to wonder at the foolish question. "Ma used to say that back at the beginning of time, God built a thousand questions but only two hundred and fifty answers, so there you are. Why do we bark at the mailman? Because, by George, cowdogs have always barked at the mailman and they always will."

Our own list of unanswered questions may not include barking at mail carriers. But which of us, backed into a corner by someone in pain, has not had to stumble through a difficult witness? "If you can tell me why your God allows an eight-year-old child to die of leukemia, then I'll believe in your God." Which of us, moreover, has not wondered from within our own life experience, "Where is God when I'm in need?

Why do the innocent suffer and the wicked prosper?" Are there not times when the cry of dereliction from the cross expresses our sense of being abandoned by a God who always seems to have more pressing business elsewhere? Do we not sometimes puzzle over the mystery of why a death must occur before there can be a redemption—if, that is, God really is the Almighty? Doesn't the triumph of the empty tomb escape us at times?

These thoughts bring us to our main question: **How can we "faith" our way through life when knowledge fails?**

Perhaps our key verse, Matthew 27:54, can point us in the right direction, for the centurion does not stop with the darkness and the pain. He is able to grasp the whole, the darkness by knowledge, the light by faith. If faith is misplaced, if there is no light, then nothing much matters anyway.

READING THE SCRIPTURE

NRSV
Matthew 27:38-54

38 Then two bandits were crucified with him, one on his right and one on his left. 39 Those who passed by derided him, shaking their heads 40 and saying, "You who would destroy the temple and build it in three days, save yourself! If you are the Son of God, come down from the cross." 41 In the same way the chief priests also, along with the scribes and elders, were mocking him, saying, 42 "He saved others; he cannot save himself. He is the King of Israel; let him come down from the cross now, and we will believe in him. 43 He trusts in God; let God deliver him now, if he wants to; for he said, 'I am God's Son.'" 44 The bandits who were crucified with him also taunted him in the same way.

45 From noon on, darkness came over the whole land until three in the afternoon. 46 And about three o'clock Jesus cried with a loud voice, "Eli, Eli, lema sabachthani?" that is, "My God, my God, why have you forsaken me?" 47 When some of the bystanders heard it, they said, "This man is calling for Elijah." 48 At once one of them ran and got a sponge, filled it with sour wine, put it on a stick, and gave it to him to drink. 49 But the others said, "Wait, let us see whether Elijah will come to save him." 50 Then Jesus cried again

NIV
Matthew 27:38-54

38Two robbers were crucified with him, one on his right and one on his left. 39Those who passed by hurled insults at him, shaking their heads 40and saying, "You who are going to destroy the temple and build it in three days, save yourself! Come down from the cross, if you are the Son of God!"

41In the same way the chief priests, the teachers of the law and the elders mocked him. 42"He saved others," they said, "but he can't save himself! He's the King of Israel! Let him come down now from the cross, and we will believe in him. 43He trusts in God. Let God rescue him now if he wants him, for he said, 'I am the Son of God.'" 44In the same way the robbers who were crucified with him also heaped insults on him.

45From the sixth hour until the ninth hour darkness came over all the land. 46About the ninth hour Jesus cried out in a loud voice, "Eloi, Eloi, lama saba-chthani?"—which means, "My God, my God, why have you forsaken me?"

47When some of those standing there heard this, they said, "He's calling Elijah."

48Immediately one of them ran and got a sponge. He filled it with wine vinegar, put it on a stick, and offered it to Jesus to drink. 49The rest said, "Now leave him with a loud voice and breathed his last. 51 At that moment the curtain of the temple was torn in two, from top to bottom. The earth shook, and the rocks were split. 52 The tombs also were opened, and many bodies of the saints who had fallen asleep were raised. 53 After his resurrection they came out of the tombs and entered the holy city and appeared to many. 54 Now when the centurion and those with him, who were keeping watch over Jesus, saw the earthquake and what took place, they were terrified and said, **"Truly this man was God's Son!"**

Key Verse

alone. Let's see if Elijah comes to save him."

⁵⁰And when Jesus had cried out again in a loud voice, he gave up his spirit.

⁵¹At that moment the curtain of the temple was torn in two from top to bottom. The earth shook and the rocks split. ⁵²The tombs broke open and the bodies of many holy people who had died were raised to life. ⁵³They came out of the tombs, and after Jesus' resurrection they went into the holy city and appeared to many people.

⁵⁴When the centurion and those with him who were guarding Jesus saw the earthquake and all that had happened, they were terrified, and exclaimed, **"Surely he was the Son of God!"**

Key Verse

UNDERSTANDING THE SCRIPTURE

Matthew 27:32-37. In Mark 15:23 the wine, mixed with myrrh, is intended as a drug to ease the victim's pain, and so it is a kindness. Jesus refuses the drug because a death on our behalf must be voluntary, endured to the end with a clear head, the will unclouded. In Matthew 27:34, however, the wine is mixed with gall. The pious women of Jerusalem would prepare the drugged wine as a charitable act. They would give the wine to the soldiers, who would offer it to the condemned. If this is the same drink as in Mark, therefore, we may assume that the soldiers have added the gall themselves in a cruel mockery. Psalm 69:21, where the NRSV translates "gall" as "poison" (though the NIV uses "gall"), may be in the background.

Matthew 27:38-44. The two men on adjacent crosses are not thieves in any normal sense of the word, for thieves break in and steal (6:19) at unexpected times when all are asleep (24:43), but they do not kill. The normal word for thief, from which *kleptomania* has entered English, is never applied to these two. The KJV translation of verse 38 has given this mistaken

impression. An entirely different word is used. They are robbers (NIV) or bandits (NRSV), the kind who attack travelers on the Jericho road (Luke 10:30). So it is possible that they are violent outlaws whose crimes include murder.

There is another possibility, however, for from the violence of the bandit the word came to be used of the irregular guerrilla soldier, the rebel, the terrorist. The word was applied to Jews who continued active and violent resistance to Roman rule and often seems synonymous with "zealot." It is in this sense that Barabbas is called a robber (John 18:40 KJV). The meaning is confirmed by the statement that Barabbas was involved in a bloody insurrection against Rome (Mark 15:7). Since Jesus was convicted by the Romans on a charge of treason, it is more probable that the three who are executed together are considered guilty of the same crime than that two ordinary outlaws are executed along with a political prisoner.

Matthew 27:45-50. The bystanders take the "Eli" ("my God") of verse 46 as a cry for Elijah to rescue him from the cross. It is possible that they have misunderstood; but, in the light of the context, it is more likely a deliberate pun as part of the mockery. The rulers had taunted Jesus with his inability to save himself. And now the bystanders taunt him with Elijah's refusal to come to his aid. Because Elijah did not die, but ascended into heaven (2 Kings 2:11), a tradition developed concerning his willingness to assist the righteous in their hour of need. More than this, Malachi 4:5-6 identifies Elijah as the messenger whom God will send before the great and terrible day of the Lord. This prophecy at last merges with messianic speculation, and Elijah becomes the forerunner. If Elijah has not come, then the Messiah cannot have come.

The irony, of course, is that the reader knows that Elijah has come and that therefore the Messiah has come; for in Matthew 11:14 John the Baptist is the Elijah of Malachi. It is not a reincarnation of the historical Elijah, however, but the Elijah mission that is fulfilled in the call to repentance and the ministry of preparation. At the Transfiguration, Elijah speaks with Jesus about the coming passion in Jerusalem (Luke 9:30-31). A suffering Messiah is thereby legitimated. But if John the Baptist is not the prophetic forerunner after all—and how can the Transfiguration visit be objectively demonstrated?—then Elijah is yet to come. In this case the taunt is a test. If Elijah takes Jesus off the cross, it will show that he is the Messiah. But if Elijah does not come, then he belongs on the cross.

Matthew 27:51-61. At the very end it is the women who remain near the cross, daring to reveal publicly their loyalty to the Crucified (27:55). The mother of the sons of Zebedee, who had once craved the places on Jesus' right and left for her sons (20:20-21), now sees crosses rather than thrones. The women's observation of the burial (27:61) is of great importance, for they provide the continuity of the witness. So when they are there on Easter Sunday morning (28:1), there can be no doubt that this is the right tomb. The other Mary (27:61 and 28:1) is Mary the mother of James and Joseph (27:56).

INTERPRETING THE SCRIPTURE

Mockery

The mockery, occurring in three separate contexts within Matthew's passion narrative, is a significant motif. It begins in the house of Caiaphas, 26:67-68, as soon as the sentence is pronounced. They, identified in Luke 22:63 as the men who are guarding Jesus, spit in his face and hit him. Then, ridiculing his popular reputation as a prophet, the guards blindfold (Mark 14:65) him and demand the names of those who slap him. Later, in Matthew 27:28-31, after Pilate's decision, the Roman soldiers continue the game. Taking up Pilate's question in Matthew 27:11, they mock royalty with the robe, crown of thorns, and reed scepter. Their sarcastic homage inevitably degenerates into spitting and hitting.

The mockery, indicating rejection, reaches its climax at the cross. The first group, those passing by on the day's business, hurl insults (NIV) or deride (NRSV) the Crucified as having promised more than he can deliver (27:39-40). Echoing the accusation at the trial (26:61), they demand a "put up or shut up" response. The verb "mock" is used of the Roman soldiers and the chief priests; but the derision of the passersby is blasphemy. Matthew uses this verb in two senses, insulting a person, as here, and insulting God, at 9:3 and 26:65. Since Psalm 22:1a provides the cry of dereliction in verse 46, the head-shaking of the passersby is probably from Psalm 22:7.

The second group, the chief priests, scribes, and elders (27:41-43), laugh off the healing miracles. He saved others from their illness, but he cannot save himself from the cross. If, on the other hand, he should save himself, the religious leaders would believe that he is their king. This one, who claims to be the Son of God, has trusted in God. So, they assert, let God rescue him if God wants him as Son. (Compare Psalm 22:8.) Finally even the two robbers (NIV) or bandits (NRSV) heap insults upon (NIV) or taunt (NRSV) him (27:44).

The passion prediction in 20:19 anticipates the mockery. Jesus, fulfilling Isaiah 53:7, actually does what he tells us to do (5:38-42). By making disciples the objects of the same verb that describes the speech of the bandits, furthermore, 5:11 suggests that our turn may come. This is aptly illustrated at Istanbul's Saint Sophia, the world's largest Christian church from the sixth century until the building of Saint Peter's in Rome. The apostles are portrayed as a line of sheep following their Shepherd wherever he goes.

Some scholars have suggested that the mockery is the conclusion of the testing, from the temptation in the wilderness (4:1-11) through the misunderstanding of the disciples (16:22-23) to Gethsemane (26:36-56).

Godforsakenness

Jesus had interpreted his own pending death as "a ransom for many" (20:28), and at Gethsemane the divine silence regarding the cup of suffering endorses that ransom. The mockery is near the end of that bitter brew and the sense of Godforsakenness in Matthew 27:46 empties the cup. Deuteronomy 31:17 warns that the Lord will forsake Israel: "My anger will be kindled against them in that day. I will forsake and hide my face from them; they will become easy prey, and many terrible troubles will come upon them." This image of God's face turning away from sin is the source of the common idea that when the Son takes the sin of the world upon himself at the cross, the Father has to look away, and that the looking away triggers the cry of dereliction.

Matthew 27:46 is a troubling verse that has been understood in four ways:

- Assuming that the quotation of the opening verse implies the whole of Psalm 22, the progression is from despair and ill-treatment at the hands of enemies to a triumphant affirmation of faith in God. It goes beyond the text in Matthew, however, in supplying material that Jesus does not quote.

- Psalm 22 speaks not so much of absence as failure to render assistance. Since the psalmist goes on to express the conviction that the Lord will ultimately give the help, the quotation is in reality a prayer for rescue. Is there no way that the cup can be withdrawn from Jesus, even now, without undermining the divine purpose? The bystanders take it this way, even if they misunderstand the source of the hoped-for deliverance.

- There is no Godforsakenness in reality, even for this moment; but the perception of the divine presence is blunted. The impact of the sins of the world upon sinlessness produces a desolation of spirit in which the communion the Son had always known with the Father appears to be broken.

- The Lutheran and Calvinist theological traditions have generally seen the cry from the cross as an accurate recognition that at this moment the Son had been forsaken by the Father. If the cross represents atonement as substitution, and if Jesus really does take the sins of the world upon himself, and if he really bears the penalty of sin in our behalf, then the penalty must be complete. The penalty for sin is not simply the death of the body, but also the death of the soul in the sense of separation from God. Only through such complete and unfathomable Godforsakenness can Christ truly take our place. If Christ is fully human, furthermore, then he must bear the penalty without even knowing how it will all come out. Anything less devalues the Incarnation. And so the Apostles' Creed includes that difficult clause about the descent into hell. Certainty is not possible, of course, or else there would not be so many interpretations; but this one takes most seriously the idea expressed in our lesson title, "The Death in Our Behalf."

Curtain

When there is nothing left in the cup to drink, a final cry of agony (27:50) signals the completion of the divine will (26:39-43). So God at last speaks in a series of stunning events; and it becomes clear, in an ironic twist, that the mockers have spoken the truth after all. The one on the cross really is the Son of God. He is thereby the King of Israel. Deity really does desire a rescue, but the rescue Jesus accomplishes is ours from sin (26:28). To rescue the Son from the cross would frustrate that desire.

God tears the curtain of the Temple in two, from top to bottom (27:51). Some scholars believe this reference is to the outer curtain, eighty feet high, that separates the sanctuary from the forecourt. It would thus be visible to the centurion—part of "what took place" (27:54). In this case the tearing of the curtain foreshadows the coming destruction of the Temple at the hands of the Romans in A.D. 70, which Jesus had predicted in 24:2. It is, therefore, a fitting conclusion to the mockery in verse 39. If, on the other hand, as most scholars believe, we take it as the curtain that separates the Holy of Holies from the rest of the Temple, it would not be visible to the centurion. The tearing, in this case, offers unrestricted access to God in Christ. (See also Hebrews 10:19-20.) This interpretation then spells the end of the sacrificial system and opens the gospel to the Gentiles. We are thus prepared for the confession of faith in verse 54.

The earthquake calls attention to the importance of this death, stressing the divine presence at the cross and pointing to its "end-of-the-world" significance. (See also the lesson for February 6.) The shock of the earthquake, which splits the rocks, breaks open the tombs around Jerusalem (27:52). The holy people (NIV) or saints (NRSV) are the righteous of Israel who lived and died before the Christ event. This action extends the Crucifixion backward in time as well as forward, thus making the same point as the descent into hell; for, according to 1 Peter 3:19 and 4:6, Jesus' descent enables the preaching to the spirits in prison. And so at Saint Stephen's Monastery in the Meteora section of Greece there is a ceiling painting of Christ bringing Adam and Eve up out of hell.

The resurrection of these saints is connected with Jesus' death, but their entrance into Jerusalem does not occur until after his resurrection. Efforts to explain the delay have not been successful. The theological symbolism, however, when divorced from a realistic explanation, is powerful; for the eternal life of the saints is tied to both ends of the death/resurrection of Christ. It is, accordingly, an effective way to stress the unity of the Good Friday/Easter Sunday experience—"You can't have the one without the other."

Confession

The text does not record the reaction of the people when they see the resurrected saints walking the streets of Jerusalem. Had such an unusual sight stimulated a confession of faith, surely we would have been told. It is, therefore, the answer to the mocking demand for a miracle in verse 42. As Luke 16:31 has it, "if they do not listen to Moses and the prophets, neither will they be convinced even if someone rises from the dead."

But the story does not end on such a negative note. There is a reaction, even if from an unexpected quarter. The centurion and his soldiers, who have the responsibility to see to it that Jesus actually dies in the prescribed manner, notice the mockery and the two cries from the cross. This would not surprise them, but they are not prepared for what happens—the sudden darkness and the breaking apart of the tombs. There is more to this than meets the eye—so much more, in fact, that it is awesome, even frightening. The fear, however, instead of inducing paralysis or flight, draws them to view the cross within a cosmic context. And so they reverse the mockery with a confession of faith (27:54) that this Jesus really is the Son of God, thus preparing us for the Great Commission (Matthew 28:16-20; see next week's lesson).

SHARING THE SCRIPTURE

PREPARING TO TEACH

Preparing Our Hearts

Today's devotional reading is from John 19:16-30. This passage is John's account of Jesus' crucifixion. As you read, be aware of the details of the story.

Next, read the background scripture for this week's lesson from Matthew 27:32-61. Look especially at verses 38-54. Again, be alert to the details of the story. Who was present? What was happening? Where did the action take place? How did people respond to Jesus? Also ask yourself: How would I have responded had I been present? How do I respond this very minute?

Pray that God might lead you to accept Jesus' death on your own behalf, on behalf of the class members, and on behalf of all persons.

Preparing Our Minds

As you have read the crucifixion stories from Matthew and John, you have been looking for specific details. You may want to continue a comparative study by reading Mark 15:21-41 and Luke 23:26-49. List details for each account and determine how they are similar and how they are different.

Look particularly at Matthew 27:38-54. Since today's lesson focuses on these verses, be sure that you have the details of Matthew's account well in hand before you teach.

Preparing Our Learning Space

Have on hand:
- several Bibles
- paper and pencils
- hymnals.

LEADING THE CLASS

(1) Introduction

One way to open this session is to read or retell the Focusing on the Main Question portion. If you do, allow students the opportunity to call out their own unanswered questions before you move to the main question.

Another way to begin is to encourage class members to report on a good, unexpected deed that someone has done in their behalf. If the class is large, ask them to divide into small groups or talk with a partner. Ask them to consider these questions:
(1) **What happened?**
(2) **How did you feel about the deed?**
(3) **What was your attitude toward the person who performed the deed?**

End the introduction by pointing out that in today's lesson we will witness the greatest deed ever done—Jesus' death on the cross in our behalf. Note that, as we shall soon see, people had varied reactions to his crucifixion. They thought that what they could see gave them all the knowledge they needed, but they were wrong. Today's main question calls us to ask: **How can we "faith" our way through life when knowledge fails?**

(2) Mockery

Point out that mockery is an important motif in Matthew's crucifixion story. As soon as Jesus is sentenced to death in Caiaphas's house, the mocking begins.

Ask a volunteer to read the accounts of mockery in today's lesson from Matthew 27:38-44. You may want to ask one person to read most of the narration, another to read the quote in verse 40, and a third to read verses 42-44 for added drama. Then ask:

(1) **Who are Jesus' tormentors at the cross?** (Three groups are mentioned: passersby; the chief priests, scribes, and elders; and the two bandits crucified with Jesus.)

(2) **How would you describe their taunts?** (Note the discussion under "Mockery" in Interpreting the Scripture.)

(3) **Given the knowledge about Jesus that these groups would have had, how do you think you might have responded to him? Why?**

(4) **Throughout all this derision Jesus holds his peace, as he tells us to do in the Sermon on the Mount (Matthew 5:38-42). In all honesty, how do you react when people are insulting you? What lessons can you learn from Jesus?**

(3) Godforsakenness

Select an expressive reader for Matthew 27:45-50.

Now ask the students to turn in their Bibles to Psalm 22, which is the source of the quotation in verse 46. If time permits, read the entire psalm aloud, but if that is not possible, read at least the first verse. Invite the students to give their own inter-

pretations of Matthew 27:46 in light of Psalm 22.

Next, lecture briefly on four ways that this verse has been understood. You will find this information bulleted in the second paragraph of "Godforsakenness" in Interpreting the Scripture.

(4) Curtain

After a volunteer reads Matthew 27:51-53, ask these two questions. You will find information to augment the students' responses under "Curtain" in the Interpreting the Scripture portion.

(1) **What is the significance of the tearing of the curtain?** (One possible meaning is that this event foreshadows the destruction of the Temple that will occur in A.D. 70. Another possibility is that the tearing of the curtain allows unrestricted access to God, thereby offering Gentiles the opportunity to hear and accept the gospel message.)

(2) **What is the significance of the earthquake?** (God is present. Moreover, the earthquake becomes the mechanism by which tombs are torn open and the dead are raised to new life. Following Jesus' resurrection, these persons are actually seen by many others in the city of Jerusalem.)

(5) Confession

Read Matthew 27:54 aloud yourself, asking the class to join you in reading the centurion's words, "Truly this man was God's Son!"

Provide a few moments for silent meditation. Ask the class to consider what it means to them to say that Jesus was God's Son. If time permits, invite some students to share their thoughts with the class. Be sure to note that this confession is not based on knowledge that can be proved but on faith.

Ask the students these questions:

(1) **How does this confession stand in stark contrast to the rest of the state-**

?

ments that people have made during the crucifixion? (The centurion and his soldiers acknowledge who Jesus is, whereas the other onlookers have mocked him because, ironically, they did not believe that he could possibly be who he said he was.)

(2) What does the entire passage of today's lesson say to you about how God acts?

(3) Do you believe that Jesus' death was in your behalf? If so, how does his willingness to die for you make you feel?

(4) What confession of belief are you willing to make?

If time permits, distribute paper and pencils. Direct the students to write a brief confession of their own faith stating what they believe about Jesus. Consider having the group stand in a circle, if this is possible in your space, and listen as several volunteers read what they have written.

To close today's session, ask students to turn in their hymnals to a hymn concerning Jesus' crucifixion. "To Mock Your Reign, O Dearest Lord" (*The United Methodist Hymnal*, no. 285) or "O Sacred Head, Now Wounded" (*UMH*, no. 286) would be especially appropriate choices because they include words based on Matthew's text.

Point out at least one of the activities below so that students might continue to engage this week's lesson in the days ahead.

HELPING CLASS MEMBERS ACT

Recommend that the students think back to a time when they had to depend upon their faith in the face of an unexplainable situation. Encourage them to recall what happened, how they responded, and what impact this event had on their faith. How do they use this experience to help others facing difficult circumstances?

Suggest that class members be aware of how they turn against leaders in the church, workplace, or government when their actions do not meet the members' own expectations. Do they forgive them, scorn them, shun them, gossip about them, or act in some other way? Ask the students to consider their response in light of the different people who stood near Jesus' cross. What lessons can they learn from the ancient observers' varied responses to Jesus?

Note that those who passed by Jesus at the crucifixion surely misunderstood the man, his mission, and his relationship with God. Recommend that students write in a spiritual journal an account of a time when they felt misunderstood and maligned. How did their faith help them to grow beyond this incident?

PLANNING FOR NEXT SUNDAY

The lessons for the winter quarter will conclude next week with a lesson entitled "The Basis of Our Authority." Here the students will consider Jesus' resurrection as recounted in Matthew 28:1-10, though the lesson focuses on the Great Commission of Matthew 28:16-20. Ask the class to read Matthew 27:62–28:20.

THE BASIS OF OUR AUTHORITY

PREVIEWING THE LESSON

Lesson Scripture: Matthew 28:1-10, 16-20
Background Scripture: Matthew 27:62–28:20
Key Verses: Matthew 28:19-20

Focus of the Lesson:
Soon after his resurrection, Jesus commissioned his disciples to share the good news with all nations.

Main Question of the Lesson:
Do we dare trust that Easter gusher enough to scatter our rose petals into it?

This lesson will enable adult learners to:
(1) be modern witnesses to Jesus' resurrection and commissioning of his disciples.
(2) recognize that Jesus is the basis of our authority.
(3) respond by being faithful to the Great Commission.

Today's lesson may be outlined as follows:
(1) Introduction
(2) Galilee
(3) Doubt
(4) Task
(5) Emmanuel

FOCUSING ON THE MAIN QUESTION

On the campus of the University of Texas in Austin there is an oil pump, placed there as a historical monument, with the name of Santa Rita #1. The state legislature had endowed the university with relatively worthless land in west Texas. In the 1920s Frank Pickrell became convinced that there was oil out there, but he could get no one to back him in his struggle to work such unproven wildcat territory. Dry hole after dry hole seemed to bear out the skepticism, and at last he came to the end of his own resources. But he persisted in his efforts to get someone else to share his dream.

At last his search for investors brought him to a group of Catholic women in New York. Their priest was so unenthusiastic that he told them if they were foolish enough to invest in Texas oil they should invoke Santa Rita, the patron saint of impossible causes. In the end they decided to follow their priest's advice while they shared Frank Pickrell's dream. And so along with the money they gave him a rose, which had been blessed by their priest, with instructions that he was to climb to the top of the derrick and scatter the rose petals over it, saying, "I hereby christen thee Santa Rita." The hole dug with their money, of course, on land owned by the University of Texas was the discovery well of the huge Permian Basin oil fields. Frank Pickrell's scattering rose petals into that gusher is one of the more dramatic images of Texas oil.

Pickrell's single-minded quest strikes a responsive chord in us, for the gospel seemed as much a lost cause as pumping money into Texas oil. And yet Pickrell continued on, dry hole after dry hole, and he kept trying to win others, sustained by the conviction that if there has been a gusher in the past there will be another one. In like manner we are commanded to continue our efforts to make disciples. There has been the gusher at Easter, and that supreme fact promises future gushers beyond the discouraging dry holes. So our main question is: **Do we dare trust that Easter gusher enough to scatter our rose petals into it?**

READING THE SCRIPTURE

NRSV
Matthew 28:1-10, 16-20

1 After the sabbath, as the first day of the week was dawning, Mary Magdalene and the other Mary went to see the tomb. 2 And suddenly there was a great earthquake; for an angel of the Lord, descending from heaven, came and rolled back the stone and sat on it. 3 His appearance was like lightning, and his clothing white as snow. 4 For fear of him the guards shook and became like dead men. 5 But the angel said to the women, "Do not be afraid; I know that you are looking for Jesus who was crucified. 6 He is not here; for he has been raised, as he said. Come, see the place where he lay. 7 Then go quickly and tell his disciples, 'He has been raised from the dead, and indeed he is going ahead of you to Galilee; there you will see him.' This is my message for you." 8 So they left the tomb quickly with fear and great joy, and ran to tell his disciples. 9 Suddenly Jesus met them and said, "Greetings!" And they came to him, took hold of his feet, and worshiped him. 10 Then Jesus said to them, "Do not be afraid; go and tell my brothers to go to Galilee; there they will see me."

16 Now the eleven disciples went to

NIV
Matthew 28:1-10, 16-20

[1]After the Sabbath, at dawn on the first day of the week, Mary Magdalene and the other Mary went to look at the tomb.

[2]There was a violent earthquake, for an angel of the Lord came down from heaven and, going to the tomb, rolled back the stone and sat on it. [3]His appearance was like lightning, and his clothes were white as snow. [4]The guards were so afraid of him that they shook and became like dead men.

[5]The angel said to the women, "Do not be afraid, for I know that you are looking for Jesus, who was crucified. [6]He is not here; he has risen, just as he said. Come and see the place where he lay. [7]Then go quickly and tell his disciples: 'He has risen from the dead and is going ahead of you into Galilee. There you will see him.' Now I have told you."

[8]So the women hurried away from the tomb, afraid yet filled with joy, and ran to tell his disciples. [9]Suddenly Jesus met them. "Greetings," he said. They came to him, clasped his feet and worshiped him. [10]Then Jesus said to them, "Do not be afraid. Go and tell my brothers to go to Galilee; there they will see me."

[16]Then the eleven disciples went to

Galilee, to the mountain to which Jesus had directed them. 17 When they saw him, they worshiped him; but some doubted. 18 And Jesus came and said to them, "All authority in heaven and on earth has been given to me. **19 Go therefore and make disciples of all nations, baptizing them in the name of the Father and of the Son and of the Holy Spirit, 20 and teaching them to obey everything that I have commanded you. And remember, I am with you always, to the end of the age."**

Key Verses

Galilee, to the mountain where Jesus had told them to go. [17]When they saw him, they worshiped him; but some doubted. [18]Then Jesus came to them and said, "All authority in heaven and on earth has been given to me. **[19]Therefore go and make disciples of all nations, baptizing them in the name of the Father and of the Son and of the Holy Spirit, [20]and teaching them to obey everything I have commanded you. And surely I am with you always, to the very end of the age."**

Ke Vers

UNDERSTANDING THE SCRIPTURE

Matthew 27:62-66. The Preparation Day is from 6:00 P.M. Thursday until 6:00 P.M. Friday. The burial, therefore, must have been completed before 6:00 P.M. Verse 62 begins with Saturday morning. The chief priests and Pharisees tell Pilate that Jesus was an impostor (27:63 NRSV) or deceiver (NIV), one who deliberately misleads others from the truth of God. In the Greek Old Testament the cognate verb is used of enticing others to serve false gods (Deuteronomy 13:6) and of the prophets who lead people astray through the influence of Baal (Jeremiah 23:13). (See also John 7:12.) The only resurrection word reported to have been spoken by Jesus in the presence of the Pharisees is the comparison with Jonah in the belly of the whale (Matthew 12:40), although it is likely that they had heard about some of the others.

Implied in the Pharisees' comments to Pilate in verse 64 is the first deception, that is, a belief in Jesus as the Messiah. This possibility had already excited the crowds, who were ready to join the Zealots in revolt against Rome whenever they thought the Messiah had appeared to lead them in battle. The commotion at Palm Sunday was a warning, and the fervor leading up to the Passover had been so potentially explosive that it had dictated

the way in which the Crucifixion had been handled. This danger appeared to have passed. But "the last deception," that Jesus had risen from the dead (27:64), would confirm to the crowd that the Messiah was indeed among them. This would be worse because it would be even more dangerous in precipitating a disastrous revolt.

Matthew 28:1-10. It is possible that the earthquake and the angelic appearance occur together while the women watch. This view is presupposed by the NRSV's "suddenly" in verse 2. It is possible that the earthquake occurred during the night and that the women see the angel already sitting on the stone. In this case the "behold" of the NKJV is the preferred translation. The Greek word is an interjection that calls attention but has no thought of time. The NIV leaves it untranslated. The stone is rolled away, of course, to allow the women to inspect the tomb, not to let Jesus out. The body has been transformed into another dimension, and so exit by the door would be as incongruous as the continued wearing of the grave wrappings. But the Resurrection must be discovered, and so the women are shown that the tomb really is empty.

The angel reassures them (28:5), explaining the emptiness of the tomb (28:6) by reminding them of Jesus' own words. (See Matthew 16:21; 17:23; and 20:19.) Their fear is now mixed with joy (28:8). In spite of the angelic reassurance, they have an uncanny sensation of fear or awe in the presence of what they cannot understand. The great joy that floods over them shows that the fear is not terror, and so they do not run as from danger, but bursting with news.

After the ordinary greeting of verse 9, the women recognize "their" Jesus at once and grasp the truth about the empty tomb. They can't just say "hello" as if nothing out of the ordinary has happened. And so, awed in their joy, they fall to the ground and touch his feet in a token of submission and worship. In verse 10 Jesus repeats the angel's injunction, but with one significant change. The angel had told them to make the announcement to "his disciples," but Jesus sends them to "my brothers."

Matthew 28:11-20. When the Roman guards come to, they know that something extraordinary has happened and some of them report to the chief priests (28:11).

They are bribed to say that the disciples stole the body while they were asleep (28:13). And if Pilate hears of this, in a court-martial for dereliction of duty the chief priests will intervene to squash the indictment (28:14). Producing the body, of course, would be the most effective refutation of the Christian claim of resurrection; but since there is no body for them to display, the lie is the next best strategy. In the middle of the second century, Justin Martyr says that this explanation of the empty tomb is still being repeated.

The giving of the covenant to Moses on Mount Sinai enriched the association of divine revelation with mountains; and so a mountain is the locale for the Transfiguration (17:1), the prayer for guidance (14:23), and the Sermon (5:1). Each of these has been considered as the location of the Resurrection appearance in verse 16. From this mountain, Jesus commissions his eleven remaining disciples. He promises to be with them as they do the work to which he has called them.

INTERPRETING THE SCRIPTURE

Galilee

Eleven out of twelve, putting Judas behind them, aim for the future by going to Galilee (28:16). It is our experience as well that someone is always quitting, that someone else is always joining, and that for the most part we never know why. So, alternately discouraged and encouraged, we too head for our Galilee, trusting that it all means more than we could ever figure out on our own.

Galilee has special meaning because that is where Jesus' own ministry had begun. The Gospel writer quotes Isaiah 9:1-2 in Matthew 4:15-16: "Galilee of the Gentiles—the people who sat in darkness have seen a great light." Thus, Matthew sees

Jesus' work in Galilee as the fulfillment of Isaiah's prophecy. (See the background scripture for December 12.) For Isaiah, Galilee symbolizes the whole Gentile world, and so beginning the ministry in Galilee anticipates its ultimate importance to the whole world. And beginning it here again, after its end in Jerusalem, pledges that the ministry cannot be snuffed out before its work is done. So to go to Galilee is to be part of Jesus' own ministry, to be inclusive in our vision and confident that our Savior controls the future.

Within Galilee itself it is significant that the meeting is to take place on the mountain where Jesus had directed them (28:16 NRSV) or told them to go (NIV). If the meaning of the verb is to send them to a particular place, they somehow know where to go even though there has been no previously mentioned instruction. If, on the other hand, the verb refers to Jesus' teaching, as Douglas R. A. Hare takes it, then "we can translate the verse: 'And the eleven disciples went to Galilee, to the mountain where Jesus laid down rules for them.' If this interpretation of verse 16 is accepted, the disciples' return to the site of the Sermon on the Mount reinforces Matthew's heavy emphasis on *doing* the will of the Father in heaven as interpreted by Jesus the Messiah (see esp. 7:21-27)."

Doubt

Jesus is waiting for them and they see him as soon as they arrive. They all worship and some of them doubt (28:17). The doubt in the presence of the risen Christ is so troublesome that it is explained away in two different ways. First, the doubt is not disbelief or the refusal to believe; rather, it is the uncertainty that the risen Christ is the same Jesus they had known in the earthly ministry. (Compare Luke 24:22, 36 and John 20:8, 11, and 24-25.) The chief objection to this explanation is the order. We would expect to find first doubt and then worship after the doubt had been dispelled. The second explanation states that if we equate this appearance with the appearance to the five hundred in 1 Corinthians 15:6, we may assume that all of the eleven worship and that some of the others doubt. But Matthew does not say that others are present, and so we end up importing data into the text that is not there. It is best, therefore, to stick with the text, dealing with worship and doubt together, and taking the eleven as the subject.

The word for "doubt" is unusual. Its only other occurrence in the New Testament is also in Matthew, and also within the context of the disciples' worshiping and doubting (14:31). In classical Greek the verb means to hesitate to make a deci-

sion; and in the nonliterary papyri of the Hellenistic period it can mean to waver from side to side of an issue because a firm decision has not been made. This is different from disbelief. The New Jerusalem Bible gives the flavor in the phrase "though some hesitated." So all of the eleven worship, and some of them doubt at the same time.

In the earlier scene where the verb is used, Peter eagerly walks on the water toward Jesus. He then becomes uncertain and sinks. Jesus rebukes his doubt and the disciples worship (14:31, 33). The change in order, doubt and worship rather than worship and doubt, is more apparent than real; for Peter's doubt is preceded by a faith strong enough to enable him to walk on water. Doubt as disbelief, of course, is incongruent with discipleship; but doubt as uncertainty strikes a realistic note. Since worship represents a specific action that follows certainty, the contrast is between worship and hesitation. The wavering then prepares the way for the Great Commission to come and the assurance that we will receive the strength to fulfill the task from the continuing presence of Christ. We are not expected to do it by our own power; it is a cosmic Christ we meet on the mountain in our Galilee.

Task

That cosmic Christ has a task for us. Authority has been given to him by God as a consequence of the Resurrection (28:18), and so he has the right to command. (See also Ephesians 1:20-23; Philippians 2:6-11; and Colossians 1:15-20.) The "therefore" of verse 19 connects the authority with the task, and the cosmic nature of the Sender's authority enlarges the extent of the task. Previously the apostles had been sent to the lost sheep of Israel (10:5-6), but now they are to go into the whole world. There has been preparation in the visit of the Magi (2:1-12), the centurion's servant (8:5-13), the

Gadarenes demoniac (8:28-34), the Canaanite's daughter (15:21-28), and the parable of the wicked husbandmen (21:33-45). Since Jesus is the son of Abraham (1:1), the promise that the nations of the world will be blessed through Abraham's descendants (Genesis 22:18) is now fulfilled.

Our task is to make disciples by baptizing (28:19) and teaching (28:20). The verbs are both present participles, highlighting an unremitting effort. We are to baptize continually and to teach the baptized continually.

Baptism marks the beginning of a Christian life. The "in" of verse 19 may be taken in two different ways. First, the NRSV and NIV have "in the name of." Only here is baptism connected with Father, Son, and Holy Spirit. Note that in Acts 2:38 the disciples baptize in the name of Jesus. The "in" means that baptism is administered by means of or under the authority of God in the three Persons. Second, the baptism may be "into the name of" (NIV margin). The name represents the person, and so here the name is God. Baptism is into the fellowship of God or the act of becoming God's property.

We are to teach others to obey everything that Christ has commanded. The "everything" probably goes beyond the Sermon on the Mount to recall pretty much everything that Matthew has written. The continual teaching suggests nurturing with more than classroom instruction. And the nurturing is "do as I do" as well as "do as I say"—for we ourselves are under the same command.

Emmanuel

Jesus' commission does at times seem like such an impossibly tall order that it fairly takes the breath away. But then the promise shores up our inadequacy and, heartened by the assurance that we are not alone, we dare to tackle our task. For our Teammate, whose very name means "God is with us" (Matthew 1:23), guarantees the reality behind the name. This presence gives us the sticking power to continue the effort to make disciples—no matter what.

Where the English translations have "always" (28:20), the Greek has "all the days." Douglas R. A. Hare comments, "We may guess that the phrase is intended to emphasize the *daily* nature of the supporting presence—'day by day by day.' The continued existence of the church despite its myriad sins of commission and omission provides the surest evidence that the promise has been kept." The final "end of the age," moreover, is an open-ended conclusion. The task and the presence will go on until the final consummation, however soon or distant that may be.

Meanwhile it is today, and we launch out, trusting (hoping?) that what we do will mean something, that Emmanuel is at least around the next corner, that he will show up when we need him. In such anxious moments I am reminded of a fellow I met in Bogotá and the story he told me. He was an American diplomat and his tale is about his tour in a Moscow plagued by shortages in everything. "So whenever you see a line you get in it. Because it means they have something for sale." On the day in question he spotted a group beginning to form up in a market area and so he rushed to get in line. "They were selling fresh fish and they had 20. I was number 18 in line and so I got one. But how would you like to be number 22?"

That story of standing in a line in the hope that something will come of it strikes a responsive chord in us, for discipleship often seems like that. We do whatever, as we feel led. But what if they run out of fish before we get there? Not to worry. No matter how long the line, Emmanuel promises that there is grace enough to go around.

SHARING THE SCRIPTURE

PREPARING TO TEACH

Preparing Our Hearts

Today's devotional reading, John 20:19-31, records Jesus' post-resurrection appearances to his disciples. The first time he appeared, Thomas was not present and, therefore, refused to believe. The second time, however, Thomas did see the Lord and affirmed his belief. John closes chapter 20 by stating his purpose for writing: "so that you may come to believe that Jesus is the Messiah, the Son of God, and that through believing you may have life in his name." Ponder your own willingness to believe that Jesus was indeed the Messiah and that he was resurrected by God. What action does your belief impel you to take?

Now look at Matthew's account of Easter morning and Jesus' commissioning of the disciples as found in the background scripture from Matthew 27:62–28:20. As you read 28:1-10, imagine yourself with the women as they find the tomb open and see the angel rolling back the stone. How might your beliefs about the Resurrection be different had you been present on that Sunday? Now think about the Great Commission that Jesus gives in verses 16-20. How do his words shape the way you live?

Close your spiritual preparation time by praying that God will guide you as you lead the class in studying this critically important Bible passage.

Preparing Our Minds

Review the entire background scripture from Matthew 27:62–28:20. Only Matthew includes the Great Commission, but you may want to read the accounts of the first Easter morning as found in Mark 16:1-8; Luke 24:1-12; and John 20:1-18. Reflect on how the details of these records enrich your understanding of the Resurrection.

Our lesson focuses, as the title reminds us, on "The Basis of Our Authority." Read the Great Commission, Matthew 28:16-20, from as many Bible translations as possible. How would you state these verses in your own words?

If possible, ask your pastor prior to the session about the number of baptisms that have been performed in the last year or so and the number of students of all ages who are enrolled in any kind of educational program in the church. Also check on the mission and outreach programs that your church supports.

Preparing Our Learning Space

If you decide to work in groups to do the activity under "Task," write the questions in that section on newsprint prior to class.

Have on hand:
- several Bibles
- paper and pencils
- statistical information on persons baptized and taught in your congregation, along with information about your mission and outreach programs
- hymnals.

LEADING THE CLASS

(1) Introduction

Begin today's lesson by reading expressively Matthew 28:1-10. Ask the students to hear the story from the point of view of Mary Magdalene and the other Mary. Then ask:

(1) Suppose you had been present with the women. What emotions might you have experienced from the time you left to go to the tomb until you returned to the disciples?

(2) How would you expect the male disciples to respond to your story?

(3) What would this experience say to you about life after death?

(4) What would Jesus' appearance say to you about Jesus himself?

Now turn to the Focusing on the Main Question portion and read or retell Frank Pickrell's story. Conclude by lifting up today's main question: **Do we dare trust that Easter gusher enough to scatter our rose petals into it?**

(2) Galilee

The rest of the lesson will focus on the Great Commission. Ask a volunteer to read Matthew 28:16-20. Better yet, have several volunteers read from different translations so that students will get a feel for shades of meaning. Note that verses 19-20 are our key verses for today. Invite the class to comment on why they believe Jesus told the eleven to go to Galilee. Here are several points from Interpreting the Scripture that you will want to make:

• Jesus' ministry began in Galilee. To have the disciples meet him there brings their travels with him full circle.

• Galilee symbolizes the whole world for the prophet Isaiah. The Gospel writer quotes Isaiah 9:1-2 in Matthew 4:15-16. Thus, Matthew shows that Jesus has fulfilled Isaiah's prophecy.

• The disciples are to meet Jesus on the mountain where Jesus had taught them how to live in the kingdom of God.

(3) Doubt

Highlight verse 17: "When they saw him, they worshiped him; but some doubted." Ask the class:

(1) Many times we say, "Oh, if I had only been with Jesus, then I would have no questions or doubts." What does verse 17 say to you about doubts?

(2) Do you think that doubting is the same as disbelieving? Explain your answer. (Note the second paragraph under "Doubt" in Interpreting the Scripture. The discussion of the meaning of the word for "doubt" in the Greek will be helpful in clarifying the difference between doubt and disbelief.)

Distribute paper and pencils. Read the following two questions aloud and invite the students to reflect on them in writing. Tell the class that you will not discuss these private thoughts.

(1) What doubts or hesitations do you have about Jesus' life and/or teachings?

(2) What beliefs do you hold so strongly that you can, in fact, worship despite your doubts?

(4) Task

Direct the class to look at Matthew 28:18. Note that God has given Jesus this authority and, in turn, that gives Jesus the right to command us. If time permits, have the students turn in their Bibles to three other passages concerning Jesus' authority: Ephesians 1:20-23; Philippians 2:6-11; and Colossians 1:15-20.

Point out that the word "therefore" in verse 19 connects the idea of Jesus' authority to the task to which we as his followers are called. Note that there is one task to be done: make disciples. To do this, we are to baptize and teach obedience to Jesus' teachings.

Share with the class the statistical information you were able to get from the pastor concerning the number of baptisms and the enrollment in all of the Christian education programs that the congregation offers. (Members of United Methodist congregations will be able to find this information in the most recent charge conference report.) Also summarize the mission and outreach programs that your church supports through contributions and/or by hands-on service. In light of this data, ask the questions below. You may want to have the whole class discuss them, or you may prefer to divide into groups and reconvene as a class to share the responses. If you choose to work in groups, write the questions on newsprint prior to class.

? (1) **What do the number of baptisms say about the way in which we as a congregation are bringing children, youth, and adults to Christ?**

(2) **What changes do we need to make? How can we go about making them?**

(3) **What does our overall enrollment in educational programs say about the scope and effectiveness of our teaching ministry?**

(4) **What changes do we need to make? How can we go about making them?**

(5) **How are we reaching out to "all nations"?**

(6) **What changes do we need to make? How can we go about making them?**

(5) Emmanuel

Matthew 1:23 and 28:20 both remind us that God is with us. Invite volunteers to speak about ways that they experience God's comforting and empowering presence "day by day."

Conclude the lesson by singing a hymn such as "Freely, Freely" (*The United Methodist Hymnal*, no. 389), "Go, Make of All Disciples" (*UMH*, no. 571), or "Lord, You Give the Great Commission" (*UMH*, no. 584).

Before you dismiss the class, be sure to suggest at least one of the ideas below so that the students will be able to live out the Great Commission in the coming week.

HELPING CLASS MEMBERS ACT

Suggest that students read the Great Commission every morning this week. Encourage them to be alert to ways that they can live it out as they go about the ordinary business of their lives.

Although not all persons are teachers by profession or calling, everyone in the class is a teacher or mentor for someone. Ask the students to list on paper the people (for example, children, team members, co-workers, neighbors, or church members) whom they teach either formally or informally. Encourage the class, as appropriate opportunities arise, to teach others by word and/or deed what Christian discipleship is all about.

The Great Commission closes with a promise of Jesus' abiding presence. Challenge class members to be aware of Jesus, especially when they are having difficulties. Urge them to give thanks each time they recognize the Messiah's presence.

PLANNING FOR NEXT SUNDAY

Next Sunday we will begin our spring unit, "Continuing Jesus' Work." This unit, which focuses on Paul's two letters to the church at Corinth, will help us recognize that the contemporary church confronts problems that are in many ways similar to those that the early church encountered. Ask students to prepare for next week's lesson, "Appeal for Unity," by reading 1 Corinthians 1:1-17.

THIRD QUARTER
Continuing Jesus' Work

MARCH 5, 2000–MAY 28, 2000

"Continuing Jesus' Work" looks at Paul's two letters to the church at Corinth. From these epistles we can get a glimpse of the challenges that confronted the Corinthian congregation. Paul wisely guides them as they work to solve their problems. Although the modern church is different in numerous ways from the one at Corinth, we confront similar problems concerning leadership, the use of diverse spiritual gifts, broken relationships, and the need for discipline within the church. Thus, Paul's words to the Corinthian church are useful for us as well.

Unit 1, "Christ the Basis of Unity," opens with a session about the need for unity within the church. The other three lessons deal with the role of the Holy Spirit as teacher, the leaders of the church as servants of Christ, and the need for discipline in the church. The study for March 5, "Appeal for Unity," is based on 1 Corinthians 1:2-17. Having heard of quarrels and divisions among the church members, Paul admonishes them to be of one mind and purpose. In the next session, "True Wisdom: A Basis for Unity," Paul speaks in 1 Corinthians 2:1-2, 4-13, and 15-16 of God's wisdom as revealed through the Holy Spirit. Those who have this wisdom will have the mind of Christ. On March 19 we will study how "Mature Leaders Bring Unity." In this lesson from 1 Corinthians 4:1-13 Paul teaches about the church and its leaders—those who are "servants of Christ and stewards of God's mysteries" (4:1). The final session in this series, "Discipline Brings Unity," looks at 1 Corinthians 5:1-13. Addressing a particular case of sexual misconduct, Paul insists that the church must enforce discipline.

The second unit, "Unity in Human Relationships," begins on April 2 with a lesson entitled "Responsibility in Marriage and Singleness." Rooted in 1 Corinthians 7:1-5 and 8-16, this lesson considers appropriate relationships between spouses and also speaks to the issues of divorce and singleness. "Let Love Lead," the session for April 9, looks at 1 Corinthians 8 where Paul addresses the matter of eating meat sacrificed to animals. He concludes that while a particular action may not be sinful, a mature Christian should lovingly refrain from such action if it will cause another to stumble. The session for April 16, "Work Together," looks in 1 Corinthians 12:4-20 and 26 at the diversity of gifts given by God for the benefit of the church. The lesson for Easter Sunday, "What About the Resurrection?" will give us an opportunity to hear Paul's teaching in 1 Corinthians 15:20-27 and 35-44 about the significance of Jesus' resurrection. This unit will conclude on April 30 with a study of the beloved teachings of 1 Corinthians 12:31–13:13. Here we will answer the question "What's Real Love?"

Unit 3, "The Glory of Christian Ministry," begins on May 7 with a lesson from 2 Corinthians 2:4-17 entitled "From Sorrow to Joy." Paul writes to the church at Corinth to tell them that they should love and forgive a member who has caused pain. "From Suffering to Triumph," based on 2 Corinthians 4:5-18, explores Paul's attitude toward the trials that he has suffered in order to proclaim Christ. In the lesson for May 21, "From Reluctance to Joyful Giving," which is found in 2 Corinthians 9:1-13, Paul encourages the Corinthians, who have already given generously, to continue to be cheerful givers. This quarter concludes on May 28 with a look at 2 Corinthians 13:1-13. In "From Confrontation to Growth" Paul challenges the people to test the quality of their own faith in Christ. Paul truly wants the Corinthian church to solve its problems before he arrives.

MEET OUR WRITERS

DR. CLIFTON BLACK

Clifton Black is Professor of New Testament at the Perkins School of Theology, Southern Methodist University, Dallas, Texas. He received his B.A. from Wake Forest University (Phi Beta Kappa, 1977), master's degrees in religion and theology from the University of Bristol (1980) and Emory University (1981), and his Ph.D. from Duke University (1986).

Dr. Black is the author of *The Disciples According to Mark* (1989), *Mark: Images of an Apostolic Interpreter* (1994), Commentary on 1, 2, and 3 John in volume 12 of *The New Interpreter's Bible* (1998), and the coeditor of *Exploring the Gospel of John in Honor of D. Moody Smith* (1996). He has published over seventy essays and reviews in over thirty-five books and journals. A teacher of pastors and laity within many denominations across the country, Dr. Black has extensively contributed to the curriculum resources of The United Methodist Church, including its popular video series, DISCIPLE. He is the author of the Abingdon New Testament Commentary on Mark's Gospel.

Dr. Black is a charter member of the Seminar on the Gospel of Mark in the international Society for New Testament Studies, an associate editor of the *Journal of Biblical Literature,* and a founding member of the editorial board of The New Testament Library of Westminster John Knox Press. He is an ordained elder of the Western North Carolina Annual Conference of The United Methodist Church. He and his wife, Harriet, have one daughter, Caroline Elizabeth.

THE REVEREND PATRICK J. WILLSON

Patrick J. Willson is a minister of the Presbyterian Church (USA) currently serving as pastor of Williamsburg Presbyterian Church in Williamsburg, Virginia. He has previously served parishes in Texas, Alabama, Mississippi, and Tennessee. Reverend Willson also served as Adjunct Professor of Homiletics at Brite Divinity School of Texas Christian University. In addition to his work as a pastor and teacher, he has written for publications including *The Christian Century, Pulpit Digest, Word & Witness,* and *Lectionary Homiletics.* Reverend Willson is married and father to two daughters.

UNIT 1: CHRIST THE BASIS OF UNITY
APPEAL FOR UNITY

PREVIEWING THE LESSON

Lesson Scripture: 1 Corinthians 1:2-17
Background Scripture: 1 Corinthians 1:1-17
Key Verse: 1 Corinthians 1:10

Focus of the Lesson:
For the sake of Christ's ministry, Paul appealed to the congregation in Corinth to end the quarrels that divided them.

Main Question of the Lesson:
On what basis can Christians hope to overcome those things that threaten to divide them?

This lesson will enable adult learners to:
(1) examine Paul's plea for unity to the Corinthian church.
(2) consider their own understandings of church unity.
(3) respond by taking a step to facilitate unity in their own church.

Today's lesson may be outlined as follows:
(1) Introduction
(2) Saints Without Halos
(3) Highest Calling or Lowest Common Denominator?
(4) The Unkindest Cult of All
(5) Whose Ministry Is It, Anyway?

FOCUSING ON THE MAIN QUESTION

Maybe not within your own congregation—God forbid that it be so!—but somewhere, somehow, in the community where you live, it has just occurred or is on the verge of happening: a Christian congregation collapses.

We have become so accustomed to church breakdowns that their oddity may escape us. Most of us, after all, consider ourselves peaceable people. Although each of us has been molded by experiences very different from those of our neighbors, still we share with them many of the same values and concerns. Most of the time we enjoy comparing our experiences with those of others; usually we are willing to talk through our differences with others in search of common ground. Given the choice, most of us prefer open handshakes over clenched fists. We would rather be hugged than shunned. Why, then, don't Christians seem able to get along with one another?

Viewed from another angle, divisions

251

within the church are scandalous. Of all communities that ought to operate on the principles of love and unity, surely the church should stand at the forefront! "You are the light of the world," taught Jesus, "let your light shine before others, so that they may see your good works and give glory to your Father in heaven" (Matthew 5:14, 16). When congregations rupture, how does that encourage Christians or anyone else to glorify God? How often do non-Christians see within the church not a beacon of hope, but a dim bulb in a darkened world?

Many of the same temptations to fall apart were experienced by the earliest Christian communities. Among these was a mission church in Corinth, Greece, to which the apostle Paul wrote around the year A.D. 54. We haven't far to read in 1 Corinthians before learning that the Corinthian church, founded only a few years earlier by Paul, was already becoming unglued. The apostle had to begin this lengthy letter with an earnest appeal that they stop quarreling among themselves, put an end to their divisions, and come together "in the same mind and the same purpose" (1 Corinthians 1:10). Well and good, we might say. But Paul invites us to dig more deeply. The main question is this: **On what basis can Christians hope to overcome those things that threaten to divide them?**

READING THE SCRIPTURE

NRSV
1 Corinthians 1:2-17

2 To the church of God that is in Corinth, to those who are sanctified in Christ Jesus, called to be saints, together with all those who in every place call on the name of our Lord Jesus Christ, both their Lord and ours:

3 Grace to you and peace from God our Father and the Lord Jesus Christ.

4 I give thanks to my God always for you because of the grace of God that has been given you in Christ Jesus, 5 for in every way you have been enriched in him, in speech and knowledge of every kind—6 just as the testimony of Christ has been strengthened among you—7 so that you are not lacking in any spiritual gift as you wait for the revealing of our Lord Jesus Christ. 8 He will also strengthen you to the end, so that you may be blameless on the day of our Lord Jesus Christ. 9 God is faithful; by him you were called into the fellowship of his Son, Jesus Christ our Lord.

Key Verse 10 **Now I appeal to you, brothers and sisters, by the name of our Lord Jesus Christ, that all of you be in agreement and that there be no divisions among**

NIV
1 Corinthians 1:2-17

2To the church of God in Corinth, to those sanctified in Christ Jesus and called to be holy, together with all those everywhere who call on the name of our Lord Jesus Christ—their Lord and ours:

3Grace and peace to you from God our Father and the Lord Jesus Christ.

4I always thank God for you because of his grace given you in Christ Jesus. 5For in him you have been enriched in every way—in all your speaking and in all your knowledge—6because our testimony about Christ was confirmed in you. 7Therefore you do not lack any spiritual gift as you eagerly wait for our Lord Jesus Christ to be revealed. 8He will keep you strong to the end, so that you will be blameless on the day of our Lord Jesus Christ. 9God, who has called you into fellowship with his Son Jesus Christ our Lord, is faithful.

10**I appeal to you, brothers, in the name of our Lord Jesus Christ, that all of you agree with one another so that there may be no divisions among you and that you may be perfectly united in mind and thought.** 11My brothers, some from Chloe's house-

Key Verse

you, but that you be united in the same mind and the same purpose. 11 For it has been reported to me by Chloe's people that there are quarrels among you, my brothers and sisters. 12 What I mean is that each of you says, "I belong to Paul," or "I belong to Apollos," or "I belong to Cephas," or "I belong to Christ." 13 Has Christ been divided? Was Paul crucified for you? Or were you baptized in the name of Paul? 14 I thank God that I baptized none of you except Crispus and Gaius, 15 so that no one can say that you were baptized in my name. 16 (I did baptize also the household of Stephanas; beyond that, I do not know whether I baptized anyone else.) 17 For Christ did not send me to baptize but to proclaim the gospel, and not with eloquent wisdom, so that the cross of Christ might not be emptied of its power.

hold have informed me that there are quarrels among you. ¹²What I mean is this: One of you says, "I follow Paul"; another, "I follow Apollos"; another, "I follow Cephas"; still another, "I follow Christ."

¹³Is Christ divided? Was Paul crucified for you? Were you baptized into the name of Paul? ¹⁴I am thankful that I did not baptize any of you except Crispus and Gaius, ¹⁵so no one can say that you were baptized into my name. ¹⁶(Yes, I also baptized the household of Stephanas; beyond that, I don't remember if I baptized anyone else.) ¹⁷For Christ did not send me to baptize, but to preach the gospel—not with words of human wisdom, lest the cross of Christ be emptied of its power.

UNDERSTANDING THE SCRIPTURE

1 Corinthians 1:1-3. To the church of God in Corinth (the capital of the ancient Roman province of Achaia), Paul writes as "an apostle of Christ Jesus by the will of God." An "apostle" refers to an envoy or emissary dispatched by another on a mission. Thus, Paul writes not as a "professional" clergyman, even less as an interfering meddler in Corinthian affairs, but as one who has received a special calling by God to preach the gospel, or "good news," of Jesus Christ (see 1 Corinthians 1:17; Galatians 1:1, 11-12). Sosthenes, Paul's "brother" (in Christ) and co-sender of this letter, may be the synagogue official whom Luke mentions in Acts 18:17.

Significantly, Paul refers to the Corinthian Christians as "sanctified" and called to be "saints." (Both terms are translations of words that share a single root in Greek.) Paul does not mean that the Corinthians are sanctimonious or hypocritically pious. In biblical tradition to sanctify, or to make holy, is to set apart someone or something in the service of God, the Holy One (see Leviticus 22:32). The Corinthians' holiness is not a unique status, achieved by their own design. They, "together with all those who in every place call on the name" of the one Lord (1 Corinthians 1:2), have been called by God and set apart in Christ Jesus. On them, as on all Christians, rest God's grace (unmerited favor) and peace (wholeness in community).

1 Corinthians 1:4-9. Paul offers an expression of thanks that is typical of his other letters (see Romans 1:8-15; Philippians 1:3-11; 1 Thessalonians 1:2-10). Notice that in 1 Corinthians 1:4-9 Paul's thanks is rendered not directly to the Corinthians, but rather to God, by whose grace that church has been "in every way... enriched" (1:5). Notice also in these verses that Paul takes a rather daring step: he thanks God for precisely those gifts that, as we shall learn later, the Corinthians have not always used wisely: speech and other spiritual gifts (see 1 Corinthians 12–14), knowledge (1 Corinthians 8), and testimony (1 Corinthians 2–4). Notice finally in 1:4-9 that Paul does not immediately focus on the Corinthians or reprimand them for their misconduct. Instead, he lovingly reminds them that their strength and endowments depend entirely, and will continue to depend, on God's own fidelity to them through "the fellowship of his Son, Jesus Christ our Lord" (1:9).

1 Corinthians 1:10-17. Paul moves to the first of many difficulties afflicting the church in Corinth: the breakdown of unity and the proliferation of divisions. That this is a major problem for the Corinthians is signaled by both the careful attention it receives from Paul until the end of 1 Corinthians 4 and the issue's reemergence in different forms in 1 Corinthians 8:1–11:1; 11:17-34; and 12–14. In 1 Corinthians 1:10-17 the primary problem appears to have been the Corinthians' cliquishness, of which Paul has learned from the people (kinfolk or other associates) of Chloe, probably a Christian woman of importance in Corinth. Factions had cropped up around various figures accorded prominence within that congregation: Paul, who founded that church (Acts 18:1-18; 1 Corinthians 2:1-5; 2 Corinthians 1:19); Apollos, a popular preacher who apparently spent time in Corinth (Acts 18:24–19:1; 1 Corinthians 3:4-6, 22; 4:6; 16:12); and Cephas, or Simon Peter (1 Corinthians 3:22; 9:5; 15:5; Galatians 1:18; 2:7-8, 11-14). Exactly what was meant by those boasting that they belonged "to Christ" (1:12) is impossible to know. In giving thanks that he baptized—so far as he can recall—only Crispus, Gaius (see also Acts 18:8; Romans 16:23), and the household of Stephanas (1 Corinthians 16:15, 17), Paul is not putting down baptism as such (see Romans 6:3-4; 1 Corinthians 12:12-13; Galatians 3:27-28). Rather, he is chiding the Corinthians for elevating their leaders on false pedestals, thereby rupturing the church's unity in Christ (1 Corinthians 1:13). Paul wants no part of any hero worship or power plays that may have erupted in Corinth; his sole mission from Christ is to preach the gospel in such a way that the authentic power of Christ's cross is in no way compromised (1:17).

INTERPRETING THE SCRIPTURE

Saints Without Halos

We began this lesson with one main question: **On what basis can Christians hope to overcome those things that threaten to divide them?** From 1 Corinthians 1:1-17 Paul's answer is clear: only on the basis of "the grace of God that has been given [us] in Christ Jesus" (1:4). For Paul, this assessment is neither empty religious jargon nor an impossible dream. God's grace, given to us through Christ, is both an inescapable fact and the church's only hope.

By addressing the Corinthian Christians as "sanctified," "called to be saints" (1:2), Paul has not for a moment forgotten that they (and he himself, for that matter: see 1 Corinthians 2:3-4) wobble on feet of clay. Nor is Paul craftily buttering up his readers before lowering the boom on them in 1:10-17. We may mislead ourselves in interpreting his intentions because of understandings of "holiness" and "sainthood" that suggest moral perfection or spiritual elitism. Historically, some Christian denominations have adopted criteria by which unusually gifted or notable persons are authoritatively recognized (or "canonized") as saints. Informally, modern Christians and non-Christians may regard a person of extraordinary charity as a saint, or see worshipers who engage in frenzied religious practices as "Holy Rollers."

In reading Paul's description of the Christians in Corinth, we need to remember the biblical understanding of sanctity and holiness: being set apart by God, for God's use. Paul is not referring here to a special order of clergy or some religious elite. Most certainly he is not referring to those who adopt a certain line of thought, or who model themselves after a particular leader (see 1:12-13). To whom is Paul referring? "To the church of God that is in Corinth, . . . together with all those who in every place call on the name of our Lord Jesus Christ" (1:2). All Christians, by their baptism, have been incorporated into God's holy church and, as *The Book of Common Prayer* states, "[made] worthy to share in the inheritance of the saints in light." As Christians we have been set apart, not by our own choosing but by God's. Our holiness is not our own, but Christ's. Our service is not of ourselves, but of the One who has called us to be the saints that indeed we are.

Highest Calling or Lowest Common Denominator?

The kind of factions to which Corinthian Christians were prone may seem to today's Christians as recognizable as the last messy meeting of our conference, synod, session, parish council, or committee on pastor-parish relations. To our eyes the biggest differences may lie in the way such conflicts are handled. For Paul it was imperative that the church in Corinth and in all places remember its primary responsibility to God, the sole source of genuine grace and peace (1:3). For only when the church remembers its true identity—"the fellowship of [those with] his Son, Jesus Christ our Lord" (1:9)—can it rise above its quarrelsome divisions and reclaim its proper vocation of unimpeachable service (1:8).

How are divisions repaired and factions defused in the modern church? Too often it seems that instead of lifting our eyes to a higher Christian vocation that transcends our individual interests—however proximately correct they are or passionately about them we may feel—we try to patch over our partisanship through political compromise, typically factored down to the lowest acceptable denominator. What course of action can we take, based on a simple majority, that will offend the fewest, pacify the powerful, and deflect concentration from hard theological questions? Given these rather different approaches to conflict-resolution, there is a fine line between who has exhibited more hard-nosed realism about the church of God: Paul, or ourselves?

The Unkindest Cult of All

The collapse of community, signaled in 1 Corinthians 1:10-17, appears to have been triggered by one of the oldest, hardiest sins within the church: the cult of personality. Perhaps your own congregation has been spared this affliction. You should not have far to travel, however, before coming to a church whose members, like so many planets pulled into solar orbit, revolve around a particular pastor, teacher, matriarch, or patriarch. Woe betide that leader's associate or successor, who might have another gift, or a different view, to offer a church that has sold itself on the exclusive validity of "our hero." Frequently, as was the case in Corinth, there are multiple solar systems within a single congregation: clusters of satellite parishioners encircling a modern "Paul" and "Apollos" and "Cephas." In the United States such a phenomenon is not uncommon among large churches with multiple pastors on staff.

How different Paul's response: in effect, "A plague on all your houses!" and in fact, "Has Christ been divided?" (1:13, the latter question obviously inviting the answer,

"No!"). Most interesting of all is Paul's flat refusal to join in the Corinthians' self-destructive game, to be seduced by those who wanted him as their own hero (1:13): "Was Paul crucified for you?" (Ridiculous!) "Or were you baptized in the name of Paul?" (Of course not!) Paul's remarks here, as well as later (1 Corinthians 3:5-9), helpfully remind us that neither he nor Apollos nor Cephas may have desired, much less have encouraged, the hero worship lavished on them by their cheerleaders in Corinth. (The same is true of many modern church leaders, appalled by the inappropriate boosterism of their fans.) Paul's comments also remind us of the great delicacy of his own position in helping the Corinthians to resolve their quarrels appropriately: for if he came on too strongly, appearing to force his readers to yield to the wisdom of his own viewpoint, he would only end up adding more fuel to a raging partisan fire.

Whose Ministry Is It, Anyway?

That, in a sense, is the question that Paul aims at Christians bent on factional bickering. It is exactly the right question: not just because it prevents Paul from being sucked into the Corinthians' quarrels and aggravating their divisions, but primarily because that question realigns the main issue, which in Corinth had become radically skewed. The careful reader of 1 Corinthians 1:1-17 realizes that this is the question that Paul has been repeatedly, emphatically, univocally answering from the letter's very beginning. The ministry is neither Paul's, nor Apollos's, nor Cephas's, nor the Corinthians'. The ministry is Christ's because the church is of God (1:2). Paul's own calling, like the Corinthians', is of Christ Jesus by God's will (1:1). The church is not a self-sanctified lord over its own destiny; the church has been made holy by Christ Jesus, our one Lord (1:2). The church's manifold enrichment, spiritual wealth, continuous strengthening, and evangelistic testimony were not the result of "the right people" joining First Church, Corinth. Rather, all these things have been pure gifts from God, whose grace is unmitigated, whose fidelity is utterly dependable, whose calling of Christians into communion with his Son is irrevocable (1:4-9). When the church, ancient or modern, comes to realize that God's ministry through Jesus Christ is the only essential and indispensable ministry, then the derivative gifts of Paul, Apollos, Cephas, all of the Corinthians, and all of us fall properly and healthily into place.

To sum up: Paul appealed to the Corinthian congregation to end their divisive quarrels for the sake of Christ's ministry, by the power of God, who enables the church to come together in authentically Christian communion. Simply patching up arguments or papering over differences is not the point, whether for Corinth or for us. At stake are nothing less than the integrity of the gospel, the true nature of the church, and the character of a ministry that proclaims the cross of Christ without emptying it of its scandalous power (1:17).

SHARING THE SCRIPTURE

PREPARING TO TEACH

Preparing Our Hearts

Today's devotional reading is found in 1 Corinthians 1:18-25, immediately after our scripture lesson. Here Paul refers to the cross as "foolishness" in the eyes of unbelievers but the power of God for those being saved. Salvation does not depend upon our wisdom but upon our belief in Jesus Christ. Sometimes we who teach think we have a bit of an edge over others.

After all, if we were not considered wise no one would attend our classes. Reflect on how your wisdom as a teacher is both a help in your spiritual walk and a hindrance. Thank God that your salvation comes not from wisdom but from belief in Jesus.

Now turn to today's background scripture from 1 Corinthians 1:1-17. As you study this passage, be alert for the ways in which Paul addresses his readers. What commendations does he give them? What are his concerns? What do you hear Paul saying to your church here?

Preparing Our Minds

Read this lesson and review the scripture passage. Find a map that shows Corinth. You may want to read about Corinth in a Bible dictionary, Bible companion, or Bible handbook so as to have a greater understanding of Paul's readers. Located near two very active seaports, the large city of Corinth was a crossroads for travelers and commercial enterprises. As the capital of the ancient Roman province of Achaia, Corinth was the home of the proconsul Gallio (Acts 18:12). Acts 18:1-17 indicates that Corinth was an important city in Paul's ministry. Sexual immorality was a major problem that Paul had to address among his Corinthian converts. In fact, the Greek verb that means "to practice fornication" is closely related to the name *Corinth*. In addition, the temple of Aphrodite and other temples dedicated to idols were located in Corinth. Since numerous religious teachings coexisted in Corinth, we can easily understand Paul's concerns that Christians not be ignorant of who they were and whose they were.

Preparing Our Learning Space

You may want to write the scenarios under "The Highest Calling or Lowest Common Denominator?" on paper prior to class.

Have on hand:
- several Bibles
- optional map showing Corinth
- newsprint and marker
- paper and pencils
- hymnals.

LEADING THE CLASS

(1) Introduction

One way to open today's session is to read or retell the Focusing on the Main Question section. Be sure to lift up today's main question.

Another way to begin (unless your congregation is currently experiencing serious conflict) is to invite the students to brainstorm causes of church disunity. List their ideas on newsprint. Make clear that you are not looking for specific details within your own congregation, but general ideas. Answers may include problems with money, disagreement over worship styles, strong personalities competing for leadership, cliques, or unwillingness to change and grow. After brainstorming, ask these questions:

(1) **What attitudes on the part of church members might cause problems to escalate rather than be resolved?**

(2) **On what basis can Christians hope to overcome those things that threaten to divide them?** (Point out that this is today's main question.)

(2) Saints Without Halos

You may want to set the stage for today's lesson by briefly lecturing on the city of Corinth and locating this important place on a map of the Roman Empire during the early Christian era.

Read 1 Corinthians 1:2. Ask:

(1) **To whom is this letter addressed?**

(2) **Name some persons who you consider saints.**

(3) **What does Paul mean by the term "sanctified," to be a "saint"?** (Paul is

?

speaking here of someone set apart by God for God's use.)

(4) How does this definition possibly change your understanding of what it means to be a saint?

Tell the students to envision what the Christian church would look like if we all took our status as "saints" seriously. Ask them to consider these questions:

?

(1) What arguments and tensions divide the Christian community? (Groups might mention divisive issues such as the place of homosexuals within the church, or vastly different interpretations of Scripture, or disagreements over positions and policies of the church hierarchy.)

(2) What messages do unresolved tensions send to unbelievers about the church?

(3) Do you see any way that these tensions might be resolved? Give some examples.

(4) If we truly considered ourselves as set apart by God for God's use, what might we be willing to do to solve our problems?

(3) The Highest Calling or Lowest Common Denominator?

Read 1 Corinthians 1:3-9. Note that Paul gives thanks for the Corinthians' knowledge, eloquent speech, and diverse gifts. In preparation for pointing out the source of their conflicts, Paul speaks about the Corinthians' highest calling.

If possible, divide the class into teams to discuss how they would creatively handle one or both of the following problems. Distribute paper and pencils to each group. Ask someone to take notes and be prepared to report on the group's ideas. Suggest that the students consider what Jesus might do as they seek a solution to the conflict. You may want to write each of these scenarios on paper prior to class for easy distribution.

Scenario 1: A youth director has been encouraging teens to take a stand for allowing the church's fellowship hall to be used as a soup kitchen on Saturday afternoons. The youth are willing to serve the homeless and underemployed persons who would come to the soup kitchen. Some upstanding church members are totally against the idea and are threatening to have this popular leader of youth fired. What are the real issues here? How can this conflict be resolved?

Scenario 2: Pastor I. M. Nice has tried hard to ingratiate herself to everyone. She has promised to lead a Sunday school class for older adults and, supposedly at the same time, to facilitate a support group for parents of young children. She obviously cannot do both. Her failure to keep her promise to both groups has alienated lots of folks, including those not affiliated with either group. Both groups had already publicized her work with them. What does this pastor have to do to continue a fruitful ministry in this congregation? How might the groups respond in healing ways? What are some possible solutions to the problem?

(4) The Unkindest Cult of All

Read 1 Corinthians 1:10-17 aloud as if you were Paul speaking to the class. Ask:

(1) What is Paul's underlying concern in these verses? (People are worshiping human personalities rather than God. They are divided into camps that support Paul, Apollos, and Cephas.)

?

(2) What are some reasons that people may be drawn toward a single personality? (Some people do have natural charisma, vision, good interpersonal skills, in-depth knowledge, or special experiences that attracts others to them.)

(3) What is the danger of focusing on an individual leader? (When that person leaves, the class or program that he or she has built may disintegrate completely. Moreover, if conflict arises and this person is somehow forced to withdraw, the church may split. Even if a particular person is associated with a certain group or program, he or she should point the group beyond the leader and toward Christ, who is the appropriate focus.)

(5) Whose Ministry Is It, Anyway?

Point out that in this section of 1 Corinthians, Paul is stating that the ministry belongs to Jesus, not to any individual or faction. The church is sanctified not by its individual members but by Jesus Christ.

If possible, ask the group to join hands in a circle. If the class is large, have them form several circles. Read aloud today's key verse from 1 Corinthians 1:10. Then go around the circle so that each person can complete this sentence: "As one of Christ's saints, I will try to...in order to bring about and preserve the unity of the church." Here you are asking each person to commit to one action that will help unify Christ's church, even in a small way.

As you remain standing in the circle, sing one or more verses of "Blest Be the Tie That Binds" (*The United Methodist Hymnal*, no. 557).

Before you dismiss the class, be sure to lift up at least one of the activities below so that class members will have ideas for putting what they have learned into action this week.

HELPING CLASS MEMBERS ACT

In 1 Corinthians 1:10, Paul appeals to the believers in Corinth to end their quarrels and reunite themselves. Suggest that class members consider situations within their own congregation where healing needs to occur so as to end a division. Encourage people to take appropriate steps to bring about unity.

In 1 Corinthians 1:2, Paul referred to the church as "those who are sanctified in Christ Jesus, called to be saints." Suggest that students begin to think of themselves and of all Christians as saints. Encourage them to note differences in how they perceive and treat people when they define them in this way.

Recommend that class members read a current article or book concerning conflict resolution. Perhaps they will be able to apply what they have learned to a situation in the church, workplace, or community.

PLANNING FOR NEXT SUNDAY

The lesson for March 12, "True Wisdom: A Basis for Unity," centers on the Holy Spirit as teacher. Ask the students to prepare for this session by reading the background scripture from chapters 2 and 3 of 1 Corinthians. The class session focuses on 1 Corinthians 2:1-2, 4-13, and 15-16.

TRUE WISDOM: A BASIS FOR UNITY

PREVIEWING THE LESSON

Lesson Scripture: 1 Corinthians 2:1-2, 4-13, 15-16
Background Scripture: 1 Corinthians 2–3
Key Verse: 1 Corinthians 2:12

Focus of the Lesson:
God's wisdom is revealed through the Holy Spirit, and those who receive that wisdom will have the mind of Christ.

Main Question of the Lesson:
Must wisdom divide?

This lesson will enable adult learners to:
(1) study Paul's understanding of the wisdom revealed through the Holy Spirit.
(2) consider how to discern the teachings of the Holy Spirit.
(3) respond by recognizing the presence of the Holy Spirit in their own lives.

Today's lesson may be outlined as follows:
(1) Introduction
(2) The Wisdom That Divides
(3) The Wisdom of God That Unites
(4) The Wisdom of God Given by the Spirit

FOCUSING ON THE MAIN QUESTION

How sad and ironic that knowledge divides us. We pursue knowledge in church school classes and individual studies. We invest in knowledge, paying increasing tuition. We trust knowledge to fashion a better world for us. We employ our knowledge to make our living and feed our family. Yet we discover to our frustration and with an accompanying sense of betrayal that what we know has a way of separating us from others. The high school English teacher and the chemical engineer scarcely have a working vocabulary for conversation, much less a meeting place.

Although the proliferation of information in our time exacerbates the division, the problem is not new. The Christians of the Corinthian congregation had also acquired wisdom. They had learned what worked and what did not work from the conventional wisdom required to get along in the first-century Greco-Roman world. They had also learned the gospel of Jesus Christ from traveling preachers. Paul had begun the church at Corinth (1 Corinthians 3:6; Acts 18), but his ministry was followed by the work of Peter (called "Cephas" here in 1:12; see also Galatians 1:18; 2:9, 11, 14) and Apollos, who carried with him the reputation of being "an eloquent man, well-versed in the scriptures" (Acts 18:24). Some of the Corinthian Christians responded favorably to Apollos's rhetoric and scriptural depth. Others were moved by the closeness of Peter's relationship to Jesus' earthly ministry and his recollections of roaming the Galilean hills with his master. Others apparently felt first loyalty to Paul's

vision of the gospel. The Corinthians learned the gospel from three instructors who, by all reports, were the premier preachers and teachers of the day. They had learned what the Scriptures taught, they had learned what Jesus did, and they had learned what all of that meant—only to the effect that they were divided by what they had learned. They knew just enough of the gospel to divide into warring factions (presaging multiplications of Protestant denominations). **Must wisdom divide?**

Responding to this situation, Paul does not offer wisdom but foolishness. He does not seek a bland common denominator to mask diversity but points to the work of the Holy Spirit so that the Corinthians themselves may discern the unity they have in Christ.

READING THE SCRIPTURE

NRSV
1 Corinthians 2:1-2, 4-13, 15-16

1 When I came to you, brothers and sisters, I did not come proclaiming the mystery of God to you in lofty words or wisdom. 2 For I decided to know nothing among you except Jesus Christ, and him crucified.... 4 My speech and my proclamation were not with plausible words of wisdom, but with a demonstration of the Spirit and of power, 5 so that your faith might rest not on human wisdom but on the power of God.

6 Yet among the mature we do speak wisdom, though it is not a wisdom of this age or of the rulers of this age, who are doomed to perish. 7 But we speak God's wisdom, secret and hidden, which God decreed before the ages for our glory. 8 None of the rulers of this age understood this; for if they had, they would not have crucified the Lord of glory. 9 But, as it is written,

"What no eye has seen, nor ear
　heard,

NIV
1 Corinthians 2:1-2, 4-13, 15-16

¹When I came to you, brothers, I did not come with eloquence or superior wisdom as I proclaimed to you the testimony about God. ²For I resolved to know nothing while I was with you except Jesus Christ and him crucified.... ⁴My message and my preaching were not with wise and persuasive words, but with a demonstration of the Spirit's power, ⁵so that your faith might not rest on men's wisdom, but on God's power.

⁶We do, however, speak a message of wisdom among the mature, but not the wisdom of this age or of the rulers of this age, who are coming to nothing. ⁷No, we speak of God's secret wisdom, a wisdom that has been hidden and that God destined for our glory before time began. ⁸None of the rulers of this age understood it, for if they had, they would not have crucified the Lord of glory. ⁹However, as it is written:

"No eye has seen,

nor the human heart conceived,
what God has prepared for those
who love him"—
10 these things God has revealed to us through the Spirit; for the Spirit searches everything, even the depths of God. 11 For what human being knows what is truly human except the human spirit that is within? So also no one comprehends what is truly God's except the Spirit of God. **12 Now we have received not the spirit of the world, but the Spirit that is from God, so that we may understand the gifts bestowed on us by God.** 13 And we speak of these things in words not taught by human wisdom but taught by the Spirit, interpreting spiritual things to those who are spiritual.

15 Those who are spiritual discern all things, and they are themselves subject to no one else's scrutiny.
16 "For who has known the mind of
the Lord
so as to instruct him?"
But we have the mind of Christ.

no ear has heard,
no mind has conceived
what God has prepared for those who
love him"—
[10]but God has revealed it to us by his Spirit.

The Spirit searches all things, even the deep things of God. [11]For who among men knows the thoughts of a man except the man's spirit within him? In the same way no one knows the thoughts of God except the Spirit of God. **[12]We have not received the spirit of the world but the Spirit who is from God, that we may understand what God has freely given us.** [13]This is what we speak, not in words taught us by human wisdom but in words taught by the Spirit, expressing spiritual truths in spiritual words.... [15]The spiritual man makes judgments about all things, but he himself is not subject to any man's judgment:
[16]"For who has known the mind of the Lord
that he may instruct him?"
But we have the mind of Christ.

Key Verse

Key Verse

UNDERSTANDING THE SCRIPTURE

1 Corinthians 2:1-5; 3:3-4, 18-20. Paul's comments are best understood as continuing his meditation on Christ as the power and wisdom of God that he began in 1 Corinthians 1:18-31. To a local congregation of Christians who have split into factions, lined up behind their favorite leaders (1:12; 3:3-4), Paul emphasizes that such conduct is utterly inappropriate to the character of the gospel that he proclaimed to them. God's power and wisdom have been disclosed, once and for all, through Christ crucified—a stunning revelation that overturns this world's criteria of authority and common sense (the "signs" asked for by Jews and the "wisdom" sought by Greeks, 1:22). Moreover, Paul reminds the Corinthians of their own less than prestigious status: God's call has

been issued to and received by those who, for the most part, have been neither wise nor powerful nor well-born. This was no accident. God deliberately selected what is foolish, weak, low, and despised, "things that are not"—namely, a crucified Messiah and the Corinthians themselves—to nullify all that this world believes to be really something (1:26-28) and to accredit the wisdom of those who become fools for God in the world's eyes (3:18-20, quoting Job 5:13 and Psalm 94:11).

Likewise, Paul minimizes himself and his own preaching during his original missionary labors among them in Corinth (probably around the year A.D. 51; see Acts 18:1-18; 2 Corinthians 1:19). Paul's proclamation of God's "mystery"—the message about the cross, which sounds moronic to nonbelievers (1 Corinthians 1:18)—was not couched in majestic, persuasive, flowery rhetoric. Instead, Paul's preaching style was inelegant and knock-kneed (1:17; 2:1, 3-4a; 2 Corinthians 10:10). What better way to proclaim nothing "except Jesus Christ, and him crucified" (2:2), what more fitting demonstration of the Holy Spirit, than for Paul to have proclaimed the gospel in such a way that the Corinthians' faith was diverted away from his skill as a preacher and redirected solely to "the power of God" (2:4b-5)?

1 Corinthians 2:6-7; 3:1-2. In 2:6 there seems to be a reversal of thought: in fact, "we Paul and other apostles do speak wisdom." Yet Paul carefully stipulates that such wisdom is only spoken to and understood by those who are spiritually mature (2:6). By contrast, the Corinthians are characterized by Paul as "infants in Christ," spiritually speaking (3:1-2). Furthermore, Paul returns to the point stressed in 1:18-31: God's supreme wisdom is cloaked in a mystery, "hidden" in the "foolishness" of the gospel (2:7; see also 1:21). The cross of Jesus Christ was no accident, no divine turning of life's lemons into lemonade. To the contrary: from eternity and before all creation, God ordained the cross as the means for "our glory," the consummation of our salvation that will be realized when this world has passed away (2:7; see also Romans 5:2; 8:18-21; 2 Corinthians 3:18; 1 Thessalonians 2:12).

1 Corinthians 2:8-16. The rest of 1 Corinthians 2 elaborates a fairly simple idea: namely, like understands like. "No one comprehends what is truly God's except the Spirit of God" and by extension, those who have received "the Spirit that is from God" (2:11-12). Nevertheless, such an idea is liable to misinterpretation unless readers understand how Paul uses the terms *spirit* and *spiritual*. By these terms Paul is not referring to thoughts or practices that modern readers might consider "pious" or "devotional." For Paul, Christians live "in the Spirit" in the sense that their lives,

flooded by the light of the cross, have been illuminated by new standards that are radically different from those by which the everyday world abides and judges matters. "The rulers of this age" (2:8; see also 2:6; 15:24-26)—by which Paul may refer to cosmic powers antagonistic to God, or to the political authorities of Paul's day, or to both—had no idea that in crucifying Jesus they were actually colluding with God in the vindication of Jesus as "the Lord of glory" (2:8) and the predesigned restoration of all those who love God (2:9, which recalls without precisely quoting Isaiah 52:15; 64:4). Such an interpretation of Jesus' death seems utter rubbish to those who view things "naturally" (a more literal translation than "unspiritual" in 1 Corinthians 2:14). For Paul, such an inability to discern God at work through the cross proves that this world has not received, and thus cannot operate in accordance with, "the gifts of God's Spirit" (2:14).

By contrast, through the Spirit God empowers Christians with gifts of discernment, "the mind of Christ" (2:15-16), by which they may perceive and act in alignment with God's unexpected but life-restorative redemption of the world through the cross of Jesus Christ (see also Romans 8:9; Galatians 4:6; Philippians 1:19). To see God at work in the cross is not the result of logic or better education ("things in words...taught by human wisdom," 1 Corinthians 2:13). Such vision owes nothing to any natural insight or achievement of our own. Nor is such vision subject to correction by this world's standards of judgment, as though human beings could presume to teach the Lord something (2:16a; see Isaiah 40:13; Wisdom of Solomon 9:13, in the Apocrypha). "The gifts of God's Spirit" (1 Corinthians 2:14) are just that: gifts. It is through the revelation to us of God's own Spirit—perhaps, as Paul suggests elsewhere, at our baptism (3:16; 6:19; 12:13; Romans 8; 2 Corinthians 1:22; Galatians 3:3; 4:6)—that Christians judge all things and are themselves judged (1 Corinthians 2:10).

1 Corinthians 3:5-17, 21-23. Paul continues to relativize his own importance and that of all human leaders in the church. He subordinates himself, Apollos, and all Christians to Christ, who subordinated himself to God (3:21-23). To make his point Paul mixes two metaphors. The first is horticultural. By preaching the gospel from which Corinthian Christianity grew, Paul "planted"; by cultivating Paul's work, Apollos "watered" (see Acts 18:24–19:1); but the church's growth in Corinth was attributable solely to God, who owns the field (1 Corinthians 3:5-9). The second metaphor is architectural. By God's grace in calling him to his apostleship, Paul in Corinth laid the only true foundation—Jesus Christ—and successive builders, like Apollos, must build on that basis with materials of highest quality (3:10-12). Great is this responsibility: the entire Corinthian congregation is nothing less than God's temple, in which God's Spirit dwells (3:16-17). Its builders, including Paul, will be called to account for the quality of their missionary workmanship on "the Day" of final judgment (3:13-15; see also 1:7-8; 5:5; Romans 2:5, 16; 13:12; 2 Corinthians 1:14; Philippians 1:6, 10; 2:16; 1 Thessalonians 5:2). "Each servant will receive wages or 'a reward' according to the labor of each" (1 Corinthians 3:8, 14)—and some of those laborers may be saved only just barely ("only as through fire," 3:15; see Amos 4:11; Zechariah 3:2; Jude 23).

INTERPRETING THE SCRIPTURE

The Wisdom That Divides

Not many of the Corinthians "were wise by human standards" (1 Corinthians 1:26). Some undoubtedly were, though it does not require much wisdom to separate people into suspicious factions. Some members of the church obviously traded with sophistication in the wisdom of the Greco-Roman world: Gaius was wealthy enough to be head of a household and host to an entire church; and the city treasurer Erastus must have been a man of means (Romans 16:23). Others, of course, had much less and perhaps were a little cowed by the wisdom that permitted persons to make their way through Corinth's corridors of power and prestige. The members of the church had received knowledge in the gospel brought to them by Paul, Peter (Cephas), and Apollos. Paul's preaching had called the church together in the city of Corinth and many members evidently felt a deep and abiding loyalty to his particular articulation of the gospel. Others had been deeply moved by the ministry of Peter, whose relationship with Jesus and story in the early Christian movement must have been both fascinating and compelling. Still others were no doubt dazzled by the rhetorical excellences of Apollos, who was known as an elegant preacher and skilled interpreter of the Scriptures (Acts 18:24). Moreover, the members of the Corinthian community had derived a sort of wisdom from their own religious experiences of the power of God's Holy Spirit in their midst. Several unsavory problems divided the community of Corinthian Christians (as we will see in later lessons), but so also were they divided by the best and most wholesome aspects of human experience. Human beings cannot long survive without learning the wisdom of the world; neither can we embrace the fullness of human life without exploring the realm of the Spirit. Still, how can we live together when what we know separated us so painfully from our neighbors?

Since our vision is limited by our own circumstances, we may think of pluralism and diversity as modern problems. In fact, this troubled community of faith we see indirectly through Paul's First Epistle to the Corinthians was probably much more diverse than most North American Protestant congregations. Here were rich and poor, those scrupulous about eating meat and those not, those ensconced within the power structures of the city and those dangling on the margins. Still, within our very familiar congregations we are aware that we approach life and faith in very different ways, and our different ways tend to separate us even in spite of our best intentions. Here sits a brother who has found new dimensions to faith on a "Road to Emmaus" retreat, sharing his experience in a chatty group of other disciples, but there is a sister reading Chicago Bulls' coach Phil Jackson's book *Sacred Hoops* and exploring Eastern meditation for what she calls "Zen Christianity." One member of the church had his deepest experience of Christ's presence while building a house last summer with Habitat for Humanity, while another felt transported into the midst of the heavenly host at a service for evening prayer when the choir sang the *Te Deum*. So different are these religious experiences that we may wonder if we are speaking of the same faith.

The Wisdom of God That Unites

Being democratically inclined we look for a common place where we may gather. Surely there must be something on which we can agree, some common ground deeper than our differences. The difficulty with this strategy, of course, is that it pretends our differences really aren't important and our particular experiences don't matter. What we have learned does matter and what we have lived through has valid lessons to teach. Instead of seeking the lowest common denominator on which to ground the unity of the church, the apostle Paul lifts us up to the highest measure of God's self-giving love and employs that as the standard for every religious insight and observance.

Paul reminds the Corinthians of his initial preaching where "I decided to know nothing among you except Jesus Christ, and him crucified" (1 Corinthians 2:2). The cross of Christ is nothing less than "the power of God" (1:18) by which the church is brought into being and continually refreshed. Such an assertion may strike us as odd if we think of the Crucifixion only as an event that took place many years ago on a day we call Good Friday, and that was located on "Place of a Skull" (Matthew 27:33), outside the walls of Jerusalem.

Unlike the Gospel writers, Paul does not locate the cross of Christ in time and space; rather, he places it first and foremost in God's design for the world. From the very beginning of all things the cross has been God's plan "for our glory" (1 Corinthians 2:7; compare Romans 9:23). The Crucifixion was not some accident, temporarily disrupting God's design, but the pinnacle and very essence of that design. By every human judgment, the execution of an innocent man constitutes a grievous miscarriage of justice; Paul's faith, to the contrary, sees the cross as nothing less than the fullness of God's mystery in public view. The wisdom the world offers may be discernible from surface appearances, but the strange wisdom of God revealed in the cross is "secret and hidden" (1 Corinthians 2:7).

Faithful Christians who find difficulty in comprehending Paul's claim for the cross as the epitome of God's wisdom and climax of God's design for the word should not be embarrassed. Were this truth obvious, Paul would have had no need to write to the Corinthians. As Paul himself makes clear, his assertion rests not upon generally accepted structures of plausibility, but on nothing less than God's own power and word. Doubtless the Corinthians initially found Paul's word of the cross as implausible as we do. (For a moment, pity, if you will, writers of curriculum whose assignment it is to make the cross humanly comprehensible: a task Paul declares impossible folly.) It takes a lifetime to stretch one's mind around the cross, a lifetime and many prayers, hymns, sermons, studies, meditations, failures, offerings, sufferings, losses and triumphs and much laughter before one can look up at the Crucified One and see—ah, yes!—the very wisdom of God.

The Wisdom of God Given by the Spirit

How does one begin this process, however? If there exists no meeting point that provides intersection between the cross of Christ and human wisdom, how do we encounter this wisdom of God that so shames our own wisdom? Clearly the problem is insoluble, impossible; but occasionally in Scripture comes an angel whispering, "Nothing is impossible with God" (see Genesis 18:14; Luke 1:37). What human wisdom cannot do, God can. That is the point of Paul's somewhat difficult explanation.

Paul argues from the basis that "like knows like." Being human we know what it is like to be human and what belongs to the human condition. Not being divine we do not know what it is to be God, nor do we know what is truly God's. Only God knows the mystery of God's work among us, but God has gracefully chosen to make known this mystery, previously "secret and hidden," but "decreed before the ages for our glory" (1 Corinthians 2:7), in the cross of Christ. To make this incomparable mystery accessible to us, God has chosen to dwell among us by the power of the Holy Spirit. By the giving of God's Spirit "we may understand the gifts bestowed on us by God" (2:12). The cross is God's self-giving through Jesus Christ. Likewise, the capacity to receive the cross is God's self-giving through the Holy Spirit. God does not provide the cross and then dare us to "Take it or leave it!" Instead, God persuades our human spirits by God's own Spirit that the cross is indeed the greatest truth and hope we may know. Even now the Spirit of God works within to open us, so that we may receive this gift.

Please note, and let there be no misunderstanding this: our difficulty in receiving this gift does not signal the absence of the Spirit from our lives. Paul is quite insistent on this matter. In the opening sentences of this letter to the Corinthians he gives thanks "that you are not lacking in any spiritual gift" (1 Corinthians 1:7). In this lesson Paul reminds us, "We have received not the spirit of the world, but the Spirit that is from God" (2:12), and "we have the mind of Christ" (2:16b). Our dilemma is not that we have not received the Spirit of God; rather, we allow the wisdom of God whispered by the Spirit to be shouted down by the clamorous wisdom of the world. The cross doesn't make sense, howls human wisdom; the cross is weak, a sign of death and curse, and no one is interested in that. The Holy Spirit confidently assures us, however, that the cross is nothing less than "the power of God and the wisdom of God" (1:24). This truth we apprehend—rather, it apprehends us—slowly, one lesson at a time.

SHARING THE SCRIPTURES

PREPARING TO TEACH

Preparing Our Hearts

Begin by reading the background scripture from 1 Corinthians 2–3. What do you hear Paul saying about spiritual wisdom? What do you hear him saying about factions in the church? What do you hear about the teachers and preachers who are working to build up the church?

Look carefully at today's devotional reading, 1 Corinthians 3:1-9, which is also part of the background scripture. As you study this passage, think about those who attend your class. Do you have some students who are clearly spiritually mature? Do you have others who are still "infants in Christ"? How do you include both of these groups in your lessons? Also think about Paul's acknowledgment that though he and other laborers have worked, only God can give the increase. As a teacher of adults, how do you see your own work in God's field? Give prayerful consideration to what you believe God is calling you to do. Pray for healing in any places of your congregation or denomination where infighting is tearing apart the church and dishonoring God.

Preparing Our Minds

Look again at 1 Corinthians 2–3. Read this lesson carefully. You will note that only selected verses from chapter 2 are used in the lesson scripture. Notice, though, that Paul's teachings on wisdom can be divided into two segments: 1:28–2:5 and 2:6-16. The first portion contrasts the wisdom of God with the wisdom of the world. Although supposedly wise persons pursue wisdom, they seek the wisdom of this world. Consequently, the message of the cross, of Christ crucified, is utter nonsense to these persons. Paul did not use eloquent words to proclaim the gospel. In his weakness the wisdom and power of God can shine through. The second portion, 2:6-16, contrasts the wisdom of mature believers with the foolishness of those who are immature. Those who are mature are guided by the wisdom of God, not the wisdom of the world.

Preparing Our Learning Space

Have on hand:
- several Bibles
- hymnals
- candle and matches
- newsprint and marker.

LEADING THE CLASS

(1) Introduction

To set the tone for today's lesson, begin the session by singing a hymn such as "Sweet, Sweet Spirit" (*The United Methodist Hymnal*, no. 334) or "Surely the Presence of the Lord" (*UMH*, no. 328). As you sing, light a candle on your worship table as a visible reminder of the presence of God's Spirit in your midst.

Ask the students these questions:
(1) **What are some sources of knowledge today?**
(2) **Bombarded by enormous quantities of information, how do you decide what you will accept as true and what you must reject as false?**

Point out that we base our values and beliefs on the knowledge that we have accepted, on what we believe to be true. However, we live in a time of great diversity, with many competing claims about truth. This diversity prompts our main question: **Must wisdom divide?**

Encourage the class to give initial responses to the main question.

(2) The Wisdom That Divides

Read aloud the second paragraph under "The Wisdom That Divides" in the Interpreting the Scripture portion. Invite the students to mention experiences that have made them deeply aware of Christ's presence in their lives. List these on newsprint. Likely, the group will note a great diversity in their responses. Ask these questions.

(1) **Do these different experiences of Christ's presence mean that one person has experienced Christ while another has not? Explain your answer.**

(2) **How do these diverse experiences help to explain the attraction of some of the Corinthian believers to a preacher like Paul, or an apostle like Peter who had a firsthand relationship with Jesus, or a learned and articulate interpreter of the word like Apollos?**

(3) **Our different approaches to faith often do divide us. But we ask again our main question: Must wisdom divide? If the answer to the question is "no," how can we be more accepting of the variety of religious experiences without insisting**

? that people must have the same experiences that we have in order to be "real" Christians?

(3) The Wisdom of God That Unites

Read aloud what Paul has to say in 1 Corinthians 2:1-2, 4-13, and 15-16. Ask the students to close their eyes and hear you as if Paul were speaking directly to them. Then ask:

? (1) **What does Paul emphasize about the wisdom of God?** (It is foolishness to those who seek wisdom from human speculation.)
(2) **How do we come to know the wisdom of God?** (The Holy Spirit teaches us.)

Ask the students to contemplate some truths that they know deep within their hearts, truths that they believe the Holy Spirit has taught them. Invite a few volunteers to share something that they know by the power of the Spirit that they could not have learned through the usual ways of gaining human knowledge.

(4) The Wisdom of God Given by the Spirit

Read these words from the Interpreting the Scripture portion:

The cross is God's self-giving through Jesus Christ. Likewise, the capacity to receive the cross is God's self-giving through the Holy Spirit. God does not provide the cross and then dare us to "Take it or leave it!" Instead, God persuades our human spirits by God's own Spirit that the cross is indeed the greatest truth and hope we may know. Even now the Spirit of God works within to open us, so that we may receive this gift.

Ask the students to work with a partner to consider these questions:
(1) **The world views the cross as a curse, a sign of death, but the Spirit says that the cross is the power and wisdom of God. What does the cross mean in your own life?** ?
(2) **How did you arrive at this meaning?**

Close the session with a prayer, asking God's Holy Spirit to continue to teach each person the wisdom of God.

Before you dismiss the class, suggest at least one activity below to help the students make the teachings of this week's lesson part of their lives.

HELPING CLASS MEMBERS ACT

Suggest that students choose a Bible passage of interest to them. Tell them to read this excerpt several times and try to discern the meaning for themselves, with the help of the Holy Spirit. Then ask them to read several commentaries on this passage, including at least one written from a theological point of view that does not reflect their own perspective. Encourage them to be open to new insights.

Recommend that class members look for situations this week in which they clearly feel the leading presence of the Holy Spirit. How did they recognize the Spirit? What did the Spirit do?

Urge students to talk this week with someone who has had a distinct experience of the Holy Spirit's leading, such as knowing that God helped them recover from a near-fatal illness. Suggest that the students find out how the person knew that the Holy Spirit was with them in such difficult circumstances.

PLANNING FOR NEXT SUNDAY

"Mature Leaders Bring Unity" is based on 1 Corinthians 4:1-13. Ask the students to read this passage and consider the qualities of spiritually mature church leaders. Challenge them to think about how these servant leaders bring about unity in the church.

MATURE LEADERS BRING UNITY

PREVIEWING THE LESSON

Lesson Scripture: 1 Corinthians 4:1-13
Background Scripture: 1 Corinthians 4:1-13
Key Verse: 1 Corinthians 4:1

Focus of the Lesson:
Mature spiritual leaders, that is, those who are servants of Christ and servants of God's mysteries, bring unity to the church.

Main Question of the Lesson:
What style of leadership befits a servant of the gospel?

This lesson will enable adult learners to:
(1) understand that Christian leaders are servants of Christ.
(2) think about how they can lead by serving.
(3) respond by making a meaningful commitment to Christ.

Today's lesson may be outlined as follows:
(1) Introduction
(2) Stewards of the Mysteries of God
(3) Judgment Belongs to the Master
(4) The Vocation of God's People

FOCUSING ON THE MAIN QUESTION

Amble the aisles of your neighborhood bookstore and notice what America is reading. Browse the business section, and you will find shelves groaning under the weight of proven guides for leadership in the workplace. Histories and biographies, by definition, chronicle society's leaders: the good, the bad, the ugly, the celebrated. Stroll over to the self-help stalls and notice the guaranteed strategies for taking charge of your emotions, your love life, your diet, your addictions. Or skim the titles on marriage, family, and parenting: Who leads, who follows, who decides? Much best-selling fiction spins yarns about power, its maintenance and corruption, in court and in hospital, at home and at work. Even in the religion section you'll find such preoccupations: nearly every year someone will plunder the Gospels for leadership tips from Jesus, cleverly disguised as media-mogul or business magnate.

We are what we read. Unless incapacitated by illness or unemployment, as adults we all are expected to exercise leadership somewhere. We are parents and homemakers, teachers, agribusiness-owners, managers, providers, programmers, secretaries, salespersons, specialists in countless crafts and trades. We have commitments to honor, quotas to reach, needs to balance, decisions to make. Although some leaders are driven by little more than self-interest, most of us want to rise above that: to do our best, set a good example, do right by those depending on us, place ourselves beyond our critics' reach. That much is clear. What's confusing is how to execute our leadership. If we are Christians, that question is complicated by Jesus' radical redefinition of authority as this world knows it: "But not so with you; rather the greatest among you must become like the youngest, and the leader like one who serves" (Luke 22:26). How many bestsellers

are devoted to the principle of servanthood? Almost none—except for the Bible, whose purchasers are not always its readers.

And so the question: **What style of leadership befits a servant of the gospel?** In this session we examine Paul's understanding of ministry. By ministry, neither he nor we shall focus on ordained clergy. Rather, Paul's reflections—applied to himself and his colleagues for his readers' benefit (1 Corinthians 4:6)—pertain to any Christian who knows herself or himself to be the beneficiary of an incomparable gift, the trustee of a wondrous responsibility, the instrument of God's blessing in a world warped by fault-finding, backbiting, and curse.

READING THE SCRIPTURE

NRSV

1 Corinthians 4:1-13

Key Verse

1 Think of us in this way, as servants of Christ and stewards of God's mysteries. 2 Moreover, it is required of stewards that they be found trustworthy. 3 But with me it is a very small thing that I should be judged by you or by any human court. I do not even judge myself. 4 I am not aware of anything against myself, but I am not thereby acquitted. It is the Lord who judges me. 5 Therefore do not pronounce judgment before the time, before the Lord comes, who will bring to light the things now hidden in darkness and will disclose the purposes of the heart. Then each one will receive commendation from God.

6 I have applied all this to Apollos and myself for your benefit, brothers and sisters, so that you may learn through us the meaning of the saying, "Nothing beyond what is written," so that none of you will be puffed up in favor of one against another. 7 For who sees anything different in you? What do you have that you did not receive? And if you received it, why do you boast as if it were not a gift?

8 Already you have all you want!

NIV

1 Corinthians 4:1-13

Key Verse

[1]So then, men ought to regard us as servants of Christ and as those entrusted with the secret things of God. [2]Now it is required that those who have been given a trust must prove faithful. [3]I care very little if I am judged by you or by any human court; indeed, I do not even judge myself. [4]My conscience is clear, but that does not make me innocent. It is the Lord who judges me. [5]Therefore judge nothing before the appointed time; wait till the Lord comes. He will bring to light what is hidden in darkness and will expose the motives of men's hearts. At that time each will receive his praise from God.

[6]Now, brothers, I have applied these things to myself and Apollos for your benefit, so that you may learn from us the meaning of the saying, "Do not go beyond what is written." Then you will not take pride in one man over against another. [7]For who makes you different from anyone else? What do you have that you did not receive? And if you did receive it, why do you boast as though you did not?

[8]Already you have all you want! Already

Already you have become rich! Quite apart from us you have become kings! Indeed, I wish that you had become kings, so that we might be kings with you! 9 For I think that God has exhibited us apostles as last of all, as though sentenced to death, because we have become a spectacle to the world, to angels and to mortals. 10 We are fools for the sake of Christ, but you are wise in Christ. We are weak, but you are strong. You are held in honor, but we in disrepute. 11 To the present hour we are hungry and thirsty, we are poorly clothed and beaten and homeless, 12 and we grow weary from the work of our own hands. When reviled, we bless; when persecuted, we endure; 13 when slandered, we speak kindly. We have become like the rubbish of the world, the dregs of all things, to this very day.

you have become rich! You have become kings—and that without us! How I wish that you really had become kings so that we might be kings with you! ⁹For it seems to me that God has put us apostles on display at the end of the procession, like men condemned to die in the arena. We have been made a spectacle to the whole universe, to angels as well as to men. ¹⁰We are fools for Christ, but you are so wise in Christ! We are weak, but you are strong! You are honored, we are dishonored! ¹¹To this very hour we go hungry and thirsty, we are in rags, we are brutally treated, we are homeless. ¹²We work hard with our own hands. When we are cursed, we bless; when we are persecuted, we endure it; ¹³when we are slandered, we answer kindly. Up to this moment we have become the scum of the earth, the refuse of the world.

UNDERSTANDING THE SCRIPTURE

1 Corinthians 4:1. This verse is not only the key for this Sunday's lesson but also the main idea that governs 1 Corinthians 4:1-13. The Christians in Corinth had put Paul and their other leaders, such as Apollos, on tall pedestals for cliquish admiration (see 1 Corinthians 1:12). Instead, Paul reminds the Corinthians of how apostles ought to be reckoned: as Christ's underlings (another way of translating *oikonomous*, the Greek word rendered in the NRSV as "servants") and as stewards or householders ("trustees" or "managers," we might say; see 1 Peter 4:10) of God's mysteries—the mysterious "word of the cross" for the world's salvation (see 1 Corinthians 2:1-2, 6-7). We might note that such a self-description does two things at once. First, it allows Paul to kick those false props out from under the apostles. Recalling 1 Corinthians 3:5-9, Paul encourages the Corinthian church to regard him and Apollos not as "top dogs" but as helpers to whom God—the true

master—has entrusted specific functions of only relative importance. Second, by identifying God and God's Messiah as the real authorities to whom apostles are accountable, Paul implicitly removes himself from the overlordship of those Christians who came to believe through him. Many modern pastors describe themselves as "serving churches." By contrast, Paul is adamant that he serves God, by whose will alone Paul was "called to be an apostle of Christ Jesus" (1 Corinthians 1:1).

1 Corinthians 4:2-5. The problem with Paul's self-description is its susceptibility to further misunderstanding and abuse by those, like the Corinthians, who were prone to self-inflation (see 1 Corinthians 4:6, 8). If Paul and other apostles are subject only to God, then what's to prevent them from acting inappropriately, then rationalizing or disowning their misconduct afterwards? Paul is well aware of that danger; hence, these remarks in 1 Corinthians 4:2-5. First, it is required of servants that they be found "trustworthy" (4:2 NRSV) or "faithful"

(NIV; see also Luke 12:42). This observation leads to Paul's second caution: the one who does "the finding" or assessment of an apostle's fidelity is the Lord alone (4:4b; compare Psalm 143:2). Whether Paul is judged by the Corinthian congregation and found to be utterly superb or completely incompetent makes no difference whatever to his self-perception. He is not concerned with his day in any human court—including any trial of his own conducting (4:3). He is not aware of any evidence against him, but that no more acquits him than (he implies) any charges brought against him by the Corinthians would be upheld (4:4a). The only day in court that concerns Paul is the day of final judgment, when Christ, presiding as judge, will illuminate all that now lies hidden in darkness and will disclose the motives buried deep in every human heart (compare 1 Samuel 16:7; 1 Chronicles 28:9; Psalm 139:1, 11-12; Jeremiah 17:10). The only praise Paul seeks, and which should matter to each of us, is the commendation that will come from God (4:5b; see also 1 Corinthians 3:5-15; 5:5, 13; 6:2-3, 9-10).

1 Corinthians 4:6-7. Paul now makes clear that he has used himself and Apollos as illustrations of his point that no one— neither the apostles nor the believers in Corinth—should be "puffed up" at another's expense (4:6; see also Romans 12:3). The proverbial saying, "Nothing beyond what is written," may have been clear in its application to the Corinthians' situation; what Paul intends by its quotation here remains a mystery to modern commentators. Fortunately, Paul's rhetorical questions in 1 Corinthians 4:7 are crys-

talline in clarity. Differences among Christians—especially those in status, as the world judges such things—are inconsequential, since everything without exception is to be received as a gift from God, not as a stimulus for bragging (see also 1 Corinthians 2:12; 3:21-22; Romans 12:6-8).

1 Corinthians 4:8-13. Here Paul's pen drips with ridiculous irony. He certainly does not believe that the Christians in Corinth "have it all," including wealth, royal power, wisdom, and strength (4:8, 10). To judge from their pompous attitudes, however, they are acting as though already they were seated on glorious thrones, with all other dominions at their beck and call (see Daniel 7:27). Well, Paul wonders aloud, where were he and the other apostles when this end-time gravy train rolled into the station? By contrast, when he reviews all the hardships that he and his colleagues are still suffering for the gospel's sake (4:11-12; see also Romans 8:35; 2 Corinthians 4:8-9; 6:4-5; 11:22-29; 12:10), Paul feels as though the apostles have been made by God a "spectacle" for the amused ridicule of all (4:9). The image summoned up here is that of prisoners of war, who in the ancient world were regularly displayed in public parades or circuses as shackled objects of pitiless scorn. Paul's last two comments echo the sayings of Jesus and the lamentations of Israel in exile. "When reviled, we [apostles] bless" (4:12b), much as Jesus admonished his disciples (Matthew 5:44; Luke 6:28; Acts 7:60; Romans 12:14). "We have become the scum of the earth, the refuse of the world" (4:13 NIV), as prophets of old had grieved (Isaiah 53:2-3; Lamentations 3:45; see also Romans 8:36).

INTERPRETING THE SCRIPTURE

Stewards of the Mysteries of God

Pull back the gray curtain of the customary English translation, "stewards of God's mysteries" (1 Corinthians 4:1), and you see a multihued and complicated social network. When Paul declares that he and the other apostles are "stewards of God's mysteries," he borrows language from the slavery system of the Greco-Roman world. That he should employ so blithely the metaphor of slavery may cause us to shudder, and with good reason.

We do well to remember, however, that Greco-Roman slavery was a vastly different social institution than the slavery of Africans in the western hemisphere. In the Greco-Roman world slaves could purchase their freedom and regularly did so; more amazingly, many who had the means to purchase freedom declined to do so. In spite of laws that forbade slaves to own property, not only did slaves own property but they themselves owned slaves who could own other slaves. Slaves digging in mines, rowing galleys, and toiling in rural areas had grim, brief lives. On the other hand, slaves attached to urban households enjoyed great freedom and were able in many instances to amass great wealth, to be treated with respect, and to hold positions of influence in the city. At the pinnacle of prestige among slaves was the steward of the household, the *oikonomos.*

When we think of "household" we should not confine our imaginations to domestic arrangements. We need to understand that a "household" in Greco-Roman culture might also include business ventures to which various clients would be attached. The *oikonomos* might represent his master or mistress in negotiations relating to the household's investments. (Many commentators speculate that "Chloe's people," in 1 Corinthians 1:11, as well as Fortunatus and Achaicus, of "the household of Stephanas" in 1 Corinthians 16:15-17, were just such *oikonomoi.*) Thus, an *oikonomos* was a slave serving a master but certainly a slave representing formidable power, a deputy to be reckoned with. This image Paul borrows to describe the apostles. Jesus also employed this metaphor in describing ministry and exhorting his disciples to faithfulness: "Who then is the faithful and prudent manager *[oikonomos]* whom his master will put in charge of his slaves, to

give them their allowance of food at the proper time? Blessed is that slave whom his master will find at work when he arrives" (Luke 12:42-43). This manager or steward—we might say the chief executive officer of the household—is responsible for the master's business and responsible to the master.

The business in question as Paul addresses the Corinthians is nothing less than "God's mysteries." Secular *oikonomoi* might manage their master's manufacturing or shipping or sales. What Paul, Apollos, and Peter oversee are the mysteries of God. They are united in accountability to a common master. They do not score their success according to the applause-meters of the Corinthian congregation. Paul describes this sense of responsibility to God: "For we are not peddlers of God's word like so many; but in Christ we speak as persons of sincerity, as persons sent from God and standing in his presence" (2 Corinthians 2:17). The mysteries demand such reverent attention because they are nothing less than God's own gift.

An exhaustive inventory of "God's mysteries" is beyond even the most faithful steward, but we can point at least to the central mystery of God's gift of reconciliation to the world through the cross and resurrection of Jesus Christ. To speak of this event as a "mystery" (1 Corinthians 2:1) is to suggest that what had been hidden has now been revealed (see also 1 Corinthians 2:7). Previously we did not know and could not know, but now God has provided the means by which we may discern God's intent for the creation and for us. This we see in the cross. That we cannot wholly say all that this means does not count against the truthfulness of the claim; indeed, glib approaches to truth only reveal their own shallowness. God had brought Paul and Apollos together as partners to tell, each in his own way, of these mysteries. To hear their preaching in such a way that listeners divide into factions, preferring one or the other messenger, misunderstands their message altogether (see also 1 Corinthians 3:5-9).

Judgment Belongs to the Master

The Corinthians evidently found something to fault in Paul's stewardship. Although many considered it unseemly to criticize another master's servants, the Corinthians did not shrink from taking on the master's role in judging Paul. The content of their criticisms is unclear, but no matter. Their criticisms, as such, are not what counts for Paul: "It is a very small thing that I should be judged by you or by any human court" (1 Corinthians 4:3a). The Corinthians doubtless thought their criticism a very large thing, just as we believe our own criticism to be weighty, wise, and of great import. A lay leader told one of this session's authors that he believed conversations over lunch after Sunday worship were of two distinct kinds: those which discussed the sermon and those which carved up the preacher along with the roast beef.

Paul appears comparatively immune to the sting of criticism that wounds so much ministry. He understands his work as a steward of God's mysteries and will not be distracted by the appraisal of human critics. His sense of ultimate accountability to God frees Paul from monitoring every response. Leadership devoted to higher principles is less likely to be distracted by petty complaints. Do not misunderstand Paul's immunity from criticism as a form of prideful self-confidence. Neither his critics' judgment nor his own finally matters; ultimately, only God's judgment matters. Human wisdom already demonstrated its bankruptcy by its assessment of Jesus (2:8). It is not likely to be more approving of Paul's preaching of the crucified Lord.

Human judgment, even Paul's own self-critique, cannot competently evaluate stewardship of God's mysteries. As a steward, Paul knows he will be judged, but judgment belongs ultimately and finally to Christ, who is more understanding of us and gentle with us than we can be when judging ourselves. Paul also understands that he has received a gift. The Corinthians seem trapped in a cycle of blaming and boasting: blaming Paul for whatever inadequacy they perceive and boasting about their own spiritual athletics. Paul simply cuts through all that folderol by asking, "What do you have that you did not receive?" (4:7b). Misused, the gift they were given to unite them in common ministry divided them into ugly factions of self-inflated claims. Paul reminds them that the proper response to a gift is thanksgiving and blessing.

The Vocation of God's People

With these gentle words Paul enacts the very strategy he describes: "When reviled, we bless; when persecuted, we endure; when slandered, we speak kindly" (1 Corinthians 4:12b-13a). This strategy is central to Christian faith. It takes its cues from the cross of Christ. The cross transforms curse into blessing. From every perspective that Paul could adopt, the cross was curse. Not only was it a human curse on an unwanted and troublesome prophet, it appeared to be God's curse as well. Hadn't the Scriptures said, "Cursed is everyone who hangs on a tree" (Galatians 3:13, citing Deuteronomy 21:23)? But Paul came to see that God had vindicated Jesus by raising Him from the dead, thereby making Christ God's own blessing to humankind. If God so transforms curse into blessing, should we not do the same?

From the very beginning of the Bible, God intended human beings for the vocation of blessing one another. God chose Abraham and Sarah, promising not only "I will bless you," but "in you all the families of the earth shall be blessed" (Genesis 12:2-3). When Jesus sent out disciples to carry His message, He sent them out to bless: "Whatever house you enter, first say, 'Peace to this house!' " (Luke 10:5). Such blessing of peace conveyed all the good things God intended to give people. Jesus also understood that not everyone would welcome the message and messenger of blessing (Luke 10:6b, 10-12). Nevertheless, the message remains the same: "Peace to this house!" He taught his disciples, "Bless those who curse you, pray for those who abuse you" (Luke 6:28). We may wonder about the wisdom of such a strategy, but such wondering presumes that we are in charge of the enterprise and qualified to critique God's plans. We are not. At the heart of the gospel is the message of blessing, and Christ summons servants to take that word to every person, every place, every circumstance, without qualification. To be a steward of God's mysteries is to bear God's blessing.

Authentic leadership in the church carries forward God's blessing spoken in the life, death, and resurrection of Jesus Christ. This blessing does not wait upon a positive response. It does not depend upon the qualifications of its messenger. It is not invalidated when it is met by curses. It does not waver or wane according to either seasons or moods. It is the very word of God that gives vision and confidence to the church's leaders, and it desires to be spoken again and again by new voices. In our worship we practice the art of blessing. "The Lord be with you!" says the liturgist; we reply, "And also with you!" As Christ's church we rehearse one another in blessing so that finally we can bless all those we meet, all those people God has chosen to bless through us. In a world where a curse is met only with a louder curse, that stewardship of blessing is real leadership.

SHARING THE SCRIPTURE

PREPARING TO TEACH

Preparing Our Hearts

Today's devotional reading is from 1 Peter 5:1-11. The author exhorts church leaders to tend God's flock willingly and to set a good example. Here it is clear that the leader is to be clothed with humility (5:5), self-disciplined, and alert (5:8). As you read this passage, think about your own leadership style. While you may not be ordained clergy, as a church-school leader you are called to give Christlike leadership to your class members. How do you think God judges the way you are leading the flock entrusted to you?

Now turn to today's lesson from 1 Corinthians 4:1-13. As you read, ask yourself how you are a servant of God's mysteries. Continue to raise this question as you prepare to teach this session.

Preparing Our Minds

If possible, read the scripture from at least three translations. How does each one enrich your understanding of the text?

Try to summarize Paul's comments in two or three sentences.

Think about how your work in the ministry of education blesses others.

Preparing Our Learning Space

Have on hand:
- several Bibles
- newsprint and marker.

LEADING THE CLASS

(1) Introduction

Open today's session by discussing the following questions. Record responses on newsprint.

?

(1) **If you were asked to write a job description for a modern leader, what words or phrases would you include?**
(2) **What words or phrases would you use to describe Jesus' leadership style?**
(3) **How would you finish this sentence: "A church leader is someone who…"?**

Point out that today's lesson focuses on church leaders and how their style of leadership affects the church. Lift up today's main question: **What style of leadership befits a servant of the gospel?**

(2) Stewards of the Mysteries of God

Invite the class to read in unison 1 Corinthians 4:1, which is the key verse for this lesson. If students use a variety of translations, have individuals read from as many different versions as possible.

Use the information under "Stewards of the Mysteries of God" in Interpreting the Scripture to help the class understand these key points:

• A steward was a trustworthy slave who managed the master's household.
• Household management also included business ventures.
• Paul and the other church leaders are to be thought of as "stewards of God's mysteries." In other words, they are to oversee God's mysteries, rather than simply overseeing household affairs.
• The central mystery entrusted to the leaders was that of God's gift of reconciliation to the world through the cross and the resurrection of Jesus Christ.
• People who hear the message of these mysteries and divide themselves into factions have missed the point.

(3) Judgment Belongs to the Master

Choose someone to read aloud 1 Corinthians 4:2-7. Note that Paul is saying that criticisms from the congregation are unimportant. What matters is God's judgment. Moreover, leaders who are devoted to higher principles—to being faithful stew-

ards of God's mysteries—are less likely to be distracted by petty complaints.

Read one or both of the situations below and ask class members to respond as they think a mature Christian leader would. If you prefer, divide the class into groups and assign one case to each group.

Case 1: Calvin Jensen, one of the active leaders at Community Church, had prayed seriously about a need that God had laid upon his heart. The community youth needed a place to go on Saturday nights and Calvin believed that the church should open its doors to them. Other leaders were incensed, protesting the cost, the possibility of damage, and the mess the youth would make that could not be cleaned before Sunday worship and church school. How would you handle this situation if you were Calvin? How might Paul's teachings in 1 Corinthians 4 help you?

Case 2: Pastor Randall's congregation had no interest in any kind of mission or outreach. Their philosophy was "We take care of our own but others will have to help themselves." The pastor preached about the need to reach out to the community, as well as to support national and international missions projects. You happen to be in a group that starts carping about the sermon and this pastor's idealist plans to support a missionary. As a mature leader, how do you respond to the group?

If you divided into groups, you may want to provide time for them to report to the whole class.

Conclude this segment of the lesson by asking:

(1) **How is a mature servant-leader's response to criticism different from the leader who wants accolades?**
(2) **What kinds of risks does one need to take in order to be an effective servant-leader?**
(3) **How do you see Paul as being a servant-leader?**

?

(4) The Vocation of God's People

Read aloud 1 Corinthians 4:8-13. Point out the irony as discussed in regard to these verses in the Understanding the Scripture portion.

Look carefully at verses 12*b* and 13. Note that the vocation of God's people is to bless others. If time permits, look at the following references to blessing:
- Genesis 12:2-3.
- Luke 10:5.
- Luke 10:6*b* and 10-12.
- Luke 6:28.

Summarize the idea of vocation in words such as these: To be a steward of God's mysteries is to bear God's blessings. Authentic leadership in the church carries forward God's blessing spoken in the life, death, and resurrection of Jesus Christ.

Provide a few moments of silence to allow the adults to reflect on their own commitment to a servant style of leadership. Encourage them to commit themselves to servant leadership in Christ's name.

Suggest at least one of the activities in the "Helping Class Members Act" section so that the students can practice what they have learned in the week ahead.

You may choose to close the session by using a familiar blessing from Numbers 6:24-26. If the students do not know this benediction from memory, read a phrase at a time and have them echo that phrase back to you: The LORD bless you and keep you; the LORD make his face to shine upon you, and be gracious to you; the LORD lift up his countenance upon you, and give you peace."

HELPING CLASS MEMBERS ACT

Challenge students who hold elected positions in the church to be very mindful of God's intentions for their congregation as they consider programs and finances. Encourage them to take a minority stand if they feel it is what God wants the congregation to do, even if naysayers speak against them.

Encourage all of the class members to lead others (whether children at home, coworkers, clients, or whomever) as humble servants. Have them think about how this servant style of leading may be different from the way that they are accustomed to leading.

Suggest that students make a list of leaders in the church or elsewhere whom they trust. Encourage them to identify the characteristics that make these leaders so outstanding.

PLANNING FOR NEXT SUNDAY

Next Sunday's session, which concludes the first unit, is entitled "Discipline Brings Unity." Ask the students to prepare by reading the lesson scripture from 1 Corinthians 5:1-13. If possible, the students should read the entire background scripture from 1 Corinthians 5:1–6:11.

DISCIPLINE BRINGS UNITY

PREVIEWING THE LESSON

Lesson Scripture: 1 Corinthians 5:1-13
Background Scripture: 1 Corinthians 5:1–6:11
Key Verse: 1 Corinthians 5:8

Focus of the Lesson:
Paul insisted that the congregation enforce appropriate discipline.

Main Question of the Lesson:
Why is discipline important in the church?

This lesson will enable adult learners to:
(1) hear Paul's concerns about discipline in Corinth.
(2) consider discipline in their own congregation.
(3) respond by addressing shortcomings in their lives that need discipline.

Today's lesson may be outlined as follows:
(1) Introduction
(2) The Lost Art of Christian Discipline
(3) Discipline as a Way of Caring
(4) What Needs to Be Disciplined?

FOCUSING ON THE MAIN QUESTION

Discipline is something that most of us associate with particular segments of our society, such as the armed forces. The fact is, however, no part of our society does or could operate without some degree of discipline. Without agreed-upon standards of conduct, plus the ability and will to implement just punishments when infractions occur, anarchy would reign. Without consensual rules of the road, automobiles would routinely smash into one another at intersections. Stripped of due process, schools, businesses, hospitals, and courts of law would come completely unraveled. Though loath to admit it, our children want fair, firm limits on their freedom and desires. With appropriate discipline by adults, youth feel secure; without it, they instinctively know they would end up troubled, jailed, or embalmed.

In general, Christians agree on the necessity of discipline. In such basic matters as sex, money, and worship, most of us would not decree that anything goes. After all, if we are going to be *disciples*, we obviously will undertake some discipline or another. When it comes to disciplining other members of the Christian community, however, that is an entirely different matter. We jump back when we hear Paul's words, "When you are assembled...you are to hand this man over to Satan for the destruction of the flesh.... 'Drive out the wicked person from among you'" (1 Corinthians 5:4b-5, 13). Paul may have been utterly certain about the right course of action, but we seldom are. Even if we are sure about what to do, we are unsure that we are the right ones to do it. "When you are assembled" sounds like the convening of the Salem witch trials. We shrink from surrendering that kind of power to any earthly council. We know too much about how grudges from the world of commerce skew the politics of the people of God. We are suspicious that those most bent on exercising discipline have personal agendas as well as a passion for righteousness in the parish. And what about the mandate of grace? If the church is not the home of "the second chance," then where on earth will we find it?

Clearly, we are confused about discipline and what that means within the context of a congregation. **Why is discipline important in the church?** If we can apply the brakes to our own insecurities and give Paul's directions to Corinth's Christians a fair hearing, he may teach us that morals and moralizing are two different things. We may also be reminded that the distance between judgment and grace is penny-slender: for discipline and nurture are but two sides of the same coin.

READING THE SCRIPTURE

NRSV

1 Corinthians 5:1-13

1 It is actually reported that there is sexual immorality among you, and of a kind that is not found even among pagans; for a man is living with his father's wife. 2 And you are arrogant! Should you not rather have mourned, so that he who has done this would have been removed from among you?

3 For though absent in body, I am present in spirit; and as if present I have already pronounced judgment 4 in the name of the Lord Jesus on the man who has done such a thing. When you are assembled, and my spirit is present with the power of our Lord Jesus, 5 you are to hand this man over to Satan for the destruction of the flesh, so that his spirit may be saved in the day of the Lord.

6 Your boasting is not a good thing. Do you not know that a little yeast leavens the whole batch of dough? 7 Clean out the old yeast so that you may be a new batch, as you really are unleavened. For our paschal

NIV

1 Corinthians 5:1-13

[1]It is actually reported that there is sexual immorality among you, and of a kind that does not occur even among pagans: A man has his father's wife. [2]And you are proud! Shouldn't you rather have been filled with grief and have put out of your fellowship the man who did this? [3]Even though I am not physically present, I am with you in spirit. And I have already passed judgment on the one who did this, just as if I were present. [4]When you are assembled in the name of our Lord Jesus and I am with you in spirit, and the power of our Lord Jesus is present, [5]hand this man over to Satan, so that the sinful nature may be destroyed and his spirit saved on the day of the Lord.

[6]Your boasting is not good. Don't you know that a little yeast works through the whole batch of dough? [7]Get rid of the old yeast that you may be a new batch without yeast—as you really are. For Christ, our Passover lamb, has been sacrificed.

lamb, Christ, has been sacrificed. **8 Therefore, let us celebrate the festival, not with the old yeast, the yeast of malice and evil, but with the unleavened bread of sincerity and truth.**

9 I wrote to you in my letter not to associate with sexually immoral persons—10 not at all meaning the immoral of this world, or the greedy and robbers, or idolaters, since you would then need to go out of the world. 11 But now I am writing to you not to associate with anyone who bears the name of brother or sister who is sexually immoral or greedy, or is an idolater, reviler, drunkard, or robber. Do not even eat with such a one. 12 For what have I to do with judging those outside? Is it not those who are inside that you are to judge? 13 God will judge those outside. "Drive out the wicked person from among you."

8Therefore let us keep the Festival, not with the old yeast, the yeast of malice and wickedness, but with bread without yeast, the bread of sincerity and truth.

9I have written you in my letter not to associate with sexually immoral people—10not at all meaning the people of this world who are immoral, or the greedy and swindlers, or idolaters. In that case you would have to leave this world. 11But now I am writing you that you must not associate with anyone who calls himself a brother but is sexually immoral or greedy, an idolater or a slanderer, a drunkard or a swindler. With such a man do not even eat.

12What business is it of mine to judge those outside the church? Are you not to judge those inside? 13God will judge those outside. "Expel the wicked man from among you."

UNDERSTANDING THE SCRIPTURE

1 Corinthians 5:1-2. The "sexual immorality" to which Paul refers translates a Greek term, *porneia,* used elsewhere by Paul and sometimes translated as "fornication" (6:13, 18; Galatians 5:19; 1 Thessalonians 4:3). Evidently, Paul has been told (perhaps by Chloe's people: 1 Corinthians 1:11) that a Corinthian Christian is living with (engaged in sexual intercourse with) "his father's wife," an idiom referring to his stepmother. By this Paul is stunned, since such conduct violates not only his Jewish sensibilities (Leviticus 18:7-8) but those of "pagans" (Gentile non-Christians) as well. Even more astonishing is the church's lack of grief over their brother's immorality, compounded by their inflated complacency in accepting this moral travesty (for Paul's views of the Corinthians' arrogance, see also 1 Corinthians 4:8; 5:6; 8:1*b*).

1 Corinthians 5:3-5. The solemnity of these verses reminds us that Paul's directions for the appropriate course of action were neither capricious nor based merely on his own scruples. This is a matter of concern for the entire church, following the apostolic judgment (5:3) of the one who first preached to them the gospel (1:1-9) and fed them with milk as a mother nurses her infants (3:1-3; 14:20; see also 1 Thessalonians 2:7). Paul's judgment is rendered and to be executed "in the name of the Lord Jesus" and with "the power of our Lord" (1 Corinthians 5:4). The Corinthian Christians may no longer abet this immorality or adopt toward it a posture of indifference; the church is to assemble itself as the church and to excommunicate the offender. That this action amounted to his being handed over to Satan (5:5) reflects Paul's Jewish tendency to personify evil as Satan, who was thought to exercise temporary dominion over this world (7:5; 15:23-28; Romans 16:20; 2 Corinthians 2:11; 11:14; 12:7; 1 Thessalonians 2:18; 2 Thessalonians 2:9) until the day of the Lord's return and final judgment (1 Corinthians 5:5; see also 1:7-8;

3:13; Romans 2:5, 16; 13:12; 2 Corinthians 1:14; Philippians 1:6, 10; 2:16; 1 Thessalonians 5:2, 4). It is unclear whether Paul believed "destruction of the flesh" (5:5) to be the literal or figurative result of the fornicator's excommunication. Two things are clearer. First, Paul regarded dismissal from the church as the removal of a protective shield, exposing Christians to satanic onslaughts. Second, the ultimate intent of such action was not the excommunicant's eternal damnation but, rather, the healing (or salvation) of his spirit (5:5).

1 Corinthians 5:6-8. Paul's stern instructions should not be mistaken as moralizing priggishness. He is concerned not only with the ultimate disposition of an offender's spirit but more generally with the impact that his immorality has upon *the entire community* of which he has been a part. Evil or malice within the church, like yeast within dough, grows secretly and insidiously (for a similar use of the metaphor, see Matthew 16:6, 11-12; Mark 8:15; Luke 12:1; Galatians 5:9). Before you know it, the whole batch has been corrupted. The church should be a place of purity, "sincerity and truth" (1 Corinthians 5:8), as symbolized by the metaphor of unleavened bread, eaten during Passover (Exodus 12:8, 15-20). Paul trumps his own metaphor by reminding the Corinthian church that it lives by celebrating a renewed Passover: Christ has been sacrificed for us, as the "paschal lamb" was slaughtered for Israel's sins in its observance of Passover (Exodus 12:1-27; compare John 1:29; 19:14-16).

1 Corinthians 5:9-13. Paul reminds his readers that he has already written to them about moral matters. (Paul's previous letter to Corinth has not survived, though some wonder if a portion of it may have been incorporated in 2 Corinthians at 6:14–7:1.) Clearly, Paul is advocating neither the church's flight from the world (1 Corinthians 5:9-10) nor its highhanded judgment of non-Christians (5:12-13a). His concern is with the preservation of the church's moral integrity (5:12).

1 Corinthians 6:1-11. Paul's conviction that Christian brothers and sisters must hold one another accountable for their evil deeds (5:11) leads him to further counsel for the Corinthians. They should not defer to secular courts, presided over by the world's "unrighteous" and "unbelievers" (6:1, 6), judgments that are properly within the jurisdiction of "the saints," Christian believers (6:1, 5-6). For Paul such an idea is ludicrous: like other Jews and Christians of that era, he thinks that believers will assist God with the last judgment (6:2-3; Matthew 19:28; Luke 22:30; Revelation 20:4), even the judgment of angels (compare Isaiah 24:21-22; 2 Peter 2:4; Jude 6). When Christians bring stain upon the church, it is the church's responsibility, through the appointment of competent judges among believers, to wash its own dirty linen (6:4). Even better would be to follow Jesus' lead by defrauding no one and enduring mistreatment by one's siblings in faith (6:7-8; see Matthew 5:39-40; Luke 6:28-30). Paul reminds Corinth's Christians that those "washed" (1 Corinthians 6:11)—probably in baptism—have been put right with God ("justified"; see also 1:30) and set apart for God's holy service ("sanctified"; see also 1:2). Having thus been fitted for God's kingdom, Christians must renounce all evil deeds (6:9-10; see also 5:10-11).

INTERPRETING THE SCRIPTURE

The Lost Art of Christian Discipline

We began to focus on this session's main question by acknowledging our ambivalence about the enforcement of discipline within the church. It has not always been so. As little as a century ago, many churches exercised discipline with deep seriousness. Following the Civil War, Atlanta became a boom town. A young man went there to make his fortune. He joined Central Presbyterian Church in the heart of town. From all evidence he quickly made an impact on the city: soon he was a business-leader in the bustling city and was elected an elder in the church. Perhaps his speedy success went to his head—who knows? Soon came murmurs that he was drinking heavily and had been observed publicly drunk on Whitehall and Pryor Streets, as church records from 1872 report in *The Church That Stayed* by John Robert Smith. The Session, that congregation's governing body, brought this to his attention. He brushed it off, explaining that he had simply overdone his physician's advice, "to partake a measure of ardent spirits for reasons of health."

The Session did not find that explanation adequate. They ordered him to appear for a trial where the pastor acted as prosecutor. The judgment: guilty. Excommunication was withheld on condition that he publicly confess his sins and pledge to change his behavior. This the young man did. He remained a member of the church, but his resignation from the Session was gratefully accepted.

Discipline as a Way of Caring

The Victorian America of Central Presbyterian Church was quite a different day, wasn't it? Churches don't act that way any more, thank heavens. Churches don't play God (well, at least not in that way). It is very difficult to imagine the threat of excommunication today, isn't it? Can you imagine anything anyone could do or say that would cause the church or elders or members to come down on a person that way? We've gotten beyond that nowadays. We've reached the point where we don't care what anybody does.

But wait, that doesn't sound right either. "We don't care"—surely we don't mean that. Or do we? We wonder what business it is of ours if he or she does whatever he or she does. It's not our business, unless of course our business is the business of caring for one another. Discipline in the early church was understood as a matter of caring for one another. If we are summoned as disciples of Jesus Christ to love our neighbor as ourselves, then our care for one another embraces even the awkward, unpleasant business of reminding one another of the discipline we have together undertaken as members of the church of Christ. What is at stake in such discipline, the early church believed, is nothing less than our own souls. Discipline was a matter of acculturating ourselves for a life appropriate to the kingdom of God. We have new customs to learn, even a new language of blessing. The extreme discipline of excommunication was undertaken in the hope that the person, recognizing the gravity of the offense, might finally be restored to the community. However outrageous Paul's rhetoric sounds regarding this matter, the intent of his prescription regarding this man is unmistakable: "So that his spirit may be saved in the day of the Lord" (1 Corinthians 5:5b).

We may be shocked by the Corinthian congregation's apparent boasting of their tolerance in this matter, but so also do we boast of the freedom we enjoy from each other. Our society gives us ample room to choose how we shall live and frowns on those who would restrict space for personal "lifestyles." Don't we boast that "It's nobody's business but my own?" and "It's a free country, isn't it?" We can live any way we want to live, and who's to tell us differently? But the fact of the matter is that we cannot live any way we want to and call it Christian. We cannot live any way we want and preserve healthy relationships in our families. We cannot live carelessly and maintain friendships. What Paul insists upon is not some small, tight, mean-spirited way of life, but a life resonant with the very best we have known. Our lives intertwine with others', and all our lives are wound round and round with the grace of God.

Paul is not inflicting some alien morality upon these people but reminding them of the truth they have already heard, believed, and accepted as the way of life. For Paul the impetus for a moral life is "our paschal lamb, Christ, [who] has been sacrificed" for us (1 Corinthians 5:7). The Easter message of death and resurrection also offers us a new way of life born out of the death of our old lives (see Romans 6:1-14). Because of what God has done, a new life is available to us (see 2 Corinthians 5:17-19). The man "living with his father's wife" (1 Corinthians 5:1) remains trapped in anachronistic habits that have no future in the kingdom that is dawning. The phrase "there's no future in this relationship" applies here, but in this case it is a purely theological judgment.

What Needs to Be Disciplined?

We can become so fascinated with this soap-opera situation of a man "living with his father's wife" (5:1) that we overlook the more ordinary vices from which Paul insists we dissociate ourselves. Paul cannot keep the Corinthians from encountering the immoralities of their world, but he can prevent them from being seduced by those immoralities that masquerade as appropriate conduct among Christians. He orders the congregation not to associate "with anyone who bears the name of brother or sister"—that is, one who would be a Christian—who steadfastly continues to be "sexually immoral or greedy, or is an idolater, reviler, drunkard, or robber" (5:11). At first glance this seems an odd list. We do not customarily consider sexual immorality and greed as equivalent. We know idolatry to have been famously forbidden (Deuteronomy 4:15-31; 12:32–13:18)—but reviling? Biblical scholars have suggested that Paul is reading Deuteronomy to the Corinthians without actually opening up the Torah scroll. The items of this vice list roughly parallel the iniquities requiring the death penalty in Deuteronomy (16:18–17:20). These sins cannot be tolerated in the community because they threaten community itself.

SIN is SIN regardless of what name you call it.

"Reviling" would appear the most harmless of Paul's list, but think of the ways that criticism and backbiting undermine the work of a community. When a constant culture of complaint infests the life of a congregation, initiative and imagination die slow, painful deaths. Just as other portions of the New Testament remind us of the power of our speaking (Matthew 5:33-37; James 3:4-10), so Paul warns the Corinthians. Our speech can be a blessing, however. We can address one another with words of care; we can invite one another to self-examination. Because we live as a community of faith, we can gently call one another to accountability. We do not need to "play God," but we do need to stop pretending our words and actions do not matter. We do not have to act as if we know what is best for everyone, but we don't have to play stupid either. That is discipline at its best—a discipline of risky, costly love.

Looking back again at the records of Central Presbyterian Church in Atlanta, there is a curious entry in 1892, twenty years after that trial previously mentioned. In 1892 the Session inserted a note to clarify its relationship with that man and its attitude toward him. They worried that earlier records " 'might make an entirely erroneous impression on anyone now reading it as to the Christian character' of this man who 'enjoys the unqualified respect and confidence of all his brethren.' " In 1892 that man was once again a prominent and dedicated elder in Central Church and a business and spiritual leader of Atlanta. Surely it is not too speculative to think that at least part of the reason the record reads as it does is that when this very confused and troubled young man needed discipline, some people went to the trouble of caring about him at a cost.

SHARING THE SCRIPTURE

PREPARING TO TEACH

Preparing Our Hearts

Begin your preparation time by reading James 3:13-18. Here James speaks about the true wisdom that comes from God. Those who are wise demonstrate by the way they live that their "works are done with gentleness born of wisdom" (3:13). Review what you have done in the past few weeks. How has your conduct revealed your relationship with Jesus Christ to others? Pray for the wisdom to make your "walk" match your "talk."

Now turn to the background scripture for today from 1 Corinthians 5:1–6:11. Look especially at the particular case that Paul writes about in 5:1-13. As you read, think about how appropriate discipline brings unity within the church. Are there situations in your own congregation that warrant discipline? If so, how might this be done with love, respect, and humility? Pray that God will guide you in teaching this important lesson that members of contemporary congregations need to hear.

Preparing Our Minds

Read today's lesson. Go back over the Understanding the Scripture and Interpreting the Scripture portions, noting additional scripture references. As time permits, look up these passages. Most of them either point to similar teachings in Paul's other letters or to the teachings of Jesus.

Preparing Our Learning Space

Prior to the class session, if at all possible, make a small quantity of bread dough that requires yeast. Put the dough in a bowl (or on a plate) so that the students can watch the dough rising. If that's not possible, bring a loaf of bread. Place the dough or bread on your altar or worship table.

Have on hand:

- several Bibles
- dough made with yeast that is in the process of rising or a loaf of bread
- newsprint and marker
- hymnals.

LEADING THE CLASS

(1) Introduction

Begin the session by reading 1 Corinthians 5:6-8. If you were able to bring some dough or a loaf of bread, be sure to point that out. Talk with the group about how this metaphor of yeast, which they can visualize in the rising dough, relates to the church. Refer to Jesus' teachings about yeast in Matthew 16:6, 11-12; Mark 8:15; and Luke 12:1. Then ask:

(1) **What point is Paul trying to make in verse 6 by using this metaphor of yeast?** (Evil or malice within the

?

church, like yeast within dough, grows secretly and insidiously.)

(2) What effect does "old yeast" have upon a congregation? (It can corrupt everyone.)

(3) What does Paul hope the Corinthians will see when he compares the church to the unleavened bread that is eaten during Passover? (The church is to be a place of purity, of "sincerity and truth" according to 1 Corinthians 5:8.)

(4) Why is discipline important in the church? (Be sure to point out that this is today's main question.)

(5) How does the metaphor of the yeast relate to today's main question? (Paul wants the people to see that they must "clean out the old yeast" (5:7). In short, they must discipline those members whose behavior threatens the moral integrity of the congregation.)

(2) The Lost Art of Christian Discipline

Choose someone to read Paul's words in 1 Corinthians 5:1-13. Then ask:

(1) What is the problem? (Paul has heard reports that a man is living with his stepmother. Moreover, the church has done nothing about this immorality.)

(2) What does Paul expect the congregation to do? (He wants them to pronounce judgment on this man, trusting that by doing so the man's "spirit may be saved" on Judgment Day.)

(3) Do you think your own congregation would censure someone for immoral behavior? Why or why not?

Read or retell the information under "The Lost Art of Christian Discipline" in Interpreting the Scripture. Ask:

(1) What do you think motivated the church in this story to act as it did?

(2) Do you believe the judgment was fair? Why or why not?

(3) What impact do you think this guilty verdict might have had on the accused?

(4) Suppose this man belonged to your congregation, what action do you think would be taken in light of his behavior?

(3) Discipline as a Way of Caring

Think about the examples of the man from Atlanta and the man from Corinth. Ask the students to discuss these questions, which you may want to write on newsprint, with a partner or team. Or read aloud the questions and assign each one to a team.

(1) What is at stake for the wayward person when the church exercises discipline? (The issue here is the person's very soul. Better to be censured, to have to "shape up or ship out," as it were, than to risk condemnation on Judgment Day.)

(2) What is at stake for the community of faith itself? (Just as yeast leavens a batch of dough, so one immoral person taints the entire church. Consequently, the church is diminished when sin goes unacknowledged within its midst.)

(3) How do you understand discipline to be a way of caring? (Just as a parent lovingly disciplines children when they choose the wrong path, so the church shows its love and concern for a member who strays.)

(4) What is the role of discipline in the life of a Christian? (Discipline helps us to know how to live as God's people within the kingdom of God.)

(5) How is our society's tolerance in allowing persons freedom to pursue their own lifestyle in tension with Paul's mandate to discipline erring church members? (We would likely say that someone else's lifestyle is not the church's business, that we are not to judge how others live. Paul, however, says that we cannot live any way we want and call our chosen lifestyle Christian.)

Bring the students back together. If time permits, you may want groups to share briefly with the whole class.

(4) What Needs to Be Disciplined?

Have the students brainstorm ideas about the kinds of offenses that they believe warrant discipline within the church. List their ideas on newsprint. Compare their ideas with 1 Corinthians 5:11.

Read the situations listed below. You may want to spend time with each one, or just focus on one or two instances. Challenge the students to figure out (1) if they would discipline the church member(s) in each of these situations and (2) how they would do that.

- One member constantly levels stinging, mostly unwarranted criticism toward both the lay and clergy leadership of the congregation.
- A church member is committing adultery.
- An elderly widow and widower are living together but choose not to marry because of the loss of income they would incur.
- A member has been convicted of spousal abuse.
- A member is an alcoholic.
- A member has been accused by an employer of embezzlement.
- One member works incessantly to make money because he (or she) likes the power and status that wealth brings.

Close this portion of the lesson by reading the final paragraph under "What Needs to Be Disciplined" in Interpreting the Scripture. Here students will see that disciplining the man in Atlanta whom they discussed earlier did, in fact, cause him to change his ways. Note that the congregation not only disciplined him but must have forgiven and forgotten his past indiscretions. They treat him with respect, not as an outcast.

If you have access to hymnals that include a Psalter, invite the class to read Psalm 51 responsively (*The United Methodist Hymnal*, no. 785). In this psalm David seeks forgiveness from God for his sins.

Before you conclude the session, lift up at least one of the activities below.

HELPING CLASS MEMBERS ACT

Encourage the adults to think about things in their own lives that warrant discipline. Some may be able to change their course of action through prayer. Others may need the help of a pastoral counselor or other professional to help them get on the right track. Recommend that they seek out whatever help seems most appropriate.

Invite the students individually to think about someone in the church who needs a friendly warning about where his or her behavior is leading. Great caution should be used here, but if a student believes that effective communication with that person is possible, he or she should go in Christian love to talk over the situation. Confidentiality is mandatory.

Some students may want to research shunning, an avoidance of flagrant sinners who have been banned from the church. This form of social ostracism is practiced among the Amish and Mennonites. Suggest that class members consider the pros and cons of this practice. In addition to 1 Corinthians 5:11, this practice of avoiding excommunicated members is commended in Matthew 18:15-17; Romans 16:17; 2 Thessalonians 3:14; and 2 John 10-11.

PLANNING FOR NEXT SUNDAY

On April 2 we will begin a new unit entitled "Unity in Human Relationships." Ask the students to read 1 Corinthians 6:12–7:16, which is the background scripture. The lesson, "Responsibility in Marriage and Singleness," will focus on 7:1-5 and 8-16.

UNIT 2: UNITY IN HUMAN RELATIONSHIPS
RESPONSIBILITY IN MARRIAGE AND SINGLENESS

PREVIEWING THE LESSON

Lesson Scripture: 1 Corinthians 7:1-5, 8-16
Background Scripture: 1 Corinthians 6:12–7:16
Key Verse: 1 Corinthians 6:19

Focus of the Lesson:
Paul taught that those who are married are to be faithful to their spouses, while those who are single are to practice celibacy.

Main Question of the Lesson:
How are we to live as faithful Christians who are also sexual persons?

This lesson will enable adult learners to:
(1) focus on Paul's counsel concerning marriage.
(2) compare biblical teaching to society's understandings of marriage.
(3) respond by considering what it means in their own lives to say that they are not their own.

Today's lesson may be outlined as follows:
(1) Introduction
(2) Reading Paul for All He's Worth
(3) You Are Not Your Own
(4) Grace to You and Peace from the Apostle Paul

FOCUSING ON THE MAIN QUESTION

Imagine signing up for a marriage enrichment weekend with members of your church. After dinner Friday night the guest speaker stands before you to say, "As for marriage, on the whole I cannot recommend it. As a matter of fact, I consider my unmarried status a real gift. Of course, if you can't control yourselves, then I suppose marriage is the best for you." Ah, Paul, you old romantic!

Paul is no romantic. Neither does he write for purposes of marriage enrichment. We are undoubtedly right to expect guidance from our church and pastors on matters regarding sexual conduct, marriage, and single life. **How are we to live**

as faithful Christians who are also sexual persons? Guidance in such weighty matters is best expressed in a relationship of mutual trust and intimate knowledge. We do not find helpful global advice that disregards particular circumstances, much less do we appreciate abstract rulings pronounced from on high. If we read 1 Corinthians as if Paul were declaiming ideal principles from the high pulpit, we miss his own struggle for words. Here Paul writes as a pastor. These sections of his letter to the church at Corinth are more like a pastor's letter to college students confused by all the promiscuity in the college dorm than a well-planned, carefully considered essay on the place of marriage, singleness, and sexuality in the Christian life.

Although there is no way of knowing how large the congregation was at Corinth, it was certainly no megachurch of thousands, largely anonymous to their pastor. Paul knew these folks. He knew people who were going up the hill to the temples of prostitution and brushing off objections by saying, "All things are lawful for me"; and he knew the ones isolating themselves from their spouses while declaring, "It is well for a man not to touch a woman." It is about *their* particular situations that he writes, not ours. That may frustrate us because we also feel beset with questions regarding marriage and singleness and sex. Paul does not speak directly to our questions, but by listening in on this conversation, perhaps we may discover something to help and guide us.

READING THE SCRIPTURE

NRSV
1 Corinthians 6:19

Key Verse

19 Or do you not know that your body is a temple of the Holy Spirit within you, which you have from God, and that you are not your own?

NIV
1 Corinthians 6:19

Ke Ver

[19]Do you not know that your body is a temple of the Holy Spirit, who is in you, whom you have received from God? You are not your own.

1 Corinthians 7:1-5, 8-16

1 Now concerning the matters about which you wrote: "It is well for a man not to touch a woman." 2 But because of cases of sexual immorality, each man should have his own wife and each woman her own husband. 3 The husband should give to his wife her conjugal rights, and likewise the wife to her husband. 4 For the wife does not have authority over her own body, but the husband does; likewise the husband does not have authority over his own body, but the wife does. 5 Do not deprive one another except perhaps by agreement for a set time, to devote yourselves to prayer, and then come together again, so that Satan may not tempt you because of your lack of self-control.

1 Corinthians 7:1-5, 8-16

[1] Now for the matters you wrote about: It is good for a man not to marry. [2]But since there is so much immorality, each man should have his own wife, and each woman her own husband. [3]The husband should fulfill his marital duty to his wife, and likewise the wife to her husband. [4]The wife's body does not belong to her alone but also to her husband. In the same way, the husband's body does not belong to him alone but also to his wife. [5]Do not deprive each other except by mutual consent and for a time, so that you may devote yourselves to prayer. Then come together again so that Satan will not tempt you because of your lack of self-control.

8 To the unmarried and the widows I say that it is well for them to remain unmarried as I am. 9 But if they are not practicing self-control, they should marry. For it is better to marry than to be aflame with passion.

10 To the married I give this command—not I but the Lord—that the wife should not separate from her husband 11 (but if she does separate, let her remain unmarried or else be reconciled to her husband), and that the husband should not divorce his wife.

12 To the rest I say—I and not the Lord—that if any believer has a wife who is an unbeliever, and she consents to live with him, he should not divorce her. 13 And if any woman has a husband who is an unbeliever, and he consents to live with her, she should not divorce him. 14 For the unbelieving husband is made holy through his wife, and the unbelieving wife is made holy through her husband. Otherwise, your children would be unclean, but as it is, they are holy. 15 But if the unbelieving partner separates, let it be so; in such a case the brother or sister is not bound. It is to peace that God has called you. 16 Wife, for all you know, you might save your husband. Husband, for all you know, you might save your wife.

8Now to the unmarried and the widows I say: It is good for them to stay unmarried, as I am. 9But if they cannot control themselves, they should marry, for it is better to marry than to burn with passion.

10To the married I give this command (not I, but the Lord): A wife must not separate from her husband. 11But if she does, she must remain unmarried or else be reconciled to her husband. And a husband must not divorce his wife.

12To the rest I say this (I, not the Lord): If any brother has a wife who is not a believer and she is willing to live with him, he must not divorce her. 13And if a woman has a husband who is not a believer and he is willing to live with her, she must not divorce him. 14For the unbelieving husband has been sanctified through his wife, and the unbelieving wife has been sanctified through her believing husband. Otherwise your children would be unclean, but as it is, they are holy.

15But if the unbeliever leaves, let him do so. A believing man or woman is not bound in such circumstances; God has called us to live in peace. 16How do you know, wife, whether you will save your husband? Or, how do you know, husband, whether you will save your wife?

UNDERSTANDING THE SCRIPTURE

1 Corinthians 6:12-20. These verses bridge Paul's concern that Corinth's Christians are hauling one another before Roman magistrates (6:1-11) and his turning toward concerns that that church had expressed about sexual intimacy and the Christian life (7:1-40). Paul begins by correcting views, attributed to him (and placed in quotation marks in the NRSV), that have distorted his own ethical position (6:12-13a). God's future destruction of both food and stomach refers either to the ultimate dissolution of all material things (7:31) or to the last judgment (3:13), after which God "will also raise us by his power" (6:14; see also 15:4, 12-22; 2 Corinthians 4:14). In the meantime, Paul's essential conviction is that our bodies, and the uses to which we put them, are not morally neutral. To the contrary: fidelity to the gospel implies the highest standards of moral, and particularly sexual, conduct. Christians' bodies are members of Christ the Lord (1 Corinthians 6:13b-17; see also 12:12-14, 27; Romans 12:4-5; compare also Genesis 2:24). Changing the metaphor, the Christian's body is "a temple of the Holy Spirit" (1 Corinthians 6:19; also 3:16). Shifting the metaphor again: because God has purchased Christians—that is, has redeemed them from enslavement to sin through Christ's atoning death for sins (see 1 Corinthians 1:30; 7:23; 15:3)—they are to glorify in their bodies God, who now owns them (6:19b-20).

1 Corinthians 7:1-7. Paul begins his reply to some issues raised by the Corinthian Christians in a letter that no longer survives ("Now concerning the matters about which you wrote," 7:1; compare the wording of 8:1; 12:1). Whether the slogan, "It is well for a man not to touch [that is, have sex with] a woman" (7:1b), is Paul's own, or another of those being bandied about by the Corinthians (see 6:12-13), is unclear. In any case Paul agrees with the principle. Why? Because Paul regards his own celibacy not as a curse but as a gift from God (7:7). However—and this is important—Paul does not regard *his* gift as *everybody's* gift. In 1 Corinthians 7:25-40 Paul advocates celibacy, and thus abstention from marriage, as a prudentially preferable way of life. Celibacy frees Christians so gifted from the anxieties of married life in a world that, as Paul (mistakenly) believed, was hurtling toward its end (7:25-31). Neither celibate singleness nor sexually active marriage is, in itself, an intrinsically superior way of life, when viewed from the perspective of the kingdom of God (in which, Paul may have agreed, there would be neither marriage nor giving in marriage: see Mark 12:25). The key point for every Christian is to claim with gratitude the particular, different gift God has given you (1 Corinthians 7:7b), to remain faithful until the end in whatever condition you have been called (7:17-24).

What of those not given the gift of celibacy? First, they should not strive for asceticism: sexual urges are too powerful and will surely lead, if not to monogamous marriage, to *porneia*, "sexual immorality" (7:2; see also 5:1-5; 6:12-20). Second, if already married, spouses should not live as celibates, which would be to deny each partner's conjugal rights. In Paul's world the husband's authority over his wife was simply assumed (see Eph-

esians 5:24; Colossians 3:18; 1 Peter 3:1, 6). The really surprising aspect of Paul's counsel in 1 Corinthians 7:3-4 is his insistence that the wife also holds authority over her husband. Here and elsewhere (7:10-11, 12-14), in a manner stunningly unconventional for his day, Paul assumes that mutuality exists between husband and wife in all such intimate matters of sex, marriage, and divorce. Likewise, married partners are free to agree on abstinence from sex for a limited period of time and for religious reasons—but only on the condition that both of them have agreed to this joint, temporary sacrifice (7:5-6).

1 Corinthians 7:8-11. Paul continues to thread his way through different possibilities. For those who have never been married, or have been widowed, Paul recommends the unmarried state. It is not mandatory, however, and definitely ought not be sought after if one's sexual urges will overcome her or his self-control (7:8-9). Explicitly drawing upon the teaching of Jesus (Mark 10:2-12), reconciliation, not divorce, of Christian believers is the order of the day.

1 Corinthians 7:12-16. Should a Christian spouse seek divorce from an unbelieving spouse? Paul has no command from the Lord in the case of mixed marriages; at best, he can offer his opinion as one with "the Spirit of God" (7:40). As elsewhere, Paul recognizes that because human life is complicated by ambiguities, no single answer can suffice. Clearly, however, a mixed marriage should not be continued if the unbeliever wants out (7:15). Equally clearly, the Christian should not fear contamination or compromise of faith by living in marriage with an unbelieving spouse. To the contrary: divorce ought not to be sought (7:12-13). Through the Christian spouse, God may secure the holiness and salvation of the unbeliever (7:14, 16). In Paul's view marriage is more than an ordained theater for sex; it is a temple through which the gospel is restoring the world (see also 6:19-20).

INTERPRETING THE SCRIPTURE

Reading Paul for All He's Worth

To learn from this scripture lesson and to read it wisely, we must be aware of two particular contexts for everything Paul writes.

First, Paul assumes that he writes at the end of the age. He can counsel new Christians, "Let each of you remain in the condition in which you were called" (1 Corinthians 7:20), precisely because he believes the time will not be long before Christ comes again in glory to make an end to such worldly distinctions as slave and free, male and female, married and single. We see this mindset most vividly as he explains, "I mean, brothers and sisters, the appointed time has grown short; from now on, let even those who have wives be as though they had none, and those who mourn as though they were not mourning, and those who rejoice as though they were not rejoicing, and those who buy as though they had no possessions, and those who deal with the world as though they had no dealings with it. For the present form of this world is passing away" (7:29-31). That Paul did not fully know the mysteries of the end does not at all diminish the value of what he would tell us, but it does signal that he would be astonished to find us reading his words in the year 2000.

Second, we are eavesdropping on a conversation. We need feel no embarrassment, for this conversation is public and visitors are welcome (1 Corinthians 14:16). Paul expected his letter to be read aloud in the gathered community of the Corinthian church. Their conversation regards matters about which they had asked Paul's guidance. The questions we would bring to Paul's attention are simply not a part of this conversation. We may be puzzled to note that Paul says not a word about love in this entire conversation about marriage. In the next chapter, "concerning food sacrificed to idols" (8:1), Paul will speak of love, but not here. Does that mean love isn't important in marriage? Certainly it is important to us, but Paul would have been puzzled by our use of "love" to describe romantic matters.

You Are Not Your Own

In spite of the years and distance of culture that separate us from the apostle Paul and his letters to the Corinthians, Paul spans the gap with a notion guaranteed to offend us, the Corinthians, and almost everyone in between: "You are not your own" (6:19). He says that first to those who continued to visit prostitutes after their conversion to Christ. They evidently believed Christian faith freed them for such things, because after all, faith was a purely spiritual matter having nothing to do with physical conduct. Now Paul works out the implications of that notion with regard to married couples who had decided their spiritual lives would be enhanced by sexual abstinence. To them Paul explains, "For the wife does not have authority over her own body, but the husband does; likewise the husband does not have authority over his own body, but the wife does" (7:4). The authority of husband over wife in the first portion of the equation would have been commonplace in the Greco-Roman world; the concomitant authority of wife over husband would have been heard as a stunning assertion. For some people, it still surprises.

We are accustomed to the notion that we are our own and that we belong to ourselves, and much of our culture and society reinforces our sense of autonomy. We seek a church that "meets our needs," we praise sermons "that really spoke to me," and we expect marriage to be personally satisfying. If my enterprise is my own personal happiness, I discover in time that I cannot achieve this goal alone. So I enlist the alliance of another person. This other person's function, then, is to assist me in my enterprise of being happy or satisfied. This is hardly a romantic image of marriage, but by no means is it remote from our experience: a few minutes spent reading the magazines located near the supermarket check out provide ample evidence for this line of thought. In marriage we select a conspirator for our happiness. The problem, of course, is that our partner has the same hopes, dreams, and aspirations for happiness. Our partner expects us to be an accessory to her or his enterprise. How unfair! They're the ones supposed to be helping us!

Though expressed in thought-forms uncongenial to us ("authority over her/his own body," 7:4), Paul's vision of conjugal mutuality invites us to a vision of marriage larger than one of personal fulfillment. (Certainly the notion that a husband has "authority" over his wife's body has been misused to justify the ugliest sorts of abuse. That we can rip a fragment of scripture from its context and employ it as a pretext for getting our own way testifies to our sinfulness and need for instruction by the Scriptures, not to a deficiency in Scripture itself.) To say that my spouse's body is under my authority is an exceedingly complicated transaction for a Christian. My "authority" has already been surrendered to another authority—that of Jesus Christ. My wants and wishes do not belong to myself alone but to Christ. Furthermore, when I wish to point to this "me" that has such authority over my spouse's person, I find that no one is home. My "me" resides under the authority of my spouse. Suddenly this notion of authority that initially sounded so arbitrary circles into a dynamic mutuality. We are coconspirators in a greater enterprise, not merely that of my personal happiness or even the happiness of our marriage, but that of God's enterprise known through Christ. God is forming a servant people.

Within this circling mutuality we may read Paul's guidance for Christians mar-

ried to unbelieving spouses. If it is hard for us to read Paul here, consider how much harder it was for Paul to write this. Paul was a Pharisee (Philippians 3:5), one devoted to a system where things were either clean or unclean, where something unclean could contaminate something clean. Here Paul sees quite the opposite dynamic at work: "For the unbelieving husband is made holy through his wife, and the unbelieving wife is made holy through her husband" (1 Corinthians 7:14a). Paul trusts the gospel's wondrous contagion. The way that disciples live and act affects the lives of others in ways we seldom suspect. Notice, too, that the effect of the believing spouse on the unbeliever is the construction of holiness, not of conversion. How surprising. Reading Paul's letters and Luke's account of Paul's missionary journeys in Acts—Luke's portrayal of how Paul preached throughout the Mediterranean world (Acts 13:13–14:28; 15:36–18:22; 18:23–21:14)—we might reasonably assume that Paul was interested in evangelism. We might also suppose that nothing was more important to him than conversion. Here Paul hopes simply for holiness. To be holy, in this respect, is to be set apart for God and for God's purposes (see also 1 Corinthians 1:2). Paul does not know how God may use these unbelieving partners, but Paul trusts in God and commends them to God's purposes. Just as he could never have guessed how God would use him (Galatians 1:11-17), so he does not now presume that God has no purpose for these unbelievers. Paul looks to the fulfillment of all things in Jesus Christ and is confident that God's dealings will be fair and full of peace.

Grace to You and Peace from the Apostle Paul

Our lives and families are not always filled with peace. Thus, Paul's word that "It is to peace that God has called you" (1 Corinthians 7:15b) is important to remember. Speaking of peace, Paul uses a word with deep resonances in the Scriptures. Far from being merely the absence of war on the earth or conflict in our families, "peace" stands for all the blessings with which God would bless us: life, health, wholeness, even happiness. The age of the righteous king's coming was seen as a time of peace (Isaiah 9:6-7; 52:7). Paul typically begins his letters, "Grace to you and peace" (Romans 1:7, 1 Corinthians 1:3). Peace figures in the blessing God gave Aaron to speak to the people (Numbers 6:26), in the message Jesus sent disciples out to preach (Luke 10:5-6), and in their own reassurance by the risen Lord (John 20:19-21). The message of the gospel can be summarized as "preaching peace" (Acts 10:36). God wills peace for the whole creation and each part of the creation—us included, even our families.

It would be a tragic misinterpretation of the apostle Paul to wade through this complicated chapter without hearing this sublime note of peace, which is counterpoint to everything that Paul says. Sometimes Paul has a word from the Lord (1 Corinthians 7:10), sometimes he offers his own best hunch (7:12), and sometimes he admits he's winging it (7:25). Of this much, however, Paul is completely certain: God has called us to peace. God has called single people and married people to peace, divorced people and remarried people to peace. Name whatever category you like; God has called all people to the peace that is God's design for the creation.

SHARING THE SCRIPTURE

PREPARING TO TEACH

Preparing Our Hearts

To begin your time of personal preparation, read 1 Corinthians 7:25-35. Here Paul speaks about family life. Remember to put his words in the context of first-century Christian believers who believed that Christ's return was imminent. Given that understanding, Paul's tendency to downplay the commitment of marriage, which would distract one from the work of the Kingdom, is quite understandable. How do you hear Paul's words?

Look now at today's background scripture from 1 Corinthians 6:12–7:16. Focus especially on 7:1-5 and 8-16. Jot down your own ideas about Paul's message concerning marriage, singleness, and divorce. Ponder what you know about the Greco-Roman world of the first century. Imagine how Paul's readers might have understood his teachings. What radical ideas was he setting forth?

Pray that you will be especially sensitive to the needs of your class as you lead this session. Some may be happily married; others, happily single. But for other group members, Paul's teachings may raise issues about divorce and possibly even abuse that they would rather not confront.

Preparing Our Minds

Read this lesson thoroughly. Review the scripture lesson. Look back at what you wrote in the previous section. Did the lesson reinforce your understandings of Paul's vision of marriage, singleness, and divorce? You may find it helpful to outline what Paul says so that you can easily refer to his points as you lead the class. What new insights did you gain about Paul's stance on these issues?

Preparing Our Learning Space

You may want to write the questions under "You Are Not Your Own" on newsprint prior to class.

Have on hand:
- several Bibles
- newsprint and marker.

LEADING THE CLASS

(1) Introduction

Begin today's session by asking the following questions. Record responses on newsprint so that you will be able to compare them.

(1) **What words or phrases would you use to define a good marriage?**

(2) **What words or phrases would you use to define a chosen life of singleness?**

(3) **Which state is better: marriage or singleness?**

Depending upon the makeup of your class, there may be much overlap in the descriptive words they use to describe marriage and singleness. Both states can offer happiness, fulfillment, and opportunities for greater closeness to God. Neither state is better than the other, though persons in an unhappy marriage may prefer to be single while those who have not chosen singleness may want to be married.

Point out today's main question: **How are we to live as faithful Christians who are also sexual persons?**

(2) Reading Paul for All He's Worth

Set the context for Paul's teaching by pointing out:

- Paul expects the end of the age to come at any time. Hence, his comments, though applicable to us, were meant for people who he thought would soon see Christ come in glory.

- Modern readers need to remember that we are eavesdropping on a conversation between Paul and a particular congregation. At the time this letter was written, marriage was not founded upon the idea of romantic love as it is for us. Hence, Paul never uses the word *love* to describe the marriage relationship as he addresses the Corinthians.

Discuss these questions:

(1) **How does one's marital state affect the work that one can do for the kingdom of God?**

(2) **What are you able to do for the kingdom of God in your present marital state?**

(3) **What might you be able to do if you were in a different state?**

(3) You Are Not Your Own

Ask the class to join you in reading today's key verse, 1 Corinthians 6:19, in unison. Also read verse 20, which says that we were bought with a price and therefore should glorify God.

Provide a few moments for the class members to meditate silently on these questions that you will need to read aloud or, if you prefer, write on newsprint prior to class:

(1) **Do I really believe that I am not my own?**

(2) **If I am not my own, to whom do I belong?**

(3) **How am I caring for my body in ways that affirm it is the temple of God's Holy Spirit?**

(4) **How am I mistreating my body?**

To conclude this meditation time, you may want to note that Paul speaks specifically about inappropriate sexual conduct as a means of dishonoring God's temple within us. Whenever we fail to practice habits that lead to health and wholeness, we mistreat our bodies. Talk with the class about other ways that people fail to honor their bodies as the temple of God's Holy Spirit. List their ideas on newsprint. Here are some things we do that are harmful: smoke; drink alcohol; overdo caffeine; abuse over-the-counter medications; eat foods high in fat and cholesterol; fail to exercise; get too little sleep; succumb to stress.

Now read aloud 1 Corinthians 7:1-5. Ask the following questions. You'll find information under "You Are Not Your Own" in Interpreting the Scripture to aid the discussion.

? (1) **What does Paul say about the relationship between husband and wife?**

(2) **How might his assertions have stunned readers in the Greco-Roman world of the first century?** (While the idea that the husband has authority over the wife was the accepted norm, the idea that the wife has authority over the husband's body would have been amazing to Paul's readers.)

(3) **We know that the idea of "authority over" has been sinfully used as a justification for abuse. How does the understanding that Christians have already surrendered their "authority" to Christ alter our understanding of "authority over"?**

(4) Grace to You and Peace from the Apostle Paul

Choose a volunteer to read 1 Corinthians 7:8-16. Ask:

? (1) **What advice does Paul give widows or single people?** (See verses 8-9.)

(2) **What does he have to say about divorce?** (See verses 10-16.)

(3) **What effect might a Christian have on a spouse who does not profess Christ?** (Be sure to note that the issue here is not conversion but holiness, according to 1 Corinthians 7:14a.)

Now ask the students to look again at verse 15. Note that "peace" stands for all the blessings with which God would bless us: life; health; wholeness; even happiness. You may want to do a Bible study with the class by looking up the references to peace noted in this section of Interpreting the Scripture.

- The age of the coming king would be a time of peace (Isaiah 9:6-7; 52:7).
- Paul greets his readers with grace and peace (Romans 1:7; 1 Corinthians 1:3).
- God told Aaron (Moses' brother) to speak peace (Numbers 6:26).
- Jesus sent the disciples out to preach peace (Luke 10:5-6).
- The risen Christ assured his disciples with words of peace (John 20:19-21).
- The gospel message is one of "preaching peace" (Acts 10:36).

The point in recognizing peace as God's purpose is that all persons, whether they are single or married, widowed or divorced, are called to the peace that God wills for all of creation.

You may want to close with a prayer of peace for all the individuals, couples, and families represented in the class.

Before you dismiss the class, be sure to lift up at least one of the activities below.

HELPING CLASS MEMBERS ACT

Encourage folks in the group who feel at peace in their current marital state (married, widowed, single, divorced) to offer an empathetic ear to others in the same state who may be having difficulties.

Suggest that parents of older children and youth talk with them about sexuality and Christian values regarding relationships between males and females.

Recommend that adults be aware of the mixed messages the media sends concerning sex, marriage, divorce, and singleness. Have them consider these messages in light of their own beliefs. Encourage them to write to sponsors of shows or advertisements that they feel are inappropriate.

PLANNING FOR NEXT SUNDAY

Suggest that the students prepare for next week's lesson, "Let Love Lead," by reading 1 Corinthians 8. During this session we will consider how actions done in love show concern for others.

LET LOVE LEAD

PREVIEWING THE LESSON

Lesson Scripture: 1 Corinthians 8
Background Scripture: 1 Corinthians 8
Key Verses: 1 Corinthians 8:2-3

Focus of the Lesson:
Love, not intellectual superiority, is to be the deciding factor when dealing with questions of faith.

Main Question of the Lesson:
When it comes to matters of Christian faith, what is most important for us to know?

This lesson will enable adult learners to:
(1) listen to Paul's teachings on love as evidenced by the way Christians are called to take into account the feelings and beliefs of other Christians.
(2) examine their own responsibility to love others.
(3) respond by helping someone to grow in the Christian faith.

Today's lesson may be outlined as follows:
(1) Introduction
(2) Concerning Food Sacrificed to Idols
(3) The God with Whom We Have to Do
(4) The Person Across the Table

FOCUSING ON THE MAIN QUESTION

The doorbell rings. At the door you find a young man, neatly dressed in a white shirt and dark tie, holding some newsprint pamphlets. With a generous smile, he begins to ask you questions about your relationship with God. Offering you a pamphlet, he suggests that it will give you the answers you may lack. As he leaves and you close the door, how do you feel?

You are sitting in a group that has been studying the Bible across many Sundays. The conversation meanders to the subject of Scripture's inspiration. Another member of the group volunteers her opinion. She chooses her words carefully. She speaks with the clarity and confidence of one who has thought long on the matter. Her answer makes sense; it seems right, at least up to a point; she expresses it with unmistakable sincerity and conviction. Why, then, are some in the group—including, perhaps, yourself—quietly fidgeting in their chairs, wishing at that moment that they could be somewhere, anywhere else than in that room?

You are a member of a tiny band of

Christian worshipers, living on a missionary frontier, surrounded by a heavily religious but thoroughly pagan world. It's supper time. The main course is meat—a rare delicacy. The man on your left passes you the platter, taking nothing from it. Observing this, the woman on your right says to him (and to you), "Go ahead, have some! Who cares whether or not it came from that silly altar in Apollo's Temple? Everybody knows that meat is meat. Eat up!" The platter is now in your hands. What do you do?

When it comes to matters of Christian faith, what is most important for us to know? And what difference should what we know make in the way we act?

READING THE SCRIPTURE

NRSV
1 Corinthians 8

1 Now concerning food sacrificed to idols: we know that "all of us possess knowledge." Knowledge puffs up, but love builds up. **2 Anyone who claims to know something does not yet have the necessary knowledge; 3 but anyone who loves God is known by him.**

4 Hence, as to the eating of food offered to idols, we know that "no idol in the world really exists," and that "there is no God but one." 5 Indeed, even though there may be so-called gods in heaven or on earth—as in fact there are many gods and many lords—6 yet for us there is one God, the Father, from whom are all things and for whom we exist, and one Lord, Jesus Christ, through whom are all things and through whom we exist.

7 It is not everyone, however, who has this knowledge. Since some have become so accustomed to idols until now, they still think of the food they eat as food offered to an idol; and their conscience, being weak, is defiled. 8 "Food will not bring us close to God." We are no worse off if we do not eat, and no better off if we do. 9 But take care that this liberty of yours does not somehow become a stumbling block to the weak. 10 For if others see you, who possess knowledge, eating in the temple of an idol, might they not, since their conscience is weak, be encouraged to the point of eating food sacrificed to idols? 11 So by your knowledge those weak believers for whom Christ died are destroyed. 12 But when

NIV
1 Corinthians 8

[1]Now about food sacrificed to idols: We know that we all possess knowledge. Knowledge puffs up, but love builds up. **[2]The man who thinks he knows something does not yet know as he ought to know. [3]But the man who loves God is known by God.** [4]So then, about eating food sacrificed to idols: We know that an idol is nothing at all in the world and that there is no God but one. [5]For even if there are so-called gods, whether in heaven or on earth (as indeed there are many "gods" and many "lords"), [6]yet for us there is but one God, the Father, from whom all things came and for whom we live; and there is but one Lord, Jesus Christ, through whom all things came and through whom we live.

[7]But not everyone knows this. Some people are still so accustomed to idols that when they eat such food they think of it as having been sacrificed to an idol, and since their conscience is weak, it is defiled. [8]But food does not bring us near to God; we are no worse if we do not eat, and no better if we do.

[9]Be careful, however, that the exercise of your freedom does not become a stumbling block to the weak. [10]For if anyone with a weak conscience sees you who have this knowledge eating in an idol's temple, won't he be emboldened to eat what has been sacrificed to idols? [11]So this weak brother, for whom Christ died, is destroyed by your knowledge. [12]When

Key Verses

Key Verses

APRIL 9

you thus sin against members of your family, and wound their conscience when it is weak, you sin against Christ. 13 Therefore, if food is a cause of their falling, I will never eat meat, so that I may not cause one of them to fall.

you sin against your brothers in this way and wound their weak conscience, you sin against Christ. [13]Therefore, if what I eat causes my brother to fall into sin, I will never eat meat again, so that I will not cause him to fall.

UNDERSTANDING THE SCRIPTURE

1 Corinthians 8:1-6. Paul's lead-in to the immediate topic—"Now concerning food sacrificed to idols" (8:1)—recalls the beginning of his comments on sexual intimacy in 7:1: "Now concerning the matters about which you wrote." Possibly in the Corinthians' letter of questions for Paul they had specifically inquired about the eating of idol-food; here, in 1 Corinthians 8, Paul gives most of his thoughts on this matter. As we shall see below, Paul's conclusion on this topic actually falls in 10:23–11:1.

In the world in which Paul and the Corinthians lived, worship was offered to many Greek and Roman gods and goddesses (compare Acts 17:22-23). In addition to remnants of a Jewish synagogue, excavations of ancient Corinth have uncovered statues of Athena and Apollo, a fountain dedicated to Poseidon, a spa dedicated to Asclepius (the god of healing), and numerous temples dedicated to Apollo, Aphrodite, and Fortuna (the goddess of cities). At such temples meat was among the sacrifices that pagan worshipers offered to their gods. Consecrated food not burned at the pagan altar was either consumed by the priests themselves, offered to the public in dining areas of their temples (1 Corinthians 8:10), or sold by the priests to Corinth's butchers, who would then resell those meats to the public (10:25). Inevitably, "food sacrificed to idols" (8:1) ended up on the tables of both Christians and non-Christians ("unbelievers," from Paul's point of view: 10:27). When this happened, there arose among some Corinthian Christians, considered by others to be "the weak" (in conscience, or unenlightened: 8:9-12), a fearful prospect: if one ate meat previously offered in pagan sacrifice, would the consumer's faith be tainted by that idol? Since Paul sternly warns Corinthian Christians away from the *worship* of idols (10:14-22)—much as a modern pastor would rush to stop the appalling participation of Christian youth in satanic rituals—the subtler question of eating meat once offered in pagan worship was understandable.

Initially, Paul shares the opinions of those in Corinth whose conscience was stronger and agrees with their theological assessments: "All of us possess knowledge" (8:1), "No idol in the world really exists" (8:4), and "There is no God but one" (8:4). Although we cannot be certain—the quotation marks do not appear in the Greek text but have been added in the NRSV—these statements appear to have been slogans of some Corinthian Christians. (The same may be true of 8:8*a*: "Food will not bring us close to God.") Though he will concede that Gentile non-Christians wrongly believe in the existence of many so-called gods and lords (8:5), as a Jew Paul disavows the potency of all idols (Exodus 20:4-5; Isaiah 46:1-13) and asserts Israel's fundamental claim that "the LORD is our God, the LORD alone" (Deuteronomy 6:4). Paul's affirmation in 1 Corinthians 8:6, which extends the claim of God's unity and claim on our lives in a distinctly Christian direction, may have originated in an early Christian creed, since its wording and style are reminiscent of other proto-creedal claims elsewhere in 1 Corinthians (10:26; 11:12; 12:3) and other New Testament writings (Romans 11:36; Colossians 1:16-17; Hebrews 2:10). We owe our existence and our ultimate allegiance to God the Father and the Lord Jesus Christ (1 Corinthians 8:6), and it is this belief that underlies Paul's earlier observation that to love God is to be known by God (8:3). Just here, however, Paul enlarges the issue of idol-meat and reframes the question, taking into account the impact of our knowledge on those whom we should be building up with love (8:2). Here, as in 1 Corinthians 13, "love" (*agape*) refers not to friendly feelings, much less romantic attraction, but to utter selflessness (see also 4:21; 16:14, 24). Because it unites Christians in consideration and care for one another, love edifies and builds up (8:1*b*; 10:23-24; 14:1-5, 12, 17, 26). On the other hand, knowledge—that arrogant, religious knowledge toward which some Corinthian Christians were inclined—inflates the ego (8:1*b*; see also 4:6, 18-19; 5:2; 13:4). Forever needing to prove one's mature knowledge is a reliable indicator of one's immature ignorance (8:2).

1 Corinthians 8:7-13. It is this realignment of what is truly important—redirecting "strong" Corinthians away from the superiority of their knowledge toward love for their siblings—that Paul works out in 8:7-13. Paul doesn't give a fig about the food as such (8:8*b*; 10:27; contrast Acts 15:28-29). His concern is, as the Corinthians' ought to be, for less knowledgeable *fellow Christians*, whose conscience is truly defiled: those wounded by guilt (8:7, 12) at the sight of reckless sophisticates abusing their liberty or rights (8:9; the rights that Paul says, in 9:4-6, 12, 18, he relinquishes for others' sake). Far from edifying the members of God's family, by parading their knowledge strong Corinthians are spurring the weak to betray their own consciences (8:10), thereby destroying siblings for whom Christ died and sinning against Christ himself (8:11-12). For Paul, the church's upbuilding always takes precedence over individual privilege (8:13; 10:28-29; Romans 14:1-23). For followers of Christ, the point is never how much you know, but always how much you love.

INTERPRETING THE SCRIPTURE

Answers right but love and concern for each other is lacking

Concerning Food Sacrificed to Idols

Although the Christians at Corinth wrote Paul a letter asking questions and sent emissaries seeking his wisdom (see 1 Corinthians 1:11; 7:1; 16:17-18), their action was not taken for any scarcity of answers in their own community. The Corinthians had answers aplenty, and with righteous vigor they hurled their answers at each other. We can probably discern some of their answers embedded in Paul's response to them: "All of us possess knowledge" (8:1), "No idol in the world really exists" (8:4), "There is no God but one" (8:4), "Food will not bring us close

to God" (8:8). With these answers and more the Corinthians bombarded each other.

Certainly their answers are fine and good and true, as far as they go. Paul had already trumpeted that the Corinthians were "not lacking in any spiritual gift" (1:7). Since he had been their teacher, Paul might agree with them that "all of us possess knowledge." Doubtless Paul would have agreed, as most of us would agree, that because "there is no God but one," it follows that "no idol in the world really exists" in the sense of an idol's having power alongside God's. That "food will not bring us close to God" might raise a lively discussion as people remember occasions when God's presence did accompany a particular meal; especially we might recall coming to the Lord's Table. Finally, though, we would concede the point the Corinthians were making: the kingdom of God is not found on a particular menu; it is not confined to one person's diet. The Corinthians have good answers and right answers, and they are proud of them. One imagines Christians speeding around Corinth in chariots with bumper stickers reading "Idols are nothing," "You can't get to heaven by dieting," and "God is One: We know!" The Corinthians know so much. Their answers are so terrific. Amazingly, these fine answers leave the Corinthians unsatisfied and asking Paul's assistance.

sin of pride

You have probably encountered people who have answers, persons who immediately know exactly what to say about everything (or so it seems). They have all the answers anyone could ever want, but you do not rejoice at this fact. It is awkward when you are a Christian and they are Christians too. As the conversation goes on, or rather as they talk and you listen, they seem to be some sort of super-Christian (that is, one with all the answers), and you feel more and more quasi-Christian (that is, one impoverished in answers). Not only do they have answers, but they have all these Bible verses ready to slam-dunk every point they make. You go to Sunday school, but you don't have all those Bible verses and answers on the tip of your tongue. You don't have all that certainty to squelch every question and eradicate all doubt. So what's wrong with you anyhow? It is hard not to wonder. But wonder about one thing more: Doesn't it seem odd that being on the receiving end of all those right answers has the effect of diminishing people rather than building them up? Does it seem funny that even though they have all these answers, the Corinthians wrote to Paul asking for something more?

Sometimes having answers is not as sat-

isfying as we think. You can have all the answers and still not have what you need. Take all these great answers they had—"There is no God but one," "Idols are not real"—wring them out, and you won't find a drop of concern for another person. Their answers were right, as far as they went. That wasn't the problem. The problem was that being right and having the right answer had become their "god," a very real idol to which they sacrificed each other. Although the Corinthian problem of eating meat sacrificed to idols may seem remote, the dynamics in their church sound painfully familiar.

The God with Whom We Have to Do

Paul would answer their questions about eating meat sacrificed to idols. But before he could do that, he understood he needed to feed people and clothe them with something richer and warmer than just one more right answer. In majestically layered language Paul tells—perhaps even sings—of one God "from whom are all things and for whom we exist, and one Lord, Jesus Christ, through whom are all things and through whom we exist" (1 Corinthians 8:6). The Corinthians squabble about who eats what and who gets to tell whom what. By contrast, Paul wraps the congregation in the biggest theological idea he can entertain and lifts people up to a higher place where they may be able to see things differently.

The elegant, possibly creedal affirmation in verse 6 is not one more "answer." Those words "answer" nothing but embrace everything. Some of the Corinthians used their answers to diminish their neighbors while they elevated themselves, but Paul's words cannot be so conveniently used. These words cannot be employed to claim turf or magnify self. Paul's affirmation properly places us in the vast wonder of God's creation. In the same instant we are dwarfed by the enormity of the vision and located in a place truly our own. The extent of what we know shrivels on the horizon of how expansively God knows us (8:2-3).

Our lives are not our own to do with as we please. Rather, they have an origin from God and a destination for serving God through Jesus Christ. Earlier in the letter Paul had dealt with a matter of sexual morality by reminding the Corinthians, "you are not your own" (6:19). Those words probably stunned the Corinthians, but for us they are nothing less than a slap-in-the face outrage to our sense of autonomy. Heralds of our consumer society announce daily that we *are* our own; that our choices are our own and no one else's; that, presumably because we live in such proprietary isolation, we desperately deserve the best we can afford. If we own ourselves and if we live to ourselves alone, it reasonably follows that we have hard work to do to get what we want and to lift ourselves above competing selves struggling for their own self-satisfaction. Paul's vision is more confident and more wholesome: our lives are a gift. We find our source and destiny in God. We are given a place in God's creation. Suddenly the question "What may I eat?" has been relocated away from my personal preference, allowing the prior question to arise: "Whose am I?"

The Person Across the Table

Paul is not content merely to reframe the issue of whether or not one may eat idol-meat. He wants the Corinthians to see what is at stake for their community. Those scrupulous about their diets and wary of the meals that have passed through various temples on their way to the market had evidently been characterized in a number of ways. They were "the weak" (so said "the strong," those with no hesitations about their diet); they possessed knowledge, but not so much as others (those who possessed sufficient knowledge to explain away difficulties about eating the idol-meat). These characterizations tended to be derogatory and diminishing. "Strong" is to be preferred in most matters, cheese and

drink being possible exceptions. We seek stronger faiths, relationships, golf swings, financial positions, health, you name it. We prefer knowing more; knowing less we remedy with study and practice. The rhetorical battle of who gets to name things had apparently been won by the carnivores of the Corinthian community.

This self-serving and slanderous manner of naming cannot stand in a Christian community, so Paul engages in a daring act of renaming which in turn calls for a reimagining of relationships. This he does by reidentifying "those weak believers for whom Christ died" (8:11). Suddenly those objects of derision, whose purpose has largely been for the self-aggrandizement of others, shine with such value that we can scarcely imagine it. So greatly are they loved by God that Christ died for them. God's estimation of these "weak believers" suddenly collides with the estimation the world gives them. Maybe they are weak, maybe they don't know as much—but they are God's, and they are Christ's by virtue of his self-giving. In *A Theology of the Cross: The Death of Jesus in the Pauline Letters*, Charles Cousar writes, "The death of Christ gives to each member a dignity and a distinction that must be honored above one's own prerogatives. Unity has to do with this mutual respect."

Paul invites us to see the person across the table differently. This person—with all of his or her particularity and peculiarity, wisdom and foolishness, strength and weakness, rightness and wrongness, righteousness and sinfulness—is so beloved of God that Christ gave his life for this person. And if that is so, can we not give a few moments' attention to what she is saying? Can we not offer patience with his way of going about this difficult business of being human? Can we not muster just a smidgen of understanding? Make no mistake: Paul is not asking us to ignore all differences, only to recognize what brings us together—the grace of God "through whom are all things and through whom we exist" (8:6).

SHARING THE SCRIPTURE

PREPARING TO TEACH

Preparing Our Hearts

Begin your preparations by reading 1 Corinthians 10:23–11:1. In these verses Paul outlines both our freedom and our responsibility for others. While it is true that believers may eat meat sacrificed to idols, this action may cause other believers who avoid such meat to stumble. The specific situation to which Paul refers here is beyond our experience. Yet you may be able to think of circumstances under which you could act with a clear conscience but someone else's faith might be damaged by your action. What are some of these instances? How do you handle them? What principles do you use to determine how you will act in such a situation?

Look now at today's lesson from 1 Corinthians 8. Here Paul is answering the question, "Is it okay for Christians to eat food consecrated to an idol?" Since most meat sold in Corinth had first been sacrificed to gods in pagan temples, some believers certainly had concerns about eating it. Other believers, however, knew that they were not worshiping idols and, therefore, had no qualms about eating such meat. In essence, Paul is saying that love is more important than knowledge. Thus, those "in the know" should avoid the meat in a spirit of loving deference to those who are bothered by eating it. In what situations do you let love for brothers and sisters in Christ override what you know so as not to cause them to stumble?

Preparing Our Minds

Read this lesson and review 1 Corinthians 8. You may want to do some additional research on food offered to idols to better understand what was happening in Corinth. Generally, part of the sacrifice was burned on the altar, another part was placed before the god, and the rest was given to worshipers to eat at the temple. Leftovers were sold in the public market. Christians might have eaten such meat with non-Christian relatives, with their trade guild, or at a dinner hosted by non-Christian friends. Those Christians who ate without impunity claimed a level of knowledge superior to that of other Christians. According to Paul, eating this meat was not a problem in and of itself. The difficulty, however, was that some Christians who had no scruples about eating the meat were harming others. Paul insisted that love, not knowledge, must be the guiding principle.

Preparing Our Learning Space

Have on hand:
- ✔ several Bibles
- ✔ hymnals
- ✔ newsprint and marker.

LEADING THE CLASS

(1) Introduction

Introduce the lesson by reading Focusing on the Main Question, one paragraph at a time. Pause to discuss the question that concludes each paragraph. Then ask these questions:

(1) **How do you feel when you are around someone who projects the image of knowing so much more than you feel you know about the Scriptures?**

(2) **What responsibilities do those who are strong in the faith have in building up the faith of those who are weaker?**

(3) **What expectations might those who are strong in the faith have of those who are weaker?**

Be sure to lift up today's main question: **When it comes to matters of Christian faith, what is most important for us to know?**

Conclude the introduction by offering a prayer that what all members of the body of Christ do will be done in love. Or, if you have access to *The United Methodist Hymnal*, read responsively "Canticle of Love" (no. 646).

(2) Concerning Food Sacrificed to Idols

Use the information regarding 1 Corinthians 8:1-6 in the Understanding the Scripture portion of the lesson to give the group an overview of non-Christian worship in Corinth. Be sure to make these points:

- A Jewish synagogue did exist in Corinth.
- Statues, temples, and other monuments dedicated to gods such as Apollo, Athena, Aphrodite, and Fortuna abounded in Corinth.
- In these temples, worshipers offered meat sacrifices to their gods.
- Worshipers ate consecrated meat in dining rooms attached to the temples.
- Priests, of course, ate some of the meat.
- The rest of the meat was sold to butchers in Corinth who then resold the meat to the public.
- Since temple sacrifices constituted the main source of meat for the entire population, consecrated meat would wind up on the tables of both Christians and non-Christians.
- This reality raised a question among some considered "weak" in the faith: If I eat meat that was offered to an idol, will my faith somehow be tainted?
- This question prompts Paul's response in 1 Corinthians 8.

Read 1 Corinthians 8 as if you were Paul speaking to the church at Corinth.

Next, ask the students to turn to this passage in their Bibles. If they use the NRSV version, they will note these sayings in quotation marks:

- "all of us possess knowledge" (8:1)
- "no idol in the world really exists" (8:4)
- "there is no God but one" (8:4)
- "Food will not bring us close to God" (8:8)

Ask these questions:

(1) **What do these sayings represent?** (These are probably responses those "knowledgeable" Christians who chose to eat meat gave when "weaker" members of the faith asked about eating food offered to idols.)

(2) **Looking at these responses from your own perspective, do you agree that they are reasonable answers? Why or why not?** (They probably are reasonable because they make the point that one's diet is not where the kingdom of God is found.)

(3) **If they do seem reasonable, why do the Corinthians feel the need to write to Paul?** (While it appears that certain Corinthian Christians had all the answers, none of them addressed the human concerns raised by those who felt uncertain about eating temple meat.)

(3) The God with Whom We Have to Do

Invite the students to look again at chapter 8 and answer the following questions. You'll find ideas for discussion in Interpreting the Scripture under "The God with Whom We Have to Do."

(1) **What does this chapter tell you about God?** (See especially verses 2-3 and 6).

(2) **Some Corinthian Christians used their "superior" knowledge to place themselves above those who were "weaker" in the faith. Where does this knowledge stand in relation to God?** (God's knowledge is so far beyond ours that what we know is dwarfed in comparison. When we claim to have knowledge, we don't really have it. Furthermore, God knows us completely.)

Note that Paul wrote in 1 Corinthians 6:19 that our lives are not our own.

Instead, we are to understand life as a gift from God. If that is truly the case, then questions regarding diet aren't really questions of personal preference, but raise the issue "Whose am I?"

Talk with the group about why it is hard for us to relinquish our personal autonomy in favor of concern for other persons, even though we must do this in certain situations because we belong to God.

(4) The Person Across the Table

Ask the class the following questions. You will find information to aid the discussion in "The Person Across the Table" under Interpreting the Scripture.

(1) Judging from 1 Corinthians 8, how do you think the people who have no problem eating meat that had been consecrated to idols would describe themselves? (Note that they would likely use positive terms, such as "strong in the faith," "knowledgeable.")

(2) How would they describe those who do have a problem eating that meat? (These persons would be seen as weak in the faith, lacking in knowledge.)

(3) How does Paul respond to those who are strong in the faith? (According to verse 11, he indicts them for destroying those "for whom Christ died.")

(4) What does Paul's response suggest about how those who are "strong" in the faith are to deal with those who are "weak"? (Stronger believers are to be patient and understanding, willing to meet the needs of others, for Christ died for all of us.)

Close this part of the lesson by asking the members to sit quietly and think about how they could help other persons whose faith is not as mature as their own. Offer a prayer that all may be sensitive to the needs of others, for whom Christ died.

Before you say good-bye, be sure to lift up at least one of the ideas below so that students may put what they have learned into action.

HELPING CLASS MEMBERS ACT

Encourage the students to reflect on how their behavior and attitudes affect the faith of someone else. What opportunities do they have to make a positive witness? Are any of their actions causing someone else to stumble? If so, what are they willing to do to change their behavior or attitudes?

Remind the class that sometimes Christians speak a language that is strange to outsiders. Words such as *salvation*, *faith*, and *grace* may not signify much to those who have not been taught what they mean. Encourage students to be mindful of their language so that they might invite non-Christians into the fold rather than inadvertently build up barriers that would keep them out.

Tell class members to take some devotional time this week to recall one incident when they set aside their own "superior knowledge" in deference to someone else. What was the situation? How did they act? How did their actions affect or influence someone else? How was their own faith strengthened by being aware of how others were responding to them?

PLANNING FOR NEXT SUNDAY

The lesson for April 16, entitled "Work Together," focuses on spiritual gifts given by God through the Holy Spirit. These diverse gifts are entrusted to us so that we might serve the church. Ask the students to prepare for this lesson by reading 1 Corinthians 12:1-30. We will especially consider verses 4-20 and 26.

WORK TOGETHER

PREVIEWING THE LESSON

Lesson Scripture: 1 Corinthians 12:4-20, 26
Background Scripture: 1 Corinthians 12:1-30
Key Verses: 1 Corinthians 12:4, 6

Focus of the Lesson:
Having provided everyone with diverse gifts to build up the body of Christ, God expects each person to use the gifts he or she has been given.

Main Question of the Lesson:
How should we think and act as diversely gifted members of the one body of Christ that we are?

This lesson will enable adult learners to:
(1) hear Paul's teaching on spiritual gifts.
(2) identify their own gifts.
(3) respond by putting their gifts to use.

Today's lesson may be outlined as follows:
(1) Introduction
(2) The Gifts of the Gift-Giving God
(3) The Body Is One and Many
(4) Paul Writes Their Script

FOCUSING ON THE MAIN QUESTION

In the middle of night, trudging to the bathroom, you stub your toe. Favoring it for the next few days, you walk a bit off-balance, only to become aware of tightness in your lower back, which in turn causes headaches and a short temper that your whole family notices. And it all began with one little toe.

In the morning of childhood, encouraged by a foresightful adult, your thumb finds middle C on a piano's keyboard. From there, the rest of your fingers press other keys. Before long the left hand learns synchronization with the right; the back, straightness to balance the arms; the feet, dexterity to operate the pedals. In time, the room is filled with beautiful music. And it all began with a thumb.

Thomas Merton, America's undisputed master of spirituality in the twentieth century, once mused, "We already have everything but we don't know it and we don't experience it. All we need is to experience what we already possess." How

---

true for the church. To the first-century church in Corinth—and to those like us who read their mail—Paul says, "Pay attention to your own body. How do you properly care for it?" For our bodies are not just our own but part of the larger body of Christ. Paul's letter prompts us to raise today's main question: **How should we think and act as diversely gifted members of the one body of Christ that we are?**

READING THE SCRIPTURE

NRSV
1 Corinthians 12:4-20, 26

Key Verse **4 Now there are varieties of gifts, but the same Spirit;** 5 and there are varieties of services, but the same Lord; **6 and there are varieties of activities, but it is the same God who activates all of them in everyone.** **Key Verse** 7 To each is given the manifestation of the Spirit for the common good. 8 To one is given through the Spirit the utterance of wisdom, and to another the utterance of knowledge according to the same Spirit, 9 to another faith by the same Spirit, to another gifts of healing by the one Spirit, 10 to another the working of miracles, to another prophecy, to another the discernment of spirits, to another various kinds of tongues, to another the interpretation of tongues. 11 All these are activated by one and the same Spirit, who allots to each one individually just as the Spirit chooses.

12 For just as the body is one and has many members, and all the members of the body, though many, are one body, so it is with Christ. 13 For in the one Spirit we were all baptized into one body—Jews or Greeks, slaves or free—and we were all made to drink of one Spirit.

14 Indeed, the body does not consist of one member but of many. 15 If the foot would say, "Because I am not a hand, I do not belong to the body," that would not make it any less a part of the body. 16 And if the ear would say, "Because I am not an eye, I do not belong to the body," that would not make it any less a part of the body. 17 If the whole body were an eye,

NIV
1 Corinthians 12:4-20, 26

Key Verse **4There are different kinds of gifts, but the same Spirit. 5There are different kinds of service, but the same Lord. 6There are different kinds of working, but the same God works all of them in all men.** **Key Verse** 7Now to each one the manifestation of the Spirit is given for the common good. 8To one there is given through the Spirit the message of wisdom, to another the message of knowledge by means of the same Spirit, 9to another faith by the same Spirit, to another gifts of healing by that one Spirit, 10to another miraculous powers, to another prophecy, to another distinguishing between spirits, to another speaking in different kinds of tongues, and to still another the interpretation of tongues. 11All these are the work of one and the same Spirit, and he gives them to each one, just as he determines.

12The body is a unit, though it is made up of many parts; and though all its parts are many, they form one body. So it is with Christ. 13For we were all baptized by one Spirit into one body—whether Jews or Greeks, slave or free—and we were all given the one Spirit to drink.

14Now the body is not made up of one part but of many. 15If the foot should say, "Because I am not a hand, I do not belong to the body," it would not for that reason cease to be part of the body. 16And if the ear should say, "Because I am not an eye, I do not belong to the body," it would not for that reason cease to be part of the body. 17If the whole body were an eye, where would where would the hearing be? If the whole body were hearing, where would the sense of smell be? 18 But as it is, God arranged the members in the body, each one of them, as he chose. 19 If all were a single member, where would the body be? 20 As it is, there are many members, yet one body.

26 If one member suffers, all suffer together with it; if one member is honored, all rejoice together with it.

the sense of hearing be? If the whole body were an ear, where would the sense of smell be? [18]But in fact God has arranged the parts in the body, every one of them, just as he wanted them to be. [19]If they were all one part, where would the body be? [20]As it is, there are many parts, but one body.

[26]If one part suffers, every part suffers with it; if one part is honored, every part rejoices with it.

UNDERSTANDING THE SCRIPTURE

1 Corinthians 12:1-3. Paul begins his ruminations on "the spiritual ones," a topic that will absorb his attention to the end of chapter 14. The introductory phrase "Now concerning" (12:1) implies, here as elsewhere (see 7:1; 8:1), that the Corinthians have specifically questioned Paul in this matter. "Spiritual gifts" is one way that the underlying Greek term may be translated; "spiritual persons" is another, equally grammatical possibility. In 1 Corinthians 12:2 Paul reminds Corinth's Christians of their former life as Gentile nonbelievers ("pagans"), once seduced by idolatry (8:4-6; 10:14-16; see also Psalms 115:4-5; 135:15-18; Habakkuk 2:18-19). In 1 Corinthians 12:3 Paul may be anticipating the larger problems surrounding speaking in tongues, which will come into focus in 14:1-40. Whether Paul hypothesizes or actually knows of frenzied Corinthians who, within the context of Christian worship, cry "Let Jesus be cursed!" is unclear. Paul is diamond-clear, and just as unyielding, that "the Spirit of God" (see 2:12) would never prompt a Christian to consign Christ to damnation. Rather, the Holy Spirit is the sole motivator for anyone to affirm that "Jesus is Lord," one of the church's earliest creedal claims (see also 8:6; Romans 10:9; 2 Corinthians 4:5; Philippians 2:11).

1 Corinthians 12:4-11. Paul emphasizes the variety of gifts distributed by God among Christians for the church's common good. As much as any verse in this section, 12:7 articulates Paul's basic criterion: "To each [member of the church] is given the manifestation of the Spirit for the common good" [or "mutual benefit of all"]. This principle has been enunciated throughout 1 Corinthians (7:35; 10:23, 33). Notice, throughout 12:4-11, the delicate balance upon which Paul repeatedly insists: within the church there are *varieties* of gifts, services, activities (12:4-6)—be they utterances of wisdom and knowledge, faith and healing, miracles and prophecy, discernment, or tongues and interpretations of tongues (12:8-10)—that are harnessed by the *same* Spirit, the *same* Lord, the *same* God (12:4-6, 8-10) who distributes and activates this abundant variety as God's Spirit chooses (12:11). It is not a matter of unity *or* diversity, either for its own sake; the critical principle is their spiritual coordination for mutual benefit.

1 Corinthians 12:12-13. Both parts of that principle are maintained, but Paul now shifts the emphasis away from that in 12:4-11. That section spotlights diversity for the sake of unity; 12:12-13 pinpoints that unity of which all diverse members partake. To do this, Paul adopts the metaphor of "the body" (12:12), an image that for at least five hundred years before

Paul had been applied by many philosophers and politicians to such entities as the universe and the commonwealth. Paul's creative contribution to this commonplace image is to "baptize" it: to adapt it with reference to the church as "Christ's body" (see 12:27). Indeed, the waters of baptism helped Paul and other early Christians to understand how different members have been united into one coherent entity: "For in the one Spirit we were all baptized into one body...and we were all made to drink of one Spirit" (12:13). The differences among early Christians—Jew and Greek, slave and free—do not evaporate, but they are relativized by the one Spirit in which all have been washed, of which all commonly drink (see also Galatians 3:27-28; Colossians 3:11; compare 1 Corinthians 1:22, 24; 7:18-19, 21-23).

1 Corinthians 12:14-26. In this long section Paul extends the metaphor of the body in two complementary directions: first, by exploring the great diversity, and thus the interdependence, of the body's members (12:14-21; see also Romans 12:4-5; Ephesians 4:4, 12, 25; 5:23, 29-30; Colossians 1:18, 24; 2:19; 3:15); second, by pointing up the honor due to seemingly less honorable members by those who are seemingly more respectable (1 Corinthians 12:22-26; see also Romans 12:15; 15:1; Galatians 6:2). Throughout 1 Corinthians 12:14-26 Paul stands conventional wisdom on its head. "The members...that seem to be weaker" (12:22) are in fact indispensable—whether one thinks of the body's vulnerable but vital internal organs, or the church's vulnerable but vital members. "Those members" thought "less honorable" or "less respectable" (12:23) are in practice clothed with greater honor and respect—whether one thinks of the body's sexual organs (compare Genesis 3:7-10) or the church's less respectable but needier members. Both the diversity and the manner of its treatment have been arranged not by us, but by God (1 Corinthians 12:18, 24). Our lives are to be conducted not in conformity with the ancient Roman or modern American ideal of radical self-sufficiency, but by sharing in others' sufferings and joys (12:25-26; also 2 Corinthians 1:7; 2:3; 7:13; 11:28-29).

1 Corinthians 12:27-30. Briefly, Paul returns to the note on which he began in 12:4-11—God's placement of diverse gifts within the one body of Christ. In parallel with the selective list of God-given abilities in 12:8-10, Paul enumerates a selective list of God-appointed functions in 12:28-30. These activities seem representative of those that were widely recognized in the early church: apostleship (see 1 Corinthians 1:1); prophecy (or "preaching": 11:4-5; 14:3-5); teaching (4:17; Acts 13:1; Romans 12:7); deeds of power (or "miracles": 1 Corinthians 12:10, 29); healings (James 5:14-15); assistance (Romans 12:8; 1 Timothy 5:10); leadership (or "wise counsel": compare Proverbs 1:5; 11:14; 24:6); and languages and their interpretation (1 Corinthians 12:30; 14:1-28). Paul's questions in 1 Corinthians 12:29-30 are obviously rhetorical: in a healthy church not all enjoy the same aptitudes and responsibilities, nor should they.

INTERPRETING THE SCRIPTURE

The Gifts of the Gift-Giving God

Most frequently we use the word "gifted" to emphasize what sets one person apart from others. Yo Yo Ma is a "gifted" cellist; Annie Dillard, a "gifted" writer; Southwest Airlines' Herb Kelleher, a "gifted" motivator. At school the "gifted" program enrolls children with the best grades and the highest aptitudes for learning. When the apostle Paul contemplates "gifted" people, he means precisely the opposite: being "gifted" is what we have in common with everyone else. Although Paul recognizes individual gifts specific to each person, he assumes each person is gifted in some way. "To each is given" certain gifts (1 Corinthians 12:7), and God works "all of them in everyone" (12:6). Paul's convictions are not generated by democratic impulses that assume equality, nor does he nod with some sort of considerate condescension that smiles tolerantly to say, "But of course we're all 'gifted,'" using our conventional sense of the word. That Paul indeed believes each of us to be gifted says less about us than it says about God. That we are "gifted" has to do with what God is doing in us, for us, and through us. God gives us many gifts for a single purpose, a variety of gifts in unity of will.

In Corinth the very gifts intended to draw people together in the unity of God's purpose have become an occasion for self-aggrandizement. Understanding themselves to be "gifted," the Corinthians preen and parade their abilities as if the gifts were ends in themselves. The important gift (mine) is what the church truly needs; less significant gifts (yours) should stand back and make room. There is one Gift-giver, but that fact is lost in the clamor of diversity. Some speak in tongues and understand themselves to be intimates of the Holy Spirit; others speak in wisdom and from a lofty perch look down on those deemed not so wise. One given the gift of administration cries out, "We need to run the church like a business!"; and one given the gift of healing invites us to pray. Everyone is quite certain that his or her gift is the most important.

Paul calls the Corinthians to lift their eyes from fascination with their gifts to recognize the generosity of the Gift-giver. At the source of the many is One; the destiny of their diversity is unity. In the meantime the individual gifts, given to each, are given for the benefit of all: "To each is given the manifestation of the Spirit for the common good" (1 Corinthians 12:7). If that is so, self-exaltation is not an actualization of a gift but a betrayal of the Giver. To call the gift my own and to trumpet its superiority over those of sisters and brothers misunderstands the gift altogether. A gift does not signal my superiority but rather shows me how I may serve God and my neighbors.

The Body Is One and Many

We read Paul's words, "The body is one and has many members" (1 Corinthians 12:12). If you yawn and think you have heard it all before, please consider that the Corinthians may have had the same reaction when the letter was first read to them. Likening a social entity to the human body was a commonplace ploy of speakers in the Greco-Roman world; the metaphor was already gray and limping while Paul was still in diapers. No criticism is implied here. Paul never asked to be measured by his originality, only by his faithfulness to Christ (4:1-4). But as a matter of fact, what Paul does with this old chestnut of the rhetorician's art is dazzlingly innovative.

The analogy of the human body was often employed as an argument to keep the lower classes pacified and in their place. Our society is an organism that works, so the argument ran, and to revolt against it would be like, well, cutting off your nose to spite your face (to borrow another proverbial use of that ancient imagery). The assertion that "our society is an organism that works" reveals as much about the speaker as the society: the society "works" for this person. The way things are organized provides food, shelter, security, health, whatever is necessary for human existence. Some Greco-Roman slaves could make the argument and did, though it is hard to imagine a nineteenth-century slave in the United States doing so. Perhaps the better-heeled and better-educated members of the church in Corinth employed the analogy of the human body in these ways to stifle the aspirations of the poorer and uneducated ones.

When Paul applies the analogy of the human body to a human society, he does so without favoring the powerful. If partiality is shown to any portion of this "body," it is to "those members of the body that we think less honorable" (12:23). He refers, of course, to those portions of the body kept clothed. Notice the stress on "we think." Each member, each part of the body has its own dignity and function in spite of what we think. Acknowledging what appears to be our inevitable human preoccupation with distinction and ranking, Paul concedes our failing yet nevertheless begs us to notice how "we clothe with greater honor...our less respectable members" and treat them with "greater respect" (12:23). It's as though he were saying: if we are to employ this analogy, let us see it through and "clothe with greater honor" those persons "we think less honorable," those whose gifts seem paltry or unimportant compared to our own.

Paul Writes Their Script

Just as Shakespeare's Hamlet staged a play to "catch the conscience of the king," so the apostle Paul becomes a playwright to touch the hearts of the Corinthian congregation. He gives lines that are uttered by feet and ears and eyes and head, voices that the Corinthians have already heard ringing in their own minds. Remember that the letter was read aloud in the gathering of the congregation for worship. The one presiding reads, "If the foot would say, 'Because I am not a hand, I do not belong to the body' " (1 Corinthians 12:15)—and over to one side of the congregation someone begins to cry softly because that is exactly how coming to church had felt for weeks: "They don't need me here." Some of us wonder if our gifts are really important, if they are indeed really gifts of a God who desires to be known as a Gift-giver. To such persons,

Paul assures, "God arranged the members in the body, each one of them, as he chose" (12:18). Others of the congregation hear their feelings mirrored, if not their words echoed, in the dialogue, "The eye cannot say to the hand, 'I have no need of you,' nor again the head to the feet, 'I have no need of you' " (12:21). Apparently, that is what the members of the Corinthian congregation were saying to one another.

The body of which these many members are a part has not been socially constructed or naturally formed, but built up by God through baptism in the Spirit. God has made the many one, and baptism has washed away distinctions that used to mean everything: "Jews or Greeks, slaves or free—...we were all made to drink of one Spirit" (12:13). Because of what God has done, we are freed from the weary dialogue of "they don't need me here"/"I have no need of you." We are given a new way of speaking to one another. Paul reminds us of the words of sympathy and the high rhetoric of rejoicing. Elsewhere, Paul invites the Christian community to "Rejoice with those who rejoice, weep with those who weep" (Romans 12:15). Here Paul simply describes the homely situation of people who walk around in human bodies: "If one member suffers, all suffer together with it" (1 Corinthians 12:26a).

Return to the dead of night. Trudging to the bathroom, you stub your toe. Favoring it for the next few days, you walk a bit off-balance, only to become aware of tightness in your lower back, which in turn causes headaches and a short temper that your whole family notices. And it all began with one little toe. Paul asks: if our bodies work thus with suffering, cannot they also work that way with rejoicing (12:26b)? If one member is honored or valued or applauded for his or her gifts, cannot that accolade spread throughout the whole body? Although we live in a world fascinated with individual achievements, we also know that there is little we do without colleagues and collaborators and conspirators of some kind. We do the best we can do and then show it to a friend, who helps us make it even better. Together we are better than we could ever be alone. Multiply that by the number of gifts given in your parish and magnify that by the infinite generosity of the God who is the Gift-giver, and reasons for rejoicing cause our hearts to swell. Measuring my own gifts, I am tempted to think them too small or to plump them up as a cushion to rest upon. Gathering our gifts together, we discern the unmistakable intent of the Gift-giver and rejoice in all that God is doing in us, for us, and through us.

SHARING THE SCRIPTURE

PREPARING TO TEACH

Preparing Our Hearts

Open your time of personal preparation by reading Paul's words to the Romans in chapter 12, verses 1-8. Here, as in today's lesson from 1 Corinthians 12, Paul speaks about the diverse gifts that are found in the "one body in Christ" (Romans 12:5). As a leader in the Sunday school, surely one of your gifts is teaching. What other gifts have been entrusted to you by the Spirit? Pray about how you are using these gifts to build up the body of Christ.

Now turn to 1 Corinthians 12:1-30. Compare what Paul says about spiritual gifts to the church at Corinth to what he wrote to the church at Rome. Ponder how the image of one body with diverse parts with varying functions is helpful to you in understanding the relationships that God intends for the church.

Preparing Our Minds

Read the lesson in its entirety and review 1 Corinthians 12, focusing this time on verses 4-20 and 26.

You may want to check the references to the body of Christ, an image that only Paul uses but one that is very important to his understanding of Christ and the church. These references include: Romans 12:4-5; 1 Corinthians 6:15, 19; 10:16-17; 12:13, 27; Ephesians 1:23; 2:16; 4:12, 16; 5:23, 30; Colossians 1:18; 2:19; 3:15.

Preparing Our Learning Space

Have on hand:
- ✔ several Bibles
- ✔ hymnals
- ✔ paper (or index cards) and pencils
- ✔ newsprint and marker.

LEADING THE CLASS

(1) Introduction

Make the opening of today's session a celebration of gifts. Begin by singing a hymn that refers to the gifts that God gives us, such as "Many Gifts, One Spirit" (*The United Methodist Hymnal*, no. 114).

Distribute paper (or index cards) and pencils. Ask the students to list one or two gifts that they feel God has given them and one or two other gifts that they believe are represented by members of the class. These gifts may include those listed in Scripture, but should be much broader, such as the gift of listening or the gift of one's presence. Tell the members not to sign their names.

Collect the papers and read several gifts at a time as if you were reading a litany. Try to read as many gifts as possible, though if the class is very large you will not be able to read them all. At appropriate intervals, cue the class to respond by saying, "Thank you, God, for the many gifts you have given."

Point out that we each have different gifts but that we are all members of one body in Christ. The challenge for us is to affirm the importance of each person's gift and find ways to work together for the glory of God. Raise today's main question: **How should we think and act as diversely gifted members of the one body of Christ that we are?**

(2) The Gifts of the Gift-Giving God

Select a volunteer to read 1 Corinthians 12:4-11.

Ask the class these questions or use these ideas to create a brief lecture about Paul's understanding of our God-given gifts.

(1) When we say that someone is gifted, what do we usually mean? (You may want to mention names of some persons gifted in different fields if the group has trouble defining "gifted" here. In our sense, "giftedness" sets persons apart from one another.)

(2) What does Paul mean when he talks about "giftedness"? (He assumes that each person has gifts. Hence, gifts are what we have in common with other people.)

(3) Why do we have gifts? (God has given gifts to build up the body of Christ.)

(4) What is Paul's concern about the Corinthians' stance toward gifts? (They pride themselves on their gifts, each person thinking his or her gift is more important than the gifts of other church members.)

(5) What does Paul say is the appropriate stance toward gifts? (God has given these gifts "for the common good" [12:7]. Therefore, gifts are not to be seen as marks of an individual's superiority but as means to serve God and neighbor.)

(3) The Body Is One and Many

Read aloud 1 Corinthians 12:12-13. Distribute paper and pencils and ask the students to write the main idea of these two verses in their own words, preferably in one sentence. Select several volunteers to read their paraphrases.

Note that speakers in the Greco-Roman world often compared groups to the human body. Read the second paragraph under "The Body Is One and Many" in Interpreting the Scripture to help the class understand how the analogy between the body and a social group was commonly used. Then ask:

(1) Other speakers used the analogy between the body and a social group in order to keep the social-order status quo. How did Paul use this same analogy? (Paul recognizes the dignity of each group. He does not favor the wealthy and powerful as secular orators do.)

(2) How are members of Christ's body to treat those members "that we think less honorable" (12:23)? (All are to be treated with equal respect, for all were "made to drink of one Spirit" [12:13].)

Brainstorm some ideas, working with the total class or in small groups. Record answers on newsprint, or have each group select a recorder who will report their ideas to the class. Use these headings to prompt the discussion:

- Gifts that the church is using right now.
- Gifts that members have that are not currently being used.
- Programs or ministries that could be instituted if people with unused gifts were tapped for leadership.

After the brainstorming, talk about how the church could be more authentically the body of Christ if all of the gifts in the church were honored and fully utilized.

(4) Paul Writes Their Script

Choose a volunteer to read 1 Corinthians 12:14-20. As this passage is being read, tell the students to imagine the parts of the body actually speaking the lines that Paul assigns to them.

Ask these questions:

(1) What happens when church members say, in essence, "Because I am not a

[?]

hand, I do not belong to the body" (12:15)? (The unity of the body is compromised. Furthermore, the smooth functioning of the body is hampered when people refuse to use their God-given gifts to build up the body.)

(2) **How could church members sincerely honor the diversity within the one body?**

Have the class consider how they would handle the following two situations. The group may want to role-play one or both of them. If you do choose to role-play, be sure to allow the class opportunities to question, agree, or disagree with the way the actors have presented the situation.

Situation 1: Mr. Holden Tate stopped coming to church. The congregation had enjoyed his rich bass voice for many years. However, when a new member was asked to sing a solo that previously would have been offered to Holden, he decided that he was no longer needed in the choir. How would you try to convince Holden that he and the new member are both important?

Situation 2: Mrs. Eleanor Best has wielded power in the church for decades. She is quick to let parishioners know how things should be done. Having held an important administrative post in a large company, she feels that she has experience and expertise that is unmatched within the congregation. After her latest power play at the board meeting, at least a third of the board members threatened to leave the church if she did not back off and let other voices be heard. You are trying to resolve this difficult situation peaceably. What do you say to Mrs. Best?

Conclude today's scripture lesson by reading 1 Corinthians 12:26. Make a list of prayer concerns and joys, which some congregations call sorrows and sunshine. Then ask class members to join you in prayer so that you may empathize with both those who suffer and those who rejoice.

Since today is Palm Sunday, you may want to close the session by singing an appropriate hymn for the day. Or, if you have *The United Methodist Hymnal,* read responsively the adaptation of Philippians 2:5-11, "Canticle of Christ's Obedience" (no. 167).

Before the students adjourn, invite them to consider at least one of the activities below.

HELPING CLASS MEMBERS ACT

Encourage the students to examine attitudes about gifts—their own and other people's. Can they identify and celebrate the gifts that God has entrusted to them? Do they appreciate the gifts God has given to others? How are they working with church members so that everyone's gifts are used to build up the body of Christ?

Suggest that class members be alert for opportunities to suffer or rejoice with members of the body of Christ. Recommend that they do something tangible to demonstrate their concern.

Invite the students to send a thank-you note to at least one church member this week. The note should express appreciation for a gift that the member has used for the good of Christ's body.

PLANNING FOR NEXT SUNDAY

On Easter Sunday we will be studying 1 Corinthians 15. Paul's writing here prompts us to consider the question "What About the Resurrection?" The lesson will focus on verses 20-27 and 35-44.

WHAT ABOUT THE RESURRECTION?

PREVIEWING THE LESSON

Lesson Scripture: 1 Corinthians 15:20-27, 35-44
Background Scripture: 1 Corinthians 15
Key Verses: 1 Corinthians 15:20, 22

Focus of the Lesson:
Just as Jesus was resurrected from the dead on Easter morning, so too his followers will be made alive in Christ.

Main Question of the Lesson:
Along what kind of horizon does Paul invite us to reflect on our own death and the death of others?

This lesson will enable adult learners to:
(1) reflect on the gospel of Jesus' death and resurrection.
(2) explore their understandings of life after death.
(3) respond by considering organ donation and planning to write or review their last will and testament.

Today's lesson may be outlined as follows:
(1) Introduction
(2) The Victory of God
(3) Because Christ Is Risen, We Shall Rise
(4) The Inevitable Questions

FOCUSING ON THE MAIN QUESTION

In late December some years ago, one of your writers returned to the town in which he had grown up. During his return he visited the cemetery in which members of his family were buried. Not far from his parents' graves, he happened to notice decorations at a nearby grave that so captured his attention that he walked over for a better look. There he found a perfectly ornamented, one-foot-tall Christmas tree. Beside the miniature tree sat an immaculately dressed stuffed bear. Both tree and bear looked fresh enough to have been placed at the grave only five minutes earlier. Peering at the inscription on the monument, he did not recognize the name of the child buried there. He was struck, however, by the dates of her birth and death: "1957–1959." In a single moment inscription, bear, and tree cried for forty years of wrenching loss.

Paul's understanding of death is just that hard and realistic. Like many of us, he may have known those whose protracted sufferings made their death seem almost like a sigh of relief. In his Epistle to the Philippians (1:21-24), Paul himself seems to flirt with such a view. Nevertheless, in 1 Corinthians 15:26, Paul speaks for us all when he refers to death as an enemy. Whatever else it may be, death is the last great enemy of all our aspirations for those whom we love, for those whom we have never known, and for ourselves. Every death creates a rupture. It leaves threads dangling, jobs incomplete, promises unfulfilled, and thoughts unvoiced for which we never managed to find the words.

We can be grateful, therefore, that the Christians in first-century Corinth were serious enough in matters of faith, and that Paul was so dedicated a pastor, that he and they peered deep into the grave and wrestled with death the same as we. We have even more reason for gratitude that Paul's reflections on death and its conquest by God survived for our edification. Unlike the well-meaning but fearful who may have tried to console us, Paul never denies death's reality. Yet because of the way Paul envisions death, we can sing with him in genuine assurance that, indeed, " 'Death has been swallowed up in victory' " (1 Corinthians 15:54). **Along what kind of horizon does Paul invite us to reflect on our own death and the death of others?**

READING THE SCRIPTURE

NRSV
1 Corinthians 15:20-27, 35-44

20 But in fact Christ has been raised from the dead, the first fruits of those who have died. 21 For since death came through a human being, the resurrection of the dead has also come through a human being; **22 for as all die in Adam, so all will be made alive in Christ.** 23 But each in his own order: Christ the first fruits, then at his coming those who belong to Christ. 24 Then comes the end, when he hands over the kingdom to God the Father, after he has destroyed every ruler and every authority and power. 25 For he must reign until he has put all his enemies under his feet. 26 The last enemy to be destroyed is death. 27 For "God has put all things in subjection under his feet." But when it says, "All things are put in subjection," it is plain that this does not include the one who put all things in subjection under him.

35 But someone will ask, "How are the dead raised? With what kind of body do they come?" 36 Fool! What you sow does not come to life unless it dies. 37 And as

NIV
1 Corinthians 15:20-27, 35-44

20But Christ has indeed been raised from the dead, the firstfruits of those who have fallen asleep. 21For since death came through a man, the resurrection of the dead comes also through a man. **22For as in Adam all die, so in Christ all will be made alive.** 23But each in his own turn: Christ, the firstfruits; then, when he comes, those who belong to him. 24Then the end will come, when he hands over the kingdom to God the Father after he has destroyed all dominion, authority and power. 25For he must reign until he has put all his enemies under his feet. 26The last enemy to be destroyed is death. 27For he "has put everything under his feet." Now when it says that "everything" has been put under him, it is clear that this does not include God himself, who put everything under Christ.

35But someone may ask, "How are the dead raised? With what kind of body will they come?" 36How foolish! What you sow does not come to life unless it dies. 37When

Key Verse

Key Verse

for what you sow, you do not sow the body that is to be, but a bare seed, perhaps of wheat or of some other grain. 38 But God gives it a body as he has chosen, and to each kind of seed its own body. 39 Not all flesh is alike, but there is one flesh for human beings, another for animals, another for birds, and another for fish. 40 There are both heavenly bodies and earthly bodies, but the glory of the heavenly is one thing, and that of the earthly is another. 41 There is one glory of the sun, and another glory of the moon, and another glory of the stars; indeed, star differs from star in glory.

42 So it is with the resurrection of the dead. What is sown is perishable, what is raised is imperishable. 43 It is sown in dishonor, it is raised in glory. It is sown in weakness, it is raised in power. 44 It is sown a physical body, it is raised a spiritual body. If there is a physical body, there is also a spiritual body.

you sow, you do not plant the body that will be, but just a seed, perhaps of wheat or of something else. [38]But God gives it a body as he has determined, and to each kind of seed he gives its own body. [39]All flesh is not the same: Men have one kind of flesh, animals have another, birds another and fish another. [40]There are also heavenly bodies and there are earthly bodies; but the splendor of the heavenly bodies is one kind, and the splendor of the earthly bodies is another. [41]The sun has one kind of splendor, the moon another and the stars another; and star differs from star in splendor.

[42]So will it be with the resurrection of the dead. The body that is sown is perishable, it is raised imperishable; [43]it is sown in dishonor, it is raised in glory; it is sown in weakness, it is raised in power; [44]it is sown a natural body, it is raised a spiritual body.

If there is a natural body, there is also a spiritual body.

UNDERSTANDING THE SCRIPTURE

1 Corinthians 15:1-11. Contrary to an attempt to *prove* a life after death—a strategy as skeptical as it is impossible—Paul begins with *faith:* faith in the good news that Paul himself had received, faith that he handed on to Corinth's believers, faith to which he encourages them to cling (15:1-3). From verses 3 through 5, Paul reminds his readers of the church's earliest tradition: Christ died for our sins (see also Romans 5:8; Galatians 1:4; 1 Thessalonians 5:10), in accordance with the Hebrew Scriptures (what modern Christians call the Old Testament: see, for example, the interpretations of Psalm 69:9 and Isaiah 53:4-12, in, respectively, Romans 15:3 and 1 Peter 2:22-25). That Christ was raised on the third day is attested elsewhere by early Christians (for instance, Matthew 16:21); that his resurrection was also in scriptural alignment is ambiguous, since neither Paul

nor any New Testament writer tells us what scripture they may have been thinking of (Hosea 6:2?; Jonah 1:17?). Notably, Paul never mentions stories of the empty tomb, known to us from the Gospels (such as Mark 16:1-8), as evidence for Jesus' resurrection, probably because the Gospel writers themselves acknowledge unsatisfactory interpretations of the tomb's emptiness (Matthew 28:11-15; Luke 24:11; John 20:2, 13-14). Rather, in 1 Corinthians 15:5-8 Paul focuses on the appearances of the risen Jesus to a large company of witnesses: Cephas (that is, Simon Peter; Luke 24:34); the Twelve (so-called even after Judas's treason); more than five hundred believers; James the brother of the Lord (Mark 6:3; Galatians 1:19); then all the apostles (envoys of the gospel beyond the Twelve). Last named in this list is Paul himself: Jesus was revealed to Paul at his calling to be an apostle (1 Corinthians 9:1; Galatians 1:15-16; compare Acts 9:3-6). As one "untimely born" (literally, a fetus incompletely formed), Paul considers himself "out of sync" with the other witnesses, least among them as an "apostolic miscarriage," because formerly he had persecuted the church (1 Corinthians 15:9; Galatians 1:13; Philippians 3:6; compare Acts 8:3). Though mediated through the proclamation of Paul and others, the Corinthians' faith in Jesus' resurrection from death is ultimately attributable to God's grace (1 Corinthians 3:10; 15:10-11).

1 Corinthians 15:12-34. With one important digression (15:20-28), all of these verses are connected by a common, argumentative thread: any claim, put forth by some in Corinth, that there's no such thing as resurrection from the dead (15:12) founders on three large rocks. First (15:13-19): such disbelief runs aground on the basic Christian confession of Christ's own resurrection (15:13, 16), which Paul preached (15:1-11, 14) and Corinth's believers accepted (15:14). If God has not raised Christ from death, horrible consequences logically follow: God is being radically misrepresented (15:15; compare 1 John 5:10) and Corinthian Christians are forever lost, most pitiably dead in their sins (1 Corinthians 15:3, 17-19). Second (15:29): if there is no resurrection, then the Corinthians' practice of surrogate baptism on behalf of the dead—whatever that may have looked like, and for whatever reason—makes no sense whatsoever. Third (15:30-34): if the dead are not raised, then the Corinthians have shamefully ripped the heart from Paul's own witness (15:33-34), proclaimed in a mission that constantly jeopardized his very life (see also 1 Corinthians 4:11-13; 16:8-9; 2 Corinthians 1:8-9; 11:23-33).

Paul will have none of this. Hence, his theologically loaded digression: indisputably, Christ has been raised by God from death (1 Corinthians 15:20-28; 6:14). Christ is "the first fruits" (15:20, 23): the earliest produce, consecrated for God's use, of a much greater harvest (see Exodus 23:19). Moreover, Christ represents a fresh start, new life for a humanity that through Adam knew only death (1 Corinthians 15:21-22; compare Genesis 2:17; 3:17-19; Romans 5:12-21). After his return from heaven, those in Christ will also be raised (1 Corinthians 15:23; 1:7-8; 1 Thessalonians 4:13-17), and all hostile dominions—ultimately, even death itself—will be subjected to Christ by God (1 Corinthians 15:24-27; Romans 8:38-39; Ephesians 1:21; Colossians 2:10, 15; 1 Peter 3:22; compare Psalms 8:6; 110:1). Last of all the Son will subject himself to his Father, "so that God may be all in all" (1 Corinthians 15:28; also 3:23).

1 Corinthians 15:35-58. Prompted by speculative questions (15:35), these verses are connected by a final theme: resurrection, for Paul, implies God's renewal of the whole of creation, including its embodied existence. To make this point, the apostle reaches back into the early verses of Genesis, which recount various embodiments of God's creation (Genesis 1:11-25; compare 1 Corinthians 15:37-43). Paul believes that flesh and blood, the perishable components of our bodies in this life, must be transformed by God into "spiritual bodies" appropriate to that imperishable Kingdom for which those in Christ will be fitted (15:44, 50-54; see also 2 Corinthians 5:4; Philippians 3:21; 1 Thessalonians 4:15-16). If we have borne the image of the first Adam—who, though living, consigned all humanity to death through sin—then we are being refashioned in the image of Christ, "the last Adam"—a life-giving heavenly spirit (1 Corinthians 15:45-49, 55-56; compare Genesis 1:26-27; 5:3; Romans 8:29; 2 Corinthians 3:18; 4:4). Wrongly, Paul assumed that this transformation would be completed during his lifetime (1 Corinthians 15:51; 1 Thessalonians 4:14). Rightly, he gives praise to God for an assured victory that gives purpose to activities now being done "in the Lord" (1 Corinthians 15:57-58; 2 Corinthians 2:14).

INTERPRETING THE SCRIPTURE

The Victory of God

Easter's hope may be obscured in the dense clouds of Paul's way of thinking and writing, and that, above all things, would grieve the apostle. Paul writes this section of the epistle not to convert people to his way of thinking or to dazzle believers with his rhetoric, but rather to give them hope and encourage them. What Paul assumes, however, remains foreign to us. His message of hope is cloaked in the language of apocalyptic, and that language cloaks his message of hope. Apocalyptic was a way of thinking very much current in Paul's day but, in its classical form, is virtually absent from our own.

Paul anticipates the final triumph of God in the creation. That hope—better, his conviction—is the foundation for the grandest statements of Paul's letters (Romans 8, for instance). Apocalyptic thinking looks for the climactic fulfillment of God's purposes for the creation. God does not ultimately intend for people to bow under injustice and oppression, but instead wills a glorious Kingdom in which each person lives in peace and harmony with God and neighbor. Petty tyrants ruling for their own purposes are alien to God's design; at the conclusion of history, Christ will reign and bring all things into an order that is just and right (1 Corinthians 15:24-25). Human life, therefore, does not find completion in the grave but in an inheritance that is unspeakably rich and wholesome, the resurrection of the dead at the end of time (15:51-52). The apocalyptic vision encompasses nothing less than the healing of the entire creation by the power, justice, love, and peace of God. That vision dazzles us with its breadth and hopefulness. How may we dare hope for so much? For Paul, the answer is seen in the resurrection of Jesus the Christ.

Because Christ Is Risen, We Shall Rise

We cannot see the fulfillment of God's design for the creation now, but this much we have seen and this much we know: Christ is risen from the dead. In that rests Paul's confidence. He reminds the Corinthians once again what he has been told, what he has told them, and what they have come to believe (1 Corinthians 15:1-8). It may sound as though Paul is saying something like, "Well, I preached the Resurrection to you, so it must be true." Instead, Paul invites the Corinthians to remember their own experience of the risen Christ. What Peter and the Twelve experienced, Paul had also come to know; through his preaching, the Corinthians discovered it for themselves. Hearing the good news of Christ's resurrection, they had come to their own conclusions.

That Jesus had walked out of a tomb one Easter Sunday morning, around twenty-five years before in faraway Jerusalem, was only the beginning of the matter. The Corinthians had known His presence and power in their own life together. One thing the Corinthians were not uncertain about was their own experience of faith. Their faith might fracture their community into warring clans; it might produce the worst sort of spiritual elitism; it might threaten to burn down the church in its zeal—but they did not lack a sense of Christ's Spirit among them. Yet what, exactly, did that mean? For some, it evidently did not extend beyond the spiritual ecstasies of the moment. Yes, they knew Christ in the present life of their community. But as for a renewed and reconstituted community of the faithful in a resurrection of the dead—well, that is a lot to believe.

The resurrection of Christ, however, seals Paul's confidence in God's plan. Christ is "the first fruits," the certain harbinger of an astonishing harvest that will undoubtedly follow. In Christ's resurrection we see God's victory over death, which presages God's total victory over everything that opposes the healing and renewal of the creation. Forces of evil and injustice may be blind to recognize it, but their future has been foreclosed. A few generations ago biblical scholars frequently likened the situation envisaged by Paul to that of the Second World War in Europe following the success of the D day landings. The Normandy invasion succeeded; though terrible battles remained to be fought, the Allied victory was unmistakably clear. Similarly, Paul takes the resurrection of Christ on Easter and from that extrapolates God's triumph for the entire creation. Already death has begun to be defeated, even though death continues its sad, self-defeating work: that futility that builds nothing, creates nothing, causes no joy, and for a gift offers only heartsickness. It is, as Paul says, "the last enemy." But death itself will finally die, because it has no future in the invincible life that God plans for the cosmos.

So vast, all-encompassing, and glorious is Paul's vision that it almost seems impertinent or selfish to ask, "But what about me?" Yes, God will obtain final victory; yes, Christ will reign over all the creation; and yes, the dead will be raised to glory. In the meantime, however, what about us? About this matter Paul has somewhat less to say, but this much is utterly clear in his letters: we are "in Christ," and those who have gone before us into death are "in Christ," and neither life nor death shall "separate us from the love of God in Christ Jesus our Lord" (Romans 8:39). Of course, it is not merely a matter of impertinence or selfishness that causes us to ask such questions. We ask on behalf of those we love. Christ has bade us love one another (John 13:34-35; 15:12-17), and because of our trust in Christ, the bounds of our love are not limited by the dimensions of life and death. We wonder about those we have loved best, whose lives have been so intertwined with ours that we scarcely can imagine any life that does not include them. Paul assures us that they are "in Christ" even as we are "in Christ"—and being "in Christ" is as good as anyone may hope for until that day when all things are transformed by grace and mercy from beyond the walls of this world.

The Inevitable Questions

The notion of the resurrection of the dead inevitably raises questions: "How are the dead raised? With what kind of body do they come?" (1 Corinthians 15:35). Such questions obviously irritate Paul, and he snaps, "Fool!" (15:36). These questions press Paul beyond where he wishes to go. They force him to speak of things for which we are given no language to speak. How could the Corinthians expect that Paul would know answers to such questions as these? If in 1 Corinthians 15:36-57 Paul says more than he knows, he does so as a pastor. When a child asks you if her long-lived, long-loved kitty is now in heaven with God, it is an occasion neither for dense theological reflection on the place of cats in the creation nor on the inevitability of mortality, but rather an opportunity for retrieving and reciting the most profound insights of faith. Faced with inevitable questions requiring impossible answers, Paul faces death square in the face and declares, "But God gives" (15:38). The initiative belongs solely to God, and from what we have already come to know of God, God may be trusted.

God gave us these bodies. There are all kinds of bodies, Paul reminds us, cataloging the creation (15:39-40). So also, in the new creation that God is fashioning, there will be bodies appropriate for a life that is abundant and everlasting. How may we think of these bodies? Paul offers an oxymoron, a contradiction of logic like "fried ice": "a spiritual body" is what we all shall receive. Paul presses language to the edges of sensible meaning, hoping that literal nonsense may generate insight into an unspeakable mystery. Obviously, we don't know what "a spiritual body" looks like or feels like to walk around in. We do know what it is to have a body; we know something of what it is to have a spirit. Though our bodies and spirits often seem at odds with themselves, we can also imagine what it might be like to have that painful chafing healed. A new creation for the cosmos requires a new creation of us (see also 2 Corinthians 5:17). That may seem impossible, but God—who creates bodies for birds to soar in air and bodies for fish to waggle in water and bodies for creatures to lope on land—may be trusted to fashion for us a suitable body in which we can enjoy a healed creation. Paul redirects our attention to the marvel of the creation. If creation shows us anything, it demonstrates God's fascination with bodies: so many different kinds of creatures, so many different kinds of bodies. Just when we think we've seen it all in *The National Geographic*, 1 Corinthians shows us a new species, an unforeseen marvel. We haven't seen it all, of course. God has vastly more in store—and unspeakably, wondrously more in store for us.

SHARING THE SCRIPTURE

PREPARING TO TEACH

Preparing Our Hearts

Begin your preparations for the Easter lesson by reading 1 Corinthians 15:12-19 and 50-57. These verses, which are part of today's background scripture, are a devotional reading to help you focus on Christ's resurrection and on the immortal bodies that we will one day put on. Think seriously about what Christ's resurrection means to you. Meditate on the awesome significance of Christ's resurrection. How is your life different because God raised Jesus from the dead? What expectations do you have for life after your mortal body dies?

Now read all of 1 Corinthians 15. This time, look especially at verses 20-27 and 35-44. What kinds of questions do you have about Jesus' resurrection? What questions might class members have? Paul's discussion about an imperishable body may sound particularly good if you suffer from physical ailments. What physical problems do you anticipate being released from when you put on this imperishable body?

Although we will not be studying any of the Gospel accounts of the Resurrection, you may want to read one or more of these accounts to prepare yourself spiritually for Easter. Check Matthew 28:1-10; Mark 16:1-8; Luke 24:1-12; and John 20:1-18.

Preparing Our Minds

As you read this lesson and follow Paul's argument in 1 Corinthians 15, you will note that he not only affirms the resurrection of Christ but also uses that event as the basis for our own hope in resurrection.

To gain new insights from 1 Corinthians 15, try to read it in two or three different translations.

Preparing Our Learning Space

Have on hand:
✔ several Bibles
✔ newsprint and marker

✔ paper and pencils
✔ hymnals.

LEADING THE CLASS

(1) Introduction

You may want to begin today's lesson by reading or retelling Focusing on the Main Question.

Another way to begin is to ask class members to complete the sentence "Death is...." Record their answers on newsprint. Invite the students to review their list to spot trends in the kinds of responses people have given. Then ask:

(1) **Why is our view of death so negative?**
(2) **What do we expect to happen to the human body after death?**
(3) **Do we expect to live on even after the human body dies? If so, why do we have this expectation?**

Wrap up this introduction by pointing out that what we believe about the Resurrection makes all the difference in how we view death. Of course, the death of a loved one or the thought of our own death brings sorrow and a sense of loss no matter what our beliefs. Yet if we believe that Jesus was resurrected, our sadness is tempered by the hope of eternal life and reunion with those whom we have been privileged to love here. As we think about how Jesus' resurrection changes our prospects for the future, we consider this main question for today's lesson: **Along what kind of horizon does Paul invite us to reflect on our own death and the death of others?**

(2) The Victory of God

Select someone to read 1 Corinthians 15:20-27. This passage is difficult, so if you have a variety of Bible translations available, call on several volunteers to read.

Note that Paul has tried to get his points across by using apocalyptic language. That is, he uses language that looks forward to the fulfillment of God's purposes for creation at the conclusion of history. At that time, God will usher in a new Kingdom, one that will be peaceable and ordered by Christ, who will bring about a just and right order. Christ will conquer all enemies, including death. In other words, all of creation will be healed by the power, justice, love, and peace of God. Paul teaches that this age will come about as a result of Jesus' resurrection.

Ask these questions:

(1) **How is Paul's teaching similar to or different from your own understanding of the hope that Easter brings?**
(2) **How does God's victory over the grave give you hope for the future?**

(3) Because Christ Is Risen, We Shall Rise

Note that Paul's teaching affirms that we are "in Christ," that because he has been resurrected we too will be raised from the dead. While we cannot comprehend what this new, imperishable body that Paul speaks of may look or feel like, we can assume that it will be an improvement over our current bodies that are subject to disease and pain.

Challenge the class to think of creative ways to describe these resurrected bodies. Perhaps one student will see a colorful balloon floating, while another will envision someone they consider particularly beautiful or handsome, and another student will see a healthy, trim, fit body. Of course, we have no language to describe the resurrected body, but prompting students to think of the best body they can conjure up will help them realize that their resurrected bodies will be even better than they could possibly imagine or describe.

Distribute paper and pencils. Read the following sentence stems aloud and give the students time to complete them.

● The thing I like best about my body right now is...
● If I could, I would change my body so that it would...

- The disease or infirmity I most fear is . . .
- I hope that my eternal body will be . . .

If you have time and wish to do so, you may want to call on volunteers to share what they have written.

(4) The Inevitable Questions

Read aloud 1 Corinthians 15:35. Invite the students to supply their own answers to the two questions this verse raises.

Now read 1 Corinthians 15:36-44 to see how Paul responds to those two questions. Note these points:

- God gave us these bodies.
- These bodies are appropriate for us within the created order.
- God will also give us appropriate bodies for our resurrected selves.
- Paul says that we will have spiritual bodies.

Divide the class into partners or teams and ask each group to discuss their beliefs about what life after death will be like. Obviously, we cannot know for certain what that eternal life will be like, but students will likely have some thoughts on this matter.

The Bible teaches that we will receive new, imperishable bodies. Our current, aging bodies are not the ones that will be resurrected. Talk with the students about organ donation. A new heart, kidney, or other vital organ could save the life of someone who needs a transplant. Suggest that class members prayerfully consider becoming organ donors and/or donating organs of loved ones so that someone else may have the gift of life in this mortal body.

You may wish to sing a hymn based on 1 Corinthians 15, such as "Sing with All the Saints in Glory" (*The United Methodist Hymnal*, no. 702) or "Christian People, Raise Your Song" (*UMH*, no. 636). Or you may prefer to close with an Easter song that is a favorite among class members.

Before concluding the lesson, be sure to lift up at least one of the activities below so that students will have an opportunity to live out their faith in the week ahead.

HELPING CLASS MEMBERS ACT

Encourage students who know someone who is grieving to visit that person and offer a listening ear and empathetic shoulder. While the mourner's tremendous loss should not be glossed over, students may find an appropriate time in the conversation to offer a word of resurrection hope.

Recommend that students who have not yet done so should consider making a last will and testament. In addition, wherever possible, adults will want to prepare a durable power of attorney for medical emergencies and other appropriate legal documents.

Suggest that students plant at least one fruit or flower seed as a sign of the new hope and life that exists as a result of the Resurrection.

PLANNING FOR NEXT SUNDAY

Next week's lesson, "What's Real Love?" looks at Paul's familiar teaching on love as found in 1 Corinthians 12:31–13:13. Invite the students to read this passage carefully and to consider how they demonstrate love for others.

WHAT'S REAL LOVE?

PREVIEWING THE LESSON

Lesson Scripture: 1 Corinthians 12:31–13:13
Background Scripture: 1 Corinthians 12:31–13:13
Key Verse: 1 Corinthians 13:13

Focus of the Lesson:
Paul explained the characteristics and value of genuine love to his readers.

Main Question of the Lesson:
What is authentic love like?

This lesson will enable adult learners to:
(1) examine Paul's teachings on authentic love.
(2) explore their own willingness to love authentically.
(3) respond by setting aside scorecards so as to love others as Christ loves.

Today's lesson may be outlined as follows:
(1) Introduction
(2) Answering the Unasked Question
(3) When Nothing Else Works
(4) The Cross and the Scorecard

FOCUSING ON THE MAIN QUESTION

Following a wedding service, frequently someone will ask, "Where can I get a copy of that thing you read about love?" The person asks, of course, about these words of Paul first addressed to the conflicted Christians of Corinth.

"It's in the Bible: First Corinthians 13."

"Really!" People are amazed. They do not expect that something so beautiful, so graceful, so perfectly lovely would be found in the pages of holy writ; and if they know anything about the Bible at all, they do not expect such from Paul. Many people think of Paul as a sort of theological thug, a heavy-handed misanthrope who subverted the sweet, gentle religion Jesus began.

What is authentic love like? This chapter's response to this often asked question is beautiful. Because it is so beautiful people raid Paul's letter to pilfer this chapter from it. They needlepoint it for the kitchen. In bright calligraphy they write and frame the words for everyone to see.

The sentiment that lifts these words out of the letter is understandable but also regrettable. Standing alone, the thirteenth chapter sounds sentimental, an idealistic

---

323

vision of love remote from the difficulty and complexity of real human relationships. We forget that the thirteenth chapter follows the twelfth chapter, and that it was written to a group of people who wanted to show each other out the door.

In the passage immediately preceding this stunning tribute to love, Paul teases his image of the body, explaining, "The eye cannot say to the hand, 'I have no need of you,' nor again the head to the feet, 'I have no need of you'" (1 Corinthians 12:21). The Corinthians were saying just that to one another: "I have no need of you." They put each other down, trumping each other's one-upmanship. The names they gave one another reflect their games: the strong and the weak, the wise and the foolish—these are hardly neutral terms. The problem was not simply that their congregation was diverse or had differences; they could not abide their differences. When every other strategy failed, they tried to discard each other: "I have no need of you." Paul shakes his head and says, "Let me show you a better way."

READING THE SCRIPTURE

NRSV
1 Corinthians 12:31–13:13
31 But strive for the greater gifts. And I will show you a still more excellent way.

13:1 If I speak in the tongues of mortals and of angels, but do not have love, I am a noisy gong or a clanging cymbal. 2 And if I have prophetic powers, and understand all mysteries and all knowledge, and if I have all faith, so as to remove mountains, but do not have love, I am nothing. 3 If I give away all my possessions, and if I hand over my body so that I may boast, but do not have love, I gain nothing.

4 Love is patient; love is kind; love is not envious or boastful or arrogant 5 or rude. It does not insist on its own way; it is not irritable or resentful; 6 it does not rejoice in wrongdoing, but rejoices in the truth. 7 It bears all things, believes all things, hopes all things, endures all things.

8 Love never ends. But as for prophecies, they will come to an end; as for tongues, they will cease; as for knowledge, it will come to an end. 9 For we know only in part, and we prophesy only in part; 10 but when the complete comes, the partial will come to an end. 11 When I was a child, I spoke like a child, I thought like a child, I reasoned like a child; when I became an adult, I put an end to childish

NIV
1 Corinthians 12:31–13:13
31But eagerly desire the greater gifts.

And now I will show you the most excellent way.

13:1 If I speak in the tongues of men and of angels, but have not love, I am only a resounding gong or a clanging cymbal. 2If I have the gift of prophecy and can fathom all mysteries and all knowledge, and if I have a faith that can move mountains, but have not love, I am nothing. 3If I give all I possess to the poor and surrender my body to the flames, but have not love, I gain nothing.

4Love is patient, love is kind. It does not envy, it does not boast, it is not proud. 5It is not rude, it is not self-seeking, it is not easily angered, it keeps no record of wrongs. 6Love does not delight in evil but rejoices with the truth. 7It always protects, always trusts, always hopes, always perseveres.

8Love never fails. But where there are prophecies, they will cease; where there are tongues, they will be stilled; where there is knowledge, it will pass away. 9For we know in part and we prophesy in part, 10but when perfection comes, the imperfect disappears. 11When I was a child, I talked like a child, I thought like a child, I reasoned like a child. When I became a man, I put childish ways behind me. 12Now we ways. 12 For now we see in a mirror, dimly, but then we will see face to face. Now I know only in part; then I will know fully, even as I have been fully known. **13 And now faith, hope, and love abide, these three; and the greatest of these is love.**

see but a poor reflection as in a mirror; then we shall see face to face. Now I know in part; then I shall know fully, even as I am fully known.

13 And now these three remain: faith, hope and love. But the greatest of these is love.

UNDERSTANDING THE SCRIPTURE

1 Corinthians 12:31. This is a bridge verse. It both concludes Paul's thoughts on the diversity of gifts within the coherent unity of the church as Christ's body (12:4-30) as well as opens up the apostle's reflections on the definitive context within which all gifts should function (thus drawing out threads of thought from 8:1-3; 12:1-3, 7). Notice that Paul introduces his tribute to love by referring to it as "a still more excellent way" (12:31b). Contrary to the heading given in some editions of the NRSV, 1 Corinthians 13 does not present love as one "gift" among others, not even as the best of gifts, but rather as the *presiding manner* or most perfect way in which all gifts should be activated and orchestrated (see also Galatians 5:6).

1 Corinthians 13:1-3. The main point affirmed in these opening verses is love's inestimable superiority—over tongues, undisputed religious virtues, and extreme sacrifices. The "tongues of mortals and of angels" (13:1) may imply a contrast between ordinary rhetoric and the ecstatic utterance ("speaking in tongues" or "angelic" speech) that Paul will consider in 14:1-40. In the "noisy gong or a clanging cymbal," some interpreters see a veiled reference to pagan rituals, which could have employed such instruments. Discernment of "mysteries" (13:2) was an apocalyptic gift, bestowed on those who interpret the secrets of God's kingdom (see 4:1; 15:51; Mark 4:11). Both mountain-moving faith (1 Corinthians 13:2) and extraordinary generosity (13:3) are familiar

biblical virtues (Isaiah 54:10; Matthew 6:2; 17:20). Without love, avers Paul, all such things amount to nothing. The "I" who speaks in 1 Corinthians 13:1-3 (and later in 13:11-12) could be interpreted as every reader or as Paul speaking of himself in an exemplary way. The apostle who boasted of his sufferings for the gospel's sake (2 Corinthians 11:30; 12:5, 9-10) would surely have heard 1 Corinthians 13:1-3 as a cautionary reminder to himself.

1 Corinthians 13:4-7. Paul characterizes love. Although he chooses not to draw the obvious connections here, the attributes of love in these verses also characterize God's love as revealed in Christ (Romans 5:6, 8; 15:3, 7-8; 2 Corinthians 8:9; Philippians 2:6-11) and the apostle's convictions of conduct appropriate for those who live "in Christ" (1 Corinthians 10:24, 32-33; Romans 15:1-2; 2 Corinthians 5:14-15; Philippians 2:3-4). In 1 Corinthians 13:4-7, as elsewhere in Paul's moral teaching (Romans 12:9-21; 13:9-10; Galatians 5:13-14), the words of Jesus lie not far beneath the surface (compare Matthew 5:43-44; 19:18-19; 25:35; Mark 10:19; 12:28-34; Luke 6:27-28).

1 Corinthians 13:8-13. Love's superiority and character have been sketched; finally Paul turns to love's permanence. By stressing the incompleteness and evanescence of prophecies, tongues, and knowledge (13:8-9), Paul relativizes the importance of those gifts over which some in Corinth have inflated themselves (1 Corinthians 4:6, 18-19; 8:1; 14:2, 13); by speaking of "childish ways" now abandoned (13:11), he subtly tweaks those in Corinth who still behave childishly (3:1-4; 14:20). Ancient Corinth was renowned for its superb bronze mirrors; yet even at their most highly polished, they cast an obscure reflection of reality. Thus Paul contrasts the enigmatic, partial view that we gain from a mirrored object (13:12a) with the clarity of vision we shall enjoy when salvation is complete (13:10; 1:7-8; compare Numbers 12:8). More important than our knowing is our being fully known—by God (1 Corinthians 13:12b; 8:3; Galatians 4:9). "The big three"—faith, hope, and love—are connected elsewhere in Pauline literature (Galatians 5:5-6; Colossians 1:4-5; 1 Thessalonians 1:3; 5:8); only in 1 Corinthians 13:13 is love underlined as the greatest of them all.

INTERPRETING THE SCRIPTURE

Answering the Unasked Question

The best things we receive we don't know how to request. No one in Corinth asked Paul to write to them about love. Everyone wonders about love but seldom do we ask about it. Asking questions about love reveals too much about us, doesn't it? One does not wish to sound naive or in need of further information about the business of loving. Earlier in the epistle Paul responds to matters the Corinthians called to his attention: "It is actually reported that there is sexual immorality among you" (5:1). He answers questions they asked: "Now concerning the matters about which you wrote" (7:1). No one, however, asked Paul, "What is real love like?"

Perhaps they asked Paul about what is most important (and, therefore, who is most important) in the church. The Corinthians were not divided only by heritage and by social and economic circumstance; they also permitted their gifts to separate them into warring factions. The gifts of God, which Paul believes could weld the church into a unity of service to Christ, have become only one more occasion for the Corinthians to bicker. Given what we know about this church, we dare not imagine any list of their contentions as exhaustive. Clearly, though, some claimed primary importance for speaking in tongues, others for prophecy, still others for faith, and some (perhaps indicating their social standing) for the sharing of possessions. "Which gift is most important?" they asked, which carries with it the accompanying but unasked question, "Which one of us is most important?" Their verbalized question masquerades as a theological concern; at its heart, however, it scrounges yet more ammunition for put-downs and one-upmanship.

Paul believes each gift mentioned to be of great importance. His letters celebrate generosity, faith, prophecy, and even ecstatic speech (see 1 Corinthians 14:5, 18-19). Without diminishing the significance of these gifts, Paul holds each of them up to the bright light of love and finds each deficient if not conceived in and expressive of love. Speech without love is only noise. Prophecy and faith without love are nothing. Generosity may stimulate both applause and boasting but without love, amounts to not much, to nothing in fact. Paul refuses to play into their network of self-aggrandizement because he has something better to offer.

When Nothing Else Works

Put-downs haven't worked; one-upmanship hasn't worked; that strategy of discarding one another has no future. When all else fails, Paul seems to say, try love. Love "bears all things, believes all things, hopes all things, endures all things" (1 Corinthians 13:7). You argue about who and what are most important, Paul seems to say. Well, I will show you.

The gifts you bring are important, just as everything that makes you special and different and the person you are is important. The talents you have, the things you know, the things you can do are important. Even more important, however, is what you have in common with every other person.

You are loved. You are the object of God's love. This seems strange to say, because nowhere in Paul's praise of love does he mention God. But those familiar with the ways in which Paul thinks and writes can see through his words to detect the shape of the cross. Paul's judgment, "love endures all things," testifies to Easter's drama. We bring out the resurrection of Jesus Christ as evidence of love's endurance. Paul is able to say love endures not because we are marvelous at loving one another, but because at Easter we have glimpsed the love of God that never surrenders and never fails.

Our love fails. This much we know. We fail in loving those people we want most and best to love. We shudder at the way we fail time and again to be loving people. Though we talk endlessly of love, most of what we call love is a craving to be loved. Something in us, however, craves also to become loving people, but we scarcely know how to begin. To become loving folk we need more than homely advice. We have heard words of love spoken again and again, and we have heard them shatter on the floor in the middle of the night, signaling our failures at loving. If all that Paul has to offer are more words, we may enjoy the poetry but need more to help us become loving.

The Cross and the Scorecard

Paul does have more than words, however. The words that he chooses sign the cross over us, revealing God's own self-giving love. That love not only shows us how to love; by being poured into our hearts by the Holy Spirit, it gives us the power we need to love one another. That the cross of Christ stands as a kind of warranty behind what is said by the apostle is evidenced when Paul declares, "[Love] keeps no record of wrongs" (1 Corinthians 13:5 NIV). The rendering in the NRSV, that love "is not irritable or resentful," is weak and bland. Paul borrows language from bookkeeping. As the New English Bible says, "Love keeps no score of wrongs."

Marriage counselors describe how couples frequently come to them with the scorecards those partners keep on each other. He has neglected to take out the garbage twelve times this month. She has callously served spinach eight times this year. It's been six months since we've made love. It's been eight months since I've heard the words "I love you." They come with scorecards, elaborate catalogs of grievances, expecting the counselor to adjudicate their complaints, tally up the scorecards, and declare a winner. If that happens, of course, everyone loses.

Life doesn't work that way. Marriage doesn't work that way. Love doesn't work that way. Sure, some things depend on keeping score. The baseball season would be far less interesting without a scoreboard. The really important things in life, however, cannot be calculated on a scorecard. They cannot even be counted. Love keeps no score of wrongs or of rights, either. Whatever victories may come our way in this lifetime can hardly be accounted for in terms of mere record-keeping. They come by grace, they come by wonder, they come in spite of more than we dare admit—but they hardly arrive by our toting up a ledger column.

The apostle Paul learned this. He had to learn it as each of us learns it. Concluding his words about love, he reflects on his life, "When I was a child, I spoke like a child, I thought like a child, I reasoned like a child" (1 Corinthians 13:11). That last comment, "I reasoned like a child," brings into play the same verb Paul used earlier when he said, "Love keeps no score of wrongs" (13:5). We might translate, "I reckoned like a child," or even "I kept score—just like a kid." Love keeps no score, however. The apostle came to this new understanding not merely through the wisdom that comes with the passing years, but by coming to know the love of God revealed in the cross and resurrection of Christ. What love is really like we know in Jesus Christ—because just there we realize that we have been fully known by God (13:12). "In Christ," Paul says elsewhere, "God was reconciling the world to himself, not counting their trespasses against them, and entrusting the message of reconciliation to us" (2 Corinthians 5:19). When Paul says God does not "count their trespasses," the verb is again the same one Paul used when he declared, "Love keeps no score of wrongs." Paul learned that if God didn't keep score, then maybe he didn't have to either. There is no future in keeping score. There is only futility.

Keeping score is doomed to failure. So also are envy, boasting, arrogance, rudeness, self-seeking, anger, and resentment doomed to failure. They cannot give us what we want. God knows we have tried. As much as we enjoy them, as much as we trust their power, they ultimately fail to give us what we want and need. When all else fails, however, love never fails.

Only love has a future.

It is not only the worst we do that fails us, but also our best. The highest gifts we bring are, in themselves, without a future. "As for prophecies, they will come to an end; as for tongues, they will cease; as for knowledge, it will come to an end" (1 Corinthians 13:8b). The best we can do, as well as our worst, pale and fail before the goodness God offers us in Christ. Paul's words in his letter to the Corinthians trace the sign of the cross over that congregation. The cross signals the death of all envy, boasting, arrogance, rudeness, self-seeking, anger, and resentment; to those whom God has claimed, however, the cross is a sign of life. If the cross is the death of all self-sufficient pretense, it is the beginning of a new way of life filled with God's love.

Only love has a future. Love is the earthly foretaste of all that God has promised us. It is a sacrament, a sign and seal, of what God finally intends for us.

SHARING THE SCRIPTURE

PREPARING TO TEACH

Preparing Our Hearts

Read 1 John 4:7-21, which contains words that you may have learned as a child: "Love one another" (4:11b), "God is love" (4:16b), "Perfect love casts out fear" (4:18), and "We love because [God] first loved us" (4:19). Recall, if you can, what these verses meant to you as a child. What ideas did you have about love based on these biblical teachings? Do you find them easier or more difficult to comprehend as an adult? If you had to summarize in a sentence or two what it means to love, what would you say?

Another familiar source of teaching on love is found in Paul's first letter to the Corinthians, 12:31–13:13. Read these beloved words with "fresh eyes"; if possible, read from a Bible translation that you do not normally use. What new insights did you gain? Close this devotional time by praying that God will empower you with love, especially as you deal with your Sunday school class.

Preparing Our Minds

Read this lesson and again review 1 Corinthians 12:31–13:13. Try to imagine writing this chapter. What concerns must have been on Paul's mind? (Look back to chapter 12 for some ideas as to the context.) What concerns might Paul's teachings address in the contemporary church? If you were asked to sum up the teachings here in one or two sentences, what would you say?

In the activity under "When Nothing Else Works," students are asked to try to understand what Paul is saying in verses 1-3. Here is some information to help you lead the discussion:

● Verse 1: The "noisy gong" and "clanging cymbal" refer to the accompaniments of pagan worship.

● Verse 2: The "faith...to remove mountains" echoes Jesus' teaching in Matthew 17:20.

● Verse 3: The purpose of handing over one's body is "to be burned," according to some manuscripts. This idea suggests a martyrdom by means of self-immolation.

● All three verses say "if I...but do not have love, I...."

● The gifts that Paul speaks about here include speaking in tongues, prophesying, having knowledge of mysteries, having faith that can work miracles, almsgiving, and making self-sacrifices.

Preparing Our Learning Space

Write the questions under "Introduction" on newsprint prior to class.
Have on hand:
✔ several Bibles
✔ hymnals
✔ newsprint and marker
✔ paper and pencils
✔ one or more commentaries.

LEADING THE CLASS

(1) Introduction

Consider opening today's session by singing "The Gift of Love" (*The United Methodist Hymnal*, no. 408), which is based on 1 Corinthians 13:1-3. If these hymnals are not available, choose another song about love among church members, such as "They'll Know We Are Christians by Our Love."

Then tell the students to pretend that they have recently moved into the community where your church is located. They are visiting your church in search of a new spiritual home. Have them answer these questions, which you will want to write on newsprint prior to the session. Divide the class into groups. You may want to assign each group just one question. Encourage them to be honest but loving in their assessment of their own congregation.

(1) **What does the atmosphere in the worship service say to you about the love that members have for one another?**

(2) **What does the bulletin, church newsletter, and/or finance report that you see posted on a bulletin board tell you about the love this congregation has for those beyond its walls? In other words, is this church reaching out to serve or is it basically focused inward?**

(3) **What does the way you are treated as a visitor (for example, perhaps someone invites you to attend Sunday school or helps you find your way around the building) say about the love that is present in this congregation?**

(4) **You have been invited to attend a small group during the week. Perhaps you will visit with a men or women's group, a committee working on an outreach project, a support group, or a choir practice. How did the way this group worked together reflect love and let you know that you were welcome?**

Reconvene the class. If time permits, hear highlights from each group's discussion.

Raise today's main question: **What is authentic love like?**

(2) Answering the Unasked Question

To help students understand what 1 Corinthians 13 is all about, help them recall the lesson for April 16 that focused on the preceding chapter. Note these points:

- There are a variety of spiritual gifts but all are given by the same Spirit.
- The purpose of the gifts is to build up the body of Christ.
- Diverse gifts exist within the one body.
- All of the gifts are important, and none is to be removed from the body.
- Members of the body are to care for each other.
- God has appointed persons with various gifts to serve the church: apostles; prophets; teachers; miracle workers; healers; leaders; people who speak in tongues.

Read aloud 1 Corinthians 12:29-31. Ask:

(1) **Based on Paul's questions in verses 29-30, what do you suppose is happening within the church?** (Possibly dissension is brewing over who has the most important gift.)
(2) **How does Paul try to remedy the problem?** (He reminds them that love provides a "more excellent way." Love is not one "gift" but rather the way in which all of the gifts should be activated.)

(3) When Nothing Else Works

Read aloud 1 Corinthians 13:1-13.

Then ask the students to open their Bibles and look at verses 1-3. Suggest that they examine the footnotes in their Bibles, commentaries, and a variety of Bible translations to understand what Paul is saying here. Distribute paper and pencils and ask the students to write these three verses in their own words. You may want to have them work in groups to do this activity. Perhaps a few volunteers will share what they have written. Close with this question:

(1) **What is the relation of other gifts of the Spirit to love?** (Note that love is foundational. It is not a gift among equally valuable gifts. Rather, all of the other gifts must be used with love or they are worthless.)

(4) The Cross and the Scorecard

Now direct the group's attention to 1 Corinthians 13:4-8. Ask:

(1) **What are the positive characteristics Paul notes about love?** (It is patient and kind.)
(2) **How does Paul describe what love is not?** (See verses 4b-6. Note that the NIV's translation in verse 5, which suggests the language of keeping track of accounts, is preferable to that of the NRSV.)

Read or retell the first and fourth paragraphs under "The Cross and the Scorecard" in Interpreting the Scripture. Then ask the students to think silently as you do this guided imagery activity about a situation in which they did keep a scorecard of wrongs.

- Close your eyes and sit comfortably in your chair. See in your mind the face of someone whom you keep a scorecard on, someone who has tallied up a number of wrongs in your eyes. (Pause)
- Think about what this person has done to cause you to keep a record of wrongs. (Pause)
- Hear these words of Paul: "Love is patient, love is kind. It does not envy, it does not boast, it is not proud. It is not rude, it is not self-seeking, it is not easily angered, it keeps no record of wrongs. Love does not delight in evil but rejoices with the truth. It always protects, always trusts, always hopes, always perseveres." (Pause)
- If you were to take these words seriously, envision how you would treat the person you've been keeping a scorecard on. How would your relationship change? (Pause)

- Ask God to empower you through the Holy Spirit to set aside your scorecard and begin to truly love this person. (Pause)
- Open your eyes when you are ready.

Conclude your study of 1 Corinthians 13 by discussing these questions related to verses 8-13.

(1) **What will happen to the gifts that the Corinthians apparently like to boast about?** (These will pass away, and only love will remain.)

(2) **What lesson does Paul offer about spiritual maturity?** (One day that which is incomplete will end, just as our childhood ways end when we become adults. We will know and be known fully. Moreover, we will be able to see clearly.)

If you have *The United Methodist Hymnal* available, turn to "Canticle of Love" (no. 646) and ask the class to read responsively to end this part of the lesson.

Close the session by suggesting at least one of the activities below.

HELPING CLASS MEMBERS ACT

Encourage students to be alert for opportunities to express God's love through their patience, kindness, and humility this week.

Suggest that class members think about the gifts that God has entrusted to them. Are they exercising these gifts lovingly? Or is there rivalry and boasting? What changes do they need to make so as to help edify the body of Christ?

Ask the adults to meditate on what they are willing to sacrifice out of love for the church. While some persons want to know what the church will do for them, those who love will want to discern what they can do to build up God's kingdom through the church.

PLANNING FOR NEXT SUNDAY

Let the students know that next week we will begin the spring quarter's third and final unit, "The Glory of Christian Ministry." The lesson for May 7 is entitled "From Sorrow to Joy." To prepare for the session, ask the students to read 2 Corinthians 1–2. Our lesson will focus on 2 Corinthians 2:4-17.

UNIT 3: THE GLORY OF CHRISTIAN MINISTRY
FROM SORROW TO JOY

PREVIEWING THE LESSON

Lesson Scripture: 2 Corinthians 2:4-17
Background Scripture: 2 Corinthians 1–2
Key Verse: 2 Corinthians 2:14

Focus of the Lesson:
Although Paul had apparently been wronged by someone in Corinth, he wrote to this church to encourage love and forgiveness.

Main Question of the Lesson:
What price must be paid for a ministry of reconciliation through Christ?

This lesson will enable adult learners to:
(1) explore Paul's teachings on forgiveness and reconciliation.
(2) consider their own ways of handling painful relationships.
(3) respond by seeking or offering forgiveness.

Today's lesson may be outlined as follows:
(1) Introduction
(2) Groping for Sense in the Shadows
(3) Forgiveness and Reconciliation
(4) The Aroma of the Marketplace

FOCUSING ON THE MAIN QUESTION

Like every flawed, human institution, the church has its fights and its ministers fall afoul of one another. At times these are tiffs. On other occasions, it feels more like war: bloody, protracted, no prisoners taken.

When the church goes to war against itself, what are the conditions for the restoration of peace? Does one side demand of the other "unconditional surrender"? Who will make the first move toward peace? Will that initiative be accepted or misconstrued? What reparations are required?

The great difficulty, of course, is that while flawed, the church knows itself to be unlike other human institutions in one critical respect: the church is *God's* creation, not our own. Through the love of Jesus Christ, Christians have been reconciled to God and have been commissioned as the church to serve as an agent through which all others may learn to stop their own fighting against God and one another. And so, when the church engages in "civil war," nothing less than the integrity of the gospel is at risk. No one knew the excruciating consequences of a church at war with itself and its leaders better than the apostle Paul. Return with us to first-century Corinth, where we shall smell not only the stench of battle, but also the hopeful aroma of a fresh peace. **What price must be paid for a ministry of reconciliation through Christ?**

MAY 7

READING THE SCRIPTURE

NRSV
2 Corinthians 2:4-17

4 For I wrote you out of much distress and anguish of heart and with many tears, not to cause you pain, but to let you know the abundant love that I have for you.

5 But if anyone has caused pain, he has caused it not to me, but to some extent—not to exaggerate it—to all of you. 6 This punishment by the majority is enough for such a person; 7 so now instead you should forgive and console him, so that he may not be overwhelmed by excessive sorrow. 8 So I urge you to reaffirm your love for him. 9 I wrote for this reason: to test you and to know whether you are obedient in everything. 10 Anyone whom you forgive, I also forgive. What I have forgiven, if I have forgiven anything, has been for your sake in the presence of Christ. 11 And we do this so that we may not be outwitted by Satan; for we are not ignorant of his designs.

12 When I came to Troas to proclaim the good news of Christ, a door was opened for me in the Lord; 13 but my mind could not rest because I did not find my brother Titus there. So I said farewell to them and went on to Macedonia.

14 But thanks be to God, who in Christ always leads us in triumphal procession, and through us spreads in every place the fragrance that comes from knowing him. 15 For we are the aroma of Christ to God among those who are being saved and among those who are perishing; 16 to the one a fragrance from death to death, to the

NIV
2 Corinthians 2:4-17

4For I wrote you out of great distress and anguish of heart and with many tears, not to grieve you but to let you know the depth of my love for you.

5If anyone has caused grief, he has not so much grieved me as he has grieved all of you, to some extent—not to put it too severely. 6The punishment inflicted on him by the majority is sufficient for him. 7Now instead, you ought to forgive and comfort him, so that he will not be overwhelmed by excessive sorrow. 8I urge you, therefore, to reaffirm your love for him. 9The reason I wrote you was to see if you would stand the test and be obedient in everything. 10If you forgive anyone, I also forgive him. And what I have forgiven—if there was anything to forgive—I have forgiven in the sight of Christ for your sake, 11in order that Satan might not outwit us. For we are not unaware of his schemes.

12Now when I went to Troas to preach the gospel of Christ and found that the Lord had opened a door for me, 13I still had no peace of mind, because I did not find my brother Titus there. So I said good-by to them and went on to Macedonia.

14But thanks be to God, who always leads us in triumphal procession in Christ and through us spreads everywhere the fragrance of the knowledge of him. 15For we are to God the aroma of Christ among those who are being saved and those who are perishing. 16To the one

Key Verse

Key Verse

other a fragrance from life to life. Who is sufficient for these things? 17 For we are not peddlers of God's word like so many; but in Christ we speak as persons of sincerity, as persons sent from God and standing in his presence.

we are the smell of death; to the other, the fragrance of life. And who is equal to such a task? [17]Unlike so many, we do not peddle the word of God for profit. On the contrary, in Christ we speak before God with sincerity, like men sent from God.

UNDERSTANDING THE SCRIPTURE

2 Corinthians 1:1-11. Following a typical greeting in 1:1-3, addressed to Corinthian Christians in the senatorial province of Achaia (southern Greece), we would expect Paul, here accompanied by his younger colleague Timothy (1:1; see also 1:19; Acts 18:5; 19:22; 1 Corinthians 4:17; 16:10-11), to offer his usual apostolic thanksgiving (see 1 Corinthians 1:4-9). Instead, in 2 Corinthians 1:4-7 Paul begins with a blessing having deep roots in Jewish worship (see Genesis 24:26-27). Noteworthy are the terms he uses to characterize God in verse 3: "the Father of mercies" (Psalm 103:13; Luke 6:36; Romans 12:1) and "the God of all consolation" (Romans 15:5). Paired with the experience of affliction (2 Corinthians 1:4), merciful consolation is a recurring theme throughout this letter (2:4; 4:8, 17; 6:4; 7:4-7; 8:2). For the apostle that consolation takes one of two forms. In 1:8-10 it is a deliverance from terrible straits. More typical, however, is the consolation Paul experiences in receiving from God the strength to endure such hardship (1:6; 4:7-9; 6:4; 12:7-10; see also Romans 5:3-5; 2 Thessalonians 1:4; Revelation 1:9). Paul receives additional comfort in knowing that his afflictions are not in vain, but for the sake of the gospel of Christ, who suffered for our healing (2 Corinthians 1:5-6; 4:10-11; Philippians 3:10; see also 1 Peter 1:11; 4:13). Following severe tribulation in Asia, a Roman senatorial province in Asia Minor (modern Turkey; 2 Corinthians 1:8-10; compare Philippians 1:12-26), Paul expresses renewed hope, confidence, and thanks for the support of Corinth's Christians (1:7, 11, 24; 7:4, 14, 16; 8:7).

2 Corinthians 1:12-14. These verses, softly defensive in tone, mark the first occurrence in 2 Corinthians of another theme running throughout the letter: Paul's personal integrity, for which he commends himself (1:12; 3:1; 4:2; 5:12; 6:4; 10:8, 12-18; 11:10, 16-18, 30; 12:1, 5-6, 9, 11). The apostle has conducted himself in good "conscience" (4:2; 5:11) and with "sincerity" (1:12; 2:17), that godly truthfulness that flouts double-dealing "earthly wisdom" (2 Corinthians 1:12; 1 Corinthians 1:17-25; 2:1-5). The Corinthians have understood—but only "in part"—Paul's motives (2 Corinthians 1:14). Full understanding must await "the end," "the day of the [return of the] Lord Jesus" (1:13-14; compare 1 Corinthians 13:12). In the meantime both Paul and the Corinthian believers may be justly proud of each other (2 Corinthians 1:14; 5:12; 7:4, 14; 8:24; 9:2-3).

2 Corinthians 1:15–2:4. Instead of paying the Corinthians other visits while en route to and from Macedonia (1:15-16), the Roman senatorial province of northern Greece, Paul sent them a letter. In these verses Paul explains his change in plans. The reason was not, as some in Corinth may have suggested, because he was wishy-washy or enthralled to "ordinary [disreputable] human standards" (1:17). Paul appeals to God's unwavering fidelity as accreditation for the apostle's own (1:18, 21, 23; compare Deuteronomy 7:9; 1 Corinthians 1:9; 10:13; 1 Thessalonians 5:24). The solidity of Paul's commitment to

Corinth, and that of Timothy and Silvanus ("Silas" in Acts 15:22, 32, 40–18:22; see also 1 Thessalonians 1:1), is matched by the strongly affirmative "Amen"—"Let it be so!"—that characterizes Christ's own integrity (2 Corinthians 1:19-20). Moreover, Paul appeals to his and the Corinthians' receipt of the Spirit: a reassuring "down payment" on the fulfillment of God's promises to them (1:20, 22; see also Romans 8:11; Ephesians 4:30). Paul is cautiously relieved that he may now acknowledge his joy in the Corinthians' faith (2 Corinthians 1:24; 2:3). Paul's only reason for deciding to bypass Corinth was to spare the Christians there "another painful visit" (1:23-24; 2:1-2). Instead, Paul wrote and sent them "a letter of tears" (2:3-4; 7:8).

2 Corinthians 2:5-11. As reconstructed in Interpreting the Scripture, Paul's strained relations with the Corinthian church had to do with someone there who caused pain during the apostle's second visit there (2:5). As that offender has now been punished (2:6), and obedience appropriate for an apostle has been reestablished (2:9), Paul pleads for the forgiveness, consolation, and reassertion of love for the offender and all concerned (2:7-8, 10). To hold a grudge would be a capitulation to evil, personified as Satan (2:11; see also 6:15; 11:14; 12:7; Romans 16:20; 1 Corinthians 5:5; 7:5; 1 Thessalonians 2:18).

2 Corinthians 2:12-17. Paul's anxiety about Corinth was not easily allayed. In Troas, a Roman seaport on the northwest coast of Asia Minor (Acts 16:8, 11; 20:5-6), "a door was opened" for Paul's evangelization (compare 1 Corinthians 16:9). Paul, however, was so worried by the delay of his Gentile coworker Titus (2 Corinthians 7:6-7, 13-15; 8:6, 16-23; 12:18; Galatians 2:3), apparently the courier of Paul's tearful letter (2 Corinthians 2:3-4), that the apostle set sail for Macedonia (2:12-13). An uneasy peace now exists between Paul and Corinth, for which he gives thanks to God (2:14). The "triumphal procession" in which Paul feels led is more ironic than it appears in translation: the reference is to imperial victory marches, in which Roman prisoners of war were forced to trudge. Such parades sometimes used the burning incense of religious rituals, which may account for Paul's use of "fragrance" and "aroma" in describing the traces of his apostolic ministry among both those "being saved" and "perishing" (2:14-16a; 4:3; compare Leviticus 1:9, 13; 1 Corinthians 1:18; Ephesians 5:2; Philippians 4:18). Paul's "sufficiency," or competence, as an apostle (2 Corinthians 2:16b; 3:5-6) depends on his personal dispatch from God (2:17; 12:19), not on the slick huckstering of a charlatan, which some in Corinth may have made Paul out to be (2:17; 4:2).

INTERPRETING THE SCRIPTURE

Groping for Sense in the Shadows

Second Corinthians 2:4-17 jars our concentration in odd ways. One difficulty in reading it is that we cannot fully understand events leading up to the writing of these verses. Another problem is easily understood but hidden from our eyes: an abundance of hurt feelings, arising from conflict in the church, causes Paul to use gentle but guarded language.

To understand what is at stake here we might attempt to reconstruct Paul's relationship with the Christians of Corinth. Preaching the cross of Christ, Paul began Christian ministry in the Roman city of Corinth (Acts 18:1-17). Later, after Paul had gone elsewhere to preach and teach, the Corinthians sent emissaries and wrote to him about certain concerns (1 Corinthians 1:11; 5:1; 7:1; 8:1; 15:12), thereby occasioning the letter we call 1 Corinthians.

Paul evidently returned to Corinth, a visit we can only guess about from an unhappy reference to it in 2 Corinthians 2:1. Something happened about which we know nothing but from which we see lingering shadows: the event was public, both Paul and the church suffered pain and humiliation, and Paul left. Another letter from Paul, not preserved by the church (one can imagine why) but referred to by Paul as the tearful letter (2 Corinthians 2:4), mobilized Paul's allies to action. The church disciplined the person who had previously instigated the public outrage, afterwards sending word of their action to Paul via Titus (2 Corinthians 7:6-7). Now Paul writes again, to continue dealing with the matter that occurred during the "painful visit" and to explain to the Corinthians why he had not visited them again (1:16-20; 2:12-13).

Forgiveness and Reconciliation

Titus's arrival with news that the relationship between Paul and the Corinthian community had been restored was obviously a source of great consolation to Paul (2 Corinthians 7:6). We might assume that that report was sufficient to end what had been a tear-filled, painful episode in the life of a congregation. For Paul, however, more consoling remained. The one who had "caused pain," not only to Paul but to the whole church (2:5), needed to be reconciled to the community of the faithful. The significance of reconciliation in 2 Corinthians cannot be stressed too strongly. In this letter more than any other, Paul highlights reconciliation as the heart of the gospel he teaches. What God was doing in Jesus Christ, Paul describes as "reconciling" (5:19); the entire activity of the church he interprets as "the ministry of reconciliation" (5:18); the preaching of the gospel is summarized, "Be reconciled to God" (5:20). Because the church has been entrusted with such a "message of reconciliation" (5:19), in 2 Corinthians 2:4-17

Paul entreats the Corinthians to find means to "forgive and console" the person who had instigated the distressful situation (2:7). This person had already been dealt with by some means of discipline, but as we saw earlier in the lesson for March 26, discipline is never understood by Paul as an end in itself but as a means to reconciliation and restoration. The "punishment by the majority [was] enough for such a person" (2:6), whatever that punishment may have been. Because that is sufficient, now it is time to "forgive and console."

In a carefully choreographed dance, Paul instructs the community. On the one hand, he insists that the painful situation, instigated by the person now punished, was not just a personal matter between that person and Paul. The humiliating event implicated the entire community of faith, perhaps even the gospel itself. Yet on the other hand, Paul asserts himself to lead in forgiveness, inviting the Corinthians to follow. The statement "Anyone whom you forgive, I also forgive" (2 Corinthians 2:10a) may sound as if he waits upon their judgment, but the grammar stresses the end of the sentence and the declaration of Paul's forgiveness. Notice: the motivation for this forgiveness is not the neediness of the offending individual but the testimony and the health of the community. It is "for your sake in the presence of Christ," so "that we may not be outwitted by Satan" (2:10b, 11). Isn't it interesting that here Satan is allied with carrying grudges, with continuing conflict—with everything except forgiveness? The situation requires forgiveness because the church has work to do, and we cannot get on with the business of being "ambassadors for Christ" and ministers of reconciliation (5:18, 20) while we haul heavy weights of grudge. Paul drops the burden of enmity so that he may embrace his brother, and invites us to do the same. Such simple but gracious gestures characterize the Christian life.

Authentic forgiveness has its own sweet

smell, something like spring, or like rain after a long dry spell—or so Paul seems to say. If we are not astonished by what Paul says here, we are just not paying attention: "Through us spreads in every place the fragrance that comes from knowing [God]" (2:14). If we associate an aroma with the church at all, we may think of the incense used in the worship of some communities. That we as the church have a distinct fragrance is a notion we have not frequently explored, and one that some may find downright shocking. A student preacher, drawing this text for an assignment, asked in his sermon, "What Does Your Church Smell Like?" No one laughed harder at that than the instructor, who had served two parishes located in close proximity to city zoos. It's a good question.

Something emanates from the life of a Christian congregation, and if it is not a distinct aroma, it is not far from it. One does not have to experience much of a church before detecting, well, a certain atmosphere that signals welcome, caring, tolerance, forgiveness—or their opposites. Nothing the preacher says from the pulpit or anyone says directly signals the presence of those qualities, but people can sense hospitality. Just as clearly, they know when they are being judged, measured, and found wanting. For Paul the fragrance in question refers not merely to our own actions and attitudes, but to what God is doing among us. It is a fragrance "that comes from knowing [God]"; it is "the aroma of Christ to God among those who are being saved" (2 Corinthians 2:14, 15). Recognizing God to be God and surrendering to Christ's purpose among us give forth an unmistakable atmosphere that something of wonderful significance is happening. We do not belong to ourselves alone but to God. Our wants do not set the agenda, but rather Christ's work of reconciliation does. In so grand a plan as God has commissioned us to fulfill, personal grudges do smell like the city zoo when compared to the sublime sweetness of God's reconciliation.

The Aroma of the Marketplace

Paul concludes with a question, "Who is sufficient for these things?" (2 Corinthians 2:16b), and an assertion, "For we are not peddlers of God's word like so many; but in Christ we speak as persons of sincerity" (2:17). He contrasts the huckster, hawking wares in the market, with the apostles' unselfish motives in proclaiming the gospel. In the marketplace merchants adorn their products with what it takes to make them sell. Television commercials insist that drinking this cola tastes of adventure, that this cologne is the fragrance of upholstered clubs and old money, that this shirt weaves its wearer into the American dream. In the cold light of dwindling church memberships, many North American parishes borrow marketing techniques. "What are people looking for?" they ask. "What do people want?" Marketing strategies provide the church with its mission.

User-friendly computers overwhelmed the personal computer market, and now user-friendly religion invites people to church. In order to succeed (and success appears to be the only meaningful measure), the user-friendly church minimizes the distance and difference from living in the world to being in the church. That strategy makes perfectly good sense, if God's purpose is to please us.

In *God in the Wasteland: The Reality of Truth in a World of Fading Dreams*, theologian David Wells has written: "The fact is that while we may be able to market the church, we cannot market Christ, the gospel, Christian character, or meaning in life....Neither Christ nor his truth can be marketed by appealing to consumer interest, because the premise of all marketing is that the consumer's need is sovereign, that the customer is always right, and this is precisely what the gospel insists cannot be the case." The gospel insists that God (not our wants) is God; that salvation is serving in Christ Jesus (not having our wants served by him); that the church has a message "sent from God" (not determined by market research). If it is disconcerting to discover that God's greatest purpose does not lie in meeting our wants, it is also a wonderful relief. How refreshing to know that there is something greater, some truth more profound, than the noisy rattle of "What I want!" It's as invigorating as a spring breeze and has a certain fragrance to it. Yes, it's the unmistakable smell of home, our home in God, who is better than what we want and more generous than all our asking.

SHARING THE SCRIPTURE

PREPARING TO TEACH

Preparing Our Hearts

Today's devotional reading is from part of the background scripture, 2 Corinthians 1:3-11. Here Paul speaks about being consoled in affliction. He was "so utterly, unbearably crushed that [he] despaired of life itself" (1:8), though the nature of this trial is not specified. Think of something, possibly related to work you have done for the church, that caused you to suffer. Perhaps you even wanted to give up on the church completely. How were you able to forgive and move on so that you could continue to do the work to which God called you?

Now continue reading today's background scripture, which runs from 2 Corinthians 1:1–2:17. Note that Paul had wanted to come to Corinth both on his way to and from Macedonia (1:15-16). He did not, however, stop in Corinth. For this reason, his critics accused him of indecisiveness. As you will note in chapter 2, Paul decides not to make "another painful visit" (2:1). He apparently had been wronged by someone in Corinth. Note that he speaks of forgiveness in verse 10. Think about broken relationships that have harmed your congregation. How has the congregation been able to forgive, heal, and go forth in ministry? If the hurt has not healed, what can you do to help bring about reconciliation?

Preparing Our Minds

Read this lesson and the first two chapters from 2 Corinthians. Look especially at the Understanding the Scripture portion. There you will find background concerning Paul's trials. Try to allow enough time to look up the passages referred to there.

Preparing Our Learning Space

Have on hand:
- several Bibles
- hymnals
- newsprint and marker.

LEADING THE CLASS

(1) Introduction

To begin today's lesson read Focusing on the Main Question. Be sure to note the main question: **What price must be paid for a ministry of reconciliation through Christ?**

Next, discuss one or more of the following realistic, though hypothetical, situations.

Situation 1: One of the influential parishioners at St. John's vehemently disagrees with the pastor's theology, though it is quite within the bounds of their denomination's teachings. The church leader is so upset that he has been rallying other persons to call for the ouster of this pastor. You see what is happening and know it will be difficult to stand against the troublemaker. What will you do? **What price** must be paid for a ministry of reconciliation through Christ?

Situation 2: You are a choir member. Another member makes a sniping remark to you about the soprano soloist who, admittedly, was not up to her usual form on Sunday. Still, she is a volunteer and this scathing criticism seems unfair. It would be easy just to agree with the critic and let the matter drop. But you don't feel that this approach is just. **What price must be paid for a ministry of reconciliation through Christ?**

Situation 3: During an Administrative Board meeting, the chair of the board of trustees declared war on the finance committee because they refused to support a project. The finance committee argued that the renovation, while nice, was unnecessary and beyond the church's financial means. The chair of the trustees really wanted this project to be adopted. You are the chair of the Administrative Board. You know the two committees, trustees and finance, must work together for the good of the congregation. **What price must be paid for a ministry of reconciliation through Christ?**

You may want to conclude the Introduction by singing a hymn that speaks of reconciliation, such as "Help Us Accept Each Other" (*The United Methodist Hymnal,* no. 560) or "Lord God, Your Love Has Called Us Here" (*UMH,* no. 579).

(2) Groping for Sense in the Shadows

Set the stage for today's lesson by using these points from "Groping for Sense in the Shadows" in Interpreting the Scripture to help the students understand what Paul is writing about in 2 Corinthians 2:4-17. You may want to present this information as a brief lecture. Consider writing the scripture references on newsprint and asking the students to turn to them as is possible within the time you have.

● This passage is difficult for us to understand because Paul does not spell out

the events that prompted him to write these verses.

● Obviously, there has been a serious conflict that has caused hurt feelings.

● Using Acts and other references from Corinthians we can reconstruct Paul's relationship with the church in Corinth.

● Acts 18:1-17 and 1 Corinthians 1:17; 2:1-2 tell how Paul began ministry in Corinth. His focus was the cross of Christ.

● After Paul left, church members at Corinth sent people to him and also wrote to him about certain concerns they had (1 Corinthians 1:11; 5:1; 7:1; 8:1; 15:12). This interaction prompted Paul to write what we call 1 Corinthians.

● Second Corinthians 2:1 indicates that Paul must have returned to Corinth for what proved to be a very unhappy visit. Although what actually happened is not discussed, apparently both the church and Paul suffered because of this event.

● According to 2 Corinthians 2:4, Paul wrote a tearful letter, one that has not been preserved.

● That letter must have caused Paul's allies to discipline the party involved. Second Corinthians 7:6-7 indicates that the church sent word to Paul about this action via Titus.

● Paul writes again to continue dealing with the matter that occurred during the "painful visit" and to explain to the Corinthians why he had not visited them again (1:16-20; 2:12-13).

(3) Forgiveness and Reconciliation

Select a volunteer to read today's lesson from 2 Corinthians 2:4-11. Then discuss these questions:

(1) **What action does Paul want the church to take concerning the person who caused the painful episode?** (Paul asserts that this person has already been punished. Now it is time to "forgive and console him" [2:7] and "reaffirm [their] love for him" [2:8].)

(2) **How is Paul's recommendation simi-**

lar to or different from the way many congregations treat someone who has created conflict?

(3) Had you been a member of the church at Corinth, how would you have responded to Paul's words about forgiveness, consolation, and love?

(4) Why does Paul believe that forgiveness is so important? (The church has ministry to do. Continuing conflict is not God's will but instead fits in with Satan's intentions.)

(4) The Aroma of the Marketplace

Conclude the scripture lesson by reading from 2 Corinthians 2:12-17. Note especially Paul's use of the metaphor that we Christians exude the fragrance of Christ. Ask:

(1) How would you describe the atmosphere in a congregation that is truly dedicated to ministry in and for Christ?

(2) What are the characteristics of individual Christians who exude this fragrance of Christ?

To close this section of the lesson, read this portion of "The Aroma of the Marketplace" aloud: The gospel insists that God (not our wants) is God; that salvation is serving in Christ Jesus (not having our wants served by him); that the church has a message "sent from God" (not determined by market research). If it is disconcerting to discover that God's greatest purpose does not lie in meeting our wants, it is also a wonderful relief. How refreshing to know that there is something greater, some truth more profound, than the noisy rattle of "What I want!" It's as invigorating

as a spring breeze and has a certain fragrance to it. Yes, it's the unmistakable smell of home, our home in God, who is better than what we want and more generous than all our asking.

Provide a few moments of silence so that the students may meditate on these observations. You may want to offer a prayer that your class members and congregation at large will, in the words of today's key verse, "through us [spread] in every place the fragrance that comes from knowing [Christ]."

Before the students leave, offer at least one of the activities below as a means of living out the teachings of today's session.

HELPING CLASS MEMBERS ACT

Suggest that students find a quiet time and place to engage in their own ministry of reconciliation. Recommend that they light a candle and read again today's scripture lesson from 2 Corinthians 2. Encourage them to "reaffirm their love" for someone who has wronged them and to forgive that person.

Recommend that students ask forgiveness of someone they have wronged. If possible, they should try to see this individual in person. If that is not possible, suggest that they make a phone call or write a note. Depending upon the situation, a small gift, such as a book or flowers, might be appropriate.

Challenge students to speak a word of good news to someone who either does not know Christ or whose life situation has made it difficult for that person to smell "a fragrance from life to life," as Paul puts it in verse 16.

PLANNING FOR NEXT SUNDAY

The many trials Paul suffered are highlighted in next week's lesson from 2 Corinthians 4. Tales of suffering are definitely part of Paul's ministry, but they are not the whole story. Through God's power one can continue to proclaim the good news. "From Suffering to Triumph" focuses on verses 5-18.

FROM SUFFERING TO TRIUMPH

PREVIEWING THE LESSON

Lesson Scripture: 2 Corinthians 4:5-18
Background Scripture: 2 Corinthians 4
Key Verses: 2 Corinthians 4:8-9

Focus of the Lesson:
Those who minister in the name of Christ will experience difficulties but will triumph through God's power.

Main Question of the Lesson:
Where do we perceive the glory of God in our afflictions and failures?

This lesson will enable adult learners to:
(1) study the trials and triumphs of Christian ministry as reported by Paul.
(2) examine their own willingness to risk difficulties for the sake of the gospel.
(3) respond by taking useful action for the kingdom of God.

Today's lesson may be outlined as follows:
(1) Introduction
(2) Strange Glory
(3) Glory Encased in Dust
(4) Glorious Dust

FOCUSING ON THE MAIN QUESTION

Of all these units on Paul's Corinthian letters, no passage may strain our credulity closer to the breaking point than 2 Corinthians 4:5-18. We have been around the block more than once. En route we have been callused by life's hard, occasionally devastating, knocks. Seeing is believing, and we are nobody's fools. When Paul suggests that our real, obvious, tormenting afflictions as Christians are featherweight in comparison with an inestimable weight of glory, now invisible but ultimately eter-nal—well, that sort of jabber may satisfy a pious eccentric. It cuts no ice with us.

Why must Paul sound at times so much like the Man of La Mancha? You remember Cervantes's Don Quixote: the genial but "muddled fool, full of lucid intervals," who dubbed himself a knight in quest of noble adventures. Dressed in rusted armor and mounted on a bony nag, Don Quixote chivalrously tilted at windmills that in his discombobulated imaginings were giants. Confused but gallant, Don Quixote selected as the mistress of his heart a peasant girl, Aldonza, and dubbed her the beauteous Lady Dulcinea. That's Paul, we may say: a poor, crazed romantic, determined to fabricate a Dulcinea from all of life's lowly Aldonzas.

But life in Christ, like great fiction, is never so simply one-dimensional. Thriving in a world invisible to others, perceiving inner beauty where others see only outward drudgery, Don Quixote acts with such valor and compassion that, in time, Aldonza recognizes within herself the Dulcinea into which she was transformed. Determined to concentrate on things unseen, to walk not by sight but by faith (2 Corinthians 5:7), so also does Paul believe that he and all servants of the crucified Messiah are being prepared "for an eternal weight of glory beyond all measure" (4:17).

Who's to say that Paul was wrong about that? About himself? About us? And so we raise today's main question: **Where do we perceive the glory of God in our afflictions and failures?**

READING THE SCRIPTURE

NRSV

2 Corinthians 4:5-18

5 For we do not proclaim ourselves; we proclaim Jesus Christ as Lord and ourselves as your slaves for Jesus' sake. 6 For it is the God who said, "Let light shine out of darkness," who has shone in our hearts to give the light of the knowledge of the glory of God in the face of Jesus Christ.

7 But we have this treasure in clay jars, so that it may be made clear that this extraordinary power belongs to God and does not come from us. **8 We are afflicted in every way, but not crushed; perplexed, but not driven to despair; 9 persecuted, but not forsaken; struck down, but not destroyed;** 10 always carrying in the body the death of Jesus, so that the life of Jesus may also be made visible in our bodies. 11 For while we live, we are always being given up to death for Jesus' sake, so that the life of Jesus may be made visible in our mortal flesh. 12 So death is at work in us, but life in you.

13 But just as we have the same spirit of faith that is in accordance with scripture— "I believed, and so I spoke"—we also believe, and so we speak, 14 because we know that the one who raised the Lord Jesus will raise us also with Jesus, and will bring us with you into his presence. 15 Yes, everything is for your sake, so that

Key Verses

NIV

2 Corinthians 4:5-18

5For we do not preach ourselves, but Jesus Christ as Lord, and ourselves as your servants for Jesus' sake. 6For God, who said, "Let light shine out of darkness," made his light shine in our hearts to give us the light of the knowledge of the glory of God in the face of Christ.

7But we have this treasure in jars of clay to show that this all-surpassing power is from God and not from us. **8We are hard pressed on every side, but not crushed; perplexed, but not in despair; 9persecuted, but not abandoned; struck down, but not destroyed.** 10We always carry around in our body the death of Jesus, so that the life of Jesus may also be revealed in our body. 11For we who are alive are always being given over to death for Jesus' sake, so that his life may be revealed in our mortal body. 12So then, death is at work in us, but life is at work in you.

13It is written: "I believed; therefore I have spoken." With that same spirit of faith we also believe and therefore speak, 14because we know that the one who raised the Lord Jesus from the dead will also raise us with Jesus and present us with you in his presence. 15All this is for your benefit, so that the grace that is reaching more and more people may

Key Verses

grace, as it extends to more and more people, may increase thanksgiving, to the glory of God.

16 So we do not lose heart. Even though our outer nature is wasting away, our inner nature is being renewed day by day. 17 For this slight momentary affliction is preparing us for an eternal weight of glory beyond all measure, 18 because we look not at what can be seen but at what cannot be seen; for what can be seen is temporary, but what cannot be seen is eternal.

cause thanksgiving to overflow to the glory of God.

[16]Therefore we do not lose heart. Though outwardly we are wasting away, yet inwardly we are being renewed day by day. [17]For our light and momentary troubles are achieving for us an eternal glory that far outweighs them all. [18]So we fix our eyes not on what is seen, but on what is unseen. For what is seen is temporary, but what is unseen is eternal.

UNDERSTANDING THE SCRIPTURE

2 Corinthians 4:1-6. A considerable portion of 2 Corinthians (2:14–6:10) is devoted to Paul's description of different aspects of "the ministry of reconciliation," which he has been given by God (5:18). The dominant theme in 4:1-18 is the stark contrast between the glory of God that irradiates Paul's apostleship and its veiled, frail appearance to an unbelieving world. This section begins and ends on the same note: Paul refuses to be discouraged, for his ministry is a gift of God's sheer mercy (4:1; compare 4:16). The apostle's denial of shameful practices and cunning falsification (4:2a) is sufficiently pointed to lead many interpreters to imagine that just such accusations had been leveled by some against Paul (see also 1:17; 2:17). Once again (compare 1:12, 18-22) Paul maintains his openness, truthfulness, and good conscience before God (4:2b). Paul's integrity is confirmed by his steadfast proclamation of Jesus Christ as Lord and himself as Christ's slave (4:5; Romans 1:1; 10:9; 1 Corinthians 12:3; Philippians 2:11; Colossians 2:6). Because Paul's deeply afflicted ministry may have been another easy mark for his critics, the apostle ripostes (4:3-4) that their cognitive blindness verifies their own subjection to "the god of this world"—Satan, perhaps (2:11; compare John 12:31; 14:30; 16:11; 1 Corinthians 2:6; Ephesians 2:2)—who has hidden the glory of Christ and his gospel before the eyes of "unbelievers," referring either to Paul's opponents (2 Corinthians 11:13-15; Philippians 1:28; 3:18-19) or to non-Christians in general (1 Corinthians 6:6; 7:12-15; 10:27; 14:22-24). In 2 Corinthians 4:6, as elsewhere in the Bible, "glory" refers to God's radiant essence, which can be apprehended by human beings only indirectly (3:18; Genesis 1:3; Exodus 33:17-23; Isaiah 9:2) and is veiled in the flesh of Jesus (John 1:14), the very image of God (see also Colossians 1:15; Hebrews 1:3).

2 Corinthians 4:7-18. Catalogs of Paul's afflictions appear throughout his letters (see also 6:4-10; 11:23-28; 12:10; Romans 8:35-39; 1 Corinthians 4:9-13; Philippians 4:11-12), but the listing in 2 Corinthians 4:8-12 is one of the apostle's most poignant. Commonplace in Greco-Roman literature, such lists were usually compiled to demonstrate a philosopher's victory over hardship. In contrast, Paul stresses that "the extraordinary power" to weather relentless adversity belongs not to himself, but to God.

Paul offers no less than four penetrating explanations for his apostolic sufferings. First, God's glorious power shines more brightly in "clay jars" (4:7), which in the apostle's day were as cheap, fragile, and disposable as are pasteboard fast-food containers in ours. Second, by giving himself up to torments for the sake of Christ, Paul carries in his body evidence of both the death (*necrosis:* literally, dead or dying tissue) and resurrection of Jesus (4:10-12). Such inner renewal within outer deterioration is perceptible only to the eyes of faith (4:16, 18). Third, Paul's endurance through suffering renews his faith in what he proclaims: that the God who restored Jesus to newness of life will do the same for Christ's servants (4:13-14; compare Psalm 116:10). Viewed along an apocalyptic horizon, current affliction is piddling when compared with the immeasurable, eternal "weight of glory" for which God's faithful servants are being prepared (4:17). Fourth, such suffering is not futile but accomplishes important goals: enhancing the church's faith, extending its witness, and amplifying thanksgiving and doxology to God (2 Corinthians 4:15; see also 1:6, 11; 2:10; 5:13; 8:23; 9:11-12).

INTERPRETING THE SCRIPTURE

Strange Glory

When Paul declares, "we do not proclaim ourselves," he is not engaging in modest demurral but pointing to the central issue: "We proclaim Jesus Christ as Lord" (2 Corinthians 4:5). Christian ministry and Christian faith are more than matters of personality. A "winning personality" may be an advantage for attracting persons to the cause of Christ; alternatively, it may be an enormous distraction, attracting attention only to a popular preacher or teacher. One need only flip through the pages of *People* magazine to be aware of the power of sheer personality. We hardly notice it when an article touts the movie star but says nothing about his newly released film. Occasionally, however, this cult of personality focuses upon a writer. From such an article we may see that writer's face, her living room and cocker spaniel; we may be informed of her partiality to pasta and Mozart—all without ever learning what she writes about. What stirs this person to spend hours in solitude, writing? What is it that her words stir in us? Such questions regarding the message retreat under the force of personality. In somewhat the same way, the Christian community in Corinth had become distracted by a cult of personality.

If Paul's ministry was not under attack in Corinth, he was at least regarded with suspicion because he seemed a poor advertisement for the gospel. During Paul's absence from Corinth, evidently something happened that caused people to wonder if his ministry bore God's blessing, vacant as that ministry was of the marks of success. Whatever happened, it must have been perfectly awful because news of it spread from one church to another. The Corinthians had heard about it, but Paul shows not the slightest hint of embarrassment: "We do not want you to be unaware, brothers and sisters, of the affliction we experienced in Asia; for we were so utterly, unbearably crushed that we despaired of life itself" (2 Corinthians 1:8). The Corinthians may have thought this debacle signaled some failure of Paul's gospel, but Paul certainly did not. The truth of the gospel is not determined by audience-response surveys. Jesus warned his disciples before he sent them out that some places would welcome them while others would brush them off with indifference or hostility. Either way, the message remained the same: "The kingdom of God has come near" (Luke 10:11; see also 10:1-12). Apostles have a message to tell, not a product to sell. As Paul puts it, "We are not peddlers of God's word like so many" (2 Corinthians 2:17).

The message shines unmistakably

because it is God's will: "For it is the God who said, 'Let light shine out of darkness,' who has shone in our hearts to give the light of the knowledge of the glory of God in the face of Jesus Christ" (4:6). This illumining word does not depend on the messenger, much less on the personality of the preacher, but creates its own light as it is told. This notion of the gospel's luminescence may perplex us. We may believe that Jesus is "the light of the world" (John 8:12; 9:5); we are less comfortable that we are "the light of the world" (Matthew 5:14); but the notion that the gospel *itself* shines gloriously may baffle us. Brilliant visions of the glory of Christ seldom appear in our Protestant parishes. Indeed, tourists in Europe and Latin America frequently find themselves put off by the gilded altarpieces of Christ in glory. Paul knows no such embarrassment. In one breath he tells the Corinthians, "we proclaim Christ crucified" and "I decided to know nothing among you except Jesus Christ, and him crucified" (1 Corinthians 1:23; 2:2), then speaks "of the gospel of the glory of Christ" (2 Corinthians 4:4). This he can do because both are true. This strange combination of cross and glory does not seem strange in the Gospel of John, where God's true glory appears on the cross (John 17:5, 22, 24). Though we associate glory with success, Paul and John see glory in the cross, a glory transforming human life.

Glory Encased in Dust

The human weakness and lack of success demonstrated by Paul do not therefore count as evidence against the truth of the gospel; it signals, rather, a power greater than human talent and success. This "gospel of the glory of Christ" (2 Corinthians 4:4) cloaks itself in earthy stuff: "We have this treasure in clay jars" (4:7). The KJV's familiar translation gets to the heart of the matter: "earthen vessels." Though we can scarcely believe such a

thing might be happening in the commonplace transactions of human life, the glory of God has chosen to come among us in human form. We may gladly affirm that in the case of Jesus, recognizing his incarnation (that is, the enfleshment of God's glory); but thinking of ourselves as human bearers of the glory of God may be more than we can manage. The distance between heaven and earth seems too great; golden images of glory seem remote from the leaden dross of our daily life. Paul assures us, however, that we are "earthen vessels" of amazing glory. God is trying to communicate something glorious through folks like you and me. This "earthy" language recalls familiar words from Genesis: "You are dust, and to dust you shall return" (Genesis 3:19). On Ash Wednesday we might hear these words as we come to worship and our foreheads are signed with the cross. In that liturgy the reminder that we are dust prepares us for another occasion when the pastor recites familiar words about death, the service of Christian burial. We are dust and to dust we shall return, but that is not half of the story. For Paul our dusty origin and dusty destiny are nothing compared to what God has in store for us.

Glorious Dust

Paul describes an extraordinary catalog of hardships for the life of those who bear witness to Jesus the Christ: "We are afflicted in every way, but not crushed; perplexed, but not driven to despair; persecuted, but not forsaken; struck down, but not destroyed" (2 Corinthians 4:8-9). We might wonder if there were not an easier way to go about this business of being an apostle, but that misses Paul's point: even—one might say especially—in extreme circumstances, the glory of God shines through. The life of Jesus shines through even the worst the world can do to God's messengers. Success does not guarantee the gospel, nor suffering either, but in every circumstance "the life of Jesus may also be made visible in our bodies" (4:10).

Just as Paul had earlier contrasted common, fragile "earthen vessels" with the rare "treasure" they contain, now he contrasts the lightness (or "slight[ness]") of "momentary affliction" with a "weight of glory" that God prepares for us (4:17). Paul's blithe confidence in the face of various afflictions is grounded in his belief that God is in fact transforming those who follow in the way of Jesus Christ. Something in us is dying—"our outer nature is wasting away"—but so also something is being born in us—"our inner nature is being renewed day by day" (4:16). More and more the life we live is the life of Jesus; less and less do we live to our former self. This is not a matter of our own moral rigor: "Every day in every way I am getting better and better and better." No: this transformation is being accomplished by God's Holy Spirit. The same Spirit that gave life to Christ now gives us a new life. So relentless is the work of the Spirit that Paul is bold to declare, "So if anyone is in Christ, there is a new creation: everything old has passed away; see, everything has become new!" (5:17). By no means is this notion of a renewed and glorious human-

ity some eccentric notion of Paul's. John the Elder, in his First Epistle, explains: "Beloved, we are God's children now; what we will be has not yet been revealed. What we do know is this: when he is revealed, we will be like him, for we will see him as he is" (1 John 3:2).

Living as a disciple of Jesus Christ is frequently a discouraging business. If the light of the gospel shines through us, we fear it is a rather dim glow, one obscured by several sins and a thousand preoccupations. We try to be loving, try to serve God and our neighbor; but the very contemplation of our attempts reminds us of things we ought to have done and didn't do, as well as of things we did and would now give anything to take back. We do not feel particularly adept at holiness; as for glory, don't mention it. Such a survey of our situation, however, misses the crucial ingredient: God is at work within us to make of us something holy and glorious, and worthy of God's eternal kingdom. Paul invites us to notice that, even if we can't see it and even if it can't be seen. Looking for what can't be seen makes no sense. Unless, of course, you look to God. Christianity is not merely what we do, but an awareness of what God is preparing in us.

SHARING THE SCRIPTURE

PREPARING TO TEACH

Preparing Our Hearts

In today's devotional reading from 2 Corinthians 6:1-10, Paul points out that salvation is available by God's grace and urges readers to respond in faith. The apostle lists the hardships that he endured (6:4-5) and links these to his virtues in verses 6-7. Note in verses 8-10 that Paul contrasts a false outer appearance with the inward truth. As you read this passage,

consider hardships that you have endured for the sake of the gospel. Also contemplate your own virtues. Finally, think about the statements of opposites with which Paul concludes this section. How do they help you understand Paul? Which of these reflect your own experience?

Now turn to 2 Corinthians 4, today's background scripture. Compare the list of problems in verses 8-9, today's key verses, with the list in 2 Corinthians 6:4-5. Think about difficult situations you have overcome in your own life. How were you able to use these hardships to witness to God? Pray that God will empower you and your students to be able to deal with whatever obstacles life throws in your way.

Preparing Our Minds

Review 2 Corinthians 4, focusing this time on verses 5-18. As already mentioned, Paul lists his afflictions both in today's lesson scripture and in the devotional reading. You may want to check these additional references to his afflictions: 2 Corinthians 11:23-28; 12:10; Romans 8:35-39; 1 Corinthians 4:9-13; and Philippians 4:11-12. Paul credits his ability to withstand these hardships not to himself but to the power of God. Be sure to examine the last paragraph of Understanding the Scripture where you will note that Paul offers four explanations for his suffering.

Preparing Our Learning Space

Prior to class you may want to write on newsprint the second group of questions under "Glory Encased in Dust."
Have on hand:
✔ several Bibles
✔ newsprint and marker
✔ paper and pencils
✔ hymnals.

LEADING THE CLASS

(1) Introduction

Open the lesson by asking the class to name as many martyrs of the Christian faith as they can. These may be persons from any historical period, including the modern era. List on newsprint these names and, where known, the reason they were killed for the faith.

If your group is unfamiliar with any martyrs, ask them to turn in their Bibles to the story of Stephen, the first Christian martyr, found in Acts 6:8–8:1a. Look

specifically at Acts 7:54–8:1a, which records his death.
Ask the following questions:
(1) **Why do people risk their very lives for the sake of the gospel?** [?]
(2) **Had you been alive during a period of persecution, do you think you would have risked your life to remain faithful to Christ? Why or why not?**
(3) **What kinds of afflictions are you willing to bear today for Christ?**
(4) **How does the fact that Christians (at least in most countries) are not persecuted affect their faith?**
Move into today's lesson by indicating that Paul certainly understood suffering. However, this suffering did not break him but rather gave him faith and hope for the future. Temporary affliction—no matter how serious—was not the last word; instead it prepared him for eternal glory.

End the Introduction by raising today's main question: **Where do we perceive the glory of God in our afflictions and failures?**

(2) Strange Glory

Ask these questions to review the quarter's work and prepare for today's session:
(1) **What do you know about the church at Corinth?** (Be sure the students make the point that this church was divided into factions as people followed different leaders.) [?]
(2) **What do you know about Paul's relationship with this church?** (Although Paul had founded the church, his relationship with them had soured between the time 1 Corinthians and 2 Corinthians was written. Paul had planned to visit Corinth according to 1 Corinthians 16:5-7, but when he did not come, 2 Corinthians 1:15-23 indicates that the people felt that he had wavered. Confidence in the apostle had eroded. Paul decided not to make "another painful visit," though he had sent a letter written with tears. Paul

apparently was wronged by someone in the congregation.)

(3) What do you know about Paul's ministry after he left Corinth? (2 Corinthians 1:8 speaks of a disaster in Asia, though the exact nature of the problem is not spelled out. 2 Corinthians 2:5-11 also records an incident that affected both Paul and the church at large. Some people wondered if Paul's preaching had failed.)

Now read or retell the information in the final paragraph under "Strange Glory" in Interpreting the Scripture. Note that the gospel message shines brightly, regardless of the personality of the bearer of that message.

Read the following story and then discuss with the students what Paul might say in this situation.

To attract more young people, Tower Church decided to hire a dynamic youth director. Although this young man had no formal theological training, his personality was electrifying. Moreover, his sporty car and well-conditioned body did not go unnoticed.

Fellowship was high on his agenda, as was drawing a large crowd. However, the youth were never challenged with the demands of the gospel. The group had plenty of discussions about current youth issues, but no Bible study to help them put these issues into a biblical context. Whenever a service project or an event that required some commitment was suggested, the director allowed—almost encouraged—the youth to vote it down. When one of the parents asked why the director did not insist that the youth become involved in mission, he responded that he wanted to be well-liked so that everyone would continue to come and bring their friends. Youth were pouring in, especially for the basketball league, the concert outings, and pizza nights. He was well-liked. Tower Church seemed to be successful in meeting its goal of attracting more youth. What would Paul have to say

about this success when held up to the bright light of the cross?

As you discuss this story of Tower Church, point out that for Paul it was the glory of the cross that was all-important. Actions were not taken to please others but to be faithful to God. When congregational groups of any age become social clubs they do not reflect the truth of the gospel, no matter how successful they may seem in terms of the numbers of people involved. The focus of any Christian community of faith must always be on proclaiming "Christ as Lord" (2 Corinthians 4:5).

Close this discussion by reading aloud 2 Corinthians 4:5-6.

(3) Glory Encased in Dust

Continue the Bible reading with 2 Corinthians 4:7-12. Ask:

(1) What are the implications for the Christian life when you consider that we are housed in "clay jars" or "earthen vessels"? (Jesus came to dwell among us in a clay jar, the incarnation of God's glory. Through the divine power, God's glory is being expressed in us as well. As Paul says in verses 10 and 11, we are "always carrying in the body the death of Jesus, so that the life of Jesus may also be made visible in our bodies...so that the life of Jesus may be made visible in our mortal flesh.")

(2) What kinds of afflictions has Paul experienced within his clay jar? (If time permits, invite the class to open their Bibles to the following passages where Paul catalogues the challenges he has faced: 2 Corinthians 6:4-5; 11:23-28; 12:10; Romans 8:35-39; 1 Corinthians 4:9-13; and Philippians 4:11-12.)

Distribute paper and pencils. Invite the students to reflect on one or both of these questions, which you may want to write on newsprint:

(1) Suppose you had an opportunity to correspond with Paul about his suf-

ferings. **What questions would you ask him? How might he respond?**
(2) **Suppose you found yourself in a situation where you knew you either had to deny your faith or face persecution. What would you do? How might Paul be a role model for you?**

Provide an opportunity for students to share their ideas either with the entire class or in small groups.

(4) Glorious Dust

Read aloud 2 Corinthians 4:13-18. Also read the second paragraph under "Glorious Dust" in Interpreting the Scripture. Emphasize the contrast between the lightness of a "momentary affliction" and "a weight of glory" that God prepares for us (4:17).

Ask the students to talk with a partner or small group about how they would try to help someone who was experiencing an affliction, such as a serious illness, job loss, broken relationship, or natural catastrophe.

Close this part of the lesson by singing a hymn concerning the trials of believers, such as "Nobody Knows the Trouble I See" (*The United Methodist Hymnal*, no. 520) or "I Want Jesus to Walk with Me" (*UMH*, no. 521).

Before the class leaves, suggest at least one of the activities below so as to provide the students with concrete ideas about living out the lesson in the week ahead.

HELPING CLASS MEMBERS ACT

Encourage the students to recall a difficulty that they have experienced. What was the problem? How did they handle it? What evidence did they have of God's power at work to resolve the problem? How did this challenge strengthen their witness for Christ?

Suggest that the class members be open to someone, especially a youth, who is having trouble putting today's problems in an eternal perspective. Youth are particularly prone to assume that a poor grade, the breakup of a relationship, or a lost game are permanent problems. Ask your group to help young people see that these temporary problems, though important today, will in time recede into the background.

Remind the adults that as Christian disciples their lives reflect a greater cause or higher purpose than just living unto themselves. Challenge persons to write a mission statement for their own lives, a statement that sums up what they feel God intends them to do and be.

PLANNING FOR NEXT SUNDAY

Our lesson for May 21, "From Reluctance to Joyful Giving," focuses on 2 Corinthians 9:1-13. This passage concerns the collection for the Christians in Jerusalem that Paul urges the Corinthians to make. Encourage students to read all of the background scripture, 2 Corinthians 9, if possible.

FROM RELUCTANCE TO JOYFUL GIVING

PREVIEWING THE LESSON

Lesson Scripture: 2 Corinthians 9:1-13
Background Scripture: 2 Corinthians 9
Key Verse: 2 Corinthians 9:7

Focus of the Lesson:
Paul taught that Christians are to give generously, cheerfully, out of commitment, and without compulsion.

Main Question of the Lesson:
What does it mean for us to give as God gives?

This lesson will enable adult learners to:
(1) study Paul's teachings on joyful giving.
(2) consider how they live out the principles of Christian giving in their own lives.
(3) respond by making a commitment to give.

Today's lesson may be outlined as follows:
(1) Introduction
(2) The Discipline of Giving
(3) The Joy of Giving
(4) The Vocation of Giving

FOCUSING ON THE MAIN QUESTION

What does it mean for us to give as God gives? How strange the paradox that we admire generosity so much but sometimes hesitate to be generous. Few things in life give us more joy than giving, yet we shyly restrain ourselves for reasons we do not always understand. By giving, we feel stronger, better, part of something larger than ourselves and perhaps more noble, but this splendid sensation is a treat to which we limit our indulgence. We love to give, yet something in us is loathe to give. We find all manner of excuses to explain this strange paradox. We're basically generous, we say, but we have to take care of ourselves first (as if we were careless at taking care of ourselves first). We wonder about the worthiness of this cause. Will our gift be invested or employed wisely and prudently? Particularly, we worry about being snookered: we will not have our generous impulses taken advantage of and misused. Scams trading off the generosity of good people offend our spirits even as they skim our wallets. These explanations for our reticence in generosity and our hesitance at giving sound reasonable enough as far as they go, but they only scratch the surface. Something more profound takes place in the strained relationship between loving to give and hating to give, between discovering enormous joy in a life of generosity and warily backing away into a self-protective posture.

The story is told of a citizen of sixteenth-century Florence, who, watching Michelangelo push a huge boulder up to his studio, asked, "What are you up to this time, Michelangelo?" To which the great sculptor replied, "There's an angel in here that is struggling to get out." Like a half-carved statue, a torso emerging out of stone, we too struggle to respond to God's call while still we are weighted heavily to the earth. To rise like an angel demands discipline, kindles joy, and announces to the world our vocation.

READING THE SCRIPTURE

NRSV
2 Corinthians 9:1-13

1 Now it is not necessary for me to write you about the ministry to the saints, 2 for I know your eagerness, which is the subject of my boasting about you to the people of Macedonia, saying that Achaia has been ready since last year; and your zeal has stirred up most of them. 3 But I am sending the brothers in order that our boasting about you may not prove to have been empty in this case, so that you may be ready, as I said you would be; 4 otherwise, if some Macedonians come with me and find that you are not ready, we would be humiliated—to say nothing of you—in this undertaking. 5 So I thought it necessary to urge the brothers to go on ahead to you, and arrange in advance for this bountiful gift that you have promised, so that it may be ready as a voluntary gift and not as an extortion.

6 The point is this: the one who sows sparingly will also reap sparingly, and the one who sows bountifully will also reap bountifully. **7 Each of you must give as you have made up your mind, not reluctantly or under compulsion, for God loves a cheerful giver.** 8 And God is able to provide you with every blessing in abundance, so that by always having enough of

NIV
2 Corinthians 9:1-13

[1]There is no need for me to write to you about this service to the saints. [2]For I know your eagerness to help, and I have been boasting about it to the Macedonians, telling them that since last year you in Achaia were ready to give; and your enthusiasm has stirred most of them to action. [3]But I am sending the brothers in order that our boasting about you in this matter should not prove hollow, but that you may be ready, as I said you would be. [4]For if any Macedonians come with me and find you unprepared, we—not to say anything about you—would be ashamed of having been so confident. [5]So I thought it necessary to urge the brothers to visit you in advance and finish the arrangements for the generous gift you had promised. Then it will be ready as a generous gift, not as one grudgingly given.

[6]Remember this: Whoever sows sparingly will also reap sparingly, and whoever sows generously will also reap generously. **[7]Each man should give what he has decided in his heart to give, not reluctantly or under compulsion, for God loves a cheerful giver.** [8]And God is able to make all grace abound to you, so that in all things at all times, having all that you

Key Verse

Key Verse

everything, you may share abundantly in every good work. 9 As it is written,

"He scatters abroad, he gives to
the poor;
his righteousness endures forever."

10 He who supplies seed to the sower and bread for food will supply and multiply your seed for sowing and increase the harvest of your righteousness. 11 You will be enriched in every way for your great generosity, which will produce thanksgiving to God through us; 12 for the rendering of this ministry not only supplies the needs of the saints but also overflows with many thanksgivings to God. 13 Through the testing of this ministry you glorify God by your obedience.

need, you will abound in every good work. 9 As it is written:

"He has scattered abroad his gifts to the
poor;
his righteousness endures forever."

10 Now he who supplies seed to the sower and bread for food will also supply and increase your store of seed and will enlarge the harvest of your righteousness. 11 You will be made rich in every way so that you can be generous on every occasion, and through us your generosity will result in thanksgiving to God.

12 This service that you perform is not only supplying the needs of God's people but is also overflowing in many expressions of thanks to God. 13 Because of the service by which you have proved yourselves, men will praise God for the obedience.

UNDERSTANDING THE SCRIPTURE

Introduction. Chapters 8 and 9 of 2 Corinthians are devoted to the subject of a collection that, throughout his ministry, Paul gathered for the church in Jerusalem. Since this collection looms surprisingly large in so many of Paul's letters (see also Romans 15:25-32; 1 Corinthians 16:1-4; Galatians 2:10), we should begin our attempt to understand 2 Corinthians 9 by recalling the importance of the collection for Paul. First, and most basically, it was prompted by genuine economic need. From both Luke (Acts 11:27-30) and the Jewish historian, Josephus, we know that severe food shortages befell Rome, Judea, and other portions of the Roman Empire during the reign of Claudius (A.D. 41–54). Second, the Christian community in Jerusalem, Judea's capital, was "the mother church" of Christianity, the center from which other Christian congregations had radiated. Therefore, to take up a collection for famine-relief in Jerusalem was an apt means of honoring a church that had played so crucial a role

during Christianity's infancy (see Acts 11:27-30). Third, it is clear from Paul's own comments (see especially Romans 15:22-33; Galatians 2:10) that he regarded this collection for "the poor among the saints in Jerusalem" (Romans 15:26) as a major ecumenical gesture of good faith, extended to Jewish Christians by the predominantly Gentile Christians among whom Paul missionized. Paul seems to have feared that upon its delivery to the Jerusalem church, this collection might be refused (Romans 15:31). Exactly how Jerusalem's Jewish Christians responded to that gift is not clearly attested in the New Testament: if the ambiguous comment in Acts 24:17 refers to the collection, even Luke does not clearly state what happened when Paul "came to bring alms to [his] nation." Much clearer is Paul's eagerness to take up the collection among Gentile Christians (Galatians 2:10), and his extensive preparations for doing so in Corinth (a city in southern

Greece: 1 Corinthians 16:1-4) and in Macedonia (the Roman senatorial province, in northern Greece, where the cities of Philippi and Thessalonica were located; 2 Corinthians 8:1-24). The apostle was convinced that through Christ Jesus, God's people had been expanded beyond Israel to include all the nations of the world. In response to the gift of God's Messiah, the Gentiles, who "have come to share in [Israel's] spiritual blessings,...ought also to be of service to [Jerusalem's Jewish Christians] in material things" (Romans 15:27).

2 Corinthians 9:1-6. Apparently writing from northern Greece, Paul informs the Corinthians down south of four things. First he bolsters their eagerness to participate in this noble undertaking (see also 2 Corinthians 8:7-15). Second he reports that he has whetted the Macedonians' anticipation of the generosity that he expects of Corinth. (The reverse of this compliment, paid to the churches of Macedonia, was expressed in 2 Corinthians 8:1-6.) Third he reminds Corinth that he is sending a delegation, consisting of his Gentile troubleshooter Titus (2:13; 7:6-7, 13-15; 8:6, 16-23; 12:18; Galatians 2:3) plus two unnamed brothers (2 Corinthians 8:18, 22; 9:3), to ready the delivery of the Corinthians' gift prior to Paul's own arrival. This "advance party" was intended to guarantee the integrity of Paul's money-raising enterprise (8:19-21) and to forestall any potential embarrassment that, upon Paul's arrival in Corinth, the church there would be asked out of the blue to "ante up" and perhaps be found wanting (9:3-5). Fourth, Paul repeatedly encourages the Corinthians' generosity through the fourfold use of the same Greek word (*eulogia*), variously translated as "bountiful gift," "voluntary

gift," "[sowing] bountifully," and "[reaping] bountifully" (compare Proverbs 11:24; 22:9).

2 Corinthians 9:7-10. Here Paul emphasizes three further points. First, the Corinthians' attitude in giving should be cheerfully generous, not grudgingly pinched (see also 8:3; Deuteronomy 15:10; Proverbs 22:8; Philemon 14). Second, Paul regards wealth positively, as a privileged blessing or grace (*charis*) from God that is intended for the thankful blessing of others (see also 2 Corinthians 8:1, 4, 6-7, 9, 16, 19; 9:14-15). Third, such generosity is a truly "good work," "the harvest of [Christian] righteousness," because it derives not from self-engendered human benevolence, but from God's own extraordinarily generous providence in supplying for our every need (see also Psalm 112:9; Isaiah 55:10; Hosea 10:12; Ephesians 2:10; Colossians 1:10; 2 Thessalonians 2:17; Titus 2:14).

2 Corinthians 9:11-15. As these verses abundantly clarify, the Corinthians' generosity is not performed for the sake of their own self-enhancement. Yes, they will be enriched, but that is a by-product of an extraordinarily intricate network of grace, or reciprocal giftedness (9:14, 15). Money is not merely pitched at human need. Its glad offering in the spirit of the Lord Jesus Christ, whose self-impoverishment enriched us (8:9), "overflows with many thanksgivings to God" (9:11-12). Through Christ-centered benevolence, Christians' ministerial service is tested (9:13), their obedience to the gospel is confessed (9:13), Christian sharing or fellowship (*koinonia*) is created and affectionate prayer is kindled among beneficiaries for their benefactors (9:14). This cycle of grace is the purest of feedback loops, for ultimately all thanks belongs to God, the sole source of an inexpressible gift (9:15).

INTERPRETING THE SCRIPTURE

The Discipline of Giving

Paul was gathering a collection from the Gentile Christian congregations scattered around the Mediterranean Sea for the relief of the Jewish Christian congregation in Jerusalem. This collection symbolically attested to the unity of Jew and Gentile in Christ. When Paul's ministry was recognized and verified by the "pillars of the church" in Jerusalem, "they asked only one thing, that we remember the poor" (Galatians 2:10). In contrast to the Gentile Christian congregations Paul had founded, the Jerusalem church was composed of people on the margins of society. Paul explained to the Romans, "I am going to Jerusalem in a ministry to the saints; for Macedonia and Achaia have been pleased to share their resources with the poor among the saints at Jerusalem" (Romans 15:25-26). Relationships between Jew and Gentile in the church remained tense, however, and Paul was by no means certain that the Jewish Christians would even accept a gift from Gentile Christians. He asked the Romans to pray "that my ministry to Jerusalem may be acceptable to the saints" (15:31).

Recognizing the outline of the situation we can think of several strategies Paul might have adopted. He might have played a sad tune on the Corinthians' heartstrings and sung a woeful ballad of suffering in Jerusalem. Most of us are moved by stories or pictures of the wretched of the earth; some of us are even moved to give in order to relieve their misery. Paul might have revved up the guilt. The wealthy of the Corinthian congregation were rich indeed; pointing out the gap between their luxury and the need of Jerusalem Christians could have achieved the desired effect of loosening the purse strings. Paul could have offered the Corinthians a trade: their money for a sense of pride at having done something for another congregation. Pride and self-worth are powerful motives for giving. Strategies like these, however, are precisely what Paul forgoes as he tells them he wants their portion of the collection "ready as a voluntary gift and not as an extortion" (2 Corinthians 9:5). He will not extort by trading on their emotions; instead, he suggests a discipline of giving. In a previous letter to Corinth, Paul had recommended a discipline of preparedness: "On the first day of every week, each of you is to put aside and save whatever extra you earn, so that collections need not be taken when I come" (1 Corinthians 16:2). Now Paul counsels the Corinthians "so that you may be ready, as I said you would be" (2 Corinthians 9:3). Yes, his letter intends to stir their preparedness, but what Paul enjoins is discipline.

Many of us prefer to give when we feel like it, when we are genuinely "moved" by the need. The trouble, of course, is that we are rightly suspicious of our feelings. Just as impulsive purchases can leave us regretful, emotion-wrought gifts may leave us feeling manipulated. Giving is best considered as a reflection of who we are and what our deepest commitments are, not as dependent on how we feel on a particular occasion. The discipline of giving flows from our discipleship, that way of life conformed to the contours of Christ's own life.

The Joy of Giving

In this discipline Paul invites the Corinthians to discover the joy of giving. "God loves a cheerful giver," says Paul (2 Corinthians 9:7). To judge from a broad reading of the Scriptures, it would seem that God loves not only cheerful givers, but grumbling, recalcitrant givers, as well as people who give not at all. Such is the embarrassment of God's grace that Luke's Gospel cheerfully concedes that God "is kind to the ungrateful and the wicked" (Luke 6:35). Giving cheerfully does not earn God's love or blessing, but those who give cheerfully find a special place in God's heart because they are so much like God. Cheerful giving replicates God's own characteristically joyous self-giving. The joy of giving is found in the giving, not in some other anticipated reward.

The equation that Paul offers, "The one who sows sparingly will also reap sparingly, and the one who sows bountifully will also reap bountifully" (2 Corinthians 9:6), has occasionally been misused to extort funds with an implied contract that those who give generously or cheerfully will receive *as compensation* a gift in return. Paul does not allow for such a contract. He does not ask the Corinthians to look for an anticipated return for themselves, but rather to focus on the harvest generated among others by their own giving. By their contribution for the relief of the saints in Jerusalem, the Corinthians participate in the life of God's kingdom. That is the harvest to be reaped. God gives us an abundance so that we may share with others, not only giving what God has given us but also living the kind of life God has lived among us in Jesus Christ.

This, quite simply, is where the joy lies. Astronauts often speak of a feeling of euphoria during their first experience of weightlessness. They feel amazingly free. So also there is a sense of joy in being one with God in participating in what God is doing in the world. No longer weighed down by anxieties and self-concern, we live as effortlessly in God's purpose as a trout swims in a stream. To shift the metaphor along the lines of G. K. Chesterton's *Orthodoxy*, "Angels can fly because they can take themselves lightly."

The Vocation of Giving

Cheerful giving, however, is not only what we are meant to do; it is what we are meant to be. We are not fashioned to pre-occupy ourselves with ourselves; we are made for sharing life together. The life we are given to live is the gift of a gift-giving God. We are not accidents abandoned in an indifferent universe; we are gifts to each other. That we have life at all is a gift. Moreover, baptized into Christ, we no longe: live to ourselves but to Christ. Our vocation is to be gift-givers.

Giving generously shows that we understand who we are and what we have been given. Giving is sacramental—an outward and visible sign of spiritual realities. As recipients of the gift of life we give thanksgiving to God. We are alive—we have won the lottery, the Publisher's Clearinghouse van has pulled up in our driveway, we've hit the jackpot—we are alive! Nothing in this world requires our existence. The cosmos could quite easily whirl on without us, but—glory be to God—here we stand and breathe. Yes, glory be to God for such a gift. Our thanksgiving to God and our glorification of God express themselves in many ways, but Paul calls our attention to the significance of our giving as a means of thanksgiving and glorification: "your great generosity...will produce thanksgiving to God through us," and "you glorify God by your obedience" (2 Corinthians 9:11, 13). Understood in this way, generous giving expresses far more than our assessment that some appeal has touched our hearts adequately, or that some need has passed inspection and is thereby qualified for our charity. Rather, our giving surges up from the depths of our theological convictions of who God is, who we are, and how we respond to the most elemental stuff of our lives. We have been given life as a gift; all that we have is a gift to be held for the short season of our lives. As Paul asks rhetorically in 1 Corinthians 4:7: "What do you have that you did not receive?" What shall we do with this immeasurable gift we have received? The Christian faith into which we were baptized teaches us to glorify God with our gifts and to share those gifts with our neighbors.

SHARING THE SCRIPTURE

PREPARING TO TEACH

Preparing Our Hearts

Today's devotional scripture is found in 2 Corinthians 8:1-15. This reading is part of a longer passage, which includes today's lesson, concerning the collection for the church in Jerusalem. See what Paul has to say about the churches of Macedonia as he appeals to the Corinthian church for financial support. If Paul were to write to your church about financial stewardship, what might he say? Where might he suggest that a collection be sent to help those in dire need?

Now look at 2 Corinthians 9, especially verses 1-13. Note that the key verse, 9:7, focuses on the idea of giving freely and cheerfully. How would you describe your own attitude toward giving? Why do you give? How has regular, systematic giving strengthened your own discipleship? Pray that God will open the hearts and minds of your students so that they will feel led to give generously to God through the church.

Preparing Our Minds

Read this lesson and review 2 Corinthians 9:1-13.

You may wish to do some background reading about the collection for the Jerusalem church. In addition to 2 Corinthians 8–9, Acts 11:27-30; 24:17; Romans 15:25-29; and 1 Corinthians 16:1-4 also speak about stewardship appeals. Galatians 2:1-10 records Paul's visit to Jerusalem when he was asked to "remember the poor" (2:10). Some scholars believe these passages all refer to the same collection, whereas others think that more than one collection is being referenced.

Note especially the principles for Christian giving that Paul maps out in 2 Corinthians 9:6-7. These principles include giving generously, cheerfully, out of commitment, and without feeling compelled to give.

Preparing Our Learning Space

Write the opinion poll for the Introduction on newsprint. Also write on newsprint the steps for creating a giving plan, which you will use in "The Vocation of Giving" portion.

Have on hand:
- several Bibles
- newsprint and marker
- paper and pencils.

LEADING THE CLASS

(1) Introduction

Post the newsprint on which you have written the following opinion poll. Distribute paper and pencils. Ask the students to complete the poll by completing each sentence. Tell them they do not need to write the beginning of the sentence; the sentence number is sufficient.

(1) I think most people give to the church because...

(2) When I give to God through the church I do so because...

(3) When I think about a finance campaign, words such as...come to mind.

(4) My attitude toward giving to support missions projects can be described as...

(5) Tithing, the giving of 10 percent or more of one's income, strikes me as...

(6) When I realize that all that I am and all that I have is a gift of grace from a loving God, I...

Allow time for the students to write their answers. Collect the papers and shuffle them to keep the responses anonymous. Then read at random responses from as many sheets as possible.

Connect this poll to today's lesson by

noting that Paul specifically asked the church at Corinth to help the poor church in Jerusalem. Paul outlines some principles for giving.

Raise today's main question: **What does it mean for us to give as God gives?**

(2) The Discipline of Giving

To help the students understand the context of today's lesson, read or retell "Introduction" in the Understanding the Scripture portion. Stress the reasons why Paul thought the collection was so important:

- A genuine need existed because there was a famine in parts of the Roman Empire, including Judea.
- Since the Jerusalem church was the church from which all others radiated, taking a collection for famine relief was an appropriate way to honor the mother church.
- Paul thought that collecting money from predominantly Gentile Christians to give to primarily Jewish Christians was an ecumenical gesture of good faith. He did not, however, know how this collection would be received.

Now choose a volunteer to read 2 Corinthians 9:1-5. Note that Paul wants the Corinthians to be ready to give what they said they would. He had already written to them in 1 Corinthians 16:2 to set aside whatever money they plan to give on the first day of the week.

Read this excerpt from Interpreting the Scripture: <u>Giving is best considered as a reflection of who we are and what our deepest commitments are, not as dependent on how we feel on a particular occasion. The discipline of giving flows from our discipleship, that way of life conformed to the contours of Christ's own life.</u>

Ask these questions:
(1) How do you perceive giving to be a reflection of your commitment to Christ?
(2) Many churches call upon members to make a pledge by estimating what they think they will be able to give in the upcoming year. How can making a pledge to give a certain percentage of your income help you to be disciplined about giving? (Be sure to note that God does not expect us to give what we do not have. Pledges made in good faith may have to be broken in the event of financial reverses. That said, a pledge enables us to be self-disciplined about setting aside money for God. When we pledge, we give God out of our firstfruits, not our leftovers.)

(3) How might finances at your own church be different if everyone were to be disciplined about giving?

(3) The Joy of Giving

Read aloud 2 Corinthians 9:6-13. Ask:
(1) What principles for giving does Paul set forth? (These principles include giving generously, cheerfully, out of commitment, and without feeling compelled to give.)
(2) Some people give because they believe their gifts serve as an "insurance policy" with God. They give because they expect to be blessed. What would Paul say about this interpretation? (Paul would agree that God abundantly blesses us. However, this blessing is not the motivation for giving but the fruit of it. We are blessed by God's grace, not by our own efforts.)
(3) What value does Paul see in giving? (Those in need will receive what they need. Those who give will participate in the life of God's kingdom. God gives to us so that we may share with others. When we give we are only returning a portion of what God has already given to us.)

Ask students to work with a partner or small team. Set a time limit. Encourage each person to tell a brief story of a time when either they gave something to someone else, or someone gave something to them. The story should include comments about how this giving or receiving was a blessing.

(4) The Vocation of Giving

Read or retell "The Vocation of Giving" in Interpreting the Scripture. Be sure to make these points:

- Life itself is the gift of a gift-giving God.
- As baptized Christians our vocation is to be gift-givers.
- When we give generously, we show that we understand who we are and what we have been given.
- Giving is a means of thanking and glorifying God for the gifts we have been given.
- Giving surges up from the depths of our convictions of who God is, who we are, and how we respond to what we have been given.

Distribute paper and pencils. Challenge the students to follow this process to begin to create a giving plan. This plan will need to be refined in consultation with a spouse or other family members. You may want to write the steps on newsprint prior to the session.

Step 1: Determine the percentage of your total income that you will give. Ten percent is the biblical standard, but for Christians this is to be thought of as the floor of giving, not the ceiling.

Step 2: Calculate the amount that percentage comes to, based on your income.

Step 3: Beginning with the church, list those organizations that you want to support.

Step 4: Decide what percentage of your total giving each organization will receive.

Conclude this silent activity by pointing out that a plan of giving helps us to be disciplined givers. It also forces us to take a look at the organizations we choose to support and can keep us from being thrown off guard by a high-pressure solicitor seeking support for an organization not on our list.

Close the session by reading the following verse of "We Give Thee But Thine Own," written by William W. How (1823–1897). This hymn appeared on page 181 of *The Methodist Hymnal* (1964). Ask the students to consider this the prayer of their own hearts.

We give thee but thine own,
Whate'er the gift may be:
All that we have is thine alone,
A trust, O Lord, from thee.

Before the students leave, lift up at least one of the activities listed below.

HELPING CLASS MEMBERS ACT

Challenge class members to review their recently completed income tax forms. How much did they give to God through the church? How do they feel about what they gave? What changes will they make?

Encourage the students to consider supporting a missionary as a class project. You may want to check with the pastor or missions committee for ideas about which persons or projects could benefit most from your support.

Invite students to meditate on why they give to God. What do their gifts mean to them? What do they mean to other people? How do they think God views these gifts? Do they expect anything from God in return? If so, what?

PLANNING FOR NEXT SUNDAY

The session for May 28, "From Confrontation to Growth," concludes the lessons for this quarter. Ask the students to read 2 Corinthians 13:1-13 to prepare. This lesson will focus on how one lives in faith.

FROM CONFRONTATION TO GROWTH

PREVIEWING THE SCRIPTURE

Lesson Scripture: 2 Corinthians 13:1-13
Background Scripture: 2 Corinthians 13:1-13
Key Verse: 2 Corinthians 13:5

Focus of the Lesson:
Paul called the congregation at Corinth to examine themselves and change their ways so as to grow spiritually and live in faith.

Main Question of the Lesson:
Under what authority, and with what kind of power, does the church of Jesus Christ live?

This lesson will enable adult learners to:
(1) recognize Paul's concern for the church as he calls the Corinthians to take stock of their lives.
(2) examine themselves to assess their own faithfulness to God.
(3) respond by making changes so as to live more faithfully.

Today's lesson may be outlined as follows:
(1) Introduction
(2) The Power of Weakness
(3) Authority to Build
(4) The Empowerment of an Authoritative Vision

FOCUSING ON THE MAIN QUESTION

Issues of power and authority abound in our time. We can call to mind more instances of the abuse of power than we would like to remember. Whether they be garishly publicized occasions of sexual harassment in the military or arbitrary pronouncements by local tyrants who reign in your office, the misuse of power lends the very word *power* a bad name. Authority in itself is also suspect. Wher-

ever we look, we discover challenges to traditional sources of authority. The very mention of "authority" raises an eyebrow or elicits a sneer, accompanied by skeptical questions of who may benefit, and who may be deprived, if the authority in question is invoked.

For Christians, things nowadays aren't much better. Most of us acknowledge "the authority of Scripture," but even that affirmation has been tainted by suspicion. We still yearn to know "what the Bible says"—why else would we be reading that book instead of John Grisham's latest?—but also we recognize that "what the Bible says" was not spoken in a vacuum of sublime disinterest. When the psalmist sings, "Give the king your justice, O God" (Psalm 72:1), we suspect that the singer has some stake in the royal enterprise. When the apostle counsels, "Wives,... accept the authority of your husbands" (1 Peter 3:1), we hear not only the words of holy writ but the voice of (probably) a man anxious about male prerogatives being eroded by changing women's roles. Christians who have been doing serious Bible study know that strategies of reading the Scriptures have changed over the years. If there were a day when preachers and teachers could pontificate "what the Bible says" and expect everyone immedi-

ately to knuckle under the pronouncement, that day has passed. We seriously want to listen to "what the Bible says"; now, however, many faithful Christians hear it as part of an ongoing dialogue between the community of faith and its Scriptures.

Clearly, issues of power and authority will not simply evaporate. Nor will they be resolved merely by shifting their implementation to those who may never have wielded such power; for history repeatedly demonstrates that, if given the chance, the oppressed are easily susceptible to becoming oppressors themselves. The question must be radically reformulated: **Under what authority, and with what kind of power, does the church of Jesus Christ live?** It is precisely with that question that Paul wrestles in this, our last session on the Corinthian correspondence.

READING THE SCRIPTURE

NRSV
2 Corinthians 13:1-13

1 This is the third time I am coming to you. "Any charge must be sustained by the evidence of two or three witnesses." 2 I warned those who sinned previously and all the others, and I warn them now while absent, as I did when present on my second visit, that if I come again, I will not be lenient—3 since you desire proof that Christ is speaking in me. He is not weak in dealing with you, but is powerful in you. 4 For he was crucified in weakness, but lives by the power of God. For we are weak in him, but in dealing with you we will live with him by the power of God.

5 Examine yourselves to see whether you are living in the faith. Test yourselves. Do you not realize that Jesus Christ is in you?—unless, indeed, you fail to meet the test! 6 I hope you will find out that we have not failed. 7 But we pray

NIV
2 Corinthians 13:1-14

[1]This will be my third visit to you. "Every matter must be established by the testimony of two or three witnesses." [2]I already gave you a warning when I was with you the second time. I now repeat it while absent: On my return I will not spare those who sinned earlier or any of the others, [3]since you are demanding proof that Christ is speaking through me. He is not weak in dealing with you, but is powerful among you. [4]For to be sure, he was crucified in weakness, yet he lives by God's power. Likewise, we are weak in him, yet by God's power we will live with him to serve you.

[5]Examine yourselves to see whether you are in the faith; test yourselves. Do you not realize that Christ Jesus is in you—unless, of course, you fail the test? [6]And I trust that you will discover that we

Key
Verse

Ke
Vers

to God that you may not do anything wrong—not that we may appear to have met the test, but that you may do what is right, though we may seem to have failed. 8 For we cannot do anything against the truth, but only for the truth. 9 For we rejoice when we are weak and you are strong. This is what we pray for, that you may become perfect. 10 So I write these things while I am away from you, so that when I come, I may not have to be severe in using the authority that the Lord has given me for building up and not for tearing down.

11 Finally, brothers and sisters, farewell. Put things in order, listen to my appeal, agree with one another, live in peace; and the God of love and peace will be with you. 12 Greet one another with a holy kiss. All the saints greet you.

13 The grace of the Lord Jesus Christ, the love of God, and the communion of the Holy Spirit be with all of you.

have not failed the test. [7]Now we pray to God that you will not do anything wrong. Not that people will see that we have stood the test but that you will do what is right even though we may seem to have failed. [8]For we cannot do anything against the truth, but only for the truth. [9]We are glad whenever we are weak but you are strong; and our prayer is for your perfection. [10]This is why I write these things when I am absent, that when I come I may not have to be harsh in my use of authority—the authority the Lord gave me for building you up, not for tearing you down.

[11]Finally, brothers, good-by. Aim for perfection, listen to my appeal, be of one mind, live in peace. And the God of love and peace will be with you. [12]Greet one another with a holy kiss. [13]All the saints send their greetings.

[14]May the grace of the Lord Jesus Christ, and the love of God, and the fellowship of the Holy Spirit be with you all.

UNDERSTANDING THE SCRIPTURE

Introduction. To understand 2 Corinthians 13:1-13, a sensitivity to its literary context is crucial. Unlike the portions of scripture that we have examined in the past three sessions, this excerpt from 2 Corinthians falls at the end of an extremely anguished and occasionally angry statement by Paul to the church in Corinth, which begins at 10:1. So starkly, abruptly different is the tenor of this material from the rest of the document (compare 7:16; 8:7; 9:1-15) that many biblical scholars consider 2 Corinthians 10–13 to be a fragment of a letter altogether different from that preserved in 2 Corinthians 1–9. In fact, some interpreters of 2 Corinthians wonder if chapters 10–13 contain a portion of that "letter of tears" to which Paul himself refers in 2 Corinthians 2:4, 9; 7:8, 12. However that may be, the material in chapters 10–13 is focused on four main

issues. The first is Paul's impassioned defense of his own apostolic ministry (10:1-18). The second is the apostle's attack against some unnamed false apostles who either passed themselves off or were regarded by some in Corinth as "super-apostles" (11:1-15). The third issue in this section is Paul's determination to boast, not of superlative activities of his own, but instead, and ironically, of all that he has suffered for the sake of Christ (11:16–12:10). Fourth and finally, in this section Paul expresses his deep concern for the Corinthian church's health as the body of Christ (12:11–13:13). The scripture on which this session is concentrated, 2 Corinthians 13:1-13, articulates the apostle's concern with final warnings, instructions, greetings, and a benediction—all directed to a very troubled congregation.

2 Corinthians 13:1-4. Paul warns the

Corinthians of a third visit that he is planning to pay them (13:1; see also 12:14)—and it doesn't promise to be a pretty one. The first visit would have been that during which he founded the small community of Christians in Corinth. Although Paul's second visit is shrouded in mystery, there are indications elsewhere in 2 Corinthians (2:1) that it was as painful as he fears his third visit will prove to be. Nor can we be sure of exactly what charge Paul demands substantiation by the biblical testimony of at least two witnesses (13:1; Deuteronomy 19:15; Matthew 18:16; 1 Timothy 5:19). Perhaps it is an accusation, lodged by some in Corinth, that Christ does not actually speak through Paul (2 Corinthians 13:3). In any case Paul canceled one potentially explosive return to Corinth out of leniency (1:23). The next time, he promises as he warned them before, he will not be lenient (13:2). Paul will deal with the Corinthians as God, working through Christ, has dealt with them: in weakness that discloses authentic power (13:3-4; see also Philippians 2:7-8).

2 Corinthians 13:5-10. These verses indicate more than Paul's peevishness in calling the Corinthians on the carpet. To the contrary, Paul's comments reveal some closely related matters that he has already touched on in his correspondence with that church. First, Paul stresses that his warnings are intended to motivate them to scrupulous self-examination and testing of their own conduct (13:5-7; see also 8:8, 22;

9:13; 1 Corinthians 11:28; 16:13). Paul earnestly wants his next visit among them to be not coercively destructive, but authoritatively edifying (see also 2 Corinthians 10:8). That is why he is "reading them the riot act" in advance, in this strongly worded letter (13:10; see also 2:3; 10:11). Second, Paul grapples with the remote chance that upon such self-scrutiny, the Corinthians will not measure up in Christ (13:5b-6). That possibility Paul cannot seriously entertain: he knows that despite all appearances, he has laid a valid foundation among them (13:7-8). Accordingly, Paul prays for their strength (13:9).

2 Corinthians 13:11-13. Paul closes this letter of chastisement with instructions that are nonetheless characteristic of other letters written under cooler circumstances. Paul pleads for the Corinthians to "put things in order" (2 Corinthians 13:11), a different rendering of a cognate verb translated in 13:9, "that you may become perfect." In other words: mend your ways. However unlikely it may be that the Corinthians will come to a common mind and be at peace, Paul refuses them neither the prayer that God's love and peace will be with them (13:11; see also Romans 15:33) nor the greetings of his Christian colleagues ("all the saints," 13:12). Neither does Paul withhold from Corinth his customary closing benediction: that Christ's grace, God's love, and the Spirit's communion may be with all of them (13:13; 13:14 NIV; see also Romans 16:16; 1 Corinthians 16:20).

INTERPRETING THE SCRIPTURE

The Power of Weakness

We began this session by grappling with a perceived erosion of "the authority of Scripture" in our day. And yet what some would regard as evidence of that rollback, the apostle Paul would find quite normal. As he begins a passage in which he will

raise issues of power and authority, Paul quotes scripture precisely for the purpose of relocating power and authority directly within the common life of people who are worshiping God and serving together in Christ. Preparing the Corinthians for his next visit, he abruptly quotes the book of Deuteronomy: "Any charge must be sustained by the evidence of two or three witnesses" (2 Corinthians 13:1, from Deuteronomy 19:15). Although it is not altogether clear why Paul reminds the Corinthians of that law at this point in his letter, the message of the citation is clear. Power and authority are not the function of one individual's personal charisma. Nor are power and authority so sublime—or so dangerous—that they must be confined to heaven. Early Christians borrowed this wisdom from Deuteronomy to order their lives (see Matthew 18:16-20; 1 Timothy 5:19), and they understood power and authority to have been given by God to the church.

Lest the "two or three witnesses" be carried away with that power and authority with which they have been entrusted, Paul goes on to describe the specific contours of Christian power and authority. Those accustomed to equating power with bombast and coercion may fail to recognize the presence of divine power. Where is the power of God demonstrated most completely? In the cross of Christ. "He was crucified in weakness," says Paul, "but lives by the power of God" (2 Corinthians 13:4). In the self-forgetful, self-giving gesture of the cross we recognize true power. Jesus died surrounded by emblems of the Roman Empire, the greatest political and military force the world had ever seen. Where is the real power in the scene of the Crucifixion? On the edge of a centurion's sword? Among the rabble of soldiers, gambling for a dying man's clothes? In the local governor's blasé shrug that Roman law doesn't matter if you've got Roman troops? Or does authentic power lie in the man who gives his life for others? To believe that the cross of Christ is "the power of God" changes everything we thought we ever knew about power. We see, even as the world sees, the weakness of Jesus on the cross. The crowds taunted him precisely because of that weakness (Matthew 27:39-44). Recognizing that weakness as the *power* of God turns our lives upside down.

Authority to Build

So enormous and encompassing is the change of heart required of us that Paul invites us, "Examine yourselves to see whether you are living in the faith. Test yourselves" (2 Corinthians 13:5). The world measures power in terms of an ability to get what you want. Does that vision of power continue to possess you? Others think of power as the ability to make yourself happy. Does such a limited horizon stunt your vision? Self-examination requires rigorous honesty and discipline. Finding fault with others is easier, a more leisurely and at times perversely pleasurable activity that hardly demands that we break a sweat. Testing *ourselves* is different. We can cheat, of course, but then we only sucker ourselves. Paul doubtless had his own judgments regarding the conduct of the Corinthians, and he might well have catalogued their shortcomings to his own advantage. Instead, he lays the yardstick of Christ beside these people and invites them to take the measure of their lives against that standard. What picture of power do I carry around in my wallet without ever thinking about it? What authorities compel me? A newspaper columnist? A neighbor's taste? Company policy or political correctness? The challenge of self-examination by the standard of Christ is an invitation to growth and maturity. Surprisingly, Paul is guardedly confident that the Corinthians will not be disappointed by their self-examination: "I hope you will find out that we have not failed" in establishing the church in Christ (13:6).

The purpose of Paul's preaching, teaching, and letter-writing was to build up the Corinthians into the church of Jesus Christ. Paul attests to this central task as he speaks of "the authority that the Lord has given me for building up and not for tearing down" (13:10). We might notice this same linkage of authority and edification also in 2 Corinthians 10:8. Authority within the church is neither arbitrary nor aimless. It has a singular purpose: the business of building up the church and edifying the faithful. In the Epistle to the Ephesians a similar sentence anchors the work of every ministry: "The gifts [Christ] gave were that some would be apostles, some prophets, some evangelists, some pastors and teachers, to equip the saints for the work of ministry, for building up the body of Christ" (Ephesians 4:11-12). Because that is the purpose of our power and authority, Ephesians continues with the warning, "Let no evil talk come out of your mouths, but only what is useful for building up" (4:29).

This image of "building up" may sound either remote or sentimentally pious, but the metaphor is not wholly absent from our culture. Perhaps it says much about our language, and ourselves, that we are more familiar with that metaphor's negative use: "put-downs" and "cut-downs"— language that by no means builds up but rather tears down. "Put-downs" are a chief source of humor in television's situation comedies. Gag-writers mine these acidic veins each week; the actors who mouth their lines slice into each other with "cut-downs" and elevate their characters with "put-downs" of others. As a result, nothing seems to change from episode to episode: we tune in each week for the same tired snarls. The fake blood is washed off the actor's face after the camera has stopped rolling; the barbed words are as disposable as this week's script.

In real life, however, it is not so. Just as bullets lacerate living tissue and vital organs, so also do "put-downs" annihilate the vitality of relationships necessary for our growth into the body of Christ. They destroy trust and respect, common purpose and joint effort. "Put-downs" and "cut-downs" breed discouragement. Paul invites us, instead, to "encourage one another and build up each other" (1 Thessalonians 5:11). Encouragement does not pretend that a person needs no further growth, nor is it uncritically blind to

imperfection. Encouragement, however, recognizes that God is doing something with this sister or that brother—something largely hidden from our eyes—and tries to point the way forward to God's future.

The Empowerment of an Authoritative Vision

As Paul says his farewell to the Christians of Corinth, he exhorts them with the most impossible of directives: "Agree with one another" (2 Corinthians 13:11). Does anyone who has worked through this thirteen-week study really believe that the Corinthians will now "agree with one another"? How can Paul be so naive? Of course the fact is that Paul does not for an instant believe that his letter is so profound that the Corinthians will suddenly shed their stubborn selfishness and be thoroughly transformed into a society without conflict. Paul places before the Corinthians an image of what the church may become in God's grace and mercy. Like the prophet Isaiah's vision of the peaceable kingdom, where "The wolf shall live with the lamb, the leopard shall lie down with the kid" (Isaiah 11:6), the apostle Paul envisages a church where people can live in peace. Such a vision dwarfs my hope of getting what I want; it overwhelms the smallness of having things done my way. Paul shows people what God wants: "Live in peace; and the God of love and peace will be with you" (2 Corinthians 13:11). The Corinthians' journey toward that outcome depends on their willingness to be guided by God's Holy Spirit. Neither they nor we will soon live in a parish where we "agree with one another"; but we shall never arrive at that destination unless and until we are ready to drop our hostile defensiveness and "Greet one another with a holy kiss" (13:12). As we go on our way—sometimes smooth, other times bumpy—we know that we travel in "The grace of the Lord Jesus Christ, the love of God, and the communion of the Holy Spirit" (13:13).

SHARING THE SCRIPTURE

PREPARING TO TEACH

Preparing Our Hearts

To begin your own spiritual preparations, turn to Acts 4:32-37. This passage presents the ideal community of faith. Communal living as described here was practiced for a time in Jerusalem. The poor were cared for because those who had resources shared them. What might life be like if modern Christian groups took care of one another to the extent that those in the early Jerusalem church did? How might your own life be different? How would such a living arrangement affect your discipleship?

Now look at today's lesson, found in 2 Corinthians 13:1-13. Here we see Paul confront the Corinthians in order to help them grow as Christian disciples. Paul makes no bones about it: he will assert his authority as an apostle in the name and power of Christ to deal with the sin at Corinth. He calls upon the people to examine their own faith. Think about your own witness. Are you "living in the faith" (13:5)? If not, seek God's guidance so that you may discern what you need to do to be more closely conformed to the image of Christ.

Preparing Our Minds

Read this lesson and review 2 Corinthians 13:1-13. Look carefully at Understanding the Scripture. Notice that some scholars believe 2 Corinthians 10–13 is part of another letter to the church at Corinth, perhaps even the letter of tears that Paul refers to in 2:4, 9; 7:8, 12. The tone of chapters 10–13 is quite different from that of chapters 1–9.

Preparing Our Learning Space

Prior to class, locate several news articles dealing with uses and abuses of power.

Perhaps you will find something about a dictator's trying to squelch his people or an extremist group's resorting to violence to force their viewpoint on others. Maybe the article will deal with abuse of power within the home. If you plan to use groups for this activity under Introduction, bring several different articles or make copies of the one that you have found.

Prior to class, you may want to write the questions for the Introduction on newsprint.

Have on hand:
- several Bibles
- optional news articles
- newsprint and marker.

LEADING THE CLASS

(1) Introduction

One way to begin the session is to summarize the news article about the use and/or abuse of power that you have brought to class. Unless the article is short, you need not read it aloud or report all the details. Be sure, though, that the students hear enough to know what the problem is and how power was used and abused.

If you prefer to deal with several articles, divide the class into groups and give each one an article.

Have the students address the following questions. If you divide into groups, write this information on newsprint and post it where everyone can see it.

(1) **What do you know about the person or group that has the upper hand in this situation?**

(2) **What is the source of that person or group's authority?**

(3) **What signs point to an appropriate use of power, or to an abuse of power?**

Close the discussion by mentioning that Paul acts authoritatively with the church at Corinth. While his words sound stern, he is neither abusing power nor relying on himself for that authority. Our main question today asks: **Under what authority, and with what kind of power, does the church of Jesus Christ live?**

(2) The Power of Weakness

Choose a volunteer to read 2 Corinthians 13:1-4. Make these points in a brief introductory lecture, or ask questions that will prompt the students to discern this information.

- Paul plans to visit with the church in Corinth a third time. Even though the second trip was a "painful visit" (2 Corinthians 2:1) that he does not want to repeat, Paul does not mince words in asserting authority in the face of wrongdoing within the congregation.
- Paul quotes scripture (Deuteronomy 19:15) in 2 Corinthians 13:1*b* to clarify the basis for dealing with wrongdoers.
- Paul will not be lenient, but the source of his power is not himself. Instead, he speaks in the authority and power of Christ.
- Paul points out that Christ "was crucified in weakness" (13:4), but is alive by God's power.
- Thus, Paul claims no power for himself, for he is "weak" in Christ, but in him the apostle has "the power of God" (13:4).

Help the class relate Paul's appropriation of Christ's power to their own lives. Read one or both of these situations and encourage the students to discuss what they would do and how they would understand their action to be rooted in the power of Christ.

Situation 1: You receive a telephone call from the police in the town where your son attends college saying that he has been charged with distributing drugs. How will you respond to the crisis? What will you say to this son who has been raised in the church and is well aware of your opposition to drugs?

Situation 2: A neighbor always seems to be fixing someone's car. There is noise at all hours and often several cars parked in front of your house. You suspect he is running a side business, but he insists that he is just doing favors for friends. What action will you take? How would you perceive this action to be based in the power of Christ?

(3) Authority to Build

Ask the class to read in unison 2 Corinthians 13:5, today's key verse. Talk with the class about Paul's strategy as revealed in this verse. Although he is clear that he will exert his apostolic authority, he would prefer that the Corinthians examine themselves and take necessary disciplinary action.

Next, read 2 Corinthians 13:6-10. Tell the students to try to imagine themselves as members of the church at Corinth as they answer these questions.

(1) How do you honestly feel about Paul exerting authority over you?

(2) How do you feel about being called to accountability?

(3) Why are you willing (or unwilling) to heed his words and examine yourself "to see whether you are living in the faith" (13:5)?

Sum up this portion of the lesson by emphasizing that Paul is using power here to build up the people, not to throw around his own authoritative weight (see 13:10). Paul could have spelled out problems and remedies in detail but instead chose to call the people to accountability. He wants them to grow toward spiritual maturity and by suggesting self-examination encourages them to do so.

(4) The Empowerment of an Authoritative Vision

Now read 2 Corinthians 13:11-13 (NRSV) or 11-14 (NIV). As the one in authority, Paul points the people toward a new vision of who they can be. Ask:

(1) How is what Paul is telling the people to do in verses 11-12 different from the way they have been living?

(2) How do Paul's words challenge your own congregation?

Before you dismiss, lift up at least one of the activities in the next section to help the students live out their discipleship in faithfulness this week.

Conclude the session by asking the group to read in unison the final verse, a benediction in the name of the Lord Jesus Christ, God, and the Holy Spirit.

HELPING CLASS MEMBERS ACT

Challenge the students to do the self-examination that Paul calls for in 2 Corinthians 13:5. They may choose to sit meditatively and listen to God in the silence. Or they may prefer to write in a spiritual journal to help them discern how they are or are not "living in the faith."

Encourage the class members to use power appropriately within the congregation. At times, they may need to speak authoritatively about a pressing issue. However, that speaking must be within Christ's power for the good of the body, not for their own self-interest. Tell them to be aware of how they use the power entrusted to them the next time they attend a church meeting.

Suggest that students think about what Paul might have to say if he were to write to your congregation. How are people living up to their high calling? What changes need to be made in order to bring the church to the vision expressed in 2 Corinthians 13:11-13? Encourage them to do whatever is in their power to move the church in a positive direction.

PLANNING FOR NEXT SUNDAY

On June 4 we will begin the summer quarter, "New Life in Christ." This series of lessons focuses on Philippians, Ephesians, Colossians, and Philemon. The first unit, "Living in Christ," opens with a lesson entitled "Living Is Christ." To prepare, ask the students to read Philippians 1:12-30, noting especially verses 12-26.

FOURTH QUARTER
New Life in Christ

JUNE 4, 2000–AUGUST 27, 2000

Our study during the summer quarter is based on four books traditionally referred to as Paul's prison letters—Philippians, Ephesians, Colossians, and Philemon. These letters contain a variety of teachings about how Christians are called to live.

The four sessions in Unit 1, "Living in Christ," focus on Paul's letter to the church at Philippi. As this unit begins on June 4, we hear Paul saying in Philippians 1:12-26 that for him "Living Is Christ." In the next lesson, entitled "Genuine Humility," Paul teaches us in Philippians 2:1-13 to have the same mind that was in Christ Jesus. Christians are to follow the example of Christ in humility, obedience, and service. In the session for June 18, "Striving to Be Christlike," Paul describes himself as an athlete who is pressing on toward the prize of the call of God in Christ. The apostle furthermore says in Philippians 3:7-21 that mature believers are to live changed lives. Unit 1 ends on June 25 with "Deep Joy." This lesson from Philippians 4:4-18 teaches that joy, gentleness, refusing to worry, and diligent prayer lead to the presence of God's peace in our lives.

The second unit, "Called to Be a New Humanity," investigates Ephesians. In this letter, Christians are called to spiritual blessings, oneness in Christ, appropriate use of spiritual gifts, and responsible living. We are also exhorted to stand firm as participants in the new community. "Claim Your Spiritual Blessings," the lesson for July 2, considers Ephesians 1:1-14. Here we are told that because of Christ we are blessed with the gifts of redemption, forgiveness, and the richness of God's grace. Ephesians 2:8-22, the passage for "Claim Your New Status," reminds the Gentile readers to whom this letter was addressed that they (and we) are now members of the household of God. Through the cross, Jesus broke down barriers and created one new humanity. "Claim Your Ministry," the study for July 16, explores Ephesians 4:1-16. The emphasis in this lesson is on the spiritual gifts that God has given for the purpose of building up the church. The next session, "Claim Your Responsibilities," looks at the teaching in Ephesians 5:1-5, 21-29 and 6:1-4. Here we are told to be subject to one another. We also will consider the relationship between husband and wife and between parent and child. This unit concludes on July 30 with a lesson from Ephesians 6:10-24, "Claim Your Power Base," which concerns the power that we have in Christ if we will just stand firm.

The summer quarter draws to a close with the unit "Christ Above All." This unit centers on the letter to the church at Colossae. These lessons emphasize the supremacy, completeness, and righteousness of Christ. Colossians 1:15-28 is the basis for the lesson entitled "The Source of Life." Here we read that God lived fully in Christ Jesus, through whom the world was reconciled unto God. "The Fullness of Life" looks at what it means to live as a mature Christian. In Colossians 2:6-19 believers are called to continue to live in Christ, "rooted and built up in him and established in the faith" (2:7). The lesson for August 20, "The Way of Life," explores Colossians 3:1-3 and 5-17 to understand how believers are to live righteously as new creatures in Christ. We conclude this Sunday school year with a study of Philemon 4-21 entitled "The Grace of Life." Here Paul writes to Philemon, asking him to welcome back Onesimus as a brother in Christ, rather than as a slave.

MEET OUR WRITER

DR. BEN WITHERINGTON

Ben Witherington III received his Ph.D. in Theology with a concentration in New Testament from the University of Durham, England. He is currently Professor of New Testament Interpretation at Asbury Theological Seminary. He has taught courses on every book of the New Testament, on the Old Testament, and on Wesley Studies at Duke University, Ashland Theological Seminary, High Point College, and Gordon-Conwell. Dr. Witherington has authored numerous professional books and articles, including *The Many Faces of the Christ: The Christologies of the New Testament* and *PaulQuest: The Search for the Jew from Tarsus.* He has also written for *Adult Bible Study Teacher Helps* and other curriculum resources.

An ordained elder in the Western North Carolina Conference of The United Methodist Church, Dr. Witherington has previously pastored churches on the Coleridge Charge and East Flat Rock Charge.

Ben and his wife Ann are the parents of Christy Ann and David Benjamin. They live in Lexington, Kentucky.

UNIT 1: LIVING IN CHRIST
LIVING IS CHRIST

PREVIEWING THE LESSON

Lesson Scripture: Philippians 1:12-26
Background Scripture: Philippians 1:12-30
Key Verse: Philippians 1:21

Focus of the Lesson:
While in prison Paul boldly proclaimed a word of hope: living is Christ.

Main Question of the Lesson:
How can we, like Paul, affirm that real living is about Christ?

This lesson will enable adult learners to:
(1) explore how Paul turned adverse situations into opportunities to live for Christ.
(2) consider their own willingness to live faithfully, especially in times of trouble and hardship.
(3) respond by proclaiming their faith even under challenging circumstances.

Today's lesson may be outlined as follows:
(1) Introduction
(2) Top Priority
(3) Handling Adversity
(4) Living on God's Time
(5) Pleasing God

FOCUSING ON THE MAIN QUESTION

The Christian perspective on life, including adverse situations, is tempered not only by a belief in everlasting life provided by Christ to those who believe in him, but also by a strong belief in God's sovereignty, which includes God's ability to work all things together for good for the believer. Since Christians do not have to see this life as the be all and end all of existence, they are freed from the need to make purely worldly matters the ultimate concern. They are freed to make living for Christ and sharing the gospel the top priority in life.

How can we, like Paul, affirm that real living is about Christ? This main question will help us to explore how Paul turned adverse situations into opportunities to live for Christ. Paul also affirmed that dying is gain, for dying is simply a matter of drawing closer to Christ and gaining an even higher form of life. We must also ask the second-order questions of whether or not we are prepared to face adverse situations and even persecution for the sake of our Christian faith, and whether we will take opportunities that come our way to turn a

detriment into a plus by following the example of Paul. We may ask if we will be reactive or proactive in the way we handle the trials and temptations we face as Christians. The examples of Christ and Paul provide the clues necessary to answer these sorts of questions as faithful disciples.

READING THE SCRIPTURE

NRSV
Philippians 1:12-26

12 I want you to know, beloved, that what has happened to me has actually helped to spread the gospel, 13 so that it has become known throughout the whole imperial guard and to everyone else that my imprisonment is for Christ; 14 and most of the brothers and sisters, having been made confident in the Lord by my imprisonment, dare to speak the word with greater boldness and without fear.

15 Some proclaim Christ from envy and rivalry, but others from goodwill. 16 These proclaim Christ out of love, knowing that I have been put here for the defense of the gospel; 17 the others proclaim Christ out of selfish ambition, not sincerely but intending to increase my suffering in my imprisonment. 18 What does it matter? Just this, that Christ is proclaimed in every way, whether out of false motives or true; and in that I rejoice.

Yes, and I will continue to rejoice, 19 for I know that through your prayers and the help of the Spirit of Jesus Christ this will turn out for my deliverance. 20 It is my eager expectation and hope that I will not be put to shame in any way, but that by my speaking with all boldness, Christ will be exalted now as always in my body, whether by life or by death. **21 For to me, living is Christ and dying is gain.** 22 If I am to live in the flesh, that means fruitful labor for me; and I do not know which I prefer. 23 I am hard pressed between the two: my desire is to depart and be with

NIV
Philippians 1:12-26

[12]Now I want you to know, brothers, that what has happened to me has really served to advance the gospel. [13]As a result, it has become clear throughout the whole palace guard and to everyone else that I am in chains for Christ. [14]Because of my chains, most of the brothers in the Lord have been encouraged to speak the word of God more courageously and fearlessly.

[15]It is true that some preach Christ out of envy and rivalry, but others out of goodwill. [16]The latter do so in love, knowing that I am put here for the defense of the gospel. [17]The former preach Christ out of selfish ambition, not sincerely, supposing that they can stir up trouble for me while I am in chains. [18]But what does it matter? The important thing is that in every way, whether from false motives or true, Christ is preached. And because of this I rejoice.

Yes, and I will continue to rejoice, [19]for I know that through your prayers and the help given by the Spirit of Jesus Christ, what has happened to me will turn out for my deliverance. [20]I eagerly expect and hope that I will in no way be ashamed, but will have sufficient courage so that now as always Christ will be exalted in my body, whether by life or by death. **[21]For to me, to live is Christ and to die is gain.** [22]If I am to go on living in the body, this will mean fruitful labor for me. Yet what shall I choose? I do not know! [23]I am torn between the two: I desire to depart and be with Christ, which is better by far; [24]but it

Key
Verse

Key
erse

JUNE 4

Christ, for that is far better; 24 but to remain in the flesh is more necessary for you. 25 Since I am convinced of this, I know that I will remain and continue with all of you for your progress and joy in faith, 26 so that I may share abundantly in your boasting in Christ Jesus when I come to you again.

is more necessary for you that I remain in the body. 25Convinced of this, I know that I will remain, and I will continue with all of you for your progress and joy in the faith, 26so that through my being with you again your joy in Christ Jesus will overflow on account of me.

UNDERSTANDING THE SCRIPTURE

Philippians 1:12-18a. Paul's discourse in Philippians 1:12-26 is called in rhetorical terms the *narratio*. Paul will inform his audience about things they were apparently unaware of prior to this time. The function of this narrative material is to provide the audience with negative and positive examples to follow in their Christian walk and witness. Paul himself provides the positive example of what it means to live for Christ, in Christlike fashion, and as if living is Christ. Paul uses rival proclaimers as the negative examples. The general aim of this letter is to bring about harmony in the Philippian congregation, which is experiencing discord (see Philippians 3–4). Therefore, Paul begins at the outset to present examples of what concordant, Christ-following behavior looks like, and what discordant, factious, rivalry-producing behavior looks like.

Although Philippians is often referred to as one of Paul's "prison" epistles, it is doubtful that he was in prison when he wrote this letter. The Greek phrase *tous desmous mou* means literally "my chains" (1:13, 17) and may simply suggest that Paul is chained to a Roman guard while under house arrest in Rome. Prison and chaining were basically not seen as a means of punishment in the Greco-Roman world; they were simply a means of holding someone until a trial resolved the legal situation.

Paul understood that his mission in life was to present a reasoned defense of the gospel to a wide variety of people, primarily Gentiles. Here Paul is speaking of how his being guarded by the elite Praetorian guard (1:13), stationed in Rome, has in fact given him access even to those involved in Caesar's household (see 4:22). Courtesy of the hospitality of the Roman system of jurisprudence, Paul has been escorted to Rome itself and placed in contact with some of the people he most desired to reach for Jesus Christ. Rather than snuffing out the proclamation of the gospel by arresting Paul, these actions have merely provided an opportunity for the good news to spread in fresh directions!

Paul lived in a world that was highly competitive, much like our own. Competition among Christian proclaimers often led to rivalry and envy (1:15). This common behavior in the ancient world often set in motion the enmity conventions that led to feuding. Paul sees this sort of behavior as unworthy of a Christian. Yet the apostle believes God can even use the wrong motives for preaching to produce the right results.

Philippians 1:18b-20. This section may suggest to many that Paul simply was an optimistic person, but in fact he was not just whistling in the dark. Paul was happy that the gospel was proclaimed, regardless of the motives of the proclaimers. He fully trusted that his own situation would be worked out as God intended and for the greater good of the advancement of the gospel. The Greek word *soteria*, which occurs in 1:19 (translated as "deliverance" in the NRSV), is normally translated as "salvation." It also has the basic sense of safety. When non-Christians of Paul's day prayed to a god for *soteria*, they were praying to be kept safe while on a journey, or kept in good health, or rescued from some difficult situation. Thus in 1:19 Paul may mean that the prayers of the Philippians will result in his safe release from chains. As 1:20 makes clear, not being put to shame by one's peers or superiors or by one's God is far more important than living or dying.

In a culture so concerned with honor and shame as the one Paul lived in, honor was of much greater value than living. Therefore, the apostle is far more concerned with doing the honorable thing of presenting a bold proclamation of the gospel than about whether he will live or die. Real living for Paul means living honorably in a way that manifests Christ and the gospel.

Philippians 1:21-26. Paul reiterates in 1:21 his basic tenet: he is in a no-lose situation. If he lives, he will be able to continue offering fruitful service for Christ. If he dies, he goes to be with the Lord, which is also a blessing, indeed a greater blessing for him personally than continuing in this life. As one commentator has remarked, it may seem strange to us that Paul speaks in Philippians 1:23 of his choosing between life and death, between release and execution. Paul obviously believes God is in control. Moreover, Paul sees himself as being on top of his situation. Even though he is under arrest, he does not assume a victim's

mentality, as so many do today. He takes what most would see as a disadvantageous situation as a further opportunity to fulfill his mission in life. In Philippians 1:23-26 Paul is expressing a desire to go beyond death into the very presence of life. Christ, in Paul's book, is the font of life itself; and since Christ is beyond the grave in heaven, dying leads paradoxically enough not to the cessation of life, but to an even higher or greater form of life.

In verse 25 Paul says he is confident that he will be released and remain with his converts to be a help to them. He evidently expects a favorable verdict. Much early Christian tradition suggests that Paul was released in about A.D. 62. The apostle seems to have had several more years of fruitful ministry before once again being arrested by Nero's troops and finally executed, perhaps around A.D. 68. Arrests and executions of Christians were not uncommon at this time because Nero used church members as scapegoats for the fire that destroyed about one-third of Rome in A.D. 64.

Philippians 1:27-30. Paul exhorts the Philippians to stand firm in the faith and share in the same struggles and suffering he has been enduring. This transitional section makes clear that the letter to the Philippians is written to an audience that Paul thinks is basically on the right track and needs to continue working out the implications and applications of their faith in daily life.

INTERPRETING THE SCRIPTURE

Top Priority

This passage is in most respects a typical missionary report sent back to some of Paul's main supporters and financial backers. The purpose of the report is both to allay fears and also to rekindle hope. Paul will make clear here that though he has endured enormous adversity and is presently under house arrest (probably in

Rome), even these adverse circumstances have provided new opportunities for him to witness to people he otherwise would not likely have reached. Moreover, his efforts motivated others to evangelize as well. Paul will also make clear that adverse circumstances and even the prospect of death can be dealt with in a positive way if Christians use hardship to take stock of what is really important in life and to choose where their ultimate loyalties and priorities ought to lie.

Christ tops the list of Paul's values. Being a citizen of the heavenly commonwealth is the highest status one could have. To understand these claims, one must realize that Paul was in one of the most shameful conditions in his society: he was a prisoner of Rome, under house arrest. Evaluated from a normal human point of view, his situation could hardly be called desirable, much less advantageous. Furthermore, Paul was a Roman citizen, and for such a person to endure these indignities unjustly would ordinarily be considered especially humiliating. Yet Paul is not troubled by the way the world would evaluate his predicament. He chooses to live in a way that pleases God, not to play to the crowd and its opinions.

Handling Adversity

Most adults realize that no human being can control all of life's circumstances. One cannot prevent many bad things from happening during the course of life, especially if one lives a long and/or active public life. Thus Christians must determine how they will react to whatever happens to them. When life throws you a lemon, will you make lemonade or simply let the situation turn you into a sourpuss? Will you let adverse circumstances make you bitter or better? Will you look for ways not only to view a negative situation positively but also to turn the situation to your advantage?

A good example of the latter is the life of the great Christian philosopher Blaise Pascal. Having spent most of his adult life quite ill and often in bed, Pascal died at a relatively young age. He took this negative situation and turned his infirmity into an opportunity to spend day after day reflecting on the meaning of life. The result was his famous *Pensées* or meditations that still inspire people today.

Living on God's Time

I once visited a farmer's wife in the hospital. She was blunt and plain-speaking. When I walked into her hospital room she said to me, "Preacher, God had to lay me flat on my back so I would look up to him." Sometimes, unfortunately, this is true of most of us. While I doubt he would have put it just this way, Paul did view adverse circumstances as an opportunity not only to realize his own mortality but also to purposely draw closer to his Maker.

After a serious illness, most people confront their own mortality. They recognize that all of us are terminal, and that the longer one lives the more one is living on borrowed time.

For many persons this can be a depressing thought; but for the Christian who truly believes in eternal life, knowing that one is living on borrowed time in this life can be a liberating experience. It can free one up to take some chances or "redeem the time" and make the most of one's opportunities to do things in the service of Christ. I am convinced that one thing that causes many older adults to have a bolder faith and a bolder witness is that for them the goal is already in sight, as it was for Paul, and they wish to be all they can be for the Lord with the time they have remaining. If you are a teenager convinced you are going to live forever on this planet, the sense of urgency is lacking and the temptation to be self-absorbed and to focus on the things of the moment is great.

I have had two relatives who lived to the ripe old age of 100, and my grandfather lived into his nineties. The first of these relatives was the main doctor on Ellis Island during the early part of this century. He worked with the incoming immigrants and later developed a milk-pasteurizing scheme for my home region in North Carolina. The other centenarian was for many years the head librarian at the University of North Carolina, who managed to turn that library into a world-class research center. In due course that grateful university named the main library after him. My grandfather, on the other hand, never went to college, but rather was a deacon in the Baptist church and fire chief for the city of Wilmington, North Carolina. When at one point I asked him why he worked so hard to live a good Christian life, he said, "Heaven is too sweet and hell is too hot to mess around in this life." He was one who had that same sort of eternal perspective that Paul had, and accordingly had his priorities straight.

What I learned from all of these persons is that the tapestry of life has many hues—some of them dark, some of them light—and that God weaves them all together for good if we place our trust in the Almighty. With such a perspective death is not a loss, but rather a gain. With such a perspective we can work vigorously and joyfully and with a purpose while we still have the light of day.

Pleasing God

Rivalry between churches is rarely a pretty sight. I once served a four-point charge where the churches were suspicious of each other, figuring one or more of the others was getting more of their minister's time than they were. They also were not happy with the way the apportionment figures were divided up among the churches. Basically these churches were close enough that they were competing for the same few new members. How could this adverse sit-

uation of suspicion and rivalry be turned into a plus? Though it cannot be said that it was a cure-all, one thing that helped is that on Sunday nights at least once a month I set up a chargewide service, with the choirs from all the churches coming and singing in one of the other church's buildings. We would share in fellowship, food, and worship, and generally a good time was had by all. Some of the suspicion and sense of rivalry fell by the wayside, and there was even a bit of friendly prodding of one another to have a better choir, or next time to bring more members to the chargewide service. Minuses can be turned into pluses when the focus is on pleasing God and helping others, especially when one has that eternal perspective that proclaims "for to me, to live is Christ and to die is gain" (Philippians 1:21 NIV).

To live in Christ means that one must live "in a manner worthy of the gospel of Christ" (1:27). Moreover, Christians must be worthy of the privilege of suffering for the gospel (1:29). In both cases Paul is stressing what a high calling and honor it is not only to be a Christian but to die for the Christian cause. We learn much about a person when we know what he or she is prepared not only to live for but also to die for. In essence Paul is urging his converts to be prepared both to live for Christ in a manner that is worthy of following him and also to die for him. Our worth is shown by the manner in which we both live our daily lives and approach death.

SHARING THE SCRIPTURE

PREPARING TO TEACH

Preparing Our Hearts

Begin your own spiritual preparation for this week's lesson by turning to another letter to the early Christian church, 1 Peter 1:3-9. Here the writer calls

us to rejoice in the salvation that is ours through Christ's resurrection. Although our inheritance is being safely kept for us in heaven, trials and suffering will come in this life. Think back over some recent experiences that have caused you to suffer. How do you respond to suffering? Do you see it as an opportunity to grow spiritually, or is it reason for bitterness and anger?

Turn now to the background scripture from Philippians 1:12-30. What do you know about Paul's present circumstances? How does he respond to this situation? What lessons can his experience offer to you?

Pray that God will lead you as you get ready to teach the class so that you will not only speak the word of truth but also live as an example of the Christian life that others will want to imitate.

Preparing Our Minds

Read this lesson and again look at the scripture, this time focusing on Philippians 1:12-26.

If possible, locate a map that includes Philippi, a city in Macedonia. Note that this city is on a major east-west thoroughfare of the Roman Empire, the Egnatian Way, which linked Italy and the East. According to Acts 16:11-13, the church at Philippi was the first one that Paul established in Europe.

The church at Philippi experienced opposition from the beginning. Thus, a main theme of this letter is courageous persistence in the faith in spite of persecution. Paul, of course, uses his own experiences with adversity to model for the readers what living in Christ is all about.

Preparing Our Learning Space

Have on hand:
- several Bibles
- optional map showing Philippi
- paper and pencils
- optional news articles about persons who have struggled successfully against enormous odds.

LEADING THE CLASS

(1) Introduction

Begin today's session by encouraging some volunteers to share stories of how they turned adversity into a witness for Christ. Here are two discussion starters, if you need them.

- A cardiac patient regularly visits other patients who have undergone heart surgery to offer inspiration and encouragement. Often the discussion during these hospital visits turns to the important role that God plays in recovery.
- A teen who at one time had been homeless mobilized a cadre of other youth volunteers to make sandwiches and take them to feed homeless people in a large city.

After stories have been shared, raise these questions:

(1) **How do most people react to adversity?** (Many react negatively with questions such as "why me?")

(2) **How might the Christian response be different?** (Christians can use adversity creatively to witness to the unfailing presence and amazing deeds of God.)

(3) **Why is the Christian response different?** (Christians live in Christ and, therefore, know that they are never alone.)

Segue into today's lesson by noting that Paul writes to the church at Philippi while he is under house arrest in Rome. He could have been angry with God, perhaps bitter that such a fate had befallen him. Instead, he chooses to see an excellent opportunity to witness for Christ, thereby spreading the gospel to the Gentiles whom he had hoped to reach.

Lift up today's main question: **How can we, like Paul, affirm that real living is about Christ?**

(2) Top Priority

You may want to locate Philippi on a map and mention that this first church that Paul had founded on European soil had experienced opposition from the very beginning.

Ask the students to follow along in their Bibles as you or a class member read aloud Philippians 1:12-26. Then ask:

(1) **Paul has said that for him "living is Christ" (Philippians 1:21). What evidence do you see in this passage to support this claim?**

(2) **What is Paul's main purpose in life?**

Distribute paper and pencils. Read the following sentences aloud and give the students an opportunity to respond in writing. I would rank Christ as the number... priority in my life. Evidence for this ranking includes.... (Here students will need to give some reasons for why they say that Christ is the first or fifth or whatever priority in their lives. As they write, some adults may be surprised to realize that the evidence they give does not support the priority they claim that Christ has in their lives.)

If time permits, you may want to have a few class members share what they have written with the entire group, or have everyone share with a partner. Close this section by pointing out that our decisions about how we live each day reflect the true priority that we accord Christ in our lives.

(3) Handling Adversity

If you were able to locate a few news articles about persons who have struggled against enormous odds and conquered adversity, read or retell at least one of these stories. Or ask class members to tell about someone they know or have read about. People such as Corrie ten Boom, Christopher Reeve, and Joni Eareckson Tada may come to mind. Then ask:

(1) **What gives people the motivation to overcome suffering?**

(2) **How has someone's strong Christian witness in the face of adversity affected you?**

(3) **How can Paul serve as a role model when you are challenged by a difficult situation?**

Note that Paul really did not seem to care whether he lived or died. While he could continue to labor for the Lord in this life, he could actually be with Christ in death. Point out today's key verse from Philippians 1:21 and then ask:

(1) **Have you ever been so crushed by adversity that you wanted to die?**

(2) **What gave you the impetus to keep fighting for life?**

(4) Living on God's Time

Read or retell all but the last paragraph of "Living on God's Time," found in the Interpreting the Scripture section. Then ask:

(1) **How has a difficult situation forced you to look to God?**

(2) **What do these examples say to us about looking at our priorities from the perspective of God's eternal time?** (You may want to read the last paragraph of this section after the students have had a chance to answer.)

(5) Pleasing God

Note that Paul mentions his rivals in Philippians 1:15-18 and again in verses 27-30. Ask these questions. If rivalries exist within your own congregation, you may want to read or retell the first paragraph under "Pleasing God" in the Interpreting the Scripture section so as to have a more neutral example.

(1) **How does rivalry affect a church?**

(2) **What was Paul's stance toward rivalry?** (Point out that he claims that no matter what the rivals' motives are, as long as Christ is preached, that is the main thing.)

(3) **How can Christians please God?** (See verses 27 and 29-30.).

Conclude the session by offering a prayer that, like Paul, we will put Christ first in our lives and be willing to do whatever is necessary in whatever situation we find ourselves to live as if Christ is our main priority.

As you close today's session, be sure to suggest at least one of the activities below so that students will have concrete ideas as to how to live out what they have learned.

HELPING CLASS MEMBERS ACT

Suggest that students who know someone who is facing adversity be open and available to that person. A gentle witness spoken in terms of "this is what God has done for me" in a difficult situation may help that individual to come to know Christ or to develop a more mature faith as a result of the problem.

Encourage class members to write down memories of a time in their own lives when they faced difficult, perhaps life-threatening, circumstances. The situation may have been caused by serious illness, loss of a loved one, war, or economic hardship. Have them call to mind not only what happened but also how they relied on God to see them through. Suggest that this story be shared with a young person as an example of how one can live in Christ no matter what the situation.

Challenge students to make a bold witness for Christ in a setting where they may be ridiculed for their faith. For example, when they hear an inappropriate joke, instead of laughing they may say that as Christians they are offended by it.

PLANNING FOR NEXT SUNDAY

Next week's lesson, "Genuine Humility," considers how we can have the mind of Christ. Ask the students to read Philippians 2:1-18. The ancient hymn in verses 6-11 will likely be familiar to the class. Encourage them to be alert for the example of humility that Christ sets before us.

GENUINE HUMILITY

PREVIEWING THE LESSON

Lesson Scripture: Philippians 2:1-13
Background Scripture: Philippians 2:1-18
Key Verse: Philippians 2:5

Focus of the Lesson:
Those who have the mind of Christ serve with humility.

Main Question of the Lesson:
What was the character of the Christ, and what should be the character of his followers who are called to be of one mind with him?

This lesson will enable adult learners to:
(1) examine the character of the Christ, the sacrificial servant.
(2) consider their own discipleship in light of Christ's example.
(3) respond by serving someone else without thought of return.

Today's lesson may be outlined as follows:
(1) Introduction
(2) An Example of Sacrifice
(3) Following the V Pattern
(4) Humility

FOCUSING ON THE MAIN QUESTION

The main question today's lesson raises is this: **What was the character of the Christ, and what should be the character of his followers who are called to be of one mind with him?** In other words, this lesson is about both Christology and discipleship and the interrelationship between the two. Obviously there are ways that Christians cannot emulate Christ. We can't, for example, die on the cross for the sins of the world as he did. Nor do we come into this world as beings who have the status and nature of a deity. Nevertheless, Paul is quite convinced that the "imitation of Christ" is possible and should be attempted by all Christians. In particular he believes that anyone can choose to assume the role and functions of a servant of others as Christ himself did.

The character of Christ was such that he was even willing to assume the position and form of the least, last, and lost of society—namely, of slaves—in order to lift up, serve, and save all persons. Paul sees this sort of self-sacrificial service as the pattern of and for the Christian life. Furthermore, he believes that this kind of service is part of what binds the body of Christ together, so that there is a unity in the midst of ethnic, social, and sexual differences. Being on the same wavelength as Jesus means cultivating a self-sacrificial lifestyle and pattern of behavior.

Though it would have been seen otherwise by many of Jesus and Paul's contemporaries, both of them thought that it took a person of strong character, not weak character, to assume the role and functions of a servant. Christ came to his human tasks from a position of divine authority and strength; and yet he set aside his divine prerogatives and status, though not his divine nature, in order to fully assume the form of a human being. In the Incarnation Christ did not become less than he was before, but more. Likewise our being a servant of others does not make us less than human or less than we were before, but more. We are called to model ourselves after Christ, who humbled himself and became a servant for our sake.

READING THE SCRIPTURE

NRSV
Philippians 2:1-13

1 If then there is any encouragement in Christ, any consolation from love, any sharing in the Spirit, any compassion and sympathy, 2 make my joy complete: be of the same mind, having the same love, being in full accord and of one mind. 3 Do nothing from selfish ambition or conceit, but in humility regard others as better than yourselves. 4 Let each of you look not to your own interests, but to the interests of others. **5 Let the same mind be in you that was in Christ Jesus,**

    6 who, though he was in the form
      of God,
      did not regard equality with
        God
      as something to be exploited,
    7 but emptied himself,
      taking the form of a slave,
      being born in human likeness.
    And being found in human form,
      8 he humbled himself
      and became obedient to the
        point of death—
      even death on a cross.
    9 Therefore God also highly
        exalted him
      and gave him the name
      that is above every name,

NIV
Philippians 2:1-13

1If you have any encouragement from being united with Christ, if any comfort from his love, if any fellowship with the Spirit, if any tenderness and compassion, 2then make my joy complete by being like-minded, having the same love, being one in spirit and purpose. 3Do nothing out of selfish ambition or vain conceit, but in humility consider others better than yourselves. 4Each of you should look not only to your own interests, but also to the interests of others.

    5Your attitude should be the same as that of Christ Jesus:
    6Who, being in very nature God,
      did not consider equality with
        God something to be grasped,
    7but made himself nothing,
      taking the very nature of a servant,
      being made in human likeness.
    8And being found in appearance as a
        man,
      he humbled himself
      and became obedient to death—
      even death on a cross!
    9Therefore God exalted him to the
        highest place
      and gave him the name that is
      above every name,

Key
Verse

Ke
Ve

10 so that at the name of Jesus
    every knee should bend,
    in heaven and on earth and
    under the earth,
11 and every tongue should confess
    that Jesus Christ is Lord,
    to the glory of God the Father.

12 Therefore, my beloved, just as you
have always obeyed me, not only in my
presence, but much more now in my
absence, work out your own salvation
with fear and trembling; 13 for it is God
who is at work in you, enabling you both
to will and to work for his good pleasure.

[10]that at the name of Jesus every knee
    should bow,
    in heaven and on earth and under
    the earth,
[11]and every tongue confess that Jesus
    Christ is Lord,
    to the glory of God the Father.
[12]Therefore, my dear friends, as you have
always obeyed—not only in my presence,
but now much more in my absence—continue to work out your salvation with fear
and trembling, [13]for it is God who works in
you to will and to act according to his good
purpose.

UNDERSTANDING THE SCRIPTURE

Introduction. Philippians 2:1-4 announces
the essential proposition for which Paul
will be arguing throughout Philippians,
namely, for Christlike behavior that produces unity in the Philippian church. This
opening is followed by an example of
what this behavior looks like in 2:5-11,
then by a concluding exhortation to exhibit
servantlike behavior based on the example
of Christ and also on the examples of Paul
and his coworkers. Philippians 2:6-11
appears to be an edited quotation of an
early christological hymn that took a V
pattern. Christ is presented as the one who
came down from above, ministered on
earth, and then returned to the right hand
of God.

Philippians 2:1-4. The translation of the
very first phrase of this conditional statement is debatable. I would translate it not
as the NRSV has it, but "If then [there is]
any appeal in [the example] of Christ...."
Paul is here setting up what he is going to
say in Philippians 2:5 and what he is following when he appeals to the example of
Christ. The phrase "any sharing in the
Spirit" presents us with the Greek concept
of *koinonia*. This word is often translated as

"fellowship," but it normally has the more
active sense of a participating or sharing
something in common with some individual or group. Fellowship would be the
result of such sharing, but Paul is speaking
about the process that produces it.

Philippians 2:5-11. Philippians 2:5 introduces the hymnic material in 2:6-11. It
indicates that the preexistent Son of God
while still in heaven made a decision
about what form his ministry would take
when he came to earth. This decision then
was acted out when he took on the form of
a servant and lived a self-forgetful life,
being obedient to God. The word form in
this case means the outward, visible manifestation of what a person truly is by
nature. Thus, Christ was in the condition
of being equal to God. He had all the
divine prerogatives and status but set
those privileges and that status aside so
that he could become a human being and
take on the form of a servant.

The first stanza of the hymn, found in
2:6-8, focuses on the downward motion
Christ took—from heaven to earth, from
being human to being a servant of
humans, from being a servant to becoming

a sacrifice, being obedient unto death on the cross. The stress on obedience unto death reflects Paul's view that Christ always acted in accordance with God's will, even to the point of giving up his life when it was required. The emphasis on obedience also mirrors the apostle's view that death on the cross was part of God's plan for Christ's life so that the world might be redeemed. Throughout this stanza the focus is on what Christ chose to do and did.

In contrast, the second stanza of the hymn in 2:9-11 focuses on the upward movement of the Christ, on what God did for Jesus because He faithfully carried out His earthly mission. The word *therefore* in Philippians 2:9 indicates a conclusion Paul draws on the basis of what has just been said. God exalted Christ because Christ perfectly followed and fulfilled God's will. The exaltation amounted not just to giving Christ an honored place in heaven but also to giving Christ the divine name *Lord*. The author is stressing that the ineffable name is one of the divine names, in this case the term *Lord*, that was granted to Jesus at his exaltation. It was at that point that he came to be known as the risen Lord. Probably the earliest and most basic confession of early Christians was that Jesus is (the risen) Lord.

Philippians 2:12-13. This passage returns to the exhortations, only this time on the basis of the example of Christ just presented in the previous passage. Philippians 2:12 is first, directed to those who are already Christians. Paul is not urging salvation by works here but rather working out the salvation one already has through God's work within. Second, the exhortation uses the plural form of "you." This exhortation is intended for the group

of Christians in Philippi so that they might help each other work out their salvation with fear and awe. Paul is not exhorting individual Christians to try to accomplish such a task on their own.

Paul is firmly convinced that God gives humans the desire, enables their will, and then provides them with the strength to carry out what God wills for Christians. Paul believes that God provides persons with the energy, impetus, strength, and determination to work out salvation.

Philippians 2:14-18. Paul speaks about the kind of behavior that leads to factions and splits within the body of Christ. He is probably thinking of the wilderness-wandering generation of the Exodus who murmured against God, and so Paul is telling his audience not to follow their example. Verse 16 envisions a scenario where Paul stands before the throne of God and boasts to God about his converts. Paul does not see this sort of boasting or taking pride in others as being in opposition to the principles of Christian humility. If the Philippians hold fast, then Paul will not have undertaken his mission—or as the athletic metaphor suggests, run his missionary race—in vain. Verse 17 presents us with another vivid metaphor: the pouring out of a drink offering over a sacrifice. Paul sees himself as the drink offering, perhaps at the point of being poured out; that is, he considers the possibility that he is about to die. Paul says that he is willing to die to make the Philippians' sacrifices a perfect and acceptable offering to God, if need be. (For a further exploration of this idea, see my commentary, *Friendship and Finances in Philippi*, Trinity Press, 1994.) The Philippians should rejoice because even if Paul loses his earthly life in the service of Christ, he will not have died in vain.

INTERPRETING THE SCRIPTURE

An Example of Sacrifice

When I was a VISTA (Volunteers in Service to America) aid in the mountains of North Carolina, on one occasion I had the opportunity to work with mountain children. It was Easter time and my task was to go out and visit poor families and try and convince the parents to let their children come to some Easter parties and functions we were planning. One extremely poor family lived way back in the woods, and their small children had never been away from home to play with other children. I was immediately struck by their young son Carl, who was about five. He was afraid, but he really wanted to come to the party and meet other children. After some persuasion the mother gave us permission to bring the truck and come get him early on a Saturday morning.

When we arrived at the house Carl was sitting on the old wooden front porch, his face scrubbed clean. He was wearing the only jacket and decent pants and shoes he had. His mother said he had been sitting there, waiting, since before dawn. As I got down from the truck and went to pick up Carl, he came up to me and handed me a large goose egg. He said it was for the other kids who didn't have any Easter eggs. Carl only had one real prize possession—his goose and what it produced—but here he was giving me a large egg for "those less fortunate." In Carl, I saw the form of one who came among us as a servant, prepared to sacrifice what he had for the good of others.

Following the V Pattern

During World War II, V was the symbol flashed by Winston Churchill and others for victory. In a sense that is what we find here in this Christ hymn that has been incorporated into the letter to the Philippians. The road to glory for Christ paradoxically involved setting aside glory, living as a human being, and enduring a humiliating death. Only after suffering and death did Jesus experience victory and receive accolades. This pattern has been one that many Christian martyrs followed, and we see in Philippians 1:20-26 that Paul himself anticipated that he would follow this path as well.

One of the issues this text from Philippians raises for us is whether or not we are prepared to die for what we believe in. Perhaps it is true that no one can be absolutely certain how he or she would respond if suddenly called upon either to renounce the Christian faith or to die. Yet it is also true that Christians can cultivate an attitude of obedience to God's will and a mindset in which we are prepared to face either living or dying with an understanding that either prospect, in God's hands, can be a rewarding one. Christ's example of self-sacrificial service can model for us not just how we should die but also how we should live. Christ shows us the importance of putting others and their needs ahead of ourselves and our own desires. This service is, of course, not a natural thing to do, but it is something that by God's grace we can accomplish.

Humility

In Philippians 2:3-4 Paul exhorts his converts not to act on the basis of selfish motives or personal ambition, but in fact to regard others as one's superiors or betters. This stance has nothing to do with having a low sense of self-worth; it is simply a matter of placing others first, which is an attitude only a person of strong character can maintain. The natural tendency is of course to be selfish and self-centered.

Philippians 2:4 has an interesting history of translation. Some earlier translators couldn't imagine Paul suggesting we should be totally self-forgetful, and so they translated the verse "let each of you look not *only* to your own interests, but *also* to the interests of others." In fact, the Greek text does not have the words *only* and *also*. Paul is not merely calling his converts to an enlightened charitable attitude that regards others and self, but to a Christlike attitude where one is self-forgetful for the sake of others.

We have come to assume that Christian humility has to do with putting yourself down, but in fact as we see in this lesson it has to do with following the example of Christ and taking on the form of a servant, deliberately taking a lower place. Christian humility has nothing to do with feelings of low self-worth, or downplaying one's own abilities. It does have to do with having true self-knowledge, knowing what one's limits and abilities truly are. A humble person knows he or she is not God, but that person also knows he or she has been created in God's image and so is a person of sacred worth with a purpose in life. If Christ is the ultimate example of humility, I can think of no person who struggled less with low self-esteem. If there ever were a confident human being it was Jesus.

Humility is an action word in the New Testament. It refers to the action of a person who knows very well that he or she is not a slave, but deliberately takes on the form and roles of a servant, stepping down in society in order to lift others up. It is interesting that the Greek word we translate as *humility* literally means to have the mind of a slave or to be base-minded. From a Greco-Roman point of view this was no virtue but rather a character flaw. Here as elsewhere, Paul takes up negative or even pejorative language and gives it a positive sense. This is emblematic of the whole way the gospel of grace and the example of Christ works, lifting up that which has been put down.

For Paul to speak about humility and then in verse 16 say that he can boast may strike us as odd until we understand what it meant in the days of the early church. Boasting had been honed to a high art form. We find it in many inscriptions on columns and buildings and in documents from the first century A.D. Boasting was not seen as a bad thing, precisely because the medieval understanding of the Christian virtue of humility did not exist. Paul believes that there is indeed a place for words of praise for others, and there is even a place for speaking proudly of what one has accomplished for Christ. The Christian is called neither to false pride nor to false modesty.

SHARING THE SCRIPTURE

PREPARING TO TEACH

Preparing Our Hearts

Spend some quiet time reflecting on the humility of Jesus, who left his exalted place to come to earth as a human being to seek, save, and serve us. What does his humility indicate about how you are to live as his follower?

Turn now to today's devotional reading from 2 Peter 3:8-18. Note that this passage speaks about the coming day of the Lord. Knowing that this day will come in God's own time, what are we to be doing in the meantime? How are we to live?

Look now at the background for today's lesson, found in Philippians 2:1-18. These words will likely be very familiar. What does Paul tell us about the humility of Christ? As you consider what Christ did, what do you think you are being called to do? Will you humble yourself? Will you obey God's voice?

Pray that God will lead you and your students deeper into the mind of Christ.

Preparing Our Minds

Review the background scripture, looking especially at verses 1-13. Read this lesson in its entirety.

Pay particular attention to the hymn in verses 6-11. These are not Paul's words, but rather assumed to be part of a hymn from the early Christian church that he has included in his letter. Notice the V pattern as discussed in this lesson.

Preparing Our Learning Space

Have on hand:
- ✔ several Bibles
- ✔ newsprint and marker
- ✔ hymnals
- ✔ optional paper and pencils.

LEADING THE CLASS

(1) Introduction

Begin today's session by asking students to brainstorm answers to the following question. Record their answers on newsprint. On the left side of the paper write the answers to the first question and on the right side record answers to the second question. That way you will have a chart for easy comparison.

(1) In what ways can we imitate Christ?
(2) What aspects of Christ's life and work are we not able to imitate?

Use information from Focusing on the Main Question to help answer these questions and round out the discussion. Or, if you prefer, use that information as a lecture to open the session.

Wrap up the introduction by singing "Dear Jesus, in Whose Life I See" (*The United Methodist Hymnal*, no. 468), or "Lord, Whose Love Through Humble Ser-

vice" (*UMH*, no. 581), or another hymn that you have available that lifts up Jesus as our model for living.

(2) An Example of Sacrifice

Read the charming story of the young boy ⌐arl, which is found in Interpreting the Scripture under "An Example of Sacrifice." Encourage the students to try to visualize this true story as you tell it. Then ask:

(1) What do you think Carl might look like?
(2) What does his desire to share his goose egg say about his character?
(3) What would you have said to Carl had you been the one who was entrusted with the egg to be given to "those less fortunate"?
(4) How is this five-year-old like Christ?

If time permits, invite class members to share similar stories of sacrifice that touched their hearts.

(3) Following the V Pattern

To hear the pattern in today's scripture lesson, assign readers as follows: reader 1: verses 1-5 and 12-13; reader 2: verse 6; reader 3: verses 7-8; reader 4: verses 9-11. As the scripture is being read aloud, ask the students to concentrate on where Christ is and on what is happening to him.

Talk with the students about the pattern that they heard. Augment the discussion with information from Understanding the Scripture. Be sure these points are made:
- Paul appeals to the Philippians to follow the example of Christ.
- Verse 5, which introduces what is thought to be an ancient hymn of the church, encourages Christians to be of the same mind as Christ.
- Verse 6 states the high estate of Christ, who was equal to God.
- Verses 7-8 show the downward pattern of Christ's descent to earth. He came as

a human being to be a humble slave who was willing to die in obedience to God's will.

- Verses 9-11 demonstrate the upward pattern, speaking about God's exaltation of Christ. All persons will come to confess, just as the early church did, "that Jesus Christ is Lord."
- Verses 12-13 call the church to work out their salvation while constantly relying on God's help.

(4) Humility

Return now to the beginning of today's text by asking the students to look at verses 3-4. If several translations of the Bible are available, ask students to read from each of them. Then invite the class members to talk with a partner or small group to discern what this passage means to them. You may want to distribute paper and pencils and ask each person to write these two verses in their own words.

Raise these questions for discussion:

(1) **What does Paul say is to be our motive for acting?**

(2) **Do you think it is possible to set aside one's own motives entirely so as to act foremost in the interest of others? Explain your answer.**

(3) **How do you define *humility*?** (Make sure the students understand that humility has nothing to do with self-deprecation or low self-esteem. Instead, Paul is referring to a Christlike attitude where one is self-forgetful for the sake of others.)

Direct the group's attention to verses 12-13. Encourage the students to comment on how these verses relate to the theme of humility. To help the class members make this connection, which at first glance may not be apparent, ask them to turn to these references to "fear and trembling" for help in discerning Paul's meaning of this phrase. (What Paul is speaking of here is humility and dependence on God.)

- 1 Corinthians 2:3
- 2 Corinthians 7:15
- Ephesians 6:5

Look next at the phrase "work out your own salvation" (2:12). As noted in the Understanding the Scripture portion, the "you" of this exhortation is in the plural. It is intended for the whole community of faith and is not to be understood as a command for one person to work out his or her individual faith. One must have a humble attitude toward other Christians in order for the group to work together.

In short, God is working through the humble and obedient, that is, those who have the mind of the humble Christ.

Conclude this section by asking the students to close their eyes and imagine what the church would be like in each of the situations you will read aloud.

- Imagine what our congregation would be like if everyone took seriously Paul's call to "do nothing from selfish ambition or conceit." (pause)
- Imagine what our congregation would be like if everyone "in humility" regarded others as better than themselves. (pause)
- Imagine what our congregation would be like if everyone let the same mind that was in Christ Jesus be in them. (pause)

While the students still have their eyes closed, offer a prayer that God will help each of you to put on the mind of Christ so that you might humbly and obediently serve God by serving one another.

As you close today's session, lift up at least one of the activities below so that students will have some ideas about how to respond to today's lesson.

HELPING CLASS MEMBERS ACT

Recommend that the students pray about one or more difficult situations that have developed in the church because an individual or group put their self-interests ahead of the best interest of the congregation.

Encourage class members to offer themselves in sacrificial service this week to at least one person in need.

Challenge the students to commit Philippians 2:5-11 to memory. If they can just learn one verse per day, while reviewing verses from the previous day(s), they will know the entire passage by the end of the week.

PLANNING FOR NEXT SUNDAY

Next week's lesson, "Striving to Be Christlike," focuses on Philippians 3:7-21. Ask the students to read all of the background scripture from chapter 3. There they will find the familiar image of Paul pressing on in Christ to reach the goal. Encourage the class members to think of a metaphor for their own spiritual journey.

STRIVING TO BE CHRISTLIKE

PREVIEWING THE LESSON

Lesson Scripture: Philippians 3:7-21
Background Scripture: Philippians 3
Key Verse: Philippians 3:14

Focus of the Lesson:
Paul encouraged believers to press on toward Christlike lives by steadfastly following Christ's example.

Main Question of the Lesson:
How shall Christians live?

This lesson will enable adult learners to:
(1) recognize that Christ is the model for all Christians.
(2) examine the way they are running the Christian race.
(3) respond by pressing on toward perfection in their own lives.

Today's lesson may be outlined as follows:
(1) Introduction
(2) Be Joyful in Suffering
(3) Focus on the Main Thing
(4) Press On to Perfection
(5) Reach the Goal

FOCUSING ON THE MAIN QUESTION

How shall Christians live? The discussion is not primarily about how one becomes a Christian, but rather about how one presses on to the goal of "perfection," by which is meant full conformity to the image of Christ. Paul will contrast two ways of pursuing this goal. The first is that practiced by some very conservative Jewish Christians, usually called Judaizers. They believe that all Christians, even Gentile Christians, should submit to circumcision and live by the Mosaic Law, including all its ritual requirements. In contrast, Paul believes that having a righteousness of our own, or adding up the sum of the laws we have kept, will never achieve the aim of perfection or full conformity to God's will. Rather, Paul believes that the Christian must live by grace and appropriate the righteousness of Christ through faith.

This status of having right-standing with God comes to the Christian not through his or her own obedience to God, but rather through the faithfulness of Christ, through what Christ accomplished on the cross for sinners. Christian life is to consist of knowing Christ and living by the resurrection power he bequeaths to believers. Paul also believes it is possible to live by faith expectantly, looking forward to the day when Christ will return and transform believers into full confor-

mity with His image by means of the resurrection from the dead (see Philippians 3:11). In other words, Christian life involves understanding that we cannot achieve perfection; it can only be bestowed upon us if in the end God in Christ ultimately and finally transforms us. Nevertheless, Paul also believes that Christians are called upon to imitate or follow the example of Christ in the meantime. To follow His example may entail sharing in Christlike suffering.

READING THE SCRIPTURE

NRSV
Philippians 3:7-21

7 Yet whatever gains I had, these I have come to regard as loss because of Christ. 8 More than that, I regard everything as loss because of the surpassing value of knowing Christ Jesus my Lord. For his sake I have suffered the loss of all things, and I regard them as rubbish, in order that I may gain Christ 9 and be found in him, not having a righteousness of my own that comes from the law, but one that comes through faith in Christ, the righteousness from God based on faith. 10 I want to know Christ and the power of his resurrection and the sharing of his sufferings by becoming like him in his death, 11 if somehow I may attain the resurrection from the dead.

12 Not that I have already obtained this or have already reached the goal; but I press on to make it my own, because Christ Jesus has made me his own. 13 Beloved, I do not consider that I have made it my own; but this one thing I do: forgetting what lies behind and straining forward to what lies ahead, **14 I press on toward the goal for the prize of the heavenly call of God in Christ Jesus.** 15 Let those of us then who are mature be of the same mind; and if you think differently about anything, this too God will reveal to

NIV
Philippians 3:7-21

[7]But whatever was to my profit I now consider loss for the sake of Christ. [8]What is more, I consider everything a loss compared to the surpassing greatness of knowing Christ Jesus my Lord, for whose sake I have lost all things. I consider them rubbish, that I may gain Christ [9]and be found in him, not having a righteousness of my own that comes from the law, but that which is through faith in Christ—the righteousness that comes from God and is by faith. [10]I want to know Christ and the power of his resurrection and the fellowship of sharing in his sufferings, becoming like him in his death, [11]and so, somehow, to attain to the resurrection from the dead.

[12]Not that I have already obtained all this, or have already been made perfect, but I press on to take hold of that for which Christ Jesus took hold of me. [13]Brothers, I do not consider myself yet to have taken hold of it. But one thing I do: Forgetting what is behind and straining toward what is ahead, **[14]I press on toward the goal to win the prize for which God has called me heavenward in Christ Jesus.**

[15]All of us who are mature should take such a view of things. And if on some point you think differently, that too God

Key Verse

you. 16 Only let us hold fast to what we have attained.

17 Brothers and sisters, join in imitating me, and observe those who live according to the example you have in us. 18 For many live as enemies of the cross of Christ; I have often told you of them, and now I tell you even with tears. 19 Their end is destruction; their god is the belly; and their glory is in their shame; their minds are set on earthly things. 20 But our citizenship is in heaven, and it is from there that we are expecting a Savior, the Lord Jesus Christ. 21 He will transform the body of our humiliation that it may be conformed to the body of his glory, by the power that also enables him to make all things subject to himself.

will make clear to you. [16]Only let us live up to what we have already attained.

[17]Join with others in following my example, brothers, and take note of those who live according to the pattern we gave you. [18]For, as I have often told you before and now say again even with tears, many live as enemies of the cross of Christ. [19]Their destiny is destruction, their god is their stomach, and their glory is in their shame. Their mind is on earthly things. [20]But our citizenship is in heaven. And we eagerly await a Savior from there, the Lord Jesus Christ, [21]who, by the power that enables him to bring everything under his control, will transform our lowly bodies so that they will be like his glorious body.

UNDERSTANDING THE SCRIPTURE

Introduction. Following the pattern of positive and negative examples we noted on June 4, Paul will again appeal to the Philippians to model themselves on Christ and other Christian leaders such as Paul himself. All of chapter 3 is part of one extended argument that continues until Philippians 4:1.

Philippians 3:1-11. The chapter begins with a theme that characterizes this entire letter: joy. While not a uniquely Christian trait, joy can and should characterize the Christian life. When Paul speaks about joy he is not referring to the effect of external circumstances on believers, or for that matter the absence of negative circumstances or situations. In Paul's view joy is produced by the presence of God in the Christian's life, and, therefore, it can exist quite apart from one's bodily state or external circumstances. Paul was a joyful person despite enduring great suffering. The word for joy in the Greek comes ultimately from the same root as the word for grace. In Paul's mind the latter is what produces the former in the Christian's life.

In Philippians 3:2 we find a warning—"beware of the dogs." Paul chose this pejorative, metaphorical language to encourage his audience to reject the overtures of the Judaizers, also known as the circumcision party. The term *dog* was often a slur word used against other ethnic groups or individuals in Paul's day (see for example Matthew 15:26). Paul uses this strong language in an effort to safeguard his converts from an influence he believed was potentially very negative and dangerous. Paul's view, as both Philippians 3:3-4 and most of Galatians show, is that the Christian already has the benefits in Christ that some might claim could be obtained by obedience to the law. Paul contrasts human actions or accomplishments with what God has accomplished for us in and through the death of Christ. However notable human accomplishments may be, they do not procure salvation, much less perfection; but the actions of Christ did in fact obtain such benefits. Thus the apostle, using himself as an example, contrasts what would be seen as a notable record and status from a Jewish point of view with what Paul had obtained through faith in Christ and his saving actions. Measured by human standards, Paul was a Hebrew among Hebrews and could even claim that he had not willfully violated God's law. Paul dramatically casts off his past accomplishments and status by calling it *skubala* in Philippians 3:8, a word that can mean spoiled food or garbage or even human excrement.

In Philippians 3:9 we find a much-debated phrase that reads literally "through faith of Christ." This phrase could mean either through faith in Christ, or through the faithfulness of Christ. Since the contrast in this passage is not between our faith and our works, but rather between our own efforts and those of Christ on our behalf, I would conclude that the proper translation is "through the faithfulness of Christ," by which is meant through what Christ accomplished for us on the cross (compare Philippians 2:8 and 3:18).

Philippians 3:10-11 makes clear that Paul does not see resurrection as something that Christians have already experienced, for example at the point of conversion, but rather something they look to obtain in the future.

Philippians 3:12-16. This passage deals with the concept of perfection, completion, or fulfillment. Paul is referring to Christians' obtaining the condition or state God always intended for them. In Paul's view this perfection amounts to being fully conformed to the image of Christ, not merely in spirit, but even in the body, by means of the experience of the resurrection.

This experience does not come in this life unless Christ should return before one dies. Like many early Pharisaic Jews, Paul believed that this experience of resurrection would occur in this world when history ended. For Paul the ultimate destiny and destination of Christians is not heaven (an interim condition inhabited until God chooses to conclude human history), but rather the kingdom of God that will one day finally and fully come on earth as it

already exists in heaven. What all this means is that in Paul's view perfection could not be obtained in our present condition in this life, but that nevertheless we should all be pressing on toward that goal of full conformity to Christ's image in conduct and character. Philippians 3:14 provides another example of Paul's use of the athletic metaphor of running to characterize Christian living. Here he refers to the finish line, and to the fact that a smart runner will not waste time and energy looking back but will concentrate on the finish line in order to obtain the prize.

Philippians 3:15 returns to the theme of how one thinks about oneself, and Paul is urging reflection before action. He says that the right-thinking Christian person will be aware of the current stage of his or her Christian pilgrimage and likewise aware that full perfection has not yet been obtained.

Philippians 3:17-21. Paul again reminds the Philippians to follow his example, which is patterned after the example of Christ, while shunning the example of "the enemies of the cross." These "enemies" preach that circumcision and obedience to the Mosaic Law must be added to faith in Christ in order to experience the pattern for Christian living. Verse 19 speaks about these enemies glorying in their shame, a euphemistic way of saying they are boasting about their private parts, and in particular about the fact that they are circumcised.

In Philippians 3:20 Paul states that the Christian's constituting government and citizenship is in heaven, not on earth. The point is that the Philippians should not be taking their cues on how to live from Greco-Roman culture but rather from Christ, who rules his people from heaven and sets the example for them. Christians are pilgrims on earth but also citizens of God's realm, and it is well to keep in mind our chief ruling principles. According to verses 20-21, the completion of salvation comes in the future when Christ returns and Christians receive a resurrection body.

INTERPRETING THE SCRIPTURE

Be Joyful in Suffering

Since Philippians is largely an argument for following good examples and shunning bad ones, we could use examples of the same sort that Paul does to illustrate and apply the principles found in this text. Stories abound that illustrate Christian qualities such as joy. Moreover, church history records numerous examples of Christlike persons, as well as of those who would turn the Christian life into something that focuses primarily on human effort and achievement rather than on grace and what Christ has accomplished for us on the cross.

One such story of joyous, Christlike persons comes to us from a legendary record. Nero decided that he would throw some Christians to the wild beasts, crucify some, and set others on fire to illuminate the nighttime sky in the Roman arena. The emperor was looking forward to the satisfaction he could obtain by again making Christians the scapegoats for the horrendous fire that destroyed about two-thirds of Rome in the summer of A.D 64. Instead of the screams and pleading in the arena that Nero expected, what he heard was the doomed Christians all singing joyful hymns to Christ and God. The story goes that this response so maddened Nero that he went down into the arena mumbling, "Why are they singing?" When he looked into the faces of some who were already dead and hanging from a cross, he noticed that some had smiles on their faces and he began to ask, "Why are they smiling? What sort of people are these?"

Paul could have told him that joy and peace and love come from the experience of Christ within, not primarily from one's external state or circumstances. Indeed, the signal witness to the reality of God's presence in these Christians' lives was their ability to sing and be joyful despite their circumstances. Such a quality is not natural, but it can be real by the supernatural grace of God working in a human life. To gain Christ is a joyous experience even when believers are called to share in his sufferings.

Focus on the Main Thing

President Maxie Dunnam of Asbury Theological Seminary has a saying, "Keep the main thing, the main thing." By this he means that it is always necessary to keep things in proper Christian perspective, neither overemphasizing less important matters nor underemphasizing more important ones. The Christian life is a matter of a proper ordering of priorities. It is important not to put the emphasis on the wrong syllable. In Paul's view, though he had many notable accomplishments and privileges while he was a non-Christian Jew, including a record for zeal and devotion for God's law that was second to none, in the eternal scheme of things all of this was eclipsed by and counted as nothing in comparison to knowing Christ and the power of his resurrection. Paul is not saying here (nor does he elsewhere) that the law, or obedience to the law, is a bad thing. He is simply stating that since Christ has come the former modes of following God's will have become obsolete or, in some cases, far less important. From Paul's perspective the problem with the Judaizers was that they did not make the main thing, the main thing. They saw obedience to the law, rather than the following of the example of Christ, as the basis of daily Christian life. Thus, they did not consider those who did not undergo circumcision and keep the whole law to be authentic Christians.

Press On to Perfection

For Paul, going on to perfection was a matter first of understanding that we are saved by grace and then patterning ourselves after the example of Christ and other positive Christian witnesses. Believers look forward to the day when they will reach the finish line and finally conform fully to the image of the resurrected Christ. In the meantime, the image Paul uses of an athlete pressing ahead, straining forward, and focusing on the finish line is valuable for the Christian life. It suggests that being truly Christlike requires our full effort, every fiber of our being. It has been suggested that in a sinful world being a Christian is like walking up a greased incline. The journey requires both maximum reliance on God and maximum personal effort just to make progress.

In 1990, 1993, and 1996 I ran three different marathons, one in Cleveland, one in Boston, and one in my home city of Charlotte. Clearly the most memorable of these was running and finishing the Boston Marathon. I still have vivid images of seeing the elite runners at the head of the pack before the race started. There were Kenyans, Nigerians, Ethiopians, Italians, Americans, and many others. None of them looked as though they had an ounce of extra body fat. All of them appeared tremendously fit and prepared for what they were about to undertake. They understood that the task was arduous and even painful, but they also knew that the potential rewards were high. Paul felt the same way about the Christian life. Though there might well be persecution and great suffering, nevertheless the eternal reward far outweighed such factors. Human suffering is both temporal and temporary, whereas eternal life in Christ begins here and now but continues on unto eternity.

While running the Boston marathon I saw numerous profiles in courage. For example I witnessed a father pushing his quadriplegic son in a wheelchair the entire twenty-six miles of the race. When I got to Heartbreak Hill a lady who was surely over seventy hollered at me, "Come on sonny, we can both make it." Even when

you have prepared for such a race and run many miles, once you get beyond fifteen miles the human body tells you in various ways that you ought to quit.

Running a lengthy race is not unlike the Christian life. Not only does it take strenuous effort to live out Christian principles and follow Christ's example, but along the way there are plenty of external hills and internal psychological blockades that would encourage you to quit. Your hills and blockades may not be the same as Paul's: you may not personally be called upon to endure persecution for Christ, but your obstacles will nonetheless be just as real and you will have just as much opportunity as Paul did to rely on God's grace to overcome them.

Reach the Goal

I shall never forget what it felt like to cross the finish line in downtown Boston. It was a beautiful day at about five in the afternoon. Thousands were standing along the side of the road cheering, and at the finish line was my best friend waiting for me as I collapsed. Although I was exhausted and every bone in my body ached, I felt tremendous joy and exhilaration. I kept repeating to myself, "I have fought the good fight, run the good race, and finished the course." All the training and effort had been worth it.

Running the race was a lonely experience. I had no friends to run with, I knew no one else in the race, and no one could run the race for me. The Christian life is also often a lonely and arduous race. One cannot cross the finish line on the basis of someone else's effort. As I reached the end, though, I had nurses wrapping me in warm blankets, my friend congratulating me, and others taking pictures. One of the things that had kept me going during the marathon was knowing that my friend Rick would be there at the end waiting for me. To me, he was an emblem of Christ who meets Christians at the end of their earthly pilgrimage, welcomes them into the heavenly commonwealth, and pronounces the words of the judge of a race, "Well done, good and faithful servant, inherit the kingdom." All the preparation and sacrifice had been worth it.

The main thing Paul wants all his converts to realize is that they have been saved by God's grace and have been called to live on the basis of that grace day by day, working out their salvation as God works in them to will and to do.

SHARING THE SCRIPTURE

PREPARING TO TEACH

Preparing Our Hearts

Our devotional scripture for this week's lesson is found in Hebrews 10:19-25 and 32-36. Here, Christians are called to approach God in faith and worship, to hold fast to the public confession of their hope, and to consider how they can lovingly help one another. Moreover, the writer of Hebrews calls readers to persevere, to keep their confidence, and to endure. What places do these words touch in your life today? How can the writer's exhortations help you to be more like Christ?

Now look at our lesson's background scripture from Philippians 3. Notice especially Paul's perspective on what most people would consider gains, as well as his viewpoint on suffering. How does the image of the race help you envision the Christian life?

Pray that you and your students may be more Christlike as you press ahead in your journey of faith.

Preparing Our Minds

Review Philippians 3:7-21, which is the major passage for today's session. Read this lesson carefully.

You have noted that Paul uses athletic imagery here. He also uses it in Philippians 1:30 where the word translated as *struggle* is the basis for our words *agonist* (one engaged in a struggle or contest), *agonistic* (argumentative), and *agony* (intense pain, violent struggle, or contest). Philippians 2:16; 3:13-14; and 4:3 also contain images related to Greek athletic contests, as do 1 Corinthians 9:24-27 and Galatians 2:2 and 5:7.

Preparing Our Learning Space

Have on hand:
- ✔ several Bibles
- ✔ paper and pencils.

LEADING THE CLASS

(1) Introduction

One way to begin today's session is to read or retell the Focusing on the Main Question section.

Another way to start is to do this imaginary exercise with the class. Ask them to sit comfortably, close their eyes, and imagine the situation that you will describe by reading this information.

See yourself step up to the starting line of a race. You look around and see everyone else dressed in running shorts and a tank top. They are all wearing fancy running shoes. No one is carrying anything. In fact, your opponents are not even wearing watches. You, however, have arrived wearing hiking boots and a heavy jacket. You have a cumbersome pack strapped securely to your back and are carrying a lunch kit.

When the gun sounds, you set off just like everyone else. Within seconds they have all shot past you. You realize you can't possibly win, but you do want to make it to the finish line. You drop the lunch kit. Soon you jettison the backpack and then the coat. Finally, you kick off the boots and run in your stocking feet. The other runners are a distant blur by now, but you persevere. Long after everyone else has completed the course, you finally cross the finish line, huffing and puffing.

You go and sit down for a few minutes to catch your breath and think. Yes, you did make it to the end, and that feels good. But somehow you weren't as prepared as everyone else.

What baggage in your life do you have to get rid of in order to press on in the race for Christ? (pause)

What protective clothing that you have wrapped around your body and soul do you need to throw off to be able to press on unfettered? (pause)

What lifestyle changes do you need to make to be prepared to run the race for Christ? (pause)

Tell the students to open their eyes when they are ready. Invite anyone who has gained new insights from this activity to share them with the class.

Move to today's lesson by mentioning that Paul calls us to press on in Christ. We are to be mature, well-prepared runners who have set aside all else to follow the example of Christ. Our main question for today is this: **How shall Christians live?**

(2) Be Joyful in Suffering

Note that in Philippians 3:1, Paul calls his readers to "rejoice in the Lord." These words may seem glib or easy to follow until we read verses 7-11. Ask someone to read these verses aloud.

Now read or retell the second and third paragraphs of "Be Joyful in Suffering" under Interpreting the Scripture. Invite students to share other stories about persons who were joyful witnesses to Christ in the face of suffering. Then ask:

(1) **What kind of impact does the witness of someone who is joyful even in the face of suffering make on others?**
(2) **What does such a witness say to you about the power of Christ?**
(3) **How does such a witness encourage you to press on to be more like Christ?**

(3) Focus on the Main Thing

Choose a volunteer to read Philippians 3:12-16. Add this quotation from Maxie Dunnam: "Keep the main thing, the main thing." Then ask:

(1) **What would Paul say is the main thing?** (Notice in verse 14 that he focuses on "the prize of the heavenly call of God in Christ Jesus.")
(2) **Paul uses action words to describe a race: "press on," "forgetting," "straining." What do these words reveal about how one gets to the goal?**
(3) **How is Paul's description of the Christian life similar to and different from the way most people that you know live?**
(4) **What changes would you need to make if you were to set your own priorities in proper order so as to "keep the main thing, the main thing"?**

(4) Press On to Perfection

Ask volunteers to read Philippians 3:10-12 from the NRSV and NIV. Also read it as it appears in the REB (Revised English Bible): "My one desire is to know Christ and the power of his resurrection, and to share his sufferings in growing conformity with his death, in hope of somehow attaining the resurrection from the dead. It is not that I have already achieved this. I have not yet reached perfection, but I press on, hoping to take hold of that for which Christ once took hold of me."

Make these points:
• The word translated as *perfection* does not mean that we never make mistakes.

Rather, it refers to "completion" or "fulfillment."

- Christians who wish to reach perfection or completion must first recognize that they are saved by grace and then pattern themselves after the example of Christ and other witnesses.
- Believers look forward to the day when they will reach the finish line and finally conform to the image of the resurrected Christ.

(5) Reach the Goal

Distribute paper and pencils. Ask the students to try to remember some goals that they had as a young adult and to list these on the paper. Call for a few volunteers to share what they have written. Now ask:

?

(1) **Who were your role models as you tried to achieve your goals?**
(2) **How many of you have reached at least one of the goals that you set for yourself in your teens or early twenties?**
(3) **How did you feel when you reached that milestone?**
(4) **What did you do to celebrate?**
(5) **How do you perceive reaching that goal to be similar to reaching "the prize of the heavenly call of God in Christ Jesus" (Philippians 3:14, today's key verse)? How is it different?**

?

If your class does not like to share personal information, read or retell "Reach the Goal" in Interpreting the Scripture.

As you close today's session, be sure to suggest at least one of the activities that students can do during the week.

HELPING CLASS MEMBERS ACT

Challenge students to meditate on Philippians 3:10-12 and discern how they are pressing on toward the goal of perfection, that is, to conformity to the image of Christ.

Encourage the class to think about persons who have been or currently are role models for them. What qualities do the students find so appealing that they want to emulate? How are these qualities reflections of Christ?

Recommend that the group members list as many similarities as they can between running a race and living the Christian life. They may also want to think of things that slow down or distract runners. This athletic image may help some persons recognize their own strengths and weaknesses.

PLANNING FOR NEXT SUNDAY

Our first unit will end next week with a lesson entitled "Deep Joy." Ask the students to prepare for this session by reading Philippians 4:4-20. If you want to get ahead in your own preparations, you may want to read the letter to the Ephesians, which we will study during the second unit.

DEEP JOY

PREVIEWING THE LESSON

Lesson Scripture: Philippians 4:4-18
Background Scripture: Philippians 4:4-20
Key Verse: Philippians 4:4

Focus of the Lesson:
Paul taught others to rejoice in Christ; for joy, gentleness, refusing to worry, and prayer lead to God's peace.

Main Question of the Lesson:
What is the secret of facing all of life's trials and triumphs with an unconquerable spirit and in a graceful manner?

This lesson will enable adult learners to:
(1) examine the positive, life-enriching attitudes that Paul writes about.
(2) explore their own willingness to be content with what they have.
(3) respond by giving thanks.

Today's lesson may be outlined as follows:
(1) Introduction
(2) The Wings of a Prayer
(3) Christian Contentment
(4) Money Matters

FOCUSING ON THE MAIN QUESTION

Paul's main aim in Philippians 4 is to provide the Philippian Christians with some basic advice as to what their frame of mind and course of life should be as they grow in Christ and endure trials and temptations. The apostle seeks to help them overcome anxieties and concerns so as not to be paralyzed by fear as to what might happen to them as a result of their commitment to the gospel. Since being Christian could make them outcasts among their own people in Philippi, whether they had previously been Jews or Gentiles, Paul must provide his converts with coping skills and techniques. Thus, the main question today's lesson raises is this: **What is the secret of facing all of life's trials and triumphs with an unconquerable spirit and in a graceful manner?**

I have recently had the privilege of knowing a student who knew the secret. This remarkable man has a terrible degenerative disease that has confined him to a wheelchair and to a life of endless visits to doctors. Yet there he was preaching in Estes Chapel and offering a profound lesson not only by his words but by the very fact that that eternal treasure was shining through his very mortal and fragile vessel. He had learned that greater is He who is in us than any of the forces the world can throw at us. He had learned that if he has Christ's presence in his life, he can endure and prevail over even the most formidable challenges. He had learned how to be content with his condition because he knew his eternal position.

READING THE SCRIPTURE

NRSV
Philippians 4:4-18

Key Verse

4 Rejoice in the Lord always; again I will say, Rejoice. 5 Let your gentleness be known to everyone. The Lord is near. 6 Do not worry about anything, but in everything by prayer and supplication with thanksgiving let your requests be made known to God. 7 And the peace of God, which surpasses all understanding, will guard your hearts and your minds in Christ Jesus.

8 Finally, beloved, whatever is true, whatever is honorable, whatever is just, whatever is pure, whatever is pleasing, whatever is commendable, if there is any excellence and if there is anything worthy of praise, think about these things. 9 Keep on doing the things that you have learned and received and heard and seen in me, and the God of peace will be with you.

10 I rejoice in the Lord greatly that now at last you have revived your concern for me; indeed, you were concerned for me, but had no opportunity to show it. 11 Not that I am referring to being in need; for I have learned to be content with whatever I have. 12 I know what it is to have little, and I know what it is to have plenty. In any and all circumstances I have learned the secret of being well-fed and of going hungry, of having plenty and of being in need. 13 I can do all things through him who strengthens me. 14 In any case, it was kind of you to share my distress.

15 You Philippians indeed know that in the early days of the gospel, when I left

NIV
Philippians 4:4-18

⁴Rejoice in the Lord always. I will say it again: Rejoice! ⁵Let your gentleness be evident to all. The Lord is near. ⁶Do not be anxious about anything, but in everything, by prayer and petition, with thanksgiving, present your requests to God. ⁷And the peace of God, which transcends all understanding, will guard your hearts and your minds in Christ Jesus.

⁸Finally, brothers, whatever is true, whatever is noble, whatever is right, whatever is pure, whatever is lovely, whatever is admirable—if anything is excellent or praiseworthy—think about such things. ⁹Whatever you have learned or received or heard from me, or seen in me—put it into practice. And the God of peace will be with you.

¹⁰I rejoice greatly in the Lord that at last you have renewed your concern for me. Indeed, you have been concerned, but you had no opportunity to show it. ¹¹I am not saying this because I am in need, for I have learned to be content whatever the circumstances. ¹²I know what it is to be in need, and I know what it is to have plenty. I have learned the secret of being content in any and every situation, whether well fed or hungry, whether living in plenty or in want. ¹³I can do everything through him who gives me strength.

¹⁴Yet it was good of you to share in my troubles. ¹⁵Moreover, as you Philippians know, in the early days of your acquaintance with the gospel, when I set out from

Macedonia, no church shared with me in the matter of giving and receiving, except you alone. 16 For even when I was in Thessalonica, you sent me help for my needs more than once. 17 Not that I seek the gift, but I seek the profit that accumulates to your account. 18 I have been paid in full and have more than enough; I am fully satisfied, now that I have received from Epaphroditus the gifts you sent, a fragrant offering, a sacrifice acceptable and pleasing to God.

Macedonia, not one church shared with me in the matter of giving and receiving, except you only; [16]for even when I was in Thessalonica, you sent me aid again and again when I was in need. [17]Not that I am looking for a gift, but I am looking for what may be credited to your account. [18]I have received full payment and even more; I am amply supplied, now that I have received from Epaphroditus the gifts you sent. They are a fragrant offering, an acceptable sacrifice, pleasing to God.

UNDERSTANDING THE SCRIPTURE

Introduction. The material in Philippians 4:4-20 is a single literary unit in two major parts, 4:4-9 and 4:10-20. From a rhetorical standpoint this material forms a two-part peroration, the concluding exhortation in an ancient speech meant to appeal to the audience's emotions and remind them of the basic content of the letter. This letter's purpose was to produce unity both among the converts in Philippi and between Paul and all these converts, and to provide resources and advice so the community could continue to endure trials and difficulties.

Paul refers to basic Christian attitudes and actions to reinforce his earlier arguments. Roughly speaking, Philippians 4:4-9 focuses on attitudes and basic actions the Philippians must continue, while Philippians 4:10-20 discusses good things they have already done for Paul for which he thanks them, but without sounding as though he is asking for more aid. Paul models the contentment he is urging his audience to cultivate as an attitude toward life.

Philippians 4:4-9. This first part of the concluding exhortation draws on both typical Christian concepts and virtues, as well as on Greco-Roman virtues with which Paul's largely Gentile audience would be familiar. Joy has been a theme throughout

this letter, but notice that Paul is not exhorting the people to *feel* joyful, but rather to praise the Lord in all circumstances. Paul knew he could not exhort human feelings, but he could appeal to his audience to undertake certain actions, no matter how they felt. Paul believes that the best and most Christian of Greco-Roman virtues should continue to be practiced by all of them. He is not calling his converts to renounce all of the values of the culture in which they grew up, but rather he appeals to such familiar ideas as being "reasonable" in order to help them make the transition to a fully Christlike life. The word *epieikes*, which I would translate *sweet reasonableness* but which the NRSV translates in Philippians 4:5 as *gentleness*, refers to a person who is generously compassionate or loving. *Epieikes* amounts to showing concern and respect for others and giving them the benefit of the doubt; hence the translation *sweet reasonableness*. This is precisely the sort of practice necessary to produce unity among a fractured group of Christians.

Philippians 4:5b-6 has often been seen as a reference to the second coming of Christ, which some scholars have assumed Paul thought would necessarily happen in his own lifetime. However, this interpretation is probably wrong. It is likely we have a paraphrase here by Paul of Psalm 145:18-19, which says "The Lord is near to those who call on him" (compare Psalms 34:17-18 and 119:151). Paul is not talking about the temporal nearness of God's coming, but rather the Lord's spatial nearness, especially when God's people pray.

Paul calls upon the Christian to offer up petitions and prayers of thanksgiving instead of being anxious about things, and he promises that the shalom or peace of God will stand sentry over the Christian's heart and life as they each do so. Not the Roman army guarding Philippi, but the presence of God provides the believer protection from harm or anxiety.

Paul believes there is a direct connection between praying, sensing God's presence draw near when one does so, and that presence conveying a sense of calm and peace to the one who prays. The peace Paul has in mind is not so much the absence of activity or strife but rather the effect of God's all-powerful calming presence in the believer's life. Paul also believes that the Christian who prays with a thankful heart and bears in mind God's previous mercies and answers prays in the right spirit.

Philippians 4:8-9 provides the reader with a list of qualities, attitudes, and virtues upon which the Christian should continuously reflect and then seek to embody. What is most significant about Paul's treatment of these virtues is not so much that he draws on terms from Greek philosophy and ethics familiar to his audience, but that he believes the example of Christ has something unique and essential to add to such discussions. In fact, he believes that the character of Christ is the context in which such terms should be defined. Thus, when Paul goes on to urge the audience to imitate him as he imitates Christ, he believes that Christ is the definition of virtue and his example lurks in the background throughout this discussion. This list of virtues may be compared to what Paul says in Galatians 5:16-26 where

he makes clear that it is the Holy Spirit that produces Christian character in the believer. Yet Paul believes that a person emulates what he or she admires, and becomes what he or she dreams or reflects on. Therefore it is critical to ponder good things and attributes.

The key term in this list from the standpoint of traditional Greek virtues is *arete.* The term literally means "excellence," but it refers to moral excellence or human goodness and was seen by Stoic philosophers as the chief aim or end to which Christians should strive. Paul believed that the world was redeemable and had some redeeming qualities that Christians should also manifest. Paul's view was that Christianity was a world-transforming—not merely a world-denying—religion.

Philippians 4:10-20. Referring to contributions, credits, and debits, this passage involves technical language taken from the language of commerce and exchange. In Philippians 4:15 we find the phrase "giving and receiving," which refers to a commercial relationship between equals. This is a different sort of relationship than that between patron and client. What Paul is suggesting is that he and the Philippians are partners in the spread of the gospel. Paul did not request the aid that the Philippians gave him, but like others involved in such ancient reciprocal situations he believed that he must give the Philippians a good return on their investment. He also wanted to make clear that they owed him nothing at this point. In Philippians 4:18 Paul moves from the commercial to a sacrificial metaphor. He is suggesting that the giving the Philippians have been doing is in fact an act of worship, like a sacrifice, and one that is pleasing and acceptable to God.

This passage also includes several verses that are often mistranslated. A good example of this is Philippians 4:13, often translated, "I can do all things in him who strengthens me." Both the context of this verse and the content of it suggest that the proper translation is "I can cope with/ endure all things in him who strengthens me." Paul then is not saying that he is superhuman and can do anything just because he is a Christian. He is instead talking about his capacity to endure want and suffering and still remain faithful to God as long as God strengthens him during the ordeal. Paul sees flexibility as a key Christian asset, being able to survive both in plenty and in want, in triumph and during suffering.

INTERPRETING THE SCRIPTURE

The Wings of a Prayer

It is often said that prayer makes a difference or prayer is powerful, but this is to mistake the means for the end. It would be more appropriate to say that the God of prayer is powerful and makes a difference, especially in difficult and stressful situations.

A United Methodist bishop tells a story of a troublesome situation he encountered while he was the overseer of one of the conferences in the Southeastern Jurisdiction. A particular church was on the verge of splitting in two over various matters. An extremely heated and contentious discussion produced no progress toward a solution. The bishop left the boardroom momentarily to make a phone call to a friend and fellow minister named Bill, who was very unlike the bishop. This bishop was not only a minister but a scholar with an earned Ph.D. and a well-known author. Bill by contrast was a lay minister without a great deal of education. Nevertheless, Bill was one of the most powerful persons of prayer this bishop had ever met.

When the bishop called Bill he explained the situation and asked him to make the fifteen-mile trip to this church and come and pray with these people. Bill came quickly, went straight into the meeting room, called for quiet, and began to pray. After twenty minutes of earnest prayer, audible groans and weeping could be heard as the barriers started to break down and people began to lay aside their hostilities. By the time Bill had finished, the church members were weeping and embracing each other. Peace had descended on the congregation, indeed a peace that defies human explanation. God had heard Bill's prayer and drawn near to all those present, and the situation had suddenly changed.

God changes things in response to our prayers. The prayers themselves do not cause the change. Prayer is not some magic wand that one can wave and make things different. Prayer is conversation with God, and it can come in various forms—petitions, thanksgiving, praise. We of course are not informing God of something God does not already know. What is happening is that we are seeking to plug into God's will for us and hear that "still small voice." God has chosen to use our prayers to aid in implementing the divine will, and so we become partners with God in the work of redemption. God is not some sort of cosmic bellhop or genie who exists to answer our every wish or command. God will frequently say no to our prayers if they are not in accord with the divine will. "No" is indeed an answer to prayer, as is "not here," or "not now," or "not with this person," or "yes, but not yet." There is no such thing as unanswered prayer when we are talking about the conversation between someone in Christ earnestly seeking the aid or guidance of God and God in Christ.

Christian Contentment

During the time Trump Tower was under construction, an interviewer asked Donald Trump, "How much is enough?"

This entrepreneur who had made many millions responded, "A little bit more." This desire for more possessions, which in the end never bring any lasting satisfaction, is one of the besetting sins of America. Greed is not a virtue. Moreover, human beings can never secure their own futures, regardless of their assets. Paul says that he has learned the secret of being content with what he has and with whatever his situation permits him to have and do. This secret involves recognizing that God is ultimately in control of human history and our individual lives.

Paul does not say that all situations Christians face are good or of God, but he does believe that God can work all things together for good for those who love God. The apostle also believes that God can give him the power to cope with whatever the world may do to him. William Faulkner, in his Nobel Prize acceptance speech, said that he believed humankind would not merely endure but prevail. Paul believed this because he believed God could and would bestow the divine resources to make both contentment and prevailing possible.

Money Matters

The Bible has often been misquoted to say, "Money is the root of all evil." In fact, 1 Timothy 6:10 says, "For the love of money is a root of all kinds of evil." Paul understood that it was not money but one's attitude and actions that determined whether money would be a blessing or a curse.

In my home congregation in Charlotte we regularly had an every member canvas. There was a relatively prosperous lawyer on the every member canvas team who visited an elderly homebound widow living on a fixed income. When he came to the house he decided just to visit with the woman and not to ask her for a pledge toward the church's budget. After a friendly conversation about what the church was doing, the lawyer prepared to leave. The woman however stopped him and said, "Let me get my pledge." When the lawyer protested and said that in her circumstances it was not really necessary, the woman rebuked the lawyer and said, "Don't you deprive me of my sharing in the ministry of the Lord. I can't go much anymore to church but I still wish to support it." This woman had the same generosity of spirit the Philippians did, even though she had very little with which to be generous. She, like the Philippians, wanted to give as a meaningful way of participating in the cause of Christ.

Paul was grateful for the Philippians' support even though he did not absolutely need it. If the maxim that how a person handles his or her money tells us a lot about the character of that person is true, then the Philippians were generous to a fault. They manifested a spirit that said that their ultimate trust was in God, not in their bank accounts. Paul proclaims that God will supply all the Philippians' needs (4:19). He does not say that God will supply all their desires or wants—and there is a difference. Pastors and laypersons should never be ashamed to ask Christians to support worthwhile Christian ministries. As one United Methodist bishop used to say, parishioners are perfectly capable of protecting their own pocketbooks. The pastor does not need to assist them in this task by failing to appeal for funds when needed, or by rejecting funds when given.

Christians are people with unconquerable spirits who need not get caught up in all the anxieties of life and let those anxieties and fears dictate their beliefs and behavior, especially as regards the way they handle their money. Believers who have their priorities straight and have a spirit open to God and God's people will understand what is really critical in the Christian life and will act accordingly. No matter what the outward circumstances may be, Christians have a continuing spirit of joy and thanksgiving in their hearts that shines forth as a witness to all.

SHARING THE SCRIPTURE

PREPARING TO TEACH

Preparing Our Hearts

Today's devotional reading from 1 Thessalonians 1:2-10 is an expression of Paul's thankfulness that the members of the church in Thessalonica had persevered in the face of persecution. Have you ever faced persecution? If so, how did you handle it? If not, what resources do you think you have to cope with persecution if it should ever come?

Look now at today's lesson from Philippians 4:4-20. Use today's main question to guide your reading: **What is the secret of facing all of life's trials and triumphs with an unconquerable spirit and in a graceful manner?** How does Paul answer this question? Judging by your actions, how do you answer it?

Pray that God will give you and your students a deep joy that abides in all circumstances.

Preparing Our Minds

Review the scripture passage and read this lesson. Think about how Paul's instructions to mature Christians apply to your students and to you personally.

In the "Money Matters" section of the lesson you will be asked to help the class take an inventory of what the church gives. Check with your church finance committee or treasurer to obtain current information needed to answer the questions in this section.

Preparing Our Learning Space

Prior to class, write on newsprint the checklist found in the Introduction. Have on hand:
- several Bibles
- newsprint and marker
- hymnals.

LEADING THE CLASS

(1) Introduction

Begin today's session by reading or retelling the story of the young man who was able to prevail over serious illness because of his relationship with Christ. You will find this information in the second paragraph under Focusing on the Main Question.

Then lift up our main question for the lesson: **What is the secret of facing all of life's trials and triumphs with an unconquerable spirit and in a graceful manner?**

Post newsprint with the following words written on it:
joy
gentleness
lack of worry
peace
prayer
thanksgiving
contentment
good thoughts
trust in God
willingness to give

Invite the students to add to the list other words or phrases that come to mind in answer to today's main question. After they have done so, note that the words you provided reflect Paul's teaching that we will be studying today from Philippians 4.

(2) The Wings of a Prayer

Select a volunteer to read Philippians 4:4-7. Encourage the students to restate Paul's comments in their own words.

Then focus on prayer. Ask the class:

(1) **How do you define prayer?** (Be sure to help the students see that prayer is conversation with God.)

(2) **What do you expect when you pray?** (Many people expect God to answer prayers in the way that they want.

[?] However, God answers in accordance with the divine will. When we pray, we are simply plugging into God's will and awaiting that "still small voice.")

(3) What relationship do you experience between prayer and the peace that "surpasses all understanding" (4:7)?

Read the story of the bishop and prayer with a troubled congregation that is found in paragraphs two and three under "The Wings of a Prayer" in Interpreting the Scripture.

Provide a few moments of silence for the students to lift up prayers of their own.

(3) Christian Contentment

Ask the following questions. You may want to record answers on newsprint.

[?] **(1) If you asked some average Americans what they needed in order to be truly content, what do you think they would say?**

(2) What kinds of feelings do people experience when they do not have whatever they believe is necessary for contentment?

Read aloud Philippians 4:8-14. Ask:

[?] **(1) What does Paul find necessary for contentment?**

(2) How is his answer different from that of the average American?

(3) Do you perceive most Americans who profess faith in Christ to hold attitudes more like those of other Americans or more like Paul's? Give some examples to support your answer.

Read again Philippians 4:13. Use the information in Understanding the Scripture in the second paragraph of the section labeled Philippians 4:10-20 to help the students understand the meaning of this verse.

Invite the class to imagine that they, like Paul, could be flexible enough to endure want and suffering and still remain faithful to God as long as God strengthens them during the ordeal. Ask:

(1) How would your way of coping with a difficult situation be different if you took Philippians 4:13 seriously? [?]

(2) What is preventing you from adopting that coping strategy right now?

(4) Money Matters

Select someone to read Philippians 4:15-18. Ask:

(1) What does Paul's response to the Philippians reveal about their attitude toward money? (Note that they [?] were ready to support Paul's ministry financially, even when no one else did. They sent contributions more than once, which indicated that they were generous. Paul says he did not "seek the gift" (4:17), so the Philippians must have given freely without being asked.)

(2) What benefits does Paul suggest will come to the church because of their gifts? (God is pleased with their offering and, according to verse 19, will satisfy their needs.)

Giving to others brings deep joy. Supporting those who labor for God is especially worthwhile. Help the class take an inventory of the giving that your own congregation does. (These questions are phrased in terms used in United Methodist churches, so you may need to revise them to fit your own denominational structure.) Write responses on newsprint. You may also want to check in advance with your finance committee or treasurer to get accurate, up-to-date information for this discussion.

(1) Where does apportionment money go? (Be sure the students realize that [?] part of this money is for World Service and conference benevolences. See *The Book of Discipline, 1996*, paragraph 249.13.)

(2) What amount of money is our congregation expected to pay? What percentage of this figure do we pay?

(3) If we are not paying our apportion-

ments in full, why? What changes do we need to make?

(4) **What national and international missions projects do we support?**

(5) **What local missions and outreach projects do we underwrite financially?**

(6) **Do you think individuals and the congregation at large experience joy in giving generously? If not, why not?**

Read the story of the woman visited during an every member canvas for an example of joy and generosity in giving. You will find this story in the second paragraph under "Money Matters" in Interpreting the Scripture.

To conclude the session, sing a hymn that reflects the deep joy that we have in Christ, even in the midst of trials and tribulations. "Come, Ye Disconsolate" (*The United Methodist Hymnal*, no. 510), "By Gracious Powers" (*UMH*, no. 517), or "What a Friend We Have in Jesus" (*UMH*, no. 526) would be good choices.

Before the students leave, suggest at least one of the activities below.

HELPING CLASS MEMBERS ACT

Recommend that the students keep a list of things for which they are thankful this week. Encourage them to include negative situations that can be turned into positives or from which they learned something. Tell them to review the day's list each night before going to bed and offer a prayer of thanksgiving to God.

Remind the group that Paul's ministry was underwritten in part by money given by the church at Philippi. Challenge them to become involved as a group in a missions or outreach project. Urge them to make a financial pledge to support such a ministry.

Ask the class members to think about what they believe they need to obtain in order to be content. Do they want a certain amount of money in their investments or savings accounts? Do they need certain persons to be involved in their lives? Must they achieve certain goals? Encourage them to reexamine these so-called needs and begin to feel content with who they are and whatever they have.

PLANNING FOR NEXT SUNDAY

Next week we will begin a new unit entitled "Called to Be a New Humanity," which delves into Ephesians. To prepare for the first lesson, "Claim Your Spiritual Blessings," the students should read Ephesians 1. Our lesson will focus on verses 1-14.

UNIT 2: CALLED TO BE A NEW HUMANITY
CLAIM YOUR SPIRITUAL BLESSINGS

PREVIEWING THE LESSON

Lesson Scripture: Ephesians 1:1-14
Background Scripture: Ephesians 1
Key Verse: Ephesians 1:3

Focus of the Lesson:
Through Christ, the people of God are blessed with redemption, forgiveness, and God's grace.

Main Question of the Lesson:
How and by what means has God provided for the salvation, redemption, and forgiveness of humankind?

This lesson will enable adult learners to:
(1) hear Paul's words of thanksgiving for blessings.
(2) claim the spiritual blessings that are theirs in Christ.
(3) respond by praising God for their blessings.

Today's lesson may be outlined as follows:
(1) Introduction
(2) God's People
(3) The Sovereign God Is in Charge
(4) God Forgives
(5) Claim Your Inheritance

FOCUSING ON THE MAIN QUESTION

In today's lesson we are called to be new people by claiming the spiritual blessings that are ours in Christ. Often in the midst of change we search for meaning and purpose in our lives. Paul tells us that because of Christ we have redemption, forgiveness, and the richness of God's grace. We have all that we need. Indeed, we are truly blessed. Unfortunately, though, all of us—perhaps most of us—do not claim these blessings. Thus, we don't live as people who praise and glorify God.

Ephesians 1 is full of heavily loaded theological terms, and its understanding depends on a reasonably clear understanding of the nature of salvation in

Christ and through his cross, as provided by the Father and applied by the Holy Spirit. The phrase "in Christ" or "in the Beloved" punctuates this entire section. In short, the focus of Ephesians 1 is on salvation, but this passage raises the "how" question: **How and by what means has God provided for the salvation, redemp-** **tion, and forgiveness of humankind?** Paul's fundamental answer is "in Christ" and by means of his death. Moreover, Paul tells us that the benefits of this salvation are provided to believers in and through the presence of the Holy Spirit in their lives.

READING THE SCRIPTURE

NRSV
Ephesians 1:1-14

1 Paul, an apostle of Christ Jesus by the will of God,

To the saints who are in Ephesus and are faithful in Christ Jesus:

2 Grace to you and peace from God our Father and the Lord Jesus Christ.

Key Verse **3 Blessed be the God and Father of our Lord Jesus Christ, who has blessed us in Christ with every spiritual blessing in the heavenly places,** 4 just as he chose us in Christ before the foundation of the world to be holy and blameless before him in love. 5 He destined us for adoption as his children through Jesus Christ, according to the good pleasure of his will, 6 to the praise of his glorious grace that he freely bestowed on us in the Beloved. 7 In him we have redemption through his blood, the forgiveness of our trespasses, according to the riches of his grace 8 that he lavished on us. With all wisdom and insight 9 he has made known to us the mystery of his will, according to his good pleasure that he set forth in Christ, 10 as a plan for the fullness of time, to gather up all things in him, things in heaven and things on earth. 11 In Christ we have also obtained an inheritance, having been destined according to the purpose of him who accomplishes all things according to his counsel and will, 12 so that we, who were the first to set our hope on Christ, might live for the praise of his glory. 13 In him you also, when you had heard the word of

NIV
Ephesians 1:1-14

[1]Paul, an apostle of Christ Jesus by the will of God,

To the saints in Ephesus, the faithful in Christ Jesus:

[2]Grace and peace to you from God our Father and the Lord Jesus Christ.

Key Verse [3]**Praise be to the God and Father of our Lord Jesus Christ, who has blessed us in the heavenly realms with every spiritual blessing in Christ.** [4]For he chose us in him before the creation of the world to be holy and blameless in his sight. In love [5]he predestined us to be adopted as his sons through Jesus Christ, in accordance with his pleasure and will—[6]to the praise of his glorious grace, which he has freely given us in the One he loves. [7]In him we have redemption through his blood, the forgiveness of sins, in accordance with the riches of God's grace [8]that he lavished on us with all wisdom and understanding. [9]And he made known to us the mystery of his will according to his good pleasure, which he purposed in Christ, [10]to be put into effect when the times will have reached their fulfillment—to bring all things in heaven and on earth together under one head, even Christ.

[11]In him we were also chosen, having been predestined according to the plan of him who works out everything in conformity with the purpose of his will, [12]in order that we, who were the first to hope in Christ, might be for the praise of his

truth, the gospel of your salvation, and had believed in him, were marked with the seal of the promised Holy Spirit; 14 this is the pledge of our inheritance toward redemption as God's own people, to the praise of his glory.

glory. [13]And you also were included in Christ when you heard the word of truth, the gospel of your salvation. Having believed, you were marked in him with a seal, the promised Holy Spirit, [14]who is a deposit guaranteeing our inheritance until the redemption of those who are God's possession—to the praise of his glory.

UNDERSTANDING THE SCRIPTURE

Ephesians 1:1-2. These two verses are known as the epistolary superscript. Though the letter as we read it claims to be written by Paul to the church at Ephesus, scholars debate whether this document is a regular Pauline letter. They also debate who the original audience was. Various of our earliest and best Greek manuscripts of the book of Ephesians omit the words "in Ephesus," and so it is possible that this letter was originally intended as a circular letter for the saints and those who are faithful in Christ. Had it been directed to a particular Pauline congregation, we would have expected the document to include the usual Pauline greetings and directions to specific converts in that locale (compare for example Romans 16), especially since Acts 18–20 suggests that Paul spent over two years in Ephesus. Thus the original text seems to have read "to the saints, those being—(here one would fill in the locale of the audience in question) and to those faithful...." Furthermore, it is possible to suggest that the word *saints* here (see also 2:19 and 3:18) refers to Jewish Christians and the reference to those who are "faithful" applies to Gentile Christians, with the latter being the main target audience of this document (as Ephesians 2:19 and 3:18 intimate).

The opening verses indicate that we are intended to see this document as a letter rather than, for instance, an early Christian sermon. It shares much in common with the beginning of other Pauline letters (see 1 Corinthians 1:1-2 and Galatians 1:1-2). Paul emphasizes his apostolic status, which he has by virtue of God's will and his own choice to fulfill this role. By using the word *saints* (or holy ones), he also emphasizes that his audience was set apart by God and called to be faithful. *Grace* and *peace* are modified forms of the Greek word for "greeting" and the Jewish greeting *shalom*, which we normally translate as "peace." Paul is greeting both the Gentiles and the Jews in an appropriate way, and at the same time suggesting that he wishes God's blessings on both groups.

Ephesians 1:3-14. These verses comprise the hymn or prayer of praise to God for redemption. While this section is often divided up into several sentences in English, it is one long (twenty-six lines in the Greek text) Greek sentence in the form of a Jewish blessing formula. Paul is not just being verbose here; his heart is overflowing in praise to God for what God has accomplished in Christ. Furthermore, this letter is deliberately written in Asiatic Greek (a more verbose style of Greek) as a piece of epideictic rhetoric. Rhetoric was the ancient art of persuasion, and epideictic rhetoric was the rhetoric of praise and blame, of honor and shame. In this case Paul is offering an ode of praise about God's work in creating the church, which encompasses Jew and Gentile united in Christ (see Ephesians 2). In the rhetoric of praise, effusiveness and hyperbole were definitely in order. The character of this document as a praise and thanksgiving document needs to be kept in mind.

Throughout this long sentence one phrase keeps coming up over and over again—"in Christ." The language of beatitude is directed to the Father for what was accomplished in and through the Son. Some of the blessings available "in Christ" for those who believe include: (1) receiving every spiritual blessing in the heavenly places; (2) being chosen in Christ before all of creation was made; (3) being set apart by God, or being holy and blameless; (4) being adopted as God's children; (5) being recipients of God's unmerited and freely bestowed favor or grace in abundant quantities; (6) receiving redemption and forgiveness for sins; (7) receiving the knowledge and understanding of God's mysterious plan of salvation for humankind; (8) receiving an eternal inheritance of which the Holy Spirit in the believer's life is both the pledge and the down payment (*arrabon* in verse 14 means basically a down payment or first installment—in short, a preview of coming attractions); (9) having the privilege of living for the praise and glory of God, not for our own praise and glory.

The language of predestination and choice in this section has often confused Christian readers. Is Paul really saying that persons have been chosen by God from before the beginning of creation to be saved, and there is nothing a human being can do to change that decision? A closer reading reveals that Paul is speaking of *Christ* as the chosen one who existed in heaven before the creation of the universe and was picked by God to bring redemption to humankind. Humans are only chosen to the extent that they are "in Christ" (that is, spiritually connected to him by being part of his "body," his faithful people). As Ephesians will go on to stress, being "in Christ" is a matter of both the grace of God and the faithful response of

human beings, a matter of both God's will and our human acceptance of God's work in our lives. Part of the point of the language of predestination is to assure Christians under fire that God will not fail in the divine purpose to redeem those who respond in faith to the good news of salvation.

Ephesians 1:15-23. Having spoken of God in Christ's part in the drama of salvation in Ephesians 1:3-14, Paul speaks of his audience's faith at the beginning of this section, only to return to the subject of God's work in Christ in speaking of what Paul wishes and prays for his audience. This is Paul's prayer of petition. The apostle characterizes his audience not only as having faith in Christ but also as loving all the "saints." The Christian life is characterized as necessarily having both a vertical dimension (faith directed toward Christ) and a horizontal one (love directed toward one's fellow believers—and others as well, of course). The audience, largely Gentile, is being informed that as they grow in their faith they should come to a deeper understanding of the riches of the inheritance they have received by becoming part of the people of God, joining Jewish believers ("saints") who already had these privileges before the beginning of the Gentile mission.

The mighty work of creating one people of God out of a world divided into Jews and Gentiles could only have been accomplished by God, and the proof that God had such power is shown by the fact that God raised Jesus from the dead. A God who can overcome death can also overcome ethnic divisions and animosities. Ephesians 1:20-23 serves as a sort of doxology to this whole section indicating that Christ has been seated at the right hand of God and rules over all forces and beings beneath him, whether spiritual or material. Both the creation and the creatures are now subject to Christ. Ephesians 1:22 makes the astounding claim that God has made Christ head over all the universe for the sake of the church, Christ's body! All of these claims and this praise are intended to encourage Christians under fire to remain faithful in their commitment to Christ and to each other, even though they were a diverse minority group.

INTERPRETING THE SCRIPTURE

God's People

Here and in Romans 9–11 Paul makes clear that Gentiles have been joined to the people of God by grace. Formerly they were aliens, not a part of the chosen people. Thus Paul begins his letter by distinguishing between the "saints" and the "faithful" in Christ. The former, being Jews, were part of the people of God originally because God set them apart; the latter, being Gentiles, joined by means of faith. This distinction is fundamental to understanding this document.

Scripture spends a great deal of time stressing that all human beings are people of sacred worth, people precious to God. This fact is made clear in a more specific way in our text by stressing the chosenness of those who are in Christ. We can begin to get a glimpse of God's boundless love when we realize that God chose us in Christ before we were ever born, indeed before the foundations of the universe. We are chosen for a purpose—to be holy and blameless before God in love. It is often said that Christians are "saved to serve," but here the stress is on the fact that we are saved to be people of integrity, making God proud and bringing God glory by reflecting the divine character on earth, just as Christ our exemplar did when he was with us. Paul is clear that humankind was created and indeed re-created in Christ for good works and to reflect God's glory. Thus, humans are not the masters of their own fate; rather, God is in control. Though it is a cliché, you cannot know who you are without knowing whose you are. We are God's.

The Sovereign God Is in Charge

Those who have read John Wesley's *Journal* will know how Wesley was always remarking on the way things worked together providentially for good. On one occasion he comments that some surly men had infiltrated a crowd of listeners while he was preaching in a field. They had come with rotten eggs in their pockets intending to pelt Wesley. Wesley observes that by a singular providence of God the crowd pressed in on these ruffians and unintentionally broke the eggs in the men's coat pockets. Wesley wryly remarked that an odor went up from them, though it was not as sweet as balsam.

No Christian can study the Scriptures long without being profoundly impressed with the accent on the sovereignty of God and the way God directs the affairs of both creation and creature. This is part of what is being stressed in Ephesians, with a special emphasis on God's being almighty to save, not merely sovereign in the abstract. God, says Paul, always had a plan to redeem the fallen creation. God was not caught by surprise when humankind fell and could not get up on its own. God does not play catch-up. The plan of salvation existed even before creation was made in the first place.

God Forgives

Paul believed that while life is often a mystery, the most fundamental mystery has been made plain to us in Christ—God loves us, indeed, so much that God had always had a plan to save us should we

410

fall. The plan involved, according to Ephesians 1:7, Christ dying on the cross as an atonement for sins so that God could provide forgiveness for those sins. In short God in the person of Jesus the Son paid the price for our sins, when it should have been us on the cross.

Some have wondered why Christ's death was necessary. Some have assumed that God could simply forgive without exacting a price. This sort of approach misunderstands the fundamental character of God, which is that God is holy Love. Not love without holiness, but also not holiness without love. Sin could not simply be forgiven, for sin is like a cancer that if not dealt with spreads and destroys the creature it dwells in. Anyone who thinks forgiveness is an exercise that cost God nothing should look closely at the cross. It cost God dearly, which shows all the more how much God loves us.

A pastor once put up a sign on his front lawn that read TRESPASSERS: (and then in very small print) *will be forgiven*. This sign captures the character of our God. God does forgive. God wants to forgive. And God wants us to forgive others as well.

Corrie ten Boom tells the poignant story of the death of her sister Betsie in a Nazi concentration camp. She was beaten by a camp guard and ended up dying shortly thereafter. As she lay on the table and saw the hatred in Corrie's eyes for her tormentor, Betsie kept saying, "No hate Corrie, only love." Years later, after her miraculous release from the concentration camp, Corrie ten Boom happened to meet the death camp guard again. On this occasion however, he came to tell Corrie that he had come to Christ and was asking her forgiveness for his horrible crime. Corrie says that at that moment she could not give it to him. She said she wrestled for some time with her feelings, but finally got in touch with the man again and said that she forgave him, but not under her own power, rather by the grace of God. Alexander Pope was right when he said "to err is human, to forgive, divine."

Claim Your Inheritance

Most of us know the story of Cain, who was marked by God (Genesis 4:14-15) so that no one would kill him. This mark was meant to ward off harm. Here in Ephesians 1:13 Paul speaks of Christians being marked by a sign of life, marked by the presence of God's very Spirit within them. Paul, when he says "marked with the seal of the promised Holy Spirit," may have in mind a document that has been sealed as authentic by a wax seal with a distinctive impression pressed into the wax. Alternately, it is possible he has in mind a brand of ownership often placed on cattle or slaves. The Holy Spirit in the believer's life not only provides life but also sets a person apart and makes clear that she or he belongs to God. The concept of being sealed may also signify the notion of protection of believers by the Spirit through their trials and temptations. By virtue of this seal, we who are God's people may claim our inheritance.

We are all familiar with the sort of rags-to-riches stories that recount how a poverty-stricken person suddenly discovers she is an heir to a great fortune through some long-lost relative, or how a child lost in infancy suddenly learns, as an adult, that he is royalty. In a sense, we have this sort of story underlying Paul's remarks in Ephesians 1:15-23. Paul says that his prayer for his converts is awareness of the richness and depth and profundity of their glorious inheritance in Christ. Not only is the future inheritance great, but the present power available to Christians is likewise great. This is made clear by the fact of Christ's resurrection from the dead. Christians must claim their great inheritance. It is rather like the case of one's having a great deal of money in the bank but never drawing on the account. Paul is urging Christians to draw on their heavenly bank account and reap the benefits of Christ's work for them.

The overall message of this entire passage may be summed up as follows: (1) God in Christ rules over all from heaven; (2) God in Christ rules and empowers the lives of believers from within by means of the Holy Spirit; (3) therefore, believers should live in faith and not be anxious about their lives as they have help available from both without and within. Paul calls us to claim our spiritual blessings.

SHARING THE SCRIPTURE

PREPARING TO TEACH

Preparing Our Hearts

Today's devotional reading is from Romans 1:8-17. Focus especially on verses 16-17: "For I am not ashamed of the gospel; it is the power of God for salvation to everyone who has faith, to the Jew first and also to the Greek. For in it the righteousness of God is revealed through faith for faith; as it is written, 'The one who is righteous will live by faith.'" What spiritual blessings does Paul speak of in these verses? How do you claim them?

Turn now to today's lesson and read the background scripture from Ephesians 1. What blessings do you find in these verses? Meditate on the way your life has been blessed by the gift of salvation. How would your life be different if you did not walk with Christ? What blessings will you appropriate more fully in your journey?

Close your devotional time with a prayer asking God to make you and your students more aware of the abundant spiritual blessings that are available in Christ Jesus.

Preparing Our Minds

Read this lesson. Review the scripture, this time zooming in on verses 1-14.

The lesson provides you with much background information about the letter itself and its possible audiences. However, you may want to do some additional research. Notice that most scholars believe Ephesians was a letter circulated among churches in Asia Minor, rather than directed specifically to the church in Ephesus.

Ephesians was thought to have been written by Paul late in his life while he was in prison. Some scholars debate the authorship, however, for several reasons. First, some words found in Ephesians are not used in any of Paul's other letters. Moreover, other words have different meanings here than the way they are used in letters that were definitely written by Paul. Second, the writing style, which includes many long sentences in the Greek, is not characteristic of Paul. Some scholars believe that these changes simply reflect changes in the way Paul thinks and writes. Many similarities do exist between this letter and Colossians. In fact, if Ephesians was penned by one of Paul's followers, that writer likely drew heavily upon Colossians, though the authorship of that letter is also debated.

Preparing Our Learning Space

Have on hand:
- several Bibles
- newsprint and marker
- paper and pencils
- hymnals.

LEADING THE CLASS

(1) Introduction

One way to begin this session is to read or retell the Focusing on the Main Question portion.

Another way to begin is to post today's main question on newsprint: **How and by what means has God provided for the salvation, redemption, and forgiveness of humankind?** Give the students a few moments to think silently about this question. Then ask them to talk with a partner or small group about how they would answer this question. Invite volunteers to share their group's ideas with the class at large. See if you can arrive at any consensus to answer the question.

Segue into the lesson from Ephesians by pointing out that Paul would answer the main question by saying that salvation is "in Christ" and by means of his death. Believers have the benefit of this salvation in and through the presence of the Holy Spirit in their lives.

(2) God's People

Read Ephesians 1:1-2. Create a brief lecture that includes the points below to help the students understand who this letter is from and to, as well as what questions scholars have raised about this letter to the Ephesians.

- Paul is an apostle, that is, one who is sent on a mission.
- God chose Paul and willed that he undertake this mission, which is on behalf of Christ.
- The letter is addressed to "saints," meaning the Jewish Christians, and to those who are "faithful," meaning the Gentile Christians.
- The letter specifies that the recipients are "in Ephesus," but this is a late addition that does not appear in the earliest known Greek manuscripts.
- Likely this letter was circulated among churches in Asia Minor. Had it been intended for a specific congregation, it would have included information directly related to that church, which Ephesians does not contain.
- Scholars debate whether this document is a regular Pauline letter.

- "Grace" and "peace" are greetings that would have appealed to Gentiles and Jews, respectively.

(3) The Sovereign God Is in Charge

Read aloud Ephesians 1:3-14. Distribute paper and pencils. Divide the class into three groups and assign one of the following questions to each group. The students may work individually and write their responses. When you have allowed time for them to write, discuss their answers.

(1) **What does this passage say to you about God?** (Answers may include: God is sovereign, forgiving, and holy. God graciously redeems us according to a divine plan conceived before the foundation of the world.)

(2) **What does this passage say about humanity?** (Humanity has been offered rich blessings in Christ that we can choose to accept by believing in him or reject. The Holy Spirit is the pledge of our inheritance.)

(3) **What does this passage say about God's relationship to humanity?** (God wants to be in a relationship with humanity, both Jews and Gentiles. God adopts us. God marks us with the Holy Spirit.)

(4) God Forgives

Use the story of Corrie ten Boom, found in the final paragraph under "God Forgives" in Interpreting the Scripture. Discuss these questions with the class:

(1) **Do you believe that it is possible for humans, under their own power, to offer forgiveness in such difficult circumstances?**

(2) **How did God bring about forgiveness for us?** (Refer to the first and second paragraphs under "God Forgives" in Interpreting the Scripture.)

(3) **What does God's forgiveness do for us?**

(4) **When we share God's forgiveness by**

? **forgiving others, what does that act do for them?**

(5) Claim Your Inheritance

In Ephesians 1:7-8, Paul says that we have redemption, forgiveness, and the riches of God's grace. In Christ, we have "obtained an inheritance" (1:11). Ask the group these questions:

? **(1) What does it mean to you to know that "in Christ" you have been redeemed?**

(2) The parable of the prodigal son (Luke 15:11-32) is a model for how God the Father unconditionally loves and forgives. How are you like the forgiven prodigal? How are you like the forgiven but resentful older brother, whom the father wants to join the party? How are you like the father who forgives unconditionally?

(3) How have you experienced God's grace in your life?

If you have access to hymnals that include a Psalter, invite the class to read Psalm 103 (at least verses 1-5) responsively. This psalm that speaks of God's blessings and benefits may be found in *The United Methodist Hymnal* (no. 824).

As you close today's session, lift up at least one of the activities below so that students may live out what they have studied this week.

HELPING CLASS MEMBERS ACT

Remind the group that because they are "in Christ" and have an inheritance, they are to glorify and praise God. Suggest that students try to develop some personal cues for praising God. For example, perhaps whenever they hear the phone ring, start the car, or finish a meal, they could give thanks to God for one blessing that they have received.

Since God has forgiven us, we are to forgive others. Encourage the students to seek out someone they need to forgive and to do so with a warm and generous heart.

Suggest that the students write in a spiritual journal whatever they consider to be their spiritual blessings. Recommend that they offer prayers of praise and thanksgiving for these blessings.

PLANNING FOR NEXT SUNDAY

Our lesson for July 9, "Claim Your New Status," is rooted in Ephesians 2. Ask the students to read this entire chapter. The session will focus on verses 8-22. Tell them to be thinking about how they experience oneness within the household of God.

CLAIM YOUR NEW STATUS

PREVIEWING THE LESSON

Lesson Scripture: Ephesians 2:8-22
Background Scripture: Ephesians 2
Key Verse: Ephesians 2:19

Focus of the Lesson:
In Christ, believers are all one in the household of God.

Main Question of the Lesson:
What are the immeasurable riches that God freely offers us in Christ and how can we claim them?

This lesson will enable adult learners to:
(1) hear Paul's call to oneness in Christ.
(2) consider their own place in the household of God.
(3) respond by setting aside differences with at least one person.

Today's lesson may be outlined as follows:
(1) Introduction
(2) Status Seekers
(3) Show Me the Money!
(4) Heroes Are Hard to Find
(5) Grace Works
(6) E Pluribus Unum

FOCUSING ON THE MAIN QUESTION

In Ephesians 2, Paul is attempting to reshape his converts' sense of their status and worth, as well as their values. He will do this in a positive way by focusing on the immeasurable riches they have in Christ in comparison to what the world offers. Though conversion had changed their basic faith orientation, it had not immediately changed all their attitudes about status and many of their values. Paul prompts his converts to reflect on what they consider riches and what gives them their sense of self-worth and status. He wants them to address today's main question: **What are the immeasurable riches that God freely offers us in Christ and how can we claim them?**

Paul's converts were constantly influenced by non-Christian culture and, therefore, were in danger of slipping back into their old ways of thinking and living. Since Paul was not present with his converts, he could not reinforce their value transformation through dialogue and discussion, so he

415

wrote to them. In this letter Paul stressed that by sharing in Christ his Gentile converts were already sharing in the rich inheritance that Jewish Christians claim.

The apostle apparently feels that his converts did not fully appreciate the riches to which they had access. They were like the riders in the Old West who were traversing the desert one evening. A voice from heaven instructed them to stop at the next dried-up creek bed and pick up stones from the creek. They were told that afterward they would be both glad and sad. Mystified, the riders nonetheless responded to the heavenly voice, somewhat halfheartedly, by picking up a few stones and putting them in their pockets. At sunrise the next morning the voice told them to take the stones out and hold them up to the light. When they did, they discovered the stones were precious gems. Then they were glad they had taken the stones they had, but sad they had not made more effort. In Ephesians Paul is holding up the precious stones the Gentiles already possessed to the light, showing them their true worth, and urging his converts to claim these riches.

READING THE SCRIPTURE

NRSV
Ephesians 2:8-22

8 For by grace you have been saved through faith, and this is not your own doing; it is the gift of God—9 not the result of works, so that no one may boast. 10 For we are what he has made us, created in Christ Jesus for good works, which God prepared beforehand to be our way of life.

11 So then, remember that at one time you Gentiles by birth, called "the uncircumcision" by those who are called "the circumcision"—a physical circumcision made in the flesh by human hands—12 remember that you were at that time without Christ, being aliens from the commonwealth of Israel, and strangers to the covenants of promise, having no hope and without God in the world. 13 But now in Christ Jesus you who once were far off have been brought near by the blood of Christ. 14 For he is our peace; in his flesh he has made both groups into one and has broken down the dividing wall, that is, the hostility between us. 15 He has abolished the law with its commandments and ordinances, that he might create in himself one new humanity in place of the two, thus making peace, 16 and might reconcile both groups to God in one body through the cross, thus putting to death that

NIV
Ephesians 2:8-22

8For it is by grace you have been saved, through faith—and this not from yourselves, it is the gift of God—9not by works, so that no one can boast. 10For we are God's workmanship, created in Christ Jesus to do good works, which God prepared in advance for us to do.

11Therefore, remember that formerly you who are Gentiles by birth and called "uncircumcised" by those who call themselves "the circumcision" (that done in the body by the hands of men)—12remember that at that time you were separate from Christ, excluded from citizenship in Israel and foreigners to the covenants of the promise, without hope and without God in the world. 13But now in Christ Jesus you who once were far away have been brought near through the blood of Christ.

14For he himself is our peace, who has made the two one and has destroyed the barrier, the dividing wall of hostility, 15by abolishing in his flesh the law with its commandments and regulations. His purpose was to create in himself one new man out of the two, thus making peace, 16and in this one body to reconcile both of them to God through the cross, by which he put to hostility through it. 17 So he came and proclaimed peace to you who were far off and peace to those who were near; 18 for through him both of us have access in one Spirit to the Father. **19 So then you are no longer strangers and aliens, but you are citizens with the saints and also members of the household of God,** 20 built upon the foundation of the apostles and prophets, with Christ Jesus himself as the cornerstone. 21 In him the whole structure is joined together and grows into a holy temple in the Lord; 22 in whom you also are built together spiritually into a dwelling place for God.

Key Verse

death their hostility. [17]He came and preached peace to you who were far away and peace to those who were near. [18]For through him we both have access to the Father by one Spirit.

[19]Consequently, you are no longer foreigners and aliens, but fellow citizens with God's people and members of God's household, [20]built on the foundation of the apostles and prophets, with Christ Jesus himself as the chief cornerstone. [21]In him the whole building is joined together and rises to become a holy temple in the Lord. [22]And in him you too are being built together to become a dwelling in which God lives by his Spirit.

Key Verse

UNDERSTANDING THE SCRIPTURE

Ephesians 2:1-10. Since the Protestant Reformation this passage has been crucial when anyone wishes to preach on salvation by grace through faith rather than salvation by works. Paul is mainly addressing Gentiles when he says "you" throughout Ephesians, while the "we" in Ephesians 2:3 refers to Paul and the Jewish Christians.

Paul begins by telling his audience that before their conversion they were dead through their trespasses and sins. "Trespasses" refer to willful violations of known commandments that are binding upon the party in question. "Sins" are immoral or unethical actions that violate God's general will for humankind. The effect of sinning is spiritual death. Paul would maintain that both Gentiles and Jews have fallen and cannot get up without the grace of God working in their lives.

Paul characterizes "the course of this world" as not basically good, but rather habitually sinful, and guided by "the ruler of the power of the air," that is, Satan (2:2). Paul envisioned Satan's dwelling place not as within the earth but rather up in the region between earth and the dwelling place of God (called the "heavenly places"

in Ephesians). Infected with a spirit of evil by means of the Evil One, the world requires a radical rescue by God, not merely a human self-help program.

Ephesians 2:3 indicates that the effects of human fallenness are universal. Not that we are all as bad as we could possibly be, nor are any unredeemable by nature, but fallenness has touched us all. All are sinners both by nature and by choice. Surprisingly, Paul includes himself and his fellow Jews as "by nature children of wrath," just like Gentiles, and so in need of salvation. The phrase "children of wrath" refers not to human temperament but rather to children destined to face the wrath of God on Judgment Day unless they repent and are saved.

Ephesians 2:4 stresses that God is rich in mercy and love toward all human beings, even though we are spiritually dead. God does not love us because of something inherently appealing about us. God's love is not directed only to something it finds attractive. Rather, it is simply the character of God to love—in spite of what we are. What was required was for God to make the spiritually dead alive again and sensitive to the positive relationship one can and should have with God. The word *grace* describes salvation. It indicates that salvation is God's undeserved blessing. We cannot get salvation the old-fashioned way—by earning it.

Ephesians 2:8-9 indicates that salvation comes by grace and through our accepting this benefit by faith. It is a gift from God, not a work or achievement of humankind. Far from being self-made persons, Ephesians 2:10 says Christians are what God has made them. We have been remade in Christ, and for a purpose—to perform good works that God had always intended for us to do.

Ephesians 2:11-22. This passage focuses on what Gentiles once were, and what they now are by grace and in Christ. As Ephesians 2:12 says, they were without Christ and were no part of God's people, Israel. They were strangers to God's covenants and estranged from the fellowship of God, without any real or living hope (of eternal life) and *atheos*—without God. This Greek word *atheos* is the origin of our word *atheist*, but it doesn't mean a person who is necessarily anti-God, or who adamantly refuses to believe in the existence of God. It refers to a person who has neither knowledge of nor relationship with God—"without God" and so alone in the world.

Ephesians 2:13 speaks of the means by which Gentiles have been brought near to God and God's people—the sacrificial death of Christ, and the spilling of his atoning blood. Christ is said to be not merely our peacemaker, but rather our peace. Ephesians 2:14-15 explains that part of the effect of Christ's death was to tear down the walls that divided Jews from Gentiles, including the Mosaic Law. Paul suggests Christ's death made that law obsolete, not because it was something bad, but because something better had superseded it, something that did not separate Jews from Gentiles.

According to Ephesians 2:15-17 the goal was not merely to stop the hostilities between Jews and Gentiles but to create one new humanity. The two groups would be reconciled into a single body of believers. Ephesians 2:19 states the high status now bestowed on Gentiles—they are now citizens in the commonwealth of God's people along with the "saints" (that is, Jewish Christians), members of the household of God. The foundation of that household is said to be the apostles and Christian prophets.

Christ is called here the *akrogoniaios*. This word could mean either the cornerstone (a stone that is part of the foundation) or, more likely, the keystone, the stone that holds two sides of an arch together from above. Throughout Ephesians there is a stress on Christ's being above in the heavenly places and ruling from above, and so the imagery of the keystone is more apt here.

With Christ as the keystone, Ephesians 2:21-22 adds that the whole structure is held together and grows up into a holy temple pointing toward Christ. Christ is the glue that holds God's people together and also causes them to grow. The goal is that we ourselves become a dwelling place for God's very presence.

INTERPRETING THE SCRIPTURE

Status Seekers

Paul lived in a highly status-conscious world. A person's honor rating was crucial to how he or she stood in society. Various factors contributed to a high honor rating: a noble family, wealth, education, citizenship, race, gender. Paul refers to all of these issues of family, race, riches, knowledge, and citizenship in order to make clear to his Gentile converts how much they have gained by becoming Christians. In regard to family, they are now a part of the household of God, a permanent family with "relatives" to be found all over, and more importantly with a "relative" in heaven who is God's right-hand man, so to speak. In regard to citizenship they now are citizens of a heavenly commonwealth and in a sense part of a new humanity through the sharing in common of God in Christ. Paul also speaks of the riches and knowledge that the Gentiles have received by becoming Christians. The point is clear—everything they could have sought or wanted in the world they now have in Christ.

Show Me the Money!

For many years an evangelist out of New York called Reverend Ike appeared on television and radio. His "Good News" was a truly American message. He preached that "the lack of money is the root of all evil." He insisted on a gospel of materialism and frequently suggested that if any of his audience was struggling with having too many things, they should just pack them up and send them to "good ole Reverend Ike" and he would remove the temptation from them!

Reverend Ike's theology contrasts sharply with Paul's. In the apostle's view Christians are not to simply capitulate to or to adopt the values of the dominant culture. Rather they are to have an alternative set of values and priorities. High status in a Christian's eyes is to be a member of the body of Christ, not a member of the jet set. Real riches amount to knowing God in Christ and God's plan of salvation for the world. This salvation indeed has a social component and involves helping to alleviate the social ills of our world, but it also involves spiritual transformation.

Heroes Are Hard to Find

It has been said you become what you admire, or to put it another way, you can tell a lot about a person by his or her heroes. Paul is suggesting in this text that those whom Christians look up to and seek to emulate are not emperors or presidents but the apostles, the prophets, and most of all Christ himself. Real status comes from serving the real Lord of the universe, not the gods or lords of this world.

Those who have an eternal perspective are not likely to get their heads turned by every new face or idea that comes down the road. My grandfather was such a person. For all of his ninety-plus years of life he was a devout member of the Baptist church in Wilmington, North Carolina. He was a deacon, always teaching or doing something for the church. He was not a man with extensive formal education; he had married as a teenager and had struggled to support his family during the Depression. He lived simply and gave much to others. He had chosen to live a life of simple Christian integrity. This is in essence what Paul is urging the Gentiles to do because he believes that they have a great heritage and a great inheritance in Christ that they can be proud of as Christians. They need not look elsewhere for status, or satisfaction, or heroes. My grandfather is one of my heroes because he embodied the attitude and lifestyle Paul speaks of here.

Grace Works

We live in a culture full of workaholics. People now are even more prone to work constantly than they were a generation ago. Technology such as e-mail and faxes not only makes instant communication possible but also creates pressure to send a response immediately. People want more, bigger, better, faster. Even purchases that used to wait until Monday are now being made on Sunday because so many stores are open.

In this sort of works-oriented culture the concept of grace seems very foreign. The notion that we are saved by grace through faith is nearly incomprehensible to some, especially in a culture that quotes sayings such as "You don't get something for nothing." It has been suggested that if we would offer salvation for sale, we would have an endless line of people waiting to purchase it; but precisely because it is offered freely, Americans are suspicious. They want to know what the catch is.

The same actually can be said about Paul's own culture. It was a culture of reciprocity where every gift came with strings attached and with a response expected. Perhaps this is why both Jesus and Paul emphasized that to be saved one needs to turn and become like a child.

Children have no problem receiving gifts. When they open one, they don't look carefully at the tag first and say, "Oh dear I'd better run to get something for my aunt because I didn't purchase her a gift." They simply know how to receive a gift, precisely because they know they are dependent on others for most of what they have and are. Many adults, however, have bought into the myth of radical independence. They don't wish to be beholden to anyone. It makes them feel uncomfortable, as if they needed something. If I may put the matter somewhat paradoxically, "grace is a hard sell" when you're dealing with such adults. They think life is about getting along on one's own, not about receiving from others. This is why Paul must accent repeatedly in Ephesians 2 that salvation comes by grace and through faith in Jesus Christ. It is not a matter of a quid pro quo (something received in exchange) between us and God.

E Pluribus Unum

When Paul envisions a united human race, he does not envision the United Nations, but rather all humankind knit together into one people by Christ. It is Christ who must both be peace and bring us peace, and it is Christ who tears down the walls of hatred, hostility, racism, and the wrong sorts of pride. To the extent that we are "created in Christ Jesus for good works" (2:10), we too are supposed to help break down barriers that divide us. A television commercial says that on the Internet there is no age, no race, no infirmities, no gender, only minds.

I am also reminded of the falling of the Berlin wall—something that no one thought would happen when it did. In a sense, Paul is saying that this is how God in Christ views the world, as a place where barriers need to be deconstructed and then society reconstructed in Christ. Those both far and near are being reconciled to each other and to God. It is a global message for all the peoples of the world. This message is uniquely suited for a world ever more rapidly becoming a global village, especially as the technology continues to accelerate. In a world moving this quickly, there is but one fixed point to which all of us can point our compasses when we look for bearings—the One who died for us and now reigns for us in heaven. We just need to claim our status as members of the household of God and take our place within Christ's family.

SHARING THE SCRIPTURE

PREPARING TO TEACH

Preparing Our Hearts

To begin your own spiritual preparations for this lesson, read John 17:1-11 and 20-23. Just prior to his death, Jesus offers this prayer for himself, his disciples, and the church universal. He prays that we will "all be one" (17:21). How does it make you feel to know that Jesus wants you and the whole church to be one in him? What can you do to promote greater unity within the church?

Look now at today's background scripture from Ephesians 2. Note especially the key verse: "So then you are no longer strangers and aliens, but you are citizens with the saints and also members of the household of God" (Ephesians 2:19). How have you claimed your status as a member of God's household? What can you do to help your students recognize and claim their own status?

Pray that God will lead you, your students, and your entire congregation into more harmonious relationships with one another and into closer communion in Christ.

Preparing Our Minds

Review Ephesians 2, paying particular attention to verses 8-22. Be sure to read this entire lesson carefully.

Practice telling the story about the riders in the Old West found in the last paragraph of Focusing on the Main Question.

Preparing Our Learning Space

Have on hand:
- several Bibles
- hymnals.

LEADING THE CLASS

(1) Introduction

Begin today's lesson by telling the story of the riders in the Old West, found in the last paragraph under Focusing on the Main Question. Ask these questions:

[?] (1) **Have you ever had an experience where you didn't really realize all that you had access to? If so, tell us about it.** (Some more mundane examples may be that persons had more insurance coverage than they had realized, or that they went to what they thought was an expensive restaurant and found that more was included in the price than they had been told by a friend.)

[?] (2) **How did you feel when you realized that you had more than you anticipated?**
(3) **Is it possible that your spiritual life includes more riches than you have thus far claimed? If so, as our main question asks, what are the immeasurable riches that God freely offers us in Christ and how can we claim them?**

(2) Status Seekers

Choose a volunteer to read aloud today's scripture lesson from Ephesians 2:8-22. Since this is a long passage, suggest that the students follow along in their Bibles.

Invite the students to read in unison today's key verse, Ephesians 2:19. Or, if members use different Bibles, have a variety of translations read. Then ask:

[?] (1) **What is the status of a stranger or alien?**
(2) **What is the status of a citizen?**
(3) **What is the status of a member of the household?**
(4) **Do you believe that some Christians cling to their outsider status? If so, why do you think this is the case?** (Answers may vary widely here. Some persons may not feel worthy to be God's child. Others may not want to get involved in the affairs of the household. Some may like to have the privilege of membership without the responsibility of caring for the rest of the family.)

Provide a few moments for the students to think silently about what value membership in the household of God has for them personally.

(3) Show Me the Money!

Share the information in this paragraph with the class. In Ephesians 2:7 (part of our background scripture), Paul speaks of "the immeasurable riches" of God's grace. As members of the household of God we are indeed rich. Yet many Christians do not acknowledge or even realize this richness. Unlike Paul, who states in verse 10 that "we are what [God] has made us," many Christians believe that who they are and what they have is the direct result of their own industry. They see themselves as self-made. In short, the values of those who see themselves as part of the household of God and those (even Christians) who do not are markedly different.

Discuss these questions with the class.

(1) **What values in our society do you see that are in tension with the values of Christians who realize that they have been saved by grace and included in God's household?**

(2) **How does claiming one's place in God's household change and clarify one's values?**

(4) Heroes Are Hard to Find

Invite students to share a few words about someone they look up to as a hero. Of particular interest are heroes who helped to shape class members' faith. To start this discussion, you may want to read or retell the information under "Heroes Are Hard to Find" in Interpreting the Scripture.

Relate this information to the lesson by pointing out that Christians who live with integrity and serve others embody the faith and pass on a precious inheritance to others.

(5) Grace Works

Direct the students to turn again in their Bibles to Ephesians 2:8-10. You may want to read or retell the information under "Grace Works" in Interpreting the Scripture.

Use the following situation as a way to talk about God's freely given grace. You will need to read this scenario aloud.

A coworker has noticed that you study your Sunday school lesson during lunch.

Her life is filled with problems that she has been unable to solve. She begins to ask you about what you believe and how you stay so calm under fire. When you get to the part about God freely bestowing grace on us, she balks at the idea. "You don't get something for nothing. There must be a catch to this," she snaps. How do you respond?

(6) E Pluribus Unum

Have the class look again at Ephesians 2:14-18 and then ask these questions:

(1) **The Bible says that Christ broke down barriers that divide us. What evidence do you have to affirm that we are one in Christ?**

(2) **What evidence do you have that there are still barriers that divide Christians, both within a particular congregation and from one denomination to another?**

(3) **What role does peace play in the reconciliation that Christ offers to us?**

(4) **What are the consequences of failing to take the oneness of Christ seriously?**

(5) **What action can you take personally (or as a group) to help Christians recognize their oneness in the body of Christ and claim their own place within the body?**

Offer this Chinese prayer for the unity of Christ's body: "Help each of us, gracious God, to live in such magnanimity and restraint that the Head of the church may never have cause to say to any one of us, 'This is my body, broken by you.' Amen."

Conclude the session by singing a hymn about the oneness of the church, such as "We Are the Church" (*The United Methodist Hymnal*, no. 558) or "In Christ There Is No East or West" (*UMH*, no. 548).

Before you dismiss the class, suggest at least one of the following activities that the students can follow through on during the week to reinforce what they have learned.

HELPING CLASS MEMBERS ACT

Encourage the students to welcome someone else into the household of God, or at least into your congregation of it. Perhaps they could offer to sit with a newcomer, invite him or her to small-group meetings or special events, or help the new person learn about what is happening in the church.

Note that in today's lesson Paul has been talking about the oneness that Jews and Gentiles alike feel in Christ. Suggest that students invite persons of different races or ethnic groups to worship and study at your church. Also suggest that your members visit some other congregations where the members are not like them.

Point out that though we are saved by grace, Paul notes in Ephesians 2:10 that God does expect us to do good works. Encourage class members to perform a random act of kindness for a stranger this week.

PLANNING FOR NEXT SUNDAY

To prepare for the session on July 16, ask the students to read Ephesians 4:1-16. This lesson, entitled "Claim Your Ministry," will examine how we are called to use our spiritual gifts.

CLAIM YOUR MINISTRY

PREVIEWING THE LESSON

Lesson Scripture: Ephesians 4:1-16
Background Scripture: Ephesians 4:1-16
Key Verse: Ephesians 4:7

Focus of the Lesson:
Each believer has been given spiritual gifts for the purpose of building up the church in unity and helping it grow toward maturity.

Main Question of the Lesson:
How can we Christians use our God-given gifts so that we may serve—rather than sever—the body of Christ by fostering its unity and growth?

This lesson will enable adult learners to:
(1) look at Paul's teachings on spiritual gifts that are to be used to build up the body of Christ.
(2) identify gifted persons who have made a difference in their lives.
(3) respond by using at least one gift to promote unity within the church.

Today's lesson may be outlined as follows:
(1) Introduction
(2) Character Counts
(3) The Essentials of Unity
(4) The Quality of Biblical Equality
(5) A Sacred Trust

FOCUSING ON THE MAIN QUESTION

How can we Christians use our God-given gifts so that we may serve—rather than sever—the body of Christ by fostering its unity and growth? In order to hone in on the main question in this lesson, it will be important to ask how one's gifts and graces may best be used so that God is glorified and God's people are edified. We need to ask these questions because it is perfectly possible for believers to abuse their gifts and act in ways that are neither godly nor conducive to church unity and growth. For example, we may think of some of the Corinthians who, according to

1 Corinthians 12–14, chose to use their gifts as a form of self-expression and self-promotion, forgetting that all gifts were given for the common good. Or we may think of the great prophet Elisha, who chose to use his considerable powers to curse and indeed destroy two young boys who had bruised his pride by shouting, "Go on up, you baldhead!" (2 Kings 2:23-24 NIV). The point is that when God gives gifts and abilities we still have the choice to use these gifts either wisely or poorly. Paul's very reason for writing this section of Ephesians and speaking of both behavior and gifts is that the latter must be used according to certain standards of conduct to please God and to be helpful to the church and world.

Paul refers to Christ's ascent into heaven because Christ's behavior provides the pattern for believers to follow in the use of their own gifts and in the bestowing of gifts and blessings on others. Notice too that people—including apostles, prophets, and indeed Christ himself—are seen as part of God's gifts to us. We are called to follow the example of Christ. We have been blessed to be a blessing to others as he was. To do so, we must claim our spiritual gifts and use them for the ministry that God has called us to undertake.

READING THE SCRIPTURE

NRSV

Ephesians 4:1-16

1 I therefore, the prisoner in the Lord, beg you to lead a life worthy of the calling to which you have been called, 2 with all humility and gentleness, with patience, bearing with one another in love, 3 making every effort to maintain the unity of the Spirit in the bond of peace. 4 There is one body and one Spirit, just as you were called to the one hope of your calling, 5 one Lord, one faith, one baptism, 6 one God and Father of all, who is above all and through all and in all.

7 But each of us was given grace according to the measure of Christ's gift. 8 Therefore it is said,

"When he ascended on high he made
　　captivity itself a captive;
　he gave gifts to his people."

9 (When it says, "He ascended," what does it mean but that he had also descended into the lower parts of the earth? 10 He who descended is the same one who ascended far above all the heavens, so that he might fill all things.) 11 The gifts he gave were that some would be apostles, some prophets, some evangelists, some pastors and teachers, 12 to equip the saints

NIV

Ephesians 4:1-16

[1]As a prisoner for the Lord, then, I urge you to live a life worthy of the calling you have received. [2]Be completely humble and gentle; be patient, bearing with one another in love. [3]Make every effort to keep the unity of the Spirit through the bond of peace. [4]There is one body and one Spirit— just as you were called to one hope when you were called—[5]one Lord, one faith, one baptism; [6]one God and Father of all, who is over all and through all and in all.

[7]But to each one of us grace has been given as Christ apportioned it. [8]This is why it says:

"When he ascended on high,
　he led captives in his train
　and gave gifts to men."

[9](What does "he ascended" mean except that he also descended to the lower, earthly regions? [10]He who descended is the very one who ascended higher than all the heavens, in order to fill the whole universe.) [11]It was he who gave some to be apostles, some to be prophets, some to be evangelists, and some to be pastors and teachers, [12]to prepare God's people for works of service, so that the body of Christ

Key
Verse

Key
Verse

for the work of ministry, for building up the body of Christ, 13 until all of us come to the unity of the faith and of the knowledge of the Son of God, to maturity, to the measure of the full stature of Christ. 14 We must no longer be children, tossed to and fro and blown about by every wind of doctrine, by people's trickery, by their craftiness in deceitful scheming. 15 But speaking the truth in love, we must grow up in every way into him who is the head, into Christ, 16 from whom the whole body, joined and knit together by every ligament with which it is equipped, as each part is working properly, promotes the body's growth in building itself up in love.

may be built up [13]until we all reach unity in the faith and in the knowledge of the Son of God and become mature, attaining to the whole measure of the fullness of Christ.

[14]Then we will no longer be infants, tossed back and forth by the waves, and blown here and there by every wind of teaching and by the cunning and craftiness of men in their deceitful scheming. [15]Instead, speaking the truth in love, we will in all things grow up into him who is the Head, that is, Christ. [16]From him the whole body, joined and held together by every supporting ligament, grows and builds itself up in love, as each part does its work.

UNDERSTANDING THE SCRIPTURE

Ephesians 4:1-3. The main verb of this sentence, *parakaleo*, could be translated as "to ask" or "to comfort," or as here "to exhort." Paul is exhorting his audience to live up to the high expectations placed on followers of Christ. In Ephesians, Paul has stressed that Christians are what they are by the grace of God, and that it is God's empowering grace and Spirit that enables Christians to live up to their calling. They are not left to their own devices.

Christians are called to live with humility, gentleness, patience, and love. These are the same character traits that describe Christ. By calling for patience and for putting up with each other, Paul acknowledges that the Christian fellowship is not made up of perfect people. Ephesians 4:3 speaks of the need for believers to make strong efforts to "maintain the unity of the Spirit in the bond of peace." God's Spirit is indeed working in the midst of the church, but the people must also make the effort to live as God intends.

Ephesians 4:4-6. This passage provides us with a brief creed based on the unifying factors that all Christians share. The trinitarian nature of this creed should be noted, with verse 4 mentioning one Spirit, verse 5 mentioning one Lord, and verse 6 mentioning one God and Father. But it is not just the trinitarian God that all Christians share in common. We also share in the one body of Christ and the same hope that is entailed in our calling.

Especially notable is the triad "one Lord, one faith, one baptism" in verse 5. Paul lived in a pluralistic world much like ours where it was believed that there were many lords and gods (see 1 Corinthians 8:5-6). Yet Paul asserts that the only Lord is the Lord Jesus Christ, the only Father is the Father God spoken of in the Bible, and the only Spirit is the Spirit of God mentioned in the Bible. Paul also says that there is only one true faith that saves, not many. Paul's conviction was that God did reveal the divine character in a final and full way in Christ, and, therefore, the gospel is not based on mere human opinions about God but rather on God's self-disclosure in Christ.

By one baptism, Paul surely means water, not Spirit, baptism, and he suggests that it is a rite not to be repeated. Baptism is a rite of initiation, and by definition, a person can be initiated into the body of Christ only once. Baptism is about that first joining of God's people.

Ephesians 4:7-16. This portion of the chapter involves a creative reflection on Psalm 68:18. The quotation in verse 8 is introduced by a remark in verse 7 that every Christian was given grace according to the measure or extent of Christ's gift. The point of this remark is threefold: (1) Christ bestowed different gifts on different persons; (2) Christ is the one who determined who gets what gift, not us; (3) it is perhaps implied that to whom more is given more is expected. The connection between this remark and the quoted psalm is the concept of God's giving of gifts.

The text of Psalm 68:18 was originally about Yahweh ascending Mount Zion after having delivered his people from their foes. In his use of the psalm, Paul probably has in mind the conquest of the spiritual forces that Christ effected through his death and resurrection (compare Colossians 2:15). Ephesians 4:9 stresses that the Christ who ascended had also previously "descended into the lower parts of the earth." This phrase may refer to the grave, but it can also mean that Christ had existed in heaven before he took on flesh. Ephesians 4:11 provides us with a brief list of the gifts Christ gave to his people whom he had left behind on earth. Similar to what we find in 1 Corinthians 12:28, Paul here says that God gave certain people to the church as gifts. Paul's point is not about the gifts people have, but rather about the gifts that certain people are. The list is not exhaustive, for Paul basically lists here only those who had some kind of communication role in the early church—apostles, prophets, evangelists, pastors, and teachers.

The role of all these persons who are gifts to the church is said to be threefold in Ephesians 4:12-13: (1) they are to bring the believers to "completion" or maturity; (2) they are to undertake the work of "service"; and (3) they are to build up the body of Christ. Thus, the translation "to equip the saints for the work of ministry" (4:12) is likely inaccurate. Paul is not speaking of what the leaders do to enable the laypersons to serve; he is speaking of how the leaders serve. Their job is to make sure that persons are fed and become mature Christians by coming to a fuller knowledge of Christ.

The condition of maturity is to be contrasted with what is spoken of in Ephesians 4:14-15. Paul says that Christians should not stay in a state of spiritual infancy forever, easily swayed by the opinions of the day and by trickery and deceit. This infancy is the characteristic of a church that does not take its teaching office and functions seriously and just repeats the same superficial messages. While the teacher or preacher is obliged to speak the truth, one must do so in love, that is, in a fashion that enables others to grow closer to Christ and to become more Christlike. When the body of Christ is working properly, the various parts all fulfill their respective roles and so promote the growth and unity of the whole.

INTERPRETING THE SCRIPTURE

Character Counts

One of the major messages conveyed by the popular *Karate Kid* movies is that a strong person is one who is able to control his actions and walk away from trouble. As Mr. Miyagi would say, "Best way to avoid trouble—not be there." The character description of the Christian found in Ephesians 4:1-3 focuses on humility, gentleness, patience, and a willingness to put up with the flaws and shortcomings of others. These attributes are seen as virtues, even though Paul's world would by and large not see humility or "gladly suffering fools" as a virtue. Meekness would have been interpreted as weakness, just as it is today. But the question is, which takes more strength of character?—to strike back when someone hurts you, or to deliberately not respond in kind, indeed even to respond to curses with blessings? Paul's focus here is on behavior that promotes family unity, that builds up the community of Christ. The use of one's gifts must also have as its goal the edification of the members of Christ's body.

The Essentials of Unity

Paul knew that his converts were a very diverse lot. They were both Jews and Gentiles, young and old, males and females, of high status and low. In the face of this diversity, Christians had to make a conscious effort to build the group, to maintain "the unity of the Spirit in the bond of peace" (4:3). Notice that Paul assumes both that the Spirit is the one who conveys God's peace and also that it is the believer's responsibility to work out that peace in the church's social relationships.

Paul was also firmly committed to the proposition that there were certain truths that all Christians in all places at all times should affirm and that affirming them together would help promote unity among God's people. The creedal fragment found in Ephesians 4:4-6 provides one such list of essentials that produce unity. It is interesting to note that this affirmation involves both things believed about God as well as things believed about the church and its practices.

A well-known author tells the story of a troubled young woman at Emory who came to him for counseling. She related to him her attempt to commit suicide. When he asked what it was that stopped her, she said that as she was about to jump off the high bridge she remembered some words,

which she thought were from the Bible. As it turned out they were part of what Christians often affirmed they believed. The counselor proceeded to ask her where she had heard those words. The girl said she could not remember. He asked her whether she had ever attended church. She said no, but then she remembered that sometimes when she was young and was visiting her grandmother in the summer she went to Bible school. "Aha," he said. This girl's life was saved literally because she remembered some elements of the Christian creed.

Paul believed that there were essential things that Christians needed to believe and affirm, and that these things could be life-giving. He believed that Christ's followers should use their gifts to convey these precious truths to others.

The Quality of Biblical Equality

Our culture affirms that all persons are created equal. While there is truth in this affirmation, one must ask, "Equal in what sense?" We are not all created with equal artistic abilities, or with equal athletic talents, or with equal intelligence, or with equal health, or with equal good looks. In all these respects we are all very different. No two persons have exactly the same gifts and graces, personality or purposes. Nevertheless, the Bible stresses that we are all equally precious in God's sight and equally created in God's image, though it also stresses (as Ephesians 4:7 suggests) that God in Christ has distributed different gifts to different human beings. We are all familiar with remarkable stories of child prodigies, such as Sarah Chang the great violinist; or Bobby Fischer the world-class chess player; or Tiger Woods, who was already a great golfer before he could even drive a car. What these stories remind us of is how unequal we are in so many ways. What we do or the skills or abilities we have are not what makes us equal.

The heart of the matter was conveyed to

me by a very elderly poor man, who when asked what he thought of the rich responded: "The way I see it, everybody comes into this world naked. Until I see someone who is born with clothes on, I'm not going to figure he's any more than me." We are all united in our humanity and in that we are all debtors to God for our very existence, for life itself is a gift. Paul would also add that a new equality can be created in Christ, in whom sexual, social, and racial differences are transcended by one's faith in Christ (Galatians 3:28).

It is interesting that Paul chooses to speak in Ephesians 4:11 not about the gifts that we have but rather about persons as gifts to the body of Christ. In particular he refers to apostles, prophets, evangelists, pastors, and teachers. I can think of numerous teachers and pastors who were certainly gifts in my life. One in particular stands out—Dr. Bernard Boyd, my religion professor at Carolina. What impressed me about him was not just his phenomenal memory for names and faces, but that he cared for his students year after year, treating each one as special.

On one occasion a distraught parent of one of his former students called him and begged him to go and talk to his son in New York. He was contemplating taking his life. Without hesitation Dr. Boyd went to be with the disturbed young man, and coaxed him into returning home and getting help for his problems. The parent had known that Dr. Boyd was the only person who could have accomplished this task. I remember his numerous stories of his experiences as a medic and chaplain during World War II. His faith was tried and found true in some of the most difficult situations human beings could ever face. Every church needs such master teachers

and pastors, for the gifts that Christ has given through them benefit us all.

A Sacred Trust

The bishop who preached the ordination sermon when I became an elder in The United Methodist Church spoke of ministers as "stewards of God's mysteries" (1 Corinthians 4:1). I was deeply impressed with his message. First he stressed that I had been given the privilege of serving in Christ's ministry. It is his ministry, not mine. I am but a steward of what properly belongs to him, and I must use my gifts in ways that comport with that fact. Second, the bishop spoke of the great mysteries and verities of the faith with which I had been entrusted. It was as if someone had handed the Hope diamond to me and told me to take care of it and show it to others. I had the responsibility and privilege of sharing precious and life-saving truths with others. As Paul once said, "Woe to me if I do not proclaim the gospel!" (1 Corinthians 9:16). I would be like a doctor withholding life-saving medicine if I did not share it. In a sense a minister's main task is to offer eternal life insurance to all comers. This insurance policy has as part of the benefits the "ones" or unifying truths and realities mentioned in Ephesians 4. Finally, in his message the bishop also stressed that we must model the way we share the gifts we have received on Christ's way of doing so. We must ever and always ask—What would Jesus do? This question, now emblazoned on garments and accessories, is perhaps the most appropriate question to ask when contemplating how and what to share with others. Jesus has entrusted each of us with gifts and a ministry. Are you doing what he would do with them?

SHARING THE SCRIPTURE

PREPARING TO TEACH

Preparing Our Hearts

As you begin to prepare your own heart for this week's lesson, turn to Ephesians 3:14-21. Here Paul is praying for the church. Use this prayer for your own class and congregation. If possible, memorize the doxology in verses 20-21 that celebrates God's glory and generosity. We will use this doxology to close the session.

Now read Ephesians 4:1-16, which is the scripture passage for this week's lesson. As you read, notice the character traits that Paul believes are important. Also consider the unity that we are called to share as members of the body of Christ. Be aware that Christ is the one who gives the gifts. Finally, recognize the kinds of gifts that Christ gives to the church and the purpose for which he gives them.

Offer a prayer that you and your students will recognize and use your God-given gifts for their intended purpose.

Preparing Our Minds

Look again at Ephesians 4:1-16. You may also want to review other lists of gifts found in Romans 12:4-8 and 1 Corinthians 12:4-11.

Think about your own spiritual gifts and those of class members. How are these gifts being used in God's service?

Preparing Our Learning Space

Have on hand:
- several Bibles
- newsprint and marker
- paper and pencils
- hymnals.

LEADING THE CLASS

(1) Introduction

To begin today's lesson, invite students to recall a pastor, teacher, or evangelist whose gifts for ministry made a real impression on them. Have the students talk with a partner or small group about this special person.

Draw the entire class back together and discuss these questions. You may want to jot down answers on newsprint.

(1) What are some words you would use to describe someone who knows how to use gifts wisely on behalf of the church?

(2) How can a person who wisely uses his or her gifts affect the church?

(3) Why do you think God gave such diverse gifts to so many people?

Move toward today's scripture passage by mentioning that the writer of Ephesians believes that God gives gifts to build up the body of Christ so that the members will be unified in Christ.

Conclude the introduction with today's main question: **How can we Christians use our God-given gifts so that we may serve—rather than sever—the body of Christ by fostering its unity and growth?**

(2) Character Counts

Distribute paper and pencils. Ask the students to list personality characteristics that promote unity within Christ's body. Provide time for the class members to jot down their thoughts.

Now ask them to turn in their Bibles to Ephesians 4:1-16 and read this passage silently. Then, they are to review their list and add new insights from the scripture.

Invite students to share what they have written. Be sure they have included these traits from Ephesians 4:1-3: humility, gentleness, patience, a willingness to put up with the flaws and shortcomings of others, and an ability to maintain peace and unity. Discuss these traits by addressing these questions:

(1) How does society generally view persons who are humble, gentle, patient,

and willing to put up with the short-comings of others? (Note, of course, that these characteristics are viewed negatively by many in our culture. They are seen as signs of weakness.)

(2) **Do you believe it takes more strength of character to strike back when hurt or to choose to exercise humility, gentleness, patience, and a willingness to put up with flaws? Explain your answer.**

(3) **What kind of character traits seem most effective to you in building up a spirit of unity within the church? Explain your answer.**

(3) The Essentials of Unity

Choose a volunteer to read aloud Ephesians 4:4-6.

List on newsprint the following words: body, Spirit, hope, Lord, faith, baptism, God, and Father. Paul tells us that there is only one of each of these. Note that some of these words relate to beliefs about God, whereas others concern the church. Paul's point was that these are truths that all Christians should affirm. Yet we know that there are and have been controversies about these essentials. Ask:

(1) **What controversies can you recall about any of these elements of a Christian creed?**

(2) **Do you agree with Paul that these are the essentials of the faith? If not, what other words would you add? Which ideas would you subtract?**

(3) **If Christians affirm these basic words, do they need to agree on the interpretation of each word? Explain your answer.** (For example, churches do not all accept each other's baptism as authentic. How can this happen if we agree there is only one baptism?)

(4) **What strategies can the church use to balance honest disagreement, especially concerning interpretation, with the need for unity in essentials?** (Respect for dialogue and sincere dis-

agreement are necessary, but members need to work together to find those basics upon which they do agree.)

(5) **How can a knowledge of the essentials of the faith be an anchor when we're in troubled waters?** (You may want to use the story of the young woman who contemplated suicide. See the third paragraph under "The Essentials of Unity" in Interpreting the Scripture.)

(4) The Quality of Biblical Equality

Direct the class members to look again at Ephesians 4:7-13. Ask these questions:

(1) **What does this passage tell you about Christ?**

(2) **What does this passage say about Christ's intentions for the church?**

(3) **If the church has been given gifts of persons who are equipped for ministry, what does that say to church members about how we are to treat the apostles, prophets, evangelists, pastors, and teachers in our midst?**

(4) **What does this passage say to those who are entrusted with gifts for ministry about their responsibility within the church?**

(5) A Sacred Trust

Read or retell "A Sacred Trust" as found in Interpreting the Scripture.

Note the importance of using the gifts in the way that Jesus would. Discuss the following situations with the group. You will need to read aloud each situation that you want to consider.

Situation 1: A pastor uses his gifts to persuade the congregation to put a lavish addition onto their building. Construction costs require them to go deeply into debt. No real programs are in place or on the drawing board for the additional space. What do you think Jesus would say to this pastor about how he has used his gifts?

Situation 2: A pastor and her staff-parish relations committee have had a serious falling out. Both expect her to leave, but not for another six months. In the meantime, she has basically been doing nothing, except preaching. Even her sermons seem poorly prepared and delivered. What would Jesus say to her about how she is using her gifts?

Situation 3: A trusted Bible teacher had become interested in some very questionable teaching. Instead of stating that what he was sharing was the teaching of a sect, he promoted the ideas as orthodox Christianity. This teaching led to confusion and disharmony within the church. What would Jesus say about how this teacher is using his gifts?

Wrap up the discussion by noting that because Christ gives gifts to build up the body, those persons called for specific ministry must not only claim their gifts but also use them responsibly.

You may want to sing the hymn "Many Gifts, One Spirit" (*The United Methodist Hymnal,* no. 114), which speaks of diversity of gifts among the oneness of the Lord.

Prior to dismissal, suggest at least one of the activities below to help the students live out what they have learned today.

To dismiss the class, use the doxology found in Ephesians 3:20-21. Ask the students to read these verses in unison.

HELPING CLASS MEMBERS ACT

Encourage students to write a thank-you note or make a phone call to someone whose wisely used gifts helped them.

Recommend that class members be alert for ways that they can support goals that a leader is trying to promote on behalf of the church.

Suggest that the adults spend time reflecting on how they have attempted to live a life worthy of their calling in Christ Jesus. They may want to write in a spiritual journal some thoughts on how they have been faithful to this call, as well as describe places where they have fallen short.

PLANNING FOR NEXT SUNDAY

Next week's lesson, entitled "Claim Your Responsibilities," looks at how Christians are called to live responsibly, especially within their families. Ask the students to prepare for the session by reading Ephesians 5:1–6:4. The session will focus on 5:1-5, 21-29, and 6:1-4.

CLAIM YOUR RESPONSIBILITIES

PREVIEWING THE LESSON

Lesson Scripture: Ephesians 5:1-5, 21-29; 6:1-4
Background Scripture: Ephesians 5:1–6:4
Key Verse: Ephesians 5:21

Focus of the Lesson:
According to Paul, believers are to live sacrificially with one another, especially within their families.

Main Question of the Lesson:
What should proper Christian relationships look like and how should they be conducted?

This lesson will enable adult learners to:
(1) study Paul's teaching on human relationships.
(2) consider how they relate to other persons, especially within their own families and the church.
(3) respond by making appropriate changes in relationships.

Today's lesson may be outlined as follows:
(1) Introduction
(2) The Marriage Paradigm
(3) Paradise Revisited?
(4) Suffer the Little Children to Come to Me

FOCUSING ON THE MAIN QUESTION

What should proper Christian relationships look like and how should they be conducted? In focusing on this main question, it is important to compare and contrast what Paul says in Ephesians 5:3-5 about how we ought not to live and how, on the other hand, we ought to live according to Ephesians 5:21–6:4. There is a proper context for sexual expression, and that context is marriage. Paul sees Christ as the example of how to love, an example that is especially well illustrated by the

Christian marital relationship. The loving relationship that Christ has for the church is to be imitated by all Christians.

There is perhaps no better way to focus on living sacrificially for others than by thinking of examples we know of such living. My grandfather provided such an example for me. He worked as a fireman. Many times when I was small and staying with him the fire alarm would go off in his house. Immediately he would race down the stairs and go off to help another person or family in distress. Once he even saved a child; he fell through a floor and walked out of a house with the child in his arms. Yet he never spoke about these things unless I asked him. He was a shy and humble man. As a public servant during the Depression, he not only supported his family of five with a meager salary but gave whatever was left to the church and to those who were less fortunate. In later and more prosperous times he continued to live simply, and gave more to others. He would often spend hours counting ballots during elections, all for no pay.

A person's character may be measured by his or her willingness to sacrifice, regardless of the circumstances. I am reminded of Paul's words: "For you know the generous act of our Lord Jesus Christ, that though he was rich, yet for your sakes he became poor, so that by his poverty you might become rich" (2 Corinthians 8:9). My grandfather was an ordinary person who had had an extraordinary experience of Christ that changed him into Christ's sacrificial likeness. He understood what it meant to live responsibly as a follower of Christ.

READING THE SCRIPTURE

NRSV
Ephesians 5:1-5, 21-29

1 Therefore be imitators of God, as beloved children, 2 and live in love, as Christ loved us and gave himself up for us, a fragrant offering and sacrifice to God.

3 But fornication and impurity of any kind, or greed, must not even be mentioned among you, as is proper among saints. 4 Entirely out of place is obscene, silly, and vulgar talk; but instead, let there be thanksgiving. 5 Be sure of this, that no fornicator or impure person, or one who is greedy (that is, an idolater), has any inheritance in the kingdom of Christ and of God.

Key Verse

21 Be subject to one another out of reverence for Christ.

22 Wives, be subject to your husbands as you are to the Lord. 23 For the husband is the head of the wife just as Christ is the head of the church, the body of which he is the Savior. 24 Just as the church is subject to Christ, so also wives ought to be, in everything, to their husbands.

25 Husbands, love your wives, just as Christ loved the church and gave himself up for her, 26 in order to make her holy by cleansing her with the washing of water

NIV
Ephesians 5:1-5, 21-29

¹Be imitators of God, therefore, as dearly loved children ²and live a life of love, just as Christ loved us and gave himself up for us as a fragrant offering and sacrifice to God.

³But among you there must not be even a hint of sexual immorality, or of any kind of impurity, or of greed, because these are improper for God's holy people. ⁴Nor should there be obscenity, foolish talk or coarse joking, which are out of place, but rather thanksgiving. ⁵For of this you can be sure: No immoral, impure or greedy person—such a man is an idolater—has any inheritance in the kingdom of Christ and of God.

²¹Submit to one another out of reverence for Christ.

²²Wives, submit to your husbands as to the Lord. ²³For the husband is the head of the wife as Christ is the head of the church, his body, of which he is the Savior. ²⁴Now as the church submits to Christ, so also wives should submit to their husbands in everything.

²⁵Husbands, love your wives, just as Christ loved the church and gave himself up for her ²⁶to make her holy, cleansing her by the washing with water through the word,

by the word, 27 so as to present the church to himself in splendor, without a spot or wrinkle or anything of the kind—yes, so that she may be holy and without blemish. 28 In the same way, husbands should love their wives as they do their own bodies. He who loves his wife loves himself. 29 For no one ever hates his own body, but he nourishes and tenderly cares for it, just as Christ does for the church.

Ephesians 6:1-4
¹ Children, obey your parents in the Lord, for this is right. 2 "Honor your father and mother"—this is the first commandment with a promise: 3 "so that it may be well with you and you may live long on the earth."
4 And, fathers, do not provoke your children to anger, but bring them up in the discipline and instruction of the Lord.

²⁷and to present her to himself as a radiant church, without stain or wrinkle or any other blemish, but holy and blameless. ²⁸In this same way, husbands ought to love their wives as their own bodies. He who loves his wife loves himself. ²⁹After all, no one ever hated his own body, but he feeds and cares for it, just as Christ does the church.

Ephesians 6:1-4
¹Children, obey your parents in the Lord, for this is right. ²"Honor your father and mother"—which is the first commandment with a promise—³"that it may go well with you and that you may enjoy long life on the earth."
⁴Fathers, do not exasperate your children; instead, bring them up in the training and instruction of the Lord.

UNDERSTANDING THE SCRIPTURE

Ephesians 5:1-5. The discussion of ethical matters had already begun at Ephesians 4:1, where Paul exhorts his readers to live a life worthy of their calling. This section simply continues that thrust and draws some conclusions. Notice in Ephesians 5:1 the call for imitation, a very normal exhortation given by a teacher to his students, as modeling and imitation were major parts of ancient education. Note the similarity between Ephesians 5:2 and 5:25.

For Paul the clearest proof that Christ loves us is that he laid down his life for us. The image of his being a "fragrant offering" conveys the idea that his death was an acceptable and pleasing sacrifice in God's eyes (compare Exodus 29:18; Ezekiel 20:41). In contrast, what is not pleasing to God is described beginning in Ephesians 5:3. Singled out is the sexual sin of fornication, along with impurity and greed. Ephesians 5:4 rules out obscene or vulgar talk, and contrasts it with giving thanks to God. This brief section ends with

the warning in verse 5 that a person who makes the habit of being a fornicator or is a covetor or is sexually impure will have no inheritance in God's kingdom. Paul is not speaking of someone who on one occasion falls into sexual sin but then repents, but someone for whom such behavior is a chosen lifestyle. Paul is saying that while good works will not get you into the kingdom of God, evil works can certainly keep you out because Christians who engage in flagrant immorality are also committing idolatry, worshiping the false gods of pleasure and desire as Ephesians 5:5 suggests. Apostasy is a deliberate choosing to violate God's will as well as a choosing to disbelieve God's word.

Ephesians 5:6-14. This section involves a metaphorical contrast between the ways of darkness and the ways of light. Paul warns against listening to the enticements of non-Christian persons; indeed, he urges Christians not to be associated with such people (compare 1 Corinthians 15:33).

Believers should not choose them as one's regular companions because of their possible negative influence.

Ephesians 5:15-20. This passage addresses the issues of life and time management. Verse 16 speaks of redeeming the time, making the most of it. Ephesians 5:18 contrasts getting drunk with wine with being continually filled with the Holy Spirit. Exuberance can characterize both conditions. The verb here does not mean to receive an additional filling by the Spirit, but rather to be filled on an ongoing basis, a state characterizing the Christian life. Instead of getting inebriated and singing drinking songs, one should be filled continually with the Spirit and sing songs and hymns exuberantly to the Lord. Christian life is characterized by an attitude that gives praise and thanksgiving to God at all times, sometimes in spite of our circumstances, sometimes because of them.

Ephesians 5:21–6:4. These verses comprise a single unit of material that continues on until Ephesians 6:9. Its distinctiveness, especially for its own time, is seldom noticed. Usually missing in such ancient advice were exhortations to the head of the household, and certainly lacking was an urging that one must exercise one's power in love. Paul, however, believed that all human beings were created equally in the image of God, and thus he reforms the existing patriarchal family structure in a variety of ways.

Note that Ephesians 5:21 and 5:22 are closely linked. In the Greek manuscripts there is no verb "submit" ("be subject") in verse 22; it is implied and carried over from verse 21. Thus, the submission of wives to their Christian husbands is but one reflection of the submission Paul requires all Christians to offer to each other. All Christians, male and female, are to be subject to one another out of reverence for Christ. The husband submits to the wife by loving her sacrificially as Christ loved the church. A relationship of mutual submission in love exists, even though the partners fulfill somewhat different roles. Notice Paul says the wife should be subject to the husband *as she would be to Christ,* which implies that if the husband models himself on Christ and loves his wife as Christ did the church, to that extent he can be submitted to. This text does not give carte blanche to dictatorial husbands or those guilty of spousal abuse. Instead Paul is trying to reform such inequities by basing the relationship on the example of Christ.

In Ephesians 5:22-33 Paul spends far more time exhorting the husband about his duties than the wife about hers. In fact, Ephesians 5:25-33 is entirely about the husband's responsibilities. Paul uses the imagery of the "wedding shower" in verses 26-27 to suggest that the husband's job is to work for the spiritual growth, sanctification, and betterment of his wife. The wife is to be loved as the husband loves his own body, and cared for in the same appropriate and meticulous manner. This notion is rooted in Paul's understanding that the husband and the wife become one flesh (Genesis 2:24); that is, they become an integral part of each other's life, and so indispensable to each other.

The considerable importance given to the comparison of the relationship of Christ and his church with the relationship of the Christian husband and wife reminds us that Paul's primary subject here is not family relationships, but rather the church (see Ephesians 5:32).

Ephesians 6:1-4 suggests children are to obey their parents. (Notice the word *obey* is not used to talk about the relationship of wife to husband.) Quoting Exodus 20:12, Paul stresses that parents are to be honored, and that those who do so are promised a blessing—long life and well-being. To honor in antiquity was understood to include providing material support for elderly parents. Finally, Ephesians 6:4 urges the father not to provoke his children to anger, but rather to bring them up in the discipline and instruction of the Lord. This regimen would be a great deal more compassionate and understanding than the usual Greco-Roman rules, which gave one the right to thrash or even kill a disobedient child. Paul tries to ameliorate the harsh aspects of ancient family life by using the model of Christ and the church as the basis for relationships.

INTERPRETING THE SCRIPTURE

The Marriage Paradigm

As is always the case, it is important to bear in mind not just Paul's position on various issues but also the direction and intention of his remarks. For example, taken out of its original social context, Paul's set of instructions to Christian husbands and wives has often been used in an oppressive fashion to reinforce the superior position of men in the family and in society, which was not at all Paul's intent. To the contrary, he was attempting to set up a more Christian and egalitarian model of family life, with Christ and Christian love being the model and ruling principle. Furthermore, Paul saw the relationship of husband and wife as a good example of the more general exhortation that all Christians should submit to one another in loving service.

The positive remarks about marriage in this section are prefaced with negative remarks about other sorts of sexual relationships. Clearly, Paul's view was that Christians should follow the dictum of celibacy in singleness and fidelity in marriage. He also believed that there was not merely an emotional and physical cost to the wrong sorts of sexual relationships but also a spiritual one. One could become a prisoner of one's lusts and find oneself outside the kingdom of God in the end.

The first section of our lesson reminds us that actions always have consequences, a lesson that we in "no-fault" America have a hard time coping with. We would like a world where one could sin with no repercussions—temporal or eternal. Contrary to this kind of thinking, God did not create an immoral or amoral world. Rather, God created a world where proper worship and proper living go together, just as improper worship and immoral actions go together. Of course, if all of Paul's converts had been perfect, he would not have needed to give such advice to them. It is a salutary reminder whenever we are prone to judge others that there but for the grace of God go I.

Perhaps the most important thing one can say about sinful behavior is that though it is self-centered it is also self-destructive because human beings were made by God to relate to and serve each other. Paul contrasts the sinful life with the Christlike pattern of self-sacrifice and faithful commitment. He tries to inculcate in his converts the attitude that "that was then, and this is now." Going back to old patterns of behavior is not a legitimate option. Instead, one should live responsibly by serving others, particularly one's fellow Christians and one's family. Christians who are "subject to one another out of reverence for Christ" (5:21) do whatever they can to help others.

Paradise Revisited?

Some have suggested that Adam and Eve had the best of all possible marital situations. He could never ask, "Why can't you cook like my mother?" and she could not say, "Do you know how many men I passed up in order to marry you?" Neither one of them had any in-laws. Yet even in those circumstances there was trouble in paradise. Marriage is no more a perfect relationship than other sorts of relationships are. In fact, it often magnifies our faults, or at least makes them more visible to our nearest neighbor, namely, our spouse.

Sometimes after the preacher has said "and the two shall become one," the couple spends a goodly portion of the rest of their adult lives trying to determine which one. Which one will be dominant? Under such circumstances it is crucial to bear in mind that Genesis 2 suggests that the desire to dominate is a result of the fall, not a part of God's plan for male-female relationships. The call to mutual submission and respect is addressed to each partner or person individually. In other words, Paul does not say, "Husbands tell your wives to submit, and tell your children to obey." Rather, the call to submit or obey is addressed individually to those in question, and they are expected to respond freely on their own, not as a result of coercion.

Paul is also suggesting here that the human marriage relationship is the closest human analogy to the relationship between Christ and his church. He of course has in mind Christian marriage when it is working properly and at its best, not when it is characterized by tyranny, oppression, and abuse. Paul seems to believe that marriage is the ultimate test case as to whether it is indeed possible for us to love our neighbor as ourselves. If we cannot love our wives or husbands as ourselves, what hope or chance is there of our loving others in that fashion? If we cannot sacrificially serve this nearest neighbor, why should we think we can do so with other more remote individuals or groups of people? I am reminded of the *Peanuts* comic strip where Linus says he loves humankind (in the abstract); it's just individuals, especially particular ones, that he can't abide.

It is indeed a sobering question, but thankfully Paul doesn't expect anyone to try and live out that relationship without divine help and grace. The third person in every Christian marriage is Christ himself, who continues to love and pour himself out on our behalf, giving us the resources we need to do what God would have us do in a marriage relationship. In this way wedlock doesn't become deadlock.

Suffer the Little Children to Come to Me

Today's Christian parents are groping for handles to help them raise their children. Certainly Christian parenting material by James Dobson or some of the better secular material by John Rosemond and others is often sought out and even discussed in church groups. Parents want to know how to communicate with their children, set boundaries, mete out appropriate punishment when necessary, help children develop a value system based on biblical principles, and find God's purpose for their lives. How is all of this to be done?

The advice Paul gives here suggests that love, understanding, and patience must characterize parenting. It also suggests that parents are not to abdicate their role as the family guides and that children are called upon to obey their parents. The catch, of course, is that the parent must relate to the child in a way that doesn't drive the child to despair or distraction. Here again asking the questions of what Jesus would do, of how Jesus would have served and led them, is crucial. We should be mindful of Christ's words that we should allow the children to come to him and not to hinder them. In short, we are not God in our children's lives. Rather we are parents who are called upon to lead them to God, and we are to so embody the character of Christ, the one who served all, so that our children will catch the vision and want to become like Christ. When we open the door to the kingdom of God for our children, we are truly claiming our responsibilities as Christian parents, just as Paul calls us to do.

SHARING THE SCRIPTURE

PREPARING TO TEACH

Preparing Our Hearts

This week's devotional reading from Ephesians 5:6-20 is actually part of the background scripture. Here Paul is warning us to be careful about how we live. We are called to be wise people who make the most of the time that we have. How are you using your time? Would God commend you for living a life filled with the Spirit and focused on the reign of God?

Now read the entire background scripture from Ephesians 5:1–6:4. Note especially our verses for today's lesson: 5:1-5, 21-29, and 6:1-4. How do you measure up to the standards of conduct set before you here? What changes do you need to make in order to imitate God more closely?

Pray that you and your students will discern ways to live responsibly and lovingly before God.

Preparing Our Minds

Review the Bible passage once again and read this lesson carefully. You may want to do some reading about the society and customs of the people to whom Paul was writing. Note that while Paul's comments hardly strike us as cutting-edge ideas, he made radical comments for his time. For example, while it would have been acceptable to tell women to be subject to their husbands, the idea of giving the husband directions about how to treat his wife would have been unique in such a patriarchal culture.

Preparing Our Learning Space

Have on hand:
✔ several Bibles
✔ hymnals
✔ newsprint and marker.

LEADING THE CLASS

(1) Introduction

Open today's session by singing about the Christian family. "Happy the Home When God Is There" (*The United Methodist Hymnal*, no. 445) would be a good choice to help the students focus on the theme of today's lesson.

Write this sentence stem on newsprint: **A Christian family...** Encourage the students to call out whatever they think best completes this sentence. Write their ideas on the newsprint.

Move into today's lesson by pointing out that Ephesians 5:1–6:4 has much to say about how we are to live responsibly, especially within our families. Our main question is this: **What should proper Christian relationships look like and how should they be conducted?**

(2) The Marriage Paradigm

Choose a volunteer to read aloud Ephesians 5:1-5. Ask:
(1) Verse 1 says that we are to be imitators of God. In what ways can we imitate God? (We are to love. Note also that 4:32 calls us to be kind, tenderhearted, and forgiving.)
(2) What kinds of behavior does Paul speak out against? (He denounces sexual immorality, greediness, obscene language, and idolatry.)

Note that in contrast to these negative images, Paul sets forth positive behaviors within the context of marriage. Call on someone to read Ephesians 5:21-29. Encourage students to make an initial response to these verses. Likely, there will be some debate, since many couples in our society would describe their relationship in different terms. Note that Paul's comments were radical for his own society.

Though he speaks of mutual submission to one another in verse 21, that ideal was likely not fully realized even in the Christian marriages of Paul's day.

Invite the students to become marriage counselors. If they were asked to give advice to the following couples, what would they say? Read each situation aloud.

Marriage 1: Jim and Julie have been married for thirty years. The parents of two grown children and three grandchildren, they have somehow drifted apart over the years. Jim and Julie seldom talk. Both are involved in their own interests. They aren't arguing with one another; they are just disinterested. What advice could you give to help them rekindle a loving, mutually affirming relationship?

Marriage 2: Lenny and Carla recently celebrated their fifteenth anniversary. Lenny is verbally and physically abusive to his wife and their three children. Carla will not leave because she loves Lenny. Moreover, she cannot afford to be on her own with the children. Lenny uses Ephesians 5:22 to remind Carla that she is to be subject to him. What would you say to help them end this pattern of abuse?

(3) Paradise Revisited?

Read or retell "Paradise Revisited?" from the Interpreting the Scripture portion. The class will likely enjoy the humor here.

Ask the students to turn again to verses 21-29 and look carefully at the relationship that is to exist between the husband and wife, and then compare that relationship to that of Christ and the church. Ask:

(1) What does this passage tell you about how Christ views and treats the church?

(2) What does this passage tell you about how the church is to relate to Christ?

(3) What do you think the church needs to do in order to be the ideal "wife" that is described in Ephesians?

Invite the students to spend some quiet time thinking about how they can enrich their own marriages and/or be a more ideal "wife" for Christ as part of the church.

(4) Suffer the Little Children to Come to Me

Turn now to the issue of responsible Christian parenting. Ask these questions. You may want to jot down answers to the first question on newsprint.

(1) What are some of the greatest issues facing adults who are trying to raise children today? (You may want to use information in the first paragraph of "Suffer the Little Children to Come to Me," found in Interpreting the Scripture.)

(2) Imagine that Jesus were a parent in the United States today. How might he handle some of the issues we have just outlined?

Note that the words from Ephesians 6:1-4 do have something important to say to parents. Read this passage aloud. Now ask:

(1) How does our society, perhaps unwittingly, undermine the relationship between parents and their children?

(2) How can your congregation help parents to do their job well?

Offer a prayer for husbands and wives, parents and children, and the church, that all may treat each other with the same love and respect that Christ offers to the church.

As you close today's session, be sure to suggest at least one of the activities below so that students will have concrete ideas as to how to live out what they have learned.

HELPING CLASS MEMBERS ACT

Call upon class members to examine their relationships with other family members and the church. Ask them to decide whether they are, in fact, being subject to one another. If they are using power inappropriately, encourage them to seek God's guidance and, if necessary, human counsel.

Encourage the students to be aware of the way they communicate with others. Are they open and loving or defensive, perhaps often putting others down rather than lifting them up? Recommend that they listen to themselves as they speak and make changes as needed.

Challenge parents and others who deal with children to set fair, consistent standards. These adults should also work with the children to help them develop a sense of right and wrong so that they can be more self-disciplined, as opposed to needing external threats of punishment to do what is right.

PLANNING FOR NEXT SUNDAY

Ephesians 6:10-24 will be the scripture reading for our lesson entitled "Claim Your Power Base." This lesson will help students recognize the resources they have available to stand firm in the Lord. Note that the following week we will begin our final unit for the summer quarter, entitled "Christ Above All." Most of the reading for that unit will be from the book of Colossians. Some class members may want to read this short letter in its entirety.

CLAIM YOUR POWER BASE

PREVIEWING THE LESSON

Lesson Scripture: Ephesians 6:10-24
Background Scripture: Ephesians 6:10-24
Key Verse: Ephesians 6:10

Focus of the Lesson:
Christians are empowered by God to stand firm against evil.

Main Question of the Lesson:
What does it take for a Christian to persevere in the faith in the midst of trials and tribulations?

This lesson will enable adult learners to:
(1) hear Paul's call to stand firm in the strength of God's power.
(2) consider their own spiritual preparedness to stand firm against evil.
(3) respond by helping someone else cope with a difficult situation.

Today's lesson may be outlined as follows:
(1) Introduction
(2) The Heart of Darkness
(3) The Full Armor of God
(4) Pastoral Concerns
(5) Persons of Perseverance

FOCUSING ON THE MAIN QUESTION

Today's lesson consists of four separate parts, all of which deal in one way or another with the issue of how Christians are to persevere under pressure. The first segment focuses on the qualities of Christian life available to us all to help fend off the assaults of the powers of darkness. These qualities include righteousness, faith, and truth, among others. The second segment focuses on prayer as a resource.

Paul tells his readers to keep alert and persevere in prayer, for prayer is a key to persevering in the faith. The third segment stresses that personal ministerial work in the form of encouraging others is a key to perseverance. The last segment emphasizes that it is God's love, grace, and peace that keeps the flames of an undying love for Christ burning in a Christian's heart.

I doubt it is an accident that Paul

stresses character when he is addressing the issue of how Christians persevere through trials. Prayer, specific tasks, and grace will help; but without Christian character, one is in all likelihood going to wilt under pressure. The strength of one's character is particularly important to Americans. We expect our community, business, and political leaders to have high moral and ethical standards. We set even higher standards for those who are called to be ordained clergy. Yet we know that all people fall short, no matter what their calling might be. How people face trials is indeed a mark of their character. Perseverance is critically important to us. Therefore, today's lesson raises the question: **What does it take for a Christian to persevere in the faith in the midst of trials and tribulations?**

READING THE SCRIPTURE

NRSV
Ephesians 6:10-24

Key Verse

10 Finally, be strong in the Lord and in the strength of his power. 11 Put on the whole armor of God, so that you may be able to stand against the wiles of the devil. 12 For our struggle is not against enemies of blood and flesh, but against the rulers, against the authorities, against the cosmic powers of this present darkness, against the spiritual forces of evil in the heavenly places. 13 Therefore take up the whole armor of God, so that you may be able to withstand on that evil day, and having done everything, to stand firm. 14 Stand therefore, and fasten the belt of truth around your waist, and put on the breastplate of righteousness. 15 As shoes for your feet put on whatever will make you ready to proclaim the gospel of peace. 16 With all of these, take the shield of faith, with which you will be able to quench all the flaming arrows of the evil one. 17 Take the helmet of salvation, and the sword of the Spirit, which is the word of God.

18 Pray in the Spirit at all times in every prayer and supplication. To that end keep alert and always persevere in supplication for all the saints. 19 Pray also for me, so that when I speak, a message may be given to me to make known with boldness the mystery of the gospel, 20 for which I am an ambassador in chains. Pray that I may declare it boldly, as I must speak.

NIV
Ephesians 6:10-24

Key Verse

[10]**Finally, be strong in the Lord and in his mighty power.** [11]Put on the full armor of God so that you can take your stand against the devil's schemes. [12]For our struggle is not against flesh and blood, but against the rulers, against the authorities, against the powers of this dark world and against the spiritual forces of evil in the heavenly realms. [13]Therefore put on the full armor of God, so that when the day of evil comes, you may be able to stand your ground, and after you have done everything, to stand. [14]Stand firm then, with the belt of truth buckled around your waist, with the breastplate of righteousness in place, [15]and with your feet fitted with the readiness that comes from the gospel of peace. [16]In addition to all this, take up the shield of faith, with which you can extinguish all the flaming arrows of the evil one. [17]Take the helmet of salvation and the sword of the Spirit, which is the word of God. [18]And pray in the Spirit on all occasions with all kinds of prayers and requests. With this in mind, be alert and always keep on praying for all the saints.

[19]Pray also for me, that whenever I open my mouth, words may be given me so that I will fearlessly make known the mystery of the gospel, [20]for which I am an ambassador in chains. Pray that I may declare it fearlessly, as I should.

21 So that you also may know how I am and what I am doing, Tychicus will tell you everything. He is a dear brother and a faithful minister in the Lord. 22 I am sending him to you for this very purpose, to let you know how we are, and to encourage your hearts.

23 Peace be to the whole community, and love with faith, from God the Father and the Lord Jesus Christ. 24 Grace be with all who have an undying love for our Lord Jesus Christ.

²¹Tychicus, the dear brother and faithful servant in the Lord, will tell you everything, so that you also may know how I am and what I am doing. ²²I am sending him to you for this very purpose, that you may know how we are, and that he may encourage you.

²³Peace to the brothers, and love with faith from God the Father and the Lord Jesus Christ. ²⁴Grace to all who love our Lord Jesus Christ with an undying love.

UNDERSTANDING THE SCRIPTURE

Introduction. There are four major parts to Ephesians 6:10-24: (1) the analogy with battle armor in 6:10-17; (2) a discussion of prayer in 6:18-20; (3) the discussion of Tychicus's role in 6:21-22; and (4) a final benediction in 6:23-24. Ephesians 6:10-20, or at least 6:10-17, forms the *peroratio*, or final exhortation and appeal to the emotions that sums up the previous arguments in the letter and attempts to reach the audience at the level of their feelings (note 6:20), with warnings about evil and about the spiritual as well as temporal dangers.

Ephesians 6:10-17. The analogy between a Christian's defenses and battle armor draws on things said in the Old Testament about God as a warrior. Our text is particularly indebted to Isaiah 59:17, which speaks of God who, because no one else would maintain justice and defeat the foe, "put on righteousness like a breastplate, and a helmet of salvation on his head; he put on garments of vengeance for clothing, and wrapped himself in a fury as in a mantle." This is probably why in our text the Christian is said to be putting on the armor *of God*. The idea here is that Christians are more or less defenseless without the resources God provides for them. This description also owes something to a Roman soldier's gear. Paul is not talking about going on the offensive against evil, but rather withstanding its assaults.

The aggressor in Ephesians 6:10-17 is the devil. Notice the stress in verse 10 on being strong, in verses 11 and 14 on standing, in verse 13 on withstanding, and in verse 16 on quenching. There is no reference here to offensive weapons such as the spear or the bow or the sling. Only the sword is mentioned in verse 17 and probably what is meant is the Roman soldier's short dagger, which was used for defensive purposes. Unlike a broad sword it was not a weapon of attack. Our author is stressing the resources Christians have to protect themselves from the powers of darkness. This is a word of comfort and reassurance to Christians under pressure and facing spiritual dangers. It has nothing to do with beginning a "deliverance" ministry, a ministry in which one seeks to go on the attack against the powers of darkness, performing rituals of exorcism and other similar rituals, even on Christians. The church has always had its exorcists, but they are few in number and are people with special gifts and spiritual wisdom. An untrained person is not being encouraged here to assume such a ministry.

The weapons that Paul thinks are available to protect the ordinary Christian are, according to verses 14-17, truth, righteousness, the gospel of peace, faith, salvation, and the word of God. These are the resources available to all Christians to use in the struggle to resist evil and proclaim peace. Verse 12 also reminds the reader that the Christian's struggles are not primarily against other human beings, but rather against supernatural evil. There is often the temptation to see other persons as the enemy, the embodiment of Evil, but this misses the larger point about supernatural evil. In Paul's view, human beings are just pawns of the powers of darkness. They are not the ultimate source of temptation or trials for Christian people. Therefore, hatred of strangers, foreigners, other races, or other nations is never justified. Rather, those in the clutches of evil must be prayed for and loved as persons for whom Christ died so that they might be set free from the sins and evil that beset them.

A Christian knows that he or she must be strong in the Lord and in God's power, not in some human source of might. A Christian is called upon to preach the "gospel of peace" according to verse 15. This is a partial quotation from Isaiah 52:7: "How beautiful upon the mountains are the feet of the messenger who announces peace, who brings good news, who announces salvation." We are empowered to seek the lost and proclaim the good news of salvation, not to attack them as if they were the source of evil.

Ephesians 6:18-20. Perhaps this passage is a continuation of the previous one, in which case the ultimate weapon of the Christian warrior is prayer. It is not just any sort of prayer that Paul has in mind, however, but prayer empowered by the Holy Spirit that indwells the believer. Notice the distinction in verse 18 between prayer and supplication. The former has in view prayers of praise and the thanksgiving, while the latter refers to petitions or requests. Christians are enjoined to persevere in prayer for their fellow Christians, including their leaders, such as Paul. Strikingly, Paul does not ask for prayer for his release but rather for prayer that he might declare God's word boldly.

Ephesians 6:21-22. Paul had coworkers who were vital to the spread of the gospel and the building up of those who had already professed their faith in Christ. Probably Tychicus is the bearer and the deliverer of this letter, entrusted with the responsibility not only to read the letter to these Christians but to add whatever additional oral remarks might be necessary to complete the task of communication.

Ephesians 6:23-24. This text includes not only a benediction that wishes peace and love from God to these Christians, but also a wish of grace for those who have an undying love for Christ.

INTERPRETING THE SCRIPTURE

The Heart of Darkness

Much has been made of late, especially in conservative Christian circles, of the role of supernatural evil in human affairs, even ordinary human affairs. This view of life has led to excesses of various sorts. If one has read such best-selling Christian thrillers as Frank E. Peretti's *This Present Darkness* and its sequels, one could come away with the impression that there is a demon under every rock, that all non-Christian people are basically possessed, and that in a no-fault world the phrase "the devil made me do it" is yet another legitimate way to shift blame for one's misconduct onto someone else. At the other end of the spectrum are those who deny there are such beings as demons or the devil. Somewhere between these two extremes is the truth that the Bible promulgates about the reality of supernatural evil.

Evil in our world is not merely human sin, or governmental corruption, or fallen structures in society, though all of these things bear witness to the reality of evil in the world. Evil also has a supernatural face that must be taken very seriously. Evil is not something to be scoffed at or dismissed; for as C. S. Lewis remarked in his classic *The Screwtape Letters*, it is a favorite ploy of the devil to put up a smoke screen so that people will begin to believe he doesn't exist.

People who scoff at the reality of evil then have a very difficult time explaining modern phenomena such as the rise to power and success of the failed Austrian painter whom we know as Adolf Hitler. Such people have no explanation for the extermination of nearly six million Jews by one of the most "civilized" of all human cultures. It is thus necessary to take seriously Paul's warning here about the powers and principalities that are not flesh and blood but that are nonetheless quite real.

The reality of supernatural evil and our great need for protection from it was brought forcefully home to me by an experience of one of my seminary roommates. One summer in the late 1970s Tim was an intern pastor in West Virginia. There, he happened to encounter a remarkable young man who was tall, friendly, and most of the time quite gentle. Yet from time to time this young man would go on a rampage downtown and destroy windows, parking meters, and a variety of other things. It was the most senseless sort of violence because he was not trying to steal anything. These activities eventually landed him in jail. Tim, as a minister, went to visit him, and became deeply concerned and disturbed because he came to the conclusion that this young man was indeed possessed. Apparently the young man had been involved in some sort of Satanic cult. Since Tim had had experience with this sort of phenomenon before, he came to visit the young man again, armed with an exorcism ritual and having prayed himself into a position of spiritual strength. As Tim went through the ritual and had the

young man name the spirit that possessed him, the man broke out in a cold sweat and was thrown up against the back wall of the jail cell by some tremendous force. After this the young man was at peace. In fact, after this the young man did not thereafter manifest any destructive behavior. Rather he reverted to the gentle and likable person he had otherwise been.

In evaluating this event, it is important to say that such cases of actual possession seem to be few and far between, but nonetheless real. They are not to be confused with the more mundane sort of physical, psychological, and emotional problems that so many human beings seem prey to. My own experience suggests that real cases of possession are rare, though there are cases where people have been deluded or deceived by the powers of darkness. As a Christian minister I find it important to rule out all normal possibilities when diagnosing a problem before reaching the conclusion that one is dealing with a case of supernatural evil. Yet equally, one must not rule out such a possibility. Human beings are not just bodies or minds or emotions. They are also spiritual creatures subject to various spiritual forces. It is naive to dismiss this truth.

The Full Armor of God

One of my favorite texts from Paul's writings is "No testing has overtaken you that is not common to everyone. God is faithful, and he will not let you be tested beyond your strength, but with the testing he will also provide the way out so that you may be able to endure it" (1 Corinthians 10:13). Our text in Ephesians 6, with its discourse on putting on the full armor of God, says much the same thing. There the writer reassures us that God is able to provide us with the strength and resources of faith to endure the onslaught of the powers of darkness. Against darkness we offer light. Against falsehood we counter with truth. Against wickedness we proffer righteousness. Against war we proclaim peace. Against bad news we offer good news. Against attacks and doubts we hold forth faith. Against lostness we preach salvation.

Perhaps the most powerful weapons of all are mentioned last in Ephesians 6:17-20 —namely, the word of God and prayer. Our lesson is clear enough that among other things it takes prayer to withstand life's trials and temptations. In regard to prayer, Paul stresses prayer enabled by the Spirit of God. Paul speaks of this matter in Romans 8 where he says that when words fail us the Spirit speaks through us to God the Father, crying Abba and speaking with sighs too deep for words (Romans 8:15-17, 26). Not only do we pray to God for others, we also pray with God's assistance for divine help.

Pastoral Concerns

Paul speaks of receiving a message from God that helps unveil the mystery of the good news. He adds that his audience should pray for him not only so that he might proclaim this message with boldness, but also that he might receive a message while preaching. Paul is here speaking of a phenomenon that has occurred repeatedly to Christian preachers, especially those preaching or sharing in a moment of trial or urgency. They have prepared their sermon, and yet when they preach something serendipitous happens. They receive new flashes of insight from God's Spirit that help to further illuminate the text and so also the audience.

Paul was essentially a pastor, and nowhere is this more evident in Ephesians than at 6:21-22. Paul does not want anyone to be worried about him and he also doesn't want anyone to be discouraged, and so he sends his assistant, Tychicus, to minister to the audience and comfort and reassure them. He is not merely the carrier of the mail or the message; he is to act as a pastor and encourage their hearts.

This letter ends with Paul's desire that God grant the readers peace, love, and grace. These attributes are gifts from God that make possible an undying love for Jesus Christ. We love because God first loved us, and poured out that everlasting divine love into our hearts (Romans 5:5).

Persons of Perseverance

Many Christians have had persons in their lives who especially manifested this undying love for Christ. Since the Christian faith is as often caught as taught, it is this sort of example that has often led people to Christ. Such was the case with me. In college I had a roommate who was an All-Conference football player, a Phi Beta Kappa student, president of the Fellowship of Christian Athletes, and on full academic scholarship. He was 6'4", blond, and handsome. He had everything going for him and every reason to be arrogant and overlook a person like me who was in essence a bookworm. Yet when I would come home at night from the library, all 6'4" were on his knees praying for me. This loving example eventually had a major impact on my life. I might well not be writing this lesson today had my friend's love not been manifest in this way.

Who we are, as well as what we say, is crucial as we bear witness for Christ. Without a doubt, one of the things that has helped me to persevere through hard times is remembering that others have found it possible to remain strong in their Christian faith despite many temptations and difficulties. The examples that led me to Christ can still sustain me in times of doubt and darkness. These examples remind me to "be strong in the Lord and in the strength of his power" (Ephesians 6:10).

SHARING THE SCRIPTURE

PREPARING TO TEACH

Preparing Our Hearts

To begin your own reflections on this lesson, read John 14:15-27. In this devotional reading, we hear Jesus promising his disciples that the Holy Spirit—the Spirit of truth—will come to them. Jesus also tells the disciples to show their love for him by keeping his commandments. How does the Spirit empower you?

Look next at Ephesians 6:10-24. These words, especially in verses 10-17, will likely be quite familiar to you and your students. Perhaps you will recall a Sunday school class from childhood in which you donned a paper helmet or other piece of the armor described here. Think about how your understanding of evil and the way that Christians stand firm against it has changed over the years. Maybe during childhood you saw evil personified in the schoolyard bully. Where do you perceive evil now? How do you stand firm against it?

Ask God in prayer to help you and your class members to be prepared to stand firm against evil.

Preparing Our Minds

Review the scripture reading and study this lesson carefully. Be sure to note, as mentioned in the Introduction to Understanding the Scripture, that we will be dealing with four different segments of scripture.

Be sure to read Isaiah 59:17, which is the source for the whole armor of God that is referred to in Ephesians 6.

Preparing Our Learning Space

Have on hand:
- several Bibles
- hymnals
- newsprint and marker
- paper and pencils.

LEADING THE CLASS

(1) Introduction

To begin today's session, invite the students to sing "Soldiers of Christ, Arise" (*The United Methodist Hymnal*, no. 513) or "Stand Up, Stand Up for Jesus" (*UMH*, no. 514). Both of these hymns are based on Ephesians 6.

Note that today's lesson is a clarion call to stand firm on the power of God in the face of evil. Ask the following questions. You may want to list ideas on newsprint.
(1) What evidence do you see that evil exists in the world?
(2) What resources do you as a Christian have to stand against such evil?
Segue into today's lesson by pointing out that the writer of Ephesians has much to say about evil and how we can combat it using the resources that God has given us.

Raise today's main question: **What does it take for a Christian to persevere in the faith in the midst of trials and tribulations?**

(2) The Heart of Darkness

Make these points about evil:
- Two extreme views of evil are present in our society. On the one hand, some believers see evil everywhere, even assuming that non-Christians are possessed by demons. On the other hand, some Christians deny the existence of supernatural evil.
- The Bible's position is between these two extremes.
  Ask these questions:
(1) How do you define "evil"?
(2) What role do you ascribe to supernatural forces of evil?

Conclude this section by reading or retelling the story of Tim, which is found the fourth paragraph of "The Heart of Darkness" section of Interpreting the Scripture. Students may wish to respond to this story.

(3) The Full Armor of God

To help the students recognize all of the resources that God's armor provides, ask one person to read Ephesians 6:10-13. Then have four different people each read one verse from verses 14-17. Prior to the reading, distribute paper and pencils. Ask the students to draw what they are hearing about how the well-armed Christian is dressed. Artistic ability is not necessary, and students will not be asked to show their work. The idea is simply to impress upon them the variety of resources at our disposal.

Next, ask the students to pick out the main resources in this passage and list them on their paper. Lists should include: truth, righteousness, the gospel of peace, faith, salvation, and the word of God.

Divide the class into teams or ask students to work with a partner. Assign each group one or more of the listed words. Encourage the groups to talk about how the word they have been assigned is a resource for them in the face of evil. Allow time for groups to share their ideas.

(4) Pastoral Concerns

Read aloud Ephesians 6:18-20. Note that "prayer" here refers to praise and thanksgiving, whereas a "supplication" is a petition or request. Ask the class:

(1) What does it mean to you to "pray in the Spirit"?

(2) How can you be in prayer "at all times"?

(3) Why does Paul ask for prayer? (Note that he is not concerned about his own predicament, only that he be able to speak the gospel boldly.)

This would be an excellent time (if you do not do so at some other time in your session) to invite students to create a prayer list. Write on newsprint the names of those needing prayer. Encourage the students to pray silently for a few moments and then offer a verbal prayer, or ask someone else to pray aloud for the persons and situations that are on the list. If your congregation has a churchwide prayer chain, be sure that the names are forwarded to someone on the chain for further prayer.

Look now at Ephesians 6:21-22. Point out that Paul is acting as a pastor by sending Tychicus to minister to the people.

(5) Persons of Perseverance

Read or retell "Persons of Perseverance" in Interpreting the Scripture. Ask:

(1) Why do you think this roommate was such a powerful witness for Christ?

(2) Who has impressed you as a person of perseverance? Why?

(3) Consider again today's main question: What does it take for a Christian to persevere in the faith in the midst of trials and tribulations?

Do this brief guided imagery exercise with the class:

● Think of a time when you were in a difficult situation, facing evil that tried your faith. (pause)

● Remember the resources you were able to call upon to get through that experience. (pause)

● Give thanks to God for those spiritual resources that enabled you to be strong and stand fast. (pause)

● Open your eyes when you are ready.

If possible, sing "I Want a Principle Within" (*The United Methodist Hymnal*, no. 410).

Ask the students to read Ephesians 6:23-24 in unison as the benediction for the morning.

Before the students depart, lift up one of the activities below so that they will have some ideas as to how to live out what they have learned.

HELPING CLASS MEMBERS ACT

Suggest that class members affirm someone they know who is coping valiantly with a challenging situation. This affirmation may come in the form of a phone call, a card, or maybe some flowers that will help lift the person's spirits and let them know that others support them in their struggle.

Perhaps some students know a crime victim who feels insecure about venturing out. Recommend that class members support this person, or others who are just as afraid in our increasingly hostile world, by offering to run errands with them.

Encourage the adults to spend extra time in prayer this week for leaders within the church and government.

PLANNING FOR NEXT SUNDAY

Next Sunday we will begin our final unit of this quarter, "Christ Above All." The lesson for August 6, "The Source of Life," is taken from Colossians 1. Ask the students to read all of this chapter for background, looking especially at verses 15-28.

UNIT 3: CHRIST ABOVE ALL
THE SOURCE OF LIFE

PREVIEWING THE LESSON

Lesson Scripture: Colossians 1:15-28
Background Scripture: Colossians 1
Key Verses: Colossians 1:19-20

Focus of the Lesson:
Jesus Christ, in whom everything was created, has preeminence in all things.

Main Question of the Lesson:
What is the source of our hope and the basis of our faith?

This lesson will enable adult learners to:
(1) hear Paul's teachings concerning the supremacy of Christ.
(2) recognize that Jesus has preeminence over all.
(3) respond by joining and remaining faithful to a Christian cause.

Today's lesson may be outlined as follows:
(1) Introduction
(2) The Pearl of Great Price
(3) Worship in the Name
(4) Universal Love
(5) The Hope of Glory
(6) Suffering for Jesus

FOCUSING ON THE MAIN QUESTION

Do you remember as a child ever wishing for a special gift for your birthday or Christmas? Can you recall what made you think that your wish would become a reality? Did you have faith in a parent, grandparent, or other significant adult who you knew would make sure that your wish came true? Just as children have faith and hope, so also do we as Christians.

What is the source of our hope and the basis of our faith? Various texts speak to us about the relationship of hope and faith. For instance, Hebrews 11:1 says that faith itself is "the assurance of things hoped for." Christian faith clearly looks forward to and is excited about what God will yet do. However the main question we will deal with in this lesson asks about the *source* of our hope and the *basis* of our faith. If we are to narrow our focus to encompass these things then we must concentrate on Christ, who is the source of our hope, and on what He accomplished, which is the basis of our faith. The material in this lesson is diverse and the christological substance of it is considerable, especially in Colossians 1:15-24.

Paul reminds the Colossians of whom and what they believe in, as well as what God in Christ has accomplished, both for them and in them. Colossians 1:13-14 and 1:21-23, respectively, emphasize the human condition before and after Jesus' reconciling work. Finally, Paul reminds his converts that there is often a cost to being a Christian: suffering. In sum, this lesson calls us to recognize that faith, hope, and love are grounded in the divine Christ and His work in creation and redemption.

READING THE SCRIPTURE

NRSV
Colossians 1:15-28

15 He is the image of the invisible God, the firstborn of all creation; 16 for in him all things in heaven and on earth were created, things visible and invisible, whether thrones or dominions or rulers or powers—all things have been created through him and for him. 17 He himself is before all things, and in him all things hold together. 18 He is the head of the body, the church; he is the beginning, the firstborn from the dead, so that he might come to have first place in everything. **19 For in him all the fullness of God was pleased to dwell, 20 and through him God was pleased to reconcile to himself all things, whether on earth or in heaven, by making peace through the blood of his cross.**

21 And you who were once estranged and hostile in mind, doing evil deeds, 22 he has now reconciled in his fleshly body through death, so as to present you holy and blameless and irreproachable before him—23 provided that you continue securely established and steadfast in the faith, without shifting from the hope promised by the gospel that you heard, which has been proclaimed to every creature under heaven. I, Paul, became a servant of this gospel.

24 I am now rejoicing in my sufferings for your sake, and in my flesh I am completing what is lacking in Christ's afflictions for the sake of his body, that is, the church. 25 I became its servant according

NIV
Colossians 1:15-28

[15]He is the image of the invisible God, the firstborn over all creation. [16]For by him all things were created: things in heaven and on earth, visible and invisible, whether thrones or powers or rulers or authorities; all things were created by him and for him. [17]He is before all things, and in him all things hold together. [18]And he is the head of the body, the church; he is the beginning and the firstborn from among the dead, so that in everything he might have the supremacy. **[19]For God was pleased to have all his fullness dwell in him, [20]and through him to reconcile to himself all things, whether things on earth or things in heaven, by making peace through his blood, shed on the cross.**

[21]Once you were alienated from God and were enemies in your minds because of your evil behavior. [22]But now he has reconciled you by Christ's physical body through death to present you holy in his sight, without blemish and free from accusation—[23]if you continue in your faith, established and firm, not moved from the hope held out in the gospel. This is the gospel that you heard and that has been proclaimed to every creature under heaven, and of which I, Paul, have become a servant.

[24]Now I rejoice in what was suffered for you, and I fill up in my flesh what is still lacking in regard to Christ's afflictions, for

Key Verses

to God's commission that was given to me for you, to make the word of God fully known, 26 the mystery that has been hidden throughout the ages and generations but has now been revealed to his saints. 27 To them God chose to make known how great among the Gentiles are the riches of the glory of this mystery, which is Christ in you, the hope of glory. 28 It is he whom we proclaim, warning everyone and teaching everyone in all wisdom, so that we may present everyone mature in Christ.

the sake of his body, which is the church. [25]I have become its servant by the commission God gave me to present to you the word of God in its fullness—[26]the mystery that has been kept hidden for ages and generations, but is now disclosed to the saints. [27]To them God has chosen to make known among the Gentiles the glorious riches of this mystery, which is Christ in you, the hope of glory. [28]We proclaim him, admonishing and teaching everyone with all wisdom, so that we may present everyone perfect in Christ.

UNDERSTANDING THE SCRIPTURE

Colossians 1:1-2. The greeting is brief and indicates that the letter is being sent by both Paul and Timothy to Christians in the Lycus valley in Asia Minor. Paul apparently did not personally convert or visit this church, which may explain this letter's more general character. Some commentators believe that Paul sent this letter to the Colossians while he was under Roman house arrest in the period A.D. 60–62.

Colossians 1:3-14. This statement about his prayers indicates Paul's concern for what the Colossian Christians will go on to do and be in the future. He speaks of "hearing" of their faith in verse 4, which suggests his lack of personal exposure to them. Verse 7 indicates that they were converted by Epaphras, one of Paul's coworkers.

Paul begins the thanksgiving section by indicating that the three cardinal Christian virtues—faith, hope, and love—are manifest among the Colossians. The phrase "the hope laid up for you in heaven" (1:5) is apparently not a reference to the attitude of the Colossians but to the basis of their hope, namely the gift of eternal life. This gift has been stored up or set aside especially for them. The gospel these converts received was future-oriented in character and brought hope to the Colossians about their own future.

Colossians 1:9-14 shows Paul's belief

that faith has an objective content; indeed, faith and knowledge go hand in hand. Through faith the Colossians have been gaining in the knowledge of God and God's will for their lives. Paul has been constantly praying that these converts would receive this understanding and wisdom. The apostle was not interested in the Colossians merely having religious experiences; he also wanted them to have an informed understanding of their faith.

Paul prays for spiritual and emotional strength for the Colossians because there is much to endure, and patience is required in order to live in a hostile world. Paul prays also that they have joy and thankful hearts even in the midst of the ups and downs of the Christian life. They have reason to praise and thank God both for the benefits they have already received from God and because they have been enabled to share in the inheritance of the saints in the light. Paul probably uses the term "saints" to refer to living Jewish Christians. Salvation is described in verse 13 as a transfer operation that places us already in the dominion of God's Beloved Son (compare 1 Corinthians 15:24). This is the only place in Paul's letters that we hear directly about Christ's dominion. The idea here is of Christ's saving reign within the believer, not of a particular place on earth. In verse 14 redemption from darkness is equated with the forgiveness of sins. If we still could not have a positive relationship with God, which is made possible by forgiveness, rescue from darkness would be to no avail.

Colossians 1:15-20. This passage, probably a quotation from an early Christian hymn, is loaded with profound theological reflections on the meaning of the Christ event. As in the hymn in Philippians 2, Christ is here seen as having a role in both creation and redemption. The former role is described in the same terms used to describe personified Wisdom in Proverbs 3 and 8–9. Verse 15 is not about Christ being the first creature born, but about His preeminence among all creation, existing in heaven before the universe was made and having a part in its creation. All spiritual and all material creatures and things were created through Christ and for him. Verse 17 indicates that Christ is the glue that holds the universe together. Not only is he first before all of creation, but he is also first in the order of redemption to experience the resurrection. Verse 19 indicates that Christ is the full expression of God and the divine character.

Colossians 1:21-23. These verses remind the Colossians of the effect of redemption on them personally—a radical change of mind, heart, and lifestyle. They were once estranged from God and did evil deeds. But through the death of Christ they are no longer in such a state or involved in such activities. The goal of Christ's dying was not merely reconciliation with God in the present but also preparation for the day of judgment, so that the Colossians would be holy and stand up to the close

scrutiny of God on that Last Day. Verse 23 states a proviso. Eternal life requires that after redemption one remain in the faith throughout the rest of one's life, without discarding the hope promised by the gospel. A person is not eternally secure until he or she has run the good race and finished as a person of faith.

Colossians 1:24-29. This passage is a reflection on redemptive suffering. Paul believes that only Christ's death provides redemption and amounts to an atonement, but he also believes that there is a certain amount of suffering God's people must undergo in this world before the end comes to pass. Paul sees himself as being like the suffering servant described in Isaiah 53, and therefore his own suffering is seen as a continuation or extension or completion of Christ's suffering in some sense. Furthermore, he believes that if he suffers more, his converts will have to suffer less. The mystery of redemption through Christ's death and then through the preaching and living out of that death in the lives of Christians is a truth that was long hidden but is now being revealed through gospel preaching. The essence or heart of this mystery insofar as it has to do with the spiritual life of the Christian is "Christ in you, the hope of glory" (1:27).

Christ is the heart of the Christian proclamation as verse 28 says, and the goal of all preaching is that people might be saved, redeemed, forgiven, and then brought to mature faith in Christ. Salvation then is both an event, beginning with conversion, as well as a lifelong process requiring the pronouncement, "I have been saved, I am being saved, I shall be saved."

INTERPRETING THE SCRIPTURE

The Pearl of Great Price

You are probably familiar with Jesus' parable of a man who is digging in a field that is not his own and finds an exceed-

ingly precious stone. Realizing its worth, he hides it again and then goes and sells everything and purchases the field (Matthew 13:44). Similarly, Matthew 13:45 speaks of the costly pearl. During the Middle Ages Bible interpreters often said that Christ Himself was the pearl of great price—both the source of hope and the basis of faith.

Certainly Paul believed this latter conclusion was profoundly true. He says in 1 Corinthians 15:12-19 that if Christ is not who the gospel claims he is, and if in fact he did not rise from the dead, then there is no basis for Christian hope in the future or foundation for faith. If Christ is not the risen Lord, Christians are not to be envied but rather to be seen as the most pitiable souls on earth, for they have believed in and trusted an enormous lie throughout the centuries. This would mean that the great figures of faith such as Ambrose and Augustine, Julian of Norwich and Martin Luther, John Calvin and John Wesley, and Dietrich Bonhoeffer and Corrie ten Boom have spent their lives living and proclaiming a delusion. It is then no trifling matter to ascertain what the real source of hope and basis of faith is in this world. On the answer to this questions hinges eternal life.

Worship in the Name

This chapter contains four of the major elements of early Christian worship. It begins with prayers, continues with a hymn text, adds some brief exhortation, and concludes with Paul's personal testimony. There is a sense of wonder in the christological hymn in Colossians 1:15-20. The same Christ who is our redeemer is also our creator, indeed the creator of all things. This sense of awe and wonder is well expressed in texts such as Psalm 8, and in stories such as the following.

It was a hot, humid August night. A couple had put their young daughter to bed rather early because company was coming over to visit and play bridge. Their friends arrived on time and the bridge game began without incident. Shortly thereafter, however, it began to blow and thunder and lightning. Concerned that her daughter might be frightened alone in the dark, the mother went upstairs to check on her. As she opened the nursery door, she found to her amazement that her daughter was standing up in her crib, bouncing. She had raised the blinds and was busily watching the storm out the window and shouting, "Bang it again, God, bang it again!"

The God who had created the wonders of creation also created a sense of wonder in this young girl and all who choose to make God's Son the basis of hope and faith for humankind. There is a sense in which Christ's coming to earth and dying on the cross is seen as the second big bang, or the second major act of God's work of creation and redemption.

Universal Love

It is hard not to gain a sense of the universal love of God from this passage. God was not satisfied to make salvation available to just some people, or even to just people, but was intent on redeeming and reconciling all of fallen and estranged creation. And it is this great love and grace that over and over again has managed to change human lives.

A businessman tells the story of how his life had gotten into a rut and lacked any joy or enthusiasm. He had just moved to a new city and his son was having a very hard time adjusting at school. The boy claimed that no one liked him. While on a plane on a business trip this businessman met some very enthusiastic young people, and he asked them what their source of energy and joy was. He wanted to know what their basis of faith and their source of hope was. The young people proceeded to share Christ with him. Accepting Christ himself, he went home and shared this newfound faith and joy with his wife and son. They too accepted Christ. Returning soon from another business trip, the man was met by his son who was no longer troubled or truculent. He raced into his father's arms proclaiming, "Guess what, Father! God has changed all my class-mates; they like me now!" Of course it was the young man himself who had really changed, and this transformation was noticed by others. The changed life has always been one of the clearest signs of reconciliation with God. People see our hope and then come to see that Christ is indeed the hope of glory or eternal life.

The Hope of Glory

In a remote part of Turkey there worked a medical missionary. On one occasion a small man near death and enduring much suffering was brought to this doctor. The missionary not only ministered to him so that he slowly regained his health but also shared the gospel of hope in Christ with him. In due course the man became both physically well and a Christian. He returned to his own village and, like many new converts, could hardly stop talking about Jesus. At one point an irritated lis-tener said to the small man: "Why should I believe you? You have never even seen this Jesus. On your own account of things he died over 1,900 years ago." Undaunted, the little man immediately responded: "To the contrary, I have seen Christ. He lives in [the doctor], and now he lives in me, giving me a hope of glory."

The basis of faith, the source of hope, the fount of love is Christ, if we will but allow His presence to fill our lives, inform our minds, reshape our wills, and guide our emotions.

Suffering for Jesus

The Christian life can indeed involve suffering, even great suffering for the faith and for others of the faith. If neither Paul nor Peter nor Jesus himself were exempt from such suffering while on this earth, there is no reason that we should expect to be. Though much of the suffering we as Western Christians endure has little to do with our Christian faith, nonetheless we have just as much opportunity as Paul or Peter to show that God's grace is sufficient in our own lives to help us triumph over and through such suffering. How you respond when the world deals you a blow shows the extent of your faith and charac-ter. It has been said that when the world throws you a lemon you have a choice—you can either become a sourpuss or make lemonade. Paul himself suggests that Christians are persons with unconquerable spirits. There may be times we have to say, "You beat me," but then we may add, "You did not defeat me because Christ is in me and gives me an unshakable hope of glory."

Paul speaks of the presence of Christ in the Christian's life as an eternal treasure in an ever-so-mortal vessel (2 Corinthians 4:7). He was probably alluding to the little clay hand-lamps that a person would carry out into the night to light the way. The funny thing about these lamps is that the thinner the vessel, the more light that gets out. When people suffer as Paul did, they become transparent; they are reduced to the very basics of life. No artifice or pre-tense can stand up to intense suffering. One not only finds out in the crucible of suffering the basis of one's hope and faith, but others will see whether Christ and that eternal treasure dwells in the sufferer or not. Pretending will be out of the question. A great Greek philosopher was once por-trayed as a man carrying a lamp into the dark of night looking for the truth, looking for an honest person. Paul suggests that we are that lamp, and that the place to look for truth, hope, and faith is within the Chris-tian life where the Christ of glory dwells.

SHARING THE SCRIPTURE

PREPARING TO TEACH

Preparing Our Hearts

Begin your own spiritual preparation by reading John 1:1-5 and 9-18. These familiar verses from the prologue to the Fourth Gospel speak of Christ as the Word who was with God in the beginning. Through Christ all things were made. He is, in fact, the source of life.

Now read today's background lesson from Colossians 1. Look especially at verses 15-28. Note similarities between this description of Christ and the one in John's Gospel. In what ways do you envision Jesus Christ as the eternal image of God? How is he the source of your hope and the basis of your faith?

Pray that you and your students will recognize Jesus as the source of life, the one above all, through whom the world was reconciled to God.

Preparing Our Minds

Read this lesson and review the scripture passage, focusing particularly on Colossians 1:15-28.

As you begin to work with Colossians, you will notice close similarities between this book and Ephesians. In fact, parts of Ephesians apparently have been drawn from Colossians. Some scholars question whether Paul or one of his followers actually wrote Colossians. They raise this question because of differences in language and style, and shifts in theological emphasis. If the apostle penned this letter, it is likely that Colossians and Ephesians were written at about the same time.

Preparing Our Learning Space

Have on hand:
- ✔ several Bibles
- ✔ hymnals
- ✔ paper and pencils
- ✔ newsprint and marker.

LEADING THE CLASS

(1) Introduction

One way to begin today's lesson is to read or retell the Focusing on the Main Question portion of the lesson.

Another way to begin is to distribute paper and pencils. Invite the students to write their own affirmations of faith about who Christ is and what he has done. Call on a few volunteers to read what they have written.

Conclude the Introduction by lifting up today's main question: **What is the source of our hope and the basis of our faith?**

(2) The Pearl of Great Price

Ask the class to look at Matthew 13:44-45. Note that during the Middle Ages Bible interpreters often said that Jesus himself was this pearl of great price—both the source of our hope and the basis of our faith.

Next, tell the class to look at 1 Corinthians 15:12-19. Then read aloud Colossians 1:15-20.

Ask these questions:

(1) **What is at stake when we are trying to ascertain the real source of our hope and basis for our faith?** (Eternal life itself is at stake. What we hope and believe in is crucial in eternal terms.)

(2) **Why can we trust Christ to be both the source of hope and the basis for faith?** (As Colossians 1:15-20 points out, Christ is the image of God, the one through whom all things were made. God dwells in him and reconciles the world to God's own self through him.)

(3) Worship in the Name

Look again at Colossians 1:15-20. Note that this hymn expresses awe that Christ our redeemer is also Christ our creator, indeed the creator of all.

Encourage the students to examine this text closely. Have them make as many statements about Christ as the text will support. Here are suggested answers. Record their ideas on newsprint that you have labeled "Christ is . . ."

- in the image of God.
- the firstborn of all creation.
- the creator of all things.
- the one for whom all things have been created.
- the one who holds all things together.
- the head of the body, which is the church.
- the firstborn resurrected from the dead.
- the one in whom the fullness of God dwells.
- the one through whom God reconciled all things.
- the one who shed his blood on the cross so that reconciliation with God could happen.

(4) Universal Love

Have the class read aloud in unison today's key verses from Colossians 1:19-20. Then ask:

(1) What does this passage say to you about Christ?

(2) What does it say to you about God?

(3) What does it say about God's intentions for all creation?

If time permits, use the story in the second paragraph under "Universal Love" in Interpreting the Scripture, which illustrates how reconciliation with God changes lives.

(5) The Hope of Glory

Select someone to read Colossians 1:21-23. If possible, have the verses read from several translations. Then ask the students to try to state in one sentence the meaning of this passage. You may want to have them write their ideas on paper and then read them aloud to a partner or the whole class.

Read the story of the medical missionary under "The Hope of Glory" in Interpreting the Scripture. Then provide quiet time so that students may meditate on these questions, which you will need to read aloud. Do not ask the students to share their thoughts.

(1) How do others see Christ living in me? What evidence do I have to support this assumption?

(2) If Christ is not readily apparent in my life, what changes do I need to make?

(6) Suffering for Jesus

Choose a volunteer to read aloud Colossians 1:24-28. Then ask the class:

(1) Since we do not suffer for our faith as Paul and the early Christians did, what do these words mean to us? (Note that we still suffer and can show the mettle of our faith through our suffering.)

(2) How does suffering help us to know the basis and hope of our faith? (In times of suffering, we can choose to put our faith and hope in Christ. We have the opportunity to go deeper into the mystery of God when we suffer. Through Christ, we can triumph over that suffering. We can then become more faithful servants because we know from experience whereof we speak.)

If possible, ask the class to read in unison the "Affirmation from 1 Corinthians 15:1-6 and Colossians 1:15-20" found in *The United Methodist Hymnal* (no. 888) to conclude the session.

Before dismissing the class, suggest at least one of the activities below.

HELPING CLASS MEMBERS ACT

Suggest that students spend some quiet time this week thinking about what they would say if they were to write a hymn to

Christ. Encourage each person to jot down ideas and, if possible, create a hymn.

Recommend that group members read about persons who have struggled and survived against all odds. Perhaps they will choose to read about victims of war, natural catastrophe, an accident in a remote place, or a serious illness. Some students may know a survivor and decide to speak with that person about his or her experience and how suffering affected his or her life and relationship with God. You may have some survivors in the class who are willing to discuss their experience with others.

Note that Paul remained faithful to the cause of Christ, no matter what the circumstances. Challenge class members to identify a church-related cause or program that they are committed to and to do something special for the cause this week.

PLANNING FOR NEXT SUNDAY

On August 13 we will continue our study of Colossians with a lesson from 2:6-19. Tell the students to be thinking about how this passage calls them to recognize the fullness or completeness of life that is theirs in Christ Jesus.

THE FULLNESS OF LIFE

PREVIEWING THE LESSON

Lesson Scripture: Colossians 2:6-19
Background Scripture: Colossians 2:6-19
Key Verses: Colossians 2:6-7

Focus of the Lesson:
All that is needed for complete, abundant life is found in Christ.

Main Question of the Lesson:
What does it take to have a full and fulfilled Christian life?

This lesson will enable adult learners to:
(1) hear the good news about fullness of life in Christ.
(2) examine their own rootedness in Christ.
(3) respond with thanksgiving to the fullness of life in Christ.

Today's lesson may be outlined as follows:
(1) Introduction
(2) Losing Focus
(3) Sects Appeal
(4) The AWOL Astronomer
(5) All I Really Need to Know I Learned ....
(6) Fullness

FOCUSING ON THE MAIN QUESTION

What does it take to have a full and fulfilled Christian life? Today's lesson from Colossians answers this question quite clearly: Christ is the necessary and sufficient basis of salvation and Christian life. One need not supplement faith in Christ with other things as means of drawing closer to God or to heaven. Spiritual disciplines are fine as expressions of faith, but they are not substitutes for Christ-centered faith.

It is possible to get distracted from the main question raised by this lesson if we focus on fulfillment in terms of our life tasks. If we ask what it takes to have a full and fulfilled Christian life, each individual will have a personal answer if we're talking about vocation. What is fulfilling for one Christian may merely be frustrating for another because he or she does not have the same gifts or graces or character.

For example, some would find a career in Christian teaching very fulfilling, whereas others would see this as an onerous burden. Some would find working with their hands to make pottery or furniture or to paint fulfilling, while others would find such work tedious and difficult. Some would find a career in public service suitable to their abilities, but others would find it unrewarding and uncomfortable. My point is that God has blessed each of us differently and given us each a different purpose in life. Therefore, if we are talking about vocation and ministry, what is appropriate and fulfilling for me may not be appropriate or fulfilling at all for another person.

Our text, however, is largely focusing on fulfillment in a different sense, a sense in which we all can share. Colossians is talking about what or who can satisfy the basic human need for a permanent relationship with God. Paul's straightforward answer to this question is Christ.

READING THE SCRIPTURE

NRSV
Colossians 2:6-19

6 As you therefore have received Christ Jesus the Lord, continue to live your lives in him, 7 rooted and built up in him and established in the faith, just as you were taught, abounding in thanksgiving.

8 See to it that no one takes you captive through philosophy and empty deceit, according to human tradition, according to the elemental spirits of the universe, and not according to Christ. 9 For in him the whole fullness of deity dwells bodily, 10 and you have come to fullness in him, who is the head of every ruler and authority. 11 In him also you were circumcised with a spiritual circumcision, by putting off the body of the flesh in the circumcision of Christ; 12 when you were buried with him in baptism, you were also raised with him through faith in the power of God, who raised him from the dead. 13 And when you were dead in trespasses and the uncircumcision of your flesh, God made you alive together with him, when he forgave us all our trespasses, 14 erasing the record that stood against us with its legal demands. He set this aside, nailing it to the cross. 15 He disarmed the rulers and authorities and made a public example of them, triumphing over them in it.

16 Therefore do not let anyone condemn

NIV
Colossians 2:6-19

6So then, just as you received Christ Jesus as Lord, continue to live in him, 7rooted and built up in him, strengthened in the faith as you were taught, and overflowing with thankfulness.

8See to it that no one takes you captive through hollow and deceptive philosophy, which depends on human tradition and the basic principles of this world rather than on Christ.

9For in Christ all the fullness of the Deity lives in bodily form, 10and you have been given fullness in Christ, who is the head over every power and authority. 11In him you were also circumcised, in the putting off of the sinful nature, not with a circumcision done by the hands of men but with the circumcision done by Christ, 12having been buried with him in baptism and raised with him through your faith in the power of God, who raised him from the dead.

13When you were dead in your sins and in the uncircumcision of your sinful nature, God made you alive with Christ. He forgave us all our sins, 14having canceled the written code, with its regulations, that was against us and that stood opposed to us; he took it away, nailing it to the cross. 15And having disarmed the

Key Verses

Key Verses

AUGUST 13

you in matters of food and drink or of observing festivals, new moons, or sabbaths. 17 These are only a shadow of what is to come, but the substance belongs to Christ. 18 Do not let anyone disqualify you, insisting on self-abasement and worship of angels, dwelling on visions, puffed up without cause by a human way of thinking, 19 and not holding fast to the head, from whom the whole body, nourished and held together by its ligaments and sinews, grows with a growth that is from God.

powers and authorities, he made a public spectacle of them, triumphing over them by the cross.

[16]Therefore do not let anyone judge you by what you eat or drink, or with regard to a religious festival, a New Moon celebration or a Sabbath day. [17]These are a shadow of the things that were to come; the reality, however, is found in Christ. [18]Do not let anyone who delights in false humility and the worship of angels disqualify you for the prize. Such a person goes into great detail about what he has seen, and his unspiritual mind puffs him up with idle notions. [19]He has lost connection with the Head, from whom the whole body, supported and held together by its ligaments and sinews, grows as God causes it to grow.

UNDERSTANDING THE SCRIPTURE

Colossians 2:6-7. Paul essentially argues that his Christian readers are to stay on the course that they began when they converted. They are not to get sidetracked by other philosophies or religious approaches to life. Since life in Christ is fully satisfying, one need not look elsewhere for spiritual succor. A life can only have one Lord, one dominating commitment and passion, and Paul insists that for the Christian Christ must be that Lord. In Greek, verse 6 uses the word *walk* (rather than *live* as in the NRSV and NIV) in Christ, which refers to following a particular course of life, in this case the pattern of Christ's life. A person who is rooted, built up, and confirmed in such a relationship and faith is one who has a deep well of spiritual resources to draw from—a well that regularly overflows and produces thanksgiving from the heart of the believer. If all of theology is grace, then all of ethics can be said to be gratitude—the response of a thankful heart to what God in Christ has done in us.

Colossians 2:8-15. There is considerable debate among scholars about Colossians 2:8 and 2:20. Does the key Greek phrase *stoicheia tou kosmou* refer to: (1) the elements of the universe (earth, air, fire, water); (2) the elementary principles of the world; or (3) the elemental spirits of the world (that is, demons)? There is ample evidence for the first two meanings in classical or New Testament Greek literature but none for the last translation. In light of the context here, which involves human traditions and philosophies, Paul probably refers to some kind of basic teaching (but compare Colossians 2:15).

In verse 8 these elementary principles of knowledge are seen by Paul as not of Christ and therefore not to be followed. It would appear from Colossians 2:16-17 that Paul has in mind matters of religious practice, such as the Jewish observance of the Sabbath, not esoteric philosophy. Yet Paul believes that any religious way of life is undergirded by a particular view of God and salvation. Thus, Paul is objecting here both to particular practices and also to the philosophy that provides their rationale.

In Paul's view, the fullness of God dwells in Christ. There is therefore no deficiency in Christ that needs to be made up for by adding other ideas or practices. Christ is no second-rate power or source of power. Rather, he is the head over every ruler and authority, whether human or supernatural. Thus, the Colossians need not submit to or placate any angelic beings or fear their malignant influence (see below on Colossians 2:18).

Colossians 2:11-12 uses vivid language to remind the Colossians about their conversion, symbolized as a circumcision and death experience—a cutting off and dying of the old self and a rising to newness of life. Baptism here is seen as symbolizing burial with Christ (compare Romans 6:4). But conversion does not just mean the end of an old way of life; it means being raised to a new way of life through faith in Christ. If God has the power to raise Christ from the dead, then surely God has the power to do the lesser deed of transforming a living person. The person outside of Christ is dead in sin and must be made alive again by God. Sin dulls and destroys the conscience and the moral and spiritual sensibilities.

Colossians 2:14 indicates that God gave us a new start by canceling the record against us—the requirements of the law of God that stands as a witness of condemnation for all lawbreakers. Paul uses the graphic image of the record of our sins being nailed to the cross with Christ and so canceled by his death, an allusion to the ancient practice of publicly listing the criminal's crimes or charges against him and nailing this record to the cross. The point is that the indictment against us was removed by Christ who endured its punishment.

The meaning of Colossians 2:15 is debated. Did Christ divest himself of the rulers and authorities when he died and went into a realm beyond the reach of human rulers, or is Paul saying that Christ disarmed the rulers and authorities by his death on the cross? Paul sees the cross not as a way of shaming Christ but as a way of shaming his executioners and those who stood against him. Paradoxically, through dying on the cross Christ triumphed over the crucifiers. Probably the verb in question here should be translated "stripped off"; that is, Christ "shed" those who sought to control, dominate, and destroy him and in fact triumphed over them through the Resurrection. Consequently, Christians need not fear such authorities any more.

Colossians 2:16-19. This section provides the practical implications of the previous argument. The Colossians are not to listen to suggestions that they should be observing certain kinds of food laws or Sabbaths or other Jewish festivals. It is not necessary to become a Jew in order to be a true Christian. Paul is concerned about the spiritual circumcision of the sinful old nature, not the physical circumcision of the body—these Jewish rituals are but the shadows or prefigurements of that which Christ and his work are the substance.

Is Colossians 2:18 speaking about participation in the worship offered by angels in heaven (see Revelation 4) in the form of ecstatic visions of heaven during worship, or is Paul actually referring here to worshiping angels? Probably the former. The apostle associates fasting and other religious rituals with such a practice, perhaps as means of preparing to receive visions. Persons who focus on such practices are not depending on Christ for spiritual stability and sustenance. Those who desire esoteric spiritual experiences more than they desire Christ are being critiqued in this text.

INTERPRETING THE SCRIPTURE

Losing Focus

When people lose focus in their Christian life, they often look for something extra, a sort of booster shot to get them excited about their faith again or to give them the sense that they are making progress in that faith.

In Paul's world, the essence of ancient religion was ritual and tradition, sacrifices, and recitation of set phrases. Since early Christianity had no temples or priests and offered no sacrifices, it is not surprising that earnest Gentile converts to Christianity would have had a hard time adjusting to a religion without such things. They would have found it quite appealing if someone had suggested that they show their moral earnestness and religious devotion by following various Jewish ritual requirements. Some persons suggested that certain kinds of visionary experiences of heavenly worship could be had as an added bonus if one fasted and performed the right rituals. Paul wishes to make clear that this sort of behavior is neither necessary nor sufficient to make them better Christians. Moreover, such behavior implies that faith in Christ alone is insufficient. Paul says, to the contrary, that Christ is all that is both necessary and sufficient to create a fulfilled and fulfilling Christian life.

Sects Appeal

This entire approach of "Christ plus" is as characteristic of various forms of sectarian behavior today as it was in antiquity. We see it for example in the case of the Mormons, who insist that Christ and the Bible are not enough; one must also read and believe *The Book of Mormon.* Similarly, the Jehovah's Witnesses insist on their particular interpretation of the Bible and their own translation of it. For Christian Scientists, Christ and the Bible are not enough; one must interpret both through the filter of Mary Baker Eddy's *Science and Health with Key to the Scriptures.*

Paul had his own problems with the "Christ plus" approach to the faith and he deals with them in this very text in Colossians. Notice, however, that Paul guards against the suggestion that he was advocating that faith was all a person needed to develop a Christian life. To the contrary, faith working through love leads to necessary deeds of both piety and charity. One must work out personal salvation that God has worked into your life, doing so with awe and reverence. Paul might have put it this way: faith in Christ works; that is, it produces the results in the Christian life that converts are seeking. Christ is not insufficient, nor does he need to be supplemented with more rituals, visions, or another holy book. But faith in Christ is like leaven in dough—it is an active agent that produces results. Put another way, Christ in the believer produces fruit in the way he or she behaves and treats others. Moreover, Christ in the believer leads to the death of the old lusts, the old bad habits. This is the natural outflow of Christ in one's life; it is not produced by practicing new religious rituals or seeking certain kinds of spiritual experiences or adopting sectarian approaches to the Christian life.

The AWOL Astronomer

William Heschel was a remarkable person in many regards. As a young man he showed great musical talent. He loved military music, so he joined the military in Hanover, Germany, in order to play in a military band. Unfortunately for him, Hanover entered a war shortly thereafter and this sensitive young musician was ill-suited to the rigors of the battlefront. In fact it frightened him so much that at first he hid from and then deserted his unit, fleeing all the way to England.

For many years all was well for William. He became a court favorite as a musician, and he pursued astronomy and made some remarkable discoveries. One day, however, things changed dramatically. A new king assumed the throne in England—George of Hanover. King George knew of the history of William Heschel and one day summoned him to a meeting at the palace at Hampton Court. William was very fearful for he knew the penalty for deserting from the German army was death. He waited for a long time in the antechamber to the throne room and became more and more afraid. Finally, one of the king's underlings came to William and said, "You are to go in, but first you must read this proclamation." Heschel, trembling, unrolled the scroll, only to find the words "You are pardoned for your previous trespasses against the crown" written there. Thereafter he was ushered into the throne room where the king greeted him and announced that he planned to knight Heschel for his many contributions to the realm and to the crown over the years.

Heschel went from a possible sentence of death to a royal status. Paul says it is much the same for us as a result of Christ's death. Because of Christ's act on Calvary the record that stood against us with its impending death sentence has been erased, our sins have been forgiven. We have been made partakers of royal status, for we are the sons and daughters of the great King, Christ. No ruler or authority or human court can finally condemn us or take away our status as saved persons because the Supreme Court of God has declared "no condemnation," pardon for sins, and indeed has gone so far as to write us into Abraham's will, so to speak, such that even Gentiles could be heirs through Christ of the promises given to Abraham, becoming part of the chosen people.

All I Really Need to Know I Learned . . .

What would you think of a person who insisted that what we learned in kindergarten is all we need to know? Several books by Reverend Robert Fulghum suggest this very thing, but Paul would have taken exception to such a conclusion. Paul says that the elementary principles of life and religion are something that Christians need to get beyond as they mature in Christ.

Christ indeed calls us to a simple faith but not to a simpleton's faith. The reality of Christ goes far beyond mere human philosophizing or human traditions. At the heart of Christianity is not a simple mystery but rather a profound one: Christ is indeed the human face of God, who came in the flesh to redeem us. Paul says it is both a necessary and sufficient truth that never becomes obsolete and needs no supplements. It is not that we need "Christ plus"; it is that the one Christ in whom the fullness of God dwells in the flesh desires more of us. We are the ones—not Christ—who have been tried and found wanting.

Fullness

Our text from Colossians has suggested that one of the ultimate keys to fulfillment in life is to be full of God in the form of the presence of Christ.

We have doubtless all known persons who were full of themselves and forgetful of others, but Paul is calling us to just the opposite—to be forgetful of ourselves and full of God in Christ. Such fullness is a great blessing and a key to contentment in life. The God-shaped vacuum in every human life is finally only truly filled by God's own presence.

If we had the whole world but were bereft of God, we would still be empty and lonely and wanting more; but if we have God we can be fulfilled and indeed quite joyful and content without a lot of life's material extras.

SHARING THE SCRIPTURE

PREPARING TO TEACH

Preparing Our Hearts

Our devotional reading is Romans 8:31-39. Here Paul expresses complete confidence in God. Having endured suffering and tribulation, Paul can say with total assurance that absolutely nothing can separate us from the love of God. How does your own experience square with Paul's view? If you have ever felt separated from God, do you honestly believe that God left you, or did you turn away?

Look now at today's lesson from Colossians 2:6-19. What is being said here about your relationship with Christ and how you are to live in him? What might endanger your relationship with Christ?

Pray that you and your class members will heed Paul's warnings about false teachings so that you will be able to live in the fullness of life in Christ.

Preparing Our Minds

Review the scripture passage and read today's lesson.

Note the warning against heretical teaching in verses 8-19 (actually continuing on through verse 23). Verses 16-18 list the harmful practices of the Colossians, which included an overemphasis on rituals, asceticism, and participation in the worship of angels. The Colossians have apparently become captives to these practices. Think about the false teachings today that try to capture Christians. Paul indicates that these erroneous teachings and practices do not hold fast to Christ, the head of the body. Notice that the false teachings have prompted church members to believe that they must engage in rituals and worship in addition to the worship of Christ. Paul insists that Christ is all-sufficient. Nothing else is needed.

Preparing Our Learning Space

Have on hand:
- several Bibles
- hymnals.

LEADING THE CLASS

(1) Introduction

Begin today's session by singing "Jesus Is All the World to Me" (*The United Methodist Hymnal*, no. 469) or another hymn that you have access to that speaks about the all-sufficiency of Jesus.

Then ask the students to talk with a partner about these questions, which you will need to read aloud:

(1) Is Jesus all that you need for a full, complete life?

(2) If not, what else do you require?

When the partners have had an opportunity to chat for a few minutes, call the class back together and prepare them to move into today's lesson. Tell them that Paul was concerned about the Colossians because they had come to believe that they needed to live ascetically and to participate in excessive rituals and angelic worship. Paul warns them against the false teaching that led them to these conclusions. Instead, he says, the church needs to be rooted in Christ. He alone is sufficient. Jesus is all that we need. All else is unnecessary.

Conclude the Introduction by lifting up today's main question: **What does it take to have a full and fulfilled Christian life?**

(2) Losing Focus

Ask the class these questions:
(1) What causes believers to lose focus in their Christian life?
(2) Where do some modern Christians turn when they want to boost their spiritual lives?

466

Next, read or retell the information under "Losing Focus" in Interpreting the Scripture to see how Paul handles the problem of loss of focus that he perceives in the church at Colossae.

(3) Sects Appeal

Use the examples of the Church of Jesus Christ of Latter-Day Saints (Mormons), Jehovah's Witnesses, and Christian Science found under "Sects Appeal" in Interpreting the Scripture. You may want to add other examples of religious groups that use the "Christ plus" approach.

Invite the class to debate this proposition: <u>By saying that Christ is all-sufficient, Paul in effect was saying that good deeds were not necessary.</u>

Bring the debate to a close by helping the students realize, if they have not already done so, that Paul would say that faith in Christ leads believers to act out of love. He is not, however, saying that works will bring about our salvation. Nor is he saying that adherence to additional books or rituals or worship practices is necessary. For Paul, the fullness of God dwells in Christ. Because Christ is the head over every ruler and authority, both human and supernatural, Christians need not worry about placating other forces, such as angels. Yet the church at Colossae and some contemporary religious groups would, in fact, argue that additions of various sorts are necessary. Groups who make this claim are in effect saying that Christ is not sufficient.

(4) The AWOL Astronomer

Choose a volunteer to read today's scripture lesson, Colossians 2:6-19, in its entirety.

Read or retell the example of William Heschel found the first and second paragraph of "The AWOL Astronomer" in Interpreting the Scripture. Then ask the class:

(1) **Imagine standing in Heschel's shoes as you awaited an audience before the king. How would you have been feeling?**

(2) **Once you read the proclamation of pardon, how would you have felt?** (Make sure that the students recognize the importance of gratitude for an undeserved pardon.)

(3) **How is Heschel's story similar to our own story as Christians?** (Use the final paragraph of "The AWOL Astronomer" to augment the discussion.)

(4) **Paul calls his readers to recognize that they were dead in their own trespasses and then were made alive and forgiven through baptism. Does this action signify fullness in life through Christ for you, or do you feel more is needed? Please explain your answer.**

(5) All I Really Need to Know I Learned...

Note that when we think about Christ as all-sufficient, as all that is needed for a complete life, some persons may assume that this approach is simplistic. Yet what Paul is saying in this passage is profound. Ask:

(1) **How can you help others who reject the message of Christ as being too simplistic?**

(2) **How can you help those who insist that rituals or other practices are necessary for "true" faith in Christ?**

(6) Fullness

Ask the class to read in unison today's key verses from Colossians 2:6-7. Ask:

(1) **What do you think are the marks of a person who lives in Christ?**

(2) **What experiences in your own life have rooted you in Christ?**

(3) **How has the church helped you to be built up in Christ and strengthened in the faith?**

(4) **Who have been important teachers in your life? These may be persons**

? known as teachers, but they may also be your parents, other relatives, even persons whom you've read about.

(5) **How do you give thanks to God for the relationship you have through Christ?**

(6) **If you do not believe you are experiencing the fullness of Christ right now, what else do you need to make that happen?**

Offer a prayer that each person will experience a complete life in Christ.

As you close today's session, be sure to suggest at least one of the activities below so that students will have concrete ideas as to how to live out what they have learned.

HELPING CLASS MEMBERS ACT

In recognition of the fullness of life that believers have in Christ, encourage the students to give thanks to God each day this week. Also encourage them to act with a thankful spirit that others can emulate.

Suggest that class members be aware of philosophies or approaches to life that offer less than the fullness of Christ. Why are these insufficient? Warn the students, though, against vilifying those persons who choose to follow these philosophies.

Recommend that individuals spend some time this week contemplating what their lives might be like without Christ. Suggest that this activity may make them more aware of the rich blessings that are theirs through faith in Christ.

PLANNING FOR NEXT SUNDAY

To prepare for next week's lesson, "The Way of Life," ask the students to read Colossians 3:1-17. In this session we will explore what it means to live in the way of righteousness.

THE WAY OF LIFE

PREVIEWING THE LESSON

Lesson Scripture: Colossians 3:1-3, 5-17
Background Scripture: Colossians 3:1-17
Key Verse: Colossians 3:17

Focus of the Lesson:
The righteous life is marked by words and deeds done in the name of Christ and in gratitude to God.

Main Question of the Lesson:
What distinguishes the Christian life from the way of the world?

This lesson will enable adult learners to:
(1) explore the essence of the true Christian life.
(2) compare their own lives to the life in Christ outlined in Colossians.
(3) respond by adjusting their lifestyle as necessary.

Today's lesson may be outlined as follows:
(1) Introduction
(2) Nothing More Beyond
(3) Garbage In, Garbage Out
(4) Besetting Sins
(5) Payback Time
(6) Biblical Illiteracy
(7) The Scout Code

FOCUSING ON THE MAIN QUESTION

What distinguishes the Christian life from the way of the world? Not only are there differences in ethical opinions but also differences in lifestyle. Consider the philosophy of life that lies behind these slogans: "the world is your oyster"; "you only go around once in life, you have to grab for all the gusto you can get"; "the one who dies with the most toys wins"; or "if it feels good, just do it." Not one of these hedonistic or materialistic approaches to life comports with what Paul urges in our lesson for today. The Christian life is distinct and distinguishable from our cultural notions of the good life. The three divisions of today's text make the contrasts between the qualities of a heavenly-minded person and of those who dwell on the things of the earth quite apparent.

A story will illustrate my point. The Christians of Estonia were, like Estonians in general, an oppressed lot during many years of Soviet domination. Many of them had a Methodist heritage and accordingly sought to make regular contact with Methodists in the United States. It is interesting that the two things they knew about Methodism in America that they identified with were *Good News* magazine, an evangelical magazine for United Methodists, and the prayer tower at Oral Roberts University. Their view was that only strongly orthodox Christians could survive and have a sense of identity in a hostile environment such as Soviet-dominated Estonia's. Consequently, they naturally gravitated toward more conservative Methodist groups in the United States.

There is a message here for us all. When the world grows cold toward the Christian faith, one had better build the flames of faith high and hot if one wants to survive the winter of our culture's discontent. This is what Paul is trying to do—steel his converts for endurance in a hostile environment.

READING THE SCRIPTURE

NRSV
Colossians 3:1-3, 5-17

1 So if you have been raised with Christ, seek the things that are above, where Christ is, seated at the right hand of God. 2 Set your minds on things that are above, not on things that are on earth, 3 for you have died, and your life is hidden with Christ in God.

5 Put to death, therefore, whatever in you is earthly: fornication, impurity, passion, evil desire, and greed (which is idolatry). 6 On account of these the wrath of God is coming on those who are disobedient. 7 These are the ways you also once followed, when you were living that life. 8 But now you must get rid of all such things—anger, wrath, malice, slander, and abusive language from your mouth. 9 Do not lie to one another, seeing that you have stripped off the old self with its practices 10 and have clothed yourselves with the new self, which is being renewed in knowledge according to the image of its creator. 11 In that renewal there is no longer Greek and Jew, circumcised and uncircumcised, barbarian, Scythian, slave and free; but Christ is all and in all!

12 As God's chosen ones, holy and beloved, clothe yourselves with compassion, kindness, humility, meekness, and

NIV
Colossians 3:1-3, 5-17

[1]Since, then, you have been raised with Christ, set your hearts on things above, where Christ is seated at the right hand of God. [2]Set your minds on things above, not on earthly things. [3]For you died, and your life is now hidden with Christ in God.

[5]Put to death, therefore, whatever belongs to your earthly nature: sexual immorality, impurity, lust, evil desires and greed, which is idolatry. [6]Because of these, the wrath of God is coming. [7]You used to walk in these ways, in the life you once lived. [8]But now you must rid yourselves of all such things as these: anger, rage, malice, slander, and filthy language from your lips. [9]Do not lie to each other, since you have taken off your old self with its practices [10]and have put on the new self, which is being renewed in knowledge in the image of its Creator. [11]Here there is no Greek or Jew, circumcised or uncircumcised, barbarian, Scythian, slave or free, but Christ is all, and is in all.

[12]Therefore, as God's chosen people, holy and dearly loved, clothe yourselves with compassion, kindness, humility, gentleness and patience. [13]Bear with each other and forgive whatever grievances

patience. 13 Bear with one another and, if anyone has a complaint against another, forgive each other; just as the Lord has forgiven you, so you also must forgive. 14 Above all, clothe yourselves with love, which binds everything together in perfect harmony. 15 And let the peace of Christ rule in your hearts, to which indeed you were called in the one body. And be thankful. 16 Let the word of Christ dwell in you richly; teach and admonish one another in all wisdom; and with gratitude in your hearts sing psalms, hymns, and spiritual songs to God. **17 And whatever you do, in word or deed, do everything in the name of the Lord Jesus, giving thanks to God the Father through him.**

Key Verse

you may have against one another. Forgive as the Lord forgave you. [14]And over all these virtues put on love, which binds them all together in perfect unity.

[15]Let the peace of Christ rule in your hearts, since as members of one body you were called to peace. And be thankful. [16]Let the word of Christ dwell in you richly as you teach and admonish one another with all wisdom, and as you sing psalms, hymns and spiritual songs with gratitude in your hearts to God. [17]**And whatever you do, whether in word or deed, do it all in the name of the Lord Jesus, giving thanks to God the Father through him.**

Key Verse

UNDERSTANDING THE SCRIPTURE

Introduction. It is occasionally charged that some Christians are so heavenly-minded that they are no earthly good. This scripture disagrees, asserting that one must be heavenly-minded precisely in order to be able to be good and useful to God and our fellow human beings while on earth.

Colossians 3:1-4. Heavenly-mindedness entails focusing on Christ. Persons who have already experienced new life in Christ know that they must focus on Christ and on the qualities of his life. Christians' lives, being so bound up with Christ, actually are elsewhere. Like a person whose home and family is in a far country, Christians live as pilgrims and strangers upon the earth. Just as a Jew who lives outside Israel will often say, "Next year in Jerusalem," so the Christian will often say, "Soon and very soon I am going to meet the King." The point is that Christ is our very life, the one who gives us joy, hope, love, and the grace to live a Christlike life. When we are apart from him our hearts are in pilgrimage. As verse 4 says, Christ's history is our destiny. Just as he now dwells in glory, immune from the onslaughts of disease, decay, and death, so also we long for a life that is safe from these things.

The Christian has died to the all-too-human ways of life that Paul outlines in verse 5. Of course Christians might be tempted to return to old ways of life. Indeed this is why Paul finds it necessary to provide the exhortation we have in this section of Colossians. Old patterns of life often die hard, even if one is in Christ. But as Colossians 3:3 makes evident, it is not just aspects of one's life that die, but the old self, the center of one's old identity. It is "you" who have died, not just a particular bad habit. Attitudes about oneself and the way of orienting one's whole thinking and pattern of living die. No longer a self-seeking and self-centered person, one must be an other-seeking and Christ-centered person.

Colossians 3:5-11. Christians must put to death longings to go back to the old way of life. What characterizes the list of sins is a tremendously self-centered approach to life. Fornication is the sexual exploitation of another for one's own self-gratification. Sexual impurity, sexual passions, and evil desires are all grounded in the fallenness of allowing one's drives to dictate one's attitude about others. Persons are reduced to objects of desire. Paul calls "greed" idolatry because at its root this sin seeks to ground one's life and security not in God but in one's own accumulated resources. Paul reminds his audience in Colossians 3:6 that there are moral and indeed eternal consequences to such attitudes and actions.

God's wrath in the present takes the form of people's being consumed by their own passions, becoming burnt-out shells of their former selves. Ultimately a person reaps what he or she sows (Galatians 6:7). Yet Paul also believes in a final Day of Reckoning that all persons, even Christians, must face.

Colossians 3:10 speaks of the new person in Christ being renewed because the new birth is only the beginning of the new life. The new self is being renewed in the image of the Creator. One must deal with and eliminate the residual effects of the old life. Though the old person may be dead, one can still be haunted by its ghost. There are still the consequences of past actions that one must come to grips with.

All human beings bear the image of God. Part of the new life in Christ is that old racial distinctions, while they still exist, are not to determine Christian identity, status, or worth in the kingdom of God. Social distinctions between haves and have nots (masters and slaves) are likewise not indicators of worth or significance. What matters is none of this but rather that we are God's set apart people, for this is what the terms "holy" and "chosen" (elect) connote (3:12).

Colossians 3:12-17. Holy people are to adopt the lifestyle of Christ. In Paul's day, as in ours, meekness was widely perceived as weakness, humility was seen as an attitude only appropriate to underlings such as slaves, and patience was not usually seen as a virtue. Rather, reciprocity was expected, whether one had received good or ill from another. Tensions exist even in Christian relationships. It is critical that we bear with one another, and when necessary forgive one another, just as the Lord has forgiven us. It is forgiveness that breaks the vicious cycle of payback. Moreover, love binds believers together in harmony.

Paul's prayer is that God's word will dwell in the Colossians richly so that they in turn can teach one another with wisdom, the gift of giving the timely, discerning word that provides practical guidance for life. Grounding in God's word generates deeply moving hymns of praise and songs of the Spirit. Perhaps many of the modern praise choruses are so shallow in their lyrics because this exhortation to be deeply grounded in the Word has not been heeded.

Verse 17 reminds us that all must be done in the name of Jesus, which means that we must ask, "Is this something Jesus would have said or done?" If it is not, we ought not to do or say it. Signing Jesus' name to a prayer without reflection on the appropriateness of its content to the character of Christ is also a mistake.

INTERPRETING THE SCRIPTURE

Nothing More Beyond

Before the voyage of Columbus, the Spanish Empire and monarchy had a motto, *Ne Plus Ultra*, which translates as "nothing more beyond," by which was meant nothing beyond the Spanish rule and realm. The voyage of Christopher Columbus shattered that notion when the New World was discovered. The motto was in due course changed to *Plus Ultra*, meaning "there is more beyond."

In a very real sense, Paul is saying precisely this to the Colossians and to us—there is more beyond and you must set your sights high. Indeed, you must set your sights on high, where Christ is. It is the task of Christians to manifest that "something beyond" the mundane or normal here on earth in order to show that Christ is real and working among us.

Garbage In, Garbage Out

A popular phrase in our computer-oriented world is "garbage in, garbage out." There is a profound truth in this phrase, and Paul in essence is saying that what you put into your mind and dwell upon will in turn affect or even determine what will come out of your heart, mouth, and life. To spend your days watching soap operas or sleazy movies or reading trashy novels that appeal to the lowest common denominator is simply to feed the fallenness that already exists in the human heart. Such actions are not harmless; they always take their toll. Since sinful behavior is addictive, you must be very careful and circumspect about what you put into your mind. It is true that "a mind is a terrible thing to waste," and we are not to waste our time and energies putting garbage into our systems.

The tale is told of a hungry falcon. One winter the bird was circling over the Niagara River looking for food. Suddenly the bird spied an ice floe with the carcass of a deer upon it. Greedily the bird swooped down on the deer, though the falcon knew that this ice floe would soon be passing over the falls. While it was feeding on the carcass, having sunk its talons deeply into the animal, the bird said to itself, "I am free, I can always fly away." Yet as it gorged itself, the bird's talons became frozen to the carcass; and so when the ice floe began to descend down the falls and the bird attempted to fly away, it was unable to do so. The falcon was killed in the fall, not because it intended to die, but because death was the inevitable consequence of its actions.

Sin affects the human life in the same way. One becomes addicted to one's pleasures or passions and cannot break away before it is too late.

Besetting Sins

One of the besetting sins of American culture, and perhaps especially of my own native Southern culture, is racism. Whether one thinks of the old hatreds whose flames the Klan has fired, or those of the neo-Nazis or white supremacist groups, or of the anti-Semitic factions in our nation, we are still dealing with sins that are woven into the very fabric of our society.

Paul was convinced that the one power that could overcome the divisions in his own world between Greek and Jew, or Hellenized person and non-Greek-speaking person, or slave and free was Jesus Christ. Moreover, Christ has the power to bring about the renewal of the universal image of God that is resident in every human. Paul's world was no less divided than ours; it is just that the lines were a little differently drawn. When one is renewed in the image of God, one realizes that one's primary sense of identity does not and cannot come from race, or social status, or intellectual gifts, or gender. If these are in fact the primary sources of one's sense of self, it is time for a reality check and a renewal of consciousness. A global village cannot survive with a tribal mentality.

Payback Time

Night after night on the evening news we hear of violence, revenge, retaliation, threats, marches, and destruction. What is singularly lacking in all of this is any discussion of forgiveness that can break the cycle of violence. I am reminded of the fact that forgiveness is still today not seen as a virtue in many quarters where a Christian ethos is not dominant and Christian values are not embraced. Forgiveness is seen as the posture of a weak person. Yet it is a key to peace and harmony in any human community. I am not suggesting that forgetting atrocity or crime is possible or even necessary. Instead, I am saying that whether or not one forgets, forgiveness is not an optional extra in the Christian life. It is the practice that makes peace and harmony possible. Furthermore, it is based in the knowledge that we ourselves have been forgiven an enormous amount by God.

It is inconsistent and wrong to receive forgiveness and yet be unwilling to give it. Indeed, the Lord's Prayer suggests that our receiving forgiveness is to some extent dependent on our willingness to bestow it. One possible rendering of 1 Corinthians 13:6 is "love keeps no record of wrongdoing." How very difficult this is, especially when you are talking about wrongs done by someone you live with. Even Christians are much more likely to react like Peter and want to ask if forgiving a person seven times isn't enough (Matthew 18:21). But Christ's answer is that we must always forgive. It is not an accident that the Lord's Prayer says "forgive us our trespasses as we forgive those who trespass against us." Forgiveness received must lead to forgiveness offered; or to put it the other way around, if we will not forgive others, we place an impediment in our own hearts to receiving forgiveness from God.

Biblical Illiteracy

The Bible is the most owned book in the Western world. It is perennially the best-selling book, even though it never makes the bestseller lists in the papers. Yet we live in an age of vast biblical illiteracy because many who purchase the Bible do not read it.

Paul would have been discouraged by this trend. He desires the word of God to dwell richly in all believers so that they will have a resource from which to draw when tough times come, when instruction needs to be given, when they want to express their faith in praise to God. The rabbis had a saying about their disciples: "To what shall we liken a good disciple? He is like a plastered cistern, never losing a single drop!" Such a person has drunk deeply from God's word and good Bible teaching and has become a great resource and storage tank of truth, a wealth of biblical knowledge. Such a person even memorizes verses and key teachings, storing them up for future use.

Perhaps it is time for us all to abandon the fast-food approach to Christian teaching and thinking and return to the older models of learning and sharing God's word. The church will always be better when its members are more biblically literate. The alternative to God's word's dwelling in us richly is God's word's dwelling in us superficially, or worse, not at all.

The Scout Code

Though Scouting does not seem as popular as it once was in the United States, it still serves as a significant socialization agency for youth who participate in it. The Boy Scouts have as part of their learned code the dictum that a scout is trustworthy, loyal, helpful, friendly, courteous, kind, obedient, cheerful, thrifty, brave, clean, and reverent. While I might want to put the last of these first, and I might want to add other qualities such as humble or loving, as Paul does in our lesson for today, I cannot fault the learning of any of these basic virtues.

What strikes me is that Scouting recognizes not only that God exists but also that there is a fundamental code of ethics and attitudes and virtues that are nonnegotiable. Paul is suggesting in our lesson that these things go naturally together. If there is a God, then there is an eternal ground for all basic ethical principles and a being who will hold us accountable for our behavior. Heavenly-mindedness does not mean having one's head in the clouds. It means knowing what God requires of us here on earth and how that differs from the ways of the world.

SHARING THE SCRIPTURE

PREPARING TO TEACH

Preparing Our Hearts

Today's devotional reading from Mark 12:28-34 focuses on Jesus' teaching concerning the Great Commandment, found in Deuteronomy 6:4-5. This commandment is the basis for the righteous way of life that Christians are expected to follow. Consider how this commandment guides your own life.

Now turn to today's lesson from Colossians 3:1-17. What do these words say to you about how Christians are to live? How do you embody this teaching in your own life? How can you help your students to live the Christian life, a lifestyle that should be easily distinguishable from the kind of life that society touts as good and desirable?

Pray that God will lead you as you prepare to teach this lesson and as you set an example before others by the very way that you conduct yourself.

Preparing Our Minds

Review Colossians 3:1-17 and this lesson.

Since the session focuses on what it means to live in ways that reflect Christ's life, spend some time thinking about what Christlike living means to you. Jesus' life manifests the qualities of compassion, kindness, humility, patience, meekness, forgiveness, love, harmony, and peace. What other qualities can you add to this list? How do you manifest these qualities in your own life? How can you help the students to manifest them?

Preparing Our Learning Space

Have on hand:
- several Bibles
- newsprint and marker
- hymnals.

LEADING THE CLASS

(1) Introduction

Begin today's session by asking students to recall slogans, perhaps from advertisers, that sum up what the good life in America is all about. List their ideas on newsprint. If you need a few discussion starters, you will find some slogans in the first paragraph of the Focusing on the Main Question portion.

Once the list is complete, invite the students to suggest words or phrases that describe the lifestyle of those who follow these slogans. Class members may use words such as hedonistic, materialistic, or self-centered.

Now encourage the students to make another list, this time using words or phrases that describe the lifestyle of those who seek to live in the image of God. Spend a few moments comparing and contrasting the two lists.

Provide a few moments of silence so that individuals may reflect on which list more closely describes their own life.

Conclude today's opening by lifting up the main question: **What distinguishes the Christian life from the way of the world?**

(2) Nothing More Beyond

Read or retell the first paragraph under "Nothing More Beyond" in Interpreting the Scripture. Then discuss with the class how the motto *Plus Ultra* ("there is more beyond") might apply to Christians. Close by reading the second paragraph of this section.

(3) Garbage In, Garbage Out

Select a volunteer to read Colossians 3:1-3.

Ask students to define the meaning of the term "garbage in, garbage out." Computer users will know that this means if you type gibberish into the computer, that is what you will get out. Now discuss these questions:

(1) **What kinds of garbage do many people put into their lives?**

(2) **What are some of the results when this garbage comes out?** (Possible answers include: people imitate violence seen on television or videos; foul language becomes acceptable speech; immoral behavior seems okay because people talk about it and act it out on television.)

Read or retell the story of the hungry falcon in the second paragraph of "Garbage In, Garbage Out" in Interpreting the Scripture. Then invite volunteers to relate this story to Colossians 3:1-3.

(4) Besetting Sins

Ask someone to read Colossians 3:5-11.

Use the information in Understanding the Scripture for verses 5-11 to create a brief lecture that contrasts the old way of life that must be put to death with the new way in Christ.

Ask the following questions:

(1) **Which of these sins that Paul says must be put to death are people— even Christians—still struggling to overcome?**

(2) **What other sins beset our society?**

(3) **What do verses 10 and 11 suggest about how the life of the Christian is to be distinguished from the life of the nonbeliever?** (Christians recognize the oneness of all persons before God and, therefore, do not make distinctions that separate persons.)

(5) Payback Time

Read aloud Colossians 3:12-14.

List on newsprint the characteristics of new life in Christ that are found in these verses: compassion; kindness; humility; meekness; patience; ability to bear with one another; forgiveness; and love.

Then discuss these questions:

(1) **How are these characteristics different from those that are seen in our society at large?**

(2) **Do you think that these characteristics are clearly evident in those who profess to be Christian? If so, how might that example influence others? If not, how might that example influence others?**

(6) Biblical Illiteracy

Tell the class to listen carefully as a volunteer reads Colossians 3:15-17. Then ask the students to state words that stood out in the reading for them. Now have the students look at this passage in their Bibles. Ask:

(1) **What is Paul telling the people they are to do?**

(2) **In general, do you feel that the people in your congregation are somewhat biblically literate? What evidence do you have for your opinion?**

(3) **What opportunities does your congregation offer to teach children, youth, and adults so that God's word might dwell in them richly?**

(4) **What might Paul say to your congregation about the way it teaches God's word?**

(5) **What changes do you need to make? What programs or models do you need to hold on to, perhaps even expand?**

(7) The Scout Code

To summarize today's lesson read or retell "The Scout Code" from Interpreting the Scripture.

Conclude the session by singing "Lord, I Want to Be a Christian" (*The United Methodist Hymnal,* no. 402) or another hymn that speaks about the nature of the Christian life.

Before you dismiss the class, lift up one of the activities below for use during the week.

HELPING CLASS MEMBERS ACT

Encourage the adults to examine their own lifestyles to see what changes they need to make in order to more faithfully reflect the characteristics of the righteous way of Christ.

Challenge students to offer forgiveness to at least one person each day this week. The offense may be minor, or it might be a major one that has caused pain for a long time.

Recommend that all class members teach someone about God this week. Teaching may take many forms. One's response to a situation, for example, teaches as much or more than whatever might be said in a discussion or lecture about a certain topic.

PLANNING FOR NEXT SUNDAY

Our Sunday school year will end next week with a lesson entitled "The Grace of Life." Ask the students to read the very short letter to Philemon to see how Paul calls us to welcome others in Christ.

THE GRACE OF LIFE

PREVIEWING THE LESSON

Lesson Scripture: Philemon 4-21
Background Scripture: Philemon
Key Verse: Philemon 6

Focus of the Lesson:
God's grace is evident in the lives of believers as they welcome others in Christ's name.

Main Question of the Lesson:
What are the costs, consequences, and Christian obligations of welcoming others, especially if these others do not appear to deserve to be welcomed?

This lesson will enable adult learners to:
(1) read Paul's plea on behalf of Onesimus.
(2) consider how they welcome others in Christ.
(3) respond by standing up for someone in a difficult situation.

Today's lesson may be outlined as follows:
(1) Introduction
(2) Welcome Back, Carter
(3) Sanctuary
(4) Modern Slavery
(5) Battle Tactics
(6) The Gift of Hospitality
(7) Small Acts of Kindness

FOCUSING ON THE MAIN QUESTION

What are the costs, consequences, and Christian obligations of welcoming others, especially if these others do not appear to deserve to be welcomed? There are several ways that one may focus on this question: (1) look at Paul's strategy as he strives to persuade Philemon to wel-come home his runaway slave, Onesimus; (2) focus on the other hints in the text that deal with the Christian's obligations to offer hospitality and give charitably; or (3) ask the hard questions of how hospitality may make the church a place where equality in Christ may be manifested, and how alienation and the harmful effects of fallen worldly structures can be ameliorated within the church setting.

In order to get a fix on the main question, consider a situation of obvious awkwardness caused by social inequality. For instance, perhaps you have entertained some important person in your home, or maybe your church hosted a famous preacher or bishop. Reflect on how you felt in this situation. How might your feelings change when you remember that this person you were entertaining was in fact your brother or sister in Christ, nothing more and nothing less? In what way should God's grace, prompting hospitable acts, be the great equalizer in socially inequitable situations?

Often in a fallen world that creates inequities there is a cost to charitable and hospitable acts. Growing up in the South in the 1950s and '60s, I witnessed the great turmoil that region went through when the public schools were integrated. One of my newfound African American friends in high school was named Willie. He was a wonderfully vivacious and likable person, and being a fellow Methodist, I and others invited him to go on retreat with our high school Methodist Youth Fellowship group. Little did we realize that there were various people in our church who would object to this hospitable act. We were seeking to act graciously and offer Christian hospitality, but there was a cost.

Paul knew in his situation that what he was asking Philemon to do had social risks. But Paul's Christian belief was that he must overcome and break down social barriers to act graciously as God does. We will see how he does this in the intriguing letter called Philemon.

READING THE SCRIPTURE

NRSV
Philemon 4-21

4 When I remember you in my prayers, I always thank my God 5 because I hear of your love for all the saints and your faith toward the Lord Jesus. **6 I pray that the sharing of your faith may become effective when you perceive all the good that we may do for Christ.** 7 I have indeed received much joy and encouragement from your love, because the hearts of the saints have been refreshed through you, my brother.

8 For this reason, though I am bold enough in Christ to command you to do your duty, 9 yet I would rather appeal to you on the basis of love—and I, Paul, do this as an old man, and now also as a prisoner of Christ Jesus. 10 I am appealing to you for my child, Onesimus, whose father I have become during my imprisonment. 11 Formerly he was useless to you, but now he is indeed useful both to you and to

NIV
Philemon 4-21

[4]I always thank my God as I remember you in my prayers, [5]because I hear about your faith in the Lord Jesus and your love for all the saints. **[6]I pray that you may be active in sharing your faith, so that you will have a full understanding of every good thing we have in Christ.** [7]Your love has given me great joy and encouragement, because you, brother, have refreshed the hearts of the saints.

[8]Therefore, although in Christ I could be bold and order you to do what you ought to do, [9]yet I appeal to you on the basis of love. I then, as Paul—an old man and now also a prisoner of Christ Jesus—[10]I appeal to you for my son Onesimus, who became my son while I was in chains. [11]Formerly he was useless to you, but now he has become useful both to you and to me.

[12]I am sending him—who is my very heart—back to you. [13]I would have liked to

Key
Verse

Key
Verse

AUGUST 27

479

me. 12 I am sending him, that is, my own heart, back to you. 13 I wanted to keep him with me, so that he might be of service to me in your place during my imprisonment for the gospel; 14 but I preferred to do nothing without your consent, in order that your good deed might be voluntary and not something forced. 15 Perhaps this is the reason he was separated from you for a while, so that you might have him back forever, 16 no longer as a slave but more than a slave, a beloved brother—especially to me but how much more to you, both in the flesh and in the Lord.

17 So if you consider me your partner, welcome him as you would welcome me. 18 If he has wronged you in any way, or owes you anything, charge that to my account. 19 I, Paul, am writing this with my own hand: I will repay it. I say nothing about your owing me even your own self. 20 Yes, brother, let me have this benefit from you in the Lord! Refresh my heart in Christ. 21 Confident of your obedience, I am writing to you, knowing that you will do even more than I say.

keep him with me so that he could take your place in helping me while I am in chains for the gospel. ¹⁴But I did not want to do anything without your consent, so that any favor you do will be spontaneous and not forced. ¹⁵Perhaps the reason he was separated from you for a little while was that you might have him back for good—¹⁶no longer as a slave, but better than a slave, as a dear brother. He is very dear to me but even dearer to you, both as a man and as a brother in the Lord.

¹⁷So if you consider me a partner, welcome him as you would welcome me. ¹⁸If he has done you any wrong or owes you anything, charge it to me. ¹⁹I, Paul, am writing this with my own hand. I will pay it back—not to mention that you owe me your very self. ²⁰I do wish, brother, that I may have some benefit from you in the Lord; refresh my heart in Christ. ²¹Confident of your obedience, I write to you, knowing that you will do even more than I ask.

UNDERSTANDING THE SCRIPTURE

Introduction. Philemon is not a purely personal letter, for its address includes a woman named Apphia (Philemon's wife?); Archippus, a fellow Christian; and the whole congregation meeting in Philemon's house. It is to be read in a public setting with the congregation present and hearing the exhortation to Philemon. With its introductory prayer and its closing benediction, the letter is suitable for use during worship.

This letter is about a runaway slave, Onesimus (which means "useful," a typical slave nickname), and his strained relationship with his Christian owner, Philemon. Paul is the mediator between the two, trying to negotiate a resolution in this grave situation. The penalty for a slave's running

away could be death. Paul, working within the fallen structures of ancient society, tries to inject grace and a more hospitable approach into these volatile circumstances.

Philemon 1-3. Paul is in chains. The translation "prisoner" may wrongly convey the notion Paul is in jail. Roman jurisprudence did not see chains or prison as a form of punishment. Someone in chains was in a holding pattern until the situation could be resolved. Notice that various people have free and ready access to the apostle (verse 23), indicating that Paul is not in solitary confinement. Verse 22 suggests that Paul expects light punishment and/or release to be imminent, which comports with the suggestion that he is under house arrest.

Rome was a haven for slaves, especially runaway slaves who could blend in readily here. A large minority of Rome's population at this time were slaves. The Roman economy depended on slave labor. The distance between Asia Minor and Rome may have led Onesimus to assume he was safe. He would hardly have thought so if he had only run from the Lycus valley to Ephesus, the nearest big city.

Ancient slavery was in many respects unlike antebellum Southern slavery. Paul is speaking about domestic or household servants in all his letters. They would be most likely to receive the best treatment, be the most educated, and be nearly full members of their households. Paul has nothing to say about slaves who worked in the mines, in rural settings, or on large farms. Domestic slaves had jobs ranging from household chores to the management of the master's estate or businesses. Often a master would free one or more of his slaves, but this was not required. Slaves could ask for freedom but they did not have any rights because according to the law they were property, not persons. Slavery is always a horrible manifestation of human fallenness, reflecting the desire to control and use other human beings, but it is important to recognize the contours of constraints on slavery in the first century in order to understand Paul's advice here.

Paul's goal is to obtain freedom for Onesimus by means of a persuasive letter to Philemon. He tries to accomplish this aim by using flattery, congregational pressure, and arm-twisting to get Philemon to do the right thing, namely, to treat Onesimus no longer as a slave but as a brother in Christ. Working within the system, Paul uses the concept of Christian hospitality within the family of faith to deconstruct the effects of slavery in and on the body of Christ. Reformation from within the community of faith, not revolution against the secular institution, is his strategy.

Philemon 4-7. In this thanksgiving prayer Paul commends Philemon's faith and love. Verse 7 says the hearts of the saints have been refreshed through Philemon's ministry. Paul prays that he may go on sharing effectively. Philemon is one of Paul's coworkers, and there is a reference here to his practical and perhaps even monetary assistance to the saints, that is, the hungry Jewish Christians in Jerusalem for whom Paul took up a collection. Paul alludes to Philemon's generosity in matters of property to introduce his request concerning Onesimus. Notice that Paul's request is postponed until later in the letter, until Philemon is softened up to hear what Paul will say on this delicate matter.

Philemon 8-16. Paul could command his coworker Philemon to act, but instead chooses to use persuasion. Paul reminds Philemon that he is an old man and a prisoner, reminders meant to make Philemon sympathetic to Paul's plight of being in chains and in need. Onesimus is called Paul's child in the faith. Onesimus has been converted not by Philemon but rather by Paul while he was under house arrest. Verse 11 is a punning on Onesimus' name. Paul is saying that "Useful" was formerly useless to Philemon, but now he is useful to both Philemon and Paul.

Paul suggests God had a plan to separate this slave from his owner so that he might come back to him no longer as a slave but as something more—a "beloved brother" in Christ (verse 16). All this prepares for the request that begins in verse 17.

Philemon 17-25. Paul first says that Philemon should welcome Onesimus home not as a slave but as he would welcome the apostle himself! He then reassures Philemon that if Onesimus had done any wrong or taken anything, Philemon should charge it to Paul's account. Paul adds, with full twisting of the arm, that Philemon owes the apostle his very eternal life! Paul uses the rhetorical trick in verse 19 of saying he will not speak of Philemon's spiritual debt to him, and thereby does so. Verse 19 originally included Paul's signature, indicating he would pay any remaining debt. Again playing on the slave's name, Paul asks for some "use" or "benefit" from Philemon. Philemon would refresh Paul's heart if he would send him the gift of a new brother in Christ to help him. This gesture would continue Philemon's practice of offering practical aid that refreshed the saints' hearts (see verses 6-7).

Finally in verse 21 Paul says he is confident of Philemon's "obedience," even though he said he wasn't commanding! Paul is certain that Philemon will do even more than he asked. In fact, Paul asks Philemon to be prepared to receive him as a houseguest even after he made such an expensive and daring request (verse 22).

INTERPRETING THE SCRIPTURE

Welcome Back, Carter

One of our past presidents whom I most admire is Jimmy Carter. Instead of simply retiring and resting on his laurels, President Carter has been the driving force behind Habitat for Humanity and a host of other projects meant to make this world a more gracious and hospitable place. President Carter has spent a good deal of his life in Plains, Georgia, and personally was prepared to pay the price for welcoming people of all races both into the Baptist church of which he has been a part and also into his business and other social relationships.

Yet there was a cost for him in the 1960s for being gracious in this way when interracial hospitality from whites to blacks was frowned upon by many. Among other things, his peanut business suffered some reverses. Yet President Carter stuck by his approach because he saw it as a matter of Christian principle.

It is easy to be gracious to our friends when there is no social cost or obstacle to overcome. Paul's letter to Philemon urges us to work to break down social barriers and dare to undertake difficult and controversial acts of hospitality in the name of Christ.

Sanctuary

According to an Old Testament practice, if a person could reach the tent of meeting and grasp the horns of the altar where God's presence was especially believed to be, that person was to be granted sanctuary and full protection from harm. This practice was adopted by modern churches in the 1980s when they offered sanctuary to refugees fleeing from oppressive regimes in Latin America, even though they were not legally authorized to live in the United States. The churches took the refugees in and cared for them until a solution to their problems could be found.

This risky offering of grace caused considerable controversy on Capitol Hill. Some would see this as an act of politics, and to be sure it had political implications, but these acts of hospitality were motivated by texts such as Philemon. The line between being faithful to a revolutionary gospel of hospitality and grace and flaunting or clearly violating the secular law is indeed very fine. Nevertheless, Paul's gospel of hospitality to all, as expressed in the letter to Philemon, had both spiritual and social dimensions and implications.

Modern Slavery

While the discussion of slavery may be difficult for us to relate to in some ways, it has not been so long since the modern industrialized nation of South Africa practiced apartheid, or for that matter since racial segregation was a regular practice in the United States. In antiquity, slavery was not a racial practice per se. Slaves could be any and all kinds of persons, even

Romans, who frequently would sell themselves into slavery to secure a better economic future. The sins of racism, classism, and social prejudice have not been abolished in our so-called enlightened times; they have just taken different forms.

Modern economic slavery is to a significant degree caused by large American companies' willingness to pay slave wages to foreign persons so they may assemble the toys, clothes, and other goods we desire to purchase cheaply. Were Americans actually willing to bite the bullet and pay more for domestic or foreign goods, we could in fact raise the standard of living of many persons worldwide. Debt, in antiquity as now, was a reality that caused people to do extreme things to get out of such a situation. The question our text raises for these sorts of cases is how Christians can act graciously to change the world in nonviolent ways so that it is in general a more hospitable place.

Battle Tactics

What tactics are appropriate to interject grace and hospitality into a fallen situation? One would deduce from this letter that Paul is not advocating a revolution against the socioeconomic system in his world, but he is proactive in working for change within the Christian community. Paul is sending Onesimus back to his owner, though he would rather have kept him. Paul is not a lawbreaker in this matter. He seeks Onesimus's freedom through a legal means—manumission by the owner. Verse 13 suggests that Onesimus could serve Paul since Philemon is not present in Rome to do so. Paul says he wants Philemon's response to be free, not forced, but he is clearly exerting all the moral and emotional pressure possible to produce the result he desires.

Think of the effect of Paul's request on Philemon's congregation, as they listen to this letter with Philemon for the first time and wait to see how Philemon will react.

This is true pressure! I wonder if we would not see these acts of persuasion as going beyond the limits of proper social conventions today. Yet that would not trouble Paul. He was prepared to be a social outcast if he could only welcome a few more people into the Kingdom and reconcile socially diverse persons in the body of Christ.

To what degree is such arm-twisting as we find in this letter appropriate as Christian behavior? Obviously, Paul feels it is acceptable to use all the legal and ethical means available to him to convince Philemon to do the right thing. Perhaps the threat to Onesimus's very life prompted these measures, for Paul certainly knew that a runaway slave could be put to death. In any case it is clear that Paul committed himself to persuasion rather than to using subterfuge or simply acting and then announcing the results.

We see here a lesson for church politics in regard to the parameters of proper behavior. The church is basically a voluntary society, and therefore moral suasion is the chief tool that should be used to produce any change in policy, direction, budget, or the like. Divine fiat is likely to backfire, especially in our mostly democratic society.

The Gift of Hospitality

One of Philemon's endearing qualities is that he had the gift of hospitality and other forms of charitable sharing. His generosity is seen not only in his willingness to host the church in his own house as verse 2 tells us, but also in his eagerness to host traveling emissaries such as Paul or his coworkers. Furthermore, there are hints of his charitable work for the saints.

In a world without hotels hospitality was one of the chief virtues of ancient culture. Hospitality had all sorts of ramifications that acts such as eating out or staying in a hotel do not have today. For one thing, the host in Paul's time would take responsibility for the well-being of his guests. If anything harmful was about to happen to them, the host would feel obliged to protect them.

New members of churches today often report that they chose to join a particular congregation because they were so welcomed, experienced such good fellowship, and felt that people took a personal interest in their lives. In antiquity, as today, hospitality was a crucial tool for sharing not only the gospel but also the other benefits of Christian life with those in need.

Small Acts of Kindness

Perhaps reading Philemon leads one to think that Paul is not speaking to us. After all, slavery is outlawed in the United States. But in fact the principles of hospitality enumerated here apply even in small ways.

Once while I was a teenager, my car broke down in the mountains of North Carolina and I hitchhiked home. I got to Yadkinville by dark but was tired. I met a Christian businessman who ran a car lot, and he graciously let me sleep in a car overnight there. I would not allow him to take me to his house because I did not want to impose on his family. Still, he was very gracious to me. I have not forgotten this small act of kindness because it kept me safe and out of the weather, and I made it home the next day. For me, this man's kindness was an example of God's grace and hospitality in action. We must go and do likewise.

SHARING THE SCRIPTURE

PREPARING TO TEACH

Preparing Our Hearts

Today's devotional reading is from James 2:1-13. As James speaks of the respect due to the poor we learn that God shows no partiality. And neither must we. How do you respect and welcome all persons?

Read all of Paul's letter to Philemon. The apostle seeks to persuade Philemon to welcome home his runaway slave, Onesimus, as a brother in Christ. Could you look with fresh eyes at someone you have seen as beneath you? How do you treat persons whose job it is to serve you?

Pray that you and your students will be able to see beyond artificial divisions among people to accept and welcome all in the name of Christ.

Preparing Our Minds

Review Philemon and read this lesson carefully. If time permits, you may want to do some additional reading about the institution of slavery within the Roman Empire during the first century.

Preparing Our Learning Space

Have on hand:
- several Bibles
- newsprint and marker
- paper and pencils.

LEADING THE CLASS

(1) Introduction

Open the session by reading today's main question: **What are the costs, consequences, and Christian obligations of welcoming others, especially if these others do not appear to deserve to be welcomed?**

Next, read aloud the second paragraph under Focusing on the Main Question. Allow a few moments for silent reflection on the questions raised in this paragraph.

Now read aloud the three ways that we may focus on the main question as found in the first paragraph of Focusing on the Main Question.

Close by reading or retelling the third and fourth paragraphs of Focusing on the Main Question.

(2) Welcome Back, Carter

Plan to read Philemon 4-21 yourself as if you were Paul speaking to the congregation that meets in your home. Then ask:

(1) Why is Paul writing to Philemon? (Paul wants his coworker Philemon to welcome Onesimus back home, not as a runaway slave but as a brother in Christ.)

(2) On what does Paul base his plea to Philemon concerning Onesimus? (Underlying Paul's letter is the principle of gracious hospitality in Jesus' name.)

Note that Paul's letter urges us to undertake difficult and controversial acts of hospitality in the name of Christ. Use the example of former president Jimmy Carter, found under "Welcome Back, Carter" in Interpreting the Scripture, to highlight the cost of such action.

(3) Sanctuary

Ask these questions:

(1) Do you believe Paul overstepped his boundaries in asking Philemon to welcome Onesimus back? Why or why not?

(2) Are you aware of modern situations where hospitality was also offered to persons fleeing oppression? If so, give an example.

Move from this question to a retelling of "Sanctuary" under Interpreting the Scripture. Note this sentence: The line between being faithful to a revolutionary gospel of hospitality and grace and flaunting or clearly violating the secular law is indeed very fine. Then ask:

(1) Under what circumstances would you be willing to violate (or have you violated) secular law to be faithful to the revolutionary nature of the gospel?

(2) What steps can you take within the law to help persons who, like Onesimus, are fleeing oppression?

(4) Modern Slavery

Discuss these questions with the class:

(1) What do you know about the institution of slavery as it was practiced in the Roman Empire during the first century? (Some information is given under "Modern Slavery" in Interpreting the Scripture and "Philemon 1-3" in Understanding the Scripture. If you have done additional reading on this topic, include that information as well.)

(2) Give examples of oppression in the modern world. (Examples include slavery in the United States, the perpetuation of prejudice through segregation, and apartheid in South Africa.)

(5) Battle Tactics

Invite the students to look closely at Philemon 4-21. Encourage them to identify all of the ways that Paul uses to interject grace and hospitality into a fallen situation. List their ideas on newsprint. You will find information to augment the discussion under "Battle Tactics" in Interpreting the Scripture.

If you prefer not to do the brainstorming, use the information under "Battle Tactics" to create a brief lecture.

(6) The Gift of Hospitality

Direct the students to turn again to Philemon. Ask them to work with a partner or small group to locate evidence in the text to support this statement that you will need to read aloud: <u>Philemon had the gift of hospitality.</u>

Invite volunteers from each team to report their findings. Use the information under "The Gift of Hospitality" in Interpreting the Scripture to round out the discussion.

In lieu of group work, consider taking the material from this section and preparing a brief lecture to help the class members understand both the importance of hospitality in the first century and Philemon's actions as a hospitable person.

(7) Small Acts of Kindness

Read or retell the example of the act of kindness done by the Christian businessman. Distribute paper and pencils. Ask the students to fold the paper in half, top to bottom. At the top they are to list random acts of kindness done on their behalf in the last week or two. Tell them to list random acts of kindness they have done for others on the bottom of the paper. Do not ask them to read their lists aloud. Instead, invite them to hold these papers as you offer a prayer that they will be able to multiply these acts of kindness so that all persons may see examples of God's gracious hospitality in action.

Lift up at least one of the activities below so that students will have ideas for living out what they have learned.

HELPING CLASS MEMBERS ACT

Encourage the students to stand up for someone who is struggling, perhaps a person who has been in legal trouble or a young person who has had a disciplinary problem in school.

Suggest that people write a note of appreciation to someone who has done a good deed for them.

Invite class members to interject grace into a fallen situation by persuading someone to do something for someone else that by non-Christian standards may seem above and beyond a reasonable expectation.

PLANNING FOR NEXT SUNDAY

To begin the new Sunday school year next week you will need a copy of *The New International Lesson Annual, September–August 2000–2001*. To prepare for the fall study, "Rulers of Israel," tell the students to read Judges 4-5, especially 4:2-9, 14-15, and 22. Our lesson, "Be an Encourager," focuses on the judge Deborah.